THE 1st INFANTRY DIVISION AND THE US ARMY TRANSFORMED

Published in cooperation with the First Division Museum at Cantigny, Wheaton, Illinois.
www.firstdivisionmuseum.org

THE 1ST INFANTRY DIVISION AND THE US ARMY TRANSFORMED

Road to Victory in Desert Storm 1970–1991

Gregory Fontenot
Colonel, United States Army, Retired

UNIVERSITY OF MISSOURI PRESS
Columbia

University of Missouri Press, Columbia, Missouri 65211
Printed and bound in the United States of America
 First printing, 2017

ISBN: 978-0-8262-2118-6
Library of Congress Control Number: 2017933331

∞™ This paper meets the requirements of the
American National Standard for Permanence of Paper
for Printed Library Materials, Z39.48, 1984.

Typefaces: Minion and Trajan

THE AMERICAN MILITARY EXPERIENCE SERIES

JOHN C. MCMANUS, SERIES EDITOR

The books in this series portray and analyze the experience of Americans in military service during war and peacetime from the onset of the twentieth century to the present. The series emphasizes the profound impact wars have had on nearly every aspect of recent American history and considers the significant effects of modern conflict on combatants and noncombatants alike. Titles in the series include accounts of battles, campaigns, and wars; unit histories; biographical and autobiographical narratives; investigations of technology and warfare; studies of the social and economic consequences of war; and in general, the best recent scholarship on Americans in the modern armed forces. The books in the series are written and designed for a diverse audience that encompasses nonspecialists as well as expert readers.

For my brothers and sisters in the 1st Infantry Division,
including spouses and family support groups.

We served together.

Duty First!

CONTENTS

FIGURES AND MAPS

FOREWORD

THERE ARE VERY few people qualified to create such a book as *The 1st Infantry Division and the US Army Transformed: Road to Victory in Desert Storm, 1970–1991*. Greg Fontenot is one of them—professional soldier and professional historian, long-serving member of 1st Infantry Division as commander in peace and war, and a staff officer with a remarkably keen eye, not only for the relationship of the division to its higher headquarters but its connection to the intellectual and technical growth of the Army, from the depths of the post-Vietnam hangover to the victory celebrations of mid-1991.

To suggest, as others have done, that the transformation of the US Army from the early seventies to the Operational Just Cause and Desert Shield/Desert Storm simply represents the "legacy of an old war" is to miss a number of very significant and profound accomplishments that are glibly passed over as being too pedestrian for comment. Greg Fontenot has ably compiled the evidence to support his position, suggestive of a massive transition from the shambles of a formation suffering a post-Vietnam malaise, to a powerful combined-arms heavy division capable of strategic deployment, modernization-on-the-move while deploying and preparing for combat, combat, and post combat activities under inhospitable environmental conditions and threat of enemy fire.

None of what happened from August 1990 to July 1991 would have been possible without a profound transformation of the total Army—active/Army Guard/Army Reserve and government civilians. This started and ended with quality soldiers, developed in a focused and rigorously enforced training system layered with a rigorous leader development program, and enhanced by a modernization program somewhat constrained by available dollars for the troops. Their leaders acquitted themselves well in combat, primarily because they had trained under conditions based upon the new AirLand Battle doctrine, a doctrine not fully resourced in low-priority divisions such as the 1st Infantry Division.

Given that the Army cannot "freeze" soldiers in place for significant periods, unit readiness is always problematic. The improvement in readiness throughout the Army from the mid-1970s through the late 1980s was profound, and it did not occur haphazardly. A long line of Army Chiefs of Staff, from Abrams to Vuono, worked long, hard, and diligently not only to transform the Army, but to create a more capable, responsible, and lethal Army with a winning spirit. Certainly it was only because the troops were capable, confident, and courageous that the deployed army and its allies prevailed in Operation Desert Storm, achieving a remarkable and fast victory with very few casualties.

There are important institutional training innovations highlighted in this book that bear emphasis: first, the creation of the National Training Center at Fort Irwin; its sister organization at Hohenfels, Germany; and the Joint Readiness Training Center (JRTC) at Fort Polk, Louisiana. In these sophisticated, instrumented, free-play maneuver facilities, featuring highly competitive opposition forces, the Institutional Army developed its leaders and soldiers as competent and capable members of tactical and operational teams.

The principal role of the training centers was to develop a more sophisticated awareness of doctrinal standards and the complexity of combined-arms warfare throughout the Army. This awareness changed the Army's appreciation of the roles of the individual soldier, as well as those of all NCOs and officers, in the application of military power on the battlefield, and it energized home-station training.

The combat-training centers provided the opportunity to all to train to the new doctrine, AirLand Battle, as if they had the programmed equipment, which in many cases the outfits did not. This imaginative training approach, plus the level of preparedness of the troops of the 1st Division saw them able to field modern equipment, some of which they had never seen, upon arrival in theater.

The 1st Infantry Division is perhaps the prime example of a unit that was low on the Army's modernization priority list but still muscled its way through an on-the-fly modernization phase, and demonstrated once again that the quality identified by John "Blackjack" Pershing in 1917–18 as "a certain spirit . . . " still existed in the ranks of the "Big Red One" in Saudi Arabia in 1991, as it does today.

From August 1990 to early November, troop tension remained high. Trained and ready soldiers, and their families, waited to learn if the 1st Infantry Division would deploy to Saudi Arabia or remain in Kansas. Emotions were mixed, and in early November the decision was made: The storied Big Red One was to be deployed from Fort Riley to combat once again. This time, the division was trained and ready. Under Tom Rhame's mentorship and strong hand, the division's competent and experienced leaders had honed their skills and those of their teams to a high level of professional practice.

I know of few accounts of the positive impact of the Post-Vietnam transformation focused on a division with the detail and breadth of this masterpiece by Greg Fontenot. Few other accounts provide such a complete picture of the entire process of strategic deployment, reorganization in theater, combat, post-combat, and redeployment.

The two constant characteristics of the US Army are change and the indomitable fighting spirit of the American soldier. *The 1st Infantry Division and the US Army Transformed* is ample evidence of the power of visionary and capable leadership from top to bottom with a clear mandate—"to transform the US Army from defeat into victory."

In this book, Fontenot gives us a look into the workings of one of our most famous, distinguished, and experienced combat divisions. He knows what he is writing about, and with every page the discerning reader will learn what soldiering is all about from a master.

Gordon R. Sullivan, General, USA, Retired

ACKNOWLEDGMENTS

I HAVE MADE A great many mistakes in my life. Not the least of them is that I believed that writing a second book would be easier than the first. Writing about the division with which I served was far more difficult than I anticipated. I am therefore particularly indebted to the many people who helped me through this project.

Colonel Paul Herbert, an old friend and colleague from the History Department at the United States Military Academy, asked me to take this on and has served as boss, coach, and editor. Without him I would never have finished. My heartfelt thanks goes also to the great research staff at the Colonel Robert R. McCormick Research Center at the First Infantry Division Museum at Cantigny in Wheaton, Illinois. Robin Kern did the publishing layout for a book I coauthored, *On Point: The US Army in Operation Iraqi Freedom*. Despite that, she agreed to edit the present volume. Mark Osterholm created the maps for *On Point* and reprised that outstanding effort here. My thanks go to everyone at the University of Missouri Press, and especially copyeditor Brian Bendlin, who helped me clarify a number of points and citations.

Insight into the Iraqi point of view is essential to this story. Such insight as this narrative contains is due to the dedication of handful of Americans and Iraqis. Colonel Stu Herrington's Joint Debriefing Center did amazing work with captured Iraqi officers. He and his soldiers enabled the Iraqis to tell their story of the invasion of Kuwait, their preparations to defend it, and the ensuing fight.

Although the Conflict Records Research Center closed in June 2015, until then it was a treasure trove of Iraqi documents. I am grateful to David Palkki and Stephanie Glass for helping me navigate that archive.

Kevin Woods at the Institute of Defense Analysis did much of the original work with the Iraqi documents and offered insights and guidance on using the records. Kevin is the author or coauthor of several important books stemming from captured Iraqi documents; equally important, he granted me access to the memoir of Lieutenant General Ra'ad Hamdani, who served in the Hammurabi Division of the Republican Guard during Operation Desert Storm. Although I do not quote his memoir, it afforded a useful glimpse into the Republican Guard. Kevin also introduced me to a senior Iraqi officer who retired from an important position in the summer of 1990 and prefers to remain anonymous; the officer shared his views on the Iraqi Army's tactics and leadership with me and remains a confidant on this matter.

Colonel Pesach Malovany of the Israeli Defense Forces Reserve helped me to understand Iraqi Army organization and operations from the Iraqi perspective; he provided translations of Iraqi articles written about the "Mother of All Battles," and is an esteemed colleague in this venture.

For a number of bureaucratic reasons, the VII Corps and 1st Infantry Division records from Operation Desert Storm were accessible neither at the National Archives and Records Administration nor at Fort Leavenworth, Kansas, where some duplicates are held. I obtained some records at one research facility, but most came from veterans or from donations by veterans to the First Infantry Division Museum at Cantigny or the 1st Infantry Division Museum at Fort Riley, Kansas.

The US Army Historical and Education Center in Carlisle Barracks, Pennsylvania, is a magnificent archive. Colonel Tom Hendrix, the director and another West Point teammate, was very helpful. Two old soldiers, Brent Bankus and Marty Andresen, the latter another West Point colleague, supported every request, pointing me to sources and providing advice.

Frank Shirer, chief of the Historical Research Branch, and the rest of the staff at the Center of Military History at Fort McNair, District of Columbia, wholeheartedly supported my work. I have used several maps originally created for Stephen A. Bourque's *Jayhawk: The VII Corps in the Persian Gulf War*, and they are beautifully done. The cartographer asked that I credit her work to the Center of Military History, and I have, but I want her to know how much I appreciate it.

The Combined Arms Research Library, Fort Leavenworth, Kansas, served as a comfortable and convivial home away from home where I could work with valuable secondary sources, professional journals, and documents that helped set the context. Rusty Rafferty helped me with doctrinal references and important studies on the Army family. Susan Plotner, the librarian for the University of Foreign Military Studies, gave her own time to help me double-check sources.

More than 150 of the great soldiers with whom I served agreed to interviews or provided materials. Some of my comrades provided copies of their journals, notes, photos, maps, and records or gave them to me outright. In each case in which originals were given to me I have, with the consent of the donor, turned them over to the First Infantry Division Museum at Cantigny. I wish to thank all of these soldiers for their help and best wishes in this effort.

Robert Smith, the director of the both the US Cavalry Museum and the 1st Infantry Division Museum at Fort Riley holds twenty-seven archive boxes of records from Operation Desert Storm. Bob bent over backward, to the point of helping me correct endnotes long distance. Flavia Hulsey and Dena O'Dell from the Fort Riley Public Affairs Office helped me access the *Fort Riley Post* archives.

Thomas Houlahan, the author of *Gulf War: The Complete History*, helped me locate several soldiers I needed to interview and provided a foil for my thinking on what the troops called Fright Night. Colonel Richard M. Swain, author of *"Lucky War": Third Army in Desert Storm*, helped to sharpen my thinking and my writing. Colonel Mike Kendall, my high school classmate and Lieutenant General John Yeosock's executive officer, allowed me access to his memoranda of meetings. Stephen A. Bourque served with me as my executive officer in the 2nd Battalion, 34th Armor. Later I urged him to write *Jayhawk*, and I am glad that I did; it is very good work. Steve advised me on several occasions, and provided me with daily staff journals of the VII Corps, 1st Division, 1-4 Cavalry, and the wartime situation reports of the VII Corps. Lieutenant Colonel John Burdan, Steve's coauthor for *The Road to Safwan: The 1st Squadron, 4th Cavalry in the 1991 Persian Gulf War*, offered corrections to errors I made.

Several persons deserve particular mention. Lieutenant General William G. Carter III read and critiqued virtually the whole manuscript, as did Colonel Kevin Benson. Colonel Chip Bircher and Lieutenant Colonels Garry Bishop, Bob Finnegan, and Bill Hedges read the chapter on "Fright Night" carefully. Colonels Jim Mowery and Mark Landrith taught me how to spell the word *helicopter* and put up with constant questions that only pilots can answer. Lieutenant General Bob Wilson and Brigadier General Dave Gross offered cogent criticism. Finally, Lieutenant General Tom Rhame gave freely of his time despite my taking a view different from his own in his role as the Division's commander.

My granddaughters Willow and Wynter have now attended three veterans' reunions and climbed all over tanks, Bradleys, and other gear at Fort Riley and at the First Infantry Division Museum at Cantigny. They are committed fans of the Big Red One and mostly good for my blood pressure.

My wife Dana shared the experience of Desert Storm, Bosnia, and various trips to Iraq and Afghanistan. She has been my best friend and most trenchant critic for forty-seven years. Thank you so much, Dana, for your love and support.

NOTE TO THE READER

When the United States entered World War I, it organized the US Army into "divisions" of about 25,000 soldiers of all arms. Of the forty-two US divisions sent to France, the first was dubbed the First Division. Now known as the 1st Infantry Division, the famous Big Red One has been on active duty ever since. One of the officers of that early First Division was the late Colonel Robert R. McCormick, who later became very wealthy and influential as the owner of the *Chicago Tribune*. He never forgot his service in World War I; he was devoted to the Division and to soldiers and veterans for the rest of his life. He left his estate in Wheaton, Illinois (named Cantigny, after the First Division's first battle) as a park, and he left his considerable fortune in a philanthropic trust, now the Robert R. McCormick Foundation. His trustees established the First Division Museum at Cantigny to tell the Division's story. One of our many activities at the museum is to support books such as this one. We were delighted to find a veteran, scholar, and author as good as Greg Fontenot and a partner as good as the University of Missouri Press. The soldiers of the Big Red One who fought in Operation Desert Storm went to war with the same anxieties, determination, and fundamental patriotism as their predecessors in all of our wars. They served with distinction, courage, and honor and they won, overwhelmingly, in a very brief campaign. Their story deserves to be told, and we at Cantigny are proud to be a part of telling it.

Paul Herbert
Executive Director
First Division Museum at Cantigny

AUTHOR NOTES

Numbered Military Units

The First Infantry Division (Mechanized) is referred to as the 1st Division, the Division, the 1 ID, and (in very few cases) the Big Red One. All other divisions are abbreviated with their number and type. Thus, 1 CD for the 1st Cavalry Division, 24 ID for the 24th Infantry Division, 82 ABN for the Eighty-Second Airborne Division, and so on.

Both Iraqi and US corps are referred to using roman numerals. (Coincidentally, the US VII Corps initially attacked the Iraqi VII Corps.) The Third Army is abbreviated as the 3rd Army.

The conventions cited above apply also to Iraqi units, except for named Republican Guard divisions, whose names I have given instead; thus, Al-Medina Armored Division and Tawakalna Mechanized Division are spelled out.

US brigades are identified by their numeral designation and, if appropriate, their branch; thus, the 1st Brigade, 1st Infantry Division is referred to as the 1st Brigade. The 207th Military Intelligence Brigade assigned to VII Corps is referred to as the 207 MI.

I refer to Iraqi infantry brigades by their numerals only; accordingly, the 110th Brigade of the 26th Infantry Division is abbreviated as the 110th Brigade. Iraqi mechanized and armored brigades are identified by numeral and branch; thus, the 18th Mechanized Brigade of the Tawakalna Division is abbreviated as the 18th Brigade or the 18 Mech Bde.

The 2nd and 3rd Armored Cavalry Regiments, which fought in Operation Desert Storm, are abbreviated as 2 ACR and 3 ACR.

Battalions composed of single type units are abbreviated by their numeral and branch; thus, the 1st Battalion, 34th Armor is the 1-34 AR. Task forces composed of more than one branch type, such as armor and infantry, are abbreviated with the branch type of the headquarters; thus, Task Force 2nd Battalion, 34th Armor, composed of two tank and two mechanized infantry companies, is abbreviated as TF 2-34 AR.

Soviet Combat Vehicles

Iraqi units fielded a great many weapons types from a great many countries, including France, the United Kingdom, and the United States, but most of its weapons were Soviet. I have used the Soviet abbreviations to identify them because that is how they were identified by US analysts. Soviet tanks are identified using US identification, with T indicating tank, followed by the model number; thus, T-72 identified the 125-millimeter armed medium tank encountered in the Republican Guard formations. The text also refers to the following Soviet combat vehicles:

BMP: Boyevaya Mashina Pekhoty (infantry fighting vehicle). The Republican Guard used the BMP-1 tracked infantry fighting vehicle armed with a seventy-three-millimeter smooth bore gun/launcher.

BRDM: Boyevaya Razvedyvatelnaya Dozornaya Mashina (combat reconnaissance patrol vehicle).

BTR: Bronetransportyor (armored transporter), a wheeled armored personnel carrier.

MTLB: Mnogotselevoy Tyagach Legky Bronirovanny (light multipurpose armored towing vehicle). The Iraqis used several variants of this lightly armored tracked vehicle; most were employed as troop carriers.

ZSU: Zenitnaya Samokhodnaya Ustanovka (antiaircraft self-propelled mount). The First Division encountered quite a few ZSU-23-4 platforms. The ZSU-23-4 is a tracked self-propelled air defense system featuring four twenty-three-millimeter cannons.

Finally, it is practically impossible to avoid using abbreviations without using even more ponderous Army titles. For all abbreviations but those referring to military rank, I explain each at first mention in each chapter; I have also provided a list of those used frequently.

ABBREVIATIONS

Note: US Army rank abbreviations apply also to the US Air Force and US Marines.

1

1LT	First Lieutenant
1SG	First Sergeant

2

2LT	Second Lieutenant

A

ABN	Airborne (Division)
ACE	armored combat engineer (vehicle)
ACR	Armored Cavalry Regiment
ACS	Army Community Service
AD	Armored Division
ADA	Air Defense Artillery
APFSDS	armor-piercing fin-stabilized discarding sabot
AR	Armor
AR Bde	Armored Brigade
ASP	ammunition supply point
AVN	Aviation

B

BCTP	Battle Command Training Program

BG	Brigadier General
BMP	Boyevaya Mashina Pekhoty, a Soviet-made infantry fighting vehicle
BN	Battalion
BRDM	Boyevaya Razvedyvatelnaya Dozornaya Mashina, a Soviet-made combat reconnaissance patrol vehicle
BTR	Bronetransportyor, a Soviet-made armored transporter

C

CARC	chemical agent resistant coating
CAV	Cavalry
CD	Cavalry Division
CENTCOM	Central Command
CG	Commanding General
COL	Colonel
COSCOM	Corps Support Command
CPL	Corporal
CPT	Captain
CSM	Command Sergeant Major
CW1	Chief Warrant Officer 1
CW2	Chief Warrant Officer 2
CW3	Chief Warrant Officer 3
CW4	Chief Warrant Officer 4

D

DIV	Division

E

EN	Engineer
EPWs	enemy prisoners of war

F

F	Forward
FA	Field Artillery

FM	Field Manual
FRAGO	Fragmentary Order
FSCL	Fire Support Coordination Line

G

GDP	General Defense Plan
GEN	General

H

HEAT	high-explosive, antitank (munitions)
HEMTT	heavy expanded mobility tactical truck
HMMWV	high-mobility multipurpose wheeled vehicle

I

ID	Infantry Division
IN	Infantry
ISU	Integrated Site Unit

J

JSTARS	Joint Surveillance Targeting Acquisition System

L

LORAN	long-range navigation
LT	Lieutenant
LTC	Lieutenant Colonel
LTG	Lieutenant General

M

MAJ	Major
Mar Div	Marine Division
MCLC	mine-clearing line charge
Mech Bde	Mechanized Brigade
Mech Div	Mechanized Division
MEF	Marine Expeditionary Force

METL	mission essential task list
MG	Major General
MI	Military Intelligence
MILES	Multiple Integrated Laser Engagement System
MLRS	multiple-launch rocket system
MP	military police
MRE(s)	meal(s) ready-to-eat
MSE	mobile subscriber equipment
MSR	main supply route
MTLB	Mnogotselevoy Tyagach Legky Bronirovanny, a Soviet-made multipurpose light-armored towing vehicle

N

NATO	North Atlantic Treaty Organization
NCO	noncommissioned officer
NTC	National Training Center

P

PADS	position and azimuth determining system
PFC	Private First Class
PKB	platoon kills battalion

R

REFORGER	return of forces to Germany
Ret.	Retired
RGFC	Republican Guard Forces Command
ROTC	Reserve Officer Training Corps
RPG	rocket-propelled grenade
RSOI	reception, staging, onward movement, integration

S

SAMS	School of Advanced Military Studies
SFC	Sergeant First Class
SGM	Sergeant Major

SGT	Sergeant
SPC	Specialist
SSG	Staff Sergeant

T

TAA	tactical assembly area
TIS	thermal imaging system
TOW	tube-launched, optically tracked, wire-guided (missile)
TRADOC	Training and Doctrine Command

U

USNS	US Navy ship
USS	US ship

Z

ZSU	Zenitnaya Samokhodnaya Ustanovka, a Soviet-made antiaircraft self-propelled mount

PREFACE

My personal history with the 1st Infantry Division, the "Big Red One," began in January 1964 when my father was reassigned from Germany to an aviation unit at Marshall Army Air Field at Fort Riley, Kansas.

The post was founded in 1854 to provide a base from which the Army could react to threats to the Santa Fe and Oregon Trails. Later it became the home of the US Army Cavalry School. The old Cavalry School campus forms the heart of Main Post; built with native limestone and sitting at the foot of a mesa, it is truly beautiful. The edge of the mesa is lined with rim rock, which made a perfect pathway for a teenage boy to look down on the old post and the World War II cantonments, which in those days remained intact: two-story clapboard barracks dominated. The mesa northwest of Main Post is called Custer Hill, which once boasted "modern" barracks built in the 1950s.

When my family arrived, the last surviving cavalry mount lived at the fort in honored retirement. I often visited Chief, as he was named, at his paddock in Camp Forsythe. He died of old age in 1968, and is buried beneath a sculpture of Frederick Remington's "Old Bill" at Cavalry Parade on Main Post. Fort Riley is steeped in history and home to a great many interesting people, then and now. In 1964, when my family moved to 3066-1 Booth Avenue, we lived a few doors down from Command Sergeant Major Theodore Dobol, who served in the 26th Infantry Regiment in every rank from private to command sergeant major. His status was such that the radio call sign for the battalion commander of the 1st Battalion was Dobol 6. J. E. B. "Jeb" Stuart, George Armstrong Custer, George Patton, Jonathan "Skinny" Wainwright, and Lucian Truscott all soldiered at Fort Riley. Future generals and Army chiefs of staff Carl E. Vuono and Gordon R. Sullivan served together in the 1st Infantry Division. The Big Red One and its traditions and soldiers, famous or not, have been an important part of my life.

I think of Fort Riley and the 1st Infantry Division as home. I lived on post with my parents and later served two tours in my own right. I graduated from Kansas State University on Saturday, May 14, 1971; the following Monday morning I reported for duty in the 1st Infantry Division. That afternoon I arrived, broke, in the motor pool of the 1st Battalion, 63rd Armor. I was broke because before I could get to my unit, I was made to buy a savings bond and memberships in the Officer's Club and the Association of the United States Army. My wife Dana and I learned to soldier in the 63rd Armor. Dana gave birth to our son Brian at Fort Riley's Irwin Army Hospital.

Dana, Brian, and I left to serve in Germany in January 1974 and returned in May 1985 with our second son, Warren, who was born in Frankfurt. We remained at Fort Riley through June 1991. I served first as the Division's plans officer from May 1985 to June 1986. Then I moved to Custer Hill, where I served as executive officer of the 1st Battalion, 34th Armor for the next year. From June 1987 until April 1989, I served at the headquarters of the 1st Brigade, first as the brigade operations officer and then as the executive officer. In April 1989, I took command of the 2nd Battalion, 34th Armor, which had just been renamed from the 1st Battalion, 63rd Armor. Dana and I had come full circle, returning to the battalion where we had started our life in the Army. That is the battalion I took to war and the one in which Dana supported families.

The Big Red One and Fort Riley captivated me then and now. I remain associated with the Division as the honorary colonel of the 34th Armor Regiment and serve on the board of the Society of the First Division. That is my background, my advantage, and my burden. I approach the task of writing about my professional home with joy and some trepidation. I am happy to tell the story of all who soldiered with the Big Red One from 1970 through the end of Operation Desert Storm. I especially want to do justice to those with whom I went to war. I feel trepidation for two reasons: I worry that I will fail to tell the story as well as it deserves to be told, and that I will fail to render as objective a judgment as possible.

Yet that is my task. I love the Division, warts and all. It is an institution worthy of admiration. Since its inception in 1917, it has served well and faithfully in each of the country's major wars except the Korean War, when it was still on occupation duty in Germany. In that time, it has done the country's bidding in North Africa, Sicily, France, Germany, Vietnam, Saudi Arabia, Iraq, Kuwait, Bosnia, Macedonia, Kosovo, Afghanistan, and across Africa and the Middle East. Its regiments are justifiably famous. The 5th Artillery dates from the American Revolution: Alexander Hamilton commanded one of its batteries, the oldest unit in the regular Army. The 16th and the 18th Regiments fought during the Civil War. The 4th Cavalry was famous in the Old West and since. The 1st Engineer Battalion is home to the original US Army company of sappers organized during the Mexican-American War . Of the combat arms units, only the armor and aviation regiments are "new"—dating from World War II in the case of the armored regiments and just before Operation Desert Storm in the case of the aviation regiments. They earned their battle streamers at places like Omaha Beach in Normandy, Soui Tre in Vietnam, Samarra in Iraq, and the hill country in Afghanistan.

The story of the Big Red One in the Gulf War is interesting in a number of ways. First, it was a singular war that literally no one expected to fight and that produced a singular outcome. Yet Desert Storm—unexpected and apparently decisive—soon faded from public memory. The Army that fought Desert Storm was an anomaly. It was postindustrial. It reflected several dramatic and historically significant trends in military history and the way the United States wages war in the modern era. Yet relatively little is known about the units and troops who fought the war. Some contemporary observers in and out of uniform describe the Army of Desert Storm, disparagingly, as a legacy force. By this they mean that because it was designed to fight the Soviets it was somehow neither modern nor relevant. In some ways this is accurate, but it fails to do justice to the characteristics of flexibility and agility of that Army and the 1st Infantry Division as it was then.

This is a war story, but it begins on a warm spring day in 1970 when a handful of soldiers brought the colors of the Division home from Vietnam. It concludes with a parade on a warm and glorious day of celebration on the Fourth of July 1991. It is the story of the Army's premier division told in the context of the development of the late Cold War Army. I approach this task in the spirit Martin Blumenson proposed in an article he wrote the year I joined the 1st Infantry Division. In it he observed, "Historians, no less than generals are human beings and therefore fallible. They too make errors. But if they do their best and if their motives are honorable, that is all anyone can ask."

I take responsibility for any errors that remain in this work. I have done my best. I pledge that my motives are honorable, if not entirely without bias.

THE 1st INFANTRY DIVISION AND THE US ARMY TRANSFORMED

INTRODUCTION

THIS BOOK IS a narrative history of the 1st Infantry Division from 1970 through the Operation Desert Storm homecoming celebration held on the Fourth of July 1991. It is an account of the Army renaissance in the late Cold War. The Army that overran Saddam Hussein's legions in four days was the product of important changes stimulated both by social change and institutional reform. The 1st Infantry Division reflected benefits of those changes despite its low priority in terms of troops and material. The Division was not an elite formation, but rather excelled in the context of the Army as an institution.

Desert Storm faded from memory nearly as soon as New York cleaned up after the ticker tape parade. In 1998 Alberto Bin, Richard Hill, and Archer Jones published *Desert Storm: A Forgotten War*, an allusion to fading interest. There were a few books that capitalized on the moment. President George H. W. Bush and Brent Scowcroft, on the other hand, collaborated to write *A World Transformed*, a clear-eyed assessment of the war and its context from their point of view. *The Generals' War*, by Michael Gordon and Bernard Trainor, may be the best of the quick histories. Richard M. Swain's *"Lucky War": Third Army in Desert Storm* is a first-rate account of planning and execution of the 3rd Army in the context of the relationships between commanders. Stephen A. Bourque's *Jayhawk: The VII Corps in the Persian Gulf War* is a well-researched and well-written account of the armored corps that made the main effort attack. Tom Carhart's *Iron Soldiers: How America's 1st Armored Division Crushed Iraq's Elite Republican Guard* is the only published account of an army division's fight. Very little has appeared since that initial burst.

After Desert Storm, the country, the Army, and the armed forces generally moved on to other things, including taking a post–Cold War peace dividend; with the dissolution of the Soviet Union, it appeared there remained no existential threats to the United States. In about four years, the active Army dropped from eighteen divisions to ten. The National Guard retained six divisions, but it too declined in size, as did the Army Reserve. All of the Army's components would have drawn down further except for the post-9/11 wars in Afghanistan and Iraq, but even so the Army is now smaller than it has been since the 1930s. Support to the civil authority in the aftermath of Hurricane Andrew, the upheavals in Haiti, and operations in Africa, Bosnia, Kosovo, and Macedonia all took resources and time. In that context, Desert Storm seemed anomalous and irrelevant. For all of these reasons, Bin, Hill, and Jones were right about it being a "forgotten war."

Whatever else it may have been, Desert Storm was not a four-day war. Soldiers, airmen, sailors, and marines began moving to the Persian Gulf in August 1990. Although no shots were fired until five months later, a great many American service members were at war. The notion that Desert Storm was a four-day war is an egregious insult to those who began to fight on January 17, 1991. Nor does this view account for the suffering in Kuwait during the Iraqi occupation. The desert war reflected the end of one era and heralded another; it was, as GEN Frederick M. Franks Jr. observed, a Janus war in which both past and future could be seen. The time is now ripe to revisit Desert Storm.

The 1st Infantry Division fought with modern equipment and with systems well past obsolescence. The application of technologies such as GPS, satellite communications, and precision munitions led some to proclaim Desert Storm the first "information-based" or "knowledge-based" war. Perhaps, but the transition was by no means complete; and that assertion, as I will show, is an exaggeration.

Several major changes to the Army began as the Vietnam War wound down. As a result, the Division that celebrated its return from Desert Storm on the Fourth of July 1991 resembled its predecessor only superficially. In twenty years, doctrine, organization, structure, and the culture of the Army had changed, and as the history of institutions go this change was rapid and remarkable. Ending the draft in 1973 brought tremendous difference to the character of soldiers and soldiering. Draftees fought in the Vietnam War, but not in Desert Storm; no women served in the Vietnam War with the Division, but many wore the patch in Desert Storm.

Of the 1,010 soldiers who served in my tank battalion task force, 1,009 of them were men. The one young woman who fought with us crossed the "death ground," as willingly as any of us to do what had to be done. She and her sisters in other units served ably, as this account will show. One of them lost her life in combat.

In Vietnam, the Division used helicopters for tactical mobility, but it fought on foot. In Desert Storm it fought fully mechanized. By 1990, it was infantry in name only; the Division fought with six tank battalions, three infantry battalions, and a cavalry squadron. It was a highly mobile, lethal force that was able to strike deep.

The change from a conscripted to a volunteer force wrought social and cultural changes as well. Conscripted soldiers were paid little and lived by strict rules that covered everything, including when to be in bed. Draftees could marry only with permission, and as a consequence, few were married. By 1991, married soldiers were the norm rather than the exception. When they deployed, their families often remained at or near the post where they served. The Army found it necessary to help families learn how to sustain themselves and to provide some family support.

Doctrine, training, and weapons changed rapidly in the 1970s and 1980s. The Army, still organized primarily around the defense of Europe in the 1970s, began to shift toward a broader concept of operations in the 1980s. This transition, although incomplete, restored the importance of offensive operations. The Army modernized, employing new weapons; for the first time in history, it had the best tank on the battlefield. It joined a great many other countries in equipping mechanized infantry with a genuine fighting vehicle instead of a personnel carrier. Laser and computer technology altered gunnery and fire support, and training transitioned from task and time to standards and conditions, all supported by first-rate simulations.

These threads are consistent throughout the present volume, but the narrative focuses on the Division from 1990 to 1991. How it prepared, deployed, rehearsed, and fought are important themes and will get their due. Planning, preparation, and execution experienced by those who served, and their families, is the means of delivery; what they experienced and felt is central to this story.

Desert Storm may have been the last large American combat operation fought by the various armed forces separately at the tactical level and jointly at the theater level. For example, tactical air control parties assigned to the Division controlled no close air support sorties during the ground attack because of decisions made at US Central Command (CENTCOM) and within the service components.

Whether or not the air component flew classic air support sorties is more or less irrelevant. What mattered is that no Iraqi aircraft could attack US ground forces. Airmen devastated Iraq's tactical reserves and damaged its strategic reserves. Air power was decisive, and the airmen assured victory; then ground troops completed their work. But the airmen fought with little regard for what tactical ground commanders wanted. In *Every Man a Tiger: The Gulf War Air Campaign*, Tom Clancy notes that "an air force is in the ordnance-delivery business, just as an airline is in the seat-delivery business." Whatever the approach airmen took, air supremacy—and, arguably, Soviet forbearance—assured success however unresponsive the air component appeared to ground commanders.

Naval operations were peripheral, but not irrelevant; maritime power certainly helped enable Desert Storm. The US Transportation Command and its components will be as important in 2090 as they were in 1990. The Division loaded six thousand pieces of equipment and cargo in Houston, Texas, and eighteen ships carried that equipment and cargo to Saudi Arabia. The 3rd Brigade, 2nd Armored Division joined the 1st Infantry Division as its third brigade, also moving by ship from Bremerhaven, Germany. Preparation to deploy and deploying are essential parts of the story.

The narrative begins by reviewing the dramatic changes in doctrine, training, equipping, and culture that occurred in the Army and the 1st Infantry Division in the 1970s and 1980s. Chapters 3–5 discuss the notification, preparation, and deployment including movement from port to northern Saudi Arabia. Chapter 6 focuses on planning and rehearsing, while executing security operations on the border with Iraq. Chapters 7–10 take the reader through the ground war. Chapters 11–13 address war termination and postwar operation and offer reflections on the war.

Although the narrative covers planning from the battalion to the division levels, it covers fighting from the company level and up. Companies and platoons fought the "close" fight directed by battalion commanders. Brigade commanders employed their brigades by designating main effort and maneuvering battalions and supporting arms. The Division planned, directed, and sustained combat operations, but once the two sides made contact there was little the Division and brigade commanders could do to influence the outcome.

Combat operations are complex; events occur simultaneously all over the battlefield. I have organized the chapters in sections to make the narrative easier to follow. During the 2003 invasion of Iraq and the subsequent occupation, the United States captured many Iraqi government and military records. I have used them to recount the Iraqi view at the strategic and operational levels. (Iraqi unit records, if they exist, are not available.) A redacted (US) VII Corps paper and debriefings of prisoners also enabled insight into the Iraqi view of the fight at the tactical level.

After more than two years, the US Army's Records Management and Declassification Agency and Freedom of Information Act offices have provided only one document in response to my request for specific records. Ironically, this document was never classified or restricted, it was one I already had. Army civil servants have been unresponsive, unhelpful, and on occasion deliberately difficult. One actually wanted to know why I needed to know the information I requested. To say the least, this attitude does not reflect the intentions of the law. After not quite two years, the National Archives and Records Administration admitted the records groups I needed were declassified. They advised that I was welcome to come to Maryland to look at the records, but they could not guarantee they were releasable. In early 2017, more than three years after my request, I learned that the Army had indeed declassified the records; alas, this came too late for me. I have relied on records in the hands of private individuals and museums. I believe I have about 70 percent of the applicable 1st Infantry Division records; I have the VII Corps fragmentary orders and essential Third Army memoranda. Newspaper accounts and more than one hundred interviews helped close the gaps.

The 1st Infantry Division enjoys a fabulous history from its first battle at Cantigny, France, in 1918 through its return from Iraq in 2014. The fighting at Desert Storm is not comparable to that at Omaha Beach and other horrific fighting in the Division's nearly one hundred years of service. Desert Storm, although comparatively short, was as violent as late twentieth-century warfare could be. In four days of fighting, the Division suffered eighteen killed and ninety-three wounded; it fought very intense battles on February 24–25, 1991, when it assaulted two Iraqi divisions, and during the night of February 26–27, when it fought elements of the Tawakalna Mechanized Division of Iraq's Republican Guard and its 12th Armored Division.

The 1st Division also played a key role at the end of the war when it seized Safwan after the ceasefire—without firing a shot. At Safwan, 1st Division troops established the site for ceasefire negotiations and supported the operation. The Division remained in the desert to defend Kuwait and provide humanitarian support. In April 1991 the troops began moving south through various stages, arriving back in the Saudi ports in May. There they prepared to ship equipment and returned home. The last 1st Division soldiers to leave Saudi Arabia departed on July 4, 1991, while those at home paraded in celebration at Fort Riley.

Gregory Fontenot
Colonel, USA, Retired
Lansing, Kansas
February 2, 2017

CHAPTER ONE

COMING HOME

Your Army is on its ass.

—Major General Donn Starry to General Creighton W. Abrams

WEDNESDAY, APRIL 15, 1970, dawned clear and cool, promising a glorious spring day. By midmorning the sun shone against a cloudless blue sky. Some six thousand soldiers stood on the tarmac of Marshall Army Air Field at Fort Riley, Kansas, to participate in a historic moment. In formation, facing north, the troops could see bleachers filled with eight thousand spectators. On a rise behind the spectators stood the native limestone buildings of the nineteenth-century cavalry post. Most of soldiers on the tarmac formed under the colors of the 24th Infantry Division (Mechanized). Divided vertically with blue and red, the 24 ID's colors featured a taro leaf. Once known as the Hawaiian Division, it fought across the Pacific Ocean during World War II and the Korean War. More recently, it had returned from service in Germany. The commanding general, MG Robert R. Linville, presided over inactivating the 24 ID and renaming it the 1st Infantry Division (Mechanized). At the conclusion of this ceremony the soldiers on the field would belong to the 1st Infantry Division and the 24 ID would cease to exist. The 24 ID's soldiers stood with the colors of her brigades and battalions in a manner similar to the legions of Rome. Adjacent to the 24th stood a smaller formation of soldiers from the 1st Infantry Division, also known as the Big Red One for the red numeral 1 on their olive drab shoulder patches. These soldiers, led by BG John Q. Henion, had just returned from Vietnam and stood with colors "cased."[1]

Henion assumed command of the Division in Vietnam in March 1970 as an interim commander. He led a guard of honor that would return the Division's colors home after five years of combat. The 347 soldiers represented every unit in the Division. They formed to return home on March 25, 1970, and conducted two departure ceremonies. They left Vietnam on April 5, 1970, and landed at Forbes Air Force Base, Topeka, Kansas, on April 6, 1970.[2]

With nearly perfect symmetry, the ceremony occurred exactly five years and one day since the Army had ordered a brigade of the 1st Division to Vietnam on April 14, 1965. The 2nd (Dagger) Brigade left San Francisco by sea on June 25, 1965. (The remaining two brigades, the division artillery and supporting units, followed in August and September.) In the intervening five years the Division served with distinction. Division units earned two Presidential Unit Citations and six Valorous Unit Awards. Fourteen units earned the Meritorious Unit Award, and nine of them received it twice. Twelve soldiers attained the nation's highest award, the Congressional Medal of Honor.[3] The Republic of Vietnam cited several for gallantry.

In the weeks before the ceremony, the commanders and staff in Vietnam worked to help soldiers at Fort Riley embrace their new identity. They sent gifts of unit patches, crests, and artifacts relating to the 1st Division. Everyone understood this transition was important. Secretary of Defense Melvin Laird, who spoke on behalf of President Richard Nixon, made it clear: "The return of the First Infantry Division from Vietnam to Fort Riley will be followed in the months immediately ahead by the redeployment [returning home] of additional thousands of American troops as our Vietnamization program marches forward."[4] The ceremony demonstrated that President Nixon fully intended to end US participation in the war. Although the ceremony had clear political implications, it was important on its own merits to those who served, including LTG Jonathan O. Seaman, who had taken the Division to Vietnam in 1965. LTG Seaman attended, as did a number of other general officers. It was important to the thousands of spectators including government officials from Kansas. The governor and the state's congressional delegation attended, including the junior senator, Robert J. "Bob" Dole.[5]

This is a narrative of the 1st Division's transition from a draftee light infantry division fighting insurgents and North Vietnamese regulars to a mechanized heavy division of the late Cold War. When the Division deployed to Vietnam, it left its two tank battalions and its armored personnel carriers behind and reverted exclusively to light infantry. In place of the two tank battalions, it received the 1st and 2nd Battalions, 2nd Infantry from the 5th Infantry Division. In Vietnam, nine infantry battalions comprised its maneuver force. They relied primarily on helicopters for mobility, but fought dismounted. LTG Seaman argued successfully for the 1st Squadron, 4th Cavalry (1-4 CAV) to retain its armored vehicles. The 1-4 CAV and a tank company attached from the 2nd Battalion, 34th Armor (2-34 AR) provided tactical mobility and mobile firepower.[6] The story reflects both the post-Vietnam doldrums and the renaissance in the Army that occurred in the 1970s and 1980s. This first chapter assesses the state of the US Army in the early 1970s and the reforms that produced a unit fundamentally different from the one that fought in Vietnam.

In the two decades that followed Laird's welcome home, the Army transitioned to an all-volunteer force, revising and revitalizing tactical and operational doctrine and the way it proposed to fight. To enable units to fight the Active Defense and AirLand Battle (the latter a complex operational doctrine that stressed attacking an enemy throughout its depth), the Army took advantage of new weapons and supporting systems. To prepare units to use those weapons, in accordance with new operational concepts, the Army revolutionized training. Live and constructive simulations replicated high-intensity combat against a well-equipped, well-trained, and well-led enemy. While it is true that this transformation stemmed in part from external stimulus, it is also true that the US Army took the need to change to heart. This chapter and the next follow the transformation of the 1st Division.

The Life of Riley

The Division that deployed to Desert Storm in 1990 bore little resemblance to the one that returned home from Vietnam in 1970. Even as the US Army drew down, the Soviet Union's combat capability continued to grow. The Army returned from Vietnam with a host of problems quite apart from money. Reductions in force (RIFs) ravaged units. The drawdown affected all ranks. When the draftees went, so too did many officers who had hoped to make a career. The RIFs got mostly "chaff," but also some of the "wheat." Further, much of the Army's equipment was obsolescent, if not obsolete, yet there was little money for acquisition. Tactical thinking about conventional war in Europe ossified while the force focused on fighting in Vietnam.

Bedraggled, underfunded, and reeling from social upheaval, the Army struggled in the early 1970s; within and without, it suffered criticism that often proved bitter. Richard A. Gabriel and Paul L. Savage, both Army officers and academics, wrote a scathing criticism of the Army, claiming "disintegration of unit cohesion had proceeded to such an extent that by 1972 accommodation with the North Vietnamese was the only realistic alternative to risking a military debacle in the field."[7] Their criticism was harsh and overdrawn, but nonetheless it was seconded by others. Briefing the results of a study on professionalism in the officer corps, LTC Walter F. Ulmer Jr. provided an equally critical assessment from within. In a briefing with senior officers he reported that "a scenario that was repeatedly described to us during our interviews for this study includes an ambitious transitory commander, marginally skilled in the complexities of his duties, engulfed in producing statistical results, fearful of personal failure, too busy to talk with or listen to subordinates, and determined to submit acceptably optimistic reports which reflect faultless completion of a variety of tasks at the expense of the sweat and frustrations of his subordinates."[8]

The critiques and questions ranged from how the Army could have commissioned the officer who perpetrated the My Lai Massacre to institutional racism. Simultaneously, the Soviet Union seemed ascendant. While the United States was embroiled in Vietnam, the Soviets modernized their enormous Army. The initial success of the Soviet Union's Arab clients in the 1973 Yom Kippur War against Israel suggested hitherto unappreciated capability of Soviet weapons and tactics; the US Army's equipment, tactics, and soldiers, by contrast, seemed inadequate.

Then CPT Bob Killebrew attended the ceremony in 1970 as Linville's aide-de-camp; that summer he would take command of a rifle company. Looking back on that time, Killebrew remarks that "people forget how unbearably screwed up the Army was in 1971, 1972, and 1973";[9] Racial unrest, drug abuse, and indiscipline plagued the Army and the Division. But Killebrew's description applied beyond 1973: the Army struggled through much of the 1970s and 1980s. The Hollow Army, as GEN Edward C. Meyer, chief of staff for 1979–83, termed it, had much to overcome.[10]

After Laird concluded his remarks, the soldiers who began the morning as part of the 24th Infantry Division now passed in review as the 1st Infantry Division and resumed their mission as part of a "dual-based" formation. Under this concept the 1st and 2nd Brigades and most of the support units served at Fort Riley. The 3rd Brigade and a bit more than one-third of the supporting structure served with VII Corps in southern Bavaria. Meeting commitments in Vietnam, NATO, and the Republic of Korea while paying for President Lyndon B. Johnson's Great Society initiatives alongside opposition to the war in Vietnam inevitably led to budget reductions. In 1970 the US Congress reduced the Army budget by 10 percent, reflecting these pressures and the logical consequence of drawing down in Vietnam. The United States could not afford to maintain the number of units it had stationed in Germany. Dual basing enabled the 1st Division to be assigned against the General Defense Plan (GDP) for Europe at reduced cost. It was a practical solution if the Division could return to Germany quickly. When the United States announced its intention to draw down troop strength in Europe, it promised to "[k]eep available substantial reinforcements to supplement a European mobilization." With that proviso, several units returned to the United States in 1968.[11]

To enable rapid return, the Army positioned equipment in Europe sufficient for several US-based divisions, including the 1 ID, which would then deploy only their troops and light equipment. This led to an elaborate system of storage facilities that maintained equipment for use by units arriving from the United States. With perfect, if awkward, precision, the Army called it Prepositioning of Materiel Configured in Unit Sets, and further obfuscated the idea by referring to it as POMCUS. NATO and the United States agreed to exercise the Return of Forces to Germany annually; reduced to the acronym REFORGER, this overarching enterprise became crucial to the Division's training regimen and culture.[12]

The 24th Infantry Division participated in the first REFORGER in January 1969; GEN Lyman L. Lemnitzer, Supreme Allied Commander for Europe, claimed the exercise demonstrated the utility of dual-based forces.[13] Less than five months after the ceremony in April, the 1st Division went to Germany for REFORGER II. There it exercised against simulated enemy Orange forces portrayed by the European-based 3rd Infantry Division. In response to an attack by Orange, the Division crossed the Main River and counterattacked to restore the border between the hostile Orange country and the friendly Blue country. The exercise ended on October 23, 1969, when the Division seized Objective Junction City, named for the garrison town adjacent to Fort Riley. The troops then road-marched to Grafenwohr Training Area in southeast Bavaria, where they test-fired all the major weapons drawn from storage.[14] Afterward, they prepared equipment for storage, returned it, and flew home.

The Army and Air Force provided the bulk of the American resources to REFORGER. Other NATO units and the German Territorial Army played important roles. These exercises rehearsed plans ranging from port operations to rear-area security. NATO executed REFORGER twenty-five times in twenty-four years. In 1973 the Division deployed to Germany twice: the first exercise began in January and the second in October.[15] The program enabled and drove training during the lean budget years of the 1970s and early 1980s. It also drove a boom-and-bust cycle in operations. In the months before an exercise, the Army brought the Division up to strength. Money afforded preparation and training that led to a peak during the exercise. On returning home, the Division drew down as the Army reassigned soldiers to higher-priority units.

This cycle caused enormous turbulence at Fort Riley. CPT Killebrew, commander B Company, 1st Battalion, 2nd Infantry (1-2 IN) through two exercises, recalls that his company "would expand (getting ready to go) and contract (on return) like an accordion." An "endless stream of guys coming back from Vietnam" joined his unit, adding to the turbulence.[16] These veterans, mostly draftees with little time remaining on their two-year service obligation, arrived and served three or four months, then got out. Generally they had no experience with mechanized infantry, so serving at Fort Riley came as shock.

Nevertheless, deployments to Germany brought more advantages than disadvantages. REFORGER shifted dollars to the Division and provided focus. Maneuvering in Germany enabled units to train for their wartime mission, which required thinking through the not inconsequential matters of getting to Germany, drawing equipment rapidly, and getting into position. The benefit is clear from the Army historical summary for 1970, which notes, "Only in exercise REFORGER II was it possible for a full division to maneuver in the field."[17] Deploying to Germany on REFORGER served an essential purpose in the national strategy.

The Army took REFORGER seriously and undertook "Intensified personnel management actions . . . to prepare REFORGER units . . . for their annual exercises."[18] But the exercise was not merely about getting to Germany. The Division exercised its role in the GDP. In *Kevlar Legions*, BG John S. Brown asserts GDP "was not just stacks of papers locked in the safes of obscure staff officers. They were organizing principles for a way of life."[19] The tens of thousands of soldiers who served became oriented to the problem of getting to Europe and getting forward to fight. Planning and exercising emergency deployment became part of the Division's culture.

The scale and scope of the exercise varied, and in some years more troops deployed than in others. Of the 1986 deployment a Division spokesman said that it amounted to, very simply, "its [REFORGER] 20,000 troops and 30,000 tons of equipment being transported from three seaports and 19 airfields."[20] Some ten thousand US Army Reserve and National Guard soldiers assigned to ninety-four different units participated that year. These units ranged from small detachments to the 32nd Separate Infantry Brigade from the Wisconsin Army National Guard. REFORGER demonstrated serious commitment.[21]

Some observers dismissed REFORGER as a movement exercise, but it was far more than that. For a number of years it provided the only venue for large formation training. When the weather permitted, the exercise included off-road, cross-country maneuvers. Umpires, using algorithms and judgment, facilitated the outcome of mock battles. These battles proved of little use in training crews and squads, but provided realistic command and control experience from platoon to corps. LTC Bill Orlov, a Vietnam veteran of the Division, soldiered at Fort Riley from 1975 to 1979; during REFORGER 1979 he commanded an infantry battalion. Of the exercise he remembers, "It was absolutely great . . . you got to soldier, hardly constrained. You got to practice your trade."[22]

LTC Orlov was right when the weather cooperated; but if it did not, the Army abandoned the field training exercise component to avoid excessive maneuver damage. CPT Killebrew experienced open maneuver in REFORGER III, but remembers that, the year before, "we mostly drove down the German highways in column."[23] COL Bill Mullen, who did three exercises, believes they had "great value for logistics and coordination. In terms of maneuver it wasn't particularly valuable."[24] On his third exercise he commanded a brigade in an "Ice REFORGER." Despite the ice, the Division drew its equipment and moved by rail and convoy to assembly areas within five kilometers of the border with Czechoslovakia. That year the field exercise included only command posts; the troops languished in the snow until they could convoy to Grafenwohr.[25]

The speed with which units arrived, drew equipment, and moved to the field was crucial and measured. Standards were exacting. MAJ Stan Cherrie, a tank battalion executive officer, believes he learned valuable lessons in complex logistics of deploying large formations under emergency conditions. Everything was evaluated and timed. "There was a stopwatch on everything that you did."[26] In 1978 Cherrie's battalion loaded ammunition under observation and, of course, it was timed. Speed was essential to execute the defense plan. First Lieutenant Gary Evans, supply officer of the 4th Combat Equipment Company, Europe, noted his company had to "have a mech[anized] infantry battalion on the road in six hours."[27] Units drew gear and moved regardless of conditions. Occasionally the Army added conditions to meet particular objectives. In 1988 the 1-34 AR drew its equipment in full chemical protective gear.

During the 1970s and 1980s, supporting the ROTC summer camp at Fort Riley was the Division's other major annual requirement. Doing so was consistent with the Division motto, "No Mission Too Difficult, No Sacrifice Too Great: As a young officer serving then, I noted in my journal, "The Division revolves around ROTC."[28] Supporting ROTC proved difficult in the early 1970s; the Army reduced in size rapidly, and what little money was available quite rightly went to units in Germany, Korea, Vietnam, and high-priority units in the United States such as the 82nd Airborne Division. As a result, the 1st Division lacked the resources to meet its obligations. Tasked to support an all-arms firepower demonstration for the ROTC summer camp in 1973, I wondered how to get it done. On Sunday, June 17, my company "[m]oved 11 tanks out to Range 29. How we'll get the other 6 required for ROTC tank gunnery I'll never know."[29] Getting tanks to run, let alone function as designed, depended on parts that were unattainable and maintenance support that was sporadic.

"Doing without" served equally well as the Division's motto. GEN Dick Cavazos, a colonel at the time and a brigade commander, claimed he learned the repair parts and maintenance systems just to survive.[30] CPT Killebrew has described his gasoline-burning armored personnel carriers as "ancient"; he had an M114 reconnaissance vehicle for his command track, but he was never able to get it to run during the year and a half he commanded. There was so little money that his unit lacked even the basics; he had no water cans to bring water to the field, and he solved the problem by buying them out of pocket.[31] Soldiers often bought things their unit needed with their own meager resources.

Both LTC Tom Fintel and MAJ Cherrie, his executive officer, had grim memories of maintenance in the 1970s. According to Fintel, "The equipment was in bad shape."[32] CPT Killebrew believed lack of funds was part of the problem, but maintenance suffered too because "none of us knew what we were doing . . . the motor pool was in disarray."[33] Old equipment and ignorance of the system played a role, but money was the chief source of frustration. Cherrie remembers that maintenance involved doing everything except ordering parts.[34] To order parts, units had to have money to commit. Without money, they prepared the paperwork, but did not submit it. If a unit's maintenance paperwork was in order, then it had a good maintenance program whether or not its equipment could move.

LT Jim Bodenheimer, who served as a tank platoon leader in 1981–82, confronted the same problems that Cavazos, Cherrie, Fintel, Killebrew, Orlov, and thousands of others had. His platoon fielded six tanks—five assigned, and one from the battalion headquarters. He could not man all six even if he only put three of the four required crewmen in each. One of his tanks was inoperable when he arrived and still inoperable when he left a year later. Still, he "could see things getting better while I was there."[35]

Lack of money for parts and too few soldiers meant supporting the ROTC required the full attention of one of the two maneuver brigades and much of the rest of the Division. The ROTC cadre ran the camp and led the training, but the Division provided the manpower and equipment to support training the two thousand cadets who came to camp each summer. Because training cadets required demonstrating techniques and firing weapons to standard, supporting summer camp enabled young officers and soldiers to see what right looked like. Further, it gave them a chance to use their equipment and fire their weapons. LTC Orlov remembers that "ROTC was not equipment intensive, but it was personnel intensive." Although the ROTC cadre led training soldiers, the Division did hands-on training with cadets. Orlov concludes that summer camp provided "leadership opportunities to young NCOs [noncommissioned officers]. It was a good mission."[36]

REFORGER and the ROTC defined the routine for more than twenty years. The NATO GDP served as an organizing principal, but less so than for the forward-based 3rd Brigade. As time wore on, the Division "Forward" became more immersed in VII Corps and less connected to the rest of the Division. At least in VII Corps, the forward brigade functioned more like a separate brigade than as part of the Division.

The Transition to the Volunteer Army

Withdrawing from Vietnam ended the cycle of back-to-back tours for career soldiers. Beginning in 1969 the United States moved by stages toward eliminating conscription and converting to a volunteer force. Opposition to the war and conscription ultimately led to ending the draft—with a whimper rather than a bang. On June 28, 1972, Nixon announced that no more draftees would be sent to Vietnam unless they volunteered;[37] by then there were relatively few troops left in Vietnam. The Army became a fully volunteer force on June 1, 1973,[38] and from that point on, those who served did so at will. The story of conversion from a draftee force to a volunteer force is part of the larger story of institutional change.

Historian Henry Gole convincingly argues that GEN William C. Westmoreland understood the Army had to change.[39] Westmoreland returned to the United States in June 1968 to become the Army's chief of staff, and instituted a number of initiatives that stimulated reform and ultimately an Army renaissance. In September 1968 he ordered a study to examine ending the draft and converting the Army to a volunteer force. In October, then candidate Nixon pledged to end the draft if elected president. Maligned for his leadership in Vietnam, Westmoreland got the Army ahead of the wave of social change. LTC Jack R. Butler led the study team that concluded that although a volunteer force was feasible, quality would be at risk; this also reflected the views of the Army leadership, which truly believed conscription was morally preferable to hiring professionals. Butler's study group also reported that pay and benefits would have to improve, and thus a volunteer force would be expensive. Finally, the group warned, "Citizens might tend to no longer feel responsible for the defense of the country."[40] In summation, the idea was feasible, but hard to implement. Although ambivalent, Westmoreland believed his options were limited: either the Army found a way to make the move on its own terms or be forced to do so without control over the process.

Transitioning to the volunteer force occurred during a period of significant indiscipline that reflected both social change and opposition to the war in Vietnam. The Army, as Killebrew observes, was "screwed up" at Fort Riley and overseas.[41] *GIs in Germany*, edited by Thomas Maulucci Jr., and Detlef Junker, analyzes the sources of unrest and indiscipline as they played out in Europe.[42] The dissent and indiscipline they describe occurred among units in the United States as well. Abuse of drugs and alcohol caused still more problems, though Jerry Kuzmarov argues in *The Myth of the Addicted Army* that the drug problem was overstated: marijuana and alcohol were the drugs of choice, but their use was not as widespread as claimed.[43] Overstated or not, officers and noncommissioned officers, from Killebrew up, understood they had a problem. In *The US Army's Transition to the All-Volunteer Force* Robert K. Griffith argues that Westmoreland and other senior officers felt the transition provided the "opportunity to regain control of the Army," and by taking the lead in the move toward a volunteer force, Westmoreland hoped to "shape the direction of the transition."[44]

In January 1970 President Nixon commissioned his own study on a volunteer force; he appointed former secretary of defense Thomas Gates to head the study and "develop a comprehensive plan for eliminating conscription and moving toward an all-volunteer force."[45] Ending the draft was no longer a question of whether to, but when. In October, at the annual conference of the Association of the US Army, Westmoreland announced an "all-out effort in working toward a zero-draft—a volunteer force."[46] He appointed LTG George I. Forsythe Jr. as his special assistant for a modern volunteer Army. Forsythe agreed, though with the proviso that he "would have a role in reforming the Army."[47]

It was Forsythe's job to determine how the Army should make the change. He considered a number of ways to make the transition work, from improving pay to relieving soldiers of the kinds of housekeeping chores that added little to combat effectiveness. Over time, the Army eliminated extra responsibilities such as that of kitchen police (KP) duty. Working half a day on Saturday went by the wayside as well, and eventually pay and benefits improved.

Westmoreland knew that in order to attain the quantity and quality of soldiers required, the Army had to expand access for minorities and women. In June 1971 he ordered LTG Walter Kerwin, the deputy chief of staff for personnel, to determine how to afford better opportunity for ethnic minorities and women. As a first step, Kerwin established an office of equal opportunity, and made choices based on analysis, feeling that equal opportunity was necessary for a volunteer force to succeed. Further, correcting injustice and promoting equal opportunity was essential to good order and discipline in the Army.[48]

How to recruit quality soldiers dominated much of the analysis and initiatives in the early years of the volunteer force. Prior to the transition, the draft accounted for 75 percent of the force. With good reason, Forsythe, like Kerwin, concluded that the Army had to recruit more minorities and women, and that women, especially, were a largely untapped source of high-quality recruits.[49] How the Army worked to recruit women serves to illustrate the transition to volunteers.

BG Mildred I. C. Bailey, a career officer in the Women's Army Corps, became its director on August 2, 1971; in her first meeting with Kerwin, he told her "to change the image of women in the Army."[50] Although he gave no specific guidance, Bailey understood he wanted more women in uniform, and with broader responsibilities. To do so required major changes in the Women's Army Corps, which was an institution of the Army but in many ways separate. Notably, the Corps did not respond with the enthusiasm feminists expected. The official history of the Corps described Bailey's dilemma simply: if the innovations the Army and feminists desired came to pass, "it would mean the elimination of the Corps. The new director was caught in the crossfire of fights *against* overexpansion and *for* the survival of her Corps."[51] However she felt, Bailey did as she was asked; overseeing the expansion of the both the number and roles of women in the Army. The pace has not slackened since. BG Mary E. Clarke, the last director of the Women's Army Corps, saw the Corps' dissolution as an artifact of the Army's commitment to "total integration of women in the United States Army as equal partners."[52]

The "integration" of women into the Army was crucial to sustaining the volunteer force. It succeeded, but not without difficulty. Fundamental changes to any culture are fraught with friction. Integrating women required fundamental changes in Army and American culture, and these changes did not occur readily. Change arrived at the 1st infantry Division in the form of 2LT Eugenia Thornton; the first woman assigned to the Division, she joined the Army because she perceived better opportunity in uniform than in the civilian workforce based on her experience job hunting following graduation from Washington College in Chesterton, Maryland. Everywhere she went, interviewers had steered her toward "women's" work,[53] but she had other ideas.

Serendipity played a role in Thornton's choice: not long after graduation, she attended a sorority sister's wedding reception at Fort Myer, Virginia, where she met COL Don Rosenblum, another wedding guest. During the course of casual conversation he suggested an Army career. Thornton liked the idea. She had already visited an Army recruiter, who had suggested enlisting, but she wanted to go to officer candidate school. Inspiration came from an advertising handout calling for female officers to serve in public relations. She vividly recalled the photo in the brochure showing a young enlisted woman at an anchor desk. Behind a camera in the foreground was a female officer holding a clipboard, and the tagline for the brochure read, "Begin as an executive." COL Rosenblum offered to look into it.[54]

He called a few days later and asked whether Thornton wanted to enlist or take a direct commission. She chose to take a commission and became part of the "first group of women to be commissioned in the Women's Army Corps, but detailed into previously all male branches."[55] Although technically assigned to the Women's Army Corps, she became an adjutant general corps officer.

Second Lieutenant Thornton arrived at Fort Riley following graduation from the Defense Information School in August 1973, excited about "beginning as an executive." She soon discovered that no one was happy to see her, because "they didn't think I should be in the Division."[56] Thornton bounced around the garrison in several jobs, while men who should have known better sought to have her replaced. Finally she returned to the Division, because the Army overruled those attempting to obstruct her assignment. As she puts it, the Army's response to staff officers' efforts to resist was "Thornton's your man."[57] The next crisis came when she deployed to Germany on REFORGER. She believes that she deployed with the Division's Public Affairs office because MG Gordon R. Duquemin made it so. According to Thornton, Duquemin "was a good man. He had the vision to know in which direction we needed to go if we went to VOLAR [volunteer Army]; we had to get women."[58]

In any case, she deployed along with PFC Connie R. Kalvick, who was assigned as her driver. The two caused quite a sensation wearing combat uniforms and using equipment with which neither had much familiarity. Wearing field gear was beyond the pale for women in 1973. Both wore shoulder length hair that protruded from their helmets; they looked out of place, but someone had to be first. They were photographed frequently, interviewed often, and occasionally permitted to do their actual jobs. Together they produced brief media buzz on two continents.

On October 13, 1973, toward the end of the first week of the maneuver, the Division suffered a horrific accident: a US Air Force fighter-bomber literally flew into the back of an M113 armored personnel carrier. The impact killed both aircrew and two soldiers, and injured two other soldiers and the farmer in whose field the crash occurred. Thornton was at the crash site when MG Duquemin arrived and called her over. She presumed he intended to send her away, but "instead, he said, 'keep the civilians and the press off the site until the Division MPs [military police] arrive.' And then he left." Thornton remained at the scene of the catastrophe with feelings of "horror," but "also *elation*, because I had been treated as a *professional*."[59]

Some of Duquemin's subordinates did not afford her that courtesy, however. Not long after, a male officer assaulted Thornton in her room in Grafenwohr. She never reported the incident because she believed nothing would be done. Her assessment is a sad indictment of the way she was received. Surprisingly, however, she blamed neither the Army nor the Division, but only the officer. She believes that what happened to her "was not a wart on the 1st Division."[60] And, in any case, she still felt serving in the Army was better than outside, because she was paid "exactly what the men got paid."[61]

Women had arrived, and they persevered. At least fifty women wore the insignia of the Big Red One on the next REFORGER. Integrating women and transitioning to the volunteer force worked, and it occurred rapidly; in a few short years, the quality of soldiers and their willingness to serve improved. Reflecting on his service at Fort Riley in the 1980s, Cherrie believes there were three reasons that things got better: "Vietnam was gone, number one. Training had a new emphasis and the volunteer Army brought the 'want-to' factor."[62] Cherrie's assessment is an exemplar of the improvement in quality that others also perceived.

Westmoreland and his team went beyond finding a way to do without the draft—*far* beyond. They reflected on incidents of fragging, lack of cohesion, and just plain bad tactical decisions in Vietnam. Most of the team members Westmoreland assembled to run the Army had served in World War II and/or Korea. All of them had served in Vietnam, but the key members "came from a generation that had cut its teeth in battalion command in World War II."[63] They believed the volunteer force needed better-prepared leadership than they had seen in Vietnam. Typical of that group, GEN Fred C. Weyand recalled that he and GEN William E. DePuy shared a determination to "establish some sort of formal education system for NCOs."[64] There was consensus among those at the top on the need to improve education and personnel management not only for NCOs but also for warrant and commissioned officers. They took these tasks on simultaneously with moving to the volunteer force, integrating women, and establishing an equal opportunity system to assure the Army got the best people and the most from them.

What Westmoreland began took several years to implement. Transition to the volunteer force, changes to the personnel system, reforming training, and professional military education took time. Westmoreland's successors as chief of staff, including Creighton W. Abrams, Weyand, Bernard W. Rogers, and Meyer, continued the effort that produced the Army of Desert Storm. The renaissance moved in fits and starts, but began with recognizing the need to change; training in race relations and in the prevention of sexual harassment developed concurrently. Changes to the personnel system included providing commanders the means to rid the volunteer force of young men and women who lacked aptitude, motivation, or proved incapable of adhering to standards. Finally, Westmoreland and his successors worked to improve the quality of leadership at all levels.

The study on military professionalism Westmoreland commissioned identified the basic complaint about officer leadership. Weyand and DePuy sought to correct leadership deficiencies they perceived in the NCOs with whom they had served in Vietnam. They aimed to restore the NCO Corps to the prestige it enjoyed traditionally. In Vietnam, polarization had occurred that pitted young draftees and junior officers against older NCOs and senior officers. Many draftees thought pejoratively of their sergeants as "lifers." Racial tensions played a role as well in the diminution of NCO authority in the Army.[65] The Army took several important steps to restore the standing of the NCO Corps officers. Westmoreland's predecessor, Harold K. Johnson, actually took the first step, establishing the position of sergeant major of the Army on July 11, 1966. His rational was simple: "if we are going to talk about the noncommissioned officers being the backbone of the Army, there ought to be an established position that recognizes that this was in fact the case."[66] Westmoreland followed up in 1971, directing the *Noncommissioned Officer Education and Professional Development Study.*[67]

The resulting Noncommissioned Officers Education System led to a professional military education system for sergeants that emulated the essential parts of the officers' education system. These included basic, advanced, and senior schools; the basis for the first two tiers already existed. In July 1972 the Army authorized the Sergeants Major Academy, whose first class met in January 1973. The Army reformed the NCOs personnel management system in

1973.[68] At Training and Doctrine Command, DePuy worked to create a culture in which "officers command units and NCOs command soldiers."[69]

The Army moved to improve officer leadership by incorporating recommendations made in the *Study on Military Professionalism* and other War College reviews of officer leadership undertaken in the early 1970s. Reforming officer education and management came later. In 1978 the Army's *Review of Education and Training of Officers* resulted in important changes to command tenure, staff officer education, and preparation for command.[70] By the mid-1970s transition to the volunteer Army was well under way, with efforts to assure that volunteers would be better led than their predecessors in Vietnam.

Transition to an all-volunteer force radically affected how things got done at Fort Riley. First and foremost, the character of soldiers and the culture of units changed. To Cherrie, the difference between troops in the early 1970s and those he encountered in 1978–79 at Fort Riley was simple. The soldiers with whom he served at Fort Riley in the 4th Battalion, 63rd Armor "wanted to be soldiers." Reflecting on his time commanding a cavalry troop in Bad Hersfeld, Germany, in 1970, he notes that he had both drug and race problems; by contrast, in 1978–79, "company commanders were not saddled with drug rehab and race issues."[71] Cherrie, who served as a recruiter in this era, believed recruiting high school graduates made a big difference as well. But recruiting high-quality soldiers was difficult at first.

To meet recruiting goals, the Army took several important and unexpected steps in addition to integrating women and appealing to minorities. In some cases these units assumed responsibility for advanced individual training; the 1 ID was one such unit.[72] Unit-of-choice recruiting, which allowed units to recruit their own soldiers, was another initiative to assure adequate end strength. The Division failed to take advantage of this opportunity. Mullen, who ran the Division's unit-of-choice operation, found it difficult because of starting late; he remembers, "We damned near turned the division inside out to get things going. We had to crash an established market [i.e., one established by other Army units]. We were at Fort Riley, and that made things hard when competing."[73] Mullen felt that because Fort Riley was literally in the middle of Kansas, it did not compare favorably to places like Fort Lewis, Washington, or even Fort Hood, Texas. But ultimately, the transition worked, and over time the quality of soldiers improved.

The transition strained the Division, but in the end the draftees went their way. The Army treated volunteers differently from how it had draftees. It eliminated things like "bed check," the six-day workweek, and other irritants; the idea was that those who volunteered deserved to be treated like professionals. In principal, the institution sought to replace soldier labor with civilians where it made sense. For example, KP duty, the bane of every soldier who did not relish scrubbing pots and pans or mucking out grease sumps, was something that young soldiers had heard of but never had to do.[74] The idea, again, was to free volunteers from tasks that did not contribute to making them more effective in combat.

All was not rosy, however. Pay and benefits for draftees were low, and they had no option but to live in barracks and could marry only with permission. Their pay was adequate—but only barely so—because they lived in barracks and ate in mess halls. Volunteers had the right to marry, but pay did not keep pace with the transition, so young soldiers who married suffered. The *Fort Riley Post* published stories highlighting the trials and tribulations of young married couples. The front-page story "Fort Riley GIs Are Moonlighting to Off-Set Low Pay and Inflation" appeared on Friday, October 12, 1979; the second page included a story with an equally grim headline, "Annual Military Pay Raise Isn't Enough: Wives Work to Help Make Financial Ends Meet."[75] Just over two months later, the *Fort Riley Post* repeated this theme in "Food Stamps Could Ease Inflationary Pains: Many Junior Enlisted Families Are Barely Surviving,"[76] a story in which one young soldier claimed, "Christmas was nothing but pure hell for us. I had to moonlight on weekends and even my wife who's six months pregnant had to get a part time job just to get through December."[77]

The transition to the volunteer force and preparing for disparate missions occurred in an atmosphere laden with the knowledge, or at least the perception, that the Army lost the Vietnam War. No amount of blaming civilian leadership or claiming "We were winning when I left" relieved the sense of failure. Many soldiers addressed the matter head on. GEN Maxwell D. Taylor, who commanded the 101st Airborne Division during World War II, posed the question directly in an article aptly titled, "Is an Army Career Still Worthwhile?" Taylor perceived threats to core "values, interests and assets" even as the Army confronted an "expanding scope of security requirements." He found plenty of reasons for a career to be rewarding, but asserted the institution needed to "restore pride and confidence in the Army itself and in doing so regain the national prestige which it has enjoyed in better days." Taylor had no patience for grousing about easing traditional standards. As he put it, "I must say I cannot get excited over such current issues as the length of a soldier's hair."[78]

Taylor was right: the Division had more important challenges than haircuts. Despite his optimism, there was plenty of angst about the transition. MG Aubrey S. Newman, a decorated World War II soldier, had reservations. He recalled the small volunteer force that served between the wars fondly and noted that "no one dislikes the draft more than I do." He added, however, that the "great Roman Empire disintegrated when it tried to buy enough soldiers to defend it."[79] Younger officers had concerns also. In March 1971 CPT Killebrew argued in *Army* magazine the difference between draftees and volunteers would be fundamental. Discipline, he believed, came from "*wanting* to soldier; cooperation from *having* to." These, he thought, were the differences between draftee soldiers and volunteers.[80]

The Yom Kippur War, October 1973

Although the Israelis eventually turned the tide, the Yom Kippur War surprised them, frightened the West, and shocked the US Army. Supported by two thousand artillery pieces, the Egyptian Army executed a dazzling assault across the Suez Canal; more than thirty thousand troops crossed in the first four hours, and about eight hundred tanks crossed the first night. The Egyptians then expanded the bridgehead under an umbrella of integrated air defense, effectively denying the Israelis local air superiority. The Egyptians repulsed a number of Israeli counterattacks with old T-55 tanks, a few modern T-62 tanks, and a great many Sagger antitank missiles. The Syrian Army attacked simultaneously in the Golan Heights. With no depth, the Israelis fought desperately to prevent Syria from gaining the Heights and, therefore, access to Israeli's interior.[81]

Equipped and trained by the Soviets, the Egyptians, Iraqis, and Syrians nearly won the day. Soviet equipment and doctrine enabled them to challenge Israel's survival.[82] Subsequent analysis of captured Soviet equipment revealed material advantages over contemporary US equipment. The T-62 armed with a 115-millimeter main gun, the Sagger antitank missile, and Soviet air defense weapons caused considerable alarm. The Sagger, in particular, concerned tankers. Even before the analysis was complete, the speed of the initial assault and the tempo of operations shocked Western observers.

That point was not lost on the Division operating in Germany on REFORGER V. The Yom Kippur War, coupled with the defeat in Vietnam, galvanized the Army. GEN DePuy, who commanded the 1st Division in Vietnam, played a key role in reforming the Army in the light of the Yom Kippur War; GEN Creighton Abrams chose him to become the first commanding general of US Training and Doctrine Command (TRADOC) on July 1, 1973. That fall, Abrams charged DePuy with studying the Yom Kippur War and determining what lessons might be learned. DePuy and others at TRADOC, including MG Donn Starry and MG Paul Gorman, acted on ongoing assessments of Yom Kippur and the Army. Together they drove intellectual change within the Army that percolated down to the lowest level. MG Gorman commanded an infantry battalion in the Division during DePuy's tenure; MG Starry commanded the 11th Armored Cavalry Regiment and worked with DePuy in Vietnam. They knew each other well and knew how to work together.[83]

Their collective assessment of the Yom Kippur War inspired several ideas. First and foremost, the Israelis demonstrated on the Golan Heights that well-trained, motivated soldiers could fight and win even when outnumbered. The success the Egyptians enjoyed with the Sagger suggested that armor no longer enjoyed a decisive advantage over infantry, even in open terrain. Slowing down the tempo of mounted attacks seemed crucial. Finally, they believed defeating the Soviets would require new equipment coupled with changes in training, manning, and doctrine.

Under DePuy, TRADOC began and sustained revolutions in doctrine and training. Concepts conceived or taken advantage of by TRADOC resulted in fielding the so-called Big Five weapons systems (the Abrams tank, the Bradley infantry fighting vehicle, the Black Hawk utility helicopter, the Apache attack helicopter, and the Patriot air defense missile system), a revolution in training and dramatic doctrinal change. These five weapons systems closed the gap or surpassed contemporary Soviet capability.

The M1 Abrams tank brought improved fire control, armor, and a fully stabilized turret enabling it to fire on the move. Although not recognized at the time, both the M1, with a 105-millimeter main gun, and the M1A1, equipped with the 120-millimeter main gun, surpassed contemporary Soviet tanks. Equipped with both a twenty-five-millimeter chain gun and a highly lethal antitank missile, the Bradley leaped ahead of the Soviet infantry fighting vehicle. The Apache clearly exceeded the capability of the Soviet M1-24 Hind attack helicopter. The Black Hawk greatly increased US Army lift and was fast. The Patriot missile system literally gave the US Army the capability of hitting Soviet missiles in flight. Synergy resulted from these weapons systems and doctrine that exploited the advantages they provided. Training concepts that aimed at performance rather than repetition further improved combat capability.[84]

The training revolution took off with the establishment of TRADOC. MG Gorman, the first deputy chief of staff for training at TRADOC, led the effort. In 1973 the Army trained much as it had in 1917, using a model called the Army Training Program, which specified the number of hours that should be spent on various tasks and emphasized repetition. Gorman reoriented training on performance against a standard defined within specific conditions. This required no extra dollars, but did require thinking about what must be done and under what conditions. Analysis of war plans led units to identifying key tasks, which constituted a mission essential task list (METL). The unit METL drove training objectives. The system required units to shape training around their METL. This systems approach also affected Army education.[85] MG Gorman's initiatives stemmed from analysis of combat operations. Analysis produced tasks, conditions, and standards.

TRADOC also set out to improve the means to evaluate performance. Within a few years, the Army went from tanks blinking headlights at each other to simulate firing to training with sophisticated simulators. Improved simulation began with a system called Real Train. It employed scopes and number placards. Soldiers used the scopes to read the numbers from target vehicles or soldiers. The "firing unit" called in the number it saw to umpires who "killed" the target. To describe this as ineffectual is an understatement, but Real Train improved on what had preceded it—which was nothing. Units learned to use subcaliber munitions instead of expensive main gun ammunition, and that enabled more frequent practice and improved outcomes. In the late 1970s and early 1980s, the Army developed high-resolution training aids. Finally, in this new approach, after-action reviews became central to training. Units learned to examine performance against discrete standards in order to see how they might improve. Performance-oriented training, better simulations, and after-action reviews dramatically improved training and altered the culture of the Army.

The Israeli experience further concentrated thinking about training. On January 8, 1974, Gorman published a report titled *How to Win Outnumbered*, a masterpiece of analysis that is compendious but succinctly done and easy to follow. Focused on tank tactics and gunnery, the report assessed how units selected, trained, and rewarded tank commanders. Gorman considered differing approaches to gunnery, such as accuracy versus speed, and reviewed factors that produced success in World War II and two Arab-Israeli wars. Gorman concluded that the way the Army selected, trained, and rewarded tank crewman was, to put it mildly, inadequate.[86]

Having identified the problem, Gorman then set about describing the solution, proposing a number of steps to improve tank crew performance. Developing a live-simulation system was essential. He argued convincingly that if the Army continued to depend on an "umpire-based" assessment of combat effects, it would lose the next fight. He wondered in his report just how umpires could assess night fights, since Field Manual (FM) 105-5, the Army manual for maneuver control, was, he noted, "mute" on that problem. He advocated the development of the Multiple Integrated Laser Engagement System (MILES) as a means to improve tactical techniques. His confidence in MILES led Gorman to assert that its effect would be similar to the brilliant innovation in naval gunnery simulations inspired by Sir Percy Scott more than seventy-five years earlier. He proposed a master gunner program to teach hand-selected sergeants how their equipment worked to a level of detail to qualify them as master trainers. He also advocated, unsuccessfully, for careful selection of tank crewman and tank commanders in particular.[87]

The MILES eye-safe laser system replaced Real Train and earlier simulations. MILES had two parts—the eye-safe laser and sensor belts. It could be mounted on virtually all weapons from rifles to tank cannons. The eye-safe laser linked directly to the firing mechanism of a weapon; when a soldier pulled a trigger he fired the laser. Potential target vehicles and soldiers wore sensors that could measure light impulses recording either a near miss or a hit. Near misses caused the MILES to emit an audible warning to a soldier wearing a harness. A similar system on combat vehicles warned crewmen of near misses. If the sensor belt detected a hit, the crew got an audible signal. A rotating amber light illuminated, showing others the vehicle had been hit. A hit on a vehicle or an individual soldier disabled their laser so the "dead" could not fire. MILES enabled tactical engagements that rewarded effective maneuver and tactical techniques. It was not perfect, however: it could not be used to simulate artillery and, furthermore, was too expensive to install on all vehicles or even all weapons. Still, MILES and the training system developed by TRADOC fundamentally changed maneuver training.[88]

MILES became the centerpiece in live maneuver training, but for the Army to gain the most benefit it needed both better training venues and better means to assess training. The development of maneuver training centers brought improved simulations and improved assessment of METL-driven training together. MG Gorman's analysis and other initiatives in training ran parallel to dynamic doctrine. DePuy's analysis of the Yom Kippur War drove his thinking about the direction in which he should take doctrine. To him, the Yom Kippur War "dramatized the difference between the wars we might fight in the future and the wars we had fought in the past. It drew our attention to those differences and to the current state of affairs in the U.S. Army."[89]

In Europe the Army would have to "fight outnumbered and win," and DePuy wondered how that could be done. Tempo and echeloning forces seemed to be at the heart of the Soviet operational concept. Soviet units planned to move steadily and rapidly, with two echelons in each formation from the battalion level up. At each level the first echelon sought weak points to be exploited by the second. Echelons provided flexibility, coupled with the capacity to mass at critical points. TRADOC's evaluation of Soviet concepts and the Yom Kippur War drove training, doctrine, and combat development explicitly.

The 1976 edition of FM 100-5, *Operations*, bore DePuy's name and reflected what he learned about the Soviets and from the Yom Kippur War. He believed tanks operating in combined arms formations would be decisive; the answer to the Soviet system included highly proficient tank crews mounted in superior tanks coupled with the means to disrupt the Soviet operational tempo. MG Starry, commanding the Armor Center at Fort Knox, Kentucky, reached similar conclusions. GEN DePuy ordered him and other branch school commandants to develop a series of "how to fight" manuals, while DePuy himself focused on the capstone manual, FM 100-5. A small group of young officers, known for the building in which they worked as the Boat House Gang, wrote the new operations manual under DePuy's personal supervision.[90]

Coordinated closely with the German Army, what emerged was called the Active Defense. It focused on winning the first battle of the "next war." Critics of the new manual abounded; they found it too tactical, too focused on defense, and oriented too much on Europe. These criticisms were not unfounded, but the controversy and the "how to fight" manuals stimulated productive debate about doctrine, how to fight, and how to train.[91] GEN DePuy appreciated the debate, though later he voiced some reservations of his own. In a 1985 letter to historian Paul Herbert, he felt the "greatest error we made was to focus 100-5 on the tactical level as opposed to the operational level."[92] Perhaps, but it inspired soldiers at all levels to think and argue about doctrine. LTG William G. Carter III, who served as DePuy's aide and in the Boat House Gang, spoke for many when he claimed it changed the Army.

In 1977 Starry took command of TRADOC from DePuy and built on the foundation his old commander had laid. He published the result in *AirLand Battle* in 1982.[93] The work represented evolution rather than revolution: Starry's thinking reflected his work with DePuy, his experience commanding V Corps in Europe, and Meyer's directives as the Army chief of staff. GEN Meyer wanted doctrine less focused on Europe and applicable worldwide. The AirLand Battle concept also reflected collaboration with the Air Force Tactical Air Command; conceptually it stressed four tenets: agility, initiative, depth, and synchronization. The new doctrine restored the balance between offensive and defensive operations. By the time TRADOC published the second iteration, the Big Five weapons systems were being fielded.[94]

DePuy's initiatives on training were as dramatic as those on doctrine. He began the work of establishing the National Training Center (NTC) at Fort Irwin, California. GEN Bernard W. Rogers commanded US Army Forces Command, while DePuy served at TRADOC. Rogers sought to acquire land that would afford training large formations. Commanders at Fort Carson, Colorado; Fort Hood, Texas; Fort Lewis, Washington; and Fort Riley were actively seeking to expand their posts for the simple reason that they had inadequate maneuver space. What had been adequate for World War II combat systems was no longer enough given the increasing range and capability of the modern weapons systems. Gorman led the way at TRADOC; in 1977 he published a statement of principle in a concept paper, *Toward National Training Centers (NTCs) for the U.S. Army*. He aimed to go beyond the need for additional training land toward a system and site that would enable joint training with the Air Force.[95]

The Army opened the NTC at Fort Irwin in 1980, but without full instrumentation, MILES, or adequate equipment and with too few troops to simulate an opposing force. The training center lacked adequate numbers of observer-controllers and visually modified vehicles to simulate enemy equipment. Even so, from the outset the NTC dramatically altered the quality of training, which now took place in the Mojave Desert against an increasingly good opposing force and under observation twenty-four hours a day for a period of two weeks. To describe the NTC as demanding fails to get at the outright shock soldiers experienced in their first rotation. Before the NTC, Army training test exercises might last three days. In the 1st Division, the pattern was to defend for two days and counterattack on the morning of the third day. Field training exercises at Fort Riley seldom lasted more than a week, and REFORGER field training exercises lasted two weeks with a two-day break in the middle. But at the NTC, units "fought" for two weeks without respite; the duration alone changed assumptions about how to train. Finally, rotations at the NTC occurred in a truly barren wasteland the size of Rhode Island.

The NTC opposing force replicated a motor rifle regiment of the Soviet Army. It used Soviet tactics and norms. The "regiment" was fast, good, and deadly with MILES. Routinely, the opposing force closed on Blue defensive positions at fifty kilometers per hour; at that rate, enemy formations traveled one kilometer in eighty seconds. Typically the regiment attacked at high speed, blanketed in smoke, on the heels of a ferocious artillery bombardment sprinkled with chemicals. Blue units had to fight with their hatches closed or hunkered down in holes wearing full chemical protective gear. The opposing forces never attacked without thorough reconnaissance and therefore often knew how Blue proposed to defend and made preparations to counter it. They were brilliant on offense and just as good on defense.[96]

Improved simulations like MILES and the NTC changed the 1st Division in an elemental way. By the mid-1980s, the Division's units were old veterans of the place, but the first opportunity to train at Fort Irwin came in February–March 1980. That first event occurred in a joint exercise called Gallant Eagle. CPL Edward Galvin concluded, "You really couldn't ask for a better place for training. It's so far from civilization and so huge you can do a lot of things out here without bothering anybody."[97] COL John Renner commanded the 1st Brigade on a rotation in January 1982. He described the rotation as "tough realistic training—One of the most important things about the training there [NTC] was the troops got to find out what it really looks like to see the 'enemy' approaching. All of a sudden from out of the smoke they appear—a mechanized rifle regiment. Now every member of the task force knows what he has to fight."[98]

There was more to the Mojave Desert than the regiment: the very terrain of the High Desert was itself a dangerous enemy, hot during the day and cold at night. PFC John Duel described the environment succinctly: "Where else can a person work in 120 degrees during the day and play at night with scorpions and rattlesnakes?"[99] Exertion quickly produced fatigue and desperate thirst. Sergeant Stephen D. Bender, a scout in the 5-16 IN, noted, "The toughest part of being out here for me was surviving in the desert, conserving water and overcoming the elements."[100] Rollover accidents in dry washes killed and injured soldiers. The flash floods that invariably followed the slightest rainfall washed away gear and threatened lives. Accidents occurred during live-fire training, and aircraft crashed. Surviving at the NTC was not a sure thing. Navigating in the desert in the day was difficult and at night nearly impossible. in response to the question, "Where are you?," LID (short for "lost in the desert") became a common retort. Living in the desert required soldiers to develop skills as mundane as taking the time to stay clean, layering clothes, and keeping arms, face, and neck protected from the sun. Sunglasses evolved from stylish accouterment to absolute necessity.

Renner's description of the regiment in the attack is accurate, but fails to capture the chilling fear it induced. In November 1984 a group of students from the School of Advanced Military Studies visited the NTC to observe training. The intent was to demystify the NTC, and it was a necessary move, because the reputation of the place had become legendary. It was perceived to be dangerous as hell, the opposing force unbeatable, and the observer-controllers implacable; it frightened more than it inspired. In the wee hours of the morning, the group clambered into the back of high-mobility, multipurpose wheeled vehicles (HMMWVs) for the ride out to a place called Red Pass. There they would observe a 1 ID unit: Task Force 4-37 AR, commanded by LTC Al Cocks.

Cocks commanded a balanced task force assigned to COL Tom Fintel's 2nd Brigade; it included two tank companies from his battalion and two companies of mechanized infantry. With its back to Red Pass, Cocks's task force defended to prevent enemy penetration of the pass. The regiment would come from the west and southwest. The enemy regiment fielded forty T-72 tanks and three motorized rifle battalions mounted on 120 BMPs. Each BMP (Boyevaya Mashina Pekhoty, a Soviet infantry fighting vehicle) carried an infantry squad and a seventy-three-millimeter rocket grenade launcher. The T-72s mounted a 125-millimeter cannon and two machine guns.[101] LTC Cocks had thirty M60 A1 tanks and twenty M113 armored personnel carriers. The M113s carried his infantry squads. The enemy outgunned and outnumbered the task force.

For the rubberneckers, two things about the trip to Red Pass stood out. First, it took forever. The small convoy drove some fifty kilometers to reach the ridge just south of the pass. The HMMWVs labored as far up the ridge as they could; the group members climbed the rest of the way in the dark, mostly by feel, until they reached the top of the ridge, stiff with cold, just as the horizon began to show light. The temperature was in the low thirties, with the wind blowing at about thirty kilometers per hour. It was, needless to say, bracing.

Finally in position, the group overlooked the approach to Task Force 4-37 AR's defense. The regiment could emerge from "the Valley of Death" or it could come through "the Whale Gap"; the latter consisted of open desert floor between a barren rocky terrain feature known as Furlong Ridge and the Whale, a dark basalt hump that rises two hundred feet or more. The regiment could, if it chose, come over the Whale, although the climb and descent were perilous.

Shortly after sunrise, the opposing forces regiment fired a simulated artillery barrage that covered the defenders; realistic flashes, smoke, and explosions produced by simulators made it look and sound like the real thing. Fortunately for Cocks and his troops, the winds that morning precluded the regiment from firing chemicals or smoke as the wind blew toward the attackers and would have hindered their attack. As the artillery impacted, the regiment thundered through the gap in a cloud of dust. As it emerged, it changed from columns of battalions to two battalions forward, abreast in columns of companies. Inexorably it bore down on Cocks's tankers and infantrymen. Those looking on were struck dumb. There seemed no chance for the Blue forces, whose artillery and return fire seemed sparse by comparison to the enemy. Yet Cocks's troops began to score kills. Amber blinking lights appeared among the enemy tanks and BMPs. Soon the whole valley floor was alive with gun flashes, "near miss" flashes, and steady blinking lights showing kills. The young officers gawking at the fight could make no sense of it. Nor could they glean any understanding from listening to the fight on a tactical radio set to Cocks's command frequency. Yet, within a half an hour, Cocks's tankers and infantrymen fought the regiment to a standstill. The regiment withdrew sullenly, firing as it went and covered by artillery.

It was astounding. Few units ever won at the NTC, and even fewer observers got to see it happen. Cocks's victory was sufficiently unusual that the 1st Infantry Division made a point of bragging about it. In its commentary on the rotation in the required annual historical summary, the Division claimed, "An outstanding performance was turned in by the 4th Battalion, 37th Armor. The 4th Battalion won more engagements than it lost and was part of the first task force to stop the OPFOR's [opposing force's] regimental attack."[102] How had this happened? According to Fintel, there were three answers. First, Cocks was an outstanding commander. Second, the training revolution had occurred. Fintel believed "old Willie DePuy" started it all; as he puts it, "By this time training task analysis had taken root out in the ranks and in the boondocks . . . the training revolution had been inculcated."[103] The NTC and the tenets of AirLand Battle focused training. Cocks "worked on the problem" at Fort Riley. Solving the problem of how to fight at the NTC would not translate everywhere, but the method of task analysis would. COL Fintel believed the transition to the volunteer force was the third reason Task Force 4-37 AR had stopped the regiment. The troops were motivated. Hard training resonated with volunteers.

The NTC had a profound effect on those who went, but the results seemed less than the Army promised. Pundits and politicians wondered what good it did since the enemy won more fights than it lost. Colonel William Darryl

Henderson wrote a detailed criticism of why the NTC did not produce the intended improvement. Chiefly, he argued, Army personnel practices precluded developing the kind of cohesive units that he claimed the Soviets and Israelis produced.[104] What the critics, including Henderson, missed is bound up in the aphorism, "Hard training, easy war." Army doctrine set a high standard. A win for a task force in the attack required it to take its objectives and remain more than 70 percent strength. In the kind of high-intensity fight simulated at the NTC, Blue often took its objectives, but not often with more than 70 percent of its strength remaining. Moreover, training ramped up or down according to performance. If a unit did well on a mission, the operations group could, and usually did, make the next one more demanding. The place was designed to train to "muscle failure." LTG Crosbie Saint, who commanded III Corps at Fort Hood, is alleged to have said of the NTC that it was "individual training done collectively." Saint was correct, but so were the critics of the personnel system. The NTC and maneuver training centers built at Hohenfels, Germany, and ultimately at Fort Polk, Louisiana, had positive benefits, but cohesion and stability in units were problems that could not be resolved at training centers.

Fighting combined arms in a live combat simulation is difficult; managing the same fight with live ammunition is an order of a magnitude more difficult. The NTC included a live-fire corridor that enabled task force offensive and defensive operations, employing small arms, missiles, tank guns, artillery, and close air support, all orchestrated by the task force staff. Live-fire training at the NTC raised the level of stress on units to that just short of combat. The live-fire phase usually lasted four days. Each unit began by drawing ammunition under combat conditions. Battalion support platoons and brigade support battalions had to upload tons of ammunition. While receiving, breaking down, and loading ammunition, the training unit built a range to calibrate weapons. Junior leaders did this work while commanders and staff reconnoitered the ground and planned. No time could be wasted, because the unit could be ordered to execute before they completed the mundane tasks of loading ammunition and calibrating weapons.

Each live-fire exercise required an attack that might take most of a day and require one or more breaching operations involving demolition. The attacking unit had to coordinate fires and bound artillery forward, all the while receiving fires with appropriate signatures from a sophisticated target array. Sometime during the operation a remotely piloted Soviet fighter made of Styrofoam would attack, necessitating the task force to defend itself. On completion of the offensive mission, the task force would transition to the defense and prepare to receive a regimental attack. This mission had slightly fewer variables as Drinkwater Lake (dry except after rainfall), the chief feature of the defensive zone, divided the avenue of approach in two.

The simulated regiment could come with a battalion on either side of the lake or stack the deck on one side or the other. There were three likely courses of action. This was no comfort to the defender, as this phase included both day and night attacks. This increased the possible permutations. The target array was extensive enough to give a compelling impression of movement as targets came up and went down. With almost no discernible ripple, enemy tanks and BMPs appeared to move toward the defenders. The regimental attack in live fire was every bit as impressive as the one Cocks's troops confronted in "force on force" operations.

LTG William G. Carter III led units at the NTC, served as assistant division commander for maneuver of the 1 ID through several rotations, and later commanded the NTC. Because of the live-fire capability at Fort Irwin, he believes the NTC taught lessons that "couldn't be learned at [the Combat Maneuver Training Center in] Hohenfels or in REFORGER."[105] Units did improve despite the claims of pundits and critics. More important, the experience shaped attitudes and directly affected how soldiers understood standards. Fort Irwin provided a crucible of bloodless combat. The benefit to soldiers individually is difficult to measure. Several generations of soldiers from private to colonel learned what getting it right looked like and how to train to get it right. Their colleagues in Europe enjoyed a less sophisticated but very capable training center in Hohenfels. Generally four battalion task forces from the 1st Infantry Division trained at the NTC each year. Going to Fort Irwin became as much a part of the routine as deploying on REFORGER.

The revolution in training changed everything the Division did, including the mundane activities associated with the emergency deployment imagined in the dual-basing concept. In the early 1970s, REFORGER preparation focused on rehearsing the equipment draw and installing batteries to prepare equipment for use. Often the Division carried rehearsal to the level of moving troops to Forbes Air Force Base to practice loading aircraft. These were elaborate efforts.

But all that changed with the training revolution. The Division initiated Operation Manhattan, a deployment exercise that incorporated the new concepts. It included rehearsing specific parts of REFORGER and training troops and staff in the processes required. In October 1979, during the first Manhattan exercise, twelve thousand troops played their parts in simulating every aspect. Army Reserve and National Guard units participated to practice their mobilization tasks.[106] The Division brought in observer-controllers from the 4th Infantry Division, which had just returned from deploying to Germany; they assessed operations during the exercise and supported after-action reviews. The training methodology applied to all tasks.[107]

The 1st Division trained to develop expertise in tactical river crossings and the reduction of obstacles. Both of these tasks required careful coordination, combined arms fires, expert engineers, and considerable control. Sequencing equipment and positioning supporting arms in the right place could be exercised, critiqued, and improved upon at Fort Riley with or without an opposing force. To practice river crossings, the Division used an inlet of Milford Lake adjacent to the training reservation at Fort Riley. Generations of soldiers have made the crossing at Milford Lake or smaller gaps inland. Rivers abounded in Europe, so practicing made sense; the Division trained to assault across rivers or gaps at least annually. CPT Dennis Rogers explained the need to practice crossing annually when he pointed out, "The majority of our soldiers have never participated in this type of exercise."[108] Recurring training events compensated for the normal turnover in soldiers.

Training on new equipment became part of the routine as the fruits of the Army's modernization effort became available. The Army fielded equipment with priority to Europe and units slated for rapid global response, such as the XVIII Airborne Corps. The Division was well down the priority list; new equipment trickled in beginning with the Multiple Launch Rocket System in 1983. By dribs and drabs the rest of the Big Five and other new equipment arrived. In 1986 the Division received the improbably named heavy expanded mobility tactical truck, which received the equally unwieldy abbreviation HEMTT, pronounced "him-it." The HEMTTs were a godsend, replacing many of the ancient cargo trucks and vastly improving cross-country mobility. Still, the Division retained many 2.5-ton, six-wheeled cargo trucks, modified with a few changes from the "deuce and a half" of World War II fame; some of these had achieved antique status, having been in active service for more than thirty years. Even so, things were definitely getting better.

The quality of equipment, troops, training, pay, and morale improved in the late 1970s and 1980s. The Division would not complete modernizing until early 1991 in the port at Ad Dammām, Saudi Arabia, but it was well on its way. The 347 soldiers who brought the colors home in 1970 would recognize unit names and the old "deuce and a half," but little else. Cobra helicopters, towed 105-millimeter howitzers, M-48 tanks, draftees, and rampant race and drug problems were long gone. The 1st Division was home, relatively well equipped, and combat ready.

NOTES

1. "Redesignation Completed," *Fort Riley Post*, April 17, 1970, 1–2. As I was a student at Kansas State University, I attended the ceremony that day. As the son of a soldier who lived at Fort Riley, I watched both the 1st and 9th Infantry Divisions deploy from Fort Riley. Two of my high school classmates' fathers

died serving in Vietnam. My own father eventually deployed to Vietnam as the 1SG of the HHC 11th Aviation Group in the 1st Cavalry Division. The Vietnam War and the 1st Infantry Division were always on my mind from the beginning until the war finally ended. See also Headquarters, 1st Infantry Division, *Operations Plan Keystone Blue Jay: Redeployment of the 1st Infantry Division: AAR*, APO 96345 (Fort Riley, KS: Headquarters, 1st Infantry Division, 1980).

2. Headquarters, 1st Infantry Division, *Operations Plan Keystone Blue Jay*, appendix 1 to annex J, J-1-1–J-1-5; see also tab A, appendix 1 to Annex J, J-1-A-1–J-1A-2.

3. James Scott Wheeler, *The Big Red One: America's Legendary 1st Infantry Division, from World War I to Desert Storm* (Lawrence: University Press of Kansas), 2007, 413–18. For the unit citations and Medals of Honor, see *Army Digest*, June 1970, 71. In March 2014 SGT Candalerio Garcia Jr. became the twelfth Big Red One soldier awarded the Medal of Honor for combat action in Vietnam.

4. Secretary of Defense Melvin Laird, quoted in "Redesignation Completed," 1.

5. Fort Riley Public Affairs videotape of the Division review conducted on July 4, 1991, First Infantry Division Museum at Cantigny.

6. Wheeler, *The Big Red One*, 418; see also chaps. 14–16 on the Division's operations in Vietnam.

7. Richard A. Gabriel and Paul L. Savage, *Crisis in Command: Mismanagement in the Army* (New York: Hill and Wang, 1978), 9. See also Maureen Mylander, *The Generals: Making It, Military-Style* (New York, Dial, 1974); Josiah Bunting, *The Lionheads* (New York: Braziller, 1972); Cincinnatus [pseud.], *Self-Destruction: The Disintegration and Decay of the United States Army during the Vietnam Era* (New York: Norton, 1981); and Dave Richard Palmer, *Summons of the Trumpet: US-Vietnam in Perspective* (San Rafael, CA: Presidion, 1978).

8. LTC Walter F. Ulmer Jr., quoted in James Kitfield, *Prodigal Soldiers: How the Generation of Officers Born of Vietnam Revolutionized the American Style of War* (New York: Simon and Schuster, 1995).

9. COL (Ret.) Robert B. Killebrew, telephone interview with the author, February 10, 2014. Killebrew graduated from the Citadel but could not take a commission due to a medical problem. He subsequently enlisted and was granted a direct commission in the Infantry. He served with the 1st Infantry Division from 1970 to 1973, briefly as a battalion operations officer in the 1-34 IN, and as aide-de-camp to MG Robert R. Linville and commander of B Company, 1-2 IN.

10. Meyer made his pronouncement in 1979 and stood by it. He elaborated on his views in an interview with David Hartman on ABC's *Good Morning America* on December 5, 1990. See also General Edward C. Meyer, *E. C. Meyer,*

General United States Army, Chief of Staff, June 1979–1983 (Washington, DC: US Department of the Army, n.d.), 146; the publication comprises extracts from speeches, letters, and papers during Meyer's tenure as chief of staff.

11. Excerpt from defense posture statement of Robert S. McNamara, *Army Digest*, July 1968, 44. See also Dr. S. L. R. Harrison, "America's 1969 Option," *NATO's Fifteen Nations*, April–May 1969, 14–16. In 1971 Secretary Laird floated the idea of reducing the Army to eleven divisions by withdrawing both Korea-based divisions. See "11 Division Plan Is Quashed," *Army*, December 1971, 6.

12. John Sloan Brown, *Kevlar Legions: The Transformation of the US Army, 1989–2005* (Washington, DC: Center of Military History, 2011), 35–37. See also bulletin, *Army Digest*, July 1968, 44; in the bulletin, the *Digest* claimed the Army would maintain "substantial reinforcements to supplement a European mobilization."

13. Lyman L. Lemnitzer, "Fulcrum for the Future," *NATO's Fifteen Nations*, February–March 1969, 72.

14. Walter Bohm, *REFORGER: Vehicles of the US Army during Exercises, "Return of Forces to Germany,"* vol. 1, *1969–1978* (Erlangen, Germany: Tankograd, 2008), 16–20. Bohm published a short history and photo essay of every REFORGER exercise from the first to the last, which occurred in 1993.

15. Bohm, *REFORGER*, 1:9, 21–27.

16. Killebrew interview.

17. William Gardner Bell, ed., *Department of the Army Historical Summary, Fiscal Year 1971* (Washington, DC: Center of Military History, 1973), 11.

18. Ibid., 10.

19. Brown, *Kevlar Legions*, 36. REFORGER and the GDP were not merely academic exercises for those who "lived" them.

20. Ginger Brown, "Guard/Reserve Vital to Mission." *Fort Riley Post*, January 3, 1986, 1.

21. Ibid.

22. COL (Ret.) William S. Orlov, telephone interview with the author, January 17, 2014.

23. Killebrew interview.

24. BG William J. Mullen III, telephone interview with the author, January 20, 2014. Mullen is a legacy of the 1st Division in more ways than one. He was born in Plattsburg, New York, where his father was assigned to the 26th Infantry Regiment, one of the 1st Infantry Division's original regiments. In 1966–67, during his second tour in Vietnam, Mullen commanded a rifle company in the 1-2 IN in the Big Red One. He commanded 1-2 IN in Fort Riley in 1972–73. He returned to command in the 1st Brigade in 1984, departing in 1986. Finally, he commanded the 1st infantry Division (Forward) in Germany in 1989–91.

25. Mullen interview. The author served as the Division's plans officer for that REFORGER.

26. BG (Ret.) Stanley F. Cherrie, interview with the author, Leavenworth, KS, February 11, 2014.

27. First Lieutenant Gary Evans, quoted in Ed Aymar, "Caring for POMCUS a Continuous Job," *Fort Riley Post*, October 16, 1981, 14.

28. Author's personal journal, May 17, 1973. The author trained as a cadet at the 1970 ROTC Advanced Camp and supported training as a lieutenant in 1971, 1973, and again in 1986 and 1988 as the executive officer of the 1st Battalion, 34th Armor and as executive officer of the 1st Brigade, respectively.

29. Ibid., June 17, 1973. June 17 was a Sunday and my wife's birthday. No one who has served in the Army will find missing holidays and family occasions unusual.

30. GEN Richard E. Cavazos, comment to the author numerous times during the two years we worked together in the Battle Command Training Program. Cavazos also commanded the 1st Battalion, 18th Infantry of the 1st Infantry Division in Vietnam.

31. Killebrew interview.

32. COL (Ret.) Arthur T. Fintel, telephone interview with the author, January 31, 2014.

33. Fintel and Killebrew interviews.

34. Cherrie Interview.

35. LTC (Ret.) Jim Bodenheimer, interview with the author, Leavenworth, KS, January 29, 2014.

36. Orlov interview.

37. Bell, *Historical Summary,* 1.

38. Ibid., 1–4.

39. Henry G. Gole, *General William E. DePuy: Preparing the Army for Modern War* (Lexington: University Press of Kentucky, 2008), 214.

40. Robert K. Griffith Jr., *The U.S. Army's Transition to the All-Volunteer Force, 1968–1974* (Washington, DC: Center of Military History, 1997), 18; regarding Westmoreland, see 17–18.

41. Killebrew interview.

42. Thomas Maulucci Jr. and Detlef Junker, eds., *GIs in Germany: The Social, Economic, Cultural and Political History of the American Military Presence* (Cambridge, MA: Cambridge University Press, 2013).

43. Jerry Kuzmarov, *The Myth of the Addicted Army: Vietnam and the War On Drugs* (Amherst: University of Massachusetts Press, 2009).

44. Griffith, *Transition*, 283.

45 Ibid., 35

46. Ibid., 52.

47. Ibid., 53.

48. Bettie J. Morden, *The Women's Army Corps, 1945–1978* (Washington, DC: Center of Military History, 1990), 261.

49. Ibid., 256. See also Griffith, *Transition*, 18.
50. Morden, *Women's Army Corps*, 259.
51. Ibid., 257; emphasis in the original. The Army dissolved the Women's Army Corps on April 28, 1978.
52. Ibid., 393.
53. COL (Ret.) Eugenia Thornton, telephone interview with the author, May 5, 2014. COL Thornton edited her original interview via e-mail on August 14, 2014.
54. Ibid.
55. Ibid.
56. Ibid.
57. Ibid.
58. Ibid.
59. COL (Ret.) Eugenia Thornton, "I'll Shoot You Myself, First: One Woman's 27 Year Journey in 'This Man's Army,'" undated PowerPoint presentation that Thornton presented for the first time in 2000. See also Bohm, *REFORGER*, 1:28–30. The maneuver phase of REFORGER V, known as Exercise Certain Charge, and the Yom Kippur War both started on October 9, 1973.
60. Thornton interview.
61. Ibid.
62. Cherrie interview.
63. Gole, *DePuy*, 214.
64. Ibid., 247.
65. Ernest F. Fisher Jr., *Guardians of the Republic: A History of the Noncommissioned Officer Corps of the US Army* (New York: Ballantine, 1994), 330–36. Fisher's work on Army NCOs is the best of its kind.
66. Harold K. Johnson, quoted in Fisher, *Guardians of the Republic*, 344.
67. This was directed by US Department of the Army, Deputy Chief of Staff for Personnel, Noncommissioned Officer Education and Professional Development Program, letter of instruction, June 16, 1971. See also Continental Army Command, "Noncommissioned Officer Education and Professional Development Study," unpublished manuscript, Defense Technical Information Center, Fort Monroe, VA, 1971.
68. Sergeant Major of the Army (Ret.) William G. Bainbridge and Colonel (Ret.) Karl R. Morton, "The US Sergeants Major Academy: The Founding," *Army*, January 2005, 41. Regarding the Enlisted Personnel Management System, see Fisher, *Guardians of the Republic*, 365.
69. Gole, *DePuy*, 247.
70. US Department of the Army, *A Review of Education and Training of Officers* (Washington, DC: US Department of the Army, 1978). Most often referred to simply as the RETO study, this effort affected all aspects of officer training

and education. See also US Army War College, *Study on Military Professionalism* (Carlisle Barracks, PA:, US Army War College, 1970).

71. Cherrie interview.

72. See Griffith, *Transition to the All-Volunteer Force*, 185–94, regarding efforts to meet quality and enlist women, and 235–36 on meeting quality while maintaining racial balance. In 1972 the Army commissioned a study titled *Army 75* that saw women as the means to reduce the burden of the draft and ultimately as part of the volunteer force. The author supported Advanced Individual Training within the provisional company of the 1-63 AR. In 1976, LTC Bill Orlov commanded a Provisional Training Battalion to train infantry advanced individual training prior to assuming command of the 1-28 IN. Orlov interview.

73. Mullen interview.

74. See Griffith, *Transition to the All-Volunteer Force*, 32–33, on recruiting incentives, and 81–84 on general efforts to improve conditions, including eliminating KP duty. The *Historical Summaries* also report incremental improvements to pay and other incentives. For a general overview of the events that produced the Army of Operation Desert Storm, see Frank N. Schubert and Theresa L. Kraus, eds., *The Whirlwind War* (Washington, DC: Center of Military History, 1995). See also Griffith, *Transitions*, chap. 9.

75. Gary Bloomfield, "Fort Riley GIs Are Moonlighting to Off-Set Low Pay and Inflation," *Fort Riley Post*, October 19, 1979, 1; Jana Easterly, "Annual Military Pay Raise Isn't Enough: Wives Work to Make Financial Ends Meet," *Fort Riley Post*, October 19, 1979), 2.

76. Gary Bloomfield, "Food Stamps Could Ease Inflationary Pains: Many Junior Enlisted Families Are Barely Surviving," *Fort Riley Post*, January 11, 1980, 1.

77. Ibid.

78. General Maxwell D. Taylor, "Is An Army Career Still Worthwhile?," *Army*, February 1973, 11, 12, 13.

79. Major General Aubrey S. Newman, "The Forward Edge: A Volunteer Army Is More Fun, But . . . ," *Army*, April 1971, 59–60. "The Forward Edge" is a column that Newman wrote for several years. Newman distinguished himself in the Pacific during World War II.

80. Capt. Robert B. Killebrew, "Volunteer Army: How It Looks to a Company Commander," *Army*, March 1971, 21; emphasis in the original.

81. For the Egyptian point of view, see Lt. General Saad el Shazly, *The Crossing of the Suez* (San Francisco: American Mideast Research, 1980); el Shazly served as chief of staff of the Egyptian Forces. See also Bren Adan, *On the Banks of the Suez: An Israeli General's Personal Account of the Yom Kippur War* (London: Arms and Armour, 1980). Adan commanded one of the three Israeli divisions

in the Sinai. Avigodor Khalani, *Heights of Courage: A Tank Leader's War on the Golan* (London: Greenwood, 1984), is a chilling account of the ferocity of the fighting on the Golan Heights. It is worth noting that Donn Starry wrote the foreword for Khalani's book. With respect to US Army lessons learned, see Paul Herbert, *Deciding What Has to Be Done: General William E. DePuy and the 1976 Edition of FM 100-5, Operations*, Leavenworth Paper 16 (Fort Leavenworth, KS: Combat Studies Institute, 1988).

82. There are ample sources for those interested in the three major stimuli that drove the Army in the early years following the end of US combat role in Vietnam. See, for example, John Romjue, *From Active Defense to AirLand Battle: The Development of Army Doctrine, 1973–1982* (Fort Monroe, VA: Historical Office, United States Army Training and Doctrine Command, 1984); Major Robert A. Doughty, *The Evolution of Tactical Doctrine, 1946–76*, Leavenworth Paper 1 (Fort Leavenworth, KS: Combat Studies Institute, 1979); General Paul F. Gorman, *The Secret of Future Victories*, III-31-III-41 (Fort Leavenworth, KS: US Army Command and General Staff College Press, 1994); and Colonel Richard M. Swain, comp., *Selected Papers of General William E. DePuy* (Fort Leavenworth, KS: Combat Studies Institute, 1994). The clearest statement of how the Yom Kippur War affected DePuy's thinking, and therefore the Army's, is General William E. DePuy, "TRADOC Leadership Conference, 22 May 1974 [at Fort Benning, Georgia]: Keynote Address by General William E. DePuy," in *Selected Papers of General William E. DePuy*, 113–20.

83. On the general rationale for the reorganization, see John Romjue, Susan Canedy, and Ann W. Chapman, *Prepare the Army for War: A Historical Overview of the Army Training and Doctrine Command, 1973–1993* (Fort Monroe, VA: Office of the Command Historian, 1993), 5–8.

84. The acquisition of the Big Five began prior to the foundation of TRADOC. TRADOC developed the concepts and structure to employ them.

85. See Romjue, Canedy, and Chapman, *Prepare the Army for War*; Gorman, *Future Victories*; Brigadier General Robert H. Scales Jr., *Certain Victory: The United States Army in the Gulf War* (Washington, DC: Office of the Chief of Military History, 1993), chap. 1; General (Ret.) Paul F. Gorman, *Strategy and Tactics of Learning: The Papers of General Paul F. Gorman USA (Ret)*, http://usacac.army.mil/cac2/CSI/docs/Gorman/index.asp; and Swain, *Selected Papers of General William E. DePuy*.

86. Deputy Chief of Staff for Training and Schools, US Army Training and Doctrine Command, *How to Win Outnumbered*, January 8, 1974, http://usacac.army.mil/cac2/CSI/docs/Gorman/03_DCST_1973_77/05_74_TanksWinOutnumbered_8Jan.pdf. This unsigned report of only seventeen pages proved an important benchmark in training both mounted and dismounted soldiers. See also the DCST section in Gorman, *Strategy and Tactics of Learning*, http://usacac.army.mil/cac2/CSI/docs/Gorman/03_DCST.asp.

87. Deputy Chief of Staff for Training and Schools, US Army Training and Doctrine Command, *How to Win Outnumbered.*

88. More detailed descriptions of MILES can be found on the Internet; see, for example, "Instrumentable - Multiple Integrated Laser Engagement System (I-MILES)," http://asc.army.mil/web/portfolio-item/instrumentable-multiple-integrated-laser-engagement-system-i-miles/.

89. Gole, *DePuy*, 240.

90. See Herbert, *Deciding What Has to Be Done.*

91. See Romjue, *Active Defense*; and Schubert and Kraus, *The Whirlwind War.*

92. Gole, *DePuy*, 262.

93. US Department of the Army, *Operations*, FM 100-5, 1982 ed. (Washington, DC: US Department of the Army, 1982). After Starry retired, the manual went through another iteration that was published in 1986.

94. See Romjue, *Active Defense*; and Schubert and Kraus, *The Whirlwind War.*

95. Anne W. Chapman, *The Origins and Development of the National Training Center, 1976–1984* (Fort Monroe, VA: US Army Training and Doctrine Command, Office of the Command Historian, 1992). See also Anne W. Chapman, *The National Training Center Matures, 1985–1993* (Fort Monroe, VA: US Army Training and Doctrine Command, Military History Office, 1997).

96. A great deal has been written about the National Training Center, but the two books that stand out are James R. McDonough, *The Defense of Hill 781: An Allegory of Modern Combat* (Novato CA: Presidio, 1988); and Bolger, *Dragons at War: Land Battle in the Desert* (New York: Ballantine, 1986).

97. CPL Edward Galvin, quoted in Lew Parson, "Gallant Eagle 80: This Is the Best Exercise of Its Kind—No Better Place to Train," *Fort Riley Post*, April 4, 1980, 1.

98. COL John Renner, quoted in Beth Howell, "Every Devil Strike Soldier Learned Something," *Fort Riley Post*, February 12, 1982, 1. This was also the first time the Division used MILES that the NTC issued. Fort Riley received MILES for home station training later, and had it by at least 1984. "MILES gunnery" became an issue: using MILES required bore sighting the laser, an entirely different skill from bore sighting for "real" gunnery.

99. PFC John Duel, quoted in Larry Rosenberg, "121st Hard At It in NTC Desert," *Fort Riley Post*, August 26, 1983, 1.

100. SGT Stephen D. Bender, quoted in Robert Henson, "Devil Strike XIII: Soldiers Comment on NTC," *Fort Riley Post*, March 18, 1988, 1.

101. The opposing forces regiment fought with Sheridan light tanks and M113 armored personnel carriers modified to resemble Soviet combat vehicles.

102. 1st Infantry Division, *Fort Riley KS, Home of the 1st Infantry Division (Mechanized): Annual Historical Supplement FY 85* (Fort Riley, KS: 1st Infantry Division), 1-1.

103. Fintel interview.

104. William Darryl Henderson, *The Hollow Army: How the US Army Is Oversold and Undermanned* (New York: Greenwood, 1990).

105. LTG William E. Carter, telephone interview with the author, December 5, 2013.

106. Jana Easterly, "Operation Manhattan, We Had It All Together," *Fort Riley Post*, October 26, 1979, 4–5. Operation Manhattan went through various iterations through 1986, after which the name changed to DEPEX (short for deployment exercise). After the REFORGER mission ceased in 1993 this effort lapsed also.

107. Easterly, "Operation Manhattan."

108. CPT Dennis Rogers, quoted in Mark Seminara, "River Crossing Exercise Challenges Soldiers," *Fort Riley Post*, September 13, 1985, 1.

CHAPTER TWO

VICTORY IN THE COLD WAR

The Cold War was a huge part of my life, because of my service in Germany.

—Commanding General Gordon R. Sullivan

When LTC Al Cocks's task force defeated the opposing forces regiment at Red Pass, it did so "unmodernized." This euphemism explains nothing and everything. Though organized in accordance with the latest concept, Army 86, it fought without the required weapons systems. It fielded M60 tanks and M113 armored personnel carriers. It should have been equipped with M1 Abrams tanks, Bradley infantry fighting vehicles, and other new equipment. Units in Europe began fielding the M1 in 1980; the Bradley, new tactical transports, radars, radios, and other equipment came soon after. The 1st Infantry Division (1 ID) did not complete fielding the M1 until the late fall of 1988 and the Bradley in the spring of 1990.

By the mid-1980s, the renaissance stimulated by refocusing on defending Europe and the observations of the Yom Kippur War was well under way. Promulgating the Active Defense doctrine achieved both more and different results than GEN William E. DePuy had imagined. It immediately provoked controversy and debate that led to dramatic improvement in doctrine, organization, and training. There are debates over when the Renaissance period in Europe began, who started it, and where it came to fruition. There can be none about the Army's intellectual renaissance. The renaissance DePuy and others began accelerated during the 1980s.

This chapter weaves the narrative of intellectual and material growth with the history of the 1 ID. It is information essential to understanding how the Division operated and looked during Operation Desert Storm. Mechanized and partly modernized, the Division immersed itself in a system of training based on task analysis. Collectively it thought critically about how it trained, and it developed systems it could apply at Fort Riley, Kansas, in order to make the transition to a combat role in the desert comparatively easy. Finally, the culture of the Division was reflected in a number of ways, both positively and negatively, in its motto—"No mission too difficult, no sacrifice too great. Duty first!"

From Active Defense to AirLand Battle

As commander of the Armor Center, MG Donn Starry played a central role in developing the Active Defense. In the summer of 1976 Starry moved from theory to practice when he was promoted to the rank of lieutenant general and assumed command of V Corps in Germany. On arrival, he began to teach Active Defense to his corps and to consider how to employ it in the Fulda Gap area of the border between West and East Germany. The General Defense Plan (GDP) presented V Corps with three very difficult problems: it had to fight outnumbered, it had very little depth, and it had to defend multiple enemy avenues of approach. Soldiers and pundits alike believed the Fulda Gap to be the most problematic area along NATO's front.

The Fulda Gap lies between the Knullgebirge, a range of low hills to the north, and the Vogelsberg Mountains to the south. It is rolling terrain that affords maneuver space for armor. If the Soviets attacked and penetrated V Corps defenses in this area, they could drive southwest to Frankfurt am Main. LTG Starry thought carefully about what was called the central battle in V Corps' sector. He led V Corps commanders and staff officers "through a series of terrain walks and simulations . . . trying to figure out if, in fact, we could defend successfully using the Active Defense doctrine and the weapons systems we had."[1]

Starry and his officers literally walked the terrain, focusing at company level. He heard from every maneuver company commander how they proposed to fight. These walks were colloquia, where he used the Socratic method to teach and learn. The lethality of modern weapons, combined with the size and expected speed of the Warsaw Pact forces, complicated the defense. The 1976 edition of Field Manual (FM) 100-5 devoted the entirety of its chapter 2, "Modern Weapons on the Modern Battlefield," to implications of increased lethality on the battlefield that had debuted in the Yom Kippur War; it forced commanders to consider the discrete components of combat against the Soviets or a Soviet-equipped force. Starry brought his own analysis to the problem and combined it with a detailed study of Soviet operational norms.[2] He made certain these studies made their way down to company commanders, and he discussed his analysis with them during these terrain walks.

Starry's terrain walks and the studies he disseminated led commanders to prepare carefully. In V Corps, officers and senior noncommissioned officers (NCOs) read the operations manual and analysis of the Yom Kippur War. They also studied the "how to fight" manuals as they were published. Preparing to brief Starry forced each commander to undertake a detailed analysis of the tactical problem he confronted. After careful study and multiple walks around their sector, they developed their concept of operations, supported by graphics depicting how they proposed to fight; these were called battle books. For those who prepared them, battle books forever changed how they thought about tactical problems; terrain analysis, weapons ranges, and weather all received due consideration in these richly illustrated works.

Starry encouraged an analytical approach to tactics. He believed that if commanders understood Soviet tactics and weapons as well as they knew their own, they could solve the conundrum of how to fight outnumbered and win. Careful analysis drove tactical thinking in the Corps. He called the result battle calculus. For example, a company commander faced with a regimental avenue of approach determined the rate at which the enemy could appear based on Soviet norms and the terrain. Armed with that understanding, he could emplace obstacles and weapons systems so he could, in Starry's words, "service the target array;"[3] this approach fit nicely with the model that emerged from the training revolution. This kind of study enabled units to derive discrete tasks and the conditions under which they might have to be done, but the approach had a downside in that it could, and sometimes did, lead to formulaic approaches. In the hands of those able to think critically, however, battle calculus was a useful framework.

In the end each company commander discussed with the corps commander how he proposed to defend. Starry took these briefings personally and led the discussions that followed. Company commanders briefed an august gathering including Starry and his commanders (battalion, brigade, and division) as well as a gaggle of senior staff officers. The terrain walks were high adventure for company commanders. Starry managed to make the experience nonthreatening to those who undertook to tell him how they would solve the problem of fighting outnumbered by five or more to one. The chief lesson was that it could be done, but there were too many bad guys coming too fast to guarantee winning.[4]

LTG Starry had continued to think deeply and critically about his perceptions of the "central battle" and his analysis of the Yom Kippur War, his thinking maturing beyond his original assessment. After walking the ground, he concluded that the problem in Europe could not be solved at the tactical level. The Active Defense was necessary, yet still insufficient; there were simply too many Soviet units coming on too many avenues of approach to defeat them tactically. Equally important, the Soviet and Warsaw Pact armies arrayed formations beyond the range the Corps could "see"—that is, beyond the range of available detection capabilities. To beat them would require attacking in depth, destroying enemy units not yet at the front, and disrupting their operational tempo. Ultimately, Starry concluded that the Active Defense was too focused on the tactical fight.

After a year at the V Corps, Starry succeeded DePuy at US Training and Doctrine Command (TRADOC). His new boss, GEN Edward C. Meyer, Army chief of staff, shared Starry's reassessment of the doctrine. Meyer also thought that the Active Defense focused too narrowly on Europe and was too heavily oriented on defense. In Starry he found a like-minded and productive colleague. Neither man rejected DePuy's work; instead they built on it. This resulted in two rewrites of FM 100-5 in 1982 and 1986. The rewrites were prompted by a new concept called AirLand Battle, a view that addressed a broader threat than the Soviets in Europe and described the "threat against which the concept is designed is typified by the Warsaw Pact in Central Europe, the larger aggregations of mechanized forces in the Middle East, or the threat from the north in Korea."[5]

Now promoted to full general, Starry altered the direction of force structure and eventually force design as he revised doctrine. He recognized that the Army had a serious structure problem: international commitments and contingency plans required more divisions than were available. President Richard Nixon's Guam Doctrine postulated a global strategy that required the nation to sustain one and a half wars simultaneously. And yet, despite this far-ranging strategy and global commitments, the US Department of Defense planned to reduce the Army from nearly 1,000,000 active-duty soldiers organized in sixteen divisions to 785,000 in thirteen divisions. Chief of Staff Creighton Abrams believed this reduction in troop strength would place the new strategy at risk, so he sought permission to organize sixteen active-duty divisions by reallocating soldiers from garrison and institutional units. The secretary of defense concurred, and the US Congress raised no objection, so Abrams moved to execute.[6]

But stripping soldiers from garrisons and institutional units was not enough; Abrams ordered TRADOC to redesign structure to create sixteen divisions within the authorized strength.[7] TRADOC had a head start, because DePuy had been looking at how to alter force design to take advantage of the Big Five weapons systems. He believed that weapons capabilities should drive force design, and the new weapons that constituted the Big Five—the Apache attack helicopter, the Black Hawk utility helicopter, the Patriot air defense missile, the Bradley infantry fighting vehicle, and the M1 tank—were on the way.[8] DePuy organized a group of officers from TRADOC and his subordinate schools. They produced the Division Restructure Study, which examined how best to organize around the new weapons.

The Division Restructure Study focused on a new design for what they called the heavy division, and optimized that division to fight in Europe against the Soviet and Warsaw Pact armies. There were a number of very good ideas that emerged from the study. It recommended increasing the leader-to-led ratio by making tactical formations smaller. This sounds counterintuitive given the frequently heard criticisms about the Army being top-heavy, but improved communications and weapons systems produced high lethality even at the small-unit level. In this light, driving the leader-to-led ratio up made sense given the potential for operating across broader fronts and in noncontiguous positions. A fixed brigade combat team of three tank battalions and two mechanized infantry battalions formed the core of the heavy division's capability. To increase available firepower, the study recommended increasing the number of howitzers in an artillery battery from six to eight and the number of batteries in a battalion from three to four. The addition of a combat electronic warfare intelligence battalion and a radar target acquisition battery improved the standard division's ability to "see deep." The study recommended the addition of a chemical company to provide chemical decontamination support and generate smoke to screen or obscure. The 1st Cavalry Division at Fort Hood, Texas, became the test base for the newly designed heavy division in 1979.[9]

Soon after he assumed command of TRADOC, Starry visited a provisional unit that was testing the ideas of the Division Restructure Study. On the basis of his visit he concluded that the study had been done too quickly and with insufficient analysis. Furthermore, he decided to shift the organizing principle from weapons systems to concepts. Equally important, he wanted to shape the concepts against "a threat laydown validated by the intelligence community."[10] Because the intelligence community would not validate a future threat beyond eight years, he focused on 1986.

Not surprisingly, Starry named the project and concept Army 86. Not so many years later when the Army, including the 1st Division, fought Desert Storm, it did so organized and trained to fight the AirLand Battle concept, a product of Army 86 that from its inception drove important doctrinal changes. A small team led by LTCs Huba Wass de Czege and Leonard D. Holder wrote the new doctrine. The Army published their work in two iterations, 1982 and 1986, both of which were called AirLand Battle.[11] Wass de Czege and Holder argued that combat operations in the modern era would be nonlinear. "Fluidity" would "characterize operations in the rear of forward deployed committed forces."[12]

The AirLand Battle doctrine defined a new way to visualize the fight. It enjoined commanders to plan and execute operations close, deep, and rear, and specified four tenets: initiative, agility, synchronization, and depth. Initiative aimed at forcing the enemy to "conform to our operational purpose and tempo."[13] Agility required friendly forces to "act faster than the enemy." Synchronization aimed at the "arrangement of battlefield activities in time, space, and purpose to produce the maximum relative combat power at the decisive point."[14] To wage AirLand Battle, commanders needed to extend the depth of the battle space through the use of air interdiction and long-range artillery because Soviet formations generated tempo and depth by attacking in two echelons. AirLand Battle sought to separate the Soviet first and second echelons in order to defeat each in detail.

In March 1981 TRADOC published the AirLand Battle concept. In addition to driving doctrine, it drove force design and weapons development; it also established requirements for capabilities that were not currently available. This reflected how Starry thought. He did not want to wait for weapons systems to be developed to design the force; to the extent possible, he wanted the concept to drive weapons development. Meanwhile, organizational design would incorporate the Big Five weapons systems as they became available. Although not among the Big Five, the multiple-launch rocket system (MLRS) would also be accounted for in force design.[15]

Although DePuy had developed the basic idea of concept driving weapons development, Starry institutionalized this approach in the Concepts Based Requirements System that remains in place today. To assure that the structure accounted for necessary capability, Starry deconstructed the essential elements and grouped them in "battlefield functions." The methodological approach required "a systematic breakdown into the division's specific tasks and subfunctions and then a reconstruction into a coherent whole or division capability."[16] For example, one of the battlefield functions, interdiction, aimed at enabling divisions to strike Warsaw Pact second-echelon formations. Thus the Army would need to organize and equip to perform the battlefield function of interdiction. That drove requirements for seeing and striking deep.

Like DePuy, Starry wanted to produce more effective tactical formations by reducing the size of companies and battalions to create more of the smaller formations to "better manage increased firepower" that the M1 tanks and the Bradley infantry fighting vehicles would bring. These two systems were developed prior to Starry's tenure at TRADOC, but they fit nicely into the AirLand Battle concept. The M1 tank brought dramatically improved fire control and improved tank gun ammunition to the fight. With the Bradley, American infantry moved from lightly armed and armored troop carriers to a genuine infantry fighting vehicle armed with a lethal cannon and antitank missile system. Army 86 also divested company commanders and their first sergeants of as many administrative tasks as possible so they could focus on fighting. Starry also moved to develop formations that were designed to fight deep; for example, he planned to organize artillery to take advantage of the deep-strike capability of the new MLRS and to use the Apache helicopter to build helicopter formations that could strike deep. The resulting design for the Division planned to incorporate "forty major weapons or new pieces of equipment that had not been procured yet, all of which would support the basic concept of AirLand Battle."[17]

Division 86 and the 1st Infantry Division

When Cocks's task force successfully defended Red Pass, the 1 ID was organizing in accordance with Army 86. By 1991 it had not completed organizing in accordance with the latest iteration of the Division design, nor was it equipped with the intended weapons. The design built organizations from the bottom up: tank platoons, for example, had four tanks assigned, and each tank had a crew of four including a tank commander, gunner, driver, and loader. Three platoons formed a company; the company commander and his executive officer each had a tank, so a tank company had fourteen tanks. Four companies formed a battalion. The battalion commander and operations officer each had a tank. Thus, a tank battalion had fifty-eight tanks. The battalion had a maintenance platoon with both mechanics and vehicle recovery sections, a support platoon, a scout platoon, and a mortar platoon. At full strength, about six hundred soldiers manned tank battalions.[18]

The mechanized infantry battalions organized on the same principle. Until the Army could field Bradley infantry fighting vehicles, each had an antitank company equipped with the tube-launched, optically tracked, wire-guided antitank missile system. Mercifully, the acronym TOW was used instead of the full name. The mechanized infantry design specified fifty-four Bradleys in each battalion. Each Bradley would have a crew of three and an infantry squad of six who could dismount and fight on foot. The infantry battalion's scout platoon had six of the Bradley "cavalry" variant. Mechanized infantry battalions had slightly more than eight hundred soldiers at full strength.

Because it was a low-priority division, the 1 ID lacked planned weapons systems or drew them late. For example, it fielded the M1 tank in 1988, years after other units. Even then, it drew used tanks from units in Europe as they replaced M1s with more modern M1A1 tanks. The aviation battalion reorganized as a brigade in 1988, but without the required helicopters; the new formation had neither the Black Hawk utility helicopter nor the Apache attack helicopter. The Division did not complete fielding the Bradley infantry fighting vehicle until 1990. As a result, it still had its TOW-equipped antitank companies when it deployed to Desert Storm. It did not have the new tactical transports, including the high-mobility, multipurpose wheeled vehicle (HMMWV) and the heavy expanded mobility tactical truck (HEMTT). These replaced a variety of older vehicles including the venerable quarter-ton truck or jeep, other light trucks, and several variations of the 2.5-ton truck. The Division did not replace the last Dodge light trucks, issued in lieu of HMMWVS, until the fall of 1990; HMMWVs and HEMTTs greatly improved cross-country mobility and cargo capacity. Nor did the Division have the latest communications equipment; it relied on single-side channel radios for communications at division level rather than the Mobile Subscriber Equipment found in units higher on the priority list.

In 1984 the Division retained an 8-inch artillery battalion rather than the longer-ranged rocket battery called for by the Army 86 design. Some alterations did not occur until the required equipment could be made available. But these impediments to applying the new fighting concept were just that—impediments. They did not preclude thinking and fighting as conceived in the AirLand Battle doctrine. Even without all the prescribed equipment, the Division could achieve the basic missions. In the offense, divisions had to "Destroy enemy security and main defensive belts," while in the defense, divisions had to "Destroy enemy 1st and 2nd Echelons."[19] The 1 ID could do most of what was expected of it even as it awaited the eventual delivery of the required equipment.

In any case, the Division had more serious problems. The truck fleet belonged in museums rather than in unit motor pools. CPT Bob Burns, a tank company commander, recalls that his 2.5-ton supply truck was nearly thirty years old.[20] Burns's colleagues in company command felt his pain, since their trucks were just as old. Much of the rest of their gear was, if not antique, at least very mature. The 1st Division was a hybrid, comprising ancient, obsolescent, and modern equipment all. Still, as mentioned, the Division's gear was good enough to get on with training to fight AirLand Battle. Finally, as a Return of Forces to Germany (REFORGER) division, it did not plan to fight with the equipment it trained with at Fort Riley;[21] since returning from Vietnam, the Division had planned on drawing well-maintained, prepositioned equipment upon arrival in Europe. No one at Fort Riley expected to depend on ancient trucks, older versions of the M1, or the venerable M113 armored personnel carriers, but CPT Burns and everyone else at Fort Riley could make do with the ancient trucks if need be.

Although the 1st Division styled itself an infantry division, it actually organized as a heavy division—of which there were two kinds. Armored divisions had six tank and four mechanized infantry battalions. As an infantry division, the 1st Division had five tank and five mechanized infantry battalions. The 1st and 2nd Brigades at Fort Riley each had two tank battalions and a mechanized infantry battalion. The 3rd Brigade, stationed in Germany and spread across several *Kasernes* (small barracks built originally for German troops) in Bavaria, included one tank battalion and two mechanized infantry battalions. The Minnesota Army National Guard provided the fifth mechanized infantry battalion.

Each brigade had a direct-support field artillery battalion. The Division artillery retained responsibility for positioning all of the artillery, including the Division's single MLRS battery and the counterfire radars organic to the target acquisition battery. The target acquisition battery enabled the Division to locate enemy artillery nearly as soon as it fired, while the MLRS extended the range the Division could strike well beyond that of the tube artillery battalions.

The Division artillery could mass-fire of all of the assigned artillery and incorporate fires of other artillery that might be assigned to reinforce.

The Division Support Command provided logistics. It assigned a forward support battalion to each brigade, and these battalions brought forward supplies and performed maintenance within their means. The main support battalion distributed supplies, provided higher-level maintenance, and supported separate units; it also tracked repair parts and calibrated tools and instruments.

The aviation brigade, the 4th Brigade, provided capability essential to AirLand Battle; it fielded a combat support aviation battalion and an attack battalion. The attack battalion organized in 1989. The 4th Brigade included the divisional cavalry squadron, and Apaches provided robust reconnaissance capability. Army 86 attack helicopter battalions had two missions—deep attack and reconnaissance. With both air and ground cavalry units, the cavalry squadron could perform reconnaissance and traditional security roles including screening, guarding, and covering. Aviation and cavalry resources were shared with the part of the Division based in Germany.

Several assigned units provided combat support; each of these sacrificed about one-third of its resources to the Division (Forward). An engineer battalion supported both breaching and preparing field fortifications though, in reality, it had few means to breach minefields and limited capability to dig in equipment and prepare obstacles. Army 86 would close the gap by providing an engineer brigade with additional resources. The planned engineer brigade did not form prior to the Division deploying to Southwest Asia. An air defense artillery battalion provided short-range air defense; it had two weapons systems, including the Vulcan twenty-millimeter Gatling gun mounted on an M113 armored personnel carrier and the Stinger surface-to-air missile. A military police company provided law enforcement and battlefield circulation support that included route reconnaissance and traffic control. It could also provide some support to rear-area security. A chemical company provided chemical detection, chemical decontamination, and obscuration via smoke generators. A military intelligence battalion rounded out combat support, providing both direct support to the brigades and general support to the Division in the form of fusion of intelligence and various electronic means of detecting enemy radars and radio networks. It needed help to see really deep; it could expect help from a corps military intelligence brigade.

When Cocks and his task force beat the regiment, MG Ronald L. Watts commanded the Division. Watts, like Cocks, commanded an "unmodernized" force, but he fully understood the intent of AirLand Battle and that the Division had to overcome its disadvantages. Previously he had served as one of the assistant division commanders; in that job he saw the struggles divisional units had in their first rotations to the National Training Center (NTC) at Fort Irwin,

California. With no Multiple Integrated Laser Engagement System (MILES) equipment to train on at home, the Division had trouble employing the only means it had to fight the opposing force regiment. But the Division obtained MILES, and Cocks's troops learned to use it. In like manner, Watts intended for the Division to learn AirLand Battle.[22]

MG Watts required that the tenets of AirLand Battle be addressed in planning operations. But planning to attack deep, at least during his tenure, proved difficult. As Watts remembers, "I believed in the AirLand Battle doctrine, for we had to attack multiple echelons simultaneously if we were to defeat the Warsaw Pact. The problem was not the doctrine; the problem was the capabilities to execute."[23] MG Leonard P. Wishart, who succeeded Watts, believed the Division "could execute the basic concepts of ALB [AirLand Battle] so long as we stayed within our capabilities and did not attempt to go beyond our limitations. Depth had some limitations; synchronization was essential, especially to go beyond the FLOT [forward line of troops], but not easy; controlling available time and judging and then accepting reasonable risk were keys to both initiative and agility."[24]

Watts and Wishart both conceived the deep fight in the terms the concept writers had imagined; that meant they believed they owned the tactical fight to defeat the first echelon. As Wishart puts it, "In my view, the really deep battle was an operational [the Army Corps'] commander's battle aimed at dealing with second and third echelon forces and seriously disrupting or metering both their movement schedules and combat effectiveness when committed."[25]

GEN Glenn K. Otis, who followed Starry at TRADOC, added another capability. In December 1982 he approved a second year at the Command and General Staff College, Fort Leavenworth, Kansas, for a select group of officers. He did so based in part on a study written by Wass de Czege, who led the team that wrote both the 1982 and 1986 versions of AirLand Battle. With the enthusiastic support of the general officer leadership at the Staff College, Wass de Czege and a small team developed a second-year course focused on operations that bridged the tactical and strategic levels. The resulting School of Advanced Military Studies (SAMS) graduated its first class of twelve in May 1984. The next year the school ramped up to twenty-four; at the end of three years' time, every division and corps had graduates planning operations in the context of AirLand Battle.[26]

On July 8, 1988, MG Gordon R. Sullivan succeeded Wishart in command. Sullivan's career might have been designed toward preparing him to command not just any division but the 1st Division in particular. Commissioned in armor from Norwich University in Northfield, Vermont, Sullivan brought his Boston Irish accent to Fort Riley and considerable experience in division and Cold War operations. He served in the 1st Division the first time as a battalion commander and chief of staff of the Division (Forward). He served a second time as the G3 Operations officer at Fort Riley, and also served at Fort Hood and in Korea. Because he was an armor officer, he served multiple tours in Europe and, like many officers of his generation, also served two tours in Vietnam.

Sullivan's tour in command is pivotal to this story. He commanded at the end of the ferment in doctrine and training that occurred after the Vietnam War. He arrived at a time when the Division had many of the tools needed to execute AirLand Battle. When Sullivan took command, the final iteration of AirLand Battle was two years old; it was an opportune time to apply the concepts in the field on the last fully mounted and largest REFORGER exercise. An inveterate note taker and sketcher of things military, his recollections and notes are a succinct and clear insight into the 1st Division's capacity to execute AirLand Battle.[27]

MG Sullivan, however, did not imagine himself coming to determine the Division's understanding and commitment to AirLand Battle. Like his predecessors since MG Robert R. Linville, his task "was to get the Division out of central Kansas to Germany to pick up its equipment and to occupy our forward battalion positions."[28] He was convinced that getting out of Kansas, deploying to Germany, and drawing equipment was "not going to happen by mistake."[29]

The Division had limitations, but it could see reasonably deep, and it had highly mobile armored formations and longer-range artillery. It could justly claim to be well trained: it had been training for and deploying to Germany frequently, and since the early 1980s it had trained at the NTC nearly every year, missing the chance only occasionally when it deployed to Germany.

Sullivan took up where he left off as G3, getting ready to deploy to Germany. The Division was scheduled to participate in the field training exercise Certain Challenge, the largest REFORGER field exercise ever. Both of the Europe-based corps, three of the four US divisions in Europe, the 1 ID from Fort Riley, two armored cavalry regiments, the Europe-based Canadian brigade group, and two German armored divisions participated. The German government also exercised two of their territorial commands responsible for rear-area security. For almost three weeks in September 1988, more than seven thousand tracked vehicles, including nearly eleven hundred tanks, trundled around Bavaria. The maneuver area was so large that, at one point, the Division ordered the 1st Brigade to break contact with the "enemy" and move south more than sixty miles. The Brigade did so, refueled, and mounted an attack to the northwest the next morning.[30]

The forward-based US V and VII Corps "fought" each other. Each employed a German armored division and a US division. Both sides attacked in depth, maneuvered, and sustained operations across long distances. Both exploited attack helicopters and fixed-wing aircraft. Certain Challenge demonstrated the scope and scale of operations the US Army and its Canadian and German allies could execute at the end of the Cold War. This is the capability the 1st Division brought to bear in Desert Storm.

Sullivan used his artist's sketchpad to record impressions, illustrate a point in a conversation, or capture his perceptions of the bloodless battles, and the sketchpad provides insight into the Army of the day. One of the pages on which he made notes is labeled "REFORGER '88 Command/Control." What follows are several pages that demonstrate how the Army intended to execute AirLand Battle. Of initiative, one of the principal tenets of AirLand Battle, he wrote: "easy to lose it—must have a good grip on intel + forces."[31] In the margin alongside that observation he wrote a further note to illustrate the point. During the early stages of an attack, the Division had encountered an opposing force cavalry platoon at 7:30 a.m. one morning. Although the attacking units "destroyed" the enemy platoon, they were unable to prevent it from reporting the skirmish. To Sullivan's chagrin, the 11th Cavalry acted more quickly than he could. By the time the Division attacked at 1:00 p.m. the cavalry had reoriented and blunted the attack. MG Sullivan's division surrendered the initiative by not moving quickly enough.[32]

On the same page he observed that "Space" did not change, but "time only diminishes," thus underscoring the utility of the AirLand Battle tenet of synchronization.[33] Arranging movement and events in time enabled effective maneuver, and maneuver, in Sullivan's mind and in the imagination of the authors of AirLand Battle, should focus on massing combat power at an opportune time and place. Simplicity and understanding time and space were keys to agility. With respect to depth, Sullivan concluded that the Division had serious gaps. The military intelligence battalion's long-range surveillance unit lacked the equipment and training it needed; furthermore, it lacked the means to report information in real time. Sullivan also believed that his division could not see deep enough. Without resolution, the Division could not fight as deep as its weapons could strike. During the deployment, the Division had shown the potential of both the AirLand Battle and the divisional structure designed to execute it.[34] The shortfalls Sullivan noted would become evident during Desert Storm.

Still, the Division came home from Bavaria on a high. Sullivan claimed, somewhat laconically given his normal effusiveness, that the troops "exceeded all standards." Indeed, they had done well; as MAJ Ulrich Schmidt, the assistant G3 Operations officer, asserted, "Big Red One soldiers did themselves proud."[35] Exercising large bodies of mounted troops in Germany is fraught with danger for the troops and civilians, sometimes resulting in fatalities. Yet the Division had only nine accidents with no fatalities in 2.6 million vehicle miles.[36] Historically, this largest REFORGER had also been the safest one for the 1st Division. David Wolsey, the Fort Riley Safety Officer, described the outcome as "phenomenal."[37] The 1st Battalion, 34th Armor passed a key test when it drew its equipment in full chemical protective gear.[38] Finally, the Division "fought" well, demonstrating that it could,— despite not being fully modernized—meet the intent of AirLand Battle.

Major General Thomas G. Rhame, Scorched Earth, and Declining Budgets

Returning to Fort Riley on the heels of a successful REFORGER was fine, but no guarantee of continued success. By this time the bloom was off the rose of President Ronald Reagan's military buildup, which had begun in 1980 with a budget increase in military spending of less than 1 percent but had grown by 10 percent in 1983 and 1984 and by 11 percent in 1985. The buildup was over by 1986; that year, the budget declined by 1 percent and continued to decline until the Gulf War. By 1989 the budget had declined for four years straight. These reductions produced real shortages. Fort Riley had already absorbed significant cuts; for a time, training was protected, but ultimately it suffered too. Some units resorted to practicing mounted maneuver in golf carts.[39] Heavy-equipment transporters moved tanks to ranges to save fuel.[40] Tank crews shared tanks when they fired tank gunnery qualification rather than each crew using its own tank. The approach seemed reasonable given that the Division assumed it would not take its Fort Riley tanks to war. If they deployed, crews would not operate the tanks with which they trained. Although the budget cuts were onerous, money for rotations to the NTC and modernization kept the Division's readiness rating afloat, if only barely.

Because MG Sullivan also commanded Fort Riley, he had good reason to be concerned with declining budgets: he was responsible for the maintenance and operations of everything from the training ranges to housing, and he had to sustain the post. Sullivan and his combined division and garrison staff retooled their effort; they focused on finding the means to assure adequate training and maintenance of facilities. He concluded that success would come by deciding the most effective use of resources the Division and Fort Riley could expect. He issued a draft master plan on March 12, 1989, in which he articulated his vision for a future in which fewer dollars would be the norm. He called the plan Republican Flats.[41]

Named for the flood plain of the Republican River that flows along the southern boundary of Fort Riley, the plan proposed ways that the post and the Division could achieve their missions while maintaining high-quality facilities for soldiers and their families. Sullivan's scheme went beyond short-term measures; it included acquiring more land to assure adequate maneuver space. Given longer ranges and higher mobility of weapons systems, Fort Riley needed more land to support maneuver training at the battalion-task force level. Any expansion had to be well reasoned—the previous land acquisition in 1965 had produced a legacy of bitterness and local opposition that had received some national backing. In 1981 the post floated the idea of acquiring still more land, perhaps aiming toward a 1950s-era plan of developing a training area of 200,000 acres.[42]

The effort went down in flames, as did the careers of several officers. No one at Fort Riley was eager to take on land acquisition. COL Gary LaGrange offered to lead the effort; since he intended to retire, he perceived no risk and thought the proposal legitimate. LaGrange had arrived at Fort Riley in the summer of 1987, and he understood the problem and the history. In November 1988, after a stint as the Division G4 Logistics officer, he assumed command of the Fort Riley garrison. He would lead the land acquisition effort and run the garrison at the same time.[43] From the beginning, LaGrange and Sullivan kept the local community fully informed. LaGrange announced the proposed acquisition in January 1989. Supporters and opponents emerged to form both local and national groups arguing for or against. Despite vocal opposition, farmers tended to favor acquisition, as they were weighed with debt at high interest rates. LaGrange conducted more than 120 meetings with community groups in which he heard public opposition, but privately the same people supported the acquisition. Staffing in the Pentagon went well. He felt reasonably confident.[44]

Republican Flats aimed to identify the most efficient means to maintain facilities ranging from a state-of-the-art multipurpose range complex to amenities such as the post exchange and the commissary. Other parts of the plan focused on retaining good soldiers and reducing drug and alcohol abuse.[45] Sullivan developed the plan, but left before it got under way. Not long after Sullivan published the Republican Flats proposal, the chief of staff reassigned him with a promotion to serve on Department of the Army staff in Washington.

MG Thomas G. Rhame succeeded Sullivan in July, after commanding the US Army Community and Family Support Center. Rhame had also been a comptroller, though he was first and foremost an infantryman. He had graduated from Louisiana State University–Baton Rouge in 1963 and as a young officer he commanded a rifle company in Vietnam. Later he returned for a second tour as a district senior adviser. Rhame had served the bulk of his "tactical unit" career in Kitzingen, Germany, where he commanded a mechanized infantry brigade, and at Fort Hood, where he commanded a mechanized infantry battalion. After brigade command, he served as chief of staff of the 3rd Armored Division (3 AD). Subsequently, he served as one of two assistant division commanders in the 3 AD, where he wore a second hat as community commander in Hanau, Germany.

Rhame had impeccable credentials as an infantryman and understood the employment of armor. The 1st Division seems to attract or perhaps create outsized personalities. Given that tradition, Rhame suited the Division and it suited him. Pulitzer Prize–winning author Rick Atkinson has described Rhame as "noisy, profane and relentless," adding that "in aggressive drive he had few peers."[46] MAJ Brian Zahn, platoon leader in Rhame's battalion, described him as great battalion commander but a "mean mother." After the famous shark movie came out, Rhame's lieutenants referred to him as Jaws.[47] He was indeed a terror, but only to those who were wrong. Known by the call sign that came with commanding the Division, Danger 6, he occasionally waxed profane, but generally for effect and never abusively. Rhame's accent demonstrated that he was a native-born Southerner; he spoke with a drawl, but listeners were more likely to take more notice of his deliberate cadence than his accent. His speech seemed measured, as if he chose each word carefully. Equally important, Rhame wasted few words; when he spoke, he did so with precision. He exuded passion and great energy, yet he also emanated a folksy, friendly quality. And, yes, he could be a mean mother.

Rhame never previously served in the Big Red One, and he was conscious of that fact. For a time, commanding generals seemed to have come exclusively from the pool of veterans. Reflecting on his selection, he observes, "I am one of those rare guys who took command of the Division who had not served in it before."[48] Whatever reticence he may have felt was not apparent, and it was equally obvious that he knew his business.

In the summer of 1989 the "life of Riley" continued much as it had since 1970. ROTC summer camp and preparation for a brigade rotation to the NTC dominated the calendar; both afforded Rhame the opportunity to assess the Division, the post, and the surrounding communities. Junction City was just across the Republican River, Ogden was literally on the other side of the north gate, and Manhattan a few miles northeast; twenty miles north, the town of Riley was adjacent to the new Multi-Purpose Range Complex. The local communities were supportive of Fort Riley and the Division. Junction City enjoyed the greatest economic benefit. Manhattan, home of Kansas State University, depended less on Fort Riley so was less enthusiastic. Ogden, a strip of small businesses and bars, typified towns that grew at the gates of Army posts. Originally a farming town, the 1965 land acquisition devastated the town of Riley. It recovered somewhat as a bedroom community and a haven for antique dealers.

MG Rhame began his assessment prior to assuming command. Before he left Washington, he visited the Kansas congressional delegation. He thought he received particularly good advice from Senator Bob Dole. A disabled combat veteran, Dole promoted the Army and Fort Riley. Rhame arrived with a clear idea of what he wanted to achieve and some insight on the surrounding communities. He believed his primary task was to "train the Division and have it ready for war where ever and when ever it comes." He also thought he could "produce a well-trained division on a well maintained post" and yet live "in harmony with its neighbors."[49] But tanks and artillery firing within yards of Riley and seven miles from Manhattan often caused complaint; harmony was not assured.

With respect to the Division, Rhame liked what he saw. He remembers that "maintenance was proper, training had the right momentum, and base ops was good. General Gordon Sullivan left me a division you would expect."[50] As Rhame made his rounds, he found the unit in good shape and on the right vector. Like Sullivan, Rhame saw himself as a steward.

In August, the 1st Brigade deployed to the NTC, affording Rhame the opportunity to see part of the Division in action. The Brigade and its slice of the combat support and logistics units moved to Fort Irwin to confront the opposing forces, as Cocks and others had before them. Just driving around the Mojave Desert in August would challenge most Americans. The soldiers of the Brigade would do so under constant stress, with little sleep and bundled up in chemical protective clothes (including rubber boots and gloves) in heat well above one hundred degrees.

Rhame had never been to the desert training site. He was familiar with the comparatively small ranges and training areas in Germany, but they could not match the NTC in simulating high-intensity operations. The Hohenfels training area in Germany, with a single maneuver corridor and maneuver space for one battalion, permitted limited maneuver; battalions at Hohenfels had an easier time of it than their counterparts at the vastly larger and more complex NTC. Perhaps as a consequence, Rhame was unimpressed by his units in the first few mock battles he saw at Fort Irwin. As he came to understand the process and the challenge at the NTC, he realized that the 1st Brigade's two tank battalion task forces were doing quite well.

Blessed with a keen analytical mind and a gift for training, Rhame drew important conclusions. "I came back from the NTC with the conviction that we could maneuver," he remembers. "We understood intelligence preparation of the battlefield. If we had anything we could do better at, it was gunnery. I thought collective gunnery could have been stronger."[51] He saw for himself that his tank crews could shoot, but he perceived fire distribution and coordination at the company and battalion levels could be improved. The live-fire corridor generated enough combinations in both offense and defense to preclude units from anticipating the fight. Gunnery alone would not produce a win; effective fire distribution would. The Division needed to improve fire distribution.

In the live-fire defense exercise the training task force confronted a regimental deliberate attack. Positioned on the edge of low hills, the friendly force faced west down a valley formed by mountains that rise several hundred feet to the north and south. The valley narrowed to no more than two kilometers just forward of the Blue force positions. It extended ten kilometers west to two narrow passes through the ridge connecting the two ranges forming the valley. Drinkwater Lake divided the valley in two unequal parts. The terrain enabled the simulated enemy regiment to attack with two battalions abreast.

Sixty BMPs (Boyevaya Mashina Pekhoty, a Soviet infantry fighting vehicle) and twenty tanks could come at thirty Blue tanks and, if "modernized," thirty Bradley infantry fighting vehicles. Thirty more BMPs and ten tanks made up the regiment's second echelon.

The "enemy" had two choices to make as it approached Drinkwater Lake. First, it had to decide how to employ the first-echelon battalions. It could attack with two battalions north of the lake, one north and one south, or it could cram both into the narrower avenue to the south. The enemy's second choice was to decide how to employ its second echelon. Soviet doctrine required exploiting success. Advancing implacably at thirty kilometers per hour, the enemy covered a kilometer every two minutes. Blue had twenty minutes to stop or kill the enemy regiment once it emerged from the passes. Ranges of tank guns and missiles effectively reduced the available time to eight minutes. The enemy could be relied upon to precede its attack with an intense artillery barrage liberally laced with chemicals. Blue could emplace obstacles to buy time. Minutes mattered, as did effective distribution of fire.

The recurring "battle" of Drinkwater Lake validated Starry's imagined central battle. To win, Blue had to solve the "battle calculus." Separating the two echelons could be achieved with impeccable timing, using good obstacles covered by accurate artillery and effective tank and missile fires. Doing so while wearing a gas mask in a tank turret with hatches closed was hard any time, but it was really hard in August. The enemy in the battle of Drinkwater never grew tired, hungry, or hot; its commander managed his simulated regiment from an air-conditioned bunker supported by superb instrumentation. He could see the fight clearly, without sweat in his eyes or tear gas searing his lungs.

His tireless "troops" could shoot too. The targets moved up and down on lifters, making them appear to move. As they approached, the enemy tanks "fired" explosive weapons simulators producing realistic signatures including sound, flash, and smoke. If a Blue force crew hit an enemy target, it "splashed" as it would if a metal-on-metal impact occurred. The "dead" target then emitted an entirely believable funeral pyre of thick black smoke. Approaching enemy BMPs fired "Smokey Sam" simulators that looked like Sagger antitank missiles. The regiment also had air support in the form of one-fifth-scale Styrofoam Soviet MiG fighters. From a tank turret they looked real. At least Blue could shoot down the Styrofoam fighters.[52]

Defending against an enemy attack at live fire is an amazing experience. Observer-trainers assessed hits on exposed Blue troops and combat systems. They used fire markers to show effect and god guns to kill. For example, if a tank crew exposed itself within range of enemy tanks when they fired, observer-controllers determined the likely effect. The controller used a god gun to shoot a laser beam at a sensor belt installed on a Blue vehicle. The god gun could trigger a near-miss warning or a hit. Only actual combat is more realistic. The battle of Drinkwater Lake promoted humility and affirmed Rhame's conviction that platoon and company fire control, not crew gunnery, was the acme of tactical excellence. Over the next year he refined maneuver and gunnery training accordingly and changed the way his units trained and prepared for the war and for rotations to the NTC.

By 1989 Fort Riley had a state-of-the-art Multi-Purpose Range Complex, which included multiple target arrays laid out around a central controlling site. The chief qualification range afforded multiple lanes and varying target sequences and arrays so that tank and Bradley crews could not anticipate where and in what sequence targets would appear. Fort Riley lacked the means and space to conduct company-level combined arms live-fire training, however, and this limited what could be done to improve fire planning and distribution.

The operations staff developed the next best thing, an exercise they called platoon kills battalion (PKB), which emulated the conditions of the battle of Drinkwater Lake. Range operations emplaced sufficient targets to simulate a motorized rifle battalion advancing at thirty kilometers per hour. PKB enabled platoons to experience the kind of stress and difficulty they could expect at Drinkwater Lake or actually fighting for their lives against the Soviets. It aimed at improving tactical gunnery and fire distribution at the platoon level and permitted company commanders to exercise tactical movement and fires within the limits of the range. The PKB exercise was unique to Fort Riley because of the comparative flexibility of the Multi-Purpose Range Complex, although other units employed similar means to train.

The first platoon fought PKB in the spring of 1990. That spring Rhame issued a training letter based on his observations of platoon gunnery at Fort Irwin and in PKB. The letter stated bluntly that "platoon fire commands are weak . . . sensing (of targets) across the platoons is weak" and added, "We have not made the large jump from individual crew gunnery to platoon collective 'war focused' gunnery."[53] In a rare moment of volubility, Rhame went on for two pages citing his disappointment; this after three of his of battalions actually "won" the battle of Drinkwater Lake and set records for excellence. The man known as Jaws, it appears, was back. The Division had performed well, but he believed it could do better. In a letter of instruction on execution of PKB issued in October 1990 Rhame drove the point home: "Platoon warfighting proficiency, achieved and sustained at home station form the bedrock of the division's maneuver combat power."[54]

For years the Division had devised ever more intricate schemes to succeed at the NTC. By the end of Rhame's first year in command, these came together in a series of exercises known as Gauntlet that brought all of the Division's resources to bear. The assistant division commander for maneuver served as exercise director. One battalion formed the nucleus of the opposing force, and another provided observer-controllers and fire markers; the aviation brigade and separate battalions provided combat support to both sides. Gauntlet replicated the NTC experience and required most of the Division's resources and soldiers. The exercise was significant: for the first time in ten years of deploying to the NTC, the Division addressed, to the extent it could, the limitations it had "fighting" at the NTC. What it did was not particularly unique, but PKB certainly gave it an edge in 1990.

While the troops trained to fight the Soviets and the opposing force at Fort Irwin, President George H. W. Bush, his national security team, and Secretary of State James A. Baker worked to manage the end of the Cold War. Secretary Baker read a paper at the outset of his tenure in the State Department that asserted, "The Soviet Union is a Great Power in Decline. As Secretary of State, our central tasks in East-West relations will be to manage the international effects of this decline productively and peacefully."[55] Secretary Baker and President Bush managed as well as anyone could have, but the United States did not really control or even manage the end of the Cold War; the Soviet Union and communist dominance of Eastern Europe unraveled faster than anyone anticipated. Baker's recollection in the fall of 1989 is succinct and accurate: "The Cold War order was crumbling before our eyes."[56]

The Cold War order had begun to come apart in the previous months. It started unraveling in Poland, when Lech Wałęsa's Solidarity movement forced the communist government to the bargaining table. In March 1989 Hungary moved to demilitarize its border with Austria. Soviet premier Mikhail Gorbachev provided openings to reduce tension worldwide. In October, Gorbachev essentially ended Soviet hegemony in Eastern Europe. On October 7 he made a speech commemorating the anniversary of the East German government in which he asserted that policy in East Germany should be made "not in Moscow but in Berlin." He doubled down in Helsinki on October 25 when he observed, "We [the Soviet Union] have no right, moral or political, to interfere in events [of satellite states]."[57] The next month young Germans began chipping away at the Berlin Wall.

There were other challenges. In June 1989 the Chinese government cracked down on protesters in Beijing's Tiananmen Square, and optimism that communism would end in China proved to be misplaced. In Panama, one-time US ally GEN Manuel Antonio Noriega became problematic. Tension had begun in 1981 when the military dictator failed to turn over command of the Panamanian military to his legitimate successor. Relations with him grew progressively worse, and in February 1988 he consolidated power in what amounted to a coup. Two US federal grand juries had also indicted him for drug trafficking.

Arguably to distract his citizens, Noriega's supporters harassed and attacked Americans in the Canal Zone in the name of Panamanian pride. In December 1988, shortly after Panamanian troops murdered an officer of the US Marines, the United States invaded.[58] Operation Just Cause removed Noriega, but managing that crisis and a "soft landing" to the Cold War were two highlights of an incredible turning point.

Even to the denizens of motor pools at Fort Riley, who could see only certain highlights, the pace of change was disconcerting. Less than twenty years earlier the Soviet Union had appeared ascendant; morale in the Army and the nation sank after the 1948 Arab-Israeli War and the fall of Saigon. Yet by the end of 1989 the Cold War, if not over, was clearly winding down and the United States seemed vindicated. In Berlin, Germans from both sides pulled down the infamous wall that had divided their city for nearly thirty years.

The 1st Division seemed to be on the sidelines at this great moment in history. Rhame spoke for most of his officers, NCOs, and soldiers when he said, "Just Cause happened and we watched with envy."[59] For many it felt as though history had passed them by. Just Cause demonstrated what the late Cold War Army could do, and the 1st Division had missed it.

Training and Resources at the End of the Cold War

Despite disappointment, training continued, although for just what was uncertain. In March 1990 the recently organized Battle Command Training Program (BCTP) arrived to run a training exercise for the first time at Fort Riley. It was a simulation-driven exercise that would enable Danger 6 and his staff to fight. The training revolution, nearly twenty years under way, had at last reached division level. As a rule these exercises pitted units in the defense against a Soviet ground attack in Germany or a North Korean attack against South Korea. LTG Frederick M. Franks Jr., the commander of VII Corps in Europe who would employ the Big Red One if the need arose, wanted to change the Division's BCTP experience; he wanted to shift VII Corps from focusing on a GDP that with the apparent end of the Cold War appeared superfluous to preparing for offensive operations. He decided on a spoiling attack against the opposing force. MG Rhame liked it; he thought Franks "did a great job pushing us to the max and getting the most out of us."[60] More important, the exercise stimulated thinking about offensive operations.

The Warfighter, as the BCTP exercise was called, included leaders down to company level. Company and battalion commanders manned the simulation workstations together, giving them time to work closely. Changing the approach from defense to offense had an electrifying effect. The opposing "Soviet" commander had previously commanded the opposing force at the NTC, where he seldom lost, but now the Division's spoiling attack confounded him, quickly overwhelming his maneuver units as they staged for their attack. Within the first few hours, 1 ID units overran regimental and divisional artillery. Turning the tables on the opposing force was great fun, and fostered bonds among brigades and between brigade and division, but perhaps the most important point is the one that MAJ Pete Lawson, the Division plans officer, made: "This exercise is the commanding general's National Training Center exercise."[61]

Training of other varieties also continued. A task force formed on the 5th Battalion, 16th Infantry (5-16 IN) ran the Gauntlet en route to Fort Irwin to participate in a light-heavy rotation (so called because the exercise combined a mechanized or heavy unit with nonmechanized or light forces) with the 101st Airborne Division. Task Force 5-16 IN beat the regiment at the battle of Drinkwater Lake, killing all but the second-echelon battalion. The live-fire controllers conceded defeat and halted the second echelon west of Drinkwater Lake. At Fort Riley, the infantry and armor battalions received the new Bradley infantry fighting vehicles and began new equipment training. Two armor battalions fired PKB.

The cadence of life at Fort Riley continued much as it had. The 1st Brigade prepared to support the ROTC summer camp: the 2nd Battalion, 34th Armor prepared for gunnery and an annual general inspection, and the 2nd Brigade began planning to go to the NTC. REFORGER was the only event not on tap for the 1 ID.[62] Other units had their share of tasks, varying from mundane details to supporting the National Guard.

In July LTC Dave Gross assumed command of the 3rd Battalion, 37th Armor; less than ten days later, it moved to the Multi-Purpose Range Complex to conduct tank gunnery. After concluding the standard gunnery tables, Gross exercised his crews in "degraded" gunnery. The M1 tank had a state-of-the-art fire-control system that combined a laser range finder, wind sensor, and onboard computer to produce results that would have appeared magical to tankers in 1970. The tank's computer used the laser range finder and wind sensor to calculate the required elevation above gun target line and the correct aim point to compensate for wind, and did all this without input from the crew. The computer also sensed turret movement and applied lead. Because the turret was fully stabilized, the gunner could track the target smoothly while moving, keeping the sight on the intended target. With this technology the gunners had only to "lase and blaze"—that is, fire the laser and then the cannon. The tank only missed when something broke or the crew made an egregious error.

Gross knew his tankers could hit targets if everything worked, but what if the turret had an electrical failure? To challenge them he induced mechanical and electrical failures, forcing his tankers to use ballistic telescopes, shoot under mortar illumination, and compute ranges based on arcane formulas used only in "degraded" gunnery. These induced failures also forced his tankers to apply "burst on target" to achieve hits. Using ballistic reticles, the gunner "choked" down on the target to determine range and then determined lead based on range. For example, firing high-explosive antitank (HEAT) ammunition at twelve hundred meters against a target moving left to right, the gunner aimed right of the target using his ballistic reticle to input the proper angle based on the range.[63] If he missed, he adjusted his sight to the apparent point at which the tracer passed the target—thus, burst on target. Gross's troops learned a lot that summer, and it stood them in good stead.

As always, the summer routine included multiple changes of command. By the end of July 1990 only two of fifteen battalion commanders had served in Vietnam: LTC Sydney "Skip" F. Baker, who had been in command of the 5-16 IN since April 1989, and LTC Robert "Bob" Wilson, who took command of the 1st Squadron, 4th Cavalry in June 1990. Both brigades also changed command. COL Lon E. "Bert" Maggart took command of the 1st Brigade, and COL Anthony A. Moreno assumed command of the 2nd Brigade; both had served in Vietnam. By the end of the summer, the soldiers who would lead the Division's Fort Riley–based brigades and battalions in Desert Storm were in command.

Also by summer's end, all but one of Rhame's maneuver battalions had trained at the NTC since his arrival. All had fired PKB once, and several had fired it twice. The Division had completed fielding the Big Five and, despite serious budget reductions, was in good shape. In good shape to do just what, however, remained the question. The Cold War sputtered out, and the Department of Defense mandated force reductions in Europe and in the United States. The future of Fort Riley was uncertain.

Although focused on training and readiness, Rhame did not forget to wear his second hat; as post commander, he managed the post with LaGrange. Because of continued budget cuts, Rhame delved into his other specialty—resource management, and in that capacity, things that cost money, saw little use, and provided low value went—as they said at Riley—"the way of the "buffalo." In fact, Fort Riley's large and occasionally rambunctious buffalo herd did go the way of the buffalo: Rhame gave the animals away in his determination to divest the post of things it could no longer afford. He also tore down an urban training site that was run-down, too small, and little used. He approached every system and facility with dry eyes and clarity: find money for essential facilities, and let go of what is not necessary. Some likened this to a scorched-earth policy, but Rhame ignored the criticism. All went well until he closed the Robert Trent Jones–designed golf course on Custer Hill. Rhame played golf, but he expected the course to sustain itself; fierce opposition led him to keep it open by increasing fees and allowing civilians access. Whether or not anyone liked his decisions, everyone had to agree that Rhame ran the post like a business.

Budget cuts, ridding Fort Riley of buffalo, miniature crises over the golf course, and other dizzying events of the year produced a fin de siècle sensation. Change and ambiguity were the order of the day. At times the ground seemed to shift, even to lurch. As fast as the Berlin Wall came down, so too did the decision to reduce the Army, and the drawdown extended beyond Europe. In the summer of 1990 the Army in Europe started shedding two of its four divisions and supporting units. The 3rd Brigade, 2nd Armored Division (2 AD) and forward headquarters as well as the 3rd Brigade, 1 ID, and forward headquarters prepared to demobilize. The drawdown began in the States as well for the 9th Infantry Division (9 ID) at Fort Lewis, Washington, and the 2 AD at Fort Hood.

Although Fort Riley was not on the "chopping block," no one there felt reassured. Rhame, for one, thought that downsizing might be in the offing. Although closer to a port than the 4th Infantry Division at Fort Carson, Colorado, or the 101st Airborne at Fort Campbell, Kentucky, the Division was in the middle of Kansas. Rhame was, he recalls, "very concerned that the division, given where it was located and it was heavy, with this thrust to get off of heavy that we would be downsized."[64] He had reason to be concerned: the end of the Cold War brought on a precipitate withdrawal from Europe. Pundits and some in the Department of Defense believed the Army was too heavy to get to prospective conflicts quickly enough given the prevalent end-of-history atmosphere. Without the Soviet threat many wondered what usefulness heavy divisions retained. While Rhame worried about the Division's survival, he also worried over reductions in force of the kind that occurred after every war. A drawdown takes on a different hue in a professional force. Rumors flew and some had a basis in truth. Thus, 1990 began with an announcement of a 15 percent cut to operations and maintenance funding. There was little reason to feel optimistic.[65] Units on post felt the secondary effects of the cut immediately as the flow of repair parts dried up.

Despite genuine concern about the future at the battalion level and below, the focus remained on training—at least within the limits of what was possible. Most of the officers commanding at the battalion level had come into the Army at the end of the Vietnam War, a time when the Army, as COL Bob Killebrew points out, was really "screwed up."[66] The lean times that defined this group of officers' early years in the Army equipped them well to find innovate ways to train. Sharing tanks, using simulations, and combining efforts all contributed to ensuring that battalions and their companies were as ready as they could be. No battalion commander at Fort Riley that summer could be found complaining about commanding a battalion during hard times; if he had, Rhame and the senior NCOs would have reminded him of his good fortune.[67] Pessimism could be found at Fort Riley, but not much of it in the battalions; while they did not have all they wanted, they had what they absolutely needed.

NOTES

1. Donn A. Starry, *Press On! Selected Works of General Donn A. Starry*, ed. Lewis Sorley (Fort Leavenworth, KS: Combat Studies Institute Press, 2009), 2:1268.

2. Starry's terrain walks obviously provided great focus for young commanders, including the author; for me it was a life-changing experience. See also John L. Romjue, *A History of Army 86*, vol. 1, *Division 86: The Development of the Heavy Division, September 1978–October 1979* (Fort Monroe, VA: Historical Office, US Army Training and Doctrine Command, 1980), 12; and John L. Romjue, *From Active Defense to AirLand Battle: The Development of Army Doctrine, 1972–1982* (Fort Monroe, VA: Historical Office, US Army Training and Doctrine Command, 1994), 24–27.

3. The process of developing battle books required drilling down on the specific weapons.

4. I commanded the 3rd Battalion, 33rd Armor, which comprised three M60 A2 tank platoons and one M60 A1 tank platoon. If war had broken out, my team would have defended just east of Bad Hersfeld, Germany. (The term *team* is used when a company attaches and detaches platoons.)

5. US Army Training and Doctrine Command, *US Army Operational Concepts: The AirLand Battle and Corps 86*, Pamphlet 525-5 (Fort Monroe, VA: US Army Training and Doctrine Command, 1981), 2. See also Romjue, *From Active Defense to AirLand Battle.* GEN William L. Creech of the Tactical Air Command and GEN Starry of the Training and Doctrine Command forged a productive partnership.

6. See Russell F. Weigley, *History of the United States Army* (Bloomington: Indiana University Press, 1984), 573; Weigley's chapter "From the Ia Drang to the Rhine, 1967–1983" provides a good overview of the institutional history of the period after the Vietnam War through the 1982 publication of FM 100-5, *Operations.* See also Richard W. Stewart, ed., *American Military History*, vol. 2, *The United States Army in a Global Era, 1917–2003* (Washington, DC: Center of Military History, 2009), 375–77.

7. John B. Wilson, *Maneuver and Firepower: The Evolution of Divisions and Separate Brigades* (Washington, DC: Center of Military History, 1998). During the crucial period in the 1970s, the Army had four chiefs of staff: Abrams, who succeeded Westmoreland in October 1972 and died in September 1974 of complications following surgery; GEN Fred C. Weyand, who succeeded Abrams and served until September 1976; Bernard W. Rogers, who followed Weyand and served until June 1979, when he was appointed Supreme Allied Commander, Europe; and GEN Edward C. Meyers, who took over in June 1979 and served until June 1983.

8. Romjue, *A History of Army 86*, 1:4.

9. Wilson, *Maneuver and Fire Power*, 380–83.

10. Starry, *Press On!*, 1256. See also Wilson, *Maneuver and Firepower*, 383.

11. Ibid.

12. US Department of the Army, *Operations*, FM 100-5, 1986 ed. (Washington, DC: US Department of the Army, 1986), 3.

13. Ibid., 15.

14. Ibid., 16–17.

15. John L. Romjue, *The Army of Excellence: The Development of the 1980s Army* (Fort Monroe, VA: Office of the Command Historian United States Army Training and Doctrine Command, 1993), 1–13. Romjue doesn't list the Big Five. The list cited here is from John Sloan Brown, *Kevlar Legions: The Transformation of the US Army, 1989–2005* (Washington, DC: Center of Military History, 2011) 16.

16. Romjue, *A History of Army 86*, 1:35.

17. Combat Studies Institute, *Sixty Years of Reorganizing: A Historical Trend Analysis*, CSI Report 14 (Fort Leavenworth, KS: Combat Studies Institute, 1999), 42. Major Glenn R. Hawkins, "United States Army Force Structure and Force Design Initiatives 1939–1989," unpublished manuscript, Center of Military History, Washington, DC, 1991.

18. The Army has standard tables of organization and equipment, but each unit is organized discretely on the basis of a modified table of organization and equipment that reflects priority and available equipment. A heavy division such as the 1st Division followed a model table of organization called AOE 8700 AXXX. The Army never realized the Army 86 design, as resources precluded fielding the formations planned. Instead, the 1st Division organized under the design concept known as the Army of Excellence.

19. Romjue, *A History of Army 86*, 1:26.

20. COL (Ret.) Robert A. Burns, interview with the author, Leavenworth, KS, April 16, 2014.

21. The prepositioned equipment sites could issue all the major end items of equipment less helicopters.

22. LTG (Ret.) Ronald L. Watts, interview by Andrew Woods, Society of the 1st Division Reunion, Colorado Springs, CO, August 22, 2008; LTG Watts, e-mail to the author, September 9, 2014.

23. Watts interview. The author served as LTG Watts's plans officer from May 1985 until April 1986. LTG Watts fully committed himself and the Division to the concepts of AirLand Battle.

24. LTG (Ret.) Leonard Wishart, e-mail to the author, September 10, 2014.

25. Ibid.

26. Kevin M. Benson, "Educating the Army's Jedi: The School of Advanced Military Studies and Introduction of Operational Art into U. S. Army Doctrine,"

PhD diss., University of Kansas, 2010, chap. 1. The SAMS remains an important component of the US Army officer education.

27. GEN Gordon R. Sullivan, interview with the author, Washington, DC, April 21, 2014. I can attest personally that GEN Sullivan used his sketchpad regularly.

28. Ibid.

29. Ibid.

30. Walter Bohm, *REFORGER: Vehicles of the US Army during Exercises, "Return of Forces to Germany,"* vol. 1, *1969–1993* (Erlangen, Germany: Tankograd, 2008), 23–29. Bohm, *REFORGER: Vehicles of the US Army during Exercises, "Return of Forces to Germany,"* vol. 3, *1986–1993* (Erlangen, Germany, Tankograd 2008), 23–39.

31. Sullivan, sketchpad and personal notes, archive, Military History Institute, Army Historical and Education Center, Carlisle Barracks, PA.

32. Ibid.

33. Ibid.

34. Ibid.

35. MAJ Ulrich Schmidt, quoted in Dave Schrecengost, "Troops Continue Redeployment," *Fort Riley Post*, October 14, 1988, 1. Sullivan's understated assertion was used in several *Fort Riley Post* headlines.

36. Dave Schrecengost, "REFORGER Safety Successful, Exceeds Goal," *Fort Riley Post*, November 23, 1989, 3. The *Fort Riley Post* sent at least one reporter to Germany with the Division and published stories of the deployment, the exercise, and the redeployment.

37. David Wolsey, quoted in Dave Schrecengost, "Based on Historical Data This Was the Safest Ever for Big Red One Soldiers," *Fort Riley Post*, November 23, 1988, 3.

38. Steve Eisenberg, "Adverse Conditions Don't Slow Division Soldiers," *Fort Riley Post*, September 16, 1988, 1, 4.

39. Cynthia Crumen, "Golf Cart Maneuvers Decrease Costs," *Fort Riley Post*, January 15, 1988, 3. In June 1988 the *Fort Riley Post* ran a story announcing a reduction in force of 215 civilian employees. The garrison commander intended to manage the cuts by freezing hiring and letting normal attrition bring down the force. See Mark M. Meseke, "Reduction in Force Impact Reduced," *Fort Riley Post*, June 10, 1988, 1, 4.

40. Janet Gohmen, "Support Battalion Makes Heavy Haul," *Fort Riley Post*, January 22, 1989, 6.

41. Headquarters, 1st Infantry Division (Mechanized) and Fort Riley, "Republican Flats—Setting the Azimuth," memorandum, February 21, 1989. GEN Sullivan's handwritten cover note, dated March 13, 1989, was appended to each copy distributed.

42. Roger W. Lotchin, "Junction City—Fort Riley: A Case of Symbiosis," in *The Martial Metropolis: US Cities in War and Peace* (New York: Praeger, 1984), 35–60.

43. See Headquarters, 1st Infantry Division (Mechanized) and Fort Riley, "Republican Flats." The information on land acquisition comes from COL (Ret.) Gary L. LaGrange, interview with the author, Manhattan, KS, June 26, 2014.

44. LaGrange interview.

45. For memos, notes, and a slick brochure on the plan, see Sullivan, sketchpad and notes, box labeled Republican Flats.

46. Rick Atkinson, *Crusade: The Untold Story of the Gulf War* (London: HarperCollins, 1994), 395.

47. COL (Ret.) Brian R. Zahn, telephone interview with the author, September 12, 2014.

48. LTG (Ret.) Thomas G. Rhame, interview with the author, Alexandria, VA, April 23, 2014.

49. Ibid.

50. Ibid.

51. Ibid.

52. Anne W. Chapman, *The National Training Center Matures* (Fort Monroe, VA: Office of the Command Historian, United States Training and Doctrine Command, 1997), 201.

53. Ibid.

54. 1st Infantry Division (Mechanized), *Platoon Kills Battalion (PKB) Situational Training Exercise: Live Fire Exercise Handbook* (Fort Riley, KS: 1st Infantry Division [Mechanized], 1990). The handbook represented codifying the program that evolved over time.

55. James A. Baker III with Thomas M. DeFrank, *The Politics of Diplomacy: Revolution, War and Peace, 1989–1992* (New York: Putnam's, 1995), 41. See also George Bush and Brent Scowcroft, *A World Transformed* (New York: Vintage, 1999).

56. Baker, *The Politics of Diplomacy*, 163.

57. Ibid., 60–61, 163. Bush and Scowcroft's *A World Transformed* is riveting on these events as well, but Baker's narrative is easier to follow.

58. Baker, *The Politics of Diplomacy*, 177–94.

59. Rhame interview.

60. Ibid. COL Eric Shinseki, later chief of staff, served as G3 Operations in VII Corps.

61. MAJ Pete Lawson, quoted in Ed Garven, "Warfighter Challenges the Big Red One," *Fort Riley Post*, March 7, 1990, 1–2.

62. Bohm, *REFORGER*, 3:40. NATO did not exercise REFORGER in 1989. REFORGER 90 took place in January 1990.

63. Both ballistic and nonballistic reticles in the M1 measured angles in mils. There are 6,400 mils in a circle; at 1,200 meters firing HEAT, lead input would be 2.5 mils of angle based on the range and an assumption that a tank target would be moving at no more than twenty kilometers per mile cross-country.

64. Rhame interview.

65. Ed Garven, "Fort Riley's 1990 Budget Absorbs Cuts," *Fort Riley Post*, February 16, 1990, 1–2.

66. COL (Ret.) Robert B. Killebrew, telephone interview with the author, February 10, 2014.

67. The author commanded at Fort Riley from 1989 to 1991. Although absolutely aware of painful decreases in funds available, Rhame found ways to assure there was just enough money for battalions to do what they had to do. My colleagues in command Harry Emerson, John Gingrich, Dave Gross, Pat Ritter, and Bob Wilson all concur (e-mail messages to the author, December 26, 2015); LTCs Skip Baker and Dave Marlin are dead, but LTC Marlin made no complaint about training resources in his war college monograph.

CHAPTER THREE

SADDAM HUSSEIN MOVES SOUTH

A more prudent despot would surely have chosen a moment other than August 2, 1990, to launch his invasion of a helpless neighbor.

—Secretary of State James A. Baker

FROM THE ARMY'S perspective, seismic shifts came at a breakneck pace in 1989 and 1990. The Soviet Union accepted the collapse of its empire with grace and seemed willing to move beyond détente—perhaps as far as rapprochement. But it was the sight of German civilians tearing down the Berlin Wall that demonstrated unequivocally the end of the Cold War. The large Army maintained during the Cold War now seemed superfluous; not surprisingly, the United States moved to reduce it significantly and quickly. Secretary of State James A. Baker's observation about Saddam Hussein's poor timing is pertinent for at least two reasons. First, if he had waited a year or so, the US Army could not have responded as it did. Most of the forces that enabled Operation Desert Storm deployed with the Europe-based VII Corps. Second, there was a surprising consensus among world powers, including the Soviet Union, that Saddam's invasion should not be allowed to stand. That moment might have passed had the dictator waited.

Life at Fort Riley in the summer of 1990 had a surreal quality. The incipient drawing down of forces affected volunteer soldiers differently from how it would have affected conscripts. The drawdown threatened the livelihood of career soldiers, but conscripts may well have rejoiced. Rumors abounded about how deep the drawdown would go and whether Fort Riley would even survive. Saddam's invasion of Kuwait astounded everyone in the 1st Division and at Fort Riley. The Department of Defense styled the immediate response to Iraq's invasion of its tiny neighbor as Operation Desert Shield, but for the time being, all of this changed everything and nothing.

Desert Shield did not include the 1st Division. The resulting ambiguity about a potential role in the conflict occupied much of the late summer and early fall of 1990. Many in the 1st Division felt sure they would eventually be called. Convictions aside, the Army shifted resources to those units bound for the defense of Saudi Arabia and away from those units it was not certain it would call. The 1st Division did what it could to prepare that fall in the event the call came.

Secretary of Defense Dick Cheney Comes to Call

None of this had yet come to pass when the 2nd Battalion, 34th Armor (2-34 AR) went to shoot qualification gunnery in July. While at gunnery, the battalion hosted Secretary of Defense Dick Cheney. The secretary had not come to visit gunnery or take briefings, but rather to talk with the troops; he wanted to explain personally the implications for them of the post–Cold War drawdown.[1] Earlier that year the Army had issued a team teaching package on how the Department of Defense intended to execute reductions in force. Secretary Cheney came to put a face on the plan, to explain the necessity of the reductions, and to see what might be done to ease the transition on those most affected.

Cheney arrived on the range late Monday morning, July 23, 1990. He proved affable and earnestly cooperative, taking a short briefing on gunnery and readiness and answering pertinent questions. Neither the secretary nor his entourage made burdensome requests. In fact, they had no special needs; they were undemanding and easy to like. After the briefing, the secretary spent the rest of the day talking to groups of soldiers from each of the companies of the battalion in turn. He easily charmed the soldiers, who felt free to ask him pointed questions, which he answered clearly and without condescension. He reassured them that their interests would be considered as the reductions occurred. They found him convincing when he asserted he cared about what happened to them.[2]

Secretary Cheney's visit had a second purpose: he also had come to meet with opponents to Fort Riley's proposed land acquisition. COL Gary LaGrange had flown to Washington to brief the secretary on the proposed land acquisition and then accompany him and the Kansas congressional delegation back to Fort Riley the next day. Instead Cheney asked LaGrange to brief both him and the Kansas delegation en route to Fort Riley.

Early the next morning, LaGrange joined Cheney, his staff, Kansas senators Bob Dole and Nancy Kassebaum, and Congressman Jim Slattery aboard a special mission airplane. Before LaGrange began, Cheney produced a briefing book delineating military installations the Department of Defense proposed for closure or realignment; Fort Riley was third on the list. Cheney's staff proposed to reassign the active duty units and make Fort Riley a National Guard and Army Reserve training center.[3]

The Kansas lawmakers offered objections, and Secretary Cheney listened, but pointed out that realigning Fort Riley was within his purview. Still, he agreed to hear the briefing. With that ominous beginning LaGrange, like the Light Brigade in the Crimea, embarked on a mission that seemed doomed. But to his immense surprise the briefing went well: despite his earlier assertion and the briefing book, Cheney did, in fact, decide to support the acquisition bid, although he did not announce his intention to the press that day.

Later, at Fort Riley, Cheney took questions at a news conference held after he met with the opposition. When queried by journalists, he was noncommittal about Fort Riley's future. Of the planned reduction of the Army he said, "No question that the US Army will be a whole lot smaller in the future than it has been in the past." On closing the post, he noted, "Everything is on the table."[4] Even so, the Fort Riley acquisition made it into the program operating memorandum, the budget-planning document, for execution in 1994.[5]

On the plane ride to Kansas, LaGrange listened in on the intelligence update to the secretary and the briefer's report that the Iraqi Army had massed on the Kuwaiti frontier. But the briefing concluded that Iraqis intended the operation as a show of force and they were unlikely to attack.[6] After Cheney departed, many at Fort Riley resumed fretting about the drawdown and the future of the post. Units continued training, although training for what, still no one knew.

A few days later, a small group of soldiers had another through-the-looking-glass experience. On Friday, July 27, 1990, five of them traveled to a reunion of the Vietnam-era 2-34 AR in San Juan Capistrano, California. On Saturday they carried the national flag and the battalion colors at the head of a welcome home parade for the Vietnam veterans of the battalion, who had returned from Vietnam in 1970. Pat Forster, who led a tank platoon in A Company during the Vietnam War, had organized the reunion for his old battalion in his hometown. The city of San Juan Capistrano fully supported the effort, issuing a proclamation that was fulsome in its praise for veterans and hanging welcome home banners along the parade route.[7]

Thus, on a clear sunny southern California morning more than eighty veterans lined up behind the color guard and the six different officers who commanded the 2-34 AR during its five years in Vietnam. When the color bearer uncased the colors, he shook out the campaign streamers the battalion had earned. Unfurling the one bearing the word *Ardennes* to its full length produced a most surprising response: a middle-aged woman ran across to the colors as fast as she could; she embraced the young man holding the colors and then took the streamer commemorating the battalion's service during the Battle of the Bulge and stroked her tear-streaked face with it. As a girl she had endured the German invasion, occupation, American liberation, and German reoccupation, and ultimately the final liberation.[8] It was truly a summer of surprises and strange occurrences.

That afternoon the color guard enjoyed celebrating with the Vietnam veterans. Tired and happy, they returned to Fort Riley the next morning, and on

Monday, July 30, they were back on the range to complete shooting. The most surreal moment of that unusual summer came mid-morning on Thursday, August 2. The battalion commander was in the control tower watching his scouts struggle a bit with their first qualification gunnery. The scout platoon had just completed transition to the Bradley; this was their first gunnery and it showed. The phone in the tower rang, and to the commander's surprise, it was his wife. More surprising still, she claimed that Iraq had invaded Kuwait. She found his subdued reaction puzzling, but it reflected the conviction that he thought she was mistaken. After they hung up he sought confirmation. The era of the twenty-four-hour news cycle had not yet begun and no one had a smartphone; confirmation came slowly, but it came. The commander called his wife back, chastened at having not entirely believed her earlier.

Most of the Division command group, some of the new commanders, and part of the staff happened to be in Germany when the news broke. They were inspecting prepositioned equipment and the ground they would defend in the event of war with the Soviet Union. The Cold War had ended, but the momentum of planning for war in Europe had not yet petered out. Surprised and not entirely believing the news of the invasion, the group continued their reconnaissance. There was really nothing they could do.

Reacting with disbelief proved common that day. The reaction at the White House, despite access to much better information, resembled that in the tower of the gunnery complex at Fort Riley and in Germany. Until the night before the invasion, President George H. W. Bush believed Saddam would not go into Kuwait. And even after learning of the attack, Bush would later write that he had "found it hard to believe that Saddam would invade. For a moment I thought, or hoped, that his move was intended to bring greater pressure on Kuwait and to force settlement of their disputes, and that he might withdraw, having made his point."[9]

Saddam surprised Kuwait and the United States—indeed, everyone. Secretary Baker heard the news in Irkutsk, Russia, where he was consulting with his Soviet counterpart, Eduard Shevardnadze. The Soviet foreign secretary had insisted over the previous months that nothing would come of Saddam's increasingly belligerent pronouncements. Even Shevardnadze found the news of the Kuwait invasion difficult to believe, telling Baker he thought it "totally irrational." Of Saddam he added, "I know that he's a thug, but I never thought he was irrational."[10]

Saddam Hussein Seizes Kuwait in a Day

Throughout the rest of the summer and fall of 1990, and many times since, various statesmen and pundits questioned Saddam's rationality. Their logic is straightforward: the dictator undoubtedly knew that his occupation of Kuwait would not be allowed to stand and that therefore he could not achieve his ends. The explanation here is that he simply behaved irrationally. The other explanation, offered at the time and occasionally still heard, is that Ambassador April Glaspie mismanaged a seminal meeting with Saddam. That explanation assumes the ambassador indicated the United States would not react to Kuwait disappearing. President Bush dismissed this theory; according to him, Glaspie "clearly spelled out that we could not condone settlement of disputes by other than peaceful means."[11]

The ambassador in no way acceded to Saddam's views. Instead, Saddam miscalculated the reaction to his invasion of Kuwait. It is equally accurate to say that both the United States and Saddam's allies, including the Soviet Union, completely misread him. Saddam and his adversaries arrived at their estimates from within the cocoon of their unique perspectives. His behavior may have seemed irrational to Shevardnadze and a great many others, but within the context of Iraqi culture, the Ba'ath system from which he drew his power, and his limited experience with international actors he behaved rationally. Saddam was implacable, tough, and determined, but also a provincial Arab from Tikrit.[12] Understanding his thinking is part of the context of the 1st Division's desert experience.

Saddam's perceptions, deceptions, the quantity of his weapons, and the size of his army influenced decision makers in the United States and elsewhere. Cunning and adept at manipulating events in Iraq, he had little understanding of how foreigners viewed him and his policies. Saddam was every bit as ethnocentric as many Western politicians. A successful conspirator, he assumed other leaders were as well; he also assumed that he was the target of conspiracy himself. His paranoia had a basis in fact: both the United States and the Soviets sought, at various times, to use him as a surrogate in their ongoing rivalry. For his part, Saddam regarded the Americans as the ultimate conspirators. In November 1979, shortly after he became president, he remarked to a group of his advisers that the United States was deeply involved in Iranian affairs, "including the removal of the Shah."[13] Equally important, outsiders often misunderstood him.

Saddam's paranoia would have served him well had it made him cautious, but he had a vision for himself and Iraq that led him to embark on a dangerous course. He imagined himself a latter-day Saladin and Iraq as the inheritor of the Assyrian civilization. In Saddam's thinking, he and Iraq had a mission to lead the Arabs: "There is no escape from the responsibility of leadership [of the Arabs]. It is not our choice to accept it or not. It is, rather, imposed on us. . . . It must be Iraq due to the fact that Iraq has everything going for it."[14]

Saddam had shown a penchant for miscalculation on foreign affairs even before he became president. In October 1978, while deputy to his predecessor, GEN Ahmad Hassan al-Bakr, Saddam arranged to have Ayatollah Khomeini of Iran expelled from Najaf, Iraq, where he lived in exile.[15] Khomeini neither forgot nor forgave; once in power in Iran, he not only rebuffed overtures from

Saddam but also went so far as to urge Iraqis to rid themselves of Saddam, whom he pronounced a deviant. For his part, Saddam seethed with desire for full control of the Shatt al-Arab waterway. Like Khomeini, he did not take kindly to personal insult. More important, Saddam perceived that Khomeini's revolution had left Iran in a weakened state—a situation Saddam hoped to exploit. In September 1980 Saddam invaded Iran, aiming to seize control of all of the Shatt al-Arab.[16]

Eight long years of the Iran-Iraq War ensued. At first the United States favored Iraq as "the enemy of my enemy." Later, to preclude Iraq becoming too strong, the United States provided limited support to Iran. Not surprisingly, Saddam complained to his inner circle about what he saw as American perfidy. One such session occurred on November 15, 1986; complaining at some length that the United States lacked morals, Saddam concluded that the Americans preferred the Iranians to the Iraqis "not because they are better looking than we are or because they are better than us, but because it is more possible to control them than us."[17] In this session, Saddam went on to wonder why the United States had forsaken Iraq. Foreign minister and deputy prime minister Tariq Aziz, the lone Christian in Saddam's inner circle, offered an alternative explanation. Aziz, who became well known globally during the 1990 crisis, suggested the Americans turned about because Iraq had publicly favored Puerto Rican independence. Even Saddam found this explanation implausible, retorting, "The Puerto Rico issue should not have a major effect on the basic politics of a country."[18] The session reveals that Saddam's closest counselors generally provided him an echo chamber, with few of them willing to stand by their own views should they differ from his.

The fighting in the Iran-Iraq War produced high casualties on both sides, but particularly among the Iranian Revolutionary Guards and the poorly trained mobs of the Basij, the militia whose members mounted suicidal attacks carrying plastic keys that allegedly would assure their admission into heaven.[19] Iran and Iraq fired woefully inaccurate Scud missiles at each other's cities, with little in mind beyond terrorizing the inhabitants. The war, which raged across a nearly seven-hundred-kilometer front and reduced several cities to rubble, occurred in three general phases. In the first, Iraq advanced nearly one hundred kilometers deep into Iran, seizing several towns, including the city of Khorramshar. The Iraqis then assumed the defensive, hoping to limit the war and reach a settlement. The second major phase occurred from 1983 to 1987, when the Iranians launched a series of counteroffensives and, in turn, advanced into Iraq, threatening Basra. It was also in this phase of the war, beginning in February 1984, that the Iraqis resorted to chemical munitions. Finally, in 1988 Iraq reduced Iran's penetrations and drove them back.[20]

Ultimately neither of the two belligerents achieved much in the long-running conflict. Each nation grew its army from a small regional force to a very large and fairly well-armed war machine. Each organized a regular army and an elite force, although Iran depended also on a large, poorly trained militia. But both of them incurred massive debts as they continuously sought to upgrade their forces and replace combat losses. Arguably, though, Saddam was the biggest loser, for he had been denied his cherished goal of taking control of the Shatt al-Arab.[21]

In a pattern familiar to those around him, Saddam managed to find cause for celebration despite the unsatisfying outcome of the war. Reminiscing about the fighting toward the end, he concluded, "What was accomplished was the highest of my hopes for this bloody route that has taken eight long years. And we have truly been able to be victors in our dependence on God."[22] Win or lose, he could not escape the war's cost: he had borrowed heavily from other Arab states to sustain his army as it struggled first to hold what it had taken and then to avoid losing part of Iraq. As the self-appointed leader of the Arabs, Iraq had, from Saddam's point of view, fought for all of them, and so he believed the others should forgive the debts he incurred in the fighting. The Saudis did just that, but Kuwait refused.[23]

Saddam, who never forgot or forgave a slight, was incensed. Further, he held a view, common in Iraq, that neighboring Kuwait was not a real country but a creation of the British. Although forced to accede to Kuwaiti independence in 1961, the Iraqis never accepted the border drawn by the British.[24] Saddam also believed the Kuwaitis were drilling for oil laterally under the disputed border, literally stealing Iraqi oil. In the end he did what he felt justified in doing: he invaded Kuwait, despite a rare show of resistance to his thinking from Tariq Aziz, who in mid-July 1990 cautioned that Iraq would "be regarded as aggressors if we carry out such an action (invasion) before we clarify it to the world."[25]

In the end Saddam invaded because he believed he could get away with it. He understood the dangers of going to war with the United States, but thought he could avoid that outcome or at least mitigate the risks. Accordingly, he and his minions made overtures to anyone who might help; Saddam even contacted the president of Iran seeking help, but couched his query in the interest of "fraternal relations with all Muslims."[26] In September, President Bush reiterated to Congress that Iraq would not be permitted to annex Kuwait; upon hearing this, Saddam observed that Bush "is beginning to warn us. He must be crazy."[27] As late as October 1990 Saddam believed the chance of avoiding war remained at least fifty-fifty.[28] He also sought to defuse the situation with the help of other Arab nations, and even some non-Arab ones; he found some support in the Soviet Union and in France. As late as November, Aziz thought the French would at least take into consideration the attitudes of the four million Arab Muslims living in France.[29]

Even if war could not be avoided, Saddam believed the United States had no stomach for it. Shortly after the invasion, he told another Arab president that "America and Israel may attack us . . . without ground forces . . . they may attack us with airplanes and missiles, (but) we will destroy them. And we will attack their fleets in the Gulf as the Kamikaze."[30] Some of what he said may have been bluster and bluff, but Saddam genuinely had confidence in the Iraqi Army's capability to wage defensive operations and in his view that the United States would avoid ground combat. He based his assessment of Iraqi defensive capability on the Iran-Iraq War. The Iraqis, fighting from sand forts with observation and firing ramps protected by barriers, mines, and obstacles, had slaughtered thousands of Iranians.[31] Saddam reasoned that his troops could do much the same against the Americans.

The American Response

Saddam never reckoned that Bush would act so decisively and rapidly. On August 5, 1990, the president responded to a question about the invasion by stating that "this will not stand";[32] but just what that meant was by no means clear. The president, like Saddam, hoped to avoid war. Richard N. Haas, then a principal in the National Security Council and a special assistant to the president, believed that it was "anything but axiomatic that the United States would decide to deploy half a million troops halfway around the world to rescue a country that few Americans could find on a map."[33]

Perhaps so, but Haas and Saddam both knew that three presidents in succession had declared security within the Persian Gulf vital to United States national interest. In his final State of the Union Address in January 1981 President Jimmy Carter had said so unequivocally: "An attempt by any outside force to gain control of the Persian Gulf region will be regarded as an assault on the vital interests of the United States of America, and such assault will be repelled by any means necessary, including military force."[34]

The implications of the Carter Doctrine grew over time, as did the means to enforce it. Both Presidents Ronald Reagan and George H. W. Bush adhered to it and issued classified directives that amplified their views.[35] In the years following Carter's declaration, the United States demonstrated its commitment by conducting operations in the Persian Gulf, including the so-called Tanker War.[36] In 1983 the United States established US Central Command (CENTCOM), oriented toward the Horn of Africa, the Middle East, and Southwest Asia. Originally CENTCOM focused on a Soviet incursion to seize the Iranian oil fields. After the Iranian Revolution, the threat assessment included Iran as a threat to the even more important oil resources of Kuwait and Saudi Arabia. By the summer of 1989 Saddam's Iraq loomed as the most likely aggressors. In November 1988 GEN H. Norman Schwarzkopf assumed command of CENTCOM and, over time, he retooled planning with Iraq in mind. Schwarzkopf's staff exercised the revised plan in July 1990 during a war game called Internal Look.[37]

In August 1990 events moved quickly and more or less as CENTCOM imagined. President Bush acted decisively, as did the Saudis. On August 5 the Saudis asked for a briefing on the threat and what the United States intended. Secretary Cheney and GEN Schwarzkopf flew to Saudi Arabia, where they briefed the Saudis and offered help in defending the kingdom. During the meeting on August 6 the Saudis accepted the US offer. That day Schwarzkopf issued movement orders, and Air Force fighters arrived in Saudi Arabia within hours; on Wednesday, August 8, the ready brigade from the 82nd Airborne Division began landing in Dhahran.[38] The United States, it was becoming increasingly apparent, intended to uphold the Carter Doctrine. The first tranche of troops deployed forces adequate to defend the kingdom, including major air, naval, and sea forces in Operation Desert Shield. Major US ground forces included the XVIII Airborne Corps and the 1 Marine Expeditionary Force. Army maneuver units assigned to the XVIII Airborne Corps included the 3rd Armored Cavalry Regiment, the 1st Cavalry Division, the 24th Infantry (Mechanized), the 82nd Airborne Division (82 ABN), and the 101st Airborne Division (101 ABN).

GEN Schwarzkopf's planners, in collaboration with the Joint Chiefs of Staff, began planning on how to eject Iraq from Kuwait if required. From the outset Schwarzkopf considered forcibly evicting the Iraqis. On August 16 he took a briefing from COL John Warden from the air staff on a retaliatory air campaign; at the conclusion of that briefing, Schwarzkopf developed a four-phased concept for driving the Iraqis out of Kuwait that included a retaliatory air campaign called Instant Thunder, followed by air attacks to suppress enemy air defenses over Kuwait, then air attacks to attrit enemy ground forces, and finally a ground attack. On August 22 the president called up selected reserves. Planning continued over the next several weeks, including how to assure success in an eventual ground offensive. That planning ultimately led to a second tranche of troops being deployed, though as of August no decision to do so had yet been made.[39]

Reaction to the movement of forces at Fort Riley reflected concern and ambiguity. Despite not being on the immediate troop list, some believed the Division would go. MG Thomas G. Rhame, despite wanting very much to deploy, was not convinced. He did not believe the Division was "a logical candidate."[40] Because the Division was not yet fully modernized, Rhame thought any additional units required would come from Europe. He "had no thought that we would be mobilized and go to war."[41]

In late August, LTC Terry Bullington, Rhame's operations officer, received a telephone call on a secure line and heard stunning news: the caller, a staff officer at the Pentagon whom he did not know, was letting him know that the 1st Division was being considered for deployment; the officer had seen several options, and every one of them "included the deployment of 1st Division."[42] Bullington reported the call to Rhame, who told Bullington he had heard nothing about it and that "we should not mention this to anyone."[43] Whatever he believed, Rhame directed his subordinates to prepare as though they would deploy. Reactions ran the gamut from those who absolutely believed they would go to those who found it impossible to believe. The two camps largely broke down along the lines of those who had served at Fort Riley for some time and those who had not. The argument for deploying held that moving quickly was something the Division knew how to do and so it made sense to send it in. That thinking was based on frequent deployments to Germany to exercise the General Defense Plan. The counterargument was that deploying to Germany had always counted on drawing equipment on arrival.

COL Lon E. "Bert" Maggart, commander of the 1st Brigade, has claimed that "all of us knew immediately we would go to war."[44] As one of Maggart's battalion commanders, another old-timer, put it, "my own assessment was that the invasion of Kuwait was so serious that the United States would ultimately go to war. Because I was so convinced this was true, I determined that afternoon, the 4th of August to tell my battalion what I believed."[45] LTC Harry Emerson, commanding the 1st Battalion, 5th Field Artillery, "assumed we were going to go."[46] CPT Juan E. Toro arrived at Fort Riley to join the 2-34 AR on Friday, August 10, in time to attend a party at the home of his battalion commander. He found an "atmosphere of anticipation."[47] Everyone he met believed the Division would go, all except his first sergeant, who said, "I think we are going to war, but right after the Boy Scouts."[48]

At the 2nd Brigade, COL Tony Moreno had been in command for all of ten days. Moreno had no insight on whether the Division would go to Saudi Arabia, but he knew he was going to the National Training Center (NTC) at Fort Irwin, California, that winter. He focused on training his staff with one eye on the Iraqis. LTC Dave Marlin, commander of the 4-37 AR, one of Moreno's two tank battalions, at first believed that nothing would come of the crisis. Marlin thought there would be the "usual saber rattling and verbal charges and counter-charges and, in the end there would be no change,"[49] but when the 82 ABN deployed he changed his mind.

LTC Dave Gross, commander of the 3-37 AR, was in the field running platoon training, and learned of the invasion from his operations officer, MAJ Paul Izzo. When Izzo told him, Gross "smiled and chuckled," and Izzo remonstrated, "Sir, this is serious."[50] LTC Gross chuckled because he recalled a conversation he had had with an intelligence officer at Fort Leavenworth, Kansas, just before he came to Fort Riley. At a briefing for Gross and others, that officer reported that Iraq had "five thousand tanks." LTC Gross had been unimpressed, as had most of his colleagues; some wondered aloud just where Iraq was.[51] Gross had dismissed the intelligence officer's assessment of the Iraqis as a threat, laughable at that time, and his own complacent attitude equally laughable in August. LTC Terry Ford, the Division's intelligence officer, not only knew where Iraq was but believed the Division would be called to go. As he put it, "within two weeks of [the invasion] it became increasingly clear . . . that if the build up continued, we were almost certainly to be one of the next units to be mobilized or to be deployed to Southwest Asia."[52] LTC Bullington felt confident enough to begin preparing to deploy, and set planners to work rewriting the Fort Riley emergency deployment plan. He named the plan Lexicon Danger and focused it on deploying to the Middle East. Doing so made sense because, he said, the "real action is in Saudi Arabia, Kuwait or Iraq. Let's just focus on it."[53]

MG Rhame acted on the same assumption. He articulated a straightforward premise: war was likely, so the Division would prepare within the means available. CPT Gene Malik, commander of the Headquarters, 1-34 AR, appreciated that approach. Rhame, according to Malik, "was a leaning forward kind of guy; I liked him a lot."[54] CPT Malik and many others at Fort Riley also liked Rhame for just that reason—he issued straightforward orders that still allowed room for initiative. Equally important, getting ready seemed prudent. Malik's colleague, CPT Jim Bell, commander of C Company of the 1-34 AR, doubted the Division would be deployed.[55] Nevertheless, Bell believed that doing what prudence dictated helped him stay focused on readiness with a purpose he otherwise would not have felt.

CPT Toro found the gap between the conviction that the Division would go to war and the facts on the ground confusing. When he took command of his tank company, it had thirty-four officers and soldiers assigned—less than half its authorized strength.[56] Toro not only had too few troops, he had too few dollars and the money situation only grew worse. About the time Toro took command, the Army began diverting money and repair parts to units en route to Saudi Arabia. On August 22 the list grew when the president authorized selected reserve mobilization. Reserve units immediately began to deploy.[57] Before the end of August, GEN Gordon R. Sullivan, the vice chief of staff of the Army, issued a directive: "All FY [fiscal year] 90 non-essential discretionary operations must be stopped and funds generated will be used to sustain Desert Shield."[58] Accordingly, units at Fort Riley could prepare as much as they liked within the limits of greatly reduced resources.

As commanding general of the Division, deploying remained theoretical for Rhame, but as post commander he had immediate obligations. COL LaGrange and his garrison troops, both military and civilian, were already at war. Fort Riley was a mobilization station where alerted reserve units assembled and deployed. Generally, these were small units that managed transportation, ammunition, other logistics functions, and medical operations. The first of these, the 545th Transportation Detachment, arrived soon after the reserve call-up on August 22 and deployed from Fort Riley on August 29. From then until the following summer, Fort Riley had units on the move. For months Fort Riley prepared units heading overseas and later demobilized them on their return.[59]

Family Support: A Volunteer Army Requirement

The ongoing deployment to Saudi Arabia highlighted an unintended consequence of the transition to volunteer units: the care of families of departed soldiers and a fundamental difference in the way the Army deployed forces. During the Vietnam War, once units deployed they remained for the duration. The Army sustained the war in Vietnam as it had in both world wars and the Korean War. Individual soldiers replaced those killed, wounded, or returned home after completing their tour. Back then the Army took little responsibility for families of soldiers; comparatively few soldiers of that era were married, and for those who were, their family members generally went home to live with relatives when units went overseas. There were exceptions, but mostly the Army had no need to concern itself with the "home front." That changed with the end of the draft, however.

The Army that deployed for Desert Shield bore only superficial resemblance to the one that had fought in Vietnam. This newer Army was composed of volunteers, many of whom were married. Units had become, in some ways, communities whose residents had different expectations from those of draftees. The institution responded to these changes as time passed. In 1983 GEN Edward C. Meyer claimed the Army had a "partnership" with families. In the middle and late 1980s, about 786,000 solders served in active duty. In 1989, 1,089,051 persons were family members of serving soldiers. They had expectations, some of which the Army believed it had an obligation to meet. For example, in 1989 it planned to spend $72.2 million building child care facilities and a further $191.6 million on other family activities.[60]

Despite committing to supporting families, by 1990 the Army had not fully closed the gap between expectations and services. Several incidents occurred that could, but did not, generate explicit Army policy. One of the most important of these occurred on December 12, 1985, when an Arrow Air charter flight crashed on takeoff from Gander, Newfoundland, killing 248 soldiers and eight crewmembers. Most of the soldiers who died were assigned to the 3rd Battalion, 502nd Infantry of the 101 ABN. The battalion was returning from a deployment to the Sinai Peninsula as part of the Multinational Force and Observers. Coping with the loss challenged the 101 ABN. Other tragedies, including combat losses in the Tanker War, stimulated the Army to develop systems for family support. Rotations to the NTC also raised awareness that something needed to done to help families help themselves. In the late 1980s some units formed family support groups to assist during training and operational deployments. They did so with little support from the larger Army institution.[61]

The Army provided some information as part of preparing prospective commanders and their spouses to serve as "command teams." In 1988 it published Department of the Army Pamphlet 608–47, *A Guide to Establishing Family*

Support Groups. At a special course for prospective battalion and brigade commanders, the Army added modules for spouses and prospective commanders to take together. The module was called Command Team Training, and its facilitators issued the Army's pamphlet and led discussions on just how to develop and sustain a family support group. Army pamphlets are not, by definition, directives; this one was instructive in how the Army imagined family support groups would be generated.

According to the pamphlet, a family support group "is a company or battalion affiliated organization of officers and enlisted soldiers and family members that uses volunteers to provide social and emotional support, outreach services, and information to family members prior to, during, and in the immediate aftermath" of extended temporary duty away from home, deployments, or training rotations.[62] But the Army provided little in the way of guidance. It was not uncommon in that era to hear senior officers talking about the Army taking care of its own. The truth of the matter is that Army spouses took care of the Army's own. At Fort Riley, that meant that volunteers helped support about twelve thousand family members. Of those, just under seven thousand lived at Fort Riley; most of the others lived nearby. Volunteer efforts included teaching family members things they needed to know in order to survive—including, for example, budget planning.[63]

In the summer of 1990 Rhame understood better than most that he had a responsibility to families. He had commanded the Army's recently created family support center, a reflection of the growing institutional awareness of the changes wrought by the transition to the volunteer force. Nonetheless, Rhame, his brigade commanders, and LaGrange thought about the problem more or less in the context of their Vietnam experience. MG Rhame's battalion commanders, on the other hand, had grown up in the volunteer Army. To them families had always been part of the Army, and they realized that those families would be looking to them for help. In this instance, the Vietnam experience was irrelevant.

Fort Riley had a secret weapon: Pearl I. Speer. As a young woman, she had graduated from a small Oklahoma college and went to work for the American Red Cross as a hospital service representative. For a year she served as a hospital field director in Vietnam, where she honed her skills in managing the provision of services to wounded soldiers and airmen. She took one more tour in the hospital at Fort Sill, Oklahoma, where she met and married a badly wounded infantry officer, CPT Bill Speer. She transitioned from a Red Cross professional to a full-time Army wife and part-time civil servant for the Army Community Services (ACS), which provided services to Army families, ranging from financial planning to relocation support designed to reduce the hardship of frequent moves. For example, nearly every military family has visited a "lending closet" during a move; these lending closets loaned basic household goods, including pots and pans, for families to use while waiting for their own items to arrive.

In the summer of 1989 Pearl Speer and her husband, now a colonel and a hospital administrator, arrived at Fort Riley. Shortly thereafter, the ACS director hired her to serve as the Fort Riley relocation manager. Soon after the invasion, Speer and her supervisor, Betty Banner, recognized that a "storm was rising."[64] Rhame, LaGrange, Banner, and Speer knew they needed to get something under way to support families of deploying units. Doing so would meet the needs of the reserve units already moving and the Division if it deployed. A requirement for units to help the US Forest Service fight wildfires also provided impetus. All the soldiers destined to support the Forest Service processed through the center, doing things such as helping soldiers and their family members prepare wills and powers of attorney. Bert Maggart believed that processing through the family support center prepared the soldiers, whether to fight fires or for "going off to war."[65]

Speer looked for good examples of how she might develop a family support program at Fort Riley. She ended up borrowing from both of the only two extant programs. To garner support she scheduled a meeting to which she invited the senior officers' spouses. When she briefed the planned effort she was met "with a lot of empty faces."[66] The ladies in attendance wanted to know, "Why are we doing this?" They pointed out that nothing like what she proposed had been part of the Vietnam experience they had all endured. Speer asked if they thought the Army should do better. To their credit, nearly all of them agreed and said they would help. Consequently, Fort Riley got a running start in developing and sustaining both a family support center and family support groups.

Many of the battalions had family support groups organized by officer's and senior noncommissioned officers' (NCOs') spouses. These groups waxed and waned more or less in accordance with deployment to the NTC, REFORGER, or other short-term missions. By the end of August, every unit was either starting or revitalizing its family support group. Peggy Waterman had a particularly large task; her husband, LTC Tom Waterman, commanded the 701st Main Support Battalion (701 MSB). With nearly twelve hundred soldiers assigned, LTC Waterman's battalion was by far the largest on post. When the 701 MSB deployed in December, 470 spouses of both sexes remained behind. LTC Waterman and his wife had little to go on beyond the notes they had taken during the precommand course and the pamphlet Pearl Speer had drafted. Armed with the same information, the 2-34 AR's family support group met on August 28, 1990, to regenerate its effort; the agenda that day dealt with everything from coping with stress to pay issues. One of the chief points was to help family members "realize they can solve their own problems."[67] Teaching self-sufficiency became the organizing principle of many family support groups.

Prudent Measures

As October wore on, the probability of deploying to Saudi Arabia rose perceptibly. LTC Bullington got more hints from staff officers in the Pentagon; LTC Ford heard from various people as well, but no one came right out and said anything. As Ford remembers, "We got a lot of phone calls from people we didn't know, from headquarters we never wanted to hear from offering us stuff."[68] An officer from the logistics staff of the 24th Infantry (Mechanized) visited Andrews to pass on lessons learned from its deployment. COL Michael Dodson, the Division artillery commander, reported "indicators" such as getting things "that you didn't expect to get in the area of supply, and maybe somebody sending you some maps or gives you authorization to do something that you hadn't expected."[69] No one said anything for certain about deploying, but the number of doubters waned through October. As Dodson notes, "All those little things [indicators] kind of helped tell us that the probability was good that we'd be going."[70]

At Fort Riley no one issued contradictory orders, so preparation continued. When the 2nd Brigade returned from the field, the 1st Brigade moved out. The 1st Brigade had two big events under way: LTC George P. "Pat" Ritter's 1-34 AR went out to shoot qualification gunnery, and the 2-34 AR drove out the first week of November to run company-level training. No one was idle. MG Rhame took most of his staff to Fort Hood to train with III Corps as it prepared for possible deployment to Saudi Arabia.

The 2nd Brigade went to work to fix equipment worn down by hard use and lack of parts. LTC Gross coped with twenty-six out of fifty-eight tanks "deadlined" for one reason or another. Most of Gross's tanks needed major assemblies, such as engines or transmissions; the Division's tanks were hand-me-downs from units in Europe, already several years old when they had arrived nearly three years earlier. As Gross remembers, "It was a pretty dismal situation."[71] LTC Marlin's tank battalion had problems too, but he thought he had a solution; he sent two of his officers, CPT Oscar Hall and 1LT Eduardo Ortega, to Fort Hood to "scrounge" parts from departing units.[72]

Thursday, November 8, found the 1st Division training at both Fort Riley and Fort Hood. More than a thousand troops were in the field at Fort Riley maneuvering or shooting. CPT Hall and 1LT Ortega were at Fort Hood scrounging parts and hoping not to be seen by Rhame or any of the Division staff, who were also there. The little mission Marlin had assigned, while prudent, exceeded his authority. That evening, as training wound down at Fort Hood and Fort Riley, the long anticipated and generally desired order came: the president announced the troop list for a second surge. These units would go to Saudi Arabia not to defend the kingdom but to provide the capability to oust Saddam from Kuwait. The Big Red One would deploy to Saudi Arabia as part of the Germany-based VII Corps.

LTG Dick Graves's efforts to prepare III Corps proved unnecessary, at least for now. As soon as he heard the news, Graves told Rhame to get his troops home so they could work on getting ready to deploy. At Fort Riley the troops in the field received the news in various ways. Out in the training area, the 2-34 AR heard it over tactical radio when the duty officer called from the battalion's headquarters. LTC Ritter and his troops, shooting tank gunnery, heard their duty officer call the control tower at the Multi-Purpose Range Complex. Most of the 3-37 AR's troops and families learned of the alert at a battalion Family Support Group meeting.[73] The news electrified 1 ID troops wherever they were.

CPT Toro told his troops at the end of what he thought was a great training day. His B Company had taken a beating the day before at the hands of a more experienced tank company led by the senior captain in the 2-34 AR. On November 8 Toro and his troops found a way to move up a gulley out of sight. They flanked their tormentors and had their revenge on C Company. As Toro remembers, he called the troops together and said, "Here's the deal, guys; we are going to take a trip."[74] There were two reactions expressed: "finally," mostly from the officers and NCOs, and "shit," mostly from the younger soldiers. Almost in unison the troops looked around sheepishly at each other and laughed. Whatever they thought, they understood what they had to do. CPT Toro believed his company came together at that moment.[75]

Despite everything, the alert surprised many young soldiers. SPC Steve Sorkness, new to Fort Riley, was amazed to find himself in the middle of Kansas; prior to receiving his orders he never thought there were any installations in Kansas, let alone one as big as Fort Riley. Sorkness's mother was worried he might be called, but he assured her, "That they won't need us." When Sorkness heard the news, he recalls, "I realized right away I lied to everyone I knew." Mrs. Sorkness responded decisively; she got in touch with SFC John T. Messer, Sorkness's section chief, and made him promise that he would get her son home safely. Messer watched over Sorkness because, he explained, "We made your mom a promise that we would keep you safe."[76]

On November 8, US Army Europe alerted the 2nd Armored Division (Forward) to deploy as the 1st Division's third maneuver brigade; this came as a surprise and had an interesting twist. BG Jerry R. Rutherford, who commanded the 2 AD (Forward), had come from the 1st Division, where he had served as the assistant division commander for maneuver for nearly three years. Warned to keep this information secret, Rutherford and his key leaders went home expecting to be told later and to have the opportunity to break the news to their troops themselves. But things did not happen that way; some soldiers and their families heard it on CNN that night, and LTC Clint Ancker, Rutherford's operations officer, heard the announcement on the Armed Forces Network the next morning on his way to work.

NOTES

1. Author's recollection.

2. Ibid. Secretary Dick Cheney proved easy to brief, easy to get on with, and very effective. Pete Williams, who accompanied him, also was very effective with the troops and with all of those who met him.

3. COL (Ret.) Gary L. LaGrange, interview with the author, Manhattan, KS, June 26, 2014.

4. Secretary of Defense Dick Cheney, quoted in Tom Skinner, "Secretary of Defense Pays Visit to Post," *Fort Riley Post*, July 27, 1990, 1; LaGrange interview.

5. LaGrange interview. The planned acquisition dropped out of the budget after Operation Desert Storm.

6. LaGrange interview.

7. As commander of the 2-34 AR, I participated in this event.

8. Author's recollection. The city turned out for a long overdue welcome home.

9. George Bush and Brent Scowcroft, *A World Transformed* (New York: Random House, 1999), 303.

10. James A. Baker III with Thomas DeFrank, *The Politics of Diplomacy: Revolution, War and Peace 1989–1992* (New York: Putnam's, 1995), 5–6.

11. Bush and Scowcroft, *A World Transformed*, 309–12. Saddam miscalculated the reaction of the United States, but he was not misled. It is equally fair to say that the United States completely misread Saddam, but then that is how many (if not most) wars come to pass.

12. The best means to understand how Saddam thought is through the ongoing effort to exploit documents and other media captured in 2003 following the collapse of his government. There are millions of pages of captured documents associated with Harmony, the code name assigned to an Army-led Department of Defense project to translate and make use of captured documents. I have made use of two of several books produced as a consequence: Kevin M. Woods, David D. Palki, and Mark E. Stout, eds., *The Saddam Tapes: The Inner Workings of a Tyrant's Regime 1978–2001* (New York: Cambridge University Press, 2011); and Kevin M. Woods, *The Mother of All Battles: Saddam Hussein's Strategic Plan for the Persian Gulf War* (Annapolis, MD: Naval Institute Press, 2008). *The Saddam Tapes* stemmed from more than two hundred hours of recordings of meetings between Saddam and key advisers. See also Kenneth M. Pollack, *The Persian Puzzle: The Conflict between Iran and America* (New York: Random House, 2004), 213. See also Baker and DeFrank, *The Politics of Diplomacy*, 262. I have also used two ethnographic studies: William G. Baker, *Arabs, Islam and the Middle East* (Dallas: Brown, 2003); and Raphael Patai, *The Arab Mind* (New York: Scribner's, 1976). Said Arburish, *Saddam Hussein: The Politics of Revenge* (London: Bloomsbury, 2001), is a credible and useful biography.

13. Woods, Palki, and Stout, *Saddam Tapes*, 22.

14. Ibid., 122.

15. Lawrence Freedman, *A Choice of Enemies: America Confronts the Middle East* (New York: Public Affairs, 2008), 152.

16. Freedman, *A Choice of Enemies*, 154.

17. Woods, Palki, and Stout, *Saddam Tapes*, 32.

18. Ibid. The first chapter of the *Saddam Tapes* is devoted to how Saddam and his advisers viewed the United States. Their views are an amazing amalgam of ignorance and naïveté, which are evidenced even in Tariq Aziz, who passed for cosmopolitan in the government of Iraq.

19. The story of the keys seems inconceivable, but appears to be true; Abbas Milani first reported it in 2007. See Kevin Sullivan, "The (Plastic) Key to Understanding Iranian Martyrdom," *Real Clear World*, May 3, 2013, 1. See also Rob Johnson, *The Iran-Iraq War* (Basingstoke, England: Palgrave Macmillan, 2011), 12.

20. See Steven R. Ward, *Immortal: A Military History of the Iran and Its Armed Forces* (Washington, DC: Georgetown University Press, 2009); for the Iraqi view, see Kevin M. Woods, Williamson Murray, Elizabeth A. Nathan, Laila Sabara, and Ana M. Venegas, *Saddam's Generals: Perspectives of the Iran-Iraq War* (Alexandria, VA: Institute for Defense Analysis, 2011). General histories include Johnson, *The Iran-Iraq War*; Shahram Chubin and Charles Tripp, *Iran and Iraq at War* (Boulder, CO: Westview, 1988); and Dilip Hiro, *The Longest War: The Iran-Iraq Military Conflict* (London: Routledge Chapman and Hall, 1991).

21. Regarding the growth of Iranian and Iraqi forces, see Chubin and Tripp, *Iran and Iraq at War*, appendixes 1 and 2.

22. Woods, Palki, and Stout, *Saddam Tapes*, 162.

23. Freedman, *Choice of Enemies*, 213–15. See also Woods, Palki, and Stout, *Saddam Tapes*, 97–98, 166–68.

24. The Ottoman Empire was one of the casualties of World War I. The victorious Allies built a cordon sanitaire around Turkey by creating new states, including Iraq.

25. Woods, Palki, and Stout, *Saddam Tapes*, 170. Perhaps buoyed by Aziz's courage, one other spoke up as well, recommending developing support within the Arab League.

26. Ibid., 105.

27. Woods, *The Mother of All Battles*, 108.

28. Woods, Palki, and Stout, *Saddam Tapes*, 35–38. These pages are from a meeting that occurred in late October with Saddam and his key advisers; Saddam's assessment of the odds of war can be found on 35.

29. Woods, *The Mother of All Battles*, 111.

30. Ibid., 95.

31. In November 2010 the author had the privilege of overflying part of the Al-Faw Peninsula with MG Vincent Brooks, who was then commanding the 1 ID. The Iraqi forts remained evident, as did one or two derelict tanks. Their siting permitted mutual supporting fires between positions. The peninsula would have afforded little or no cover and no concealment to attacking Iranian units; there is little wonder that Saddam overestimated what his units could achieve.

32. Bush and Scowcroft, *A World Transformed*, 333.

33. Richard N. Haas, *War of Necessity, War of Choice: A Memoir of Two Iraq Wars* (New York: Simon and Schuster, 2009), 63.

34. Ibid., 21.

35. Reagan published his guidance in Nation Security Decision Directive 114, "U.S. Policy Toward the Iran-Iraq War," November 26, 1983. On October 2, 1989, President Bush signed National Security Directive 26, "U.S. Policy Toward the Persian Gulf."

36. The Tanker War broke out between the United States and Iran in 1987. Ward, *Immortal*, argues that crisis came because while the Iraqis could ship oil overland and obtain war materials through ports on the Gulf, Iran could not. Iran began attacking ships carrying war materials. Ultimately Kuwait sought help from the United States that led to Kuwaiti tankers flying US flags and traveling under US escorts. An undeclared naval war occurred in 1987–88 that culminated when the USS *Vincennes* shot down an Iranian airliner in July 1988. See Lee Allen Zatarain, *Tanker War: America's First Conflict with Iran, 1987–1988* (Philadelphia: Casemate, 2008).

37. General H. Norman Schwarzkopf with Peter Petre, *It Doesn't Take a Hero: The Autobiography* (New York: Bantam, 1992), 289–92.

38. Ibid., 295–310. See also Bush and Scowcroft, *A World Transformed*, 334–36.

39. Schwarzkopf, *It Doesn't Take a Hero*, 317–25. On the machinations that led to the second tranche of troops, see Colin Powell with Joseph E. Persico, *My American Journey* (New York: Random House, 1995); and Bush and Scowcroft, *A World Transformed*.

40. LTG Thomas G. Rhame, interview with the author, Alexandria, VA, April 23, 2014.

41. Ibid.

42. COL (Ret.) Terry W. Bullington, "The First Infantry Division in Desert Shield/Desert Storm: Notes by Terry Bullington," undated letter to the author, received June 16, 2014.

43. Ibid.

44. MG (Ret.) Lon E. Maggart, "Eye of the Storm (Duty First)," unpublished manuscript, 1992–97, 18.

45. Ibid. The 2-34 AR is the unit to which Maggart refers; it returned from the field on August 4, 1991.

46. COL (Ret.) Harry Emerson, e-mail to the author, January 30, 2014.

47. LTC (Ret.) Juan E. Toro, telephone interview with the author, October 8, 2014.

48. Ibid.

49. Lieutenant Colonel David W. Marlin, "History of the 4th Battalion, 37th Armored Regiment in Operation Desert Shield/Storm," unpublished manuscript, US Army War College, Carlisle Barracks, PA, 1992, 18, 39–40.

50. BG (Ret.) David F. Gross, telephone interview with the author, August 13, 2014.

51. Ibid.

52. LTC Terry Ford, G-2, 1st Infantry Division, interviewed by MAJ Thomas A. Popa, Fort Riley, KS, July 23, 1991, DSIT-C-064.

53. LTC Terry Bullington, G-3, 1st Infantry Division, interviewed by MAJ Thomas A. Popa, Fort Riley, KS, July 24, 1991, DSIT-C-067.

54. Eugene J. Malik, telephone interview with the author, September 22, 2014. Malik commanded the headquarters and headquarters company of the 1-34 AR during Operation Desert Storm.

55. LTC (Ret.) James A. Bell, telephone interview with the author, October 1, 2014.

56. Toro interview.

57. See Schwarzkopf, *It Doesn't Take a Hero*, chap. 17. See also US Department of Defense, "Operations Desert Shield/Desert Storm," timeline, http://www.gulflink.osd.mil/timeline/time2.htm.

58. MG Gordon R. Sullivan, quoted in "Non-Essential Spending Curtailed," *Fort Riley Post*, August 31, 1990, 11.

59. "Unit Deploys, Others Prepare," *Fort Riley Post*, September 7, 1990, 1.

60. United States Army Military Personnel Center, slide presentation, Worldwide Conference, December 1985. The Meyer quotation is referenced in the conference slide deck, and the projected spending comes from the program operating memorandum included in the slide deck. In 1984 the Army highlighted its efforts by declaring that year the Year of the Army Family.

61. As the Army transitioned to the volunteer forces, sociologists, psychologists, and anthropologists (among others) studied the ramifications of the transition, including its effect on families. An early attempt to examine that problem is Florence W. Kaslow and Richard I. Ridenour, eds., *The Military Family: Dynamics and* Treatment (New York: Guilford, 1984); for a more recent study, see Karen Houppert, *Home Fires Burning: Married to the Military for Better or Worse* (New York: Ballantine, 2005). For a study on marriage and the military from 1996 to 2005, see Benjamin R. Karney and John S. Crown, *Families under Stress: An Assessment of Data, Theory and Research on Marriage and Divorce in the Military* (Santa Monica, CA: RAND, 2007),. The percentage of married soldiers declined from a high of just under 70 percent to 60 percent;

the downward trend began in 1998, apparently reflecting increasing deployments, including the mid-1990s Bosnia and Kosovo operations.

62. US Department of the Army, *A Guide to Establishing Family Support Groups*, Pamphlet 608–47 (Washington, DC: US Department of the Army, 1988).

63. The author has been unable to find definitive statistics for the number of family members at Fort Riley. Army-wide statistics from the United States Army Military Personnel Center's Worldwide Conference in December 1985 suggests that the number would have been just under twice the total number of soldiers. Apparently there were fewer than might have been expected at Fort Riley. COL LaGrange recalls that there were about twelve thousand family members, a number he claims he will never forget as families and their needs were his greatest challenge. LaGrange interview.

64. Pearl I. Speer and COL (Ret.) William L. Speer, interview with the author, Milford, KS, June 25, 2014.

65. Maggart, "Eye of the Storm," 19; LaGrange interview; author's recollections.

66 Speer interview.

67. BG (Ret.) John S. Brown, Mary Elizabeth Brown, BG (Ret.) Lloyd T. Waterman, and Peggy Waterman, interview with the author, Denver, September 25, 2014. Dana H. Fontenot also shared with me the family support group formation planning meeting minutes from August 28, 1990. The 2-34 AR needed to reorganize its family support group, as the one it had previously was defunct.

68. Ford interview; Bullington, "The First Infantry Division"; Bullington interview.

69. COL Michael Dodson, Commander, Division Artillery, 1st Infantry Division, interviewed by MAJ Thomas A. Popa, Fort Riley, KS, July 24, 1990, DSIT-C-068.

70. Dodson interview.

71. Gross interview.

72. Marlin, "History of the 4th Battalion, 37th Armored Regiment," 49–51.

73. Gross interview.

74. Toro interview.

75. Ibid.

76. SFC (Ret.) Steven M. Sorkness, telephone interview with the author, September 23, 2014.

CHAPTER FOUR

GETTING THERE

Planes, Trains, and the *Jolly Rubino*

We will deploy a well-trained Division of proud, disciplined soldiers.

—Major General Thomas G. Rhame

MG THOMAS G. Rhame and his staff returned from the III Corps exercise at Fort Hood the morning of November 9, 1991. At 2:30 that afternoon, Rhame convened what he thought of as a caucus; the meeting included his principal staff officers and battalion and brigade commanders. He began by sharing what little he knew for certain. He believed that the 3rd Brigade 2nd Armored Division (Forward) would deploy from Europe to round out the Division. The 1st Division (Forward) was too far in the process of deactivating to go. The 2 AD (Forward) was organized like the 1st Division (Forward); BG Jerry Rutherford, commander of the 2 AD (Forward), had served as assistant division commander of the Big Red One for nearly three years, so Rhame thought Rutherford and his unit would meld easily. He estimated the Division would be loading equipment on trains for movement to the Port of Houston on or about December 1. He had been told the Division would exchange its 105-millimeter main gun M1IP tanks for 120-millimeter main gun and more heavily armored M1A1 tanks upon arrival in Saudi Arabia. It was even possible that units might not ship tanks from Fort Riley at all.[1]

After detailing what he knew, Rhame and his team "caucused . . . on what we were doing and where we were going, what we had to get done and what we had to prioritize."[2] The discussion ranged from what had to be shipped and what new equipment might arrive to how to incorporate newly assigned soldiers. They also considered how to generate opportunities to train while planning simultaneously for the mission. The caucus was free ranging, but not aimless. MG Rhame kept the discussion on track and avoided speculation about questions that could not yet be answered. He made one important decision and allowed chance to make a second: since the port in Saudi Arabia was in friendly hands, Rhame decided to send COL Bob Shadley's logistics units overseas first. To everyone's surprise, and even some bitterness, he decided on a coin toss to determine which brigade would go first. COL Lon E. "Bert" Maggart won, and the 1st Brigade would go before COL Tony Moreno's 2nd Brigade.[3]

Sending the Division Support Command first was a far more important decision than which maneuver brigade moved first. Sending the logistics units first assured the maneuver units would be adequately supported upon arrival. This would enable them to unload more quickly, move more rapidly to tactical assembly areas, and be able to fight soon thereafter. Without logistics in place the combat units had little capacity to operate. MG Rhame could make this choice because the XVIII Airborne (ABN) Corps was already on the ground and able to provide security for the VII Corps as it arrived.

Most histories of combat operations, including those devoted to Operation Desert Storm, fail to review the actual business of preparing and deploying. Operational deployments tend to be chaotic and frustrating, even painful. Moving thousands of people and thousands of pieces of equipment efficiently and effectively is a complex undertaking. Mistakes made in sequencing are difficult to overcome. The present study is not a history of the deployment, but understanding the scope and scale of the effort to prepare and move to Saudi Arabia is necessary and an important part of the story. How the Division arrived and sorted itself out at the port is a tribute to the determination of the troops to get the job done, and their story deserves telling. The tremendous efforts of those who never left Fort Riley but nevertheless worked hard to get the Division equipped and deployed also are worth describing here.

As both post and division commander, Rhame set both the garrison and division staffs to work on the long list of things to do and to find answers to the even longer list of questions. Key players included COL Fred Hepler, the Division's chief of staff, and LTC John Andrews, LTC Terry Bullington, LTC Terry Ford, and LTC Ollie Schierholz; these four primary staff officers ran logistics, operations, intelligence, and personnel, respectively. A graduate of the School of Advanced Military Studies (SAMS), Hepler had what Rhame described as a SAMS mind. By that he meant Hepler could make sense of complex matters and manage collective efforts to solve them. COL Hepler coordinated the work of the primary staff. MG Rhame also relied on BG William G. Carter III, his assistant division commander for maneuver. Easygoing, direct, and supportive, Carter was the perfect foil to Rhame.

Preparation and Planning

MG Rhame made another important decision that better enabled preparation: He turned over command of Fort Riley to COL Gary LaGrange. That allowed

Rhame to focus on getting the Division ready and freed LaGrange to focus on running Fort Riley as it prepared to deploy the 1st Infantry Division (1 ID) and continued to deploy Army Reserve and National Guard units. The garrison staff operated post activities, ranging from housing, the hospital, and transportation (including the rail yard). Ordinarily, the garrison commander ran routine operations but deferred to the Division commander and took directions from him. When Rhame turned over command of the post to LaGrange, Fort Riley became a platform for deployment rather than an auxiliary of the Division. COL LaGrange then decided how best to support the Division and meet the post's obligations to other deploying units, tenets, and families.

Until Rhame turned over command of Fort Riley, the Division and garrison shared several key staff billets. For example, Bullington served both as the Division and garrison operations officer. Now that Rhame wore only one hat, so too did Bullington and his peers on the staff. LaGrange needed to reconstitute the garrison staff without the officers who served as primary staff officers in the Division. This would have had to be done once the Division deployed, but it was better to do it early than late. The garrison staff was fairly robust. The only reorganization needed was to replace the dual-hatted staff principals. COL LaGrange decided he needed a soldier in his operations shop to replace Bullington. Accordingly, he moved LTC John Allard from the Directorate of Logistics to become director of operations. Allard's civilian deputy became the director of logistics. COL Steve Whitfield, the director of engineering and housing, and COL Bill Speer, Irwin Army Hospital administrator, became indispensable, as did Bob Fuentes, the installation transportation officer. COL Whitfield achieved incredible results literally within days.

COL Arnie Daxe, commander of the US Army Correctional Activity, provided valuable assistance. COL Daxe's organization was 850 strong; most of his troops were soldier prisoners who were earning their way back into the Army. Correctional activity troops supported operations on the railhead, worked alongside Whitfield's engineers to build shelving in shipping containers to store parts for shipment, and worked on a host of other tasks. COL Mike Eskew, the deputy commander of the 3rd ROTC Region, and his staff assisted. All over the post, civilian employees, senior officers, noncommissioned officers (NCOs), and soldiers from nondeploying units served in the Fort Riley operations center or took over the roles of the departing soldiers. Speer believed LaGrange's leadership was essential. According to him, LaGrange "imbued" everyone with a sense of duty to the post and the troops.[4]

The garrison and the Division confronted an enormous task. In 1968, when the Army withdrew the 24 ID from Germany and stationed it at Fort Riley, it did so planning to deploy the troops by air. On arrival in Germany, they would draw prepositioned equipment and move to their General Defense Plan. Units at Fort Riley had exercised this concept for more than twenty years. For all of those years, the 24 ID and then the 1 ID remained near the bottom of the priority list for equipment. The Army viewed the equipment at Fort Riley as training equipment only; modernizing it was not a high priority. For this reason, many assumed the 1 ID would not be called for Operation Desert Shield. CPT Randy Shannon, an artilleryman in the 4th Battalion, 5th Field Artillery (4-5 FA), who served as the fire support officer to the 3rd Battalion, 37th Armor (3-37 AR), was among those who doubted that the Division would be alerted. His reasoning was straightforward: "Our wartime equipment set is in Germany. They're not going to send us to war with worn out stuff."[5] CPT Shannon was both excited and astounded by the order to go.

LTC Bullington's decision in August to rewrite the deployment plan proved fortuitous. The new plan, Lexicon Danger, dramatically altered more than twenty years of planning. Instead of moving only troops, and only by air, the Division would move equipment by rail to a port and then by ship to Saudi Arabia. Only then would the troops fly overseas. The implications of this change went well beyond shipping gear. Basic ammunition loads would also be shipped from Fort Riley rather than drawn from ammunition depots in southwest Germany. Basic ammunition load is a concept for determining the mix of ammunition, by type and quantity, a unit will use; units decide on the basic load based on anticipated missions. In this case units would have to decide on what ammunition they needed and/or wanted, submit requisitions, and then load tons of it on fighting vehicles within the cramped quarters of unit motor pools.[6] Loading ammunition on combat vehicles while loading shipping containers required an almost balletic choreography. Trucks offloading pallets of ammunition had to come and go while troops moved about loading ammunition and shipping containers. It is hard to exaggerate the difficulty of shipping everything compared to moving only troops.

CPT Shannon's assumptions proved partly accurate. The Army did not intend to send the Division to war with "worn-out stuff." Instead it intended to modernize the Division, and to do so in less than a month. A tidal wave of new equipment flowed in, along with teams eager to teach the troops how to use it. MG Rhame was amazed; as he recalls, "I did not understand the power of the United States Army to modernize in a hurry."[7] He also found the process of modernization on the fly "a little overwhelming . . . it was a constant stream of stuff all of which had to be [painted] brown by the time it left."[8]

How to accommodate receiving new equipment and in what sequence to do things began after the "caucus" on November 9. There was almost too much to do and too little time in which to do it. Each of the commanders varied his approach somewhat. In the 1st Brigade, COL Maggart "gathered my commanders in the brigade Conference room and reiterated the Commanding General's intent as well as my own. After innumerable REFORGER [return of forces to Germany] deployments, I knew this would be a snap if we took each phase of the operation in turn and maintained focus on the objective."[9] Maggart told his commanders they would meet daily to review progress, assess what needed to be done next, and share information. Despite what Maggart thought, none of his commanders and troops thought getting ready to go was a snap.

The list of things to do and to decide never seemed to grow shorter, and changes seemed to come faster as the clock ticked on. Everything big and small used up time, some of it wasted. For example, the matter of how many of the new Army rations MREs (meals ready-to-eat) would be carried by each soldier consumed much time and energy. Since World War II, the planning standard had been for soldiers to carry three days' rations. At some point a directive emanated from the Division requiring each soldier to carry five days' rations. Fifteen hefty brown bags of food now had to be divided among each soldier's two duffel bags, a rucksack, and the soldier's person. With everything else the soldiers had to carry with them, this directive was patently impossible. Yet the idea could not be buried until multiple fruitless demonstrations had been carried out proving there was no room. Finally the debate ended where it began: the troops would carry three days' rations just as they had for several decades. Thus, only nine of the cursed, bulky brown bags had to be borne by the troops, but two of these were to be carried in cargo pockets too small to hold them.[10]

The ink had not yet dried on Lexicon Danger before the Division began issuing fragmentary orders to amend previous orders as information changed; these FRAGOS, intended to clarify and inform, sometimes had the opposite effect. In 1990 e-mail was virtually unknown at Fort Riley. Although there were quite a few personal computers, there were very few government-owned computers. Thus, the Division printed and issued FRAGOS on paper. Despite control measures designed to assure everyone got each order, the system sometimes failed. If a World War II veteran visited the headquarters of the 1 ID in 1990 he would have recognized most of the communications and office equipment; radios had improved a great deal since World War II, but typewriters and papers still dominated offices. COL Maggart, one of the few who did have a computer, still had to manage preparation using index cards, notepaper taped to the wall of his conference room, and notes made on "butcher paper." Maggart groused, "All of this planning could have easily been done on a computer with a sophisticated scheduling program."[11] Alas, that fall, computer-generated spreadsheets could be found in very few places at Fort Riley.

Relying on analog communications produced confusion in a number of ways. Most commonly, confusion ensued when orders did not arrive at the same time in every headquarters. For example, someone from the Division would call inquiring if unit A had complied with the latest FRAGO without referring to the order's serial number and date-time group. The recipient of the phone call often had not yet seen the order and assumed the caller was speaking about one that had been received. The resulting discussion led to more confusion and sometimes anger and distrust. It got so bad that LTC Dave Marlin and several of his fellow battalion commanders met periodically for coffee in order to compare notes. According to Marlin, "It was fascinating finding out the different guidance and instructions being issued to battalion commanders in one brigade."[12] The disparity between brigades was obviously great.

Deployment preparation developed in three phases. The first included those things that had to be done prior to rail loading equipment; the second involved moving to the railhead and loading equipment and cargo; and the third involved everything that could be done after the equipment had been shipped. During this phase only limited training was possible, but the focus shifted to final preparations for soldiers and families. All of this activity occurred simultaneously with learning the mission. Planning for combat operations continued while units trained as well as they could. For example, tank and Bradley gunnery simulators went into use twenty-four hours a day. Crews squabbled over access to simulators the way a later generation might fight over access to the family Xbox.

COL Shadley believed the Division made two vitally important logistical decisions. First, Andrews, the logistics staff officer, approved the purchase of 319 twenty-foot vans with chassis that enabled them to be towed. Focused on defending Germany, Army logistics units were not fully mobile; the main support battalion could not move its equipment and spare parts in a single lift. The forward support battalions were better off, but not by much. The 319 vans Andrews bought were still not enough to enable full mobility, but they were a big improvement.[13]

COL Shadley thought buying the Magellan GPS was the other great decision. Many believe it was the best prewar decision made. LTC Bullington made that choice; during one of several calls he received before the alert, an Army staff officer suggested that he "look at getting a global positioning system for use by the Division."[14] Shortly after that call, he read an advertisement in *Army* magazine for the Magellan GPS and, as he remembers, "off we went."[15] He called the manufacturer and bought Magellan's entire current inventory of a dozen bright yellow devices and contracted for more. In an ironic twist, after the war the Army investigated him for not using the correct procedure for the purchase, but fortunately no one interfered beforehand.[16]

General H. Norman Schwarzkopf's Commanders Meeting

A few days after the commanders' caucus, Rhame was summoned to meet with GEN H. Norman Schwarzkopf, commander in chief of CENTCOM, and the other American commanders. Rhame, his aide CPT Steve Payne, and his plans officer MAJ Don Osterberg flew to Saudi Arabia from Forbes Field in Topeka. On November 14 Rhame and twenty-one other American generals gathered to hear Schwarzkopf's guidance. The group included CENTCOM's three-star

Army, Navy, Air Force, and Marine component commanders. Two Army corps commanders, LTG Gary Luck and LTG Fredrick M. Franks Jr., rounded out the three-star group at the meeting. The Marine officers commanding the 1st Marine Division (1 Mar Div) and the 3rd Marine Air Wing also attended, as did seven Army division commanders, including Rhame. MG William "Gus" Pagonis, Schwarzkopf's logistician, rounded out the two-star attendees. A few brigadier generals completed the galaxy of stars and a handful of more junior officers crowded the back of the room.[17]

Schwarzkopf brought his subordinates together to describe his intentions and concept for defeating the Iraqis. The general, famous in the Army for his temper and equally prone to histrionics, had worked himself up into a "ferocious state."[18] In *Crusade: The Untold Story of the Gulf War*, an excellent account of Operation Desert Storm, Rick Atkinson described GEN Schwarzkopf as "the most theatrical American in uniform since Douglas MacArthur."[19] "Stormin' Norman" shared some of MacArthur's other undesirable traits: he bullied and badgered subordinates, yet was himself supersensitive to perceived slights. He was nonetheless an impressive speaker, and on November 14 he gave one of his best performances. In his self-proclaimed "ferocious state," Schwarzkopf aimed to have every commander present "embrace his mission and be breathing fire by the time he went out the door."[20]

MG Rhame took meticulous notes, and they show that Schwarzkopf gave about 75 percent of the briefing himself. He was, Rhame recalls, "the dominant presence in the room."[21] GEN Schwarzkopf articulated four strategic goals. First and foremost among them was to liberate Kuwait and restore the legitimate government. Second and third included defending US interests and those of our Arab coalition partners. The last required the destruction of Iraqi forces necessary to attain the stated goals. MG Rhame understood liberating Kuwait to be "the central focus."[22]

GEN Schwarzkopf proposed to fight in four phases. During phase 1, coalition air forces would attack Iraqi command and control, achieve air superiority, and destroy Iraqi theater logistics. Curiously, the air components would execute phase 2 simultaneously with phase 1. In phase 2 the air forces would fight to gain theater-wide air superiority. Phase 3 would focus on battlefield preparation—that is, attacking Iraqi tactical units within Kuwait. Finally, in phase 4, the ground forces would attack. GEN Schwarzkopf planned for his four ground corps—the VII Corps, the XVIII ABN Corps, the II Marine Expeditionary Force (MEF), and the Arab Corps—to attack in "corridors."

Schwarzkopf wanted the II MEF to attack north along the Persian Gulf coast toward Kuwait with an aim of "tying up Saddam's forces."[23] Just what that meant the general did not say, and no one asked; presumably he meant to keep the Iraqis from moving freely. He planned for the Arab Corps to attack in parallel on the Marines' left flank. Farther west, the VII Corps, of which the 1 ID would be a part, would attack to destroy the Iraqi Republican Guard. Here Schwarzkopf was specific: he did not want the Republican Guard defeated or pushed out of Kuwait; he wanted it utterly destroyed. To ensure that none of the Republican Guard escaped, he wanted the XVIII ABN Corps, attacking in the far west, to block the major highway that stretched along the south side of the Euphrates River from Basra to Baghdad. LTG Franks, commander of the VII Corps, thought Schwarzkopf's briefing was a "masterful presentation, in format and in motivational language. No one there could possibly have a question about what he was supposed to do."[24] MG Rhame's notes were precise—he understood the grand outline, but did not yet know his mission. This was an ambitious plan that depended on carefully coordinated timing.

Following the session with Schwarzkopf, Franks met with his subordinate commanders. These included MG Ronald H. Griffith of the 1 AD, MG Paul "Butch" Funk of the 3 AD, Rhame, and COL Don Holder of the 2nd Armored Cavalry Regiment (2 ACR). They reviewed the main operational task: destroying the Republican Guard. GEN Schwarzkopf expected to launch the ground offensive in mid-February, so they had a sense of how much time they had. Planning with a general outline of the mission could now begin.

Afterward Rhame and Osterberg took time to do a reconnaissance of the area. They also visited MG Barry R. McCaffrey, whose 24 ID, part of the XVIII ABN Corps, had served in the desert for several months. Rhame wanted to hear McCaffrey's views on the mission before them. MAJ Osterberg thought McCaffrey and his team were "genuinely happy" to see them and glad to have more "heavy" forces en route.[25] MG McCaffrey shared lessons learned ranging from how to live in the desert to maintaining tanks and Bradleys in a difficult environment. He also provided his unfettered evaluation of the Iraqis.

MG McCaffrey believed the Iraqis were far less capable than the intelligence community claimed; he remembers thinking, "These people can't deal with us."[26] He told Rhame the coalition would win decisively and do so within thirty days, but he did expect high casualties. He estimated his division would suffer about two thousand killed and wounded. In retrospect that sounds horrific, but McCaffrey's estimate seemed optimistic at the time. Various experts appeared on television claiming the Iraqis would seriously challenge US and coalition forces. While watching television in the desert, McCaffrey heard one expert claim the attack to retake Kuwait would be the bloodiest fight in US history since Normandy. There was, he recalls, "tremendous anxiety about the fourth largest Army in the world."[27] Nonetheless, Rhame felt buoyed by McCaffrey's confidence.

Soon after the session with McCaffrey, Rhame returned to Fort Riley to continue preparing to deploy and to begin operational planning. Shortly after he got home, Franks called from Germany, where the VII Corps was stationed. Franks thought the 1st Division might be best suited to make the initial attack.

He based his thinking on the experience Rhame's brigades had at the National Training Center (NTC), where they routinely attacked against prepared defenses. Franks asked whether Rhame would take the mission to penetrate the Iraqi fixed defenses, and Rhame agreed immediately. Now the Division had a clear mission: it would make a deliberate attack against prepared enemy positions defended by complex obstacles. Once the penetration was achieved, the rest of the Corps would pass through the breach.[28] MAJ Osterberg, who remained in Saudi Arabia to stay abreast of planning in theater, could now begin planning with clear focus.[29] He could also collaborate with both CENTCOM and VII Corps planners prior to returning home.

Preparing and Modernizing

Prior to the alert, Rhame got a head start on another problem. In September, on his own initiative, he decided to repaint the Division's equipment the color of sand. After the alert, the painting effort went from normal routine to twenty-four hours a day, seven days a week. Despite the early start, Fort Riley did not have the means to paint six thousand pieces of equipment in less than a month. The Directorate of Logistics had a paint shop, but it could not meet the demand, so the post staff contracted facilities at Mobile Traveler, a small company that built pickup truck campers and recreational vehicles, and found other small contractors to help. Still, demand outpaced resources. To close the gap, the two maneuver brigades each built a temporary paint shop.[30]

To complicate matters further, the Army required a special paint, chemical agent resistant coating (CARC). Designed to reduce corrosion and penetration from poison gas, the coating posed a hazard to those who handled it or breathed its fumes, and protective overgarments and breathing apparatuses had to be used when applying it. The paint crews also had to submit to frequent blood testing to determine whether they had inhaled or absorbed dangerous chemicals. Despite every effort to protect the outside atmosphere, a haze of potentially lethal CARC paint could be found in the enclosed bays where painting occurred.[31]

Despite numerous problems, various contractors and soldiers finished painting in less than thirty days using nearly eight thousand gallons of CARC. It was a hell of an achievement, done with little time to plan and little room for error. The great painting adventure produced the first outpouring of patriotic volunteerism. The post fire department pitched in with great enthusiasm. The Division could not buy enough protective overgarments, so the fire department gave up virtually all of its suits. The firemen also gave freely of their time to assure the troops operated safely.

People everywhere wanted to help in the predeployment efforts, and every unit had an anecdote. For example, in the 4-37 AR, 1LT Phillip Corbo's parents happened to be in Fort Riley visiting when the Division was notified to deploy. His battalion was struggling to build storage to move maintenance equipment.

His father pitched in. He spent nearly a month at Riley building storage boxes for high-mobility multipurpose wheeled vehicles (HMMWVs), shelving for maintenance vans "liberated from Fort Hood," and storage for the maintenance platoon. Corbo's mother volunteered with the Fort Riley family support group.[32] That's the way it was that fall—a little like a patriotic movie from the World War II era.

Patriotic fervor could not solve the problem of repairing broken equipment and getting antique trucks ready to deploy. That would take money and parts. Once alerted for Saudi Arabia, the Division's fortunes changed dramatically. An artillery battalion gleefully reported, "Maintenance priority jumps to 0-1 [highest] from 0-13 [lowest]. Now we are getting the parts to fix our equipment. All of a sudden we've become important."[33] Now, with access to parts, the troops repaired or rebuilt equipment at an impressive rate; instances of broken-down gear went from 30 percent to less than 10 percent.[34] Parts flowed in, as did outside help, including a "quick fix" team from Army Materiel Command, which COL Shadley contacted and where his old commander and mentor served as operations officer. COL Shadley unabashedly called MG Thomas B. Arwood for help getting critical parts. Arwood recalls that one night after a late call, he wished he had "had a two-star general to chase parts for me when I was a DISCOM [Division Support Command] commander."[35]

Several units practically rebuilt their ancient 2.5-ton trucks. Every tracked vehicle in the 1 ID underwent a track inspection to determine how many miles remained before requiring replacement, and the troops installed new track on every vehicle that inspectors concluded had fewer than five hundred miles remaining before the track became unserviceable. All of the battalions replaced a significant amount of track. The 4-37 AR, for example, replaced track on about twenty of its fifty-eight tanks.[36] Changing track on a tank is heavy work: each block of tank track weighs sixty-four pounds, and each tank has eighty blocks on a side; laying it out requires a lot of space. All of this had to be done simultaneously with painting, loading ammunition, and a host of other tasks required before shipping out. The motor pools at Fort Riley looked like disturbed anthills for about three weeks.

Painting and fixing equipment proved a challenge, but shipping thousands of tons of equipment generated plenty of work as well. Assuring that the rail yard at Fort Riley could support loading became a major task for COL Steve Whitfield and the post engineers. Most of the infrastructure to support rail movement across the Army dated from World War II. Focused on fighting in Europe, the Army had not maintained rail yards at stateside posts. According to Whitfield, the railhead at Fort Riley was "completely inadequate."[37] Fort Riley only had two docks and two long tracks for loading. The railhead had no yard engines and no way to turn a train around. When trains departed the railhead, they went all the way to Solomon, Kansas, forty-five miles west and south, in order to then turn south toward the ports. The requirement to shuttle trains to Solomon made timing at the rail yard even more critical, and the yard could not physically support the planned shipping schedule.[38]

COL Whitfield had to build a facility adequate to the task. The post engineers, aided by division troops, improved docks, built dirt ramps at the ends of spurs, and emplaced assault bridging to provide a firm base for earthen ramps. The engineers also brought in light sets to provide illumination so the troops could load around the clock. Their jury-rigged system worked: at the peak of loading, the troops and rail support teams loaded 214 cars in a day. Rhame recalls with pride that even with jury-rigged docks, his troops could load faster than the Army could deliver rail cars.[39]

New equipment began to arrive by rail even as the engineers worked to enlarge the rail yard, further complicating their work, but they got the job done anyway. On November 27 the fruits of the great effort to improve the rail yard paid off: the 701st Main Support Battalion began loading that morning, only nineteen days after the alert.[40] US Army reserve deployment-control units ensured accurate documentation and marking to facilitate tracking material in transit. Bob Fuentes and his team supervised the staging, loading, and documentation; he aimed to "move the 1st Infantry Division in safe and organized manner for them to arrive in country prepared to fight."[41]

Fuentes did not fully realize his aspiration to see the Division move out in an "organized" manner. Senior NCOs ran the operations to unload new equipment as it arrived and to load and ship equipment once the Division began to deploy. SPC John Tabb's battalion assigned him to the rail-load detail, partly because he had come from a unit in Germany and had considerable experience loading trains. As SPC Tabb remembers, "The railhead operation was crazy";[42] none of the units at Fort Riley had the experience of Tabb's outfit in Germany, where US units often moved to training areas on trains.

Furthermore, most units in Europe had "German tie-down," which featured purpose-built chains that could be tightened using a ratchet-like device and metal blocks with teeth on the bottom. The process was simple; one member of the crew guided another, who drove the tank or any other vehicle onto a flat car. Once in place, the crew placed the blocks, rapped them with a hammer, and installed and tightened the tie-down chains; the task could be done in minutes. German rail yards were also well lit and well built. In US Army Europe, companies of fourteen tanks routinely loaded and tied down in about a half hour. At Fort Riley, units sometimes loaded a handful of vehicles bound for the NTC but seldom loaded more than once a year. SPC Tabb found things at Riley "chaotic" because the equipment was inadequate and "the movement control piece was out of practice."[43]

Even as Whitfield's engineers worked to improvise rail infrastructure at Fort Riley, the Army shipped hundreds of pieces of new equipment by rail and road.

In less than a month, the Division received, processed, and learned how to use 1,274 new vehicles. Nearly every five-ton cargo truck was replaced. Units that still had commercial light trucks turned them in for HMMWVs. The Army also provided more than 2,600 brand new pieces of optical gear, ranging from night-vision devices to binoculars. Thousands of new Beretta nine-millimeter pistols replaced the venerable M1911 A1.45-caliber pistols. Those soldiers who would draw Berettas learned how to clean and maintain them, and then they learned how to shoot them.[44]

None of the tasks associated with getting new gear was particularly difficult, but each took time. In-transit visibility was managed by visual inspection of shipping labels. No bar codes or scanners supported the effort in 1990; the entire process was managed by hand. The scale of the effort tended to outpace the means to track inventory and movement. Managing inbound and outbound shipments required physical inventory. For example, the Division logistics shipped ten thousand different parts in its inventory of spares, and much of that inventory was managed by hand.[45] Each new piece of equipment came with documentation, manuals, and requirements for parts to be stocked. Some of the new pieces of equipment arrived with spare parts, and some did not; those that did required documentation to acquire and stock spare parts. Dealing with the avalanche of new equipment required the work of both the Division and post staffs.

The 4th Brigade's experience exemplifies the modernization effort. Between November 9 and early December, when the Brigade loaded, it replaced its light-wheel vehicle fleet, drew nine-millimeter Beretta pistols, and modernized the helicopter fleet's aircraft survivability equipment. These improvements included infrared jammers, infrared suppression kits, improved radar warning receivers, and hover infrared reduction systems that reduced the heat signature of the Brigade's UH-1 Huey helicopters. The 4th Battalion, 1st Aviation (4-1 AVN) also replaced two of its oldest first-generation UH-60 Black Hawk helicopters with updated versions.[46]

Altogether, the Division fielded twenty-four entirely new pieces of equipment in less than a month's time. (The Beretta pistol counted as a single new piece of equipment, but thousands of them were involved.) New equipment required training, and in some cases that training occurred before the equipment arrived. That was the case for training on the M1A1; because the Army planned to issue M1A1 tanks in Saudi Arabia, the Division conducted "roll over" training for the tank battalions. Training to transition to the M1A1 from the M1 is not difficult, the main gun being the chief difference between the two tanks. M1 tanks fired fixed 105-millimeter ammunition. The propellant and projectile were one piece, with the propellant contained in a metal casing. When the gun fired, the projectile went down range while the casing ejected on counterrecoil. The A1 fired 120-millimeter combustible ammunition. When the gun fired, the projectile went down range and the casing burned, leaving only an "aft cap." Still, roll over training took precious time.

The sense of too much to do and too little time to do it in was pervasive. At first, everyone worked pretty much around the clock, but eventually Rhame mandated rest for the troops. He decreed the workday would run from 7:00 a.m. to 8:00 p.m.—except on Sunday, which was to be a day off. He permitted one exception: painting would continue in shifts twenty-four hours a day, seven days a week, until everything was sand brown. Commanders and senior NCOs found they had to work longer hours, but at least the troops got some rest. One day off a week had the additional benefit of enabling soldiers to have some time with their families.

In mid-November the pace of operational planning began to take shape around a clear mission. With Rhame having agreed to conduct the attack to penetrate Iraqi defenses, the Division could focus. LTG Franks estimated the attack would occur somewhere in a diamond-shaped mapmaker's creation called the Neutral Zone. The center of the Neutral Zone lies about two hundred kilometers west of the Persian Gulf coast and just northwest of the Saudi town of Hafir al-Batin. That placed the attack corridor west of the Wadi al-Batin, a shallow valley that runs from north to south along the western edge of Kuwait and the most significant geographic feature of southern Iraq. Although rugged at its southern extremity, the wadi formed a natural avenue of approach to the north.

Although the Army and the Division issued pamphlets and handbooks that described how the Iraqis planned to fight, they conveyed little useful intelligence—that is, specific information about Iraqi units and locations. The documents asserted the Iraqis were far more capable than they proved to be in practice. The Division's own booklet claimed the Iraqi Army was a "battle hardened force."[47] Planning focused on a deliberate attack against prepared positions, although nearly everyone thought of the problem as an obstacle-breaching exercise.

A breach requires the attacking force to attack through obstacles under fire. If the Iraqis were as good as the intelligence suggested, then attacking through obstacles against prepared defenses posed a daunting task; if the Iraqis lived up to their reputation, it would be bloody. Despite gloomy intelligence assessments and even gloomier prognostication by experts, some believed otherwise—Barry McCaffrey, for one, but soon others came to share that view. One evening in November, LTC Pat Ritter happened to see a television report of Saddam Hussein visiting one of his forward units. The camera followed while an Iraqi soldier showed Saddam at a machine gun emplacement. The fighting position had no overhead cover and appeared to be no more than two and a half feet deep. LTC Ritter's confidence grew, because he felt sure that "you don't take the president of your country to a crappy unit."[48] LTC Ritter kept his views to himself, while the intelligence apparatus maintained a chorus about Iraqi excellence. MG McCaffrey's assessment of the Iraqis did not appear in the threat handbooks. Regardless of the quality of the estimates, the Division had a clear mission and a threat against which to prepare. Preparing against a worst-case scenario had the advantage of forcing consideration of every means to mitigate risks.

In addition to planning for the breach, units had to figure how to function in the desert. To that end, the Army sent a General Dynamics Corporation team to Fort Riley to train soldiers in the maintenance of equipment. The briefing focused on sustaining the M1 tank in the harsh environment of the Arabian Peninsula. COL Maggart's brigade took the briefing on November 15. The General Dynamics technical representatives reviewed maintenance techniques and how to avoid damage due to sand and dust. Some of the advice seemed trivial, such as the team urging that engines be placed on a tarpaulin or engine stand when working on them rather than on the ground. Such commonsense advice was akin to suggesting that troops wear rubber boots when it rained. On the other hand, units readily took advice on how to inspect seals, use access panels to minimize exposure, and clean air filters.[49]

On November 23 the 1st Brigade took what Maggart described as a "no shit" information briefing on how to operate in the desert from COL Greg Giles. Giles arrived fresh from commanding a 101 ABN brigade in the Saudi desert to give practical advice on how to function and prepare for combat. He suggested some things that seem mundane in retrospect a quarter century later, but all of his advice found eager listeners. One idea stood out: Giles recommended that units have gatherings that focused on managing fear. These sessions proved powerful for young soldiers, many of whom had not been in the Army for very long.[50]

Planning occurred at all levels. Despite the lack of detailed information, a lot could be done at the conceptual level. The Division had insufficient information on where it would attack and too little intelligence on specific Iraqi units to do detailed planning. It could, however, run rock drills on the problem. A rock drill is a conceptual exercise based on applying doctrinal solutions to missions that are as yet hypothetical. It is a "what-if" drill done by professionals based on what is known early in the planning process. By mid-November the Division knew it would do a penetration attack against prepared defenses somewhere in the Neutral Zone west of the Wadi al-Batin. The likely enemy forces would be light infantry supported by tanks. An important rock drill occurred in late November in a maintenance bay of a 1st Brigade motor pool; the Division's commanders, from the company level up, gathered around a terrain board laid out on the floor on which blocks ("rocks") representing friendly and enemy units could be moved about.

MG Rhame and his team brainstormed on how each of the two brigades would do its part. His concept required the 1st and 2nd Brigades to attack to penetrate the enemy. Once they had done so, they would pass the 3rd Brigade forward to continue the attack. This drill occurred without BG Rutherford's units. Their part would have to be fully developed and rehearsed when the whole Division assembled in Saudi Arabia.[51]

Fundamentally, the discussion revolved around an assumed Iraqi defense based on how the Iraqis defended during the Iran-Iraq War. MG Rhame used this gathering to solicit ideas from his commanders and to build cohesion. He also used the session to motivate junior commanders. While most of Rhame's officers and NCOs had executed attacks against prepared defenses at the NTC, none had participated in a brigade or division attack of any kind. They understood the basics of breaching obstacles in an attack against a prepared defense, but no one had attempted anything on this scale since World War II. Not surprisingly, they had some anxiety about how it would go.

MG Rhame had settled on a basic concept for this operation: he intended to attack with two brigades abreast, and each would assault with two battalion task forces. Further, he proposed to mass combat forces on a narrow front, and to precede the attack with an intense artillery bombardment. COL Maggart and COL Moreno each discussed his part of the operation, and soldiers moved blocks of wood marked with unit designations to show movement and relative positions.[52] COL Mike Dodson reviewed how he would position supporting artillery. MG Rhame called on battalion and company commanders to ensure he heard their views. The rock drill was informal, much as the commanders' caucus had been, but the discussion drove home the scale and importance of the operation; there was a clear sense among those in attendance that they were witnessing a historic moment.

CPT Bob Burns, who would command one of the assault companies, found the experience intense. He believed he understood what Rhame intended and felt that the "war game" demonstrated that "leaders trusted leaders." He found the effort to "figure out the mechanics of how we are going to do that [penetration attack]" compelling. A brief interlude with Rhame made the strongest impression. MG Rhame placed his hands on Burns's shoulders, looked into his eyes and said, "Bob I have to have the breach. You have to get the breach for me." CPT Burns recalls that at that moment "I was prepared—maybe not willing, but prepared—to lose my company, but I was going to get the breach."[53] CPT Burns left as Rhame had intended—motivated. COL Moreno, an older hand, felt confident rather than inspired. By this point in the planning process, he had settled on his concept. His brigade had gone over its plan several times and tested it in simulation. COL Moreno recalls that he "felt real good about this."[54] Regardless of how Burns and Moreno felt, getting beyond conceptual planning to specifics would have to wait until the Division and VII Corps arrived in Saudi Arabia.

Two other events brought greater clarity to the problem. First, the Division leadership had the opportunity to see a film made at the NTC that showcased new capabilities to breach obstacles. The film advocated specific tactics, techniques, and procedures. COL Moreno and some of his leaders had visited the NTC during the production and had seen firsthand what the center advocated. Meant to teach the best method for attacking a position protected by obstacles, the video failed dramatically. Nearly everyone who saw it decided that what they saw was, if not insane, not the best way to do business. LTC Ritter wondered why the attackers dismounted their infantry and assaulted the trenches in much the same way as the British did at the Somme River in 1916.

Specifically, the NTC advocated dismounting infantry and assaulting the trenches on foot. In the video, each infantry squad carried a little orange pennant meant to mark its progress as it moved down the trenches throwing grenades and firing machine guns. The demonstration did look like what the British infantry had attempted in the summer of 1916. Not given to historical analogy, Maggart thought it looked "far too complicated, involved many more dismounted infantrymen than I had available, and worse, [it] would have resulted in more casualties than I was willing to accept."[55] COL Wesley Clark, who developed the video, noted how complicated the effort was and that it had taken two of his opposing forces companies three weeks to develop and practice before they could run the demonstration. The video was harrowing to watch. COL Moreno, who saw the effort in person, reached the most explicit conclusion: "Son of a bitch, that's a way to kill kids."[56] Not surprisingly, the Division's leadership rejected the NTC solution.

The second major event that affected planning the attack occurred during M1A1 "roll over" training. Because the Army planned for the 1 ID to exchange its M1 tanks for M1A1 tanks on arrival in Saudi Arabia, the tank battalions went through introductory training on the M1A1. CPT Bob Stavnes, who led the New Equipment Training Team from the Army Materiel Command, brought seventeen M1A1s and a number of pieces of Soviet equipment, including a T-72 tank, to Fort Riley for training and familiarization. Intelligence specialists came along to brief the capabilities of the Soviet weapons. Saddam's Army was equipped with a variety of Western and Soviet weapons, but his tank fleet was almost exclusively Soviet or Chinese versions of Soviet tanks. The intelligence analysts who briefed on the Soviet gear assured their listeners that the T-72 was every bit the "bogeyman" they insisted it was. They claimed the T-72 main gun round could penetrate US tanks at greater ranges than US tanks rounds could penetrate it.[57] They insisted that American and coalition units would have to maneuver to obtain flank shots in order to have any chance at all. The T-72s, they asserted, would give the Iraqis a significant advantage. This was not news; various military and civilian analysts had long claimed that US tanks were inferior to Soviet armor and that, in any case, the M1 used too much fuel and was too complicated to stand up well against Soviet-built tanks. CPT Stavnes remembers thinking that the analysts "were well convinced of their point of view."[58]

They undercut their assertions, however, by allowing the troops to inspect the equipment for themselves. On examination, the T-72 revealed itself to be inferior to the M1 in a number of ways. The T-72 relied on infrared night vision, had a primitive fire-control system, and put ammunition propellant in the crew compartment. The M1 had a thermal imaging system that did not depend on projecting infrared light to see but instead gathered images based on heat signatures. The M1 had an effective fire-control computer linked to a laser range finder, and its crew compartment was separated from ammunition storage. When asked to demonstrate the T-72's self-digging capability, the briefing team readily agreed. After a half hour of great gouts of blue smoke and lots of noise, the T-72 scraped a shallow hole no more than a foot deep; no one who had the opportunity to see the vaunted T-72 or watch it dig came away impressed.[59]

Most important, the T-72's lack of thermal imaging capability afforded a significant advantage to US tanks. Depending on conditions, the T-72 could see no more than about twelve hundred meters at night. M1 tank crews, on the other hand, could expect to see much farther and identify targets accurately at about fifteen hundred meters. American tank crews could expect to fight far more effectively at night than their counterparts and enjoyed some advantage in resolution during daylight hours. Those who saw the Soviet gear for themselves felt more confident and paid less attention to the gloomy forecasts of both official and unofficial experts on Soviet armor and the Iraqi Army.[60]

Meanwhile, in Garlstedt, Germany, the 2 AD (Forward) prepared to deploy and began planning in parallel with Rhame's Division without the advantage of being able to collaborate directly. As a part of a dual-based division, the Garlstedt unit comprised a bit more than a third of the 2 AD. It had the 2 AD's 3rd Brigade, a rump division staff, and a share of the combat support and service support resources. Thus it had both a brigade commander and Rutherford, who served as the 2 AD (Forward) commander. From the outset Rutherford had to cope with two serious personnel problems. On November 11, COL V. Paul Baerman, commander of the 3rd Brigade, learned he would not be able to deploy. Although a "real warrior and a superb leader," Baerman was an insulin-dependent diabetic.[61] His supply of properly stored insulin could not be assured, so he would have to be replaced. Also, an unsavory situation had arisen in the 4th Battalion, 3rd Field Artillery (4-3 FA): the officers lacked confidence in their commander, to the point that several claimed they would not go to war with him. Although very upset with their attitude, Baerman did not believe the commander could recover their loyalty and so relieved him on November 15. The next day, Baerman gave up command of the 3rd Brigade to COL David Weisman.[62] COL Baerman remained in command of the "subcommunity" at Garlstedt, where he made a crucial difference in supporting deployed soldiers and families in much the same way LaGrange did at Fort Riley. Replacing the commander of 4-3 FA came later. It must have seemed like things were unraveling in Garlstedt.

There was significant confusion over when the Garlstedt units would deploy and in what capacity—some of it caused by Rutherford himself. On November 22 Franks visited Garlstedt. Rutherford approached him about using his unit as a separate brigade. As an alternative to providing a third brigade to the 1st Division, this idea had little merit. Rutherford did not command an independent brigade. His unit was designed to fight as part of the 2 AD when that unit arrived in Germany to support the NATO General Defense Plan. Rhame needed a third brigade. Accordingly, the 2 AD (Forward) took its place in the 1 ID order of battle. BG Rutherford accepted reality gracefully and rejoined the Division he had left a year earlier.[63]

The Garlstedt contingent enjoyed several advantages. It was fully modernized and it was in Europe, where it had access to the robust war reserves of US Army Europe. COL Weisman's two tank battalions had the newest M1A1 heavy armor tanks, armed with 120-millimeter main guns and better armor than the M1 or the standard M1A1. The Brigade also had relatively new M-2 Bradley infantry fighting vehicles, and it also received upgrades and new gear, including mine plows and rollers as well as the M9 armored combat earthmover—an armored bulldozer designed to keep up with tanks. The Brigade had begun to transition to the new communications system, mobile subscriber equipment, but that was incompatible with the 1st Division's obsolescent system. The 1 ID (Forward) provided its signal platoon, which had compatible equipment, with the parent division. COL Weisman also needed air defense augmentation, because his brigade had only shoulder-launched air defense missiles. The 1st Division's 2nd Battalion, 3rd Air Defense Artillery (2-3 ADA), equipped its C battery with Vulcan twenty-millimeter air defense cannons. Combining two units not originally planned for combination caused some pain. At least in Garlstedt, they did not have to paint; that was deferred for execution in the desert.[64]

Garlstedt, like other US Army garrisons in Germany, had no significant local maneuver space or ranges. Units in Europe rotated to two major maneuver and firing facilities about once a year; therefore, training after the alert required much more coordination and time than at Fort Riley. These problems did not deter 2AD (forward) from training, however; it employed many of the techniques its teammates used at Fort Riley, including tactical seminars and rock drills. After the alert, units ran dismounted exercises, practicing formations and literally walking through actions on contact, as well as other battle drills. Like units at Fort Riley, troops at Garlstedt used their unit conduct of fire simulators twenty-four hours a day, seven days a week.[65]

Somewhat to its surprise, the 3rd Brigade experienced virtually the same enthusiastic support from nearby communities as the troops at Fort Riley enjoyed. For the most part, the local German communities appreciated their Americans and showed it. The city manager of nearby Osterholz-Scharmbeck wrote Rutherford to assure him that "during the absence of the troops, the City of Osterholz-Scharmbeck will continue its efforts to truly be a home to its American citizens and will do everything possible to support and help the Americans remaining here."[66] Each of the battalions had a partnership with a nearby German Army unit, and these units helped where they could; they even mounted guard for the Americans.[67] Further, Americans experienced random acts of kindness from Germans they met. Students from the University of Bremen and some other outsiders sounded the only sour note, showing up "a couple of times" to demonstrate against the deployment.[68] Many American soldiers thought of Germany as a second home, and many Germans appreciated their presence as guarantors of the peace and part of their shield if war broke out with the Soviet Union.

Making up for personnel shortages and replacing those who could not be deployed was difficult. Every unit bound for Saudi Arabia had to do find a way to do so. Arguably, no unit or commander faced a greater challenge than the Garlstedt-based 4-3 FA and LTC Robert L. "Lanny" Smith. LTC Smith arrived in Germany in 1986 and held several important positions in the 3rd ID artillery. On Saturday, November 24, he took a call that changed his life and that of his family in a fundamental way. He was told to report to Garlstedt the following day to take command of the 4-3 FA in the wake of his predecessor's relief. Packing in haste, Smith, his wife Sally, and their two daughters made the all-day drive to Garlstedt, arriving about 11:00 p.m. the next day. BG Rutherford and COL Weisman were waiting for him.

Rutherford and Baerman told Smith that he needed to take command immediately and that he had a problem on his hands; Rutherford summarized the issues that had resulted in the relief of the previous commander. Although Baerman had relieved the battalion commander because he thought things had gone too far for him to recover, he also believed the battalion's officer leadership was a major part of the problem. They had come to believe they were running the battalion.[69]

After hearing this grim news, Smith asked for directions to the battalion headquarters so he could take command as required—immediately. He walked to the battalion headquarters and found the basement conference room, where the battalion's officers were waiting. As he came in, they all rose. He took his seat, but left the officers standing for "a minute or two." Finally he asked them to be seated. He told them who he was and gave them a homework assignment. They were to read Herman Wouk's *Caine Mutiny* and tell him what they learned. They would reconvene the next morning at 5:00 a.m. Smith then left to settle his family. That night the 4-3 FA's officers scurried around trying to find a copy of the book. At one point they contemplated breaking into the library. Fortunately, one of the officers' wives owned a copy. They duly skimmed the book. Early the next morning they reported to Smith that "had we been loyal to our commander we probably could have gotten through this, but we weren't loyal."[70] With that LTC Smith said, "Great! Lesson learned. Let's go to work."[71]

There were other problems. Although the battalions at Fort Riley and Garlstedt included authorized battalion surgeons, none were assigned; the Army assigned doctors to hospitals, not battalions, and planned to provide doctors as required on deployment. When the alert occurred, the system worked mostly as designed. CPT James M. Goff Jr.'s experience provides an example. In 1990 he was serving as general medical officer at Fort McPherson, Georgia, while waiting to enter a surgical residency. The day before Thanksgiving 1990 his supervisor ordered him to Fort Riley to serve as a battalion surgeon. He arrived at the end of November or the first week of December as the last doctor to join the Division and reported to the 2-34 AR for duty as battalion surgeon. When reporting, Dr. Goff thought it best to play the role of Army officer. As he put it, he did things "most doctors don't do, I reported correctly."[72] He cut his hair close and reported as he had learned to do in the ROTC. He recalls that it "was wild. Everything was in motion. There was zero instruction from any part of the medical command of what you should and shouldn't have."[73] Dr. Goff did what everyone else did. He figured it out and did a superb job with too little time and too much to do.

In addition to Goff, hundreds of soldiers arrived at Fort Riley, some only a few days before they deployed. Some of them joined their units in the desert a few weeks or days before the ground offensive began. West Point roommates 2LT Brian Cook and 2LT Mark Camarena went to basic armor officer training at Fort Knox, Kentucky, together. Both had orders to report to Fort Riley on completion of the basic course. Cook took a three-day leave and arrived at Fort Riley on December 17, where he was assigned to the last available tank platoon in the 4-37 AR. Camarena took a longer leave so he could visit the woman he would later marry; he arrived on Christmas Eve 1990 and joined the 1-34 AR as the assistant logistics officer. By the time Camarena arrived, the post literally had run out of field gear, and he had to travel to two different installations to get all of his equipment. A day or so after Christmas, he flew to Georgia, drew a gas mask and chemical protective overgarments at Fort Benning, and flew back to Fort Riley the same day. Like virtually every other soldier who arrived in the flurry of activity just before deployment, he found the experience disorienting. According to Camarena, "No one could remember [my] name. I was known as the extra lieutenant."[74] To add to his dilemma, he had nowhere to live. He was more fortunate than most late arrivals, because he had an aunt and uncle who lived in nearby Manhattan, Kansas. He spent his last few days in the States with relatives. Second Lieutenant Jim Enicks also arrived late and had nowhere to live; he slept on another platoon leader's couch.

Arriving during the chaos of deployment was even more unsettling for young soldiers and their spouses. Pearl I. Speer, the wife of COL Bill Speer, witnessed their difficulty and worked hard to get them settled and able to cope. One young couple in particular stuck in her mind. The day they arrived, Linda Rhame and several other senior officers' wives were with Pearl Speer at the family support center. A young private came into her office, and "behind him was a weeping child woman."[75] They had just driven across country from their home in the South. The young woman had become pregnant before they were married and her parents promptly threw her out of their home. The young man had married her and then joined the Army so he could provide for her and their child. They arrived ignorant of the fact that the unit he was joining was bound for Saudi Arabia. Pearl Speer sat the young private down and walked him through what he needed to do. Meanwhile, "Lin Rhame held [the young woman] and let her cry."[76] Pearl Speer, with Linda Rhame's help, got the two of them organized. Pearl Speer would later visit the young woman several times while her husband was away and watch her confidence grow; she bore the baby and "went from a wailing child to a strong, brave Army wife."[77] Not every story turned out that well, but many of them did because Pearl Speer, Linda Rhame, and a host of other Army spouses helped them learn to cope. Some of the volunteers were the spouses of senior officers or NCOs, but most were young people who rose to the occasion. Pearl Speer also thought things worked because commanders had come around to supporting the idea of family support. As a consequence, most units left good rear detachments in place to aid families during the deployment.

LTC Bob Wilson and the 1st Squadron, 4th Cavalry (1-4 CAV) had an unusual problem with both personnel and material implications. While other battalions worked to reconstitute platoons or rebuild companies, the 1-4 CAV had to build a cavalry troop from scratch. It had only one of its two authorized cavalry troops because Alpha Troop was in Germany with the 1st Division (Forward) that was deactivating. With the drawdown under way, the Army reassigned A Troop to Fort Riley, but without soldiers. The day after the alert, Wilson reactivated A Troop under the command of CPT Kenneth Pope. He and the Division then went after troops and equipment. On November 22, with the process well under way, Bullington called Wilson, saying, "Bob, the division is going to draw 249 M1A1 tanks in SWA [Southwest Asia]. This is nine more than we were expecting and I am wondering if nine tanks might be directed to the squadron. Does this track with anything Fort Knox has been working on?"[78] Wilson had just come from Fort Knox and knew that the Armor School there wanted to add tanks to the cavalry. He called the documentation section at the Armor School, which duly sent a "test" table of organization, which the Division used to justify giving nine tanks to the squadron. In fact, six would have been the right number, but the Division took all nine tanks offered. Wilson assigned three tanks to A Troop and six to B Troop.[79] The cavalry would not only have tanks but more than it was supposed to have if and when the test table of organization was approved.

The drama of organizing a unit and deploying it almost immediately played itself out across the Division in newly formed platoons and fleshed-out companies. MG Rhame remembers, "The Division motto (no mission too difficult, no sacrifice too great, duty first) was very much on our minds."[80] Many of these units did not form completely until after the trains had been loaded and shipped to the port. Some soldiers saw their new platoon or company as a whole for the first time when they assembled in Saudi Arabia.

Finally troops started leaving for Saudi Arabia. On November 27 a liaison party including a tactical planner, a logistician, and an interpreter departed. The Division support command started flowing on December 5, and the Division advance party flew on December 10. Danger Forward, the tactical command post, the commanding general, advance parties of the 101st Military Intelligence Battalion, and the 2-3 ADA left on December 12. The remainder of the advance parties departed on December 15. The main body of troops began deploying on December 18, and the last of them flew on January 28, 1991. Troops from Garlstedt began flying on Christmas Eve, and their main body closed in Saudi Arabia on January 5. Units conducted casing the colors ceremonies that marked their official departure. These ceremonies were followed by the final more poignant farewells in a hangar at Marshall Army Airfield, where the troops were sequestered. Buses duly arrived and loaded the troops for the hour or so ride to Forbes Field in Topeka, where they boarded aircraft for the long trip to Saudi Arabia.

Listing departures and noting the process does little justice to the deployment. The scope of things that had to be done in a very short time, together with the scale of the problem, made the deployment to Saudi Arabia an epic of the genre. It was "the biggest fastest [movement] of troops in the history of the United States."[81] Some 15,180 soldiers deployed from Fort Riley, including 12,049 from the 1st Division and 3,131 from other units. They flew on 110 aircraft. Fifty-one Air Force C-141 transports and twenty-eight Boeing 747 airliners accounted for more than half of the aircraft used.[82] The 3rd Brigade traveled from Germany by air as well. One airline pilot quipped that there were so many aircraft in the air on the transatlantic crossing he thought he could walk on them.[83]

Equipment moved by rail to Houston, Texas, on thirty-four trains pulling nineteen hundred rail cars with more than six thousand pieces, including vehicles, trailers, and containers. On arrival in Houston, stevedores and soldiers, designated as supercargo, loaded thirteen ships. The 4th Brigade's helicopters flew to the port where they were "shrink wrapped" and loaded. The thirteen ships ranged from relatively modern US Ready Reserve Fleet vessels to an aging, rusty Italian flagged "roll on/roll off" ship named the *Jolly Rubino*. Whatever their vintage and registration, the ships moved more than 66,000 short tons of equipment and supplies to the Persian Gulf port of Ad Dammām, Saudi Arabia. The Danish container ship *Adrian Maersk* arrived first, on January 7, 1991, having loaded on December 7, 1990. The last ship, the MV *Cape Diamond*, loaded on December 28 and arrived on January 26.[84] The 3rd Brigade traveled by rail and road in Germany from Garlstedt to Bremerhaven, where it loaded on three ships, one each on December 30, December 31, and January 4. Two of them, the MV *American Falcon* and the USNS *Regulus*, arrived in Ad Dammām on January 17. The *Saudi Makkah* arrived in Al Jubayl, north of Ad Dammām, on January 18.

Each vessel included a handful of troops and an officer who had the task of assuring the cargo remained securely tied down and supported unloading on arrival. First Lieutenant Charles G. Hahn, the 4-3 FA's battalion motor officer, commanded the supercargo aboard the *Regulus*, a roll-on/roll-off fast sealift ship some 946 feet long and displacing 55,000 tons. Hahn and a dozen other soldiers worked for the captain of the *Regulus* on her second voyage from Bremerhaven.[85] The *Regulus* departed on January 4, bound for Ad Dammām with more than thirteen thousand tons of the 3rd Brigade's equipment. First Lieutenant Hahn learned a great deal on the trip. First, he learned that the rumor of no alcohol on ships was just that; one of the merchant seamen drove the lesson home when he wheeled a shopping cart full of liquor aboard. The no-liquor rule apparently applied to ships with USS as their prefix, but not those with USNS. The sailors were, according to Hahn, "a rough crowd," consisting mostly of a "bunch of grizzled old guys who were there to make a living."[86]

Hahn and the rest of the supercargo had plenty to do as the *Regulus* made her way down the English Channel across the Bay of Biscay. Famed for rough weather and rough water, the bay did not disappoint. Several times a day, Hahn and his men made their way through the vehicle compartments to check tie-downs to preclude the cargo from shifting. Crossing the Bay of Biscay was, in a word, terrifying. The ship pitched, rolled, and yawed. Howitzers strained against the chains that secured them while the hull creaked, groaned, and flexed. It was, remembers Hahn, "horrible."[87] Nevertheless, he and his soldiers arrived safely in Saudi Arabia, where they joined the rest of the Division and prepared go to war. SPC Will Parrett may have described what would come next as well as it could be said; on his departure for Saudi Arabia he observed, "We know we are properly trained for our mission in the Middle East, but that is only half of it. The other half, the most important part, is focusing our minds on the hardships to come in the desert."[88]

NOTES

1. Multiple sources, but chiefly the author's notes from that meeting, and MG (Ret.) Lon E. Maggart, "Eye of the Storm (Duty First)," unpublished manuscript, 1992–97, 23.

2. LTG (Ret.) Thomas G. Rhame, interview with the author, Alexandria, VA, April 23, 2014.

3. Multiple sources, but chiefly the author's notes from that meeting, and Maggart, "Eye of the Storm," 23.

4. Multiple sources, but chiefly the author's notes from that meeting; Maggart, "Eye of the Storm," 23; and Pearl I. Speer and COL (Ret.) William L. Speer, interview with the author, Milford, KS, June 25, 2014.

5. LTC (Ret.) Randy S. Shannon, interview with the author, Wyandotte, KS, October 14, 2014.

6. Motor pools are enclosed spaces that include some garage-like maintenance bays, some office space, and storage for parts and tools. Mostly they are concrete parking areas designed to park a battalion's tanks, Bradleys, and other equipment with just enough space to move in and out.

7. Rhame interview, April 23, 2014.

8. Ibid.

9. Maggart, "Eye of the Storm," 23.

10. Author's notes.

11. Ibid.

12. Lieutenant Colonel David W. Marlin, "History of the 4th Battalion, 37th Armored Regiment in Operation Desert Shield/Storm," unpublished manuscript, US Army War College, Carlisle Barracks, PA, 1992, 45.

13. MG (Ret.) Robert D. Shadley, telephone interview with the author, August 1, 2014; LTC John Andrews, G-4, 1st Infantry Division, interview by MAJ Thomas A. Popa, Fort Riley, KS, July 24, 1991, DSIT-C-066. See also Headquarters, 1 ID (M) DISCOM. *Desert Shield/Desert Storm Support Operations* (Fort Riley, KS: Headquarters, 1 ID [M] DISCOM, 1992).

14. COL (Ret.) Terry W. Bullington, "The First Infantry Division in Desert Shield/Desert Storm: Notes by Terry Bullington," undated letter to the author, received June 16, 2014.

15. COL (Ret.) Terry W. Bullington, telephone interview with the author, October 29, 2013.

16. Linda Hoeffner, interview with the author, Fort Riley, KS, October 31, 2013. In 1990 Hoeffner worked for Bullington in resource management. She sought approval through contracting at Forces Command. With the irrefutable logic of government bureaucrats, Forces Command contracting told Hoeffner that the devices could not be bought because they were not on the Division's authorized equipment list. In the end, Magellan shipped several hundred devices to Bahrain. One of Bullington's staff officers drove from Ad Dammām across the causeway over the strait between Saudi Arabia and Bahrain and picked them up.

17. General H. Norman Schwarzkopf with Peter Petre, *It Doesn't Take a Hero: The Autobiography* (New York: Bantam, 1992), 380–84; Tom Clancy with General Fred Franks Jr., *Into the Storm: A Study in Command* (New York: Berkley, 2004), 190–96; COL (Ret.) Donald Osterberg, telephone interview with the author, October 14, 2014. See also Richard M. Swain, *"Lucky War": Third Army in Desert Storm* (Fort Leavenworth, KS: US Army Command and General Staff College Press, 1994).

18. Schwarzkopf, *It Doesn't Take a Hero*, 380.

19. Rick Atkinson, *Crusade: The Untold Story of the Gulf War* (London: HarperCollins, 1994), 1.

20. Schwarzkopf, *It Doesn't Take a Hero*, 380–81.

21. LTG (Ret.) Thomas G. Rhame, telephone interview with the author, October 21, 2014.

22. Ibid.

23. Schwarzkopf, *It Doesn't Take a Hero*, 382.

24. Clancy, *Into the Storm*, 193.

25. Osterberg interview.

26. Ibid.

27. GEN (Ret.) Barry R. McCaffrey, telephone interview with the author, March 10, 2014.

28. Rhame interview, October 21, 2014; LTG (Ret.) Thomas G. Rhame, telephone interview with the author, November 7, 2014.

29. Osterberg interview. Osterberg came home for a few days over Thanksgiving, but returned soon after with his planning team. They came home for good in May.

30. The 2-34 AR established the paint shop in the 1st Brigade, while the 4-37 AR did the same in the 2nd Brigade.

31. Maggart, "Eye of the Storm," 27–28. Marlin, "History of the 4th Battalion, 37th Armored Regiment," 46–49.

32. Marlin, "History of the 4th Battalion, 37th Armored Regiment," 50–56.

33. Headquarters, 4th Battalion, 5th Field Artillery, "Faithful and True: Operation Desert Storm Journal," unpublished manuscript, Fort Riley, KS, n.d.

34. 1st ID (Mechanized), "Big Red One: Logistics Readiness: Deployment through Reconstitution," briefing, January 13, 1992.

35. Shadley interview.

36. Marlin, "History of the 4th Battalion, 37th Armored Regiment," 59–60.

37. COL (Ret.) Steven K. Whitfield, telephone interview with the author, November 4, 2014.

38. Ibid.

39. Ibid; Rhame interview, October 21, 2014. Rhame's assertion is correct. Robert S. Korpanty, PE, *Rail Deployment at CONUS Installations during Operation Desert Storm*, MTMCTEA Report OA 91-4a-26 (Fort Eustis, VA: Military Traffic Command Transportation Engineering Agency, 1992), 13, shows the maximum achievement at Fort Riley.

40. Carl Cartwright, "Rail Loading Underway," *Fort Riley Post*, November 30, 1990, 1.

41. Patrice Macan, "Vehicles Loaded," *Fort Riley Post*, December 7, 1990, 4.

42. LTC John D. Tabb, telephone interview with the author, October 30, 2014. After his enlistment, Tabb went to college and returned to the Army as a commissioned officer.

43. Tabb interview. See also Korpanty, *Rail Deployment*, 13. A loading cycle consists of loading, tying down, and cycling cars. Fort Riley averaged no more than two loading cycles in a day, which looked good compared to other posts, but none of them impressed.

44. COL Myron Kryschtal, "Desert Logistics," postwar briefing, n.d. See also 1st ID (Mechanized), "Big Red One."

45. Kryschtal, "Desert Logistics."

46. COL (Ret.) Philip L. Wilkerson, telephone interview with the author, October 22, 2014. COL Wilkerson commanded the 4-1 AVN.

47. Headquarters, 1st Infantry Division (Mechanized) and Fort Riley, *Iraqi Threat Handbook* (Fort Riley, KS: Headquarters, 1st Infantry Division [Mechanized] and Fort Riley, 1990).

48. COL (Ret.) George P. Ritter, telephone interview with the author, August 4, 2014.

49. Maggart, "Eye of the Storm," 26; Ritter interview. I learned things about the M1 tank that day that I believe helped my unit prevent damage to our tanks. I have found sufficient reference to these briefings elsewhere to believe this conclusion applies across the 1 ID.

50. Giles's advice about fear made a particular impression on me. I discussed fear with every unit in my task force. The Army did not immediately alter the

rotation of commanders, which had the effect of removing experienced commanders in the months prior to the war itself.

51. Maggart, "Eye of the Storm," 40–41; COL (Ret.) Robert A. Burns, interview with the author, Leavenworth, KS, April 16, 2014.

52. Maggart, "Eye of the Storm," 41.

53. Burns interview.

54. COL (Ret.) Anthony A. Moreno, telephone interview with the author, August 12, 2014.

55. Maggart, "Eye of the Storm," 90 (see also 40–41); Ritter interview.

56. Moreno interview. The video is titled *The Breach and Assault*, and can be viewed at https://www.youtube.com/watch?v=oI0Vprf7Fbo.

57. The author can attest to this. See also Major James K. Morningstar, "Points of Attack: Lessons from the Breach," *Armor*, January–February 1998, 9.

58. COL Robert P. Stavnes, telephone interview with the author, October 8, 2014.

59. Maggart, "Eye of the Storm," 42; author's notes; McCaffrey interview (regarding pundits' views). The author induced the analysts to show off the T-72's capacity to dig; it was truly underwhelming.

60. This assertion cannot be quantified, but instead reflects the author's impression and that of his key leaders. Other battalion commanders report similar responses.

61. LTC Clinton J. Ancker, "2nd Armored Division (Forward) and the Gulf Conflict," unpublished manuscript, Naval War College, Newport, RI, n.d.

62. Ibid., 40.

63. Just when this decision was made is unclear. Shifting the UK 1 AD to the VII Corps from II MEF muddied the waters. The Marines needed a large armor formation. In the end the 2nd Brigade, 2 AD, from Fort Hood met that need.

64. Ancker, "2nd Armored Division (Forward)," 25, 27–28, 31. The Forward Division concept left open questions about how to meld the formation when the rest of the Division arrived.

65. COL (Ret.) George T. Jones, telephone interview with the author, March 11, 2014.

66. Ancker, "2nd Armored Division (Forward)," 53.

67. Jones interview; BG (Ret.) John S. Brown, interview with the author, Denver, September 25, 2014.

68. Ancker, "2nd Armored Division (Forward)," 54.

69. Ibid., 51; COL (Ret.) Robert L. Smith, telephone interview with the author, October 7, 2014; COL Charles G. Hahn, telephone interview with the author, October 30, 2014.

70. Smith interview.

71. Ibid.

72. CPT James M. Goff Jr., telephone interview with the author, September 28, 2014.

73. Ibid. Dr. Goff served as the surgeon in the author's battalion and proved to be a very good Army officer as well as a really good doctor.

74. COL Brian C. Cook, telephone interview with the author, September 10, 2014; LTC (Ret.) Mark J. Camarena, interview with the author, Leavenworth, KS, October 22, 2014.

75. Speer and Speer interview.

76. Ibid.

77. Ibid.

78. LTC Robert Wilson, "Tanks in the Division Cavalry Squadron," *Armor*, July–August 1992, 6.

79. Ibid. See also Stephen A. Bourque and John W. Burdan III, *The Road to Safwan: The 1st Squadron, 4th Cavalry in the 1991 Persian Gulf War* (Denton: University of North Texas Press, 2007), 23. Wilson assigned six tanks to B Troop because the troop commander had been in command for a while. This made CPT Pope's task of organizing and training A Troop a bit less difficult.

80. Rhame interview, April 23, 2014.

81. Author's notes.

82. 1 ID (Mechanized), untitled AAR charts, n.d.; these are backup charts for a briefing. COL Gary LaGrange, Fort Riley garrison briefing presented at Fort Benning, GA. A handwritten note suggests that LaGrange gave this briefing on March 15, 1991.

83. Canadian airline pilot Joe Oakley, comment to the author when both were students at the National Defence College of Canada in the fall of 1991.

84. COL Gary LaGrange, Fort Riley Garrison briefing, Fort Benning, Georgia, n.d. (probably March 15, 1991); James K. Matthews and Cora J. Holt, *So Many, So Much, So Far, So Fast: United States Transportation Command and Strategic Deployment for Operation Desert Shield/Storm* (Honolulu, HI: University Press of the Pacific, 2002), appendix 10, 288, 297.

85. Matthews and Holt, *So Many, So Much, So Far, So Fast*, 128. USNS *Regulus* made her first round trip between December 6 and 17, 1990, carrying over nine thousand tons of gear belonging to 1 AD and VII Corps artillery.

86. Hahn interview.

87. Ibid.

88. SPC Will Parrett, quoted in Lori Stephens, "Discipline Key to Mental Preparation," *Fort Riley Post*, November 30, 1990, 1.

CHAPTER FIVE

HEADING FOR THE BADLANDS

After five meals and five movies, we landed in Saudi Arabia.

—Fourth Battalion, Fifth Field Artillery Unit Journal

The road between Dammam and TAA Roosevelt consisted of vast empty spaces punctuated with vehicle wreckage from accidents.

—First Lieutenant Jay C. Mumford

I swear to God we are ready. We are ready to fight America.

—Saddam Hussein

WHEN PRESIDENT GEORGE H. W. BUSH announced the deployment of the VII Corps and supporting troops, he galvanized both the American and Iraqi armed forces. Alerting and moving the VII Corps to Saudi Arabia provided GEN H. Norman Schwarzkopf and the coalition that President Bush had formed the capacity to drive Iraq from Kuwait by force. Diplomacy remained possible, but time was fast running out. Saddam Hussein, despite his bluster about fighting, hoped to find a way out of the crisis without fighting and believed he might succeed and achieve at least some advantage. The window for a diplomatic solution began to dissipate as the VII Corps deployed.

Iraqi Estimates and Dispositions

Saddam's intelligence organization, the General Military Intelligence Directorate (GMID), may have shared his aspirations, but not his optimism. From the beginning of the crisis, GMID assessed the Americans as likely to attack. In August the directorate concluded that the "continuous concentration of

American troops in the region affirms the intention of the Coalition forces to launch the attack."[1] The Iraqis surmised the attack might be exclusively from the air in the beginning. Toward the end of August, the directorate asserted, "While waiting for more troops to arrive, the Americans will mainly depend on their air superiority."[2] Following Bush's announcement in November, GMID concluded, "The American administration is serious about attacking Iraq."[3] Despite his public pronouncements, Saddam took these warnings seriously and acted on them throughout the crisis.

The Iraqis sought to improve their estimates by using the reconnaissance resources they had. These included oblique photography, signals intelligence, and side-looking airborne radar.[4] They also used agents to ascertain the location and activity of coalition forces. The Iraqi diplomatic corps exploited their contacts as well. In August 1990 the air attaché in Belgrade reported on a contact between the Palestinian military attaché and the director of Yugoslav intelligence. According to the Palestinian attaché, the Yugoslavs believed the United States would attack as early as the end of August. The Iraqis also interviewed line crossers and monitored Western media.[5]

Schwarzkopf made draconian threats to his staff about security, but someone, possibly in government, talked. A great many people knew the basic outline. In any case, the media either learned or deduced the general outlines of Central Command's (CENTCOM's) campaign plan. In an article in the *International Herald Tribune*, Leslie Gelb wrote, "Everyone seems to know that the likely scenario calls for US and British forces to wheel around Kuwait and cut across the southern part of Iraq toward Basra."[6] The CENTCOM concept of an attack around the Iraqi Army's western flank was an open secret. The Iraqis simply found the idea of a great wheel around Kuwait unlikely.

Although Saddam used the Republican Guard Forces Command to seize Kuwait, he did not employ it to defend his newly acquired "nineteenth province." Instead, he withdrew the politically reliable, mobile, and well-equipped Republican Guard and positioned it to the north of Kuwait and southwest of Basra as a strategic reserve. From this position the Guard could respond rapidly to a coalition attack into Kuwait or north along Kuwait's western boundary. Relatively immobile infantry divisions formed the front line. To the rear of the front-line formations, they established tactical reserves, and they positioned operational reserves farther to the rear.[7]

Initially the Iraqis established a forward defense along the Kuwait-Saudi border employing techniques generally similar to those they had employed in the Iran-Iraq War. Each of the forward infantry divisions deployed with two brigades up and one back. Each of the brigades dug in its three infantry battalions and supporting weapons including tanks. Generally, each infantry brigade could count on a tank company in support. Each of the forward corps controlled several front-line divisions. Each also had at least one mechanized or armored division as a tactical reserve. In December, the Iraqis formed a corps headquarters they called Jihad. It moved into the theater just northwest of Kuwait as an operational reserve. The Jihad Corps controlled the 10th and 17th Armored Divisions (ADs). As the buildup of coalition forces continued, the Iraqis worked to improve their positions and extend their main line of resistance west into southern Iraq.[8]

Their method of extending west followed an easily discernible pattern. As divisions repositioned or new divisions extended the line, they refused their western flank. They did so by positioning at least an infantry battalion of each division oriented to the west supported by the division's reserve located to their rear or north. In September an unidentified Iraqi division extended the defenses well to the west by deploying some one hundred kilometers west of the triborder region. To their east, the Iraqi 26th Infantry Division (ID) positioned two brigades to defend the Iraqi right flank west of the Wadi al-Batin. It was here that the 1 ID attacked them in February 1991.[9]

Over the course of several weeks the Iraqi VII Corps worked to close the gap between its units and the main line of resistance in Kuwait. The efforts of its divisions were inconsistent. Some built complex obstacles including minefields, wire, antitank ditches, and in a few cases trenches filled with oil that could be set ablaze. Many of them did not establish complex obstacles; some failed to dig in adequately or develop sufficient overhead cover for fighting positions. In some places, local conditions confounded Iraqi troops' efforts to dig because bedrock lay only three feet or so below the surface. In any case, they did not build the kind of positions described in US Army threat handbooks. Iraqi units certainly could build complex obstacles and impressive defensive positions, as they had demonstrated in the Iran-Iraq War, but they failed to do so west of the Wadi al-Batin. The lack of adequately prepared positions chiefly stemmed from inadequate supervision of hastily raised conscript units and inadequate resources including mines, wire, and obstacle materials. Farther east, where they had more time and resources, their defenses were better.[10]

In September and October 1990 the Iraqis studied six possible "enemy" courses of action. These included a seaborne attack from the Persian Gulf supported by an attack northward along the coast. An attack more or less into the teeth of the Iraqi defense midway along Kuwait's boot heel comprised the second course of action. The third assumed an attack north, along the western edge of the boot heel. Their analysts imagined an attack northeast from the bend in the southern boundary of Kuwait as the fourth course of action. The fifth course of action assumed an attack northeast from the southwest corner of Kuwait just east of the Wadi al-Batin. Finally, the Iraqis considered an attack up the Wadi al-Batin feasible.[11] The Iraqis also positioned forces to defend the Al-Faw Peninsula against an amphibious assault.[12]

The Iraqi Estimate of Coalition Courses of Action

The Iraqis reinforced the defense of Kuwait throughout the fall, expanding their Army to do so. Saddam's ministry of defense increased both the regular army and the Republican Guard; it added four divisions to the Guard order of battle, although only two moved south. After Bush announced the deployment of additional US forces, Iraq moved ten more divisions into the theater. This reinforcement raised the number of deployed troops to about 500,000. They were organized in at least forty-one divisions, though there may have been as many as fifty-five. Infantry divisions comprised the bulk of the newly created formations. They were poorly equipped and not well trained. They were used to thicken defenses and close gaps. Three regular army armored divisions arrived to combine with units already in the theater to beef up the operational reserves. The three armored divisions raised the number of tanks available to 4,200. The newly arrived 17 AD and the 51 ID (Mechanized) provided mobile forces to back up three infantry divisions and one infantry brigade defending the coast north of Kuwait City. The 12 AD arrived in December 1990. That unit combined with the 10 AD, under control of the Jihad Corps, oriented on the Wadi al-Batin. In January 1991 the Iraqis formed yet another corps, with headquarters in Nasiriyah, Iraq. Called West Euphrates Corps, it controlled two divisions defending southern Iraq.[13]

Iraqi planners clung to two flawed assumptions: first, they believed the US would mount an amphibious assault as part of the coalition campaign; second, they were convinced the Americans would attack up the Wadi al-Batin. They had perfectly good reasons for their conviction. CENTCOM retained an amphibious capability, suggesting the possibility of amphibious assault. GEN Schwarzkopf never intended to land Marines in Kuwait, but he kept Marines afloat and worked to deceive the Iraqis into believing an amphibious assault was coming. Just as he intended, the Iraqis honored the threat. Despite US media alleging a great flanking maneuver to the west, the Iraqis found that option implausible based on the sheer difficulty of maneuvering and navigating west of Wadi al-Batin. Featureless desert is an inadequate description of that ground. It was absolutely barren. In accordance with the CENTCOM deception plan, the US VII Corps positioned no units in the west until shortly before the attack. The 1st Cavalry Division (1 CD) moved into the area in February and conducted operations designed to create the impression the coalition attack would come up the wadi.[14] For all of these reasons, the Iraqis reinforced their defenses oriented toward the wadi and along the coast. By the time the 1 ID began arriving in Saudi Arabia, Iraqi reinforcements were either on the way or in the positions they would occupy on the day the ground offensive began.

Operational Planning in the US VII Corps, December 1990

Although MG Thomas G. Rhame returned to Fort Riley after the CENTCOM briefing on November 14, MAJ Don Osterberg, his plans officer, remained to work with his counterparts in the VII Corps, the XVIII Airborne (ABN) Corps, the 3rd Army (the US Army component command that would control the two Army corps), and CENTCOM. Osterberg came home for a few days in late November, long enough to pack and say good-bye to his family. Because he remained with the planners, he had a feel for the planning effort in the theater. Understanding how other units saw the problem provided context for the Division planners.

The tempo picked up when the Division began to deploy. In late November, a small logistics liaison team deployed first. When assistant division commander for maneuver BG William G. Carter III flew on December 12, he brought operations officer LTC Terry Bullington and the Division planners with him. Carter took his command post, Danger Forward, with him. Rhame flew from Fort Riley on December 16; the next day the advance party, Danger Forward, and the commanding general arrived at the port of Ad Dammām.[15]

Carter and Danger Forward immediately began work on the myriad tasks required to receive arriving units. Osterberg and the planners continued planning the attack, accompanying Rhame to a VII Corps commanders' conference on December 18. LTG Frederick M. Franks Jr. briefed the Corps' mission, his assumptions, intelligence estimate, operational concept, and intent. He made several planning assumptions: he assumed coalition air superiority prior to the attack and that coalition air forces would wear down the Republican Guard to 50 percent strength and the remainder of the enemy to 75 percent strength; and, most important, he assumed that the coalition supporting attacks would fix the enemy in Kuwait. Schwarzkopf's plan depended on the attack in the east "tying up Saddam's forces."[16] The CENTCOM deception plan also constrained the VII Corps in important ways. Schwarzkopf forbade units to move west of the Wadi al-Batin until he authorized it. The VII Corps attack, the main theater effort, would emanate from west of the wadi. Not being able to build up logistics stocks west of the wadi would inhibit a rapid advance into Iraq. Long turnaround times to bring up fuel and ammunition would effectively force a slow advance.

The Corps had a pretty good overall picture of the Iraqi defenses, although without much detail.[17] Of vital interest to Rhame, the VII Corps estimated that "[t]he enemy defensive line gets weaker the further west you go." The Corps also assessed the Iraqi front-line infantry divisions as fundamentally immobile.[18] Franks expected the enemy to defend in belts with the Iraqi 26 ID (Forward) and the 16 ID and 12 AD to their rear. Franks's concept called for the 1 ID to conduct a deliberate attack to penetrate the 26 ID (located in the Neutral

Zone northwest of Hafir al-Batin and west of the Wadi al-Batin) and clear an area sufficient to enable forward passage of the remainder of the Corps in column. He directed that the penetration occur on a frontage of no more than sixteen kilometers using two brigades in the assault. To pass the rest of the Corps forward, he wanted eight lanes cleared within eight hours. Franks envisaged the operation unfolding in six phases:

1. Getting through the ports and moving to the tactical assembly area rapidly.
2. Training and preparing in the tactical assembly area for about three weeks and then moving to an attack position.
3. Breaching the enemy defenses.
4. Defeating the tactical reserve.
5. Destroying the three divisions of the Republican Guard.
6. Defending northern Kuwait once the Iraqis had been ejected.[19]

MG Rhame wrote down the corps commander's intent verbatim. The corps commander wanted to "position a well-sustained three division plus armored cavalry regiment [force] in a concentration area to fight a mobile Airland Battle [i.e., applying the tenets of the 1986 doctrine for AirLand Battle] clearly to destroy Republican Guards. I want to attempt to locate and exploit gaps in the enemy's defensive obstacle system so we can exploit. I want to confuse the enemy as to time and place of our attack. We will breach his defense. We will pass tailored combat elements through the breach quickly. We will envelop tactical reserve divisions. Rapid tempo, minimize casualties. Mass ground and air repeatedly. Deep operations focus on tactical reserves."[20]

Franks planned to attack at first light. MG Rhame preferred to attack at night and asked for a midnight attack time, but Franks said no. The attack would go in just before sunrise.[21] The die was cast, and after this session, little of importance changed from Rhame's perspective. Osterberg and his planning team could focus their effort on specific Iraqi divisions dug in a few kilometers west of the Wadi al-Batin. All that remained was to get the Division ashore in Saudi Arabia and move up-country to get the final preparations under way. After the meeting, Rhame briefed Bullington and gave his guidance to the planners. He then flew home that evening to close out the deployment at Fort Riley. That did not take long. On December 21 the Division conducted a departure ceremony during which Rhame and CSM Fred Davenport cased the colors of the Division. Rhame, Davenport, the Division planners, and the rest of the Division headquarters company departed for Saudi Arabia the evening of December 26, arriving on the morning of December 28.[22]

While Rhame closed out at Fort Riley, Carter got on with preparing to receive the Division when it arrived in the forward area. He moved Danger Forward to the VII Corps Tactical Assembly Area (TAA) Juno, in northern Saudi

Arabia, on December 20. COL Bob Shadley and the early arriving logistics troops received their equipment in Ad Dammām on December 19 and 20. Immediately afterward, they convoyed north to establish the division support area and get the supply chain working. TAA Juno (see Map 1) was an area designated on a map rather than an actual place; it lay east of King Khalid Military City, astride the Trans-Arabian Pipeline road. Roughly a hundred kilometers wide and nearly twice as long north to south, it enclosed featureless desert. Within TAA Juno, the Corps assigned each of its divisions a piece of ground. The 1st Division's TAA Roosevelt lay just east of the village of Al Qaysumah and north of Tapline Road. The Corps could move into TAA Juno securely, because Saudi units screened the frontier to the north. Two Egyptian divisions, a Syrian division, the XVIII ABN Corps, and various other coalition forces occupied defensive positions along the coast and south of the Kuwait border.[23]

On his way north, Carter visited MG Barry R. McCaffrey and the 24 ID in that division's defensive positions some two hundred kilometers northwest of Ad Dammām. Like Rhame before him, Carter received a clear-eyed assessment of enemy capability from McCaffrey. He then continued on to TAA Roosevelt, and Osterberg and the planners followed on December 23. By Christmas Eve, Danger Forward had established adequate command and control to receive the Division while continuing to plan the attack. COL Shadley and essential elements of the Division Support Command had also closed. LTC Tom Waterman's 701st Main Support Battalion (701 MSB) set up so they could support arriving units.[24] Carter, Bullington, and the planners could work in a secure area and receive units as they arrived.

Escaping the Port

Anyone who has traveled by air to an overseas destination knows how disorienting it can be. You arrive tired, dirty, and disheveled. You must find your bags, process through customs, and perhaps drive in an exotic place, all without adequate rest. However unpleasant, the typical international traveler's experience pales by comparison to what soldiers endure during the process known as reception, staging, onward movement, and integration—the stages a deploying unit must pass through that parallel those of an arriving international traveler. The difference in scale, of course, is huge. Nearly fifteen thousand soldiers in the 1st Division arrived with weapons and baggage, and each soldier's baggage included two duffel bags as a minimum.[25] All six thousand pieces of cargo shipped from Fort Riley came through the same port as well. All fifteen thousand soldiers needed a place to sleep, food to eat, basic amenities, and somewhere to assemble their equipment, repair it as necessary, and marshal convoys before moving about five hundred kilometers to TAA Roosevelt.

Doctrinally, MG Gus Pagonis's 22nd Support Command (22 SPT CMD) had the responsibility for receiving arriving troops and getting them to where they needed to go. But Pagonis had too few units under his direction to do the job, because both Schwarzkopf and LTG John Yeosock, the Army component commander, wanted to minimize the number of troops in the theater. To achieve that goal, the Army leaders chose to accept logistic risk; specifically, they did not bring in sufficient logistics units to run reception and theater logistics for two corps. Pagonis needed help; on November 9 he called Franks and asked him to provide troops to help with the reception, staging, and onward movement mission. Franks agreed. First he sent the 2nd Armored Cavalry Regiment (2 ACR) to secure TAA Juno. COL Ed Simpson, the VII Corps deputy chief of staff, went next to establish the corps forward command post.[26]

To assist the 22 SPT CMD with reception and staging, Franks tapped his West Point classmate and friend BG Bill Mullen, who commanded the 1st Division (Forward). Although in the process of deactivating, Mullen still had most of his troops and could take the mission. Franks gave him succinct and clear guidance: "Do everything possible to help the Corps get into the desert ready to fight."[27] Mullen's 3rd Brigade, commanded by COL Stephen D. Wesbrook, began moving almost immediately. To reduce the appearance that there was any ramping up of the numbers of troops in theater, the 3rd Brigade did not appear on any lists of deploying units. Therefore, it had no deployment orders; it was, in a manner of speaking, unofficial. As Wesbrook creatively recalls, "1500 hundred Big Red One and attached soldiers literally hitch hiked [*sic*] with the Air Force, infiltrating into Saudi Arabia in small groups."[28] This was an absurdity, but it served to keep the "official" number of arriving troops down. The deception satisfied the 3rd Army and CENTCOM. Wesbrook's troops arrived just ahead of the Corps and met the first Corps troops to arrive "officially" on December 2. The first ship docked on December 5.[29]

The Brigade's footprint grew rapidly into a full-fledged port support activity. In that capacity, the 3rd Brigade assumed virtually the entire mission of reception and staging, taking on all of the support tasks, from running housing and transportation to offloading ships and staging equipment. The 3rd Brigade also contracted buses to meet flights at the nearby arrival airfield. On the heels of that assignment, the mission grew yet again when Franks asked Mullen to assume command of the VII Corps (Forward). With that increment, the task now included taking charge of onward movement. Now the 3rd Brigade would arrange convoys and transportation to move units to the field. BG Mullen arrived in Saudi Arabia on December 28 and assumed command of the VII Corps (Forward), thus bringing general officer clout to the problem of running the Corps.

Mullen's arrival freed the 3rd Brigade to focus on execution. COL Wesbrook organized two port support activity task forces. LTC Russell L. Honoré commanded a task force built around his 4th Battalion, 16th Infantry Brigade, and it ran the port support activity at Ad Dammām under the operational control of the 7th Transportation Group (7 TRANS GRP), whose business this was; the group had the expertise, but it needed extra hands. Honoré's soldiers unloaded, staged, and moved arriving VII Corps equipment; they also housed and fed units until they departed the port (as Honoré puts it, he ran a "bed and breakfast"). LTC Myron Griswold's Task Force 3-34 AR, organized around his tank battalion, performed the same function at the smaller port of Jubayl north of Ad Dammām.[30]

With only fifteen hundred troops to operate two ports and two staging areas, Honoré and Griswold needed arriving units to help. Occasionally an arriving battalion commander refused to support one of their requirements; more than one argued that the port support activity commander had no authority to ask them to do anything. Honoré and Griswold used persuasion and threat as required. Sometimes they had to make good on a threat to take the issue to the next level. They also occasionally received what Honoré, an infantryman, described as "stupid-ass tanker orders"—that is, orders that could not be executed.[31] One such order mandated that no one was to sleep on the ground, yet there were too few cots to go around. The only thing to do was say "Yes, sir" and move on. At least in Ad Dammām most of the troops slept in large tents, under army canvas, or in an apartment complex, the Khobar Towers. In Jubayl, almost everyone slept under canvas courtesy of a US Navy mobile construction battalion (of the Sea Bees) that built tent pads and erected tents for incoming soldiers.[32]

Contractors provided some basic amenities. These included locally built hand-washing stations, outdoor latrines, and showers. The latrines were ubiquitous; they could be found at pier side, in staging areas, in living areas, and wherever else they might be needed. Better still, enough were built to move some to the tactical assembly areas. The shower units had reservoirs made of tin and filled with salt water. The water might warm up some during the day, but usually when it emerged from the gravity fed showerheads it was tepid at best, and after sundown it was freezing cold.

The port support activity had no means to feed the great number of troops passing through. Contract caterers served meals, mostly with good results. On January 8, however, a caterer at Ad Dammām served a meal with unfortunate results. Approximately eighty soldiers suffered salmonella poisoning after eating what the troops called Iraqi attack chicken. CPT Jim Goff, the battalion surgeon of the 2-34 AR, along with his medics, treated symptoms and administered fluids to the victims of what he remembers as a "two-bucket" disease. Several really sick soldiers had to be evacuated to the nearby 85th Evacuation Hospital.[33]

According to Mullen, effectively supporting arriving units depended on synchronizing air arrivals with ships. Given the limitations of the port and available transportation surges, last-minute changes would generate chaos and tax the capacity of the port support activity. More than 107,000 VII Corps troops arrived at three arrival airfields. Ships did not arrive as planned, resulting "in long delays in the reception area awaiting equipment, overconcentration in staging areas, lost training opportunities and extra risk [of Scud missile attacks] to soldiers."[34]

With all they had to do, the port support activity task forces properly focused their main efforts on unloading ships. COL Dan Whaley's 7 TRANS GRP assisted with expertise and oversight, but tankers and infantrymen from two task forces unloaded and marshaled equipment in unit sets. This may sound simple, but like most things in a combat zone it was not. Despite attempts to combat load the ships, none were so loaded. Combat loading aims for effectiveness at the port of debarkation rather than efficient loading: what needs to come off first is loaded last. As a minimum, ships would load intact units. But ships were loaded without regard to unit integrity; transportation officials in the ports of embarkation focused on efficiency for loading rather than effectiveness on arrival.[35] Equipment and supplies were loaded to optimize use of space aboard the vessels, regardless of which unit owned them. Peacetime focus and peacetime rules trumped effectiveness in the ports.

Loading without regard to unit integrity complicated marshaling, staging, and onward movement. Marshaling equipment and containers consumes a lot of space; both ports had marshaling areas, but neither had sufficient space to cope with six thousand pieces of equipment inbound from Fort Riley and nearly eleven hundred more from Garlstedt, Germany. The port in Ad Dammām was the bigger of the two ports, about six kilometers long and five kilometers wide. Warehouses and piers consumed most of that area. Shuffling equipment around Ad Dammām, let alone at the small port, would have driven deck handlers on an aircraft carrier to distraction. Everything that came off ships needed to be parked in unit sets. Once equipment arrived and the port support activity unloaded, units could stage for onward movement.

In Ad Dammām, CPT Dave Cavaleri and his tank company made this happen. With masterful understatement, he describes the mission as "unsettling" because "we didn't know how to prepare for it . . . we had nothing, we had nobody to tell us how to do this."[36] To understand the problem he and his soldiers confronted requires some simple arithmetic. An M1 tank is slightly more than ten meters long and just under four meters wide. Cavaleri's company unloaded all 243 tanks shipped from Fort Riley. As they did so, his soldiers parked the tanks in unit sets. These included fourteen tanks per company, fifty-eight tanks per battalion, 116 tanks per brigade, and so on. Consider that, if parked end to end, the line of tanks from a single brigade would exceed one kilometer, but the staging area was barely a kilometer long and far narrower. Lining up tanks was not the end of it, however; space had to be found for fuel trucks, ammunition trucks, ambulances, command post tracks, and a host of other pieces of rolling stock. The fact that few units had their gear on a single ship and ships often arrived days apart compounded the problem and created delays. CPT Cavaleri and his troops managed the problem with meticulous attention to detail, continuously shifting vehicles to accommodate departures and arrivals. The staging area soon resembled a matrix formed of vehicles parked nose to tail with barely enough space to walk between the columns.[37]

Nothing could be done without coordination between the 7 TRANS GRP and arriving vessels. In this case, that meant one young specialist (an Army enlisted rank between private first class and sergeant) from the 7 TRANS GRP "was the only guy who could negotiate with the ship's crew."[38] He was good at what he did, but could only be on one ship at a time. Only after he concluded arrangements with the ship's crew could the soldiers detailed to unload go to work. Often they discovered a vehicle they were not licensed to drive. In a few cases, they even found vehicles they had never seen. "They kind of figured it out," remembers Cavaleri, and drove off whatever they found. Despite all the headaches, the unloading crews got it done. According to Cavaleri, "We just faced down problems."[39] His laconic conclusion described the chief method of the 1 ID (Forward). From Mullen to the most junior private, they "faced down problems."

Cargo also arrived by air, sometimes accompanied by troops, sometimes not. In late January 1991 the last Division flight arrived at the airport in Ad Dammām. The Air Force cargo craft carried the Division personnel staff section's sergeant major, forty-five soldiers, and a number of cargo pallets. The aviation brigade's handheld long-range navigation (LORAN) devices were on one of these pallets. As the aircraft approached, it aborted the landing due to an immediate warning of an inbound Scud missile.[40] The aircraft circled until the threat passed. On board, everyone masked in the event the Scud had a chemical warhead. When the aircraft landed, the aircrew sent the passengers off the airplane at full speed. Then they shoved the pallets out and departed forthwith. Subsequently the pallets "disappeared."[41]

Brigade executive officer LTC Dave Wildes and his logistics officer set off to find their lost pallet of LORAN devices and learned of a "frustrated" cargo lot where undeliverable cargo was stored. Cargo generally ended up in the lot because it lacked unit identification codes and/or clear shipping labels. On arrival, they found a handful of 24 ID soldiers who somehow had become responsible for managing the place. Wildes remembers being stunned; the lot was "an image from *Raiders of the Lost Ark*. Acres of pallets, all uniform in appearance."[42] The enterprising soldiers devised a system designed to make it possible to find cargo. They grouped the lost shipments by division designation. Unfortunately there were at least four divisions with the number 1 in their designation. Wildes and the brigade staff officer had no recourse but to look until they found their missing pallet.[43] Sometimes only patience would allow a problem to be "faced down."

Ad Dammām and Jubayl shared one characteristic: both were hives of activity, much of it dangerous, and just sleeping at one of the ports was risky. One of the 1st Brigade's tank battalions lived in an enormous German festival tent on a quay. It had arrived on New Year's Eve and departed for the assembly area on January 12. During the nearly two weeks they stayed in port, a large ammunition ship nearby unloaded day and night. The tankers worked, ate, and slept within close proximity to a truly dangerous operation. Yet dangerous cargo was not the only peril soldiers confronted in the port; riding on buses driven by local nationals was hair-raising. As one soldier noted, "It was our first experience with bus racing and demolition derby as a combined sport."[44] First Lieutenant Jay Mumford described the port as "a scene of organized chaos, as Humvees, tanks, 5-ton trucks, cranes, buses, . . . camel-burger vendors, odd engineer vehicles, M113s and every other type of armored vehicle in the army inventory rumbled from point A to point B."[45] If the port was a dangerous place to live, it was an even more dangerous place to work. Miraculously, only one soldier died during unloading operations, on January 7; she fell from one of the piers and, loaded down with her equipment, weapon, and ammunition, went straight to the bottom of the harbor and drowned before rescuers could find her in the murky water.[46]

Mullen's troops worked hard to provide the necessary support. Despite their best efforts, nothing about transiting through the port was easy. Although the vast majority of the troops arrived at a nearby airport, all of them needed to be near the port so they could prepare their equipment for onward movement. The port at Ad Dammām, although comparatively large compared to the one at Jubayl, could by no means accommodate the number of troops who needed to be there. Originally the 3rd Army estimated no more than 17,000 soldiers in the port at a time, but the number rose to 43,000 because ships did not arrive as planned. Honoré managed space for soldiers at Ad Dammām and at two other sites: the Khobar Towers apartment complex twenty-five kilometers away, and a factory complex thirty kilometers away. LTC Griswold managed space at Jubayl and at a tent city nineteen kilometers from there. Neither port support activity had sufficient transportation; units needed to work at the ports to ready their equipment, but found it difficult to get to and from the ports. In despair of getting a ride to and from Khobar Towers, an artilleryman resorted to hitchhiking with a cardboard sign that read "port." This "worked to and from the port, and so the hobo transit was formed."[47] LTC Don Schenk got around by putting "a ton of miles" on his "leather personnel carriers." Schenk was housed at Khobar Towers, but getting to and from the port was too difficult. He chose to stay at the port and slept where he could.[48]

Most of Weisman's brigade staged in Ad Dammām, but one of the three vessels docked in Jubayl. His brigade operated split between two ports that were nearly sixty kilometers apart. The brigade also had not been able to paint its equipment in Germany. His troops shuttled their gear to painting stations where contractors painted eleven hundred pieces of equipment.[49] There was no time for reflection or planning, and barely enough time to get everything done.

In addition to unloading and getting ready to move north, COL Lon E. "Bert" Maggart's brigade turned in its old tanks and received new M1A1s. This process took only a day or so, but it could not begin until ships arrived. The 2-34 AR troops arrived on New Year's Eve and the 1-34 AR on New Year's Day. Although the intent was for ships and troops to arrive within a day or so of each other, that seldom happened, and it did not happen in this case. Some of the 2-34 AR's tanks had come in, so that battalion began receiving its equipment on January 7. The Italian transport ship *Jolly Rubino* and the *American Eagle* arrived that day with the rest of the two tank battalions' equipment. CPT Cavaleri's troops unloaded both ships rapidly. The 2-34 AR executed "roll over" two days later, and the 1-34 AR drew their new tanks on January 12.[50] Ready to load on January 11, the 2-34 AR confronted the task of finding heavy-equipment transporters that could haul its tanks nearly five hundred kilometers to TAA Roosevelt.

LTC Bob Wilson's 1st Squadron, 4th Cavalry (1-4 CAV) drew M1A1s in the port and also transitioned from the basic cavalry variant of the Bradley infantry fighting vehicle to a newer version with better fire control, armor, and fuel stowage. Additionally, CPT Ken Pope finished organizing A Troop after arriving in Saudi Arabia with a handful of soldiers and a guidon. Now he had to complete manning and equipping. Soldiers flowed in, but Wilson also made deals with other units for help—for example, obtaining some tankers from the Division's tank battalions. Hard work and frequent intervention by COL Jim Mowery and later Rhame helped get the gear and people the troop needed. Frustration abounded, but eventually A Troop went from a gleam in Wilson's eye to reality when the last trooper joined on February 14.[51]

Despite frustration with the port, the Fort Riley–based troops appreciated their colleagues from Mullen's Division Forward. As Don Schenk recalls, "There was nothing easy about being there [in the port] . . . the one bright spot was the 3rd Brigade of the 1st Infantry Division. . . . When you walk up to a guy and the patch on his left shoulder is the same as yours, it is a good thing."[52] Cavaleri, Griswold, Honoré, Mullen, and others had all served at Fort Riley; they wanted to help, and it showed. In some ways, the two ports were a reunion of the 1st Division: soldiers ran into old friends everywhere they turned. Nevertheless, the one thing every soldier wanted most was to get out of the port. To Schenk, the first priority was answering the question, "How do we get out of here?"[53] The port felt like a target—and it was.

Life in the port became more difficult when the air war began on January 17. Assuming the Iraqis would respond to the air attack with chemical weapons, everyone in the port donned chemical protective overgarments and masks. The next day they masked again, pulling on overgarments and rubber boots to the wail of air raid sirens. Not long after the sirens wound up, a Patriot air defense missile battery launched a missile with a thunderclap. Startled troops gazing overhead witnessed the incredible when a Patriot missile destroyed an inbound Scud over Ad Dammām. The next day, as a 4th Battalion, 5th Field Artillery (4-5 FA) convoy prepared to move, Patriot air defense missiles destroyed "several Scuds." A Patriot launch and interception is an amazing sight, and the artillerymen were duly impressed. As their journal noted, "The war seemed to bring the ADA [air defense artillery] back to a level of respectability."[54] Inbound Scuds eradicated any lethargy that remained among those in the port. After January 17 it was easy to think of getting out of the port as a matter of life or death.

Dispersion of equipment over several ships, delays in arrival, maintenance, and availability of transport all contributed to stringing out the time spent trying to leave the port. The experiences of the 5th Battalion, 16th Infantry (5-16) IN and the 2-34 AR illustrate the problem. The infantry arrived in Saudi Arabia on December 29 and 30; the tankers arrived New Year's Eve and New Year's Day. The bulk of the 5-16 IN headed north on January 10 and 13, but the last of them did not leave until January 14. Although ready to move on January 11, the 2-34 AR had to wait for heavy-equipment transporters. Its first convoy did not depart until January 12, and the last 2-34 AR soldier did not leave until January 20. The first ship carrying the Division's equipment arrived on January 7, and the last on January 26, yet Rhame's last troops did not reach the assembly area until February.[55] Getting out of the port remained hard to do.

Despite the trials and tribulations, Mullen's troops had reason to take pride in their achievements. Their mission began on December 1, when the first of them arrived to support the VII Corps (Forward). Ultimately they assumed the full scope of supporting reception, staging, and onward movement. On February 18, when they finished the job, they had unloaded and staged more than fifty thousand vehicles. They housed and supported 107,000 VII Corps soldiers transiting through the port and thousands more from other units. They managed, to the degree that could be done, nine hundred convoys. They had "faced down problems."[56]

Getting out of the port was not an end in itself, but rather the first step on the road home. Reception, staging, and onward movement ended when the last units left the port. The next step took place at TAA Roosevelt, where tactical integration occurred. This included assembling units, rehearsing, and preparing for combat. The Corps estimated the attack would occur in mid-February. Getting out of the port at the end of January meant that the Division had three weeks or less to get ready. Preparation included generating sufficient intelligence to enable a deliberate attack. The Corps and Division needed time to develop tactical information from which analysts might develop accurate intelligence.

Mad Max and the Thunderdome: Getting to Tactical Assembly Area Roosevelt

LTG John Yeosock, commander of the 3rd Army and all the Army forces in the theater, considered an enemy-spoiling attack down the Wadi al-Batin the most dangerous possibility because such an attack threatened the Trans-Arabian Pipeline road. Known simply as Tapline Road, the route traveled east to west along the Trans-Arabian Pipeline all the way to Jordan. CENTCOM required the road to position forces for the offensive. The Arab Corps, located west of the wadi during the buildup of forces, would have to move east to reach its attack positions. Meanwhile, The XVIII ABN Corps would move west to get to their attack positions. LTG Franks's VII Corps would attack north and parallel to the wadi, so using the VII Corps to defend the area made sense. On January 7 COL Don Holder's 2 ACR, BG John Tilelli's 1 CD, and a brigade of the 101 ABN defended the area. Tilelli's units moved from just south of Tapline Road into the wadi, a brigade from the 101 ABN defended the airfield at Al Qaysumah, and the 2 ACR defended east of the wadi. The 1 AD and 3 AD were still transiting the port. The VII Corps could expect no additional help until 1st Division units arrived. On January 9, the 3rd Army reported that three Iraqi divisions were moving south toward these defenses.[57] Fortunately, the alarm proved false.

Everyone wanted to get forward. Frustration about getting on the road often generated fruitless activity in what LTC Skip Baker, commander of the 5-16 IN, called "the rush to get the hell out of the port,"[58] something not so easily done. The US Army has carefully considered and clearly written doctrine that describes exactly how onward movement should occur. Units assess their transportation requirements and request what they need, and the controlling headquarters assigns priorities, processes clearances, and tasks transportation units. Movement-control units issue "march credits" that account for the number and size of vehicles to avoid a bumper-to-bumper snarl. If all goes as planned, trucks show up where and when they are needed. Units load their equipment, form convoys, and depart. But in this instance, this elegant system failed miserably; too many units trying to move on too few transports produced chaos.

Soon after arriving, Mullen concluded the transportation system could not be made to work as designed. He ordered Wesbrook to designate a "single officer . . . [to] take charge of all ground transportation management elements."[59] Wesbrook sent for LTC George Higgins, commander of the 1-16 IN. Higgins hitched a ride from Germany and assumed responsibility for making sure the right transport was available in the right sequence to move tracked vehicles and cargo. He also had to find buses and stage them to move soldiers. Track crews and infantry squads could not ride in fighting vehicles loaded on trucks. Higgins has described the problem of finding qualified drivers for contract buses as "insolubly problematic." In fact, he was supposed to coordinate transportation, but there was no one with whom to coordinate. "The unhappy bottom line is that there was no organization that took 'ownership' of this part of the transportation conundrum."[60]

CENTCOM complicated matters by ordering the XVIII ABN Corps to reposition at nearly the same time as the VII Corps. The Airborne Corps' four divisions competed for the same transportation. There were fewer than five hundred heavy-equipment transporters in the theater, and no one could say for sure how many could actually haul tanks. The M1 tanks weighed more than sixty tons and truly required heavy-equipment transporters. Only those transports brought by the US and Egyptian armies were known to be adequate. In mid-January the US and Egyptians had 226 transports available, but this number was insufficient to complete the task. Civilian transports, often of dubious capability, closed the gap. There were nearly two thousand US and British tanks that needed to be moved in a very short span of time.[61]

Every commander of every battalion, his brigade commander, and his generals all wanted transport as soon they unloaded their ships. Into this morass LTC Higgins dared to tread. Urbane and meticulous, Higgins now had to learn the patience of Job. Daily he convened a "transportation allocation meeting" at the port of Ad Dammām. "Based on priorities received from [headquarters] 1ID F [Mullen's unit], I allocated available transportation resources—for both the ports of Jubayl and Damman [*sic*]."[62] Every meeting was chaotic. Often he had help he did not need. Instead of Division transportation officers making their needs known, "ADCs [assistant division commanders], chiefs of staff and G-4s (logistics officers) showed up," all lobbying for their needs to be met.[63] Merely allocating resources was insufficient. Transports failed to show, had maintenance problems, or were "'diverted,' 'high jacked,' or otherwise misdirected to units who should not have moved to the TAA when they moved."[64] Confusion and misappropriation stemming from a lack of discipline on the part of the very officers expected to maintain it led the VII Corps to observe, in marvelously bureaucratic language, that "less than optimum use of transportation assets is lengthening the deployment of units and forward movement of ammunition."[65] Helpful observations from the Corps headquarters helped not at all.

To overcome the chaos, most senior commanders remained in the port until they were able to get the bulk of their units moved. BG Jerry Rutherford arrived on January 4. Rhame was glad to see him not only because he was an "old first ID guy" but also because Rutherford was "a Tiger" and just the guy to have running operations in the port.[66] A man of boundless enthusiasm and fearsome determination, Rutherford exuded energy and joi de vivre except with those found wanting. Years earlier he had earned the nickname Ricochet; this epithet was not meant disparagingly, but as an accurate comparison to the high-speed, high-energy cartoon character Ricochet Rabbit. He proved effective due to his energy, personality, and his knowledge of the commanders and soldiers in the Division. Rutherford was everywhere, encouraging some and prodding others. He pitched in by "appearing on site" and "getting involved."[67]

Even if tank transports showed up when and where they were promised, there was no guarantee they could haul a tank. Most of the transports were Saudi owned and driven by third country nationals, almost none of whom spoke English. Hand and arm signals, a few phrases, and trial and error served to determine whether a given truck could handle the load. Maggart ascertained that "the only way to find out if they [transport] could support the weight of the vehicle being loaded was to drive up the ramp. If the load was too great, the trailer broke or buckled and the owner became animated and vocal. The crew loading the vehicle then backed off and another vehicle was driven on. The whole process was mad."[68]

The madness proved dangerous as well. The very first tank Maggart watched drive onto a transport "completely lifted the truck attached to the trailer off the ground. The soldier who was ground guiding the tank on the trailer was hurled 10 ft into the air. He was unhurt, but mad as hell."[69]

Finding buses proved even more difficult. Contracts were let for about three hundred buses. Each had seats for forty passengers, but no room for baggage. They were therefore inadequate for heavily burdened soldiers, each of whom had at least a large rucksack. When Higgins assumed responsibility for managing buses, he found "no intelligent guidance, no coherent plan, and no sensible C2 [command and control system] in place."[70] The contractors failed to produce enough drivers to make the long round trips to and from the tactical assembly area. In the end, units provided drivers who were supposed to drop their passengers off and return their buses to the port. Higgins thought this a naive plan, and he was right: a considerable number of buses disappeared into the desert, and several were found abandoned—one of them with its engine still running.[71] Finding transports and buses to haul crews made Higgins's life difficult, and it was no picnic for his customers either.

Despite everything, Baker's battalion managed to load, stage, and get enough transport to begin moving on January 10. MAJ Brian Zahn led this first convoy northwest up a modern six-lane highway. At first the route for the nearly five-hundred-kilometer trip looked promising, and the convoy traveled at a good pace. About 120 kilometers out, the route turned west on to the narrow two-lane highway with no shoulders that was Tapline Road. Oliver Wendell Holmes famously described war as an "incommunicable experience"; driving on Tapline Road in January 1990 was the very definition thereof. The horrific scenes in the Mad Max movies set in postapocalyptic Australia are an approximation of what it was like to drive Tapline Road. Averaging only thirty or thirty-five miles per hour, convoys stretched out of sight and merged with other convoys to form an endless stream of trucks, buses, tankers, light-equipment transporters (called low boys), and heavy-equipment transporters, and a few locals going about their lives. The traffic moved bumper-to-bumper in both directions.

Wrecks and derelict vehicles littered the road; many of the derelicts showed evidence of violent collisions that had resulted in fiery destruction. A 4-5 FA convoy happened on one of many such nasty accidents. Just before the convoy happened on the scene, a heavy-equipment transporter collided head on with a high-mobility multipurpose wheeled vehicle (HMMWV); the accident killed one soldier and injured four others. Local contract drivers ignored convoy discipline or simply drove in accordance with the principle *inshallah*— if God willed it, they would survive. But often God chose not to intervene. One such accident involved an oil company tanker that rear-ended a stopped bus loaded with troops. That accident injured thirty people. Getting to the tactical assembly area required courage, endurance, and luck.[72]

Zahn and about 150 infantrymen moving in trucks, buses, HMMWVs, and low boys departed about 8:00 a.m. on January 10. Saudis and third country nationals drove the transports hauling Bradley infantry fighting vehicles. Along the way one driver stopped his vehicle on the road, got out and set about brewing tea. Everyone behind him stopped. Zahn cajoled and then finally threatened the driver to get him back on the road. That Zahn got the recalcitrant driver to give up his tea break is a tribute to the sincerity with which he communicated his threat—he drew his weapon and pointed it at the man.[73]

Few convoys arrived intact. Some transports arrived days late due to maintenance. Others arrived late because their civilian driver became lost or stopped at a roadside café. With only a sketch called a strip map as a guide, the 2-34 AR's first convoy departed Ad Dammām at 3:30 p.m. on January 12. The convoy included buses and fifty-six tanks loaded on heavy-equipment transporters of dubious and distinctly unmilitary origin. Only twenty-two of them arrived at the convoy release point at 3:30 a.m. the next morning; the rest trickled in over the next three days.[74]

CPT Jim Bell, who led the first 1-34 AR convoy, recalls it as "a goat screw to the max."[75] Bell could get no one to give him either a map or a strip map. Finally, Honoré drew a strip map for him. With some idea of the route, Bell departed, leading what he believed was a convoy of sixteen heavy-equipment transporters carrying fourteen tanks from his company and two belonging to the battalion headquarters. Buses hauling his troops followed. The convoy drove in a heavy downpour that caused poor visibility. At a rest stop he realized his convoy had grown; an artillery major approached and announced he was part of the convoy, a fact hitherto unknown to the convoy commander.[76]

After a short halt, Bell led his growing convoy to the *convoy release point*, a term meant to suggest a place where units could stop and sort themselves out prior to moving into their assembly area. While the term conveys a sense of order, in this case a unit convoy release point usually turned out to be a soldier standing by the side of the road with a cardboard sign. One version of the sign featured a Big Red One patch drawn with a felt-tip marker on the back of an MRE (meal ready-to-eat) box. At the bottom of the patch someone had scrawled "convoys stop here." CPT Bell found his convoy release point when he saw such a sign. He arrived with all sixteen tanks, but without the buses carrying the troops. Whether the buses were lost or broken down he did not know. The heavy-equipment transporters needed to return to the port. Bell and one or two sergeants with him unloaded all of the tanks and parked them. They hoped to see some crews soon.[77]

LTC Clint Ancker, who led the 3rd Brigade, 2 AD headquarters, had an even more difficult experience. It had rained throughout the previous night and was raining when his convoy left on the morning of January 13; already damp from sleeping in leaky canvas tents, the troops drove in rain all day. As night fell, they approached the area where they should have found their convoy release point. LTC Ancker expected someone from the brigade quartering party to be on the lookout for them. He found no one waiting, and "no signs except for the hand lettered cardboard signs that announced the turn off for various units."[78] In pouring rain the convoy drove on, and Ancker soon realized it had overshot its release point. He turned the convoy around and headed back the way they had come, stopping at every sign. After a fruitless search, Ancker decided to lead the convoy to nearby Logistics Base Alpha. On the way in off the Tapline Road, a bus carrying troops became mired in sand made gooey by the constant rain. A passing wrecker crew stopped to help, but instead of freeing the bus, the wrecker broke the bus's windshield and pulled off its bumper. At about this time, Ancker received a radio message warning of an impending five-division assault by the enemy. Because he could not communicate, the warning did not seem prudent. Ancker elected to bed the troops down where they were. Truly frustrated, he bummed a ride with some military police that happened by and made his way to the Division Support Command headquarters, where he slept part of the night sitting up in a metal chair; at least there he would have ready access to information. The warning of an attack proved false,[79] and the next day Ancker recovered the convoy and finally found the brigade assembly area.

Manning a convoy release point proved nearly as frustrating as finding one. CPT Gene Malik, commander of the Headquarters and Headquarters Company, 1-34 AR, had that task. Malik went down to the convoy release point daily and waited there all day, "hoping someone from 1-34 was coming."[80] With no communications with the port, he had no idea when the next convoy might show. Soldiers in every unit shared experiences like those of Ancker, Bell, and Malik. The experience of convoying to the tactical assembly area was not only incommunicable, but also fraught with ambiguity and uncertainty. Existential questions abounded: Would we get there? Would we find the convoy release point when we did get there? Were the Iraqis going to attack? One commander who led a convoy to the tactical assembly area wrote that anyone who drove the route to the tactical assembly area earned "a combat patch, as surely the body count will suggest." He went on to add, "The truth is we made it because we wanted to."[81]

Tactical Assembly Area Roosevelt: Integration

Arriving at the tactical assembly area was cause for celebration. Just moving to the assembly area reduced some of the danger from some threats. Units dispersed in assembly areas made poor targets for Iraqi Scud missiles and short-range rockets. Because the coalition amassed enormous ground and airborne defenses, the Iraqi Air Force posed little threat. Terrorist attacks remained a possibility, but a conventional ground attack posed the most likely threat. Moreover, as the Division arrived it could help meet the threat of attack down the Wadi al-Batin.

By nightfall on January 13 most of COL Bert Maggart's brigade had arrived, though he had not. Maggart and LTC Pat Ritter, commander of the 1-34 AR, were still in the port trying to extract the last of the brigade. That night the Division ordered the 1st Brigade to get into position to stop an anticipated large Iraqi attack coming down the Wadi al-Batin. The Brigade had little to work with; although nearly all of the 5-16 IN troops had arrived, they had no means to fire their twenty-five-millimeter Bushmaster automatic cannon. LTC Baker had followed the Lexicon Danger plan to the letter. The plan's order required that units remove the bolt and track mechanisms that enabled the Bradley cannon to fire and that firing pins be removed from tank main guns. The order had been issued in accordance with peacetime rules because railway and shipping lines feared a weapon being fired accidentally; neither wanted to move fighting vehicles with ammunition aboard, let alone fighting vehicles whose weapons could be fired. Most battalion commanders ignored the order or at least shipped the mechanisms with their vehicles. Baker had not only obeyed that order but also had packed bolt and track mechanisms in a shipping container, just as Lexicon Danger specified. Naturally, the container did not arrive before the battalion left the port; if committed, Baker's troops would fight with small arms only.[82] The fact that Baker had followed the Division order did not mollify Rhame. He was most decidedly not amused to learn that the only Bradleys available to him could not shoot; peacetime rules and thinking had effectively neutered the 5-16 IN.

The 2-34 AR had twenty-two tanks that arrived early that morning. None of the tanks had a complete load of main gun ammunition. The battalion had full loads for its 7.62-millimeter and .50-caliber machine guns. No main gun ammunition had been issued in the port—there had simply been no room to do so. The Corps planned to issue ammunition for the 120-millimeter main gun in the assembly area. Earlier on January 13 the battalion obtained ten rounds of high-explosive antitank ammunition per tank; this was far short of the usual full load of forty rounds. A handful of equally disadvantaged tanks from 1-34 AR were available. LTC Harry Emerson's 1-5 FA, also on the scene, did have ammunition. In this sorry state, without a clear command link and no idea that the 1 CD was in the area, the 1st Brigade prepared to move out and fight. Thankfully, the Iraqis did not attack that night.[83]

Even without responding to false alarms, there was more than enough to do. On January 16 Rhame issued five priorities of work in the assembly area:

1. Get Organized.
2. Calibrate or zero tanks.
3. Get countermobility equipment (mine plows and rollers) mounted and begin training on how to use it.
4. Continue planning and conduct rehearsals.
5. Train.

Maggart arrived that day and took stock of how things stood. Nearly all of the 5-16 IN and 2-34 AR had closed the assembly area. Fifteen of Ritter's tanks arrived that day, so he had forty-three of his fifty-eight tanks. Bravo Troop 1-4 CAV had arrived, and the 2nd and 3rd Brigades were starting to move as well. Organizing the force could be said to be under way.[84]

Getting organized required finding equipment and people that had not yet arrived but were known to have left the port. This took days. It also meant getting ammunition. The Corps ordered units to load in tiers based on ammunition availability. Naturally, unloading ammunition from the ships that brought it, reloading it on transports, and hauling it to the assembly area where it could be issued all took time. There was less ammunition available than required. Friction in this process included inane peacetime requirements. For example, commanders had to provide a signature card authorizing someone in their unit to sign for ammunition on their behalf. Some logistician decided commanders should also provide a letter explaining why they needed ammunition, but then failed to make that requirement known. At least one unit made the long trip to the ammunition supply point only to return empty-handed for want of the required papers. This absurdity led the irate battalion commander to pen a note purportedly from his mother to the logistician explaining why her little boy wanted bullets.[85] The logistician got his note, and the battalion got its bullets, but peacetime rules and peacetime thinking continued unabated even as war approached.

Learning how to use the new mobility gear was a more straightforward task. Unlike ammunition, the mine rollers and plows were available and issued with minimum bureaucratic procedure. All three brigades drew the suite of equipment designed to enhance mobility. The 1st and 2nd Brigades focused on developing tactics for employing plows, mine rollers, and mine rakes in the planned penetration attack. The Garlstedt contingent worked to develop basic skills to effect breaches of hasty defensives positions from the march or "in stride." Units also revisited training at the platoon and company levels to integrate new soldiers and several newly formed platoons. The 1-4 CAV also had to finish forming A Troop before it could begin to train.[86]

It was difficult work, but most soldiers reveled in it; they were finally in the field, doing what they had come eight thousand miles to do. LTC Dave Marlin spoke with relief about getting to the assembly area. From Marlin's perspective, "Battalion Commanders did not have command of their battalions from the time they left Ft. Riley until they arrived in the TAA."[87] He very much wanted to get back in command of his battalion. CPT Juan E. Toro, new in the command of his company, thought "the preparation was fun."[88] Part of the "fun" included cross-training: clerks learned to serve as tank crewmen, and so forth. The idea was to achieve depth in the event of casualties. The troops also learned how to live in the desert. Those who had trained at the National Training Center already understood how hard it was just to survive in the desert, but those who had not had to learn to do more than survive; they had to thrive in order to do their jobs effectively.

To describe the northern desert of Saudi Arabia as a harsh environment is to engage in understatement. The temperature swung fifty or more degrees every day: at night it could be in the twenties, yet it reached the seventies during the daytime. Everyone wore long underwear, and most put on a sweater before they dressed in their desert camouflaged uniform. A lined desert parka, scarf, and gloves completed the ensemble. As the day wore on, layer after layer came off, but by late afternoon all the layers were back on.

No one had anticipated day after day of cold driving rain. Water stood everywhere in puddles wide and deep enough to qualify as ponds. Troops complained, "This is supposed to be the desert, but it rains more than Fort Riley!"[89] Weather and all that sand made staying clean difficult. To keep total troop strength to the absolute minimum, no shower and bath or laundry units deployed. The Division bought plastic washtubs and issued them at a rate of one for every nine or ten troops; the troops washed themselves and their clothes in these tubs. At not quite three feet in diameter and about a foot deep, the tubs were barely adequate. They came in three colors: hot pink, turquoise, and sky blue; watching a column of tanks or Bradleys rumble by sporting hot pink tubs seemed ironic, even comical, and it was certainly at odds with the sand-colored paint that had been so laboriously applied.

Field latrines came in three varieties. Although they were not much to look at, those built in the port and hauled forward were the most comfortable. They were large wooden boxes made of plywood walls just over waist high; a screen sufficed for the rest of the wall. Each latrine had a roof and a single door. Inside users found a wooden bench with three holes. Really nice ones had plastic toilet seats, though most did not. Under each hole lay the bottom third of a fifty-five-gallon oil drum. Early each morning a "detail" of soldiers serviced the latrines. They dragged out the barrels, added diesel fuel, and set the contents alight; one soldier per barrel stirred constantly to assure everything burned. The location of company assembly areas could be discerned from a long distance by the grayish black pyres of the morning waste disposal operation. Burning the contents of the drums reminded those who had served in Vietnam of the many reasons they were happy when that war ended.

There were never enough of the plywood latrines. The second common facility featured 1.5-liter plastic water bottles cut and driven into each other to form a tube. The resulting tube was then jammed several inches deep into the ground as urinals for male troops. Once the ground war started, soldiers used a third kind of facility—field expedient cat hole latrines—or they shoveled dirt over whatever they had to do. Privacy did not figure into the equation; there was no such thing in the desert. Many young men found the lack of privacy entertaining. It was not uncommon for someone to be cheered on and coached during the use of field expedient facilities.

Women, on the other hand, did value privacy, and achieved a modicum of dignity by sheltering behind ponchos held by their friends. Most young men respected the privacy of their female colleagues. Those who did not soon learned to do so at the behest of their fellow soldiers regardless of gender.

Bathroom problems, discomfort, and surviving in the desert all became side issues in the early hours of January 17, when the air war began. Duty officers in command posts in the assembly areas, in the ports, and in the life-support areas awakened their commanders and units. In the ports and areas where the troops lived, everyone was ordered to "mission oriented protective posture 1." This was easy enough to do and a task soldiers trained at frequently. Soldiers, so ordered, opened sealed bags containing coated, charcoal-laden protective overgarments and put them on, also making sure they had their masks. COL Mowery of the 4th Brigade was still in the port that morning. Awakened at 2:00 a.m., Mowery and the twelve hundred soldiers in the facility with him put on their overgarments; most went back to sleep. At 2:30 a.m. the Division duty officer awakened Mowery to make sure he knew the air war had started. Again Mowery tried to go back to sleep. About 3:00 a.m. Rutherford came by to check on the Brigade, and Mowery got up for the third time. After Rutherford left, Mowery gave up on sleeping. This proved wise, as the air raid sirens went off at 3:30 a.m., forcing everyone in full chemical protection, mission oriented protective posture 4, which entailed donning the gas mask and arranging the hood to protect the neck.[90] Next the soldiers put on rubber gloves with liners and finally protective rubber shoes over their combat boots. Now encased fully in chemical protective clothing from head to toe, they hoped for the best.

Things happened more tranquilly in the tactical assembly area. SPC Gary Green was on guard that night, and around 1:30 a.m. he "heard what seemed to be hundreds of jets flying overhead. I quickly checked my wrist compass and thought 'oh shit!' they are headed north, towards Iraq. Seconds later I witnessed red lights illuminate the horizon. I thought to myself, 'the waiting is over.'"[91] CPT James K. Morningstar arrived in the assembly area "with nine tanks, knee deep in mud in pitch darkness around 0300, 17 January, in time to watch the first air attacks scream overhead on their way to Iraq."[92] Later that day, one of the first 2-16 IN convoys arrived at their convoy release point. CPT Mark Samson met the convoy with, "Welcome to the war zone. They're bombing Baghdad. George started it."[93]

The Iraqis had a far less tranquil experience. The day before the attack, BG Ra'ad al-Hamdani anticipated the difficulties to come. He spoke to the troops of his 17th Brigade of the Hammurabi Republican Guard Division, exhorting them to do their duty and reminding them that "history always spoke favorably of those who died defending their homeland."[94] A few hours later, a panic-stricken soldier awakened Hamdani by shouting, "The planes are above us!"[95] Hamdani thought the war "was too easy to start and only God knows when it will end, and what will be the fate of our country and our people."[96] For coalition troops, the air campaign consisted mostly of gawking at contrails or watching air-to-air refueling and occasional muted sounds of distant bombardment. Iraqi troops, on the other hand, suffered; those who were not bombed soon fell short in food and water. Moving around day or night was dangerous; life under aerial bombardment drove the Iraqis underground and seems to have destroyed what little initiative the front-line units had.

Multitasking: Combat Operations and Assembly

After reacting to the news that the war had started, the soldiers moved on with what had to be done; there was, after all, plenty to do, and looking for flashes on the horizon would not get it done. On the morning of January 17 the 2-34 AR drove south of Tapline Road to Jayhawk Range, a makeshift gunnery range, to zero tanks. MG Rhame was out and about the first day of the air war; at 9:00 a.m. he visited the 1-4 CAV. Earlier that morning he had ordered Shadley to establish the support area in the Division forward area from which the attack would be mounted. Rhame was looking for Wilson to discuss moving B Troop west to provide security for the Division Support Area when Shadley moved. LTC Wilson, however, had not yet left the port, nor was his operations officer present. Accordingly, Rhame gave instructions to CPT Lianne Tedesco, the assistant operations officer, and went on to visit other units.[97]

Specifically, Rhame told Shadley to "start sliding the division [support command] over that way [to the forward assembly area], and don't screw up and mess up the MSR [the main supply route—Tapline Road], and don't get caught doing it."[98] Rhame needed Shadley to get a logistics base established prior to the attack, but had to move cautiously to avoid compromising the CENTCOM deception plan. In fact, nothing was supposed to be located west of the wadi. GEN Schwarzkopf had made dire threats toward anyone who did anything that might reveal the planned "left hook" that would come west of the Wadi al-Batin. Yet no operations could be mounted without establishing the means to sustain them. Logistics preparations had to be made; Shadley gave the task to Waterman and his 701 MSB. About the time Rhame visited the 1-4 CAV, MAJ Sylvia Marable, the 701 MSB support operations officer, headed west with an advance party and a handful of military police. Marable and her troops traveled just over 120 kilometers west of TAA Roosevelt, arriving at the planned site of the Division support area that afternoon. They immediately went to work; getting set up would permit the Division Support Command to stockpile supplies needed to support the Division when it attacked. That night Shadley made a radio call to Marable. It took some time, as she was far enough west that he had to relay through three other stations. Once he made contact he asked if she needed anything. Marable replied, "Yes, the cav squadron. I'm a speed bump out here."[99]

Marable's assessment was quite accurate. She and the troops with her had only light weapons; her military police were few in number and also lightly equipped. Her troops could fight off an Iraqi patrol, but not much more. There was literally nothing but fifty kilometers of sand between the logistics advance party and the Iraqi front lines. Iraqi outposts were no more than fifteen or twenty kilometers north. The Iraqi units had the means to conduct spoiling attacks. Indeed, the VII Corps remained concerned they would do just that. Clearly a lightly defended logistics installation would make a juicy target.[100] At the same time, putting troops too far north might reveal the left hook.

The planned forward assembly area lay nearly in the center of the Neutral Zone. The Neutral Zone appeared on maps as an elongated diamond northwest of the town of Hafir al-Batin. The Saudis had built a berm, ten or twelve feet high, from east to west through the center of the Neutral Zone. On their side of the berm they had also dug an antitank ditch several feet deep. The berm marked the de facto boundary between Saudi Arabia and Iraq. They also built small forts at intervals. One of these small border posts, which looked like a slightly smaller version of the one shown in the Gary Cooper classic *Beau Geste*, sat almost in the middle of the lengthy border berm that cut through the Neutral Zone. The Wadi al-Batin ran south to north at the eastern corner of the Neutral Zone. In contrast to the absolutely flat ground at TAA Roosevelt, the ground in the Neutral Zone sloped downhill from south to north. North of the berm the ground gently sloped up again. Several trails and unimproved roads cut across the Neutral Zone as well. Although not as featureless as the tactical assembly area, the environment in the Neutral Zone was just as harsh.

Just south of Marable's burgeoning logistics base, VII Corps engineers moved in to build roads and infrastructure at would become Corps Logistics Base Echo, which the Corps sited at the southernmost corner of the Neutral Zone, just north of Tapline Road. Although constrained by CENTCOM's direction to keep combat formations east of the Wadi al-Batin consistent with the deception plan, both Franks and Rhame knew they must establish logistics bases early enough to build up the supplies to sustain the attack. Obviously they had to secure those bases. On January 20 Rhame ordered Wilson to provide security for Marable and the Corps units to her rear. MG Rhame wanted Wilson's cavalry on the move not later than January 22. The Corps countermanded that order because of concern about moving armored vehicles west, but then doubled back to allow it. They had to have the bases and they had to be secured. MG Rhame met with both Wilson and Mowery, Wilson's brigade commander, on January 24 and ordered them to execute.[101] Wilson had only B Troop available. The air cavalry troops and A Troop had not yet left the port. For good or ill, the 1-4 CAV would enter the zone of action to execute their first combat mission in dribs and drabs over the next few days.

CPT Mike Bills led B Troop's Bradleys and tanks west later the same day with orders to establish a screen north of the logistics areas. Cavalry units do three kinds of security missions: screening, guarding, and covering. A screen is designed to preclude direct observation of the formation being screened. In this case, that meant preventing Iraqi patrols from getting close enough to find the Corps and Division logistics bases. By definition, screening meant avoiding decisive combat. In short, B Troop would not fight to the death in this mission but would delay until help arrived. Bills and his troop arrived at Division Support Area Junction City in the afternoon. Marable could tell him little about the enemy situation. Accordingly, B Troop moved north, employing advancing-to-contact tactics. Doctrinally, that meant moving with a small force forward so if the troop encountered the enemy, Bills could develop the situation with as few soldiers forward as possible. B Troop reached its screen line safely. Bills knew that his troop could not effectively screen the forty kilometers of frontage assigned, but until A Troop and the two air troops arrived, Bills's troopers had to do what they could.[102]

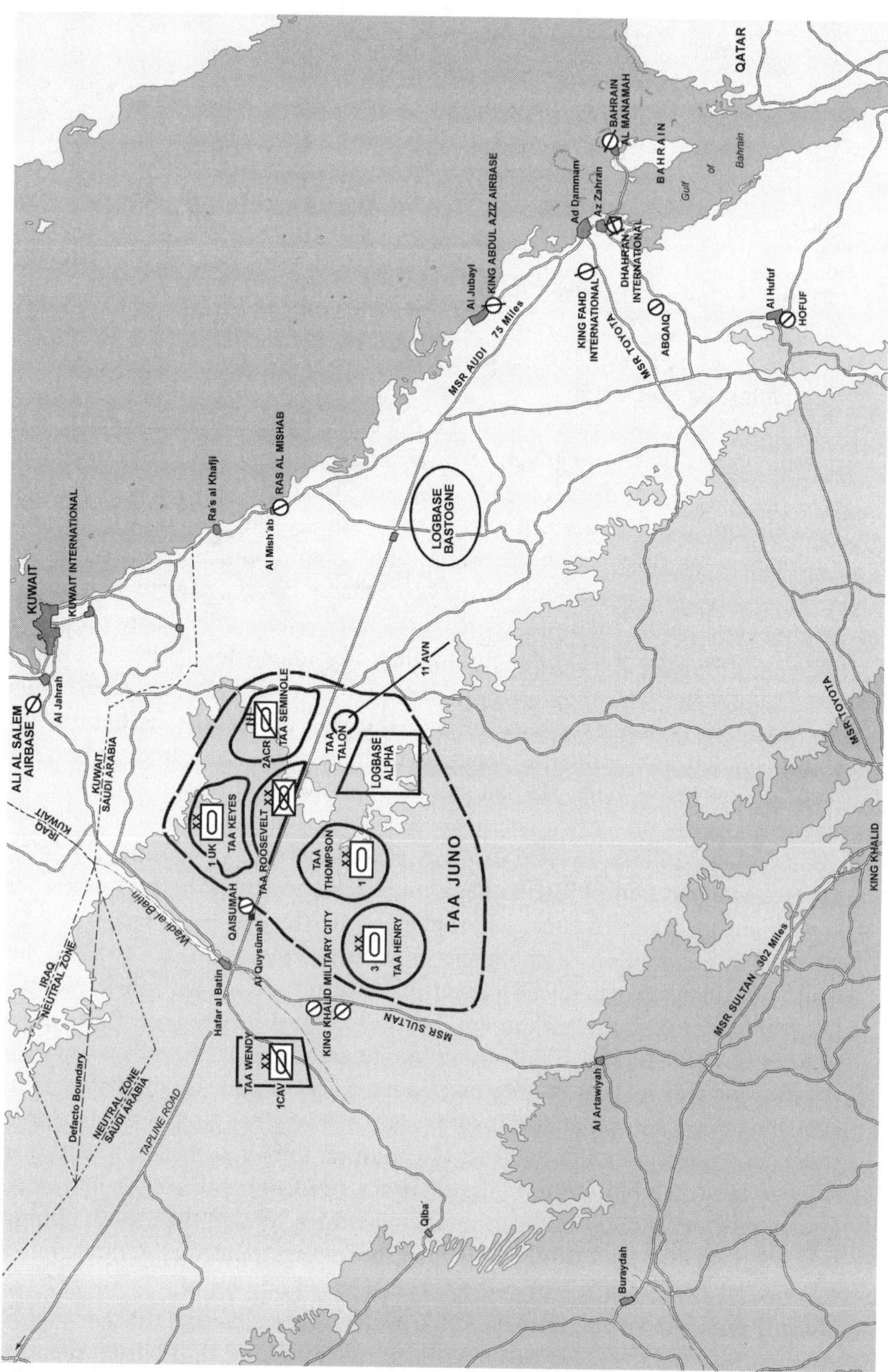

MAP 1. VII Corps Tactical Assembly Areas and Logistics Bases, January 1991. Recreated from Map 6, Stephen A. Bourque, *Jayhawk! The VII Corps in the Persian Gulf War.*

Bedouins moving around the area created confusion and anxiety. Although the Saudi government had ordered them to evacuate, many of the fiercely independent nomads chose not to leave. These shepherds had long since abandoned camels as their primary means of transportation in favor of light trucks. Bills's cavalry might reasonably wonder if Bedouins or Iraqi soldiers drove a light truck they happened to see moving in their direction. Late on January 24 the VII Corps authorized the rest of the cavalry squadron to thicken the screen as it arrived. The air troops and squadron tactical command post moved on January 25. Still not fully manned and by no means fully trained, Pope's A Troop followed the next day.

Bills and his cavalrymen were well trained and eager, but like everyone else in the Division they were green. The National Training Center experience, as challenging as it had been, could not replicate the uncertainty and ambiguity that confronted B Troop when they became the first Division unit to take on combat mission in twenty years. Barely able to communicate because of the distances involved, the troops lacked any reliable combat information about the Iraqis or their intentions. They had little or no information about the Saudi border troops, who were still manning their *Beau Geste* forts. They did know that the 1 CD had moved up to defend the wadi thirty-five kilometers east. Bills had to run the screen and coordinate with the 1 CD and the Saudis; he also had to determine if wandering light trucks contained Bedouins or Iraqi reconnaissance. He may have made Marable feel safer, but he and B Troop had plenty to be concerned about.

On January 26 Bills traveled east and established contact with the 1-7 CAV, the westernmost unit of Tilelli's Division. On his way back he encountered a Toyota pickup truck and moved to intercept it. The driver evaded, and Bills pursued in his Bradley, reaching speeds of forty miles per hour. Even so, he could not catch the truck. His gunner fired warning shots with their twenty-five-millimeter Bushmaster cannon, but still the Toyota sped on. Bills called one of his outposts and ordered them to intercept. SSG Michael Cowden successfully maneuvered his Bradley on a course to do so, and also fired a warning shot, but to no avail. When the Toyota raced on, Cowden's gunner fired a single round into the rear end of the truck. In addition to being a hell of a shot, this stopped the truck but did not kill the driver. Bradley crews are taught to fire a ranging shot followed by two rounds to assure a hit and then three rounds to destroy the target. Cowden and Bills showed restraint that demonstrated the kind of competence required in uncertain conditions; others might have killed the man driving that truck. SSG Cowden's crew collected the thoroughly cowed driver and turned him over to the military police at the division support area who in turn handed the man over to the Saudi police. After questioning him, the Saudis released the man, who apparently was just as he claimed: a

Bedouin tribesman who had gone to visit family and become curious about the Americans.[103]

COL Mowery reflected on this first contact in his journal. He thought the incident very much like what he had experienced in Vietnam, "when we had free fire zones and the locals would go out and farm it anyway because if they did not they would starve. Here the Bedouins do not recognize governments and take their chances." Mowery didn't believe the man was a spy, but believed that "we have to keep them out of our area."[104] Uncertainty about just who was in the area combined with false alarms to make life interesting.

After dark that day, Mowery flew up to the cavalry command post, bringing with him LTC Terry Bullington, the Division operations officer, and LTC Terry Ford, the Division intelligence officer, who wanted to meet with Wilson. On the way Mowery eavesdropped on B Troop's command radio net. According to Mowery, "The previous event of firing on the Bedouin had made them all see ghosts. . . . They had eight vehicles to their front in one sector and an unknown number of vehicles to their front in another sector."[105] Mowery dropped down on their net to help them settle down and then investigated their contacts. One contact proved to be a VII Corps long-range surveillance unit that was looking for the squadron command post in order to coordinate. They had not called in to announce their visit and were seen north of the screen line. Wandering around the desert in other units' zones of action, without coordination, put soldiers at risk; this was dangerously sloppy and a mistake made far too often. Despite knowing better, many soldiers made careless mistakes in the early going. Mowery thought B Troop had performed well, but still had "some settling down to do."[106] Despite showing some symptoms of "buck fever," the Quarter Horse, as the 1-4 CAV styled itself, had done well. On January 28 Pope's A Troop took up its place on the screen line.

Everyone sought to learn from Wilson and his troops, since they had the first opportunity to execute a real mission. After visiting the 1-4 CAV, one commander concluded, "Cav is learning how to fight cheaply. They are in a low threat environment but are in contact." With a touch of envy, Wilson's compatriot concluded, "They have take[n] 4 PWs (prisoners of war) and learned a great deal about fire control. Chiefly, the key is to have a plan on distribution of fire and rigorously discipline the force on rules of engagement. Bob Wilson, 1-4 CDR is doing a good job of bringing the squadron up to speed while on a war footing."[107]

The Division's war started slowly as troops found their way out of the port and made the march up-country. The great military theorist Carl von Clausewitz has described the chief problem confronting soldiers: "Everything in war is very simple, but the simplest thing is difficult. The difficulties accumulate and end by producing a kind of friction that is inconceivable unless one has experienced war."[108] Certainly everyone who went through either port could testify to friction there. LTC Wildes searching for three days to find containers is ample proof that the simplest things were indeed difficult in Ad Dammām. LTC Ancker could attest to friction in convoys. And CPT Bills and B Troop discovered that small matters accumulate to make the simple difficult. Attempting to stop a truck to ask the driver his intentions led to a shooting incident that could have led to an unnecessary death. CPT Bills, SSG Cowden, and B Troop demonstrated competence stemming from effective training. No matter how well trained, however, they remained as yet unschooled in combat. That too would come, and at a price.

NOTES

1. Kevin M. Woods, *The Mother of All Battles: Saddam Hussein's Strategic Plan for the Persian Gulf War* (Annapolis, MD: Naval Institute Press, 2008), 128.

2. Ibid.

3. Ibid., 129. From the outset of the crisis, GMID believed the Americans would attack.

4. Ibid., 129.

5. Ibid. The author considers it likely that the Iraqis obtained satellite data, but found no supporting evidence. See Conflict Records Research Center, various military telegrams, memoranda, and intelligence reports on the First Gulf War, SH-MISC-D-000-901, 26; regarding the interview of two Saudi line crossers, see also 40. In this instance the Iraqis were more concerned about the intentions of these two men than whether they knew anything.

6. Leslie Gelb, quoted in Lawrence Freedman and Efrain Karsh, *The Gulf Conflict in 1990–1991: Diplomacy and War in the New World Order* (Princeton, NJ: Princeton University Press, 1993), 391.

7. See Kenneth Pollack, *Arabs at War: Military Effectiveness, 1948–1991* (Lincoln: University of Nebraska Press, 2002), chap. 3, which argues that the Iraqis largely abandoned Soviet operational techniques after the October War of 1973.

8. Ibid., 137–40. See also Stephen A. Bourque, *Jayhawk: The VII Corps in the Persian Gulf War* (Washington, DC: Center of Military History, 2002), 74.

9. Overhead imagery showed flanking positions at regular intervals, none of which were occupied on February 24, except for those in the 26 ID. COL (Ret.) James L. Stockmoe, telephone interview with the author, November 18, 2014.

10. Ibid.

11. Brigadier General Robert H. Scales Jr., *Certain Victory: The United States Army in the Gulf War* (Washington, DC: Office of the Chief of Staff, United States Army, 1993), 139, fig. 22.

12. The source of this assessment is COL Pesach Malovany, a retired Israeli Defense Force Intelligence officer and the author of *The Wars of Modern Babylon: A History of the Iraqi Army from 1921 to 2003* (Lexington: University Press of Kentucky, forthcoming).

13. The actual images and estimates remain unavailable. The best source for understanding dispositions of Iraqi forces against which the VII Corps fought is G2, VII Corps, "The 100-Hour Ground War: How the Iraqi Plan Failed," May 4, 1994; this unclassified document is heavily redacted. See also Scales, *Certain Victory*, 160–61; and Woods, *The Mother of All Battles*, 142. COL Malovany is the chief source concerning formation of West Euphrates Corps grouping and the timeline for Iraqi units; he believes the Iraqis eventually fielded fifty-five divisions in theater subordinate to ten corps headquarters. As many as seventeen divisions remained in Iraq oriented on Iran or the Kurds.

14. Richard M. Swain, *"Lucky War": Third Army in Desert Storm* (Fort Leavenworth, KS: US Army Command and General Staff College Press, 1994), 89.

15. COL (Ret.) Donald A. Osterberg, telephone interview with the author, October 14, 2014; Headquarters, 1st Infantry Division (Mechanized), *Operation Desert Shield and Desert Storm Command Report* (Fort Riley, KS: Headquarters, 1st Infantry Division [Mechanized], 1991), 1–2; LTG William G. Carter III, telephone interview with the author, November 16, 2014; COL (Ret.) Terry Bullington, telephone interview with the author, November 20, 2014. See also 1st Infantry Division (Mechanized), "Operation Desert Shield/Storm Briefing," September 17, 1991. Rhame returned to Fort Riley for a few days and then returned to the theater immediately after Christmas; LTG (Ret.) Thomas G. Rhame, telephone interview with the author, November 6, 2014. The dates reported in the command report and shown in the briefing are different from those Rhame recorded in his journal. MAJ Osterberg, who like COL Fred Hepler was a graduate of the School of Advanced Military Studies, could not recall when he flew, but did recall that he flew with Danger Forward.

16. General H. Norman Schwarzkopf with Peter Petre, *It Doesn't Take a Hero: The Autobiography* (New York: Bantam, 1992), 382.

17. Rhame interview, November 6, 2014.

18. Ibid. Quotations are drawn directly from Rhame's personal journal, from which he read.

19. Ibid. LTG Franks made other assumptions than those noted here, but they are not vital to understanding the planning effort. The enemy situation proved inaccurate as more information became available, but the data available on December 18 were good enough to plan against.

20. Rhame interview, November 6, 2014.

21. Ibid.

22. The 1st Infantry Division Museum at Cantigny in Wheaton, IL, has a 1 ID Public Affairs video of the departure ceremony. Dates come from MG Rhame's journal, e-mail to the author, December 31, 2015.

23. Bourque, *Jayhawk*, 76–80. VII Corps logistics units had already begun to arrive at Logistics Base Alpha, which lay south of Tapline Road and about twenty kilometers south of TAA Roosevelt. TAA Roosevelt was named after BG Theodore Roosevelt Jr., the son of President Theodore Roosevelt; the younger Roosevelt served with the 1st ID in both world wars.

24. Carter interview; Bullington interview; Headquarters, 1 ID (M) DISCOM, "Desert Shield/Desert Storm Support Operations," January 15, 1992, A-1.

25. Approximately twelve thousand soldiers deployed from the 1 ID; the rest were part of the 2 AD (Forward).

26. Tom Clancy with General Fred Franks Jr., *Into the Storm: A Study in Command* (New York: Berkley, 2004), 224–29. Yeosock supported Pagonis; the VII Corps needed to help itself. Regarding VII Corps forward, see Clancy, *Into the Storm*, 236. Pagonis organized the supporting organization extemporaneously; the Army designated the pickup team that he formed 22 SPT CMD in December 1990.

27. BG William J. Mullen III, "Desert Shield/Desert Storm," e-mail to the author, October 7, 2013.

28. Ibid.

29. Ibid. See also Headquarters, 1st Infantry Division (Forward), *Desert Shield/Storm After-Action Report: VII Corps Debarkation and Onward Movement* (Fort Riley, KS: Headquarters, 1st Infantry Division [Forward], 1991), A-4-1–A-5-1.

30. LTG (Ret.) Russell L. Honoré, telephone interview with the author, August 29, 2014; COL (Ret.) Myron J. Griswold, telephone interview with the author, November 5, 2014.

31. Honoré interview.

32. Honoré and Griswold interviews.

33. CPT James M. Goff Jr., telephone interview with the author, September 28, 2014; 1LT Gregory G. Glaze, 2nd Battalion, 34 Armor journal.

34. Headquarters, 1st Infantry Division (Forward), *Desert Shield/Storm After-Action Report: VII Corps Debarkation and Onward Movement*, 7. The risk Mullen alluded to in his report can be seen in the loss of twenty-eight soldiers killed by a Scud impacting in the port on February 25, 1991.

35. Headquarters, 1st Infantry Division (Forward), *Desert Shield/Storm After-Action Report: VII Corps Debarkation and Onward Movement*, 10–11, appendix 8 to annex A.

36. LTC (Ret.) David P. Cavaleri, telephone interview with the author, October 30, 2014.

37. Ibid.; author's personal observation.

38. Cavaleri interview.

39. Ibid.

40. The Scud is a Soviet SS1 short-range ballistic missile. Iraq fired forty-six Scuds into Saudi Arabia and forty-two at Israel; most were Scud B, the second version of the SS1, but some were Iraqi variants.

41. COL (Ret.) David Wildes, interview with the author, Washington, DC, April 25, 2014.

42. Ibid.

43. Ibid; Wildes remembered that the process took at least two days.

44. Headquarters, 4th Battalion, 5th Field Artillery, "Faithful and True: Operation Desert Storm Journal," unpublished manuscript, Fort Riley, KS, n.d., 14.

45. 1LT Jay C. Mumford, "Rangers in Iraq: Task Force Ranger, 2nd Battalion 16th Infantry in the Persian Gulf War, 10 November 1990 to 12 May 1991," unpublished manuscript, August 31, 1991, 13.

46. Honoré interview. See also MG (Ret.) Lon E. Maggart, "Eye of the Storm (Duty First)," unpublished manuscript, 1992–97, 59–60.

47. Headquarters, 4th Battalion, 5th Field Artillery, "Faithful and True," 19.

48. BG (Ret.) Donald F. Schenk, telephone interview with the author, November 8, 2014.

49. Headquarters, 1st Infantry Division (Forward), *Desert Shield/Storm After-Action Report: VII Corps Debarkation and Onward Movement*, A-19-1.

50. Maggart, "Eye of the Storm," 62; author's personal journal; James K. Matthews and Cora J. Holt, *So Many, So Much, So Far, So Fast: United States Transportation Command and Strategic Deployment for Operation Desert Shield/Storm*. Honolulu, HI: University Press of the Pacific, 2002), 288; COL (Ret.) George P. Ritter, interview with the author, August 4, 2014.

51. Stephen A. Bourque and John W. Burdan III, *The Road to Safwan: The 1st Squadron, 4th Cavalry in the 1991 Persian Gulf War* (Denton: University of North Texas Press, 2007), 44–48.

52. BG (Ret.) Donald F. Schenk, telephone interview with the author, November 15, 2014.

53. Ibid.

54. Headquarters, 4th Battalion, 5th Field Artillery, "Faithful and True," 28.

55. Headquarters, 1st Infantry Division (Forward), *Desert Shield/Storm After-Action Report: VII Corps Debarkation and Onward Movement*, A-11-1; Matthews and Holt, *So Many, So Much, So Far, So Fast*, 288, 297. These dates are inclusive of the 2 AD (Forward) contingent.

56. Headquarters, 1st Infantry Division (Forward), *Desert Shield/Storm After-Action Report: VII Corps Debarkation and Onward Movement*, 1.

57. Clancy, *Into the Storm*, 240–41. Regarding initial positions of the forces in October, see Bourque, *Jayhawk*, 24, and regarding defending Tapline Road, 74–80. The 1 CD had only two assigned brigades.

58. LTC Skip Baker, quoted in Maggart, "Eye of the Storm," 62.

59. Headquarters, 1st Infantry Division (Forward), *Desert Shield/Storm After-Action Report: VII Corps Debarkation and Onward Movement*, 19.

60. "Ground Transportation Management for VII Corps during Operation Desert Shield/Desert Storm," n.d., attachment, MG (Ret.) George Higgins, e-mail to the author, November 21, 2014.

61. Swain, *"Lucky War,"* 157; Bourque, *Jayhawk*, 81–83; Higgins e-mail.

62. Higgins e-mail.

63. Ibid.

64. Ibid.

65. VII Corps Fragmentary Order 32–91, January 9, 1991.

66. LTG (Ret.) Thomas G. Rhame, telephone interview with the author, December 19, 2014, quoting from Rhame's personal journal, January 4, 1991.

67. LTG (Ret.) Jerry A. Rutherford, telephone interview with the author, December 16, 2014.

68. Maggart, "Eye of the Storm," 61.

69. Ibid., 64.

70. Higgins e-mail.

71. Ibid.

72. Headquarters, 4th Battalion, 5th Field Artillery, "Faithful and True," 28. See also Bourque, *Jayhawk*, 82.

73. COL (Ret.), Brian R. Zahn, telephone interview with the author, November 22, 2014.

74. Ibid; author's journal. The 1-34 AR, the last of the 1st Brigade maneuver battalions, took even longer to dribble in. On January 16, fifteen of the battalion's tanks arrived, bringing the total on hand to forty-three of fifty-eight. Broken-down heavy-equipment transporters, flat tires, and drivers stopping to rest, drink tea, or visit a mosque all contributed to numerous delays. See CPT Jim Stockmoe, ed., *1st Brigade, 1st Infantry Division: Desert Shield/Storm History* (Fort Riley, KS: 1st Brigade, 1st Infantry Division, 1991), 28, 137.

75. LTC James A. Bell, telephone interview with the author, October 1, 2014.

76. Ibid.

77. Bell's experience was typical for convoy commanders in the 1 ID.

78. LTC Clinton J. Ancker, "2nd Armored Division (Forward) and the Gulf Conflict," unpublished manuscript, Naval War College, Newport, RI, n.d., 97.

79. Ibid., 96–98.

80. CPT Eugene J. Malik, telephone interview with the author, September 22, 2014.

81. The quotation is from a report by the author written on March 15, 1991. See also Stockmoe, *Desert Shield/Storm History*, 27.

82. Maggart, "Eye of the Storm," 62; Zahn interview.

83. Author's notes; Maggart, "Eye of the Storm," 65–67.

84. Stockmoe, *Desert Shield/Storm History*, 137; author's personal journal, notes from commanders' meeting, January 16, 1991; Ancker, "2nd Armored Division (Forward)," 98–99.

85. Author's personal journal. This absurd incident occurred with the 2-34 AR ammunition section.

86. Author's personal journal, January 16, 1991. Maggart, "Eye of the Storm," 70.

87. Lieutenant Colonel David W. Marlin, "History of the 4th Battalion, 37 Armored Regiment in Operation Desert Shield/Storm," unpublished manuscript, US Army War College, Carlisle Barracks, PA: 1992, 138.

88. LTC (Ret.) Juan E. Toro, telephone interview with the author, October 8, 2014.

89. Mumford, "Rangers in Iraq," 15.

90. COL James Mowery, "Saudi Journal," 34.

91. Headquarters, 4th Battalion, 5th Field Artillery, "Faithful and True," 25.

92. Major James K. Morningstar, "Points of Attack: Lessons from the Breach," *Armor*, January–February 1998, 9.

93. Mumford, "Rangers in Iraq," 14.

94. Woods, *The Mother of All Battles*, 181.

95. Ibid.

96. Ibid. Hamdani would later command II Corps of the Republican Guard Forces Command during the US invasion of Iraq in 2003.

97. Bourque and Burdan, *The Road to Safwan*, 61–62.

98. MG (Ret.) Robert D. Shadley, telephone interview with the author, August 1, 2014.

99. Ibid.

100. Bourque, *Jayhawk*, 149–50. Bourque and Burdan, *The Road to Safwan*, 67–68. On January 30 the Iraqis demonstrated their capacity to execute limited objective attacks when they seized Al Khafji, Saudi Arabia.

101. Bourque and Burdan, *The Road to Safwan*, 68–70. Mowery, "Saudi Journal," 44–45.

102. Bourque and Burdan, *The Road to Safwan*, 68–70.

103. Ibid., 71–72.

104. Mowery, "Saudi Journal," 48.

105. Ibid.

106. Ibid., 49.

107. LTC Gregory Fontenot, commander's note, February 3, 1991, in 1LT Gregory G. Glaze, 2nd Battalion 34 Armor Journal. This was a handwritten journal used to provide context for the formal staff journal and is a supplement to that effort.

108. Carl von Clausewitz, *On War*, trans. and ed. Michael Howard and Peter Paret (Princeton, NJ: Princeton University Press, 1984), 119.

CHAPTER SIX

ALARUMS AND EXCURSIONS

First Contact with the Enemy

Don't let the CG [Commanding General] know something you don't.

—Colonel Fred Hepler

Enemy sees us better than we thought; avoid physical, electronic detection.

—Major Don Osterberg

I remember from Vietnam what new guys are like the first days of combat: They see things; shoot things that are not there; shoot at friendly personnel.

—Colonel Jim Mowery

OPERATION DESERT STORM was not, as often portrayed, a four-day war. The first battle experience of the 1st Division since Vietnam occurred in January 1991, weeks before the ground offensive began on February 24, 1991. In the Division's introduction to combat, some soldiers made mistakes from which they learned; others made mistakes that killed their comrades. The troops learned, as their predecessors had, that combat required them to attempt multiple tasks simultaneously while in danger of their lives. The experience often leads to vivid memories, but not always to accurate recollection. The intent here is to divine what happened from competing accounts and ambiguous documentary evidence in order to communicate something of Oliver Wendell Holmes's "incommunicable" experience.

No matter how well prepared they are, combat can surprise the best soldiers. After surviving Scud attacks in the port and the harrowing convoys to the tactical assembly area, the troops had to learn how to thrive in the desert. They had to thrive, not merely survive, because they also had to learn how to use new equipment. And they had to do this while preparing for an attack in the company of soldiers, some of whom they had known for only a few days or weeks. If that did not prove challenging enough, they had to mount combat operations, preparing the ground over which they expected to attack.

Iraqi Estimates and Dispositions

Since the fall of Baghdad in 2003 it is possible for one to access Iraqi records, although the picture remains incomplete and is in some areas murky. More clarity will come eventually, but what is now known permits at least some insight on how Iraqi commanders perceived the situation as it developed in 1990–91. Ironically, the Iraqi VII Corps defended the ground through which the US VII Corps had to attack to reach the Republican Guard. If many observers and intelligence analysts overestimated the Iraqi capability and Soviet weapons before Desert Storm, afterward many underestimated Iraqi operational acumen. Saddam Hussein's field commanders made reasonable operational decisions given their limited capacity to see the battlefield. They understood the limitations of their weapons systems. US experts both in and out of uniform claimed the Iraqi T-72 M1 tank was superior to the M1 Abrams tank. The Iraqis, on the other hand, held conferences to determine how to cope with the Abrams. Unlike American pundits and intelligence officials, they understood that the Abrams was superior to all of their tanks.[1]

Iraqi planning remained dynamic as the conditions on the ground changed. The Iraqis reacted to the additional US buildup both by stiffening and extending their defenses. They added units and developed reserves at the tactical and operational echelons. For example, each of the forward corps had a tactical reserve and additional mobile forces formed operational reserves. They remained convinced the coalition would likely attack up the Wadi al-Batin, possibly supported by an amphibious assault into Kuwait. Their dispositions reflected their thinking. In the west, the Iraqi Jihad Corps, composed of the 10th and 12th Armored Divisions (ADs), were located just south of the Republican Guard astride the northern end of the Wadi al-Batin. In other words, the Jihad Corps were positioned literally astride the northern exit of the wadi. In the east, the Iraqi II Corps retained two mobile formations, the 17 AD and the 51st Infantry Division (Mechanized). Five divisions of the Republican Guard Forces Command (RGFC) formed the theater reserve. According to the Iraqi official history, these units were "known to be highly trained, to have excellent spirits which won the admiration of the Iraqis, Arabs and foreigners."[2] LTG Ayad Futayyih Khalifa al-Rawi articulated three tasks for the Republican Guard. First, it would conduct "operations to abort the enemy's attacks in the depth of regions where he is mobilized."[3] In simpler terms this task dictated spoiling attacks. Second, the Guard troops were to counterattack anywhere the enemy achieved a foothold. Finally, they had to be prepared to defend Basra as required.[4] Al-Rawi's concept did not assume success, but rather anticipated contingencies.

MG Ahmed Ibrahim Hamash's VII Corps lay astride the ground over which LTG Frederick M. Franks Jr.'s VII Corps would attack. Hamash had good credentials both as a soldier and as a regime loyalist; he had won his spurs in the Iran-Iraq War, commanding armored units at the brigade and division levels, including the Medina Armored Division. In April 1988 he had been promoted to major general and assigned to command the Iraqi VII Corps.

The Iraqi high command used the VII Corps to extend the Iraqi defenses westward from the Wadi al-Batin some 120 kilometers. Most of Hamash's units arrived in the fall and were in place in November. Five of the six divisions assigned were nonmotorized infantry divisions; most of these divisions were understrength and not well trained. The infantry divisions arrived in the theater at about 80 percent strength, with no more than eight thousand soldiers; desertions thinned them further, with some apparently shrinking to five thousand or less. The 52 AD was the VII Corps' only mobile force; it formed in December 1990 by combining three brigades from three different corps.[5]

Hamash deployed his five infantry divisions abreast. His 27th Infantry Division (27 ID) defended the wadi, while the 25 ID, 31 ID, 48 ID, and 26 ID extended the line west in that order. Each of the divisions defended with two brigades forward and one in depth. Each had a reconnaissance battalion and a tank battalion. The 27 ID defended on a fairly narrow frontage of ten kilometers, but the other forward divisions defended frontages of nearly thirty kilometers. Hamash had little choice given the ground he had to cover. To respond to tactical penetrations, he had the hastily formed 52 AD commanded by BG Sakban Turki Mutlik. Mutlik deployed his three brigades well to the rear of the front line, where they could react to an advance north along the wadi or against a penetration of the front line.[6]

The 26 ID anchored the right or western flank of the Iraqi VII Corps exactly where Franks intended to penetrate. Accordingly, the 26 ID became the object of rapt attention. It defended with two brigades abreast across a frontage of nearly thirty kilometers. The 110th Brigade defended on the right or west, and the 434th Brigade on the Iraqi left or east. The 806th Brigade refused the right flank from a position nearly fifty kilometers to the north.[7] It could neither support nor be supported by the forward brigades. Both forward brigades had a tank company in reserve, antitank guns, and artillery in support. At full strength, the 26 ID would number between seven and eight thousand strong, but probably fielded fewer than five thousand troops in February 1991.[8] The deployment reflected the relative immobility of Iraqi infantry divisions and

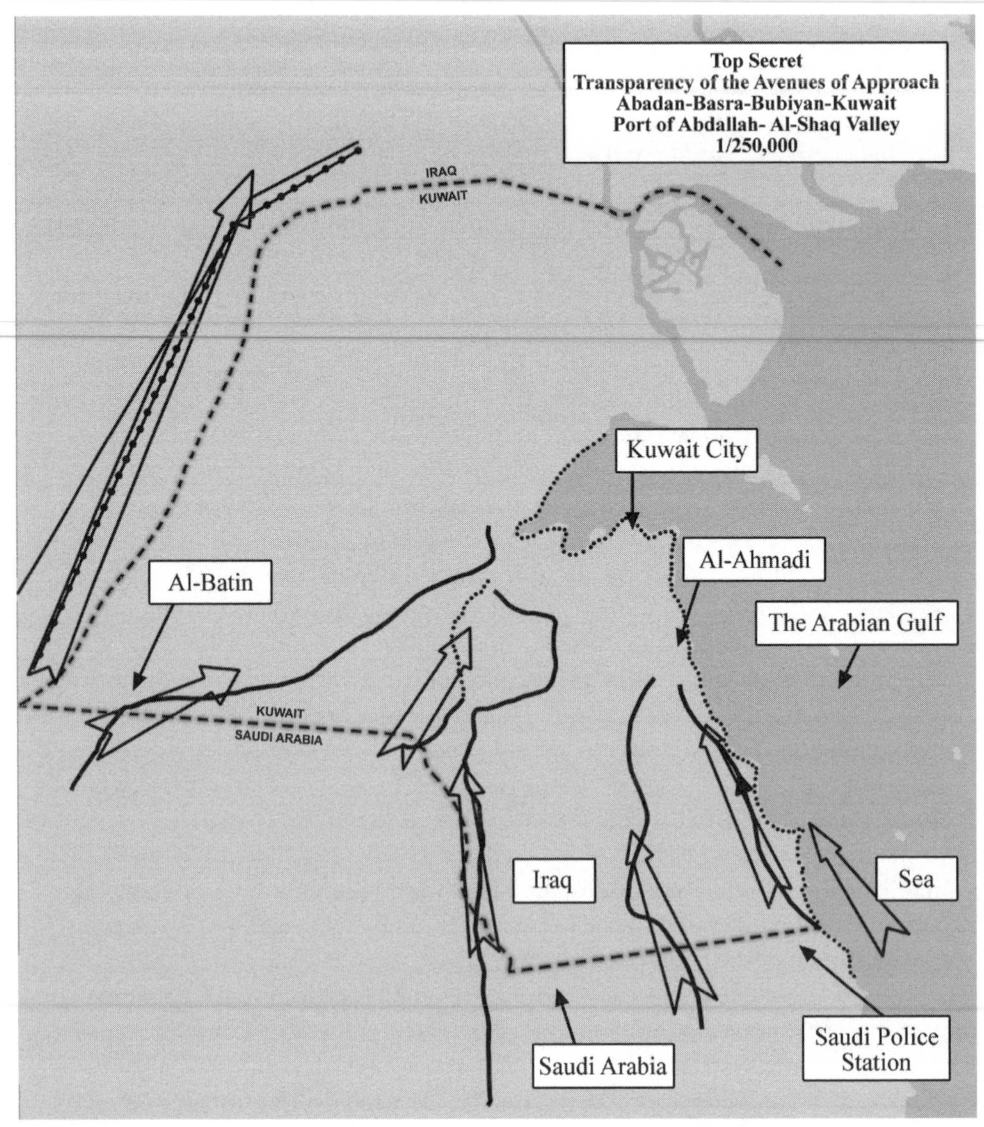

MAP 2. Iraqi Estimate of Coalition Avenues of Approach. Reproduced from a captured Iraqi Document found in Harmony Folder, ISGP-2003-00033503, courtesy of Kevin M. Woods.

inadequate resources. The VII Corps front-line divisions, including the 26 ID, did not defend in depth nor did they build complex obstacles or the triangular defensive positions that worked against Iran.[9]

Early in January the General Military Intelligence Directorate (GMID) determined that a coalition attack, if not inevitable, had become very likely. Saddam met with his key advisers on January 13 to decide what to do. They discussed many issues, including destroying Kuwaiti oil infrastructure if the coalition attacked. Saddam planned to destroy the wellheads and oil infrastructure when the coalition struck. He also released his missile forces to launch conventional attacks as soon as the coalition invaded. Saddam received an intelligence update on US ground forces. Among other things, the man giving the briefing reported a large number of American units "heading toward Hafir al Batin" and amplified the report by noting that Tapline Road was the primary route.[10] Saddam wondered whether Iraqi helicopters could attack the road. The forthcoming answer was circumspect, but amounted to a negative, and no such attack was attempted.[11] Although they could do nothing about it, the Iraqis had detected the US VII Corps moving into its assembly areas. Just what they concluded from this information is not yet known, but it may have confirmed their impression of an attack along the wadi. That impression is consistent with the deployments they made and their understanding of navigation hazards in the desert. A wide "left hook" just did not seem plausible to the Iraqi high command given the difficulty of navigating in the desert. In any event, Saddam ordered Iraqi forces to go on full alert the next day, January 14—one day before the United Nations deadline for Iraq to withdraw from Kuwait. If Iraq failed to meet that deadline, coalition forces could use force to compel Iraq to withdraw.

Planning the Attack: The US VII Corps and 1st Infantry Division

Planning the attack on the Iraqi 26 ID was only one of many things that had to be done in Tactical Assembly Area (TAA) Roosevelt, but it drove everything else. Planning extended beyond breaching the Iraqi front line. That mission was the first step on the way to the decisive fight against the Republican Guard and ultimately to going home. Planning also had to be balanced with establishing adequate logistics to sustain arriving units while building up stockpiles to support the actual attack. As troops arrived in driblets, newly formed platoons and other small units needed time to train new arrivals. Units needed time to prepare weapons and equipment that had been shipped some eight thousand miles. The Army continued to issue new equipment even in the forward areas. None of these tasks could wait—nor could finishing the operational plans.

MAJ Don Osterberg and his plans team had been at work either at the port or at TAA Roosevelt since the VII Corps commanders' conference on December 18. Although MG Thomas Rhame had flown home that evening, he returned in the early morning hours of December 28 to focus on planning and preparing the Division for the attack. The basic mission and Rhame's concept had remained unchanged since the mid-November "rock drill." The Division would attack on a narrow front with two brigades abreast. The initial assault had to breach the defenses and go deep enough to prevent direct and indirect fires into the passage lanes through which Corps units would pass forward.

Field Manual (FM) 71-100, *Division Operations*, defined four forms of offensive maneuver: frontal attack, envelopment, penetration, and infiltration. Although the Division operations manual described infiltration as a form of maneuver, it asserted that infiltration would generally be used by one part of a division while the remainder employed another form of maneuver. The 1 ID employed every one of these forms of maneuver during the ground offensive except infiltration. In a frontal attack, units attack more or less equally spread across an enemy's defenses. FM 71-100 stipulated that frontal attacks were employed against a weaker enemy force or "to fix an enemy force in position to support an envelopment or penetration."[12] The manual described the envelopment as an attempt "to avoid the enemy's main defensive strength by passing around his identified main defensive positions" to attack his flank or rear.[13] Double envelopment and turning movements were variations of envelopment. Finally, a penetration attack is mounted on a narrow front. A division conducting a penetration attacked "through the enemy's principal defensive position to divide the enemy force to allow it to be defeated in detail. The division exploits through the penetration deep into the enemy's rear areas."[14] This is what Rhame intended.

The lexicon for Army operations went beyond forms of maneuver in the offense to describing five types of offensive operations. These included movement to contact, hasty attack, deliberate attack, exploitation, and pursuit. In Operation Desert Storm, the 1 ID conducted all of these operations. The Division planned its first operation as a deliberate attack employing penetration as its form of maneuver. According to the operations manual, "A deliberate attack is planned in detail and is expensive in terms of manpower, equipment and supplies. . . . A deliberate attack involves overcoming strong enemy forces in established positions and is undertaken after a time-consuming reconnaissance, acquisition and development of targets and analysis of all other factors affecting the situation."[15]

Planning under way since mid-November had matured considerably by the end of December; the basic concept and many of the details were in place. On January 1 Franks hosted another conference to hear his commanders' concepts. Of this meeting Rhame noted in his personal journal, "Today is set aside for Div[ision] Cdrs [Commanders] to back brief the Corps Cdr."[16] The meeting began with Franks making some key points. He described the January 15 United Nations deadline as unyielding. Specifically he said, "Indications are we are going to use force. It is not a matter of whether but when."[17] Franks believed time was short, and it was unlikely everyone would complete all that they hoped to accomplish. LTG Franks wanted the Corps' operations oriented on the enemy rather than terrain. Finally, he wanted to maintain a fast pace.

Rhame briefed commanders on his vision of the operation using the six phases designated by the Corps. In phase 1, the Division would occupy TAA Roosevelt and build combat power. In phase 2, the Division would move to defensive sectors south of the border berm. In phases 3, 4, and 5, he envisioned three discrete offensive operations respectively: penetrating the enemy defenses; supporting the defeat of tactical reserves, including passing forward the United Kingdom's 1st Armoured Division (UK 1 AD); and acting as corps reserve in support of the attack on the RGFC.[18] MG Rhame reported that he planned to attack with two brigades on a narrow front supported by artillery firing some 89,000 rounds against specific Iraqi targets. The 1st and 2nd Brigades would initially drive five kilometers deep as measured from the enemy forward line. That depth would assure that no enemy remained within direct-fire range of the breach lanes. Subsequently, the 3rd Brigade, 2 AD, would pass through the assault brigades and attack to a depth of fifteen kilometers followed by the two assault brigades expanding to the same depth. During the attack, the Division would clear and mark eight lanes and do so within four hours, as ordered.[19] Clearing the enemy to the depth planned and generating eight lanes would facilitate passage of the UK 1 AD to attack east and then pass the rest of the corps forward.

Rhame conceived of the breach and passage as though it were a river crossing. This made sense, because river crossings are similar to assaults through obstacle belts and routinely practiced in NATO. Control measures were well understood across the alliance and thus were familiar to the VII Corps and the British. Army doctrine asserted that, when attacking through major obstacles, "the effect is similar to the significance of a major river."[20] The VII Corps divisions were well practiced at river crossing, and the tight control measures facilitated managing the enormous numbers of vehicles and troops that would pass through the breach. Still, it made sense not to assume too much given that 1 ID and the UK 1 AD had not worked together previously.

Rhame thought the briefing went well and noted Franks's assessment—"Looks good."[21] There were a great many other issues discussed, but maneuvering the remainder of the VII Corps around the Iraqi right flank rather than passing through the breach took center stage. Originally, Franks planned for the entire Corps to pass through the penetration, but he rightly focused on the end state that GEN H. Norman Schwarzkopf and LTG John Yeosock specified: destruction of the Republican Guard. Franks therefore wanted to maneuver three divisions into position to attack each of the Republican Guard divisions in turn; those three divisions had to arrive together, and rapidly. Finding a way to avoid passing all of them through the narrow breach would better enable the Corps to meet Schwarzkopf's intent.

LTG Franks did not decide that day whether to go around the breach to the west or through it with the entire Corps, so how the 2nd Armored Cavalry Regiment (2 ACR), 1 AD, and 3 AD would maneuver remained unclear. The UK 1 AD had less ambiguity; it would pass through the Big Red One and turn east to envelope the enemy from the west. The 1 ID's mission remained unchanged. Rhame found some of the discussion frustrating, as the two armored division commanders, MG Ronald H. Griffith of the 1 AD and MG Paul E. Funk of the 3 AD, lobbied for more resources. To Rhame, the Corps commander and his staff appeared to give little thought to either the 1st Division or the UK 1 AD subsequent to the breach. Rhame groused in his journal about the Corps' handling of logistics: "Logistics are the long pole in the tent here. No one seems to care."[22] Rhame also recorded with pleasure the best line of the day. MG Rupert Smith, who commanded the UK 1 AD, provided some comic relief when he said of himself and his unit, "Trained in Europe, dressed for the jungle [a reference to Britain's lightweight uniforms] and fighting in the desert."[23]

Less than a week later, Franks brought his team together again for a seminar to settle the final Corps plan. Although the 1st Cavalry Division (1 CD) was the Central Command (CENTCOM) reserve, BG John Tilelli attended, because joining VII Corps subsequent to the initial attack was one of his possible missions. From January 6 to January 8, the Corps' commanders and staff met at the Corps headquarters in King Khalid Military City; Franks described the three-day effort as a "plans and issues session."[24] Here the Corps settled most of the remaining tactical issues. Franks did not alter the basic operational concept he had settled on in November, but he did make two important changes regarding the two armored divisions. Franks wanted his two US armored divisions to avoid a lengthy and complicated forward passage of lines. He felt confident that although the 26 ID had refused its flank, he could get around to the west. From there, the two tank divisions could move north far more rapidly than by going through the penetration. To make this work, he either needed Tilelli's division assigned to the Corps or some other means to free up the 3 AD from defending the Wadi al-Batin against a spoiling attack. For the same reason, he needed to determine whether there was sufficient room between the planned penetration and the western corps boundary with the XVIII Airborne (ABN) Corps for the two divisions to move north abreast rather than in column.[25] LTG Franks deferred that decision until he could see the ground for himself.

Franks believed he had to have three divisions in the fight against the Republican Guard. That remained a central problem because of his estimate of the casualties the 1 ID would sustain in the penetration attack.[26] If the 1st Division took a lot of casualties, then the Corps would have only the two US armored divisions to attack the Republican Guard. Therefore, he hoped to get

Schwarzkopf to give him Tilelli's division. Since the end of Operation Desert Storm, some have criticized the Army generally and Franks specifically for his conviction that he needed three divisions to attack the Republican Guard. Yet during the run-up to the war, no one predicted the rapid, low-cost victory that would occur. Many assessments of casualties and the likely performance of coalition forces were downright gloomy: unofficial estimates of casualties ranged as high as twenty thousand. The intelligence community and various experts contended that the T-72 in the hands of Iraqi soldiers, hardened in the war with Iran, would be more than a match for the coalition.[27] In an article written just before the ground attack, Richard Jupa and James Dunnigan described the Republican Guard as "tenacious veteran fighters who take pride in their role as the fire brigade that pinches off penetrations of the Iraqi line."[28]

Schwarzkopf, whose postwar criticism of Franks was particularly harsh, believed his own planners' estimates were optimistic. They estimated casualties at two thousand dead and eight thousand wounded.[29] Yet after the fact he found Franks too deliberate and overly concerned about enemy potential. During the "plans and issues" seminar, Franks lacked the hindsight Schwarzkopf enjoyed when the latter penned his self-aggrandizing memoir. In January 1991 Franks and the VII Corps had only the information available at that time, including dour casualty estimates and pessimistic assessment of the capacity of US weapons and units against the "battle-hardened" Iraqis and the vaunted T-72 M1 tank.

Franks's commanders arrived at King Khalid Military City without hindsight either. Each brought key planners. Rhame's team included COL Mike Dodson, the Division artillery commander; LTC Terry Bullington, operations officer; LTC Terry Ford, intelligence officer; and, of course, the Division's plans officer, MAJ Don Osterberg. Nothing is easy in war, including just going to meetings. Each morning Rhame's delegation departed at 5:30 a.m. in order to arrive by 8:00 a.m. It backtracked in the evening, leaving at 5:00 p.m. The drive took the delegation part way on the suicidal Tapline Road and then south on the equally harrowing highway from Hafir al-Batin to King Khalid Military City.

The day before the seminar began, Rhame's team prepared by reviewing the assault plan in detail. Important issues remained, including final intelligence estimates, techniques on using new equipment for breaching minefields, and specific tactics the two assault brigades would use. But the scheme of maneuver was set.[30] They arrived at King Khalid Military City prepared for the long days that reviewing the Corps plan would entail.

On Sunday, January 6, the commanders reviewed the first two phases of the operation. CENTCOM had the equivalent of four corps for the attack, but none were positioned where they needed to be. The Arab forces, Marines, and XVIII ABN Corps that composed the initial defensive forces defended across the Saudi border with Kuwait and Iraq. With the VII Corps arriving, CENTCOM could begin to move units to their final assembly areas in preparation for the ground offensive. This meant the Arabs forces had to move east from their original defensive positions while the two US corps moved west and avoided detection. The commanders began by discussing how the VII Corps would move westward from the tactical assembly areas into their final assembly areas.

They also discussed the actual assault. All but the 2 ACR and the 1 ID would move into forward assembly areas. The cavalry regiment and 1 ID would move into defensive positions along the border berm to preclude the Iraqis from interfering as the rest of the Corps assembled to the rear. The commanders settled on a sequence of movement: the 1 CD (the CENTCOM reserve) would move first ultimately to defend the wadi. The 3 AD, 2 ACR, 1 ID, UK 1 AD, and finally 1 AD would follow, in that order. Each of these units would move one hundred kilometers or more in a highly choreographed sequence in order to assure steady and secure movement.

Detailed planning was absolutely crucial given the enormous size of the VII Corps. At more than 140,000 soldiers, the Corps was about 40,000 stronger than the Army of the Potomac at Gettysburg.[31] The Corps was huge in comparison even to a World War II corps. In that war, a corps usually controlled three to five divisions and ranged from 80,000 to 100,000 soldiers strong. A full-strength World War II corps of two armored divisions and an infantry division would field 526 tanks organized in six tank battalions and about thirteen thousand infantry in fifteen infantry battalions.[32]

In contrast, the VII Corps had twenty-five tank battalions assigned, which together fielded 1,447 tanks. The 2 ACR had another 126. There were a few others scattered about in command groups, and nine in the 1-4 CAV. The VII Corps was an incredibly potent and large ground force. The Jayhawk Corps, as it had been known since inception in World War I, also had sixteen infantry battalions, each of which had about eight hundred infantrymen on their rolls. The infantry moved on 707 infantry fighting vehicles; thirty-two artillery battalions fielding thirty-six eight-inch howitzers, 576 155-millimeter howitzers, 108 MLRS launchers, and eight separate rocket batteries with thirty-five more launchers would provide fire support. This large number of weapons systems does not include air defense artillery, cavalry fighting vehicles, other combat support vehicles, and the thousands of logistics vehicles the corps required. The 1st Division, for example, had 115 five-thousand-gallon tankers to keep all of its thousands of vehicles moving. Each of the divisions had an aviation brigade, as did the Corps. Effectively, Franks and his commanders had their own tactical air force. COL Don Holder's cavalry regiment had its own air force, as did each of the divisional cavalry squadrons. LTC Bob Wilson's two air cavalry troops each fielded six OH-58 scout helicopters and four AH-1 Cobra gunships.[33]

Moving the Corps required dynamic management of fuel resources; on the move the VII Corps consumed about 2.5 million gallons per day. Keeping the

Corps supplied with fuel was no small problem. To solve it, fuel trucks either had to get ahead of moving units, units had to refuel on completion of the march, or some combination of both. In any case, fuel trucks also had to be replenished on the move. Whether fuel was cached or tankers were sent back to a previously established fuel point, effective coordination and movement control was essential. Hiding the movement of thousands of vehicles and several refueling operations from the Iraqis would be, to say the least, problematic.[34] Spending the first morning of the seminar thinking this through made good sense and resulted in planning intermediate logistics staging bases for critical supplies—fuel in particular.[35]

On the afternoon of January 6 the focus shifted to phase 2, the assault. According to Franks, during phase 2, "The point of main effort for the Corps is in the breach."[36] Rhame felt that point got lost; he found the discussion frustrating as the Corps staff and others continued to introduce issues he believed were settled. At one point there was discussion about having the 3 AD cross in front of the 1st Division as part of a deception effort. Franks planned to use the 3 AD in the Wadi al-Batin to conduct feints in support of the CENTCOM deception plan. To get the 3 AD moving north would require it to move either around or in front of the 1st Division. With respect to the idea of an armored division crossing his division en route Rhame wrote, "They need to keep the plan simple."[37] Dodson had doubts as well; he thought the plan had "weak points," and these included "ineffective feint, fragmented combat power."[38] The Corps commander also made a boundary change that complicated matters and reassigned some engineers that had been promised for the breach. Rhame's notes for the day reflected his frustration with the process and his concern about a follow-on mission. He confided his thoughts in his journal: "Major things from this day. More attention is being given to the western envelopment . . . very little attention currently being shown in 1 ID, [UK] 1 Armored Division and this thing we call LOGISTICS!"[39] Although frustrated, Rhame could see the wisdom in the western envelopment. With respect to the loss of engineers and the boundary change, his journal entry read, "We will go with what we have."[40]

On the second day, January 7, the Corps commanders and staff discussed the defeat of enemy tactical reserves. The 1 ID had no clear mission during this phase, but Rhame desperately wanted one. He was not the only commander concerned about getting into the fight following the breach; BG John Tilelli said to Franks, "Don't forget about us."[41] MG Rhame found the day went slowly and the competition for resources was tiresome; he wrote, "Everyone wants more. All should learn to operate with what they have. If you are not the main effort you should not get much."[42] Much of the discussion revolved around getting the Corps main body around the Iraqi right flank. COL Dodson found the day frustrating as well; his notes report "poor understanding of the main effort," and he believed the plan a "logistical nightmare."[43] From the perspective of Rhame's delegation, the discussion meandered away from the intended focus.

January 8, the third and last day of the meetings, brought several interesting developments and resolution of important questions. LTG Yeosock, the 3rd Army commander, had grown concerned about an Iraqi preemptive attack down the Wadi al-Batin and decided to make defensive arrangements. Specifically he wanted the VII Corps to defend north of Tapline Road, but the Corps had not yet closed on its tactical assembly area and thus had few units available. Yeosock assigned Tilelli's 1 CD and 2nd Brigade, 101 ABN, to VII Corps to defend the Wadi al-Batin and the approaches to Hafir al-Batin.[44] Tilelli's troops would defend the wadi and feint against Iraqi positions in support of the CENTCOM deception plan. That would free up the 3 AD. Yeosock had solved both the problem of the 3 AD moving quickly after the breach and from having to move around or across the 1 ID.

Franks reviewed central features of his intent. First and foremost, he wanted the Corps to "maintain momentum" and to "mass on one RGFC Div[ision] at a time."[45] Osterberg's note reflects Franks's dilemma. Although he wanted to attack all three Republican Guard divisions simultaneously, as of January 6 he could only count on having the 1 AD and 3 AD available. If he could not be certain of attacking them simultaneously, he would attack them sequentially. Franks was most concerned about the Republican Guard. The Tawakalna, Medina, and Adnan Divisions were positioned north of the exits of the Wadi al-Batin, oriented southwest. They could be attacked one at a time if necessary. Franks still believed the 1st Division would be unable to join the attack immediately following the breach.[46]

In the final concept Franks retained the penetration but elected not to pass the entire Corps through it. The British would pass through, turn east, and roll up the Iraqi right flank. The cavalry regiment would pass west of the breach, followed by the two US armored divisions, following either in column or abreast. With the scheme of maneuver settled, Franks assured his commanders he would publish the Corps order on January 14. This would allow time for them to plan their operations.[47] Franks focused most of the discussion on destroying the Republican Guard; the discussion was, according to Rhame, "An Armor show, great diagrams, very few examples of massed combat power and no mission for the 1 ID."[48] After pressing COL Stan Cherrie, the Corps' operations officer, for an explanation, Rhame learned why he had no follow-on mission. It was simple: "Corps does not expect to be able to use us until D+4. They believe we will be chewed up with battle losses and possibly contaminated from a chemical strike."[49] The Corps estimated losses might be as high as 25 percent. Rhame remained determined not to be left behind because he believed the Division would be in shape to continue.[50]

BG Buster Glosson, the air component command operations officer, briefed the air plan that afternoon. Of the air campaign briefing Rhame wrote "these guys are very confident."[51] Glosson promised to destroy 50 percent of the Republican Guard; all of Iraq's chemical, biological, and radiological capability; all of Iraq's Air Force; and to do "major damage to his [Saddam's] leadership, command and control."[52] Rhame's operations officer thought Glosson cocky, noting that the "inference to me was all you ground guys have to do is drive through and occupy the ground."[53] The airman's effusive confidence was not the highlight of the day. The last briefing galvanized Rhame and his officers. BG John Stewart, the 3rd Army intelligence officer, provided a "splendid assessment of the enemy situation."[54] Stewart proffered a sobering estimate of the enemy positions as he anticipated they would be on February 1.[55]

Rhame was not downhearted, because Stewart "provided us detailed intelligence on the 26 ID where we want to breach."[56] The planners thought it was a breakthrough; now they had real intelligence with which to work. Stewart offered reasons for concern as well; he believed the Iraqis might launch a preemptive attack toward King Khalid Military City and Hafir al-Batin. Such an attack "would be a Corps attack of at least four divisions." He reported, "The signs are there. We must be prepared."[57] Stewart further surmised the Iraqis had detected the arrival of the VII Corps. As evidence, he cited their repositioning two divisions farther south. One, the 12 AD, moved in to the rear of the Iraqi 31 ID about fifty kilometers northeast of the planned penetration attack. It would be in position to counterattack. He confirmed that the 26 ID had refused its right flank. Worse still, he anticipated the Iraqis would use artillery-fired chemicals in response to the penetration within four hours, and he estimated they would employ longer-range rocket-delivered chemical munitions within twenty-four hours. Rhame concluded, "Our fight will be more difficult." With tongue in cheek he added, "Not bad, we will get to defeat the 26th ID, 36th and possibly the 12 AD."[58]

In addition to a "splendid assessment" from Stewart, the Division received an even better gift from the British. GEN Rupert Smith provided images, taken by a British remotely piloted vehicle, showing the Iraqi front lines where the assault would occur. The British contribution enabled the final touches to the plan. As Rhame put it, "We can now focus."[59] According to Bullington, the imagery the British provided electrified the staff; "It gave us for the first time pictures of what [units and ground] we were looking at."[60]

During the seminar, someone made a discovery that Bullington found even more surprising. The seminar occurred in a building at King Khalid Military City that Bullington believed once housed a theater intelligence unit, because he could explain what happened no other way. One of the staff found photo imagery of the 1 ID's attack sector in a burn bag—that is, a container of classified trash awaiting destruction. The photos had been discarded because they were uninteresting at the theater level.[61]

Why was it that images the 1 ID needed were marked for destruction, and why was it the British who provided the first images of the Iraqi position? The mostly likely reason is that intelligence organizations generally satisfy their chief customer first. Thus, theater intelligence units focused on what GEN Schwarzkopf wanted although they were supposed to provide support to the subordinate units as well. BG John Stewart was an exception to that reasonable bias in favor of the next higher headquarters. To him, "The single most important objective . . . was to focus all intelligence endeavors downwardly from [the 3rd Army] through it [higher headquarters] to the Captains, Lieutenants and Sergeants who fight the war."[62]

Despite Stewart's conviction, the 3rd Army, VII Corps, and 1st Division often failed to get intelligence in the hands of captains, lieutenants, and sergeants. Neither Stewart nor his colleagues at the corps and division levels had the means to disseminate information rapidly. In 1991 intelligence and orders were distributed in hard copy; imagery could not be distributed electronically and moved in bulk. At one point the Corps military intelligence brigade delivered a pallet load of imagery-based overlays to the Division. The intelligence staff divided the overlays into packets for the brigades. Still another courier had to carry them to each brigade, and so on all the way down to the troops. All of this took precious time.

As promised, the VII Corps issued operations plan Desert Saber on January 14. Franks's order specified "a deliberate breach with precision and synchronization resulting from precise targeting and continuous rehearsals."[63] The breach constituted the first step in the means to destroy the Republican Guard. Franks's concept had evolved; originally he had thought he would have to move the entire Corps through the breach, but now the breach would enable the UK 1 AD to attack east to roll up the Iraqi VII Corps and preclude the 52 AD from interfering with the main body of the US VII Corps as it moved around to the breach and headed north. Franks described this idea succinctly: "Once through the breach, I intend to defeat forces to the east rapidly with one division as an economy of force and pass three divisions and the ACR as point of main effort to the west of that action to destroy the RGFC in a fast-moving battle."[64] Rhame's staff published operations plan Scorpion Danger on January 19.

Scorpion Danger envisioned six phases:

1. Occupy TAA Roosevelt, build combat power.
2. Move to defensive sectors.
3. Attack to penetrate enemy forward positions, conduct forward passage of the UK 1 AD.
4. Corps Reserve, attack to defeat tactical reserves.

5. Corps Reserve, destroy RGFC.
6. Defend northern Kuwait.

The mission, not in the least prosaic, proclaimed, "At BMNT [begin morning nautical twilight], G+1 attacks, as VII (US) Corps main effort, to penetrate Iraqi defensive positions: defeat enemy first tactical echelon forces and conduct the forward passage of VII (US) Corps' forces. On order, continue the attack in zone to destroy the RGFC."[65] Even at the time, the order seemed anticlimactic. So much planning had occurred in parallel that published plans amounted to historical artifacts that reflected what had already been done. Subordinate plans followed in rapid succession. For example, the 1st Brigade issued its plan on January 22; Task Force 2nd Battalion, 34th Armor (TF 2-34 AR) issued its plan four days later.[66] Parallel planning enabled the rapid production of subordinate unit plans.

Beyond Survival in the Desert

However anticlimactic, the orders were not irrelevant. They provided details that enabled precision and synchronization. What remained to be done was to turn theory into fact literally by practicing or rehearsing under a range of conditions. Preparing for the attack became the primary activity during phase 1—to occupy TAA Roosevelt and build combat power. The troops had to learn how to use new equipment including mobility equipment such as mine rakes, rollers, and plows none had seen previously. Most important, the Division had to develop the enemy situation to the point that it could effect "precise targeting." Just how much time remained to prepare no one knew; the only thing everyone felt sure of was that there was no time to waste. Everything from equipment to ammunition seemed to be arriving late. Dodson spoke for many when he confided in his journal, "Some fear of attacking before we are ready."[67]

Preparation to fight included satisfying basic needs ranging from food to shelter. Dealing with the basic necessities had been, to some extent, settled in the port. The Division hauled to the desert plywood "outhouses" built in the ports, along with washtubs and other amenities purchased locally. At least one battalion augmented the tubs by buying hundreds of toilet plungers. When a soldier applied the plunger with force, it agitated the water in the tub so that some suds were generated.[68] Just how well this worked is debatable; at least clothes smelled clean after having been briskly stirred about in soapy, muddy water. The Division Support Command brought food, water, and basic amenities. Eating meals out of brown MRE (meal ready-to-eat) bags washed down with water, MRE cocoa, or MRE instant coffee sufficed to sustain life, but lacked in interest, taste, and variety.

In addition to MREs, Division Support Command supplied meals called tray packs. These represented two trains of thought in the Army's ideas on tactical

1st Infantry Division Task Organization

1st Brigade
Task Force (TF) 5-16 Infantry (IN)
1-34 Armor (AR)
TF 2-34 AR
1-4 Cavalry (CAV) **1**
1-5 Field Artillery (FA) (155, SP)
4-3 FA (155, SP) **2**
A/2-3 Air Defense Artillery (ADA) (-)
46 Chemical Company (CHEM CO)
1/12 CHEM CO (Decontamination) (DECON)
1/5/12 CHEM CO (Reconnaissance) (RECON)
9 Engineer Battalion (EN BN)
Four (4) Ground Surveillance Radar (GSR)/Teams (TMs)/B/101 Military Intelligence (MI)
1/1 Military Police Company (MP CO) (-)
6/1 MP CO **4**
1/B/121 Signal (SIG)
101 Forward Support Battalion (FSB)
Tactical Air Control Party (TACP)

2nd Brigade
TF 2-16 IN
TF 3-37 IN
4-37 AR
4-5 FA (155, SP)
5-18 FA (203, SP) **4**
1-17 FA (155, SP) **4**
B/2-3 ADA (-)
84 CHEM CO
2/12 CHEM CO (DECON)
2/5/12 CHEM CO (RECON)
1 EN BN
317 EN
Four (4) GSR TMs/B CO/101 MI
2/1 MP CO (-)
2/B/121 SIG
201 FSB
TACP

Division Artillery (DIVARTY)
142 FA BDE
DIVARTY
2-142 FA (203, SP)
1-142 FA (203, SP)
1 (UK) AD **3**
2 Field Regiment (FD Rgmt) (155, SP)
40 FD Rgmt (155, SP)
26 FD Rgmt (155, SP)
32 Heavy (HVY) Rgmt (203, SP)
39 HVY Rgmt (Multiple Launch Rocket System) (MLRS)
75 FA Brigade (BDE) **3**
1-158 FA (MLRS)
4-27 FA (MLRS)
E/333 FA (Target Acquisition) (TA)
D/25 FA (TA)
B/6 FA (MLRS)
Target Acquisition Radar System (TARS)/D/4-1 AV
TM/B/121 SIG

Division Support Command (DISCOM)
701 Main Support Battalion (MSB)
95 Maintenance (MAINT) CO (Calibrate)
25 Ordnance (OD) Detachment (DET) (Missile Maintenance) (MSL MAINT)
120 OD DET (MSL MAINT)
PLT/A/121 SIG
Army Material Command (AMC) Liaison Officer

Division Troops
2-3 ADA BN
12 CHEM CO (-)
PLT/323 CHEM (DECON)
176 EN BN
249 EN BN
317 EN BN
246 EN DET

1st Infantry Division Task Organization (continued)

3/2nd Armored Division

TF 1-41 IN
2-66 AR
TF 3-66 AR
4-3 FA (155, SP)
C/2-3 ADA (-)
4/C/2-5 ADA
Platoon (PLT)/CHEM CO (DECON)
D/17 EN
Four (4) GSR TMs/B/101 MI
4/12 CHEM (Smoke)
PLT/502 Military Police (MP) CO
4/B/121 SIG
498 FSB
TACP

4th Brigade

1-1 Aviation (AV)
1-4 CAV (-) (On Order)
4-1 AV (-) (Provisional)
F/1 AV
3/B/121 SIG (-)

118 MP BN
84 EN DET (Terrain)
548 EN DET (Terrain)
101 MI BN (Communications Electronics Warfare Intelligence) (CEWI) (-)
DET/101 MI
EH-60/D/4-1 AV
Limited Procurement Urgent - Ground Station Module (LPU-GSM)/A/2 MI BN
1 MP CO (-)
972 MP CO
Tm/B - J CO/6 MP (Criminal Investigation Division) (CID)
121 SIG BN
12 CHEM CO (-)
DET 507 Tactical Air Warfare Center (TAWC)
OL-G/7 Weather Squadron (SQDN)
DET 8/5 Weather SQDN
DET 7/5-7 Tactical Air Control Wing (TAIRCW) (USAF)

Task Organization changed as mission changed. *Source: 1st Infantry Division AAR*

1. Breach then Division Control
2. Breach then 3rd Brigade
3. Reinforcing 1st Infantry Division during breach
4. Breach then other VII Corps units

feeding: first and foremost, the Army sought to reduce the number of soldiers handling and preparing food; second, it wanted to reduce as much as possible the need to store and transport perishables. Although they were served hot, or at least warm, tray packs—or T-RATs, as they were called—had even less appeal than the widely loathed MREs. Tray packs were literally meals packaged in trays of entrees, vegetables, and desserts that could be heated in Army mobile kitchen trailers.

These trailers featured steam tables enabling unit cooks to heat the tray packs and serve hot coffee. Tray packs arrived in pallets containing a single type of meal. The Army had also divested itself of most of its capacity to "break" rations—that is, to divide rations to assure such variety as was available were issued equally to all units. So what did this mean in practice? Tray packs came in ten different menus for the evening meal. But because of the paucity of soldiers assigned to manage rations, the 1st Division received only four different evening meals in five months. Consequently, some units ate shrimp creole and rice for weeks on end while others ate nothing but chili and macaroni. COL Shadley could do little about variety. Whatever arrived on a pallet was consumed until another pallet arrived that might or might not contain a different offering. The lack of variety occurred for all meals. Not surprisingly, soldiers vividly recalled what their units ate nearly twenty-five years later. Shadley's troops did what they could by supplementing the detested tray packs with fresh eggs and other fresh food when possible. The Division Support Command's postwar after-action review summarized the sentiment about food with masterful understatement: "Much consternation existed with regard to type of meals and variety available."[69] Shadley and his support troops bore the brunt of barbs and criticism, but could do little but suffer bad jokes, ill temper, and, like everyone else, eat the same meal every day.

When fresh food arrived, it was cause for immediate celebration and enthusiastic comment in journals and letters home. Whether they ate shrimp with rice from a tray pack or spaghetti and meatballs from a brown bag, no one starved. But no one got fat, either. Most of the troops were hungry all of the time, and nearly everyone lost weight. Second Lieutenant Matt Green's letters home focused on food: "Apparently I was starving to death, because all the letters contain a strong thread of all the foods I was dreaming about and what a huge joy it was to finally get one of those MOREs [meals operational ready to eat—an extemporized tactical meal developed when the Army began to run short of MREs] instead of the standard 12 original MREs."[70] Journals, letters, and even official documents reflect the importance of food and the frustration of eating the same thing over and over. Troops appreciated anything done to perk up a meal. Units bought pita bread and other supplements in nearby Saudi towns when they could.[71]

Only sleep seemed more important than food. Most units arrived at TAA Roosevelt with few tents. Tents cost money, of which the 1st Division had little. Upon arrival in the theater, money became plentiful. Units bought what they could, including Bedouin tents that kept the troops more or less dry, but finding ways to stay dry in the desert was not a problem anyone had anticipated. Those soldiers who had made multiple rotations to the National Training Center (NTC) assumed California's Mojave Desert was more or less like all other deserts. Not so. It seemed to rain almost constantly in the northern Saudi desert. Getting out of rain that fell sideways mixed with blowing sand was important. Cold, wet, exhausted troops do not stay healthy and do not fare well in combat. Units found ways to provide shelter for their soldiers. Those contemplating bivouacs in the desert that winter might imagine rows of tents, as in World War II, but they would be mistaken. The assembly areas featured ramshackle collections of Bedouin tents, lean-to shelters, misappropriated cargo parachutes, and huts made of ammunition boxes. The assembly areas looked more like depression-era hobo jungles than the uniform bivouacs ubiquitous in movies.

Despite the almost comical appearance of their homes in the field and the tiresome sameness of what they ate, the troops got on with why they had come: to make final preparations to go to war. Preparation for any attack in the desert included addressing navigation. No one wanted to be LID—lost in the desert. Before the alert in November 1990, the 1st Division had only a handful of ways to navigate in the desert, most of which were risky. A compass heading and an odometer worked reasonably well for getting from one point to another. This method required the navigator to dismount and move away from his vehicle to get out of its magnetic field. It was possible to buy "marine" compasses that compensated for magnetic fields. The Army did not have such compasses as part of its standard equipment.

Helicopters were blessed with on-board compasses that worked. Some had Doppler navigation systems; these depended on beginning from a known point, and when they were updated periodically were reasonably accurate. Artillery units in particular depended on accurate locations from which to base their firing data. They too had a system known by yet another acronym, PADS, which stood for position and azimuth determining systems. The VII Corps artillery had a survey capability that established PADS data in the port and then moved it forward incrementally. Division artillery then built on that data. If artillerymen knew where they were, they could then find direction by a number of means including celestial methods. Long-range navigation (LORAN) provided still another means. Developed during World War II, LORAN depended on transmitters sending signals from fixed sites and was accurate. The desert in Saudi Arabia and Iraq was blessed with a good grid of LORAN transmitters to support the oil industries.

Of all the navigation aids and methods, one outshone the others and in the minds of many soldiers proved decisive. The global positioning system, or GPS, gave coalition forces a tremendous, maybe even a decisive, advantage. Today GPS has become ubiquitous in its use by civilians, and it has improved to the point that even telephones have GPS mapping; it is perhaps the only abbreviation equally well known in or out of uniform. In 1990 the Magellan GPS was remarkable, but it was clunky compared to what is available today. Even so, in the winter of 1990–91 it seemed like magic. Additionally it came with "selective availability," a feature that induced up to a one-hundred-meter circular error to preclude the civilian system to be used as a targeting tool. Few if any soldiers knew about selective availability, so they were puzzled when their Magellan GPS units seemed a little off. Additionally, there were too few satellites to assure twenty-four-hour access.[72] Even though Magellan got its users only to within a hundred meters of where they intended to be, that was miracle enough in the truly featureless desert of northern Saudi Arabia and southern Iraq.

Although Bullington had placed the order for the Magellan GPS units prior to deployment, very few arrived before the Division deployed; the bulk of the Magellans arrived just in time to be issued in the tactical assembly area. CPT Gene Malik drew his Magellan GPS in mid-January in the middle of the night when someone at Brigade headquarters called him to the command post to pick it up. He was to use it to lead the few 1-34 AR tanks and Bradleys that had arrived to respond to an expected Iraqi attack. He stood in a driving rain, using a flashlight to read the instructions, believing he would need it later that night in combat. Thankfully, the warning of an Iraqi attack proved to be false. Although he was relieved that he did not go to war that night, Malik came to believe, as did many others, "If there was a secret weapon of the war, GPS was it."[73] Accurate position location led to accurate navigation, all of which enabled the famous "left hook." GPS may have been the most important new technology introduced in Desert Storm. It confounded the Iraqis, who never really believed a left hook or any major movement through the open desert possible.

With decent means to determine location, other important tasks could be undertaken. Arriving artillery units could stop at a surveyed point near Tapline Road and load their PADS or use their newly acquired Magellans to determine their location. With PADs and/or GPS units, howitzers could be laid more precisely on the intended direction of fire, and this was key to firing accurately. The Division artillery had just transitioned to the Tactical Fire Direction System (TACFIRE), an artillery computer system. TACFIRE could make calculations rapidly and support fire planning rapidly, but it depended on accurate location. Each of the arriving artillery battalions fired their howitzers to verify the firing data in their ballistic tables. Calibrating assured that the projectiles struck where the firing data predicted they would, but all of this had to begin with the ability to determine location accurately.

Tankers and mechanized infantry undertook a different course, but also calibrated their guns. The process began with bore sighting—aligning the sight and the bore so the gun pointed where the sight did. Successful gunnery must account for a number of variables including cant, barometric pressure, wind, temperature, and superelevation—the arc a round must travel above the line of sight. Gunnery is a matter of physics and some arcane math. The M1 tank is blessed with onboard computers and sensors that account for all of these variables except barometric pressure. Tankers and artillerymen both depended on weather reports for the data they needed to assure accuracy. Bradley gunners managed accuracy by firing a ranging round and adjusting the strike of the rounds by a process called burst on target; they literally adjusted their sight picture to where the ranging round went. The second part of calibration required shooting to verify that rounds struck where the gun was aimed. For that, everyone needed a range.

To support direct fire calibration, VII Corps engineers built a range south of Tapline Road. Here tanks and Bradleys could calibrate and fire basic platoon gunnery exercises. This was necessary for the 1st Brigade, since it had drawn new tanks in the port. The 2nd and 3rd Brigades also needed to shoot since none of their crews had fired the main tank-killing round called service sabot. The armor-piercing fin-stabilized discarding sabot rounds featured a long rod depleted uranium penetrator. The penetrator of the 120-millimeter M829A1 sabot round is twenty-six inches long with a diameter of slightly more than an inch. The term *sabot* refers to a collar made of four segments or petals of ceramic material around the penetrator enabling the round to fit tightly in the 120-millimeter gun tube. When the round is fired, the petals fly apart and the sabot is discarded. There were sabot rounds for both the 105-millimeter on the basic M1 and 120-millimeter main guns found on the M1A1. Bradley twenty-five-millimeter cannons also boasted depleted uranium penetrators. The 105-millimeter and 120-millimeter penetrators traveled at more than a mile a second. A kinetic energy round, sabot achieves kills by penetrating armor. The penetrator imparts enormous heat and energy, with catastrophic results on the target. After bore sighting, tank and Bradley crews verified "zero," assuring that rounds struck where the gunner aimed.[74]

Crews applied to their computer the data for the round they would fire. This process was called "applying fleet zero." Crews then fired to confirm zero. If the first round struck other than where it was aimed on the target panel, the crew fired two more rounds to get a "grouping" and then moved the sights to the center of the grouping. Once the gun struck the panel where aimed, the gun had been zeroed or calibrated. Generally the system worked as designed. Of the process SFC Michael Schulte, at that time a battalion master gunner, observes, "If the systems were functional and if you set it up properly it [fleet zero] worked like a champ."[75] Tankers were astounded by the performance of the service sabot. As LTC Pat Ritter, then the commander of the 1-34 AR, notes, "That thing was so impressive" that he and SFC Richard Howard, his master gunner, adjusted their sights to fifteen hundred meters. The standard in 1990 for battle sight against an armor threat was to travel with a sabot round loaded at preset range of twelve hundred meters.[76] Setting the battle sight at fifteen hundred meters demonstrated faith in the accuracy of the round at longer ranges.

The 4th Brigade undertook similar exercises. Its attack battalion (1-1 AVN) experienced some problems initially, but soon resolved them. Calibration took place rapidly, and with few problems. The Division attack battalion's first Apache attack helicopter arrived in the assembly area on January 19. By January 24 all eighteen had arrived and completed calibration.[77]

The obvious question is, what would the results have been without time to calibrate or zero weapons? For one thing, US gunnery would have been far less effective. Zeroing weapons does two things: first, it assures they perform at their optimum; second, and perhaps more important, crews that have the opportunity to test-fire weapons are far more confident than those who do not. For the crews and platoons that had not trained together, firing a few basic platoon gunnery exercises was essential to developing trust and confidence in each other. Calibration, zeroing, and shooting are essential tasks in assembly areas, and they met the intent of "build combat power."

Building combat power also required meeting a need that had not occurred to Maslow. The troops may move on their stomachs, but a mechanized division moves only if its vehicles run. Every piece of equipment sat idle for as much as five or more weeks in a port of embarkation, in the hold of a ship, or in a holding area on arrival. Vehicles left sitting do not fare well. Even newer M1A1s, many of which were not new, sat in the port until issued. Not surprisingly, maintenance problems abounded. Logistics in Desert Shield/Storm proved uneven. MG Gus Pagonis commanded the extemporized 22nd Support Command (22 SPT CMD). Pagonis enjoyed very good press in the United States for having performed a logistics miracle in the desert. He celebrated his success in *Moving Mountains*, a business leadership book based on his effort in the desert; it enjoyed considerable publishing success, but found few enthusiasts among those who served in the 1st Division.

In fairness, the Army and CENTCOM made choices that directly affected the capacity of 22 SPT CMD to support operations. Using an extemporaneous headquarters like the 22nd contributed to the problem, but there was much more. None of the units, from maneuver battalion to theater logistics, had adequate transportation. Automation systems varied between units and some had no automation. Shadley's Division Support Command managed to sustain the Division in fuel, food, ammunition, and water, but barely. It was able to manage because the Army issued trucks above its authorization. LTC Ed

Buffington's 101st Support Battalion (101 SPT BN) had only seven of its ten authorized five-thousand-gallon fuel tankers. Shadley augmented Buffington with a reserve unit that brought thirteen more. Without augmentation, Buffington could not have kept the Brigade refueled.[78] The Army had reduced logistics organizations to maintain more combat units. The VII Corps logistics command was also shorthanded, in part because it was assigned to US Army Europe. In Europe, local hires augmented corps- and theater-level maintenance. Obviously, none of these people deployed to the theater.

Supply distribution, particularly that of repair parts, absolutely hampered operations. Simply put, the repair parts system failed. First Lieutenant Jay C. Mumford, the author of the 2nd Battalion, 16th Infantry journal, described the problem and the solution thoughtfully and without the emotion found in other after-action reviews: "Viewed from any angle, Class IX [repair parts and major assemblies] was a major problem in the KTO [Kuwait Theater of Operations]. The parts were simply not available at the front."[79] To solve the problem, officers and sergeants spent time "scuttling around the Division AO [area of operations] and beyond in search of parts. Troops even made almost a dozen trips all the way back to port looking for needed parts."[80] LTC Dave Marlin opined that on a scale of 1 to 10, logistic support merited a 1; he claimed that only 6 percent of his requisitions were filled. LTC John Gingrich reported 5 percent filled. One tank battalion reported processing 5,300 requisitions, less than 10 percent of which were filled.[81]

Scrounging for parts solved only a part of the problem. Most units deployed with ample amounts of unauthorized excess, because it was an article of faith that getting parts in the field proved all but impossible. At the NTC, observer-controllers coached and evaluated units on their capacity to process requisitions, but no one seemed to coach the logisticians on filling requisitions. CW2 James "Jim" D. Logan, a battalion maintenance technician, noted that he and his colleagues in the other battalions deployed with a "stash." Logan made numerous trips to the port, to King Khalid Military City, and to logistics bases in the field looking for parts. Generally he found parts at each of these places and people willing to give them up, but as he remembers, "No one knew what they had."[82] It is true that Pagonis had a mountain of parts, but if they could not be found and were not distributed, they were of little use.

Shadley understood the problem, but he never could solve it. In his after-action report, he claimed a satisfaction rate of 19 percent on requisitions. The difference between what he claimed and what units believed resulted from how requisitions were managed and not because either the battalions or the Division Support Command intended to mislead. The Division Support Command Report concluded, "Logistics automation problems and inability to provide in-transit visibility coupled with limited transportation assets at all levels to push repair parts, resulted in very little class IX reaching the division."[83] This was absolutely true.

Resupplying the troops as boots and clothing wore out proved equally frustrating. Getting a pair of boots turned out to be more difficult than the biblical story of a camel getting through the eye of a needle. Soldiers literally walked out of boots and wore out underwear. Some weeks after the end of the war, the 2-34 AR was offered as many pairs of size 44 boxer shorts as it would like. What was puzzling is why the Army even stocked sizes that big, as anyone that large would surely be discharged as overweight. Of that problem Shadley wrote, "There was limited to no resupply of organizational clothing and individual equipment (OCIE) [everything from sleeping bags to field jackets]. When equipment was destroyed in combat, there was no means to replace OCIE lost by soldiers."[84] For all of these reasons, building combat power had to be done without parts or new underwear. Units made do, and preparation went on.

Rehearsal sites were crucial and required engineers to build them. LTC Steve Hawkins's 1st Engineer Battalion (1 EN) closed on TAA Roosevelt on New Year's Eve 1990. In the first week of January, it began building a breach rehearsal site under BG William G. Carter III's supervision. The Division had two engineer battalions to support the breach—the Division's organic battalion, the 1 EN led by Hawkins, and the 9 EN, led by LTC Rich Jemiola, provided direct support to the two assault brigades, the 2nd and 1st Brigades, respectively. Both engineer battalions built "enemy" positions protected by obstacles, including training minefields to allow tactical unit training and rehearsals. The site Carter had Hawkins build was large enough for a full-scale division rehearsal.[85]

The engineers practiced with three new pieces of equipment essential to overcoming antitank ditches, wire obstacles, and minefields. These included the armored combat engineer vehicle, or ACE. The Army fielded the ACE as a light bulldozer that could keep up with the M1 tank. It turned out to be very good at breaching defensive berms, collapsing bunkers, and filling tank ditches. It was not very good for digging in equipment. The ACE had one crewman and no radio; these were major drawbacks in an assault. The Army also modified two venerable engineer vehicles. The combat engineer vehicle (CEV) had been around since the 1960s, and the Army developed mine rakes for installation on some of the CEVs. The rakes looked a bit like mine plows, but rather than cutting blades that would go deep and push mines aside, they had comparatively slender tines. Engineers designed them to "rake" up small mines that might pass through the larger blades of a mine plow. The final new piece of kit, the mine-clearing line charge (MCLC), could be mounted either on a trailer or on the chassis of an armored vehicle–launched bridge. This was a tank chassis that could be equipped to lay a scissors bridge. Used to mount the MCLC rather than the bridge, the army awarded it a new label, AVLM, for armored vehicle–launched MCLC. This gadget used a rocket to launch an explosive line that uncoiled behind the rocket as it flew down range to lie across an obstacle. Once the rocket delivered the charge, the crew detonated it. The resulting blast would destroy mines, clearing a path one hundred meters long and eight meters wide. A two-man crew operated the system, but like the ACE, it had no radio.[86]

All six of the tank battalions received mobility equipment as well. Each of the twenty-four tank companies drew three mine plows and one mine roller. Each plow had twelve blades; six were centered over each of the two tracks, with a small roller called a dog bone between the two sets of blades. The blades cut deeply enough to force mines up and away from the tank's tracks, and the small roller would serve to detonate mines that might come up between the two banks of blades. Although the troops had seen this equipment prior to deploying, none had trained with it. The mine roller was just what it sounds like: a heavy roller attached to the front end of a tank. The tank pushed the roller ahead of it, and the roller was heavy enough to detonate mines and thus locate the edges of minefields or it could be used to proof a plowed lane by rolling the lane. No detonations equaled a proofed lane.

The 2-34 AR and 3-37 AR led the experimentation that followed. Each of these two tank battalions would attack as balanced task forces of two tank and two mechanized infantry companies. The four resulting balanced task forces formed the nucleus of the Division assault echelon. The 2-34 AR began arriving at TAA Roosevelt early on January 13. By the end of that day, CPT Grant Steffan's Alpha Company, 9 EN, had built an Iraqi platoon defensive position for the task force to use for training and rehearsals.

The 2-34 AR began practicing with mine plows and rollers the next day. Over the next few days, the battalion tested different approaches to determine what worked best. Troops began by using three mine plows in a wedge. This method was unsatisfactory, because plows occasionally pushed mines to the side and into the lane just plowed by a preceding mine plow. So the 2-34 AR tried plowing in echelon, in column, in double lanes and other combinations. On January 18, COL Lon E. "Bert" Maggart, the brigade commander, invited Rhame and Franks to see what the battalion had decided. They and a "cast of thousands" spent a couple of hours watching several different methods and debating the options. CPT Bob Burns, commander of C Company, 2-34 AR, ran the event and explained the reasoning behind each of the options. It was a remarkable occasion in which every person involved with this crucial part of the attack plan played a role, from tank driver to Corps commander. They all understood getting this right could spell the difference between success and failure. No one held back; discussion flowed freely. LTG Franks inspected the furrows left by mine plows and observed the efforts as closely as Sherlock Holmes would a crime scene.[87]

The scheme that the 2-34 AR recommended featured a tank company clearing two lanes simultaneously. Two plows cleared one lane in column, followed by the CEV rake. The third plow cleared a second lane, with the mine roller following to proof it. The roller then turned and proofed the first lane. In each lane, an engineer squad followed to mark the lane. Over four days of intensive effort, the battalion arrived at several other conclusions. Mine plows could maintain a steady eight-to-ten miles per hour. The plows could drive through two belts of triple-strand barbed wire and a belt of mines 250 meters deep in times that varied from as long as two minutes and fifteen seconds to as a little as one minute and thirty seconds. Both of these are a very long time under fire in a minefield, but far faster than anyone believed possible before the experiments. The battalion also found that the mine plows could plow as far as they had fuel to go and they could maneuver with reasonable agility. Mine rollers, on the other hand, were not so agile; they had trouble turning. Later that same day, the 2-34 AR published a short lessons learned paper to share with the other tank battalions.[88]

LTC Dave Gross's 3-37 AR arrived in the assembly area a few days later and, like the 2-34 AR, turned immediately to working on the problem. The two battalions exchanged some information via their respective brigades. Like the 2-34 AR, the troops of the 3-37 AR had no basis for comparison, so they repeated some experiments to see for themselves what worked. MAJ Paul Izzo, Gross's operations officer, recalls of their method that "it was trial and error."[89] Through trial and error the two battalions and the two brigades produced similar solutions. Both brigades organized for the assault with two balanced task forces, each with two tank companies and two mechanized infantry companies. The two infantry battalions used the systems developed by the tank battalions with which they were paired. Subsequent to learning how to employ plows and rollers, the assault battalions incorporated the engineers to work out how to combine the capability they brought. In the 1st Brigade, the task forces planned to employ combat engineer rakes in the second of the two lanes each plow platoon would clear. Infantry followed the plow tanks to assault the enemy defenses. ACEs, line charges, and engineer squads trailed the assault echelon to clear mine belts and reduce obstacles, bunkers, and trenches. The only major difference in the two brigades was that the 2nd Brigade brought the line charges up closer in their assault formations.[90]

Marking cleared lanes proved far more difficult than figuring out how to clear them in the first place. No single system existed to enable marking a lane as a breach occurred. Since the plan ultimately called for sixteen lanes, this problem was not trivial. The Army had several extemporized systems, but none worked particularly well, and some put engineers at risk. In the end, the lanes themselves stood out so well that the bigger problem was to mark the approaches so that the lane entrance could not be missed. The Division came up with the answer: each lane would be marked beginning three kilometers out with a four-by-eight-foot plywood panel painted red with a white letter identifying

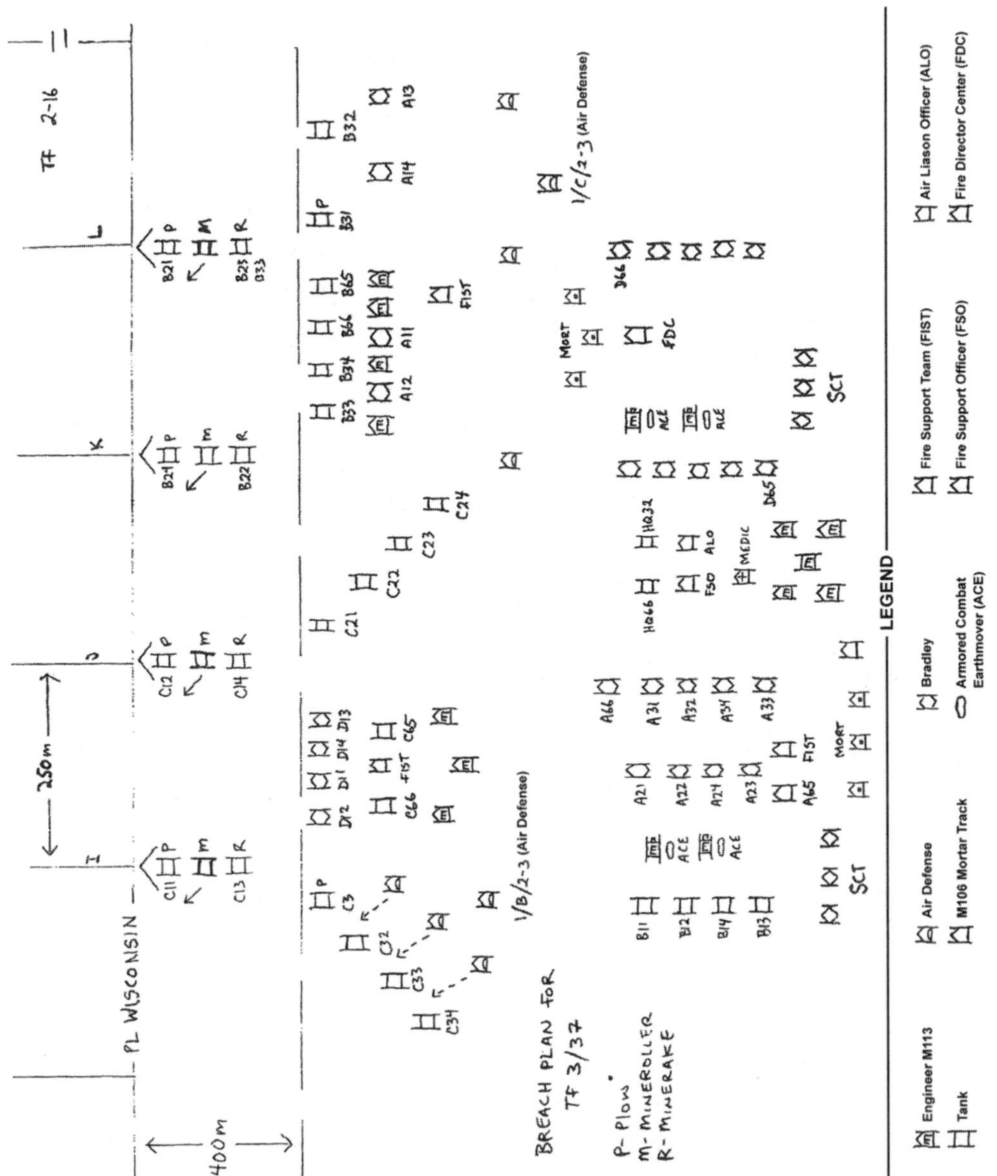

MAP 3. A reproduction of Task Force 3-37 Armor graphic showing the planned attack formation for the breach operation on February 24, 1991. The graphic shows the planned positions of individual vehicles in the formation. Courtesy of BG USA Retired David F. Gross.

the lane. What stood out about the preparation for the breach is not how units solved problems but how often they refined their respective solutions and the number of times they practiced to get it right.

Practicing and rehearsing are not the same exactly. Units practiced drills such as reaction to enemy contact, but rehearsed their parts in the planned assault. The difference is simple. Practice aims to perfect general techniques or tactics by doing them over and over; in rehearsals, explicit assigned tasks are repeated in the expected sequence and in varying conditions. The idea is to assure that if improvisation is required, it is done on the basis of fully understanding the intended outcome. Rehearsals went beyond the basic tasks that maneuver units expected to perform. For example, units developed techniques to evacuate damaged vehicles and practiced until they felt confident. Then they rehearsed in context, such as a battalion-level rehearsal of the breach. The division practiced all manner of techniques ranging from battalion tactics on the move to chemical decontamination, all with hitherto unheard-of intensity and commitment.

Tension could and did result from rehearsals. During preparation for a rehearsal, CPT Jim Goff, a battalion medical platoon leader, had a heated exchange with a company commander who refused to provide the number of soldiers Goff requested to simulate wounds for an evacuation rehearsal. Referring to the doctor, the company commander offered the view, "I don't need some rear-echelon motherfucker telling me how to run my company." Dr. Goff responded that the belligerent commander was an "infantry officer, because the brightest thing he had ever done was assemble and disassemble an M-16."[91] Both got to their feet, but were immediately restrained by the battalion's two majors. The battalion commander intervened with the result that Goff's medical platoon got to practice against the worst-case estimate. Prudence and a lieutenant colonel's oak leaves carried the day.

Constant practice of tactics, techniques, and procedures both day and night produced results. Things seemed to come together, and the feeling of being ready for what lay ahead became palpable. Jim Enicks, then a tank platoon leader, recalls, "Everything was going on without a lot of radio traffic . . . everything was moving with purpose."[92] Even before the intelligence preparation was complete and the orders fully revised, the assaulting forces had rehearsed to the point that their anticipated tasks had become second nature.

Phase 1 continued practically until the ground assault on February 24 and overlapped with phase 2, the move to defensive sectors. The 2 ACR moved from the port first in order to screen the VII Corps as it occupied the assembly areas. The possibility of an Iraqi spoiling attack, which galvanized LTG Yeosock into assigning the 1 CD and a brigade of the 101 ABN to defend the approaches to Hafir al-Batin, also affected the logistics buildup. When Rhame ordered

Shadley to establish the Division Support Area to support the attack, he effectively began the transition to phase 2.

MAJ Sylvia Marable's preparation of Division Support Area Junction City is an example of the overlap in phases 1 and 2. The arrival of the 1st Squadron, 4th Cavalry was part of phase 2. CPT Mike Bills, commander of B Troop, established the screen on January 25. LTC Bob Wilson's two air troops arrived that same day. CPT Ken Pope and A Troop calibrated weapons on January 25; they took their place on the screen line the next day.[93] With Wilson's cavalry squadron in place, Marable and her team breathed easier. In fact, the Iraqi high command ordered Hamash's VII Corps to probe south to identify what forces lay opposite his and to provoke a reaction that might reveal coalition intentions. After several false alarms, the 1st Division had become, if not jittery, hyperalert. Combat veterans in the Division thought perhaps they had seen this before. Mike Dodson's journal noted several reports of possible preemptive strikes. Of the alarm on January 13 that had Malik standing in the rain to learn how to use his GPS unit, he wrote, simply, "tensions high."[94] On January 14 he wrote a lengthier assessment: "Tension [over possible Iraqi attack] remains high. Corps and above planning badly flawed concerning how/where to build combat power. Would have laagered units close to port until combat power was built then moved forward."[95]

Rhame had a serious problem. His division needed to secure its own and the Corps' logistics bases west of the Wadi al-Batin while defending Tapline Road, assembling and preparing its units (the last of which arrived in the assembly area on January 28), and rehearsing the attack. Rhame had to find troops to bolster the Quarter Horse without hampering other critical tasks too badly. He wanted to use COL Dave Weisman's 3rd Brigade, but it would close last, so he dealt with the problem in stages. LTC Wilson got the task of forward security under way first.[96]

The piecemeal arrival in the assembly area seemed risky to many of the arriving troops because it was. The alarm on January 13 sent ripples of fear among the handful of tankers and infantrymen available to respond. The VII Corps intelligence staff believed the 12 AD, 17 AD, and the Republican Guard Tawakalna Mechanized Division capable of mounting attacks west of the Wadi al-Batin.[97] The Iraqi 26 ID's patrol activity in the direction of the Quarter Horse screen, forward of the Division Support Area, exacerbated unease. For most of January, there were too few troops in position to respond to an attack of any size. Accordingly, every time an alarm sounded, the handful of units available took it seriously. There were Syrian and Egyptian troops in position to screen the frontier when the VII Corps moved in; their presence offered no solace to the Americans, as the Corps had no idea there were friendly troops around. The situation improved when the 3rd Army assigned Tilelli's 1 CD to the VII

Corps. The 1 CD moved in north of Tapline Road to the rear of the Syrian 9 AD. The Egyptian 3rd Mechanized Division was forward as well, but both the Syrians and the Egyptians needed to move east to get in position for the ground offensive. The Syrians cleared out on January 21 and headed east, followed by the Egyptians. For a short time no combat forces screened the frontier.[98]

Rushing about in response to false alarms seems foolish in retrospect, but it was deadly serious then. How serious became apparent on January 19, when the Iraqis attacked, seized, and for a short time held the Saudi border town of Al-Khafji. Taking the small town located near the coast, just one hundred kilometers north of Tapline Road, sent a shock through CENTCOM. The danger posed by Iraqi probes and outright attacks remained a real concern until the last VII Corps combat units arrived from the port. That happy event did not occur until the 3 AD closed on February 11. The danger subsided further when the 1 ID occupied defensive positions just south of the border berm.[99] In the meantime, Rhame and Franks accepted risks to the Division Support Area and Corps Logistics Base Echo. Nevertheless, support troops began stockpiling ammunition, fuel, and food in preparation for the attack.

Although well trained, the Quarter Horse and every other battalion in the Division had no combat experience. Not surprisingly, the cavalry got excited when first confronted with tactical decisions. Iraqi patrols made an appearance virtually every night. LTC Wilson's soldiers had to differentiate between expectations and actuality; every unit new to combat has to learn that it is possible to see what you expect rather than that what is there. Avoiding confirmation bias in combat requires patience, yet the Army focused on speed in contacts and gunnery. Learning when to make haste slowly comes by critically assessing experience. Wilson's troopers got a head start in learning hard lessons.

On the night of February 1 they had another contact that reflected just how much they had to learn. That night they reported seeing tanks. MG Rhame called the aviation brigade to respond with Apache attack helicopters. COL Mowery, already airborne and en route from visiting his British counterpart, monitored the call. Mowery coached Wilson and LTC Ralph Hayles, the attack helicopter battalion commander, to be certain "that both had a perfect grasp of the situation before the Apaches moved out to kill the enemy."[100]

Mowery wanted them to take their time in prosecuting this first combined contact. After all, no one was actually shooting. As time wore on, however, Rhame became quite heated and profane about just how long it was taking to get the Apaches in contact. Mowery told Rhame he wanted to avoid an incident of friendly fire. To that Rhame remarked, "Dragon 6 [Mowery's call sign] has a very good point, forget everything I said for the last twenty minutes."[101] Rhame recognized he needed to back off, and he did.

LTC Hayles and his wingman got in position over the cavalry at 10:45 p.m. They made visual contact with B Troop and turned west, flying along the forward trace bound for A Troop, which was south of the perceived enemy activity. Hayles intended to search for the enemy from above A Troop's screen line. Onboard threat sensors alerted him to air defense radar illuminating his aircraft and identified the radar source as a Soviet-made ZSU-23-4, a tracked vehicle with four twenty-three-millimeter antiaircraft cannons. His wingman, CPT Stephen M. Schiller, reported he too was being illuminated by ZSU-23-4 radar.[102] To the west, about 3,500 meters away, Hayles could see possible targets where he expected A Troop to be. He asked Schiller if he could identify the targets, but Schiller could not. LTC Hayles then decided they would make the approach from a different direction. As they repositioned, someone fired at them. Schiller saw a single strand of orange tracers; he took this to mean a Bradley had fired, because a ZSU would have had four streams of tracers, one from each of its four cannons. Although the cavalry later denied firing, it is possible—even likely—that one of the Bradleys had fired given what Schiller saw. On the other hand, CPT Bills, commander of B Troop, also took fire. He reported seeing green tracers (green was consistent with Soviet weapons, and thus Iraqis). Just who shot at Hayles and Bills is unclear, but it is likely that Iraqis did some of the shooting and possibly all of it.[103]

Obviously something was amiss. Wilson, as the commander on the scene, called a cease-fire. The two Apaches winged it south without further incident. A postmortem revealed that the ground surveillance radar supporting B Troop apparently triggered the Apache sensors. Furthermore, with its radar dish up, the ground surveillance radar track looked a lot like a ZSU. After reviewing the gun camera tapes, both Hayles and Schiller concluded that they could not effectively identify targets at 3,500 meters or more. The gun camera had much better resolution than the nighttime Apache targeting viewer, and it also had far better resolution than a pilot peering through night-vision goggles. The key lesson was that night sights, on both helicopters and ground combat vehicles, were inadequate for being certain of identification at extended range.

In any case, the Quarter Horse needed help, and it was on the way. The day before the shooting incident Rhame organized the Combat Command Carter, which would form the second increment for establishing adequate defenses to protect logistics, Tapline Road, and the Division staging areas. Rhame tapped BG Bill Carter to command the brigade-size grouping and named it for him. Combat Command Carter formed around the Quarter Horse, the 3-37 AR, the 1st Battalion, 5th field artillery (1-5 FA), and assets from LTC Rod Moore's 101st Military Intelligence unit (101 MI). Choosing Carter made perfect sense. As the assistant division commander for maneuver, he came with his own command post—Danger Forward. Carter knew each of the battalion commanders well, and he was smart, unflappable, and proven in combat. LTC Dave Gross, the second maneuver battalion commander, had proven himself effective during the series of exercises known as Gauntlet in the fall. LTC Harry

Emerson's 1-5 FA filled out the team. Emerson had demonstrated technical and tactical competence during several NTC rotations, and with a year in command he was the most experienced commander in Carter's makeshift outfit. LTC Emerson blended well with Carter, who was effervescent, and with Wilson and Gross, who were taciturn by comparison.[104]

Rhame envisioned Combat Command Carter as a temporary measure, as each of its assigned battalions needed time to prepare for the assault. He planned for the 3rd Brigade to assume the mission as soon as it was able. Finally, the 1st and 2nd Brigades would assume the defense just before the ground attack. Meanwhile, Combat Command Carter would secure the forward sector to "guard critical logistic/C2 [command and control] nodes, deny enemy recon and provide early warning of preemptive enemy attack."[105] As Rhame put it, "I intend to thicken our forward security south of PL [phase line] Cherry to ensure sufficient combat power is available to counter enemy attacks against DSA [Division Support Area] Junction City, ASP 2 [ammunition supply point] or LOGBASE E [Logistics Base Echo]."[106] Danger Forward, the 3-37 AR, the 1-5 FA, and supporting attachments moved on February 3, joining the Quarter Horse that evening.

With Combat Command Carter in place, the Corps now had three brigade equivalents securing the frontier. BG Tilelli's 1 CD defended with two brigades extending from a road junction just east of the Wadi al-Batin to its boundary with the 1 ID some fifty kilometers west. COL Randolph W. House's 2nd Brigade defended the wadi and the road junction in the east. COL House's brigade fielded two tank battalions and one mechanized infantry battalion. COL George Harmeyer's 1st Brigade, also composed of two tank battalions and one mechanized infantry battalion, defended the open terrain to the west.[107]

Combat Command Carter moved in with Gross's TF 3-37 AR on the right, to the east. Gross tied in with Harmeyer's troops. His task force of two mechanized infantry company teams and two tank company teams screened along thirty kilometers. Wilson's two ground cavalry troops extended the screen another thirty kilometers west. Wilson's cavalry was organized and trained to do security missions, including screens. For Gross's task force, a security mission was a secondary mission within its capacity, but one not routinely practiced. Before ordering him to go, Rhame asked Gross point-blank whether he believed he could execute the mission. Gross replied that he could, but would need a little time to get ready; MG Rhame gave him twenty-four hours. Gross demurred, believing he needed more time, and Rhame put it simply: "Get your shit together and get ready to move out."[108] That settled it.

LTC Gross had to organize the screen and communicate the basics to tankers and infantrymen who had not practiced the mission. Screening forces provide early warning, but Rhame wanted more. His order specified that Combat Command Carter would transition to a guard mission if the Iraqis did more than probe. If that happened, then Carter and his troops had to provide the Division "with early warning, reaction time and maneuver space."[109] In short, Rhame expected Combat Command Carter to defeat anything short of a divisional attack. In that event they had to buy time for help to reach them.

The 26 ID defended the ground opposite Combat Command Carter. On Carter's eastern flank, Tilelli's 1 CD confronted four Iraqi divisions, with the 48 ID defending the ground just east of the 26 ID. Ironically, the respective boundaries of the two Iraqi Divisions aligned nearly exactly with that between Combat Command Carter and the 1 CD. With Combat Command Carter in place, the logistics infrastructure to support the ground offensive could take place in relative safety. Having contact with the enemy would afford the opportunity to further develop information and intelligence on Iraqi defenses. It was equally certain that there would be combat actions. Hamash had orders to probe, and Tilelli orders to feign attacks to portray preparations for an attack up the wadi. Eventually the 1 ID would have to cut gaps in the border berm. With both sides determined to test the other, skirmishes were inevitable. In the process the Americans, at least, would learn a lot. But to their sorrow, they would soon learn some lessons the hard way.

NOTES

1. Kevin M. Woods, *The Mother of All Battles: Saddam Hussein's Strategic Plan for the Persian Gulf War* (Annapolis, MD: US Naval Institute Press, 2008), 174.

2. Conflict Records Research Center (CRRC), *Report on Republican Guard Fighting in Kuwait in 1st Gulf War*, CRRC SHDDWN-D-000-346.

3. Woods, *The Mother of all Battles*, is essential to understanding what the Iraqis perceived; G2, VII Corps, "The 100-Hour Ground War: How the Iraqi Plan Failed," May 4, 1994, is helpful as well. The 513 MI Brigade supporting the 3rd Army published debriefings of captured Iraqi senior officers, colonel and higher, that provide context.

3. CRRC, *Report on Republican Guard Fighting*, 5.

4. Ibid.

5. G2, VII Corps, "The 100-Hour Ground War," 18.

6. MG Hamash gave an interview that was published in *Al-Jumuriya*, an Iraqi newspaper, on January 30, 1994; COL Pesach Malovany of the Israeli Defense Forces provided a précis of the interview. Dispositions taken from a number of sources, including Stephen A. Bourque, *Jayhawk: The VII Corps in the Persian Gulf War* (Washington, DC: Center of Military History, 2002); G2, VII Corps, "The 100-Hour Ground War"; and an undated 1 ID intelligence overlay, published probably in late January or early February 1991, that shows both the 26

ID front-line trace and the 48 ID front-line trace, although the estimate incorrectly identified the 48 ID as the 25 ID.

7. Bourque, *Jayhawk*, map 13, 190–91; G2, 1 ID, sketches, compiled from various sources. Iraqi soldiers from the 110th Brigade captured by the TF 3-37 AR and debriefed on February 11, 1991, provided confirmation of unit identifications.

8. G2, VII Corps, "The 100-Hour Ground War," 27–29. Desertion and bombing reduced the strength of committed units. The actual strength of the Iraqi 26 ID may never be known accurately.

9. The author has corresponded throughout this effort with an Iraqi major general who retired shortly before Desert Shield but who asked that his name not be cited. He believes that many of the front-line units had not been fully reconstituted following the war with Iran and that the quality of these units—in particular, the infantry units—was not very good.

10. Woods, *The Mother of All Battles*, 180; regarding the alert, see 176.

11. Ibid., 180.

12. US Department of the Army, *Division Operations*, FM 71-100 (Washington, DC: US Department of the Army, 1990), 4-15. Since the publication of the Active Defense doctrine in 1976, the Army had become one that read field manuals and used doctrinal terms.

13. US Department of the Army, *Division Operations*, 4-10.

14. Ibid., 4-13.

15. Ibid., 4-27.

16. LTG (Ret.) Thomas G. Rhame, telephone interview with the author, December 16, 2014. Rhame read journal entries to the author in a series of telephone interviews.

17. Ibid.

18. Ibid. See also "Big Red One Operations" (briefing, n.d.)

19. Rhame interview, December 16, 2014. See also Tom Clancy with General Fred Franks Jr., *Into the Storm: A Study in Command* (New York: Berkley, 2004), 287, which doesn't mention the January 1 session but focuses instead on the session facilitated by the Battle Command Training Program at Hafir al-Batin, January 6–8, 1991; Bourque, *Jayhawk*, 189–99; and Brigadier General Robert H. Scales Jr., *Certain Victory: United States Army in the Gulf War* (Washington, DC: Office of the Chief of Staff of United States Army, 1993), 149.

20. US Department of the Army, *Division Operations*, 6-14. Regarding river crossing doctrine, see 6-12–6-15. The 1 ID and all NATO units routinely practiced river crossings.

21. Rhame interview, December 16, 2014.

22. Ibid.

23. Ibid.

24. Clancy, *Into the Storm*, 287. King Khalid Military City is a Saudi base south of Hafir al-Batin.

25. Clancy, *Into the Storm*, 287–89. On January 8, the 3rd Army assigned the 2nd Brigade, the 101st ABN and the 1 CD to VII Corps to defend the northern Tapline Road.

26. Clancy, *Into the Storm*, 287–88.

27. Regarding casualty estimates, see Bourque, *Jayhawk*, 184–85. Pundits including William S. "Bill" Lind and Edward Luttwak consistently offered pessimistic estimates about the outcome, but so did the Army.

28. Richard Jupa and James Dunnigan, "The Republican Guards: Loyal Aggressive, Able," *Army*, March 1991, 61. With selective memory, postwar critics abounded who found that the Army, in particular, failed. COL Richard M. Swain, "Reflections on the Revisionist Critique: Ground Operations in the Gulf War," *Army*, August 1966, 25–31, is a well-executed riposte.

29. General H. Norman Schwarzkopf with Peter Petre, *It Doesn't Take a Hero: The Autobiography* (New York: Bantam, 1992), 356.

30. LTG (Ret.) Thomas G. Rhame, telephone interview with the author, December 19, 2014. See also Headquarters, 1st Infantry Division (Mechanized), "Operation Desert Shield and Desert Storm First Look Chronology of Events," March 14, 1991. COL (Ret.) Terry W. Bullington, "The First Infantry Division in Desert Shield/Desert Storm: Notes by Terry Bullington," undated letter to the author, received June 16, 2014.

31. MAJ Donald A. Osterberg, personal journal, notebook 4a. See also Bourque, *Jayhawk*, map 12, and 175.

32. Regarding World War II structure, see John B. Wilson, *Maneuver and Firepower: The Evolution of Divisions and Separate Brigades* (Washington, DC: Center of Military History, 1998), chap. 7, esp. 185 and 186, chart 20. See also Simon Forty, *American Armor: 1939–45 Portfolio* (Harrisburg, PA: Stackpole 1981).

33. LTG Robert Wilson, e-mail to the author, January 3, 2016. Each of the divisions had an AH-64 attack helicopter battalion. The 1-1 AVN fielded eighteen AH-64 Apache attack helicopters, thirteen OH-58 scout helicopters, and three UH-60 Black Hawk utility helicopters. The 4-1 AVN general support aviation battalion assigned to the 1 ID fielded six UH-1 utility helicopters, six OH-58 D scout helicopters, three EH-60 intelligence collectors, and fifteen UH-60 Black Hawk utility helicopters. COL James L. Mowery, e-mail to the author, January 3, 2016.

34. The author developed the numbers shown for GEN Frederick M. Franks Jr. during a tour as the chief of the command-planning group at US Training and Doctrine Command (TRADOC), Fort Monroe, VA. The numbers for the UK 1 AD come from official sources and conversations with COL Charles

Rogers, the British liaison officer to TRADOC, who commanded a mechanized infantry battalion in the UK 1 AD.

35. See COL Wilson R. Rutherford III and Major William L. Brame, "Brute Force Logistics," *Military Review*, March 1993, 61–69. See also LTC Peter S. Kindsvatter, "VII Corps in the Gulf War: Deployment and Preparation for Desert Storm," *Military Review*, January 1992, 2–16.

36. Osterberg, personal journal, notebook 4a, January 6, 1991.

37. Rhame interview, December 19, 2014; quoting from Rhame's personal journal, January 6, 1991.

38. COL Michael L. Dodson, personal journal, January 6, 1991.

39. Rhame interview, December 19, 2014.

40. Ibid.

41. Clancy, *Into the Storm*, 288.

42. Ibid. Osterberg took few notes that day. His notes focused on what 1 ID planners had to do, but he wrote down language that Franks used.

43. Dodson, personal journal, January 7, 1991.

44. Ibid., 288.

45. Osterberg, personal journal, notebook 4a, January 8, 1991.

46. Regarding positions of the Tawakalna, see G2, VII Corps, "The 100-Hour Ground War," 110–11; there are also maps that show positions. See also Bourque, *Jayhawk*, map 20, which shows the Tawakalna positions; and Clancy, *Into the Storm*, 287–90.

47. G2, VII Corps, "The 100-Hour Ground War," 110–11. See also Clancy, *Into the Storm*, 287–90.

48. Rhame interview, December 19, 2014, quoting from Rhame's personal journal, January 8, 1991.

49. Ibid. D is the first day of operations; thus, "D+4" is the fifth day.

50. Ibid. The author is unaware of anyone in the Division who accepted the VII Corps estimate.

51. Rhame interview, December 19, 2014, quoting from Rhame's personal journal, January 8, 1991.

52. Ibid.

53. COL (Ret.) Terry Bullington, telephone interview with the author, January 2, 2015.

54. Rhame interview, December 19, 2014, quoting from Rhame's personal journal, January 8, 1991.

55. Ibid.

56. Ibid.

57. Ibid.

58. Ibid. Rhame's journal entry misidentified the 31 ID as the 36 ID. In any case, the 31 ID was a front-line division of the Iraqi VII Corps and occupied fixed positions about thirty kilometers east of the intended breach site. The

designation of the Iraqi 12 AD as a tactical reserve of the VII Corps is mistaken. The 52 AD was actually the division located north of the 31 ID. The 52 AD, formed in December, did move south to exactly where Stewart estimated it had; see Bourque, *Jayhawk*, 355. The Iraqis almost certainly knew of the arrival of the VII Corps.

59. Rhame interview, December 19, 2014, quoting from Rhame's personal journal, January 8, 1991; Bullington interview.

60. Bullington interview.

61. Ibid. This story came up in nearly every interview with Bullington.

62. BG (P) John F. Stewart Jr., "Operation Desert Storm: The Military Intelligence Story, A View from G2 3d US Army," unpublished manuscript, April 1991, 5.

63. GEN Frederick M. Franks Jr., "VII Corps in Desert Storm," presentation to the School of Advanced Military Studies, Fort Leavenworth, KS, n.d.

64. Ibid.

65. Extracts of Scorpion Danger, untitled 1 ID Desert Storm, briefing, n.d. Although the plan for Operation Scorpion Danger has been declassified, it has not been officially released. The author has a copy of the plan, but it is missing the applicable pages; thus the need to cite this briefing.

66. CPT Jim Stockmoe, ed., *1st Brigade, 1st Infantry Division: Desert Shield/Storm History* (Fort Riley, KS: 1st Brigade, 1st Infantry Division, 1991), 339. This plan was superseded on January 25 with the order Desert Storm 4, putting the plan in effect as an order. Desert Storm 4 updated instructions as well. See also 2-34 AR, Order DS-4-91, January 26, 1991.

67. Dodson, personal journal, January 7, 1991.

68. LTC (Ret.), James D. Dowdy, interview with the author, Fort Leavenworth, KS, December 9, 2014. LTC Dowdy served as logistics officer in the 2-34 AR.

69. Headquarters, 1 ID (M) DISCOM, "Desert Shield/Desert Storm Support Operations," January 15, 1992, 3. Bearing in mind that the 1 ID ate catered meals on the way into the theater and on the way out, the scale of the Division Support Command effort is remarkable.

70. LTC (Ret.) Matt Green, e-mail to the author, December 23, 2014.

71. Dowdy interview.

72. The author found them so unreliable that he used a compass and odometer. The Air Force tactical control parties did have accurate GPS devices. The 1 ID used the Magellan 1000M GPS receiver.

73. CPT Eugene J. Malik, telephone interview with the author, September 22, 2014.

74. SFC (Ret.) Michael G. Schulte, telephone interview with the author, November 5, 2014. Master gunners were specially trained soldiers, expert in the physics and mechanics of their particular weapons system.

75. Schulte interview. Some tanks did need to be zeroed.

76. COL (Ret.) G. Patrick Ritter, telephone interview with the author, August 4, 2014.

77. COL James Mowery, personal journal, 37, 45. The process for calibrating the cannon on helicopters is similar to that for tank. The 1-1 AVN had some trouble with Hellfire missiles based on a technical error.

78. LTC Edwin L. Buffington, Commander 101st Forward Support Battalion, 1st Infantry Division, interview by LTC William H. Taylor, Carlisle Barracks, PA, December 13, 1991, DSIT-MHI-003.

79. First Lieutenant Jay C. Mumford, "Rangers in Iraq: Task Force Ranger, 2nd Battalion, 16th Infantry in the Persian Gulf War, 10 November 1990 to 12 May 1991," unpublished manuscript, August 31, 1991, 20.

80. Ibid.

81. LTC David W. Marlin, Commander, 4th Battalion, 37th Armor, 2nd Brigade, 1st Infantry Division, interview by COL Terry L. Nienhouse, Carlisle Barracks, PA, November 8, 1991, DSIT-MHI-026; LTC John R. Gingrich, Commander, 4th Battalion, 5th Field Artillery, 1st Infantry Division, interview by COL Terry L. Nienhouse, Carlisle Barracks, PA, November 18, 1991. DSIT-MHI-013; Headquarters, 2nd Battalion, 34th Armor, "Operation Desert Storm AAR," March 8, 1991, 13.

82. CW4 (Ret.) James D. Logan, telephone interview with the author, August 3, 2014.

83. Headquarters, 1 ID (M) DISCOM, "Desert Shield/Desert Storm Support Operations," January 15, 1992, 6, Q-1.

84. Ibid., I-5.

85. Regarding task organization, see 1 ID Operations, briefing, n.d. The 3rd Brigade, 2nd AD had D Company, 17 EN in direct support. The Corps further augmented the 1 ID with the 176th Engineer Group, which brought with it two combat engineer battalions heavy; these were construction battalions, and played no role during the breach. Terrain analysis engineer detachments also supported the Division. See also 1st Engineer Battalion, "Desert Storm: January 17, 1991–April 11, 1991," unit journal, n.d.

86. The ACE and MCLC proved effective, although the MCLC had a number of misfires. The chief complaint about the ACE is that it had a single crewman and no radio. See Thomas Houlahan, *Gulf War: The Complete History* (New London, NH: Schrenker Military, 1991), 147–50, 276–79. See also Vernon Lowrey, "Initial Observations by Engineers in the Gulf War," *Engineer*, October 1991, 42–48.

87. Author's personal journal; MG (Ret.) Lon E. Maggart, "Eye of the Storm (Duty First)," unpublished manuscript, 1992–97, 75.

88. 2-34 AR, "Mine Plow Exercise: Lessons Learned," January 18, 1991. This mimeographed paper included sketches of the various options considered,

concluding that the "double lane" option worked best. The 2nd Brigade sketch may be found in Headquarters, 2nd Brigade, 1 ID (M), 2nd BDE Opord 3-91, appendix 2 to annex F.

89. COL (Ret.) Thomas Connors, BG (Ret.) David Gross, and MG (Ret.) Paul Izzo, oral history group interview by Andrew Woods, McCormick Research Center, First Division Museum at Cantigny, Wheaton IL, January 22–23, 2011.

90. 2-34 AR, "Mine Plow Exercise"; 3-37 AR, sketch, (n.d.). A variation of the 3-37 AR method can be found in Major James K. Morningstar, "Points of Attack: Lessons from the Breach," *Armor*, January–February 1998, 10.

91. CPT James M. Goff Jr., telephone interview with the author, September 28, 2014.

92. LTC (Ret.) James L. Enicks, telephone interview with the author, December 17, 2014.

93. See Stephan A. Bourque and John W. Burdan III, *The Road to Safwan: The 1st Squadron, 4th Cavalry in the 1991 Persian Gulf War* (Denton: University of North Texas Press, 2007), chap. 6.

94. Dodson, personal journal.

95. Ibid.

96. 1st Infantry Division (Mechanized), Fragmentary Order (FRAGO) 52-91, "Forward Security," January 21, 1991.

97. VII Corps, Fragmentary Order 34-91, "Defense of Wadi al-Batin," January 10, 1991, includes this estimate.

98. Bourque, *Jayhawk*, 141; see also 122–28. Some of the confusion and lack of confidence resulted from poor coordination on the part of the 3rd Army and CENTCOM over where the Arab units were and just what they intended. The Syrians exacerbated this problem by training weapons on Americans when they saw them; they even detained COL Shadley for a short while.

99. See Bourque, *Jayhawk*, 86–99, on building combat power in the corps assembly area.

100. Mowery, personal journal, 57.

101. Ibid. See also Bourque and Burdan, *The Road to Safwan*, 77–78.

102. ZSU stands for Zenitnaya Samokhodnaya Ustanovka, which translates as "antiaircraft self-propelled mount."

103. CPT Stephen M. Schiller, "Fratricide in Operation Desert Storm," unpublished manuscript, Infantry School, Fort Benning, GA, June 25, 1993; Mowery, personal journal, 57–58. See also Bourque and Burdan, *The Road to Safwan*, 77–78.

104. BG William G. Carter III, telephone interview with author December 5, 2013; BG William G. Carter III, telephone interview with the author, November 16, 2014. Carter had been a key player in GEN William E. DePuy's doctrine work as a charter member of the Boat House Gang that did much of the writing of the Active Defense operations manual. See also FRAGO 52-91, 1.

105. This is taken from the mission statement in FRAGO 52-91, 1.

106. Ibid. Phase Line Cherry lay south of the border berm. Combat Command Carter eventually operated north of Phase Line Cherry, but short of the border berm.

107. Bourque, *Jayhawk*, 141–48. Bourque has done a good job laying out the complex movements of coalition forces in January–February 1991.

108. Connors, Gross, and Izzo interview.

109. Ibid.

CHAPTER SEVEN

CUE THE CURTAIN

First Battles and Battlefield Preparation

Patience my ass, I want to kill something.

—Major General Thomas G. Rhame

The more days I spend in the desert, the more I am amazed at the harshness of the environment.

—First Lieutenant Jeffrey K. Sanson

Combat command carter's arrival on the Saudi-Iraq border effectively shifted combat operations from extemporaneous efforts to screen Corps and Division logistics bases, to defending the border, to permitting phase 2 operations. During this second phase of operations the VII Corps divisions would move to their final assembly areas and prepare to attack. The 1st Infantry Division (1 ID) and 1st Cavalry Division (1 CD) would provide security for artillery raids designed to degrade and destroy the Iraqi VII Corps artillery. The 1 CD would conduct demonstrations and feints to convince the Iraqis what they were already inclined to believe—that coalition forces would mount a major attack along the Wadi al-Batin. This phase of operations would end when the ground offensive began. Both LTG Frederick M. Franks Jr. and MG Thomas G. Rhame's commanders' reports suggest an eagerness to get on with it. Even without the benefit of reading what senior commanders had to say, the sense of irresistible momentum toward the attack was widespread.

As planned, Rhame rotated units through the defense mission, thereby enabling them to learn by doing and assuring adequate time to complete preparations for the attack. First contact with the Iraqis illustrated the superiority of American units, but revealed their inexperience as well. Units made mistakes that in one instance resulted in Americans killed and wounded. Mistakes generally stemmed from inexperience, but personalities and technical problems were also factors.

During phase 2 the Division completed battlefield preparations for the attack. These preparations included refining intelligence based on gaining tactical information in contact with the enemy and information provided by the VII Corps. With improved intelligence the Division and Corps developed sufficiently accurate targeting data to enable effective artillery raids and improved results from coalition air attacks. Better intelligence enabled refined tactical planning for the attack to breach the enemy defenses. Finally, stockpiling ammunition and other necessary supplies to sustain the attack occurred during phase 2.

The Iraqi VII Corps situation deteriorated during the first half of February. At the outset, the coalition air campaign focused on strategic targets; later the airmen struck operational reserves such as the Republican Guard. Finally, the campaign broadened to include front-line units. Air attacks further eroded the condition of MG Ahmad Hamash's units, already poorly equipped and short of supplies. One of the division logisticians in Hamash's corps told his American captors that by the time he was captured on February 27, he had only ten operational supply trucks left from a fleet of eighty.[1] The air campaign was a resounding success in weakening the already fragile front-line divisions; once it had begun, the Iraqi high command ordered Hamash to probe south of the Saudi Border to provoke a response. The warnings of attacks down the Wadi al-Batin issued by the US VII Corps in January 1991 may have stemmed from these probes. But other than rattling the nerves of arriving US VII Corps units, the Iraqi probes achieved little. After the war Hamash claimed his corps maneuvered to distract the coalition from detecting the attack at Al Khafji. There is little evidence that his units maneuvered far enough south to give the impression of an attack in the west. Iraqi VII Corps units continued to patrol, but with little perceptible result.

Developing Intelligence: February 1–17, 1991

By the end of January, Franks's Corps was in position to complete preparation for the ground offensive. Rhame confided in his journal that the Division knew "all we need to know to execute a successful breach."[2] Yet at the same time he felt that intelligence remained "sketchy." However contradictory this sounds, it made sense. Thanks to several sets of imagery, the Division knew the positions of the Iraq front-line defenses in depth but still needed to refine that information to permit precise targeting and maneuver. Rhame expected Combat Command Carter and later Task Force Iron to acquire tactical information about the enemy.[3]

Despite several warnings and the unsettling attack on Al Khafji, neither Combat Command Carter nor TF Iron believed an Iraqi preemptive attack likely. Both believed that if the Iraqis mounted an attack, it would most likely

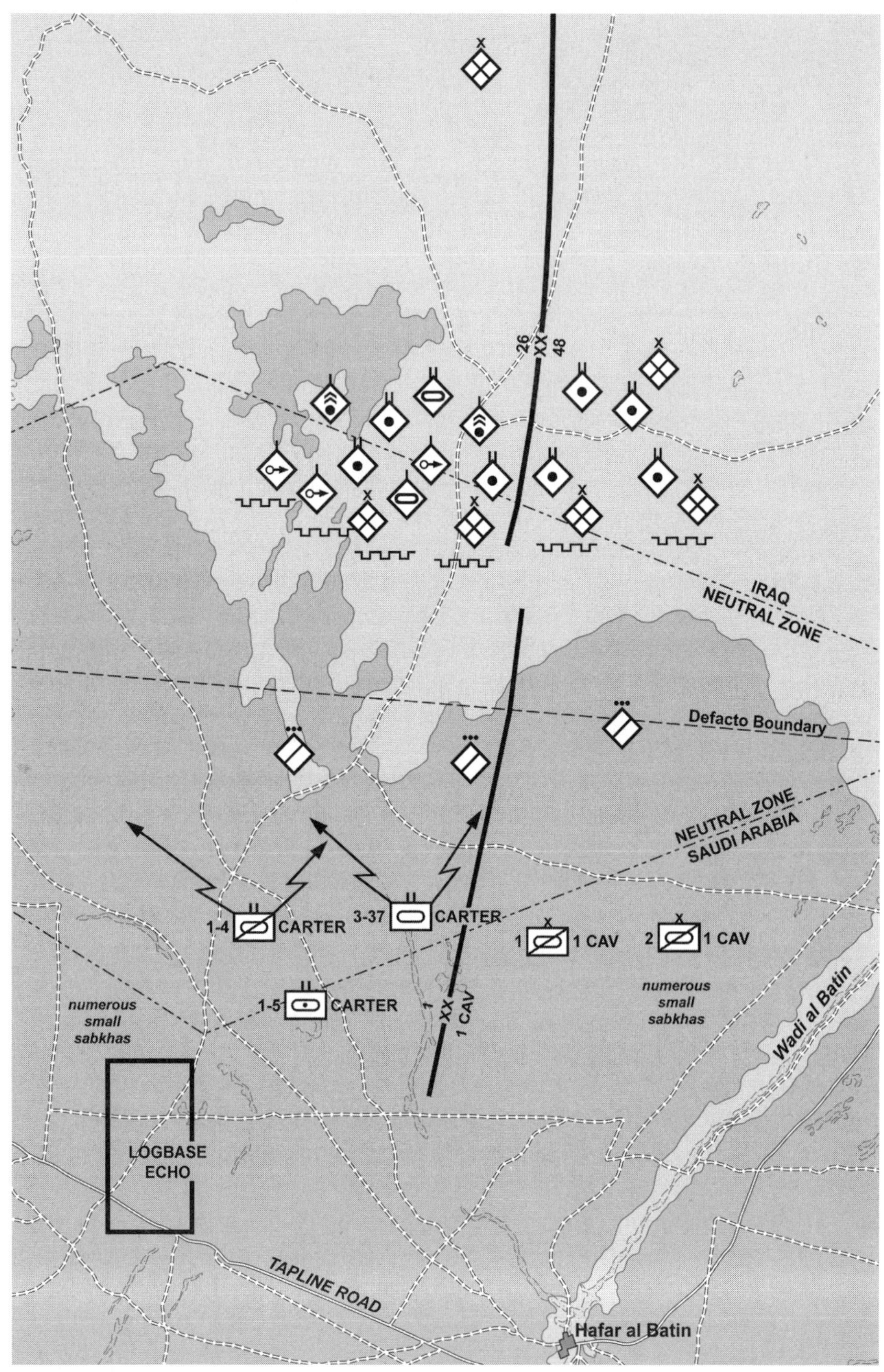

MAP 4. Positions of Combat Command Carter, February 3–15, 1991. Recreated from Map 10, Stephen A. Bourque, *Jayhawk! The VII Corps in the Persian Gulf War.*

come down the Wadi al-Batin rather than against Combat Command Carter. And both were confident—with good reason—of ample warning. Airborne radar provided the means to detect Iraqi movement. The Joint Surveillance Targeting Acquisition System (JSTARS) sometimes generated false alarms, but it proved generally effective.[4] Furthermore, Rhame and BG William G. Carter III had formed an impression of the opposition. Carter knew his ad hoc brigade faced reserve infantry divisions, for which he had low regard. As he remembers, these "were not front-line [first-rate] divisions."[5] From this time until the ground attack, the Division would defend the frontier forward of its final assembly areas. MG Rhame remained committed to rotating the brigades through the security mission so that they might gain experience in low-risk combat operations, even while they made their final preparations.

The list of things that still needed to be done remained daunting, but what seemed a distant goal in early January was now within reach. Intelligence officers needed to develop targeting data and turn raw data into the kind of intelligence that battalions and companies could use. The assault battalions needed enemy intelligence down to the platoon level, including accurate information on obstacles and defensive minefields. The Division wanted to fire a program of artillery raids to attack enemy artillery and other targets of specific interest such as air defense and armor. Intelligence preparation included developing accurate locations to these targets.

Refining the intelligence picture was near the top of the list of things to do, but it proved difficult. MG Rhame's contradictory assessment about knowing enough to execute the breach, yet believing intelligence was sketchy, accurately described the problem. By the end of January the 1 ID had enough imagery to know the design of the enemy's defenses and could see their entrenchments. But the imagery had not undergone geolocation and mensuration. Simply put, pictures do not reveal locations. Geolocation has little to do with the natural world; it is an application of imagery to maps. Mensuration is measuring the objects in images; this lets one determine, for example, the length of trenches. Moreover, images, however compelling, do not communicate intentions, morale, or capability, and minefields and wire obstacles usually cannot be seen. Contact with the enemy, capturing a few of them, or physical reconnaissance, was central to learning more.

The final intelligence products had to be distributed at the platoon and company levels, a task that proved far more difficult than developing the intelligence in the first place. Neither the VII Corps nor the 1st Division had adequate means to reproduce and distribute intelligence. Complicating matters, the Corps had little access to national intelligence systems, because the priority remained on finding Scud launchers and strategic targets. Worse still, even when information became available, there were no maps on which to post it. BG Carter describes the map problem succinctly: "We didn't have diddley."[6] BG

Carter concluded, "We had a terrain appreciation that was a hundred percent wrong based on national geographic maps."[7] First Lieutenant Jeffrey K. Sanson had no maps at all; as a tank platoon leader, he wondered how "they expect[ed] me to do my job without the tools necessary to the trade."[8] Soldiers produced jury-rigged alternatives—for example, lining blank sheets of paper with grid marks consistent with those on a map. Most Army tactical maps use grid coordinates rather than longitude and latitude to find location. These grids included an x-axis, or easting, and a y-axis, or northing. Eastings, though north-south lines, are measured from west to east, and northings are west-east lines measured south to north. These grid sheets soldiers developed allowed them to plot known locations without reference to terrain.[9]

The logistics of distributing maps exacerbated the matter. Enough maps were available to enable battalions and brigades to plan, but there were not enough for execution. Units worked around the problem, effecting a variety of solutions. CPT Jim Stockmoe, the 1st Brigade intelligence officer, had anticipated the problem; shortly after the alert in November, he had the print plant at Fort Riley, Kansas, make a thousand copies of the 1:250,000-scale maps. That decision saved a great deal of frustration and provided a stopgap. Although maps are a supply rather than an intelligence function, CPT Stockmoe took on the map problem further. He and one of his sergeants reasoned that the supply system helps those who help themselves; accordingly, they went to the Division Support Area and sifted through two stake-and-platform truckloads loaded with maps "to obtain those that we felt were needed to conduct future operations."[10] Stockmoe did not solve the problem entirely, but he helped to alleviate it. The 1st Brigade fought part of the ground offensive with the black-and-white 1:250,000-scale maps printed at Fort Riley.

Seeing the terrain is part of intelligence preparation of the battlefield. Seeing the ground and understanding the lay of the land is essential to the process of estimating how an enemy might defend it. All maps are essential, but three-dimensional maps are even better, as they make it easier to see the lay of the land. No three-dimensional maps were available, so SGT David "Dusty" Rhodes built a highly detailed three-dimensional terrain board to 1:50,000 scale. He did so by laminating sheets of cardboard together and cutting them along map contour lines that showed elevation. This required some thoughtful mathematics to increase the size of the model without sacrificing accuracy. The result impressed those who used Rhodes's product. Analysts and commanders called it the Holy Grail because they had long searched for some means of visualizing the terrain. SGT Rhodes's map helped everyone visualize the terrain and facilitated planning the assault. The other brigades used different approaches, but all developed some means to visualize their battle space.

Before arriving in the theater, the intelligence officers assumed the Iraqis would develop the triangular defensive positions like those they had built to defend the Al-Faw Peninsula during the Iran-Iraq War. By early December 1990 it was clear the Iraqis had opted for a static linear defense supported by mobile reserves in each corps, with theater-level reserves positioned in depth. To develop accurate targeting and planning information, the Corps and Division used multiple sources. These ranged from satellite imagery to signals intelligence. Even at the national level, intelligence was problematic. The Corps obtained satellite imagery by sending two imagery analysts back to the United States to get it. Two VII Corps analysts traveled via Frankfurt, Germany, to the Intelligence Threat Analysis Center near Washington, DC, where they picked up copies of the images the Corps needed and returned carrying the digital files, which were too large to be sent by the electronic means available to the VII Corps in 1991.[11]

The Corps' 207th Military Intelligence Brigade (207 MI) had organic means to collect images, signals, and electronic intelligence. These included airborne platforms, ground-based platforms, and long-range surveillance units. Together the 207 MI and the VII Corps intelligence section had a robust analytic capability. Coupled with the images brought back from Washington, the Corps, supported by the 207 MI, had developed a good picture of how the Iraqis had arrayed their defenses.

Intelligence analysis is a process of human interaction, and comparing notes between the echelons worked best. In this instance LTC Terry Ford, the Division's intelligence officer, led the effort at the top. CW2 Phyllis Fitzgerald, Ford's order of battle technician, and her analysts attempted to identify enemy units and organization from available raw data. Others on the intelligence team estimated how the Iraqis proposed to fight. At the 1st Brigade, CPT Jim Stockmoe led a small intelligence cell, including CPT Dave Shade, 1LT Pat Filbert, and the formidable "Dusty" Rhodes. Finally, CPT Ken McCurry led the intelligence section of Task Force Second Battalion, Thirty-Fourth Armor (TF 2-34 AR), which included one other officer, three noncommissioned officers, and a single enlisted soldier.[12]

In early February, Fitzgerald and her analysts could not yet identify enemy units with absolute confidence, but they were getting close. But even when they did arrive at answers on unit identity or, more important, information such as precise locations, they had trouble disseminating what they knew. Passing information digitally had not come of age in 1991; in the VII Corps units, most information moved on paper. Getting intelligence and graphic portrayals of information to units depended on copying acetate overlays using a commercial blueprint reproduction system. These machines worked wonderfully in an architect's office on the fifteenth floor of a high-rise office building in Houston, but they did not always flourish in the desert. Once these blueprint copies were made and distributed, they too had to be copied. To get the results into the hands of the troops, intermediate headquarters reversed the process:

they copied the blueprints by hand on to acetate using methods that medieval monks had pioneered. Reproducing analysis could be done on copy machines, dot-matrix printers, or alcohol-based mimeograph systems such as those used by schoolteachers at the time. CPT Marv Meek's experience as assistant operations officer at the battalion level was typical: once the 1-34 AR planning staff had completed their operations plan for the breach, Meek spent two days reproducing by hand the required acetate overlays.[13] Copies then had to be distributed by couriers via vehicles or helicopters.

Developing Intelligence in Contact

The 1st Battalion, 4th Cavalry (1-4 CAV) obtained better results. Before Combat Command Carter arrived on station, the cavalry captured—or, more accurately, accepted the surrender of—four Iraqi soldiers. Rhame recorded their story in his journal, writing that they were deserters, or "line crossers," led by a corporal who had earlier served in the war with Iran. The corporal and his privates walked south until they encountered B Troop, which fired warning shots; then the four surrendered. CPT Mike Bills's troopers discovered that the Iraqis had hastily buried grenades they were carrying; from this they concluded that the four were patrolling rather than deserting. Rhame did not find that explanation convincing; the three privates, all age fifteen or sixteen were, in Rhame's opinion, "too young to be soldiers."[14] Of greater interest was that the prisoners reported they expected to encounter Syrians or Egyptians. All four described the coalition bombing as very effective. They further claimed that forty of the eighty men in their company had deserted.[15] BG Carter's assessment that the enemy opposite the 1 ID was not the first team seemed borne out.

In accordance with their orders, Iraqi VII Corps units did patrol, but they never came deep enough to grapple with Carter's troops. Despite orders to go far enough south to provoke a response, they did not do so. It appears that neither Hamash nor his subordinate commanders were assured these patrols would do as ordered. At the same time, LTC Bob Wilson and units that joined the defense later were "told not to do aggressive recon."[16] With the Americans operating to preserve security and avoid revealing their presence, and the Iraqis unwilling or unable to do as ordered, few contacts resulted, though alarms and reports of activity in the wadi continued. On February 1 the US VII Corps reported that the Egyptian Corps had intercepted an Iraqi radio conversation regarding a planned attack into the Wadi al-Batin. Allegedly, the Tawakalna Mechanized Division of the Republican Guard Forces Command would make the attack.[17] But the attack never materialized.

With a single notable exception, the Iraqis stayed on their side of the border berm. In the early morning hours of February 1, two days before Rhame ordered the formation of Combat Command Carter, the Iraqis attacked a small Saudi border post. Located about fifteen kilometers north of the westernmost scout team of the Quarter Horse (1-4 CAV), it sat right on the border near a small collection of tin-roofed shacks called As Samwah. Here Bedouins occasionally gathered to receive grain for their sheep and other supplies from the Saudi government. There had been no coordination or information about the border guards, so the cavalry was unaware of the little fort or that there were about fifty Saudi border guards assigned there. When the Iraqis attacked, the Saudis ran south and stumbled into A Troop's positions at about 3:15 a.m. CPT Ken Pope's troopers fired warning shots at the ragtag convoy of light trucks, which immediately stopped. The Saudis told the cavalry that Iraqi soldiers had driven them from their post, but Pope didn't take them at their word. His troopers disarmed and detained the intruders, only to learn the next morning they were indeed Saudi border troops. They were released with apologies.[18] CPT Pope's soldiers had behaved with restraint that belied their inexperience. They could have fired on the unidentified trucks, but they had thought better of it.

On February 4 Rhame wrote, with some satisfaction, that the Quarter Horse destroyed an Iraqi scout car the previous night. But when the sun came up, the scout car proved to be an abandoned bulldozer with bright paint that an airborne scout weapons team had mistaken while looking at it through night-vision goggles. Part of the bulldozer's roll cage had been bent in such a way as to look like a gun: what the crew thought they were seeing is what they expected to see.[19] This would happen again and again. Night-vision devices are not foolproof, and low-resolution thermal images can at times look like whatever a soldier expects to see.

The revelation that the cavalry had attacked a derelict bulldozer produced nervous laughter, because everyone understood that what happened to the cavalry could happen to them. Seeing what soldiers thought made sense and/or what they expected to see proved problematic throughout the 1 ID's operations in the Gulf.

The next night, LTC Dave Gross's TF 3-37 AR made its first contact when ground surveillance radar reported a moving column of vehicles. Originally estimated to be as many as forty vehicles, the contact turned out to be, in Gross's words, a "camel herd, nationality unknown."[20] Ground surveillance radar detects movement very well, but it is not very good at target identification. Because Gross understood that, he did not immediately order the column to be taken under fire. Instead he readied his task force for a fight against what looked like a large enemy formation and maneuvered a tank platoon in position to make positive identification. The tankers correctly identified the moving target indicators seen on radar as camels wandering across the task force front.[21] LTC Gross showed patience and maturity; the task force was not being fired at, so he developed the situation and learned there was no threat.

Not everyone in Operation Desert Storm did as Gross did. The situation on the border required commanders to think, prepare their forces, and finally, if necessary, to shoot. All of this meant being patient during potentially dangerous encounters. This went against the grain of training, which tended to emphasize deciding quickly and firing first. Exercises at the Army's National Training Center training had tempered the emphasis on speed, but that bias had not disappeared.

February 5 proved busy throughout the VII Corps. The most interesting development occurred east of Combat Command Carter. Near the Wadi al-Batin, an Iraqi observation post fired on a 1 CD Cobra attack helicopter. BG John Tilelli's division responded with a carefully choreographed combined arms attack. The artillery began by destroying the observation post with a laser-guided artillery round. Next, a Cobra gunship destroyed a truck parked near the outpost, to prevent any survivors using it to flee. Finally, a battery of artillery completed destruction of the observation post and nearby buildings. This violent response fit nicely with Tilelli's mission to portray preparation for an attack from the Wadi al-Batin. The cavalry division patrolled aggressively and mounted raids on Iraqi positions right up until the ground offensive began.[22] Iraqis never changed their estimate that the coalition would make a supporting attack up the Wadi al-Batin.

Although operating under constraints designed to prevent active contact, Combat Command Carter continued to take prisoners. On February 6 Wilson took a prisoner personally. During the early morning hours, one of A Troop's scout teams and ground surveillance radar detected activity near the abandoned village of As Samwah, just south of the Saudi border post. Wilson chose to investigate personally. At sunup he flew with an airborne scout weapons team in one of the squadron's OH-58 scout helicopters. Upon arrival over the village neither Wilson, his pilot, nor the crew of the accompanying Cobra gunship saw anything. Wilson ordered the Cobra to recon by fire (firing a few rounds hoping to cause a response). After the gunship fired its recon rounds, an Iraqi soldier appeared, waving his arms. Wilson had his pilot land, and the squadron commander disembarked and took the Iraqi soldier prisoner. He bound the man and left him there, and then he and the scout weapons team flew to A Troop, his closest ground unit. Wilson, still airborne, led a scout section of Bradleys back to recover the prisoner and to clear the village.[23] They did so without incident.

Later, A Troop reported seeing renewed activity in As Samwah. Because no vehicles were supposed to be that far forward, Wilson decided to send a UH-1 Huey helicopter with a five-man patrol led by MAJ Bill Wimbish, his executive officer, to investigate. At the last minute, the Headquarters troop commander joined the expedition. The patrol found nothing, but their activity produced a volcanic eruption from the Division commander. Rhame liked Wilson and thought him a first-rate commander, but he was furious that Wilson had just violated his orders on two counts. First of all, the 3rd Army, VII Corps, and he had all ordered tracked vehicles not to venture close enough to the border to be detected. Bringing Bradleys within a kilometer of the border violated both the spirit and letter of these orders. Equally important, Rhame believed he had been clear about the role of battalion commanders.[24] Commanders' roles did not include taking prisoners personally.

Rhame had told his battalion commanders what he expected of them at the caucus he had held back in the States on November 9. Among other things, he had ordered them to fight using their battalions, not their weapons systems. Now one of his best officers had violated that guidance. After barking at Wilson, he made the rounds to remind his battalion commanders just what their job entailed and what it did not. Rhame's message was simple: personal heroics were not part of their job description; they were to fight using their unit as a whole. Each of those officers with whom Rhame met felt certain the commanding general had singled them out personally. Rhame wanted aggressive commanders, but not foolhardy ones. He understood Wilson's motivation, but needed his commanders to remain focused.[25]

Combat Command Carter continued to have adventures that once again proved military theorist Carl von Clausewitz's assertion that in war everything is difficult. On the night of February 7–8 a remotely piloted vehicle overflew Combat Command Carter. Supposedly the VII Corps had no such airborne platforms. Two nights later, the little aircraft returned. Assured by the Corps that no such friendly aircraft were about, Carter asked for weapons release so he could have the unmanned aircraft shot down. What ensued would have embarrassed the Keystone Kops. After what seemed a very long time, during which the little airplane circled overhead, Corps granted permission to fire.[26]

First, the Quarter Horse fired machine guns and missed. Then TF 3-37 AR fired a Stinger shoulder-launched air defense missile and missed. The airplane moved off, but later returned so that TF 3-37 AR could miss yet again. Frustrated, Gross made the unconvincing argument that the duration of time to get weapons release led to the failure to hit the irritating little airplane. Meanwhile, the 207 MI complained to the VII Corps that friendlies were shooting at their remotely piloted vehicle. The Army had, it turned out, deployed an experimental aerial surveillance system with the VII Corps. Despite the Corps' claims to the contrary, the airplane belonged to the same Corps. Clearly, coordination, terrain management, and air defense needed work.[27] It is reasonable to wonder just why the 207 MI appeared to be reconnoitering friendly positions, but whatever the reason, they indulged in the practice several times.

Intelligence Estimates and Rehearsals: February 1–17, 1991

Both the Corps and the Division learned from these embarrassing mistakes. Learning how to operate and coordinate with a large number of units across vast distances and in combat conditions cannot be fully done in simulation or at a training center. That said, overcoming friction and learning how to function at the scale of brigade, division, and corps came comparatively cheaply in the weeks along the Saudi-Iraq border. Combat Command Carter learned not only how to operate but also a lot about the opposition. While the combat command operated under tight restrictions on patrolling that made it difficult, Iraqi patrols and line crossers did provide useful information. Perhaps the best such information on the opposition came from seven Iraqi soldiers captured on February 11 by one of Gross's infantry companies. These seven came south apparently intending to desert. They confirmed information gleaned from other Iraqi soldiers taken by both VII Corps units, reporting coalition bombing effective, morale low, and desertions high. Further, these men provided detailed information on how their unit was organized, the depth and layout of its trench works, and the unit's identity. All seven were assigned to the 110th Brigade, 26 ID. All of them were Kurds, only two of whom spoke Arabic.[28]

The Kurdish conscripts helped confirm other unit designations, including the 434th Brigade, which occupied the line on their left, and the 806th Brigade located to their north. According to them, the 110th Brigade was severely understrength. Companies in the 110th Brigade ranged from as low as a third of assigned strength to just over one half. This and other information helped CW2 Fitzgerald fill in blanks on her order of battle. Meanwhile, armed with updated imagery and prisoner reports like these, CPT Stockmoe, CPT McCurry, and their counterparts in the other brigades had necessary details to refine intelligence preparation.[29]

The information from these seven unfortunates made its way around the Division. Most of what they provided confirmed what the intelligence staff believed. Since early February, the Division had estimated Iraqi morale as low, and the prisoners added credence to that assessment. Mistaken information still made it into intelligence estimates. The 1st Brigade and the rest of the 1 ID vacillated about the identity of their opposite number. The 2nd Brigade published a graphic of enemy positions based on imagery dated January 22. In that graphic, brigade intelligence correctly identified the Iraqi 26 ID, but later the Brigade misidentified the 26 ID as the 48 ID.[30]

Unit identify was of little importance since the Iraqi units across the border from the VII Corps were similarly organized and of uniformly low quality. Because the Iraqis lacked concealment and made almost no use of camouflage, intelligence officers knew the location of enemy positions down to the platoon level. Thanks to captured soldiers, the assault brigades also knew to some degree the enemy's strength, how they were equipped, and what battle damage they had incurred. For example, the Division estimated COL Tony Moreno's 2nd Brigade would attack the Iraqi 434th Infantry Brigade, which defended with nine companies abreast and one in depth. The 434th Brigade had a tank company in reserve with one platoon forward. It may also have had a fourth platoon from the 26 ID's tank battalion. Three batteries of Soviet-made 130-millimeter howitzers positioned well forward provided the artillery support. The brigade also had a single Soviet-made SA9 air defense artillery missile battery.[31]

Based on reports from Gross's prisoners, the Division believed COL Lon E. "Bert" Maggart's 1st Brigade would assault the 110th Brigade. LTC Ford's intelligence analysts estimated that the 110th Brigade fielded nine companies, although it actually had ten; it employed a tank company in reserve with two additional tank platoons positioned forward to support front-line troops. Three batteries of 130-millimeter howitzers and an SA9 air defense battery rounded out the 110th Brigade; the Brigade oriented three of its companies to the southwest and west to avoid offering an open flank. The 806th Brigade, the third of the 26 ID's brigades, was dug in well to the rear and oriented west. Finally, three batteries of howitzers positioned to the rear of the forward brigades provided general support fire.[32]

The intelligence overlays had errors in identification, but they showed enemy positions very accurately. Units planned, rehearsed, and assigned targets using them. The Division could also take satisfaction in knowing its enemy had suffered at the hands of the coalition's air force; it appeared likely that the front-line units had been reduced by as much as half. Finally, the enemy's positions did not seem as formidable as anticipated.[33] Focus in the breach effort shifted to refining intelligence and targeting.

MAJ Don Osterberg and the planners moved on to look beyond the breach toward an eventual attack on the Republican Guard Forces Command. In February, the planners worked on refining three contingency operations plans named Jeremiah I, II, and III.[34] Rhame did not intend for the Division to be left behind licking its wounds at the breach.

In February the focus of rehearsal and training changed. Before then the focus had been at the platoon and company levels; that made sense because platoons and companies could practice assaulting trenches and actions on contact without detailed information. Operations plan Scorpion Danger, published on January 19, had the detail brigades needed to complete their basic plans. In turn, they published their supporting plans by the end of January. Now the focus of rehearsals shifted to battalion and brigade. For example, the 1st Brigade executed a logistics rehearsal on February 1 to examine how it would move its huge logistics train, referred to as the whale, through the breach lanes. Moving the whale was no small matter, so LTC Dan Magee, the executive officer, and LTC Ed Buffington, the support battalion commander, took pains to plan and practice the move on a large outdoor terrain model.[35]

COL Dave Weisman's 3rd Brigade did its first high-level rehearsal as a "table top" exercise looking for flaws in the planned execution sequence.[36] COL

Moreno's 2nd Brigade executed a mounted rehearsal on February 4 with Rhame looking on. The brigade achieved mixed results, but that is the point of rehearsing: it is practice for execution. Mistakes reveal flaws in planning, training, or both. Learning and improved execution resulted from effective rehearsal.[37] The First Infantry's units rehearsed until they got it right.

Preparing Logistically

COL Bob Shadley's Division Support Command had perhaps the most to do. His troops had established four corps artillery resupply points in which to cache artillery and other critical ammunition that needed to be stocked prior to the assault. Located within fifteen kilometers of the border berm, the caches would cut the distance for resupply during the breach operation by more than half. The stockpiles had to be sufficient to sustain the initial assault and enable rapid transition. COL Shadley's troops eventually stocked more than thirty thousand 155-millimeter rounds, ten thousand eight-inch rounds, and one thousand rockets.[38] During the course of the ground offensive, thirteen battalions of tube artillery, three rocket battalions, and two rocket batteries drew ammunition from the caches.

In coordination with the Division staff, Shadley stocked common-use ammunition for the maneuver units in the form of a rolling ammunition transfer point to support each maneuver brigade. He loaded twenty "stake and platform" trailers of high-demand ammunition and divided them among the three forward support battalions. This gave the brigades ready-made resupply.[39]

Every logistics shortfall that the 1 ID experienced during Desert Storm stemmed from two basic problems. The first of these was that the Army had no effective means to track supplies or parts as they moved through the logistics pipeline. COL Shadley and his battalion commanders knew very well the value of in-transit visibility, but lacked the tools to do it. Barcode markers that could be scanned or radio transponders common today simply were not available; the answer was to stock as far forward as possible. Generally, if the Division Support Command did not have whatever it was, finding it was nearly impossible. Presuming that required parts or supplies could be found, hauling them proved equally problematic.

The second problem was the woeful lack of transportation that characterized logistics in Desert Storm. LTC Tom Waterman, who commanded the 701st Main Support Battalion, proved himself a master of understatement when he described the distribution problem as "a transportation challenge right from the get-go."[40]

BG Jerry Rutherford, the assistant division commander whose portfolio included logistics, exemplified what worked: "You go down and get involved."[41] He knew all the players in both the 1 ID, where he had preceded Carter, and in the 2 AD (Forward), which he had commanded. Energetic to the point of hyperactivity, Rutherford appeared wherever and whenever he thought his intervention would help. COL Shadley was experienced and kept his cool, thinking things through and documenting each step. No matter what, he persisted, as did his troops. He understood the challenge of sustaining the Division in an offensive operation; he also knew that the Division would not stop "until we get our feet wet or see an American flag."[42] That is, the attack would continue across northern Kuwait to the Persian Gulf. As February wore on, stocks of critical supplies piled up in the Division Support Area and aboard the rolling stock of the forward support battalions.

Persistence and determination could do nothing, however, to solve the problem of scarce and hard-to-deliver repair parts, including engines, transmissions, and other major assemblies. Soldiers made do while maintenance technicians and mechanics roamed the desert, like Bedouins, in search of parts. The postwar Division Support Command after-action review described the problem in classic desiccated military prose: "Logistics automation problems and inability to provide in-transit visibility coupled with limited transportation at all levels to push repair parts, resulted in very little Class IX [repair parts and major assemblies] reaching the division."[43] The problem reflected a systemic problem in Army logistics: parts arrived in Saudi Arabia and disappeared into a morass of storage sites.

There were a handful of key people who worked to find and move parts. LTC Jim Talley, an old 1 ID hand, provided indispensable support to all of the units in the theater. LTC Talley, well known as a logistics operator, had retired in 1989 from his last assignment as the commander of the Division Material Management Center, but in fall 1990 he was asked to return to active duty. Ultimately he was tasked to manage major assemblies (engines and transmissions) for the 22nd Support Command (22 SPT CMD). In the beginning that included taking as spares the usable engines and transmissions from the M1s the 1st Brigade had turned in. LTC Talley bent to his task with a will.

Talley and handful of other commissioned and noncommissioned officers found major assemblies and worked to get them where they were needed. There were others who became indispensable, including Ernie Dykes, a civilian Army logistician and one-time tank mechanic in the 5th Battalion, 33rd Armor (5-33 AR) at Fort Knox, Kentucky. Dykes seemed to be everywhere at once and could find parts or knew where a part might be. LTC Pat Ritter, commander of the 1-34 AR, had served with Dykes at Fort Knox and believed him to be a hero; his name came up often as a potential source for critically required parts. Dykes and others like him did what they could to solve the nearly intractable problem of parts distribution; they acted with energy and some success to close gaps in the system through sheer hard work and untiring effort. Yet some troops went to war with weapons systems that were not fully operable. Infantrymen, artillerymen, and tankers did what they had to do to get in the fight. Some soldiers went to war with tanks that would move and shoot but had no working radio, yet they made do.[44]

Morale and the Home Front on the Eve of the Ground Attack

Frustration in the desert over food, parts, and continual rain seemed mild compared to frustration over mail—or, rather, the lack of it. Getting mail forward suffered from the same transportation problem that inhibited moving parts and other supplies: there were simply too few trucks or helicopters to haul it. "Any Soldier" mail, which invited Americans to show their support for the troops by addressing a note or letter to Any Soldier, compounded the problem. People at home relished the opportunity to demonstrate their support, but Any Soldier mail overwhelmed the system. Frustration with the lack of mail became as ubiquitous, and every bit as irritating, as the lack of variety in meals. Erratic mail service created problems, both in the desert and at home. In the absence of the ability to communicate, young families tended to imagine the worst. Mail moved slowly both to and from the theater and exacerbated everything from managing finances to coping with loneliness.[45]

A handful of satellite phone sites had been established along Tapline Road, but the trip to the phones took an hour each way. On arrival, troops waited in line, often for more than hour. When they finally got to a phone, they had a five-minute limit. One commander avoided going to the phone until his troops had a chance to make a call; when he finally called home, he took a tongue lashing from his wife, who had no need to hear of his undying love but did need to put several rumors to rest. Several chagrined commanders had similar experiences. From then on, they tried to get the word back one way or another.[46]

Family support groups helped immensely. They attempted to stem the tide of rumor by supplying facts to nervous parents, spouses, children, and significant others. Family support groups existed to educate young spouses and family members on just how to use the services available and to help them learn to get along on their own. Providing and managing information was perhaps their most important role. Nearly every unit published newsletters to provide information ranging from how to use government services to unit activity in the desert. Some units published newsletters prior to the alert, but did so without government support for reproduction and mailing. During Desert Storm, the Army paid for reproduction and mailing of newsletters to facilitate separating fact from fiction. Newsletters varied from Army Public Affairs–produced efforts such as the *Sandblaster*, published in Garlstedt, Germany, for the 2 AD (Forward) to newsletters produced by volunteers.

Family support groups also produced newsletters that combined articles written by volunteers and official reports; most appeared monthly. The 2-34 AR family support group typified these battalion-level efforts; it transitioned from peacetime production of a quarterly newsletter to a monthly newsletter in January 1991. Keeping families informed in the time before global e-mail and satellite phones was hard to do. In this instance, the commander serially numbered his official input to the newsletter. Thanks to the indifferent mail service, his third offering arrived before the first and second. Even with the confusion, families appreciated the effort; the newsletter had 650 subscribers—about fifty more than soldiers assigned to the battalion. Newsletters provided valuable information and maintained a sense of connection between those in the field and those at home.[47] By reducing the stress at home, these simple and short communiqués also reduced stress in the field.

Learning by Doing

As February wore on, the connection with the home front became more and more tenuous. To preserve operational security, the Corps imposed restrictions on media access. There were some media present in the Division, but they could not release stories without clearance. As the time to move to the forward assembly area approached, restrictions grew. Accordingly, the Division stopped access to telephones on February 13.[48] That same day, the VII Corps published Fragmentary Order (FRAGO) 119-91, ordering the move to the forward assembly areas beginning on February 14. That order effected the transition from building combat power to final preparation for the assault.[49]

Movement into forward assembly areas signaled the end of Combat Command Carter's mission. BG Carter's troops prepared to turn over security operations to TF Iron, which was built around COL Weisman's 3rd Brigade. LTC Wilson had one concern he believed needed to be addressed before TF Iron arrived: the Quarter Horse continued to perceive activity in As Samwah, but the squadron was too far south to intervene effectively or to be certain of what they saw. LTC Wilson knew the plan called for the Division to move into the area that Combat Command Carter had cleared. He knew TF Iron would move right up to the border, fifteen kilometers farther north. TF Iron's purpose was to cut lanes in the border berm to prepare the way for the attack. It would then clear the ground farther north. If there were enemy troops in As Samwah, they posed a threat to the task force as it moved forward. He sought and received permission to clear the village yet again, and to occupy it so the enemy could not return unmolested.

LTC Wilson had no infantry and too few cavalrymen to clear even the small collection of shacks at As Samwah, so Carter tasked LTC Gross to give up one of his rifle companies. Gross sent D Company, 2nd Battalion, 16th Infantry (2-16 IN), which Wilson ensured had more than enough firepower to get the job done. He ordered Pope and A Troop to support by fire and placed the squadron's mortars and Cobras on call. He implemented tight controls over fires to avoid a repetition of the earlier incident when the squadron narrowly avoided a fratricide between ground troops and Apache helicopters. Carter shared that concern. Although Wilson would supervise execution, Carter asked company commander CPT Mark Hammond to brief his concept for the operation. Hammond's plan was sound and relatively simple: he proposed to leave one Bradley platoon in position to support by fire or maneuver as required, and he intended to sweep the village with his remaining two platoons. Because Hammond also had concerns about fire discipline, he specified that no one would shoot unless fired upon. Carter thought the plan adequate, but warned the young officer to be wary of firing on the shacks, as rounds would travel right through them and endanger anyone on the other side.[50]

On February 14, D Company moved into As Samwah. What followed added no laurels to the Division. No Iraqis fired, yet firing broke out almost immediately. LTC Wilson, monitoring the infantry company's radio net, immediately called a cease-fire. When the dust settled, it turned out the infantry had wounded three of their own: an M16 bullet struck one soldier, a fragment from a grenade wounded a second, and the third cut his hand on something. And yet, there were no Iraqis in the ramshackle collection of huts. Medics treated the wounded and prepared them for evacuation, but the inbound air ambulance had no secure radio. Transmitting in the clear would surely afford the Iraqis the chance to do damage, so the wounded were evacuated by ground ambulance.[51]

Once again an inexperienced unit had made mistakes. Although well trained in open warfare, D Company had no training for fighting in a built-up area. Even a small village presented a challenge to an unprepared unit. Tin-roofed shacks in a village have to be cleared as methodically as high-rise buildings in an urban center. Instead D Company troops fired indiscriminately and compounded the matter by throwing at least one grenade into a shack. CPT Hammond's supporting platoon and the cavalry averted worse by exercising restraint.[52] Of the incident Rhame wrote in his journal, "This is out of control. What a way to start a war."[53]

TF Iron arrived later that afternoon, and Combat Command Carter's tenure ended. The Quarter Horse now reported to TF Iron. LTC Harry Emerson and LTC Gross returned to their brigades. COL Weisman brought in the TF 1-41 IN, commanded by LTC Jim Hillman. An experienced commander, Hillman had two tank companies and two infantry companies as the core of his combat power. LTC Lanny Smith's 4th Battalion, 3rd Field Artillery (4-3 FA) provided support.[54]

While events unfolded along the border, the rest of the Division moved as well. FRAGO 119-91 ordered the VII Corps into forward assembly areas in order to prepare for "offensive operations."[55] Every soldier in the Corps had anticipated that move, and most were eager to go. By late afternoon on February 14, units had prepared to meet their movement times. What no one imagined is what an impressive sight it would be. Advance parties moved almost immediately on receipt of the order. The 1 ID moved the following morning. Those who saw the thousands of vehicles on the move from the air found the sight awe inspiring. Even those whose view was limited to what they could see from a tank or Bradley turret thought it impressive. COL Maggart, traveling with his brigade, imagined it as "an enormous land battleship . . . I was so struck by the massive speed and power of the brigade moving across the desert, like Gen. Patton in an earlier time, that I felt sorry for the Iraqis."[56] The Division moved about 115 kilometers, completing the move with very few incidents after nightfall on February 14.[57]

Two incidents deserve mention, however. At about 5:00 p.m. on February 13, while en route to their staging area, soldiers in TF 2-34 AR observed gold tracers over the horizon to the north. The US Army uses red tracers, so these were not American, but whose they were was unclear. The firing continued for several minutes, accompanied by a couple of explosions that sounded like thunder in the distance. Pyres of black smoke drifted away after each one. Several minutes into this sound and light show, a Scud missile broke the horizon looking for the world like a space shuttle launch. Within seconds soldiers could see flashes from bomb strikes followed by a possible secondary explosion. The source of the gold tracers became clear—Iraqi air defense artillery had fired at attacking coalition fighters. At midday on February 14 another Scud blew up over Hafir al-Batin, raining debris over a wide area.[58]

The arrival of the Division in its forward assembly areas completed the transition from phase 1 (building combat power) to phase 2 (moving to defensive sectors). During phase 2, the 1 ID made final preparations for the ground offensive. TF Iron would cut lanes through the border berm and clear the ground north of the border of enemy surveillance. Just how deep it would go had not been determined. COL Dodson's Division artillery would orchestrate a series of artillery raids focused on known and suspected artillery positions; COL Shadley's troops would continue to stockpile ammunition and search for parts, and the remainder of the Division would execute final rehearsals. Subsequently, the 1st and 2nd Brigades would relieve TF Iron a few days prior to the ground offensive. The cavalry squadron would then join the 1st Brigade for the assault, and the 3rd Brigade would reassemble as the Division reserve. On the evening of February 14 there was a sense of satisfaction and anticipation.

TF Iron's first night on the berm passed uneventfully, but a pattern emerged that marked the arrival of yet another well-trained but inexperienced unit. LTC Hillman's troops were seeing things in the dark. COL Dave Weisman and LTC Clint Ancker had both served in Vietnam, but very few of their subordinates and none of their battalion commanders had. Just as the 3-37 AR and 1-4 CAV had to get over the "willies," so too did TF 1-41 IN; in fact, its soldiers actually were seeing things, but their interpretation of what they saw was suspect. As mentioned, soldiers expecting or fearing enemy activity are subject to "confirmation bias."

Following up at daylight on supposed "contacts" revealed that "there was nothing there, no bodies, no equipment, or even indications of Iraqi presence."[59] As Ancker put it, "We later determined some of the activity [reported] was simply the tricks played on thermal sights by differential cooling of junk on the desert floor. Metal and other kinds of material on the desert floor would cool at a different rate from the desert itself when the sun went down."[60] Hillman and his troops were learning the same lessons their predecessors had to learn.

On the evening of February 14, COL Jim Mowery and LTC Ralph Hayles returned to the 3rd Brigade command post to coordinate with Weisman, Ancker, and Hillman on how the attack helicopter battalion would support TF Iron. They had met once before on February 11, when they had reviewed how the attack battalion would operate. Ancker took careful notes. Among other things, Mowery, citing his earlier experience with the 1-4 CAV, asked the Brigade to turn off ground surveillance radar when the Apache helicopters arrived, because the Apaches' radar warning system confused US ground surveillance radar with enemy ZSU-23-4 air defense radar. Mowery and Hayles were very specific about when they would or would not engage targets. Ancker wrote in his journal that the 4th Brigade "will not fire if they can't positively ID TGT [target]." The aviators reported they had been fired on previously when operating with the Quarter Horse, but "did not return fire" because the target could not be positively identified. Ancker noted that both were confident there would be little chance of fratricide.[61]

That evening they discussed coordination measures to assure effective and safe support of the ground troops. Hillman reviewed his operations plan and provided a copy of graphics that illustrated the disposition of TF 1-41 IN. They reviewed how to pass targets and how the Apaches could increase the effective range of target acquisition. Finally, they reviewed the plan for the next day.[62]

Mowery wrote of the meeting of February 14 that the Apaches "will go very well."[63] He had every reason to be confident. He believed Hayles was a first-rate commander who had improved with the experience gained working with Wilson. Hayles remained confident, having declared in an interview a few weeks earlier, "I have high confidence that we won't shoot any coalition forces."[64]

Elsewhere in TF Iron the troops reported enemy activity, but nothing much materialized. During the night the 4-3 FA fired a mission against a suspected enemy mortar position that may or may not have been there. At first light on February 15, MAJ Mark Landrith, 1st Battalion, 1st Aviation (1-1 AVN) operations officer, flew to the TF Iron command post, from where he would ensure that Weisman got the support he needed. At 8:30 a.m. that morning, LTC Smith reported battle damage from a mission fired during the night, and noted two BDRs. In answer to the inquiry of just what BDRs were, he answered "Big Desert Rats."[65] That was the last light moment in a busy day. At 11:00 a.m. the Quarter Horse launched two scout weapons teams, one in support of Hillman and the other for the squadron's ground troops. At 11:30 a.m. the artillery fired a short bombardment on suspected enemy targets. At noon, the Quarter Horse and TF 1-41 IN advanced, each supported by five armored combat earthmovers to cut lanes through the berm and begin the process of clearing the Iraqi security zone.[66]

The armored dozers went to work under cover of a smoke screen. Within fifteen minutes the Quarter Horse and TF 1-41 IN had cut gaps in the berm, entered Iraq, and headed north toward the day's limit of advance, a phase line five kilometers north of the berm. The Division estimated the zone in which the Iraqis maintained combat outposts or surveillance outposts would be fifteen to twenty kilometers north, but almost immediately, the Quarter Horse encountered Iraqi security forces. B Troop, moving on the 1-4 CAV's right, silenced Iraqis firing on them from an earthen fortification and fired on an Iraqi mortar position as well. The Iraqis manning the mortars decamped north in a light truck. A Troop, on the left, ran off a group of Iraqi troops from their outpost.[67]

Later that afternoon Hillman's troops observed enemy retreating north beyond the range of their weapons. Weisman asked for Apaches, and Landrith called for and guided in a flight of them. CPT Tim Linderman, commander of A Company, maneuvered his flight directly above the ground unit that made the report. From there he could see the enemy, but they were beyond the ten-kilometer maximum range of his laser range finders and thus out of range to shoot.[68] With the enemy north of the limit of advance, the Apaches could not pursue.

TF Iron encountered little further resistance. One of the Apache crews detected what they thought was a BMP (Boyevaya Mashina Pekhoty, a Soviet-made infantry fighting vehicle). They launched a Hellfire missile, but it went awry and flew harmlessly north.[69] The Iraqis did fire a few ineffectual rounds of artillery. To stay abreast of the tactical situation, Weisman and Ancker followed the advance. Ancker brought along the last set of colors hauled down as the US Army withdrew from what had been the Cold War confrontation line. Ancker flew this flag from the antenna of Weisman's command track.[70]

Methodically clearing the ground, TF Iron reached the limit of advance, Phase Line Minnesota, by midafternoon. The Quarter Horse and TF 1-41 IN took up hasty defensive positions and prepared to continue the advance on February 16. As the ground troops settled, Linderman's helicopters landed at a patch of desert near TF Iron's command post to confer with Landrith.

Landrith wanted to review the gun camera tape to determine if he could tell why the Hellfire had misfired. After the Apache that fired the errant missile wound down, he climbed up on the forward avionics bay and opened the gunner's door so he could see the recording. What he saw was a clear view of "a moving heavily loaded Bradley."[71] Perhaps there was a problem with the Hellfire, but there was definitely a problem with the Apache crew. They had misidentified the Bradley as a Soviet-made BMP. The only good news was that the copilot/gunner had "screwed up the switch positions so badly, that there was no way the missile was going to hit anything he was aiming at."[72] That night, Landrith reviewed the recording with both Hayles and Linderman, who led the flight. LTC Hayles was "livid. He grounded both members of the firing crew indefinitely and was contemplating even more serious action against them."[73] Because this was the second instance of a potential fratricide due to misidentification, Hayles and Landrith were deeply concerned.

At 3:00 that afternoon, Rhame met with his brigade commanders to discuss the timeline for the next forty-eight hours and to review the next day's operation. Rhame intended for TF Iron to clear the zone seven kilometers farther north. He was content with the day's operation and believed it vital to continue, but worried that the Corps might yet halt the operation. There was a lot of marching and countermarching among the VII Corps, 3rd Army, and Central Command (CENTCOM) units. Rhame asserted "What is happening across the Corps' front is not synchronized."[74] Because this was so, he thought LTG Franks might call off the operation.

The Corps had a lot to synchronize. Most of it was still moving into forward assembly areas. The 1 CD had been on the border since January 22 and in frequent contact with the Iraqis. On February 14 it carried out "berm busting" operations to reinforce its portrayal of the main attack coming out of the Wadi al-Batin. In a series of small contacts, the cavalry division destroyed observation towers and trucks and captured 170 Iraqi troops. BG Tilelli's troops, like Rhame's, crossed into Iraq on February 15. Crossing the border provoked a fight with security forces of the Iraqi 48 ID just east of the far less aggressive 26 ID. The 48 ID put up a fight and laid mines where they expected the cavalry to come if they continued north.[75]

MG Rhame's concern about the operation the next day proved prescient. At 5:30 p.m. Franks told him that the Fire Support Coordination Line (FSCL) would not be moved farther north as previously planned; it would remain one kilometer forward of the 1 ID front-line trace until 5:00 p.m. on February 17. This effectively canceled the next day's operation. Generally, firing beyond the FSCL required minimal coordination. Inside the FSCL, the ground commander controlled fires. CENTCOM chose to redefine the FSCL. During Desert Storm, fires beyond the FSCL had to be cleared by the Air Force. No one could shot without its explicit approval.[76] Moving units forward of the FSCL was not in the cards, as they would not be able to even use mortars with Air Force approval. In effect the FSCL had become a boundary. Unhappy but undaunted, Rhame resolved to "take the war to the Iraqis tomorrow by doing an artillery raid with

MLRS [multiple-launch rocket system] and cannon artillery."[77] Always part of the plan, the raids could still be executed, albeit without the benefit of moving the artillery as far north as planned. The raids would be fired from positions south of the line that TF Iron had occupied along Phase Line Minnesota.

There the Quarter Horse and TF 1-41 IN defended frontages of thirty kilometers each. The actions that the TF 1-41 IN took that afternoon exemplify a hasty defense by a balanced task force. Six of Rhame's ten battalion-size formations organized as balanced combined-arms task forces, meaning they had two tank companies and two mechanized infantry companies. Examining the techniques Hillman used is useful to understand both the capabilities and limitations of a fully modernized battalion task force.[78] LTC Hillman's company commander began by identifying the boundaries of their sectors. Next they "staked in" their combat vehicles using metal pickets to mark their left and right limits. They also established target reference points by marking the direction and elevation to targets determined by reference to the map. Each crew made a range card or sketch of their left and right limits and targets. These could then be added to "sector sketches" and combined at the platoon and company levels to enable effective fire control.[79]

That evening Hillman trooped the line to check his infantrymen and tankers. He spent most of his time on his right or eastern flank with his scout platoon. The scouts had responsibility for maintaining contact with the cavalry division on the right. The 1 CD remained in Saudi Arabia so they were to the TF 1-41 IN's right and well to its rear. To maintain contact, Hillman's scouts deployed in a sharp curve shape, almost like a fishhook, to ensure there were no uncovered avenues of approach along the Division boundary. LTC Hillman and his scout platoon leader worked to position the six Bradley scout tracks where they could cover the ground and yet see each other. With nearly fifteen kilometers to cover, this took some doing. Once again Hillman reminded his units to be certain of their target before they fired.[80]

Not much happened that first night. One of Hillman's companies reported seeing enemy tanks, but no contact developed.[81] The next day, despite not continuing the advance, TF Iron and the rest of the Division found plenty to do. COL Dodson coordinated artillery to meet Rhame's intent "to take the war to the Iraqis." Franks and Rhame both believed artillery raids, designed to attack Iraqi artillery, were essential. Coalition air forces had focused on gaining air superiority, on strategic targets, and finally on targets nominated through joint targeting boards. So far, however, VII Corps had not hit many targets.

Franks did not believe he was getting adequate support from the Air Force. In particular, he worried that the Iraqis might fire chemical munitions. They had done so against their own people, so it seemed unlikely they would balk at firing chemicals at Americans. Specifically, what he did not want to have happen was to have "the Big Red One get in the breach and get a lot of chemical

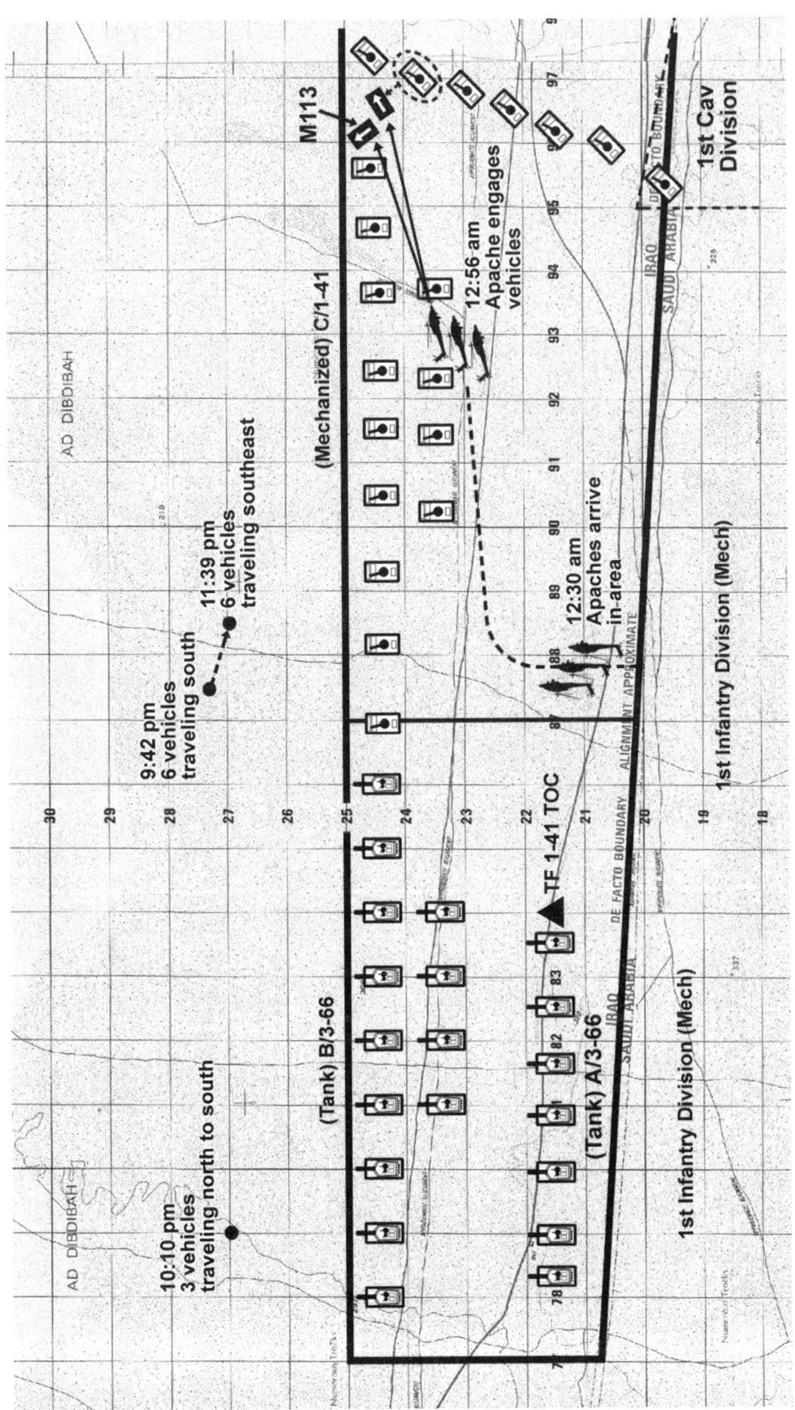

MAP 5. Positions of Iraqi and US combat forces at 12:56 AM, February 17, 1991, when the Apache Fratricides occurred. Reproduced from GAO Report Operation Desert Storm: Apache Helicopter Fratricide Incident—GAO-OSI-93-4 June 1993.

and scattered mines dumped on top of it."[82] He wanted to destroy any enemy artillery that could range the breach, but found it a "constant struggle" to get the air component to bomb his targets.[83] The Corps estimated the Iraqis had eighteen battalions of tube artillery (some estimates showed twenty-two battalions) and eighteen multiple rocket launchers that could range the planned breach.[84] Soviet-made 122-millimeter and 130-millimeter howitzers comprised the bulk of that artillery; with ranges of more than fifteen kilometers and twenty-seven kilometers, respectively, they constituted a significant threat. Although the rocket launchers were the 107-millimeter rather than the more fearsome 122-millimeter gauge, they constituted a serious threat as well.[85]

COL Dodson planned on using his own artillery and 142 FA from the Corps to destroy enemy artillery that could range the breach. The 142 FA fielded two eight-inch howitzer battalions. To obtain enough ammunition for them to fire the raid, Dodson had to borrow ammunition from the British. The supply system did deliver "just enough MLRS [ammunition] in to continue the mission." The 142 FA Brigade fired eight hundred volleys of eight-inch rounds, and three MLRS batteries fired four hundred rockets in the initial raid.[86]

Ammunition supplies remained too low to fire the raids as conceived. MG Rhame complained in his journal that one of the three Corps ammunition resupply points had only been filled to 20 percent capacity. There was a shortage of some ammunition at the same time units were force-issued ammunition they were unlikely to use. There were plenty of mines, for example. Mines might be laid if the Corps had to go on the defense, but they were unlikely to use mines during the attack.[87]

Ammunition shortages did not irritate as much as the inability to determine what, if anything, the artillery raid of several hours had achieved. LTC Lanny Smith's tongue-in-cheek reporting of killing desert rats demonstrated the general inability to determine battle damage. Rhame observed with some wonder that there was "No reaction at all." He was puzzled by the lack of enemy reaction. He concluded his thoughts on the day by noting, "I would love to know if we hurt him."[88] The Division had few means to assess whether it had hurt the Iraqis. This problem extended across the theater. CENTCOM could count sorties and bombs dropped, but even tapes could not accurately reveal the results.

Despite Franks's concern over air support, the air forces were doing their part. The VII Corps air support operations cell kept the Corps abreast of the air campaign via an irreverently and unofficial situation report called the "Daily Queep." The airmen's daily report revealed the difficulty airmen had in assessing results; it was, to put it colloquially, "smart-assed," but nonetheless accurate. On February 16 the humorists in blue claimed that if a fighter pilot begins by saying, "This is no shit . . . then you can believe at least 10% of the story." The "Queep" for the day eventually got to the point; it listed 210 sorties against Iraqi VII Corps and another 170 at deeper targets, including the Iraqi Republican

Guard.[89] What it did not and could not say accurately is what the sorties had achieved.

Air attacks against the Iraqi VII Corps began in late January and focused on MG Ahmad Hamash's reserves. In the second week of February, the strikes grew in intensity and frequency. Eventually the air forces attacked daily. The pressure rose when the air component commander, LTG Chuck Horner, shifted his enormous resources to "shaping" the battlefield. Controversy over which corps got what sorties flown remained, but Horner's airmen struck Iraqi VII Corps targets every day, including artillery targets.[90] With daily artillery raids added to the bombing, the Iraqis had little or no respite.

At sundown on February 16, TF Iron settled in for their third night defending the forward assembly area and their second night in Iraq. Although TF 1-41 IN was new, the Quarter Horse could claim to be grizzled veterans. South of TF Iron, the 1st and 2nd Brigades were preparing to occupy positions along the frontier. Newly received imagery caused some adjustments to evolving attack plans at the low tactical level, but mostly confirmed earlier analysis.[91]

During the course of the evening, three different officers from Tilelli's division appeared in the TF 1-41 IN's area. LTC Hillman described them as "sightseers." They were innocent—they merely wanted to see the ground forward of them. Even so, he ran them off; he did not want people, friendly or not, roaming his area in the dark.[92] Both the Quarter Horse and TF 1-41 IN reported enemy activity. At 8:09 p.m. the Iraqis fired a single artillery round that impacted two hundred meters southwest of TF 1-41 IN's command post. Hillman moved it to avoid any adjustments the Iraqi artillery made. At 9:42 p.m. C Company, Hillman's easternmost company, reported six enemy vehicles to their front. The enemy soon disappeared, but reappeared at 11:39 p.m. moving southeast. Shortly afterward C Company saw three enemy vehicles some two kilometers farther east, moving east.[93]

The enemy appeared to be moving generally east across the front using terrain to mask their movement. Although Hillman dismissed some earlier reports as "random" sightings, this one seemed legitimate, and his command post tracked this group for about two hours. What they were up to was not clear; he thought they might have been resupplying outposts rather than trying to probe his positions. His infantrymen identified the enemy vehicles as American-made M113 armored personnel carriers. The Iraqis had captured M113s from Kuwait. Convinced they had positive identification, Hillman cleared his infantry to shoot. They fired antitank missiles "at a range of nearly 4,000 meters but with no observable effect." Believing the enemy beyond effective range, Hillman called for Apaches.[94]

Earlier in the evening CPT Dan Garvey had prepared his Apache company to support TF Iron, but at 9:30 p.m. Garvey had scrubbed the mission due to weather conditions. Lack of moonlight and high winds blowing steadily at thirty knots and gusting higher, produced blowing sand that made flying particularly dangerous;[95] the mission would not occur in the absence of critical need. Not long after, however, Garvey was told the mission was back on. CPT Stephen M. Schiller expected to fly on Garvey's wing as briefed. But Garvey told him that Hayles had said to "get my wing man." Garvey took that as an order for him to fly with his regular wingman crew, CW 2 Kelly Gulker and CW 1 Steve Grady, instead of Schiller's crew.[96]

LTC Hayles did not want to execute, and he said as much. He "indicated that he did not want to go on the mission and that he did not want any of his pilots to go, because he was concerned about the proximity of the targets to the friendly forces."[97] The last grid coordinates reported placed the targets less than three kilometers north of TF 1-41 IN's Bradleys and thus well within range of their antitank missiles. To Hayles there seemed no urgent need to use Apaches. Nevertheless, TF Iron asked for help. COL Mowery believed the obligation to the ground troops outweighed Hayles's reservations and thus ordered the mission.[98]

Because of his reservations, Hayles believed he needed to fly. He would do so in his normal position of gunner-copilot. He and his pilot had trouble even finding their aircraft in the murk produced by the overcast and the blowing sand. On boarding their aircraft, each of the gunner-copilots entered the reported target grid coordinates into his fire-control computer, while the pilots got the aircraft ready to go. Just lifting off that night was difficult; one of the helicopters almost crashed. Nonetheless, by 12:10 a.m. three Apaches had taken off and were headed toward TF Iron. The three included Garvey without his wingman, Hayles and his pilot, and Gulker and Grady.[99]

MAJ Scott Knobel, TF 1-41 IN's executive officer, briefed Hayles en route. He described the targets as two enemy vehicles moving west to east reported at grid coordinate NT 915270. He told Hayles the infantry believed they had hit one of them. At 12:30 a.m., using the call sign Gunfighter 6, Hayles reported arriving at the rear of TF 1-41 IN. The Apaches apparently flew in along the 88 easting north-south map grid line that divided the 1:50,000-scale map sheets into squares of one kilometer on a side. They came that way maneuvered toward the grid where the enemy had first been seen. Approaching from the south, they identified the screen line, but saw no targets. Hayles set out to look at NT 915270, as Knobel had asked. The Apaches did not withdraw south and then head east in order to return north perpendicular to the screen line as planned. Instead they flew northeast, closing on the screen line as they came. About this time Garvey, using the call sign Blue 6, activated his gun camera recorder. From that moment on a recording was made of what Garvey could see through his Target Acquisition and Designation System and what could be heard, including voice communications, internal crew communications, and multiple synthetic voice warnings of enemy air defense radar. Soon after, Hayles and the third helicopter crew called sign "Blue 5" to turn on their recorders.[100]

As he flew northeasterly Hayles reported, "And north-south 29er. Looks like they're driving away from you on the 29." Grid coordinates are read right and up; thus, the first three numbers of a six-digit grid coordinate refer to north-south lines on a map, the second three to east-west lines. Hayles was referring to the east-west grid lines: the 29 ran east and west some four kilometers north of the screen line. Weisman believed these vehicles to be those reported at NT 915270, but perhaps moving away, as Hayles reported. He responded using his call sign, Iron Deuce 6: "Go after 'em. That's your target." This transmission was followed almost immediately by the first of several warnings of enemy antiaircraft radar. The three crews, flying in high wind and hearing repeated audio warnings of enemy radar, believed they were about to engage and perhaps be engaged by enemy ground forces. Apparently Hayles never asked Hillman or Knobel to verify whether the ground surveillance radars had been turned off, and Knobel did not think to tell him. The Apache's sensors "read" friendly ground surveillance radar as enemy air defense radar. Having discussed this with the 1-41 IN leadership previously, Hayles may have assumed the radars had been shut down. Blue 6 then asked Gunfighter 6, "What is their front line trace, east-west grid line? Gunfighter 6 answered, "They're on the 22, 23 grid line. So you can shoot anything north of the 25."[101]

Over the next minute or so, Gunfighter 6 and his team, along with TF 1-41 IN and TF Iron, all collaborated to locate the enemy and establish the location of friendly forces. But three things happened to confound them. First, Hayles was focused on the targets he could see; he perceived they were moving when it was in fact his aircraft drifting in high winds that led to that illusion. One of the pilots remarked to his gunner/copilot on intercom, "It's a [expletive deleted] to fly."[102] Second, Hayles believed he was oriented north when he was oriented northeast. The vehicles he saw were a Bradley and a ground surveillance radar M113 at the eastern end of the screen line, where it bent to the south. The main body extended east to west just south of the 25 grid line. The two tracks Hayles could see were nearly due east of his position and south of the 25 grid line at approximately grid coordinate NT 962247. This was nowhere near the grid reported for the enemy at NT 915270.[103] Further, the two tracks appeared to be separate from the screen.

Third, the final and most serious problem was that when he reported the location of the suspect vehicle to the ground commanders, Hayles mistakenly read the target grid he had manually entered into his system and not the grid his target acquisition and detection system was computing. His display showed the correct grid, but he mistakenly read the stored grid three times. During the discussion on the location of these two vehicles, Garvey actually read the correct grid when Hayles asked him to confirm the location. Garvey noted that "when I NAV and store it, I get greater than 9524 vicinity. It doesn't . . . it's not coming out right."[104] His sensors reported the correct grid coordinates, but

Garvey believed his commander must be right and his own equipment wrong. The third aircrew did not intervene.

Some fifteen minutes after arriving on station, Hayles remained concerned and troubled by the setup. His radio transmissions reveal uncertainty and apprehension; Hillman and Weisman sound excited, wanting the target prosecuted. Ralph Hayles was on station to support them, and so he did. Fighting the wind, he had his pilot close on the target. Just before he fired he said over the radio, "Boy, I'm going to tell you, it's hard to pull this trigger. Back me up a little bit here. Tell me—I'm firing 070 [compass direction—northeast] 3,800 meters." No one offered to back him up nor contradict him. Still confusing the stored grid with the actual grid, Gunfighter 6 fired. With the missile en route he said on his intercom, "I hope its enemy," followed seconds later by "—'cause here it comes." The missile flew straight and true. He reported the first target destroyed and tracked over to the second and fired. The second missile flew straight and true and destroyed the second target. When he noticed two survivors walking away from the burning tracks, he directed another Apache to move in and fire a thirty-millimeter cannon. Just then Hillman, using call sign Stalwart 6, called Weisman: "Iron Deuce, Stalwart reporting that maybe friendly vehicles may have been hit. Over." Hayles said, "Roger. I was afraid of that. I was really afraid of that."[105]

Heartsick, Hayles realized he had killed or wounded several other Americans. Mowery told him to remain on station, as the ground troops still had targets. Both Hillman and Weisman proposed to continue the mission.[106] Several minutes later, the two ground commanders remained uncertain about who destroyed a scout platoon Bradley, killing two soldiers and wounding three more. When the Bradley got hit, the soldiers in the adjacent ground surveillance track bailed out, but were wounded by the blast when the Hellfire missile struck their M113. Several soldiers on the ground saw the missiles fired and watched them all the way to impact. Second Lieutenant Danny Strickland saw the "missile in flight before it hit the Bradley."[107]

Soldiers in the 1 CD saw it all as well; LTC Jim Gunlicks, the operations officer called LTC Terry Bullington to tell him that 1st Division units were shooting at each other. By the time Hayles headed back to his assembly area, it was pretty clear he had destroyed the two tracks. If there were enemy troops out there that night, they concluded their business unscathed. Monitoring the engagement, Rhame and Bullington thought they had fratricide, but they wanted to be sure before saying so. COL Stan Cherrie, the operations officer at the VII Corps, talked to both of them. He wrote in his journal, "My sensing is that division knows there has been a fratricide in their hearts, but will not admit it."[108] Cherrie understood that there was no intent to deceive but rather a desperate hope to be mistaken.

A hard lesson of combat is there are no "time-outs." Hillman's troops evacuated their dead and wounded and continued the mission, and the Iraqis continued to probe. Later that night TF Iron detected and fired on an enemy mortar position. Nothing decisive occurred, and around 3:00 a.m. activity petered out. That marked the end of the misery for the night. Meanwhile, Mowery sent LTC Dave Wildes to the attack battalion to begin a preliminary investigation.

The next morning Rhame wrote in his journal, "Today is the worst day I have had in the Army." This is a surprising statement given what he had seen as a combat veteran in Vietnam. It reflects how deeply self-inflicted wounds hurt and how deeply he felt his responsibility. He knew Hayles had fired the missile; of that he wrote, "Why he was shooting is beyond me. I wish he would have been commanding instead of shooting."[109] COL Mowery's journal reflects his disappointment: "To make a long story short everything that could go wrong went wrong and Ralph Hayles personally launched two hellfires on two friendly vehicles . . . killed two U.S. soldiers and wounded six . . . he should have been supervising and not fighting and this probably never would have happened."[110]

When Mowery watched the tapes and listened to the recordings, he heard and saw the tragedy unfold. He brought the tapes to Rhame at 8:15 a.m. The recordings revealed the error quite clearly. Later that day, Mowery's preliminary report summarized the tragedy in a single page. The accident happened for several reasons, but chief among them was that Hayles kept reading the stored grid rather than the one generated when he ranged the target. The preliminary report noted that "lasing the target convinced the gunner, over all other information—especially the heading tape [showed easterly heading rather than northerly heading] that he was in fact laid on an enemy vehicle at NT 915270 when in fact he was laid on a [friendly] target at NT 950240."[111] As long as he read the stored grid and not the generated grid, lasing the target did not matter.

The preliminary and subsequent reports, including the General Accounting Office's otherwise outstanding report, underestimate several contributing factors and put the onus on Hayles. By doing so these reports miss an important point. It is true that Rhame told each of his commanders to fight their battalion and not their weapons system. Citing this instruction is accurate, but it releases others from their responsibility. What happened was, in part, an Army failure. The review of Hayles's performance at Fort Hood, Texas, specifically criticized him for "centralized control" and "allowing little initiative."[112] The fact is that Hayles prospered in the Army by taking charge personally and not affording freedom of action to subordinates. His mistake reflects on both the Army and the 1 ID.

Equally important, the prosecution of the contact that night went beyond what was necessary. The Iraqis operating forward of Hillman's task force fired at no one and were beyond the range of his organic antitank missiles. They were not a proximate threat either to the mission or the troops on the screen line, yet there was an urgency about attacking them. What happened that night happened partly because it was a first battle of inexperienced commanders. That is not to say they were not able. Weisman was a proven combat leader, but this was his first fight as a brigade commander. Hillman worked through that difficult night calmly, but he too had never fought his battalion. Hayles was as yet relatively inexperienced. Subsequently he claimed he would not have fired on his own, "but fired on the urging and pestering of a ground commander senior to me who I was working for."[113] The radio transcript supports his argument, albeit without addressing the key fact that he reported the wrong target location at least three times.

Finally, Hayles saw what he expected to see. He suffered that night from confirmation bias. Humans make decisions based on their perception of the environment; further, they routinely cycle through possible courses of action using "mental simulation." Psychologist Gary Klein defines confirmation bias as "the search for information that confirms your hypothesis even though you would learn more by searching for evidence that might disconfirm it."[114] Clearly Hayles felt like something was not right, but rather than acting on his intuition he acted on his perceptions—skewed because he kept referring to stored grid coordinates. He did ask for a check when he announced an azimuth of 070 and a range of 3,800 meters. That should have alerted him to his error since the reported targets were almost due north of the screen line. The position of the scout Bradley and ground surveillance radar vehicle made them appear separate from the screen line. He was told to look for two vehicles away from the screen line. He made the facts fit what he expected to see.

The remainder of February 17 passed without incident, except in 1-4 CAV's sector. In midafternoon the squadron target acquisition radar reported an artillery impact north of B Troop. The operators believed the shot had come from an Iraqi mortar. SSG Alvin Fugate led a scout section toward the reported mortar position, and found two Soviet-made BRDMs (Boyevaya Razvedyvatelnaya Dozornaya Mashinas, combat reconnaissance patrol vehicles). Fugate fired antitank missiles, but missed. Faithful to the Iraqi pattern in the days before, the BRDMs withdrew.[115]

As if things were not going badly enough, an MLRS crew made things worse. Artillery fired multiple raids that day. All went well, with "One exception—1 MLRS fired wrong data."[116] It was truly egregious. The crew fired 180 degrees out. Hundreds of bomblets impacted, practically on and between the 1-34 AR's scout platoon and one of its tank companies. Surprisingly, no one was hurt by this near miss. When Rhame went to visit LTC Pat Ritter and his troops, Ritter was, to say the least, upset. He told Rhame, "General, fifty meters either way, and I would have been asking for a new scout platoon or a tank platoon for

Alpha Company."[117] To add insult to injury, Dodson wanted him to guard the unexploded bomblets until they could be cleared.

Alarmed by the fratricide, Franks ordered Rhame to withdraw early. Mercifully, the night of February 17 passed quietly, and the next day TF Iron withdrew. As Rhame had planned, his other ground maneuver brigades had moved up to the berm. COL Maggart's 1st Brigade occupied a sector on the left or west. COL Moreno's 2nd Brigade moved in on the right. The Quarter Horse headed south toward passage points through the 1st Brigade. The rest of TF Iron headed toward the 2nd Brigade.

In the east, Smith's artillery led the way followed by Hillman's infantry. A tactical withdrawal requires more deliberate effort than does an advance. Withdrawing units move by bounds, with part of the force oriented toward the enemy at all times. Withdrawing units also must move to previously coordinated passage points. As TF 1-41 IN approached the berm, the companies hit passage points where they formed columns to go through the lanes. CPT Bill Hedges designated a staging area for his tank company about fifteen hundred meters north of the berm.[118]

CPT Hedges chose a small hillock he thought his platoons could easily find. When he arrived with the trail platoon he found the company coiled up close together; the troops were on the ground, talking and smoking and entirely complacent. Bone tired, he settled in for a few minutes to gather his thoughts. And then, with a start, he realized his tanks were bunched up. He immediately ordered his unit to spread out. Just as he got his people moving, the previously quiescent Iraqi artillery dumped twelve or more rounds in and around them. His gunner, SSG Tony Appelget, had not yet gotten back in the turret, and as he lowered himself through the loader's hatch, a fragment from one of the artillery rounds rebounded off the deck of the tank and struck him in the back of his neck. Fortunately, the fragment was nearly spent, so the wound was superficial. The company cleared the beaten zone and passed through the berm. CPT Hedges learned a valuable lesson: he had selected a place for his troops to rally based on it being recognizable, but the Iraqis could see these places too and had preregistered targets on many of them. Others would later learn this lesson on their own.

The Iraqi artillery also fired on CPT Roy Peters, who commanded one of Wilson's air troops. Peters observed impacts some distance from where he hovered in his helicopter. Destroying helicopters with artillery is not impossible, so Peters moved. Subsequently, he saw artillery impacts where he had been. Meanwhile, A and B Troops began passing through the gaps in the border berm. As A troop completed passing, the crew of an OH-58C observation helicopter reported they were going down. They crashed in the area A Troop had occupied, so Pope and part of his troop went to the rescue, securing the site and recovering the crew. Neither LT Tom Schwartz nor his observer, SPC Steven Dunn, was injured. A Troop secured the site until the wreckage could be recovered. It crossed the border late that afternoon.[119] With that, the Quarter Horse closed on the aptly named Tactical Assembly Area Respite, where they would have a rest from nearly a month of combat operations.

Of the day's events Rhame wrote, "Today was a better day . . . we will totally confuse this guy. He doesn't know what we are doing now."[120] Never depressed for long, he found that the decision to withdraw made sense given the news that G-Day, the day the ground offensive would start, had been postponed. It now appeared the ground offensive would begin on Saturday, February 24. Rhame's focus turned to final preparation for the assault. He also had to decide what to do about Hayles. BG Carter did the internal investigation February 17. The results confirmed Mowery's preliminary investigation. MG Rhame wanted another night to think about it, but decided the fratricide would "be dealt with sternly." He wrote in his journal, "We owe it to our soldiers to do better than allow other Americans to kill them."[121]

The news of the fratricide went through the Division at high speed. Right on the heels of that news came the news of artillery hitting Hedges's tank company and the helicopter crashing. Now the previously uncommitted 1st and 2nd Brigades defended the border. Curious and hoping to learn what went wrong, the two brigades would soon have their first battle experience.

NOTES

1. Regarding the debriefing of the Iraqi 27 ID logistics officer, see COL Stu Herrington, director, Joint Debriefing Center, briefing presentation, 513 MI Bde Joint Debriefing Center, 1991.

2. LTG (Ret.) Thomas G. Rhame, telephone interview with the author, February 2, 2015, quoting from Rhame's personal journal, February 3, 1991.

3. Rhame, interview, February 2, 2015, quoting from Rhame's personal journal, February 2, 1991.

4. JSTARS is synthetic aperture radar mounted on a modified Boeing 707; it is able to track movement of units over a wide area. The radar generates what analysts call "snail trails"; from these estimates can be made of the size of the unit moving. On several occasions, JSTARS analysts generated false reports based on their interpretation of the data. Nevertheless, this was a very useful system at the corps level and above.

5. LTG (Ret.) William G. Carter III, telephone interview with the author, February 8, 2015.

6. LTG (Ret.) William G. Carter III, telephone interview with the author, November 16, 2014; Franks quotations from Carter. See also Clancy, *Into the Storm*, 257.

7. LTG (Ret.) William G. Carter III, telephone interview with the author, December 5, 2013.

8. Jeffrey K. Sanson, "Alpha Co. 3rd Bn, 37th AR, Ironhorse," unpublished manuscript, June 23, 1991, 8.

9. There are a number of good sources online that will enable the reader to understand how such grids are used; see, for example, Army Study Guide, www.armystudyguide.com. The grids used in Desert Storm were generated from the NATO Military Grid Reference System.

10. MAJ Jim Stockmoe, "Brigade Intelligence Operations in the Gulf War, Then and Now," unpublished manuscript, n.d., 3.

11. COL (Ret.) Gary E. Phillips, telephone interview with the author, February 10, 2015. Phillips served as the operations officer of the 207 MI, which supported the VII Corps.

12. LTC Ford's cell included many more analysts of different stripes; CW2 Phyllis Fitzgerald happened to be the locus for developing the enemy order of battle.

13. Marvin L. Meek, personal journal, January 25–26 and February 11, 1991.

14. Rhame interview, February 2, 2015, quoting from Rhame's personal journal, February 1, 1991.

15. Ibid.

16. LTG (Ret.) Robert Wilson, telephone interview with the author, February 6, 2015.

17. 1st Infantry Division Main, G3, Operations, daily staff journal, February 1, 1991.

18. Stephen A. Bourque and John W. Burdan, *The Road to Safwan: The 1st Squadron, 4th Cavalry in the 1991 Persian Gulf War* (Denton: University of North Texas Press, 2007), 76–77.

19. Rhame interview, February 2, 2015, quoting from Rhame's personal journal, February 4, 1991; Wilson interview; Bourque and Burdan, *The Road to Safwan*, 84.

20. Lieutenant Colonel David F. Gross, "The Breach of Sadam's [*sic*] Defensive Link: Recollections of a Desert Storm Armor Task Force Commander," unpublished manuscript, US Army War College, Carlisle Barracks, PA, 1992, 32; see also Bourque and Burdan, *The Road to Safwan*, 86.

21. COL (Ret.) Thomas Connors, BG (Ret.) David Gross, and MG (Ret.) Paul Izzo, oral history group interview by Andrew Woods, McCormick Research Center, First Division Museum at Cantigny, Wheaton, IL, January 22–23, 2011.

22. Bourque and Burdan, *The Road to Safwan*, 87–89.

23. Stephan A. Bourque, *Jayhawk: The VII Corps in the Persian Gulf War* (Washington, DC: Center of Military History, 2002), 142. The deception effort played to the Iraqi predisposition.

24. Bourque, *Jayhawk*, 142; Rhame interview, February 2, 2015; Wilson interview.

25. Wilson interview.

26. Bourque and Burdan, *The Road to Safwan*, 90–92; BG (Ret.) Stanley F. Cherrie, interview with the author, Leavenworth, KS, February 10, 2015; COL (Ret.) Gary E. Phillips, telephone interview with the author, February 10, 2015. As Corps G3 operations officer, Cherrie managed terrain and air space in the VII Corps.

27. Bourque and Burdan, *The Road to Safwan*, 90–92.

28. TF 3-37 AR, message 27 to DTAC, 1 ID, dated 111849ZFeb 91. This standard message appears as a single document in the collection at the Robert R. McCormick Research Center, First Division Museum at Cantigny, Wheaton, IL. The message was sent on February 11, 1991, at 5:49 p.m. Greenwich Mean Time; local time was three hours ahead.

29. Ibid.

30. Data drawn from Diazo-generated overlays issued by the 1 ID and the 2nd Brigade, author's possession. Copies are now available at the Robert R. McCormick Research Center, First Division Museum at Cantigny, Wheaton, IL.

31. Ibid.

32. 1 ID graphic intelligence overlay, 1st Brigade operations and intelligence graphic, February 17, 1991, and 110th Brigade orations graphic, February 25, 1991, author's possession.

33. Stockmoe, "Brigade Intelligence," shows that the Division had a very good understanding of the condition of the Iraqi 26 ID.

34. MAJ Don Osterberg and the planners had in fact transitioned soon after the publication of Scorpion Danger on January 19.

35. MG (Ret.) Lon E. Maggart, "Eye of the Storm (Duty First)," unpublished manuscript, 1992–97, 108–9.

36. COL (Ret.) Clinton J. Ancker, "2nd Armored Division (Forward) and the Gulf Conflict," unpublished manuscript, Naval War College, Newport, RI, n.d., 119.

37. Rhame interview, February 2, 2015; MG Rhame visited the 2nd Brigade rehearsal.

38. Headquarters, 1 ID (M) DISCOM, "Desert Shield/Desert Storm Support Operations," January 15, 1992, P-II-1–P-II-3.

39. Ibid., 5.

40. MG (Ret.) Lloyd T. Waterman, telephone interview with the author, October 28, 2014.

41. LTG (Ret.) Jerry A. Rutherford, telephone interview with the author, December 16, 2015

42. COL (Ret.) Larry Githerman, interview with the author, Fort Riley, KS, November 20, 2013. Githerman served as Shadley's executive officer.

43. Headquarters, 1 ID (M) DISCOM, "Desert Shield/Desert Storm Support Operations," 6.

44. COL (Ret.) George P. Ritter, telephone interview with the author, August 5, 2014; author's notes; LTC (Ret.) James R. Talley, telephone interview with the author, November 6, 2014.

45. Mail taking eighteen to twenty days to reach Army post offices in Germany became a frequent complaint in the VII Corps commander's daily reports.

46. This paragraph reflects my personal experience and that of several of my colleagues in command.

47. COL (Ret.) V. Paul Baerman provided a bound collection of issues of the *Sandblaster*; it is rich with personal interest stories written about the forward deployed soldiers. That kind of story for Fort Riley–based troops appeared in the *Fort Riley Post*. Information on the 2-34 AR newsletter stems from the records kept by Dana H. Fontenot. The 2-34 AR newsletter included Spanish-language notices to assure that those who spoke little or no English had access to basic information.

48. Several sources reference the last day of access to phones as February 12. First Lieutenant Jay C. Mumford, "Rangers in Iraq: Task Force Ranger, 2nd Battalion, 16th Infantry in the Persian Gulf War, 10 November 1990–12 May 1991," unpublished manuscript, August 31, 1991, 21.

49. VII Corps, Fragmentary Order 119-91, "Execution of PH II (Movement to FAA's [*sic*] and Sectors)," date redacted.

50. Bourque and Burdan, *The Road to Safwan*, 93. LTG (Ret.) William G. Carter III, e-mail to the author, March 1, 2015. CPT Hammond's name appears on the roster for D Company, 2-16 IN that is published in Mumford, "Rangers in Iraq," 78.

51. Bourque and Burdan, *The Road to Safwan*, 94.

52. Ibid.

53. Rhame interview, February 2, 2015.

54. For a timeline, see 1 ID Desert Storm (briefing, n.d.); After the war the 1 ID gave virtually the same briefing multiple times, all are undated. The title used varied but all contained the same charts as that cited here; several versions may be found at the Robert R. McCormick Research Center, First Division Museum at Cantigny, Wheaton, IL. See also Bourque and Burdan, *The Road to Safwan,* 95; Headquarters, 1st Infantry Division (Mechanized), "Operation Desert Storm First Look Chronology of Events," March 14, 1991; and Lieutenant Colonel James L. Hillman, "Task Force 1-41 Infantry: Fratricide

Experience in Southwest Asia," unpublished manuscript, US Army War College, Carlisle Barracks, PA, 1993.

55. VII Corps, Fragmentary Order 119-91, "Execution of PH II."

56. Maggart, "Eye of the Storm," 131.

57. The VII Corps sequenced the move over several days. In Clancy's *Into the Storm*, 295, Franks recalls that the move began on February 16 and ended two days later. Bourque, *Jayhawk*, 174–75, reports that the move occurred February 15–17, with the 1 ID moving on February 15. Headquarters, 1st Infantry Division (Mechanized), "Operation Desert Storm First Look," 6, and several briefings report moving on February 14; various personal journals, notes, and unit chronologies all report moving on February 14.

58. Author's notes; Maggart, "Eye of the Storm," 130–33.

59. Ancker, "2nd Armored Division (Forward)," 131, and, regarding thermals, identification of targets, and friendlies, 131–33.

60. Ibid.

61. LTC Clint Ancker, personal journal, February 11, 1991. ZSU stands for Zenitnaya Samokhodnaya Ustanovka, which translates as "antiaircraft self-propelled mount." In this case, it comprised four twenty-three-millimeter cannons.

62. COL (Ret.) James L. Mowery, "Saudi Journal," February 14, 1991. See also Ancker, "2nd Armored Division (Forward)," 126. In this postwar manuscript, Ancker wrote that according to Mowery and Hayles, "there was no chance of fratricide." It is easy to believe they may have said that as both of these officers exuded confidence.

63. Mowery, "Saudi Journal," February 14, 1991.

64. Rick Atkinson, *Crusade: The Untold Story of the Gulf War* (London: HarperCollins, 1994), 318. Atkinson amplified his assessment of Hayles by reporting that many on the division staff regarded Hayles as "a cowboy."

65. MAJ Mark S. Landrith, "History, 1st Battalion, 1st Aviation Regiment, 4th Brigade, 1st Infantry Division, Desert Shield/Desert Storm," unpublished manuscript, n.d., n.p. [18]; Ancker, personal journal, February 15, 1991.

66. Bourque and Burdan, *The Road to Safwan*, 96, 128. While Bourque and Burdan report that Smith fired on a small group of Iraqi trucks, Ancker refers to the mission as a preparation fire. In any event, there clearly were Iraqis just north of the border berm.

67. Bourque and Burdan, *The Road to Safwan*, 96–97.

68. Landrith, "History," n.p. [19].

69. 1-1 AVN, note transcribed by MAJ Dan Pike, executive officer, February 15, 1991; Mowery, "Saudi Journal," February 15, 1991.

70. Ancker, "2nd Armored Division (Forward)," 129.

71 COL (Ret.) Mark S. Landrith, e-mail to the author, March 9, 2015, referring to details in his "Unit History."

72. Ibid.

73. Ibid.

74. Ibid.

75. Ibid. See also Bourque, *Jayhawk*, 143. The Iraqi 25 ID proved much more aggressive than the 26 ID.

76. Just how the controversy over the FSCL came about is not essential to the story of the 1 ID, but the Division understood that the truth had changed regarding the FSCL and shared that understanding with the VII Corps. See COL Michael Dodson, Commander, Division Artillery, 1st Infantry Division, interview by MAJ Thomas A. Popa, Fort Riley, KS, July 24–25, 1991, DCSIT-C-068..

77. Ibid.

78. The six maneuver battalions organized as balanced combined arms task forces included the 2-16 IN, 5-16 IN, 1-41 IN, 2-34 AR, 3-37 AR, and 3-66 AR. The 1-4 CAV was organically organized as a combined arms air-ground team except, unlike regimental cavalry squadrons, it did not have organic infantry squads in its troops.

79. COL (Ret.) James L. Hillman, interview with the author, Fort Meade, MD, April 23, 2014. See also Ancker, "2nd Armored Division (Forward)," 131; and US Department of the Army, *Tank Gunnery*, FM 17-12 (Washington, DC: US Department of the Army, 1972), chap. 6.

80. Hillman interview.

81. 2-66 AR, S-2, daily staff journal, February 15, 1991. Since the 2-66 AR remained in the forward assembly area, this entry reflects a spot report monitored on the Brigade Operations and Intelligence net.

82. LTG Frederick Franks, Commanding General, VII Corps, interview by unidentified person, October 31, 1991, DSIT-MHI-011.

83. Ibid.

84. VII Corps, "Air-Ground Operations in Desert Storm," briefing, n.d., reports eighteen battalions. Bourque, *Jayhawk*, 161n49, asserts that the Iraqis had twenty-two battalions opposite the Corps. He draws that number from G2, VII Corps, "The 100-Hour Ground War: How the Iraqi Plan Failed," May 4, 1994.

85. G2, VII Corps, "The 100-Hour Ground War," tab L. There was at least one 155-millimeter howitzer battalion located in the 48 ID, to the northeast of the planned penetration. The Corps G2 believed that the battalion supported the Iraqi VII Corps Reserve. The author believes they were positioned to fire on coalition forces coming north in the Wadi al-Batin.

86. COL Michael L. Dodson, personal journal, February 16, 1991; Rhame interview, February 2, 2015, quoting from Rhame's personal journal, February 16, 1991. The MLRS batteries that fired included the 1 ID's organic rocket battery and batteries from the Corps artillery.

87. Rhame interview, February 2, 2015, quoting from Rhame's personal journal, February 13, 1991. The 2-66 AR completed drawing its load on February

15, 1991. See 3rd Brigade, 2nd Armored Division (Forward), daily staff journal, February 15, 1991, 1738.

88. Rhame interview, February 2, 2015, quoting from Rhame's personal journal, February 16, 1991.

89. VII Corps, "Air Support Operations Center," daily situation report, February 16, 1991. The air component had so many sorties that eventually they managed to strike VII Corps targets. VII Corps, "Air-Ground Operations in Desert Storm," is duly grateful for the efforts of the air component. From the author's perspective, anything the air forces killed could not kill Americans. The situation in the desert in 1991 was ideal for air power.

90. Tom Clancy with General Chuck Horner (Ret.), *Every Man a Tiger* (New York: Putnam's, 1999), 466–76. The chief problem with air support to ground forces in Desert Storm resulted from GEN H. Norman Schwarzkopf's decision to retain command of the ground component. As a consequence, LTG John Yeosock spoke for the US Army, LTG Walt Boomer for the US Marine Corps, and GEN Khaled bin Sultan commanded the Arab Joint Forces. See Richard M. Swain, "*Lucky War*": *Third Army in Desert Storm* (Fort Leavenworth, KS: US Army Command and General Staff College Press, 1997), chap. 6. Swain's book is a dispassionate assessment of the irritants between the air component and the US Army.

91. 1 LT Gregory G. Glaze, 2nd Battalion, 34th Armor journal, February 16, 1991. The author asked 1LT Glaze to keep this journal and offer his own views of operations. Glaze made entries nearly every day, and the author added entries periodically.

92. Hillman interview.

93. US General Accounting Office, *Operation Desert Storm: Apache Helicopter Fratricide Incident* (Washington, DC: US General Accounting Office, 1993), 30; 3rd Brigade, 2nd Armored Division (Forward), daily staff journal, February 17, 1991. Until a complete Army record is available, the GAO report remains the most accurate account of what happened that night, and indeed it is the best investigation of any fratricide incident in the history of the 1st Infantry Division. It is unfortunate that the GAO did not undertake an investigation of every fratricide incident in the 1st Division and in Operation Desert Storm. The Division and the armed forces generally failed to investigate fratricides as rigorously as the GAO did. The armed forces performed brilliantly in Desert Storm, but could have learned far more from what happened than they did.

94. Hillman, "Task Force 1-41." In his monograph, Hillman reports the target as three enemy vehicles. In the interview with the author he remembered only two targets. The difference is that when LTC Hayles arrived on the scene he reported seeing two vehicles—the ones that he fired on proved to be friendlies. What is absolutely certain is that Hayles never saw the targets that Hillman wanted him to attack.

95. US General Accounting Office, *Apache Helicopter Fratricide Incident*, 34.

96. CPT Stephen M. Schiller, "Fratricide: Operation Desert Storm," unpublished manuscript, US Army Infantry School, Fort Benning, GA, June 25, 1993, 11.

97. US General Accounting Office, *Apache Helicopter Fratricide Incident*, 34.

98. Ibid., 30. I have used only times listed for the TF 1-41 IN, because log times for the 1-1AVN, the 4th Brigade, and the GAO report *Apache Helicopter Fratricide Incident* conflict.

99. US General Accounting Office, *Apache Helicopter Fratricide Incident*, 34–35.

100. Ibid., 36.

101. Ibid., 64. Appendix 5 of the GAO report is a combined transcript from intercom, radio, and information displayed on the aircraft monitor.

102. US General Accounting Office, *Apache Helicopter Fratricide Incident*, 67; bracketed text in the original.

103. Ibid., 33; the author has determined the grid coordinate from the GAO sketch in appendix 2. The grid is approximate, because the sketch was not drawn to scale.

104. For details on how the target acquisition and detection system worked, see US General Accounting Office, *Apache Helicopter Fratricide Incident*, 36–37.

105. US General Accounting Office, *Apache Helicopter Fratricide Incident*, 72–82.

106. Ibid., 84; discussion about whether the enemy did the damage can be found at 85–97.

107. LTC (Ret.) Jacob "Danny" Strickland, telephone interview with the author, August 7, 2014.

108. COL (Ret.) Terry W. Bullington, telephone interview with the author, October 29, 2013; COL Stanley F. Cherrie, personal journal, February 16, covers events through the early morning hours of February 17.

109. LTG (Ret.) Thomas G. Rhame, telephone interview with the author, February 3, 2015, quoting from Rhame's personal journal, February 17, 1991.

110. Mowery, "Saudi Journal," February 17, 1991.

111. 1st Infantry Division, "Firing Incident O/A 0100 17 February 1991," memorandum for commander, February 17, 1991.

112. US General Accounting Office, *Apache Helicopter Fratricide Incident*, 49n1.

113. Ibid., 48.

114. Gary Klein, *Sources of Power: How People Make Decisions* (Cambridge, MA: MIT Press, 1998), 273. Klein is a well-known commentator on recognition primed decision making or deciding on the basis of pattern recognition.

115. Bourque and Burdan, *The Road to Safwan*, 102.

116. Dodson, personal journal, February 17, 1991.

117. COL (Ret.) George P. Ritter, telephone interview with the author, August 5, 2014.

118. LTC (Ret.) William H. Hedges, telephone interview with the author, November 30, 2014.

119. Bourque and Burdan, *The Road to Safwan,* 103–4.

120. Rhame interview, February 3, 2015, quoting from Rhame's personal journal, February 18, 1991.

121. Ibid.

CHAPTER EIGHT

ONCE MORE INTO THE BREACH

Wow! Forty days of bombing and we still aren't moving.

—Major General Thomas G. Rhame

Confidence in the Task Force is high.

—First Lieutenant Gregory G. Glaze

It was exactly what AirLand battle doctrine was supposed to look like.

—Second Lieutenant Joseph Reed

My greatest worry was that a mine would explode under me.

—Specialist Bruno Berry

At about 4:00 p.m. on February 18, 1991, a scout from the Task Force 2nd Battalion, 34th Armor (TF 2-34 AR) peered through the optics of his Bradley and saw an Iraqi soldier emerge from a spider hole. The Iraqi stood about one kilometer north of the frontier and two kilometers northwest of the Bradley on the 1st Division's far left flank, well west of the ground Task Force (TF) Iron had cleared. The scout could see the Iraqi stretching; apparently he had not seen the scouts move in nearby. Ordered to fire only if fired upon, the scout platoon leader, 1LT John McCombs, asked for permission to shoot. When granted, one of McCombs's Bradleys fired a short burst from a twenty-five-millimeter Bushmaster cannon. The rounds fell short and the Iraqi fled into a second bunker nearby. McCombs's platoon watched the bunker throughout the night. Stung that his platoon had missed on its first attempt to strike the enemy, McCombs intended to remedy this at first light and follow up with a dismounted patrol.

Neither McCombs nor the enemy soldier he chased underground knew the ground offensive would start in less than a week. They both had their own tasks. McCombs aimed to kill the Iraqi or drive him off, so he could not report what he saw. The Iraqi soldier was part of the security zone west of the ground TF Iron cleared when it swept north. His job was to detect and report. He had certainly detected; whether he ever reported is unknown.

From VII Corps' perspective, a great deal remained to be done; completing logistics preparation and whittling down MG Ahmed Ibrahim Hamash's front-line units and his tactical reserve topped the list. During this last week before the commencement of the ground offensive, the Division focused on precluding any last-minute discovery of its intentions and on final preparation for the breach of the Iraqi 26 Infantry Division (26 ID). The preparation included mentally preparing for what lay ahead. Finally, on February 24, 1991, the 1st Division attacked.

Iraqi Estimates: February 18–23, 1991

Despite Saddam Hussein's earnest efforts to find a way to avoid a major ground offensive, the Iraqi high command understood a coalition attack had moved from likely to certain. The General Military Intelligence Directorate (GMID), relying largely on human intelligence—line crossers, attachés, and even the Western media—had concluded as much by February 14, reporting that an attack was "imminent."[1] Iraqi intelligence perceived that the uptick in cross-border operations and artillery raids presaged an attack. It had also received information from "advance reconnaissance units." In early February, Iraqi reconnaissance detected US special operations forces and elements of the XVIII Airborne (ABN) Corps operating in the western desert. The Iraqis also detected the two American corps moving west of the Wadi al-Batin.[2]

Iraqi intelligence had not deduced the date of the attack, but starting in mid-February it provided or received almost daily warnings. On February 15 the Iraqi embassy in Jordan opined the attack would come on the February 18. On February 16 the GMID reported "more than 1000 tanks and vehicles, in addition to different types of weapons, missiles and thousands of soldiers" west of the Wadi al-Batin.[3] As late as February 16 the intelligence directorate still believed the coalition would attack on more than one axis and make the main effort up the wadi. Two days later, however, it produced a new estimate that outlined in general terms the actual course of action.[4]

The estimate did not accurately identify the objective of the "left hook," but it correctly predicted it would envelope the Iraqi positions in Kuwait and southeastern Iraq. The directorate believed that the attack would emanate from Arar, a town located in the far northwestern corner of Saudi Arabia; it estimated an axis from Karbala and Al-Hillah to Baghdad. This was much farther west and far more dangerous to the regime than GEN H. Norman Schwarzkopf's left hook. The directorate further concluded that the coalition aimed "at isolating our forces in the South and Southwest of the Euphrates River." Given Saddam's lack of enthusiasm for bad news, the director concluded his estimate with a courageous assessment. LTG Sabir 'Abd al-'Aziz al-Douri concluded that the coalition scheme was such that "we could not possibly overcome."[5] It is unclear what Saddam made of this estimate or what could have been achieved in the short time that remained, but the positions and orientation of the Republican Guard Forces Command and the Jihad Corps served well enough to react to the left hook as actually executed. Positioned to respond to an attack north along the Wadi al-Batin, Iraqi reserves would have found it far more difficult to respond to the attack the GMID imagined. Neither the Republican Guard nor the Jihad Corps moved farther west, so perhaps Saddam did not agree with the estimate.

Whatever the Iraqi high command knew, little of that intelligence made its way from Baghdad to any of the line divisions in southern Iraq and Kuwait. The coalition had serious difficulty disseminating intelligence products. Yet by comparison to that of Iraq, the coalition's system worked like clockwork. Iraqi prisoners taken before and during the assault had no idea who was across from them; most believed they faced Arab units. Division commanders in the Iraqi VII Corps knew little more than their rank and file. Fearful of using electronic means to communicate, and largely unable to move freely because of bombing, the Iraqi 26 ID and its sister formations had little idea of what was coming and seemed disinclined to gain information by patrolling aggressively.[6]

Defense of the Border and Final Preparations: February 18–23, 1991

The 1st and 2nd Brigades assumed the defense of the border and passed TF Iron southward as they withdrew back into Saudi Arabia. As the 1st Brigade moved forward, 1LT Keith Markham's tank platoon passed by one of the logistics bases and noticed "a huge number of coffins stacked up."[7] Seeing the coffins did nothing for the soldiers' morale, but it did remind them they were going into harm's way. COL Lon E. "Bert" Maggart's 1st Brigade occupied a gentle rise two kilometers south of the berm, and could see over the berm and cover its approaches. In this position, Maggart's troops defended slightly more than twenty kilometers of the border and prepared for the impending assault. LTC Greg Fontenot's TF 2-34 AR defended the western flank of the Division. Task Force 5th Battalion, 16th Infantry (5-16 IN), commanded by LTC Skip Baker, defended the sector east of Fontenot's unit. Both task forces consisted of two tank and two mechanized companies.[8] TF 5-16 IN also boasted an antitank company composed of tube-launched, optically tracked, wire-guided (TOW) antitank missile launchers mounted on M113 chassis. These contraptions were called improved TOW vehicles. LTC Pat Ritter's 1-34 AR occupied positions to the rear in reserve. LTC Bob Wilson's 1st Squadron, 4th Cavalry (1-4 CAV) had withdrawn to the rear to rest and prepare to attack under Maggart's operational control.

COL Tony Moreno's 2nd Brigade defended nearly twenty kilometers of the border on the right. LTC Dave Gross's TF 3-37 AR tied in with Baker on his left. LTC Dan Fake's TF 2-16 IN defended the border on Gross's right. LTC Dave Marlin's tank-pure 4-37 AR defended on Fake's right and maintained contact with a tank battalion from the 1st Cavalry Division (1 CD) on its right. The two forward brigades assumed the defense to prevent Iraqi reconnaissance from interfering with final preparations for the attack. When ordered, they would attack from these positions to penetrate the Iraqi 26 ID. The 1st Battalion, 1st Aviation unit (1-1 AVN) continued to support operations with eight Apache helicopters flying in the daytime and sixteen dedicated to nighttime. MG Thomas G. Rhame assigned priority of support to the 2nd Brigade.

Of the third iteration of his plan to secure the forward assembly areas and to permit stockpiling supplies, Rhame wrote, "1st and 2nd Brigades will be tested [by] getting used to being up front and I will rest the 1-41 [INF] and the Quarter Cav."[9] MG Rhame planned to rotate as many of his battalions as possible through the security missions in order to enable a "shakedown" or "test" in a comparatively low-threat environment. The rotation scheme permitted his maneuver brigades the same opportunity. Seven of the ten ground maneuver battalions "shook down" prior to the attack; three did not have that opportunity. In the 1st Brigade, Ritter's tank battalion remained in reserve, although one of his companies spent two days on the line. In the 3rd Brigade, neither LTC John S. Brown's nor LTC George T. Jones's tank battalions got into an active sector or skirmish before the onset of the ground offensive.[10] The Quarter Horse (1-4 CAV), the Division's tenth ground maneuver battalion, had a month's experience in combat operations. The attack helicopter battalion, although not a ground maneuver battalion, counted as the eleventh maneuver battalion; like the Quarter Horse, it had one month's experience.

The 1st Brigade had a busy first night on the line. According to Maggart, his brigade fired "every weapon in the Brigade that night against a variety of targets real and imagined, except for [the] tank main gun."[11] At sunup on February 19, McCombs's scouts attempted to revenge their failure of the day before. They scored several hits on the bunker they had seen the lone Iraqi enter the night before. Because the bunker glowed hot in their thermals throughout the night, they believed their nemesis had remained inside. After hitting the bunker with twenty-five-millimeter canon rounds, McCombs led a dismounted patrol out to investigate. The patrol found not one bunker, but three. The hole from which the Iraqi soldier had emerged created considerable interest. He had dug a hole into the side of a little rise so that he had to slither in; once inside, he lay prone

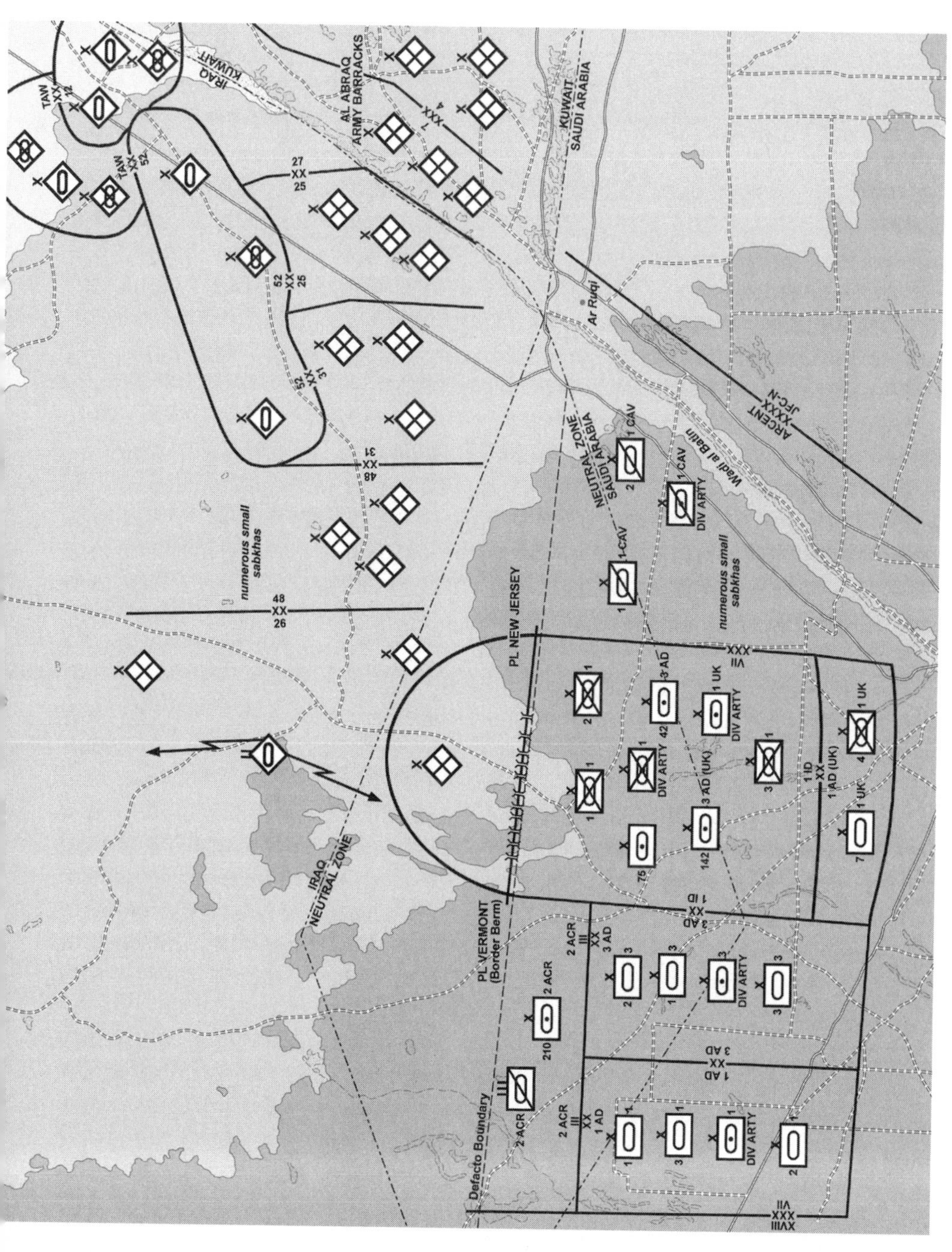

MAP 6. Final preattack positions of VII Corps, February 23, 1991. Recreated from Map 6, Stephen A. Bourque, *Jayhawk! The VII Corps in the Persian Gulf War.*

to observe. The other bunkers were larger and contained the remains of meals, some equipment, and trash.[12] The Iraqi soldier they had seen the evening before had left, but the heat signature in the bunker suggested he and the rest of the outpost's occupants had not been gone long.

There was still plenty to do that cool, breezy morning. Both brigades patrolled on foot and no farther than one kilometer north of the border. That kept them south of Central Command's (CENTCOM's) Fire Support Coordination Line. COL Bob Shadley's Division Support Command worked in earnest to stock and maintain the ammunition that COL Mike Dodson's artillery needed to sustain an ambitious artillery raid program and a very big preassault bombardment. COL Weisman's 3rd Brigade moved into a reserve position south of the brigades on the berm. LTC Jim Hillman's task force needed to rest and recover from the ugly fratricide it had endured; LTC Lanny Smith's artillery had earned a rest as well.

The attack battalion labored under the shadow of the ongoing investigation of the friendly fire incident, but Rhame did not let the battalion languish for long. MAJ Mark Landrith, the battalion operations officer, briefed the Corps commander on February 20 for the nighttime mission into Iraq to be executed two nights later. LTC Phil Wilkinson's 4-1 AVN also flew both day and night to support logistics, intelligence collection, and command and control missions. The 4th Brigade also prepared to move farther forward to assure responsive support once the Division launched the ground attack.[13]

Of immediate interest to the Division artillery was cleaning up the mess made by the multiple-launch rocket system crew that fired on Ritter's battalion while continuing the raid program. Many of the small bomblets spewed around the 1-34 AR had not exploded. The errant crew fired six rockets, so that meant there were hundreds of unexploded bomblets, each of which could kill or maim, strewn throughout the area. COL Dodson investigated the incident with support from VII Corps artillery, and concluded he had no choice but to relieve both the section chief and his gunner and discipline both.[14] Meanwhile, LTC Scott Lingamfelter directed the actual cleanup operation. An explosive ordnance disposal unit blew up the bomblets where they were, as they were too dangerous to handle. Combat engineers buried the rocket motors where they fell. This was dicey work, but no one got hurt. The artillery also ramped up the raid program and did so more effectively than previously. As COL Dodson noted at the time, "Coordination is improving. OPS/Intel [operations/intelligence] is getting in the swing."[15] LTC John Gingrich's battalion fired 530 rounds on February 17, and 182 rounds the next day. Though Gingrich's troops admitted to being nervous, "everyone did their jobs"; the battalion "worked initial bugs out of the system and refined our ability to get steel on target."[16] LTC Harry Emerson's 1st Battalion, 5th Field Artillery (1-5 FA) also fired that day, as did its reinforcing battalion from Corps artillery.

With everything else that had to be done, Rhame had to decide what to do about the fratricide. He had seen the gun camera tapes and listened to the radio and intercom exchanges the morning after the tragedy. He asked BG Bill Carter to do the investigation. Carter began early on February 17 and completed his report the next evening; his investigation made it clear that LTC Ralph Hayles had made serious mistakes and had not followed Rhame's directive to lead his battalion rather than fight as a helicopter gunner. That night Rhame wrote in his journal, "I and I alone will decide." He was very clear with his commanders about what he expected of them. His conviction about what happened when commanders did not meet those obligations was equally clear: "Dumb things happen when leaders fail to exercise proper command and control." Rhame "spent the day [February 18] on LTC Hayles's case";[17] he carefully reviewed Carter's report in the company of LTC Warren Hall, the Division staff judge advocate—that is, the Division's lawyer.

COL Jim Mowery feared the worst. That Hayles had killed other Americans was indisputable. Although he had been encouraged by the ground commander to shoot, and had flown in truly difficult conditions, it remained hard to see why he fired. As noted, just before the tragedy he transmitted over the radio, "Boy, I'm going to tell you, it's hard to pull this trigger," which raised a big question: With no one under fire, and with doubts in his mind, why had he fired? COL Mowery thought Hayles a "first class commander who has done a great job." He also thought changing commanders at this late date would not serve either the attack battalion or the Division. He went to see Rhame at 9:30 a.m. on February 19 and pleaded his case. Afterward Mowery wrote, "I talked to the CG [commanding general] for quite a while, but I think his mind is made up. The CG has lost trust and confidence in Ralph and I am pretty sure he will relieve him."[18]

COL Mowery could not let it go, and he spoke to Rhame a second time. At the end of that conversation, Rhame told Mowery he wanted both a written statement from Hayles and to meet with him. Mowery wrote at the time, "If Ralph plays his cards right, and writes his statement well he can set the stage for a good discussion." He reviewed Hayles's statement at 3:00 p.m. He thought it shallow, and likely to "set the stage for disaster." Hayles met with the commanding general at 7:30 p.m. Afterward, Hayles told Mowery that "the meeting was very ugly and that he thought he would be relieved." Rhame had empathy for Hayles, but very little sympathy. "He is a distraught officer. Good man, made a terrible leadership mistake." It was clear to Rhame that Hayles "[d]isobeyed my orders on how battalion commanders are to provide for command and control and synchronization. Killed two soldiers of the United States."[19]

At 2:00 p.m. on February 20 Rhame called Mowery and told him Hayles was relieved of command immediately. Things moved rapidly thereafter. The Army had already slated LTC Ron Reichelderfer to assume command of the battalion after Hayles. Reichelderfer had deployed with the Division and was serving as the 1st Division liaison officer to the VII Corps. COL Mowery sent a helicopter to pick him up at the Corps command post and went himself to tell Hayles. Having expected the news, Hayles had already packed.[20]

Word of Hayles's relief reverberated in the Division. None of his peers was surprised. Rhame had, after all, made clear what he expected of his commanders. Isolated by distance and focused on their own affairs, not much discussion occurred among commanders or even within units. What little came out revealed few had sympathy for Hayles. Few could imagine themselves in Hayles's shoes. As one of his own soldiers put it, "Colonel Hayles was not relieved for that friendly fire accident. . . . He was relieved for failure to obey a direct order."[21] The full effect of Hayles's relief is hard to assess, but one aspect of it was to raise the expectation that each subsequent incident of fratricide would be subjected to a rigorously thorough investigation. But in retrospect, in the minds of many soldiers the Division did not meet that expectation.

In any case, there was little time for reflection. The forward task forces had tried to learn from Combat Command Carter and TF Iron. It appeared, for example, that the Iraqis fired flares to illuminate the lanes their patrols used to cross their defensive obstacles. Triangulation showed that the nightly light show occurred just over the Iraqi front line at roughly the same time each night. Enemy combat patrols did come south, but failed to close the border. Direct-fire engagements seldom occurred; often firing mortars at the enemy was enough to drive them off. Dealing with contacts and learning by doing were the background to final planning and preparation.

The Plan in Context

Neither the deliberations of the Iraqi high command nor those of Hamash's VII Corps troubled the 1st Division troops. The Iraqi 26 ID, on the other hand, captivated them and their commanders. Two things remained uppermost in the minds of the commanders of the assault units: Do we know where the 26 ID units are? Do we know how badly we have hurt them?

Just how badly the Iraqis had been hurt remained unknown, but there was enough information to make informed estimates. The air component had shifted some of its resources to attack front-line units at the end of January and ramped up that effort in February. Beginning on February 17, Division and Corps artillery joined in the effort. Pilot in-flight reports and prisoner debriefings provided the best feedback on effectiveness. The VII Corps air support operations group provided a daily litany of crass jokes and witty asides along with actual, usable information. By mid-February, the authors of the unofficial situation report called the "Daily Queep" were reporting significant battle damage to the enemy front-line divisions. The air operations officers also could provide the number of sorties flown against various Iraqi units, but determining effect remained problematic. Both CENTCOM and the 3rd Army tracked and debated battle damage assessments. At the start of the ground attack, the 3rd Army estimated air and artillery strikes had reduced the Iraqi VII Corps to 50 percent effectiveness or less. No one could make that assessment with absolute confidence. Analysts could conclude that front-line units suffered low morale. Prisoner reports to that effect seemed entirely plausible based on their appearance: they were dirty, ill equipped, and clearly not particularly capable.[22]

The Division also knew with a high degree of certainty the dispositions of its target. In January and February, LTC Terry Ford's analysts published overlays that showed Iraqi positions down to the platoon level in those units the two assault brigades would attack. These overlays stemmed from detailed analysis of imagery and electronic intelligence coupled with combat information gleaned from prisoners. CW2 Phyllis Fitzgerald and her analysts developed orders of battle for the units targeted in the breach, others in Hamash's Corps, and the Republican Guard. She and the rest of the Division's intelligence troops provided a good picture of the 110th and 434th Brigades of the Iraqi 26 ID. Thanks to them, the combat units knew where the enemy was. The orders process that began in a motor pool at Fort Riley, Kansas, in mid-November 1990 now culminated on the basis of good and improving intelligence. By the end of January, plans and orders were published down to the task force level. All that remained was to refine targets, make adjustments based on new information, and rehearse ad infinitum.

LTC Gross thought his own concept for the attack ironic, observing that the "organization for combat and scheme of maneuver resembled the organization and tactics of our former enemy, the Soviet Army."[23] Soviet soldiers would have recognized the technique of attacking on a narrow front with at least three-to-one odds at the point of penetration supported by overwhelming artillery. Nevertheless, Rhame's concept had the imprimatur of US Army doctrine because both shared some basic principles with its counterpart. His concept reflected exactly what had been imagined in FM 71-100, *Division Operations*; in the field manual a penetration is indicated "when the enemy is overextended, weak spots in his position are detected, terrain and observation are favorable, strong fire support is available, or an assailable flank is not available."[24] The authors of the manual would have been hard pressed to find a situation better suited to making a penetration. The Iraqi 26 ID, perhaps at half strength, defended about twice the frontage it could defend effectively at full strength. It fielded far less combat power than did the US 1 ID and essentially could not maneuver. The open desert denied it both cover and concealment. To support the attack, Rhame would have the equivalent of six brigades of artillery. In every way the situation supported making a penetration attack.

To increase his advantage, Rhame narrowed the frontage of the attack to about eighteen kilometers. The opposition, on the other hand, defended nearly thirty kilometers. Each of the assault brigades further narrowed the initial point of penetration to no more than two kilometers. Together the four lead task forces would attack with 116 tanks and about a thousand infantrymen in 116 Bradley infantry fighting vehicles against no more than eight hundred lightly equipped enemy infantrymen supported by fewer than thirty tanks. After the assault echelon penetrated the enemy, 116 more tanks from the reserve tank battalion in each brigade would expand the breach. The assault brigades would carry the attack deep enough to drive the enemy beyond direct-fire range of the actual breach. Next, Rhame would commit 116 more tanks and fifty-eight Bradleys in Weisman's brigade. Together the three brigades would drive the enemy beyond artillery range. Rhame and his brigade commanders had stacked the odds in their favor.

There were differences between the US and Soviet approaches to tactical operations. MAJ Tom Connors, Gross's executive officer, described the most important one: "Every platoon leader knew this plan. So if it all went to shit, any platoon leader could run with it, which is not the Soviet model."[25] If things went as planned, the Iraqi 26 ID would cease to exist as a fighting formation no later than the second day of the attack.

Each of the four assault task forces approached the problem based on assigned tasks, terrain, enemy, proximity of friendly units, and the concept of each of the commanders. Each had to clear and mark four passage lanes for following forces. They also had to expand their penetration through the depth of the enemy front-line brigades and laterally to afford adequate space for the four passage lanes and to preclude the enemy from placing direct fire on them. In 1991, Army operations doctrine stressed the primacy of clearly articulating intentions and concept. This is another point where US Army doctrine parted company with Soviet thinking. Soviet forces applied high levels of "troop control" and planned operations using "norms." They took a scientific approach, featuring mathematical calculations of force ratios and statistical norms for rates of March. The US Army, on the other hand, believed that if a commander communicated intent clearly and concisely, soldiers in the unit could execute with or without communications or even the commander. GEN William E. DePuy's and GEN Donn Starry's influence underlay this thinking. The doctrine reflected both American culture and the Army's aspirations about soldier initiative. Finally, both DePuy and Starry believed the intensity of combat against Soviet forces would require the US Army to fight without tight control.

Gross published his operations order on February 13. When he briefed it, he told his soldiers to "punch a hole through the first defensive line; kill or capture the enemy that get in the way; and protect the breach from enemy direct fire, so follow-on forces can get through the hole."[26] His written concept flowed less eloquently: "TF 3-37 conducts a deliberate attack in zone with two tank teams abreast breaching two lanes each and penetrate enemy defensive positions along PL [Phase Line] Wisconsin."[27]

Fontenot specified the technique he desired in greater detail. He planned to maneuver at least a company to attack each enemy platoon. With the exception of the first objective that could only be attacked frontally, his concept asserted, "We will seek to clear the enemy from the zone by attacking his positions from the flanks or rear. The key to minimizing casualties is to seek flanks and maintain momentum. Movement is the key to survivability." Finally, "we must conserve resources. I expect to operate two days with the fuel and ammo we are able to carry."[28]

Gross and Fontenot differed slightly in intent, but they were fundamentally the same conceptually, as were those who led the other assault formations. With orders in hand, units rehearsed everything from evacuating the wounded from tanks and Bradleys to platoon battle drills right up until the day before the attack. Many of the troops were eager, but others harbored doubts. As 1LT Markham, the platoon leader who had seen the stacks of coffins, recalled, "All of us thought the odds were such if we got wounded we would be lucky."[29] Despite growing evidence that air and artillery were hurting the enemy, the Division still believed the Iraqis would have considerable capacity to resist. To begin with, they would enjoy the benefits of being the defender—the Division had to come to them. Equally important, the historical record showed that bombardment rarely reduced the enemy or their obstacles as much as was hoped. The Division had done what it could to mitigate risks, but nonetheless expected casualties. At the 3rd Army, the staff estimated twenty thousand killed and wounded across the theater of operations in the first five days.[30] No one believed the Iraqis would defeat the attacking forces, but few believed casualties would be low. Shortly before the ground attack, one young officer posed a question in the journal he maintained for his unit: "Who are the 85% of the people in America favoring a ground war? We are definitely the 15% opposed."[31]

However individual soldiers felt about the imminent start of the ground offensive, all of them felt the atmosphere electric with anticipation. There was a palpable sense of expectation generated by reports of operations underway elsewhere. The 1 CD and a few Marine units, far to the east, were conducting raids and feints to deceive the Iraqis on the direction of the attack, to test defenses, or to reduce obstacles. The date for the attack, or G-Day, had not yet been set, but clearly it would be soon. On February 19 LTG Frederick M. Franks Jr. ordered BG John Tilelli to conduct a reconnaissance in force "to determine his [Iraqi] composition, his disposition and his intent."[32] Tilelli assigned the mission to COL Randolph W. House and the 2nd Brigade. One of House's infantry companies crossed the berm that night to identify crossing sites and to search for mines. The company-size patrol returned safely with little to report. The next day the Brigade penetrated the security zone of the Iraqi 31 ID, which was defending just west of the Wadi al-Batin.[33]

The Iraqi 103rd Brigade fought effectively. Supported by antitank guns and tanks, the 103rd ambushed House's troops. In the ensuing fight the Iraqis destroyed three combat vehicles and damaged a fourth. The Iraqis also killed three Americans and wounded nine others.[34] Until this skirmish, no VII Corps unit had encountered the main enemy defenses. Because the Iraqis expected the main attack to come up the Wadi al-Batin, the defending 31 ID enjoyed resources that divisions farther west did not. Its obstacle belt rivaled the complex obstacles systems detected farther east. This engagement had a sobering effect on the 1st Division. It appeared the Iraqis could fight.

The Cavalry Division's probe of the Iraqi defense is best understood in the context of the overall operational plan. In the west, the XVIII ABN Corps planned to begin with the 6th French Light Armored Division seizing the As Salman Air Base. The 101 ABN would airlift its brigades by helicopter in stages all the way to the Euphrates River to cut off the main highway from Basra to Baghdad. On their right, the 24 ID would attack to the same highway to interdict the escape route from Kuwait. In the east, the Marines and Arab forces would attack north. Franks's VII Corps would attack to penetrate the Iraqi VII Corps over the course of two days. On G-Day, when the ground offensive began, the Corps would kill or drive off the enemy in their security zone. On G+1, the 1 ID would complete the breach and pass the UK 1 AD forward. The British would then attack east and roll up the Iraqi VII Corps as it went. The 2nd Armored Cavalry Regiment (2 ACR) and the two US armored divisions would bypass the breach and the Iraqi defenses to the west and head north toward Corps Objective Collins. There they would turn east and be joined by either the 1st Division or the 1 CD to destroy the Republican Guard. This option assumed the Guard would remain where they had been positioned in December. Richard M. Swain, the 3rd Army historian, points out that the timing of the attack in the west worked against Schwarzkopf's concept of freezing Iraqi reserves by attacking in the east.[35]

Artillery raids, air bombardment, and final preparation consumed the last few days before the ground offensive began. At the VII Corps, Franks issued daily orders for cross-border attack helicopter and artillery raids to continue whittling away at the points of attack and against Hamash's reserve armored division. Franks's fragmentary order 128-91, issued at noon on February 20, specified, "Increased G-Day operational sequence activities continue with artillery raids. Berm preparations, patrolling, and AH-64 raids planned across the front."[36] Even the most indolent and careless Iraqi analyst could not help but conclude the attack would come soon. Operational planning settled down as execution ramped up.

Final Preparations: February 20–23, 1991

On February 20 Rhame met with his brigade and separate battalion commanders. Among other things, he told them the ground attack would likely go "on or about 24 February."[37] Later that day, Reichelderfer, Hayles's successor, participated in a briefing to the corps commander on a cross-border mission, given by Landrith, his operations officer. Franks approved the mission for execution on February 22.[38] That afternoon Rhame visited with the battalion to assure them of his trust and confidence. COL Mowery thought he "gave a great talk."[39] Dodson continued the raid program. That day, the UK forces fired twenty missions, expending some 1,560 eight-inch rounds and 155-millimeter rounds, as well as eighty-four rockets.[40] COL Maggart met with COL Don Holder to review flank coordination. Holder's 2 ACR would attack to the west of the 1st Division with the two US armored divisions following him. Holder and Maggart arranged how they would maintain contact during the advance. COL Moreno's troops maintained their watch on the frontier and practiced still more; COL Weisman's brigade did likewise. He, the brigade staff, and commanders spent all day on a map exercise "going over everything in the executions matrix again."[41] In his diary, Rhame observed, "We are getting much more air into our friends in front of us. Between us [artillery raids] and the Air Force he [the enemy in the Iraqi 26 ID] must really be hurting."[42] Finally, at 10:30 p.m. on February 20, Franks called to confirm that the ground offensive would begin in a little more than seventy-two hours, at first light on Sunday, February 24, 1991.[43]

The moment anticipated since November 1990 had come. The Division Support Command and 2nd Corps Support Command continued to deliver ammunition to support raids and cache enough artillery ammunition to support the two and a half hours Dodson planned for the final artillery preparation. By the end of the next day, logistics troops had stockpiled nine thousand short tons of ammunition; that would be more than enough to finish the raids and do anything else that needed doing.[44] The artillery fired thirty-three missions on February 22 and seven more the next day. They fired 1,584 eight-inch and 155-millimeter rounds and 132 rockets on February 22 and another 972 rounds and 108 rockets the next day.[45] Back on the berm, life continued apace. At first light on February 22, Baker's infantry took three more prisoners who had walked seventeen kilometers south to escape the war.

There remained only precombat inspections of equipment and a final review of plans to assure that all was ready. The concept Rhame had developed in November endured, albeit with adjustments as more information became available. He had organized each of the three maneuver brigades to support his concept and assure they had what they needed. The 1st and 2nd Brigades each had an entire engineer battalion in support. LTC Rich Jemiola's 9th Engineer

Battalion (9 EN) continued to support the 1st Brigade, while LTC Steve Hawkins's 1 EN supported the 2nd Brigade. All three brigades had an air defense artillery battery. The brigades had chemical reconnaissance, decontamination, and smoke platoons as well as military police and ground surveillance radar. Finally, each had its own support battalion to provide logistics and maintenance support.

MG Rhame's scheme envisioned a two-and-a-half-hour preparation bombardment to suppress and destroy enemy targets. The number of targets and the desired effect drove the length of the preparation. To strike all of the targets with the desired effect, Dodson planned to fire eighty thousand rounds over the course of the two and a half hours. Three things had changed since Rhame had developed his concept. First, and most important, Franks had decided not to pass the entire Corps through the penetration. Only the UK 1 AD and Corps artillery would pass through the breach. Second, the number of lanes the Division would clear had grown from eight to sixteen. This meant no mines and no enemy able to interdict the lanes with direct fire. At just over twelve feet wide, the lanes would handle both tracked and wheeled vehicles. Third and finally, the attacking units knew with high fidelity where and how the Iraqi 26 ID proposed to defend.

The 26 ID had made few alterations to its positions since arriving in late December. It defended with two brigades forward, the 110th Brigade in the west and the 434th Brigade in the east. The 806th Brigade occupied positions roughly fifty kilometers northwest of the two forward brigades and was oriented west. Each of the two forward brigades had three battalions arrayed with two battalions forward and one back. The 26 ID also had a tank battalion originally composed of thirty-six tanks. Two of the tank companies occupied positions in the rear of the infantry brigades from where they could counterattack against penetrations. The enemy division also had light-armored cars and supporting air defense and field artillery. Overhead imagery and videos from the Corps' remotely piloted vehicles enabled 1st Division intelligence analysts to conclude the enemy trench system was shallow and narrow; the trenches appeared to be no more than chest deep.[46]

The 26 ID appeared to be second rate at best. On February 20 Rhame wrote, "we will have a fight on our hands, but he [the enemy] will be very weak." The next day, the sixth in a row of artillery raids and air strikes, he surmised, "today we really beat him up." The last day before the assault Rhame estimated, "we have him at less than 50% strength. I don't think there's more than four tanks left in front of the 26th Division and only 15–20 artillery pieces left in his sector."[47] Despite Rhame's confidence, soldiers manning the plow tanks and lead vehicles in the assault prepared for the worst. When CPT Tim Norton, who commanded a tank-heavy company team, reassigned missions among his platoon leaders he thought, "I was signing his [the platoon leader's] death warrant."[48]

While Norton prepared for the worst, the Iraqi high command believed the ground offensive had already begun. Iraqi histories generally assert that the ground attack began on February 21. Cross-border sweeps, patrols, and aggressive probes by the 1 CD led the Iraqis to believe the ground offensive was under way. In the east, the Iraqi 7 ID believed it had defeated a combined arms attack involving armor and artillery. Pleased with the result, "The Army commander called to present his appreciation to the soldiers for their resistance, and he gave a [commemorative] gun to each soldier."[49] On February 22, the Iraqi 26 ID reported forcing coalition forces to withdraw from contact; in southern Kuwait, the Iraqi 14 ID allegedly defeated a ground attack. So if the Iraqis believed that the ground war had already begun, at this point they also thought they were succeeding. This gave credence to the Iraqi leadership's belief that the Soviet Union would succeed in arranging a cease-fire that would enable Iraq to negotiate a withdrawal.[50]

February 23, the last day before G-Day, was—like all other days before it—busy, but it was also especially fraught with trepidation. CPT Juan Toro noted that "nothing was done grudgingly."[51] CPT Jim Bell felt confident; he believed in his leaders, from Franks to Ritter, and felt that "I would go to hell for any of these folks."[52] Leaders felt their responsibility acutely. SFC Ralph E. Martin, who led Jim Bell's third platoon, considered himself personally "responsible for the [other] 15 solders" in his platoon. CPT James K. Morningstar commanded a tank company team in one of the assault formations, and on the evening of February 23 visited his combat engineers; looking back upon it later, he found it "hard to express the feelings you go through when you look at men that you know may be killed the next day while under your command."[53] That evening soldiers made peace with what lay before them. Chaplain Gerald D. Bacon spent part of that last night before the attack with CPT Curt Torrance's company. He described the tone of the evening eloquently, if romantically, as like "the mood in Gethsemane. Our tankers would rather they didn't have to drink of this cup; yet they would willingly do so. No one in the battalion has refused the cup today."[54]

That night the commanders and key leaders of TF 2-34 AR watched a video of the trenches they would attack in the morning. The video had been taken by a remotely piloted vehicle from the 207th Military Intelligence Brigade. It may have even been the same one that Combat Command Carter had tried to shoot down before it was made aware that the 207th had drones. In the video, the Iraqi troops were "plainly visible"; the enemy was no longer an abstract concept, but now real people like themselves. Equally important, the video showed the "trenches are not as formidable as we thought."[55] For his part, Rhame was ready to go; in his journal he wrote, "We are about, at last, to be set free."[56] The attack battalion flew another mission that night, crossing the border at 9:30 p.m. It reconnoitered the ground to the north, "destroyed two vehicles and shot up a few a few enemy troops in the bunker line—all without loss." The battalion crossed back into Saudi Arabia at 1:10 a.m. COL Jim Mowery concluded his journal entry that night by writing, "The reality of it all [the imminent attack] is apparent everywhere."[57]

The Approach: February 24, 1991, 3:30 A.M. to 2:30 P.M.

The ground offensive began at 4:00 a.m. when the French 6th Light Armored Division attacked with a brigade of the 82 ABN in support toward As Salman Air Base. In the east, the Marines attacked at the same time, having asked for and received permission to attack early to reduce obstacles in their area. How Schwarzkopf believed this consistent with his plan is difficult to see. Arab forces assigned to Joint Forces Command East attacked at 6:31 a.m. The 101 ABN began moving by air at about 6:30 a.m., bound for an objective about halfway to the Euphrates River. Arab forces in Joint Forces Command North on the western flank of the Marines would attack later in the day. Scheduled to attack at first light, the 1st Division started moving the short distance to the berm at 5:00 a.m. No one could yet see any dawn sunlight; it was cold that morning, with rain and fog, and pitch-black.

SFC Jeff Hein, an infantry platoon sergeant, noted in his journal, "0330—first call, get up and pack up the gear and prep [prepare] to move. The mood is somber as the chemical over garments are opened and put on. The rain that held off all night now begins to fall and the wind picks up. Infantry weather."[58] Hein was right—in this instance, infantry weather favored the attacking infantry and their comrades in tanks by concealing their approach. Coming out of the south and southeast, the wind benefited the attackers, because if the Iraqis used gas, it would drift back toward themselves.[59]

Military theorist Karl von Clausewitz has described the litany of things that could go wrong in war as friction, and in the US armed forces, Murphy's law is often cited to account for unexpected error. Both Murphy and friction were afoot that morning. COL Tony Moreno had just received a brand new Bradley infantry fighting vehicle, and when his team had transferred their gear, they failed to transfer Moreno's map with the Brigade's graphics. Moreno, who stressed to his commanders that everyone had to know his part, operated that day without graphics, but never missed a beat, having committed the graphics to his formidable memory.[60]

Although the team members knew their location, finding the cuts or lanes TF Iron had made in the berm proved problematic. As Clausewitz has noted, in war the simplest things are difficult. Mythology recited with some pride among veterans asserts that the Division crossed the line of departure—the berm—at 5:38 a.m., though only one unit, TF 2-16 IN, reported crossing at that time, and none reported 5:31 a.m., the time the Division had planned to cross. TF

2-34 AR reported its scout platoon crossing too early, at 5:27 a.m. MAJ Jack Crumplar, the task force operations officer, described the conditions created by moonset and rain: "It was so dark I didn't realize I had gone through the gap [in the berm]."[61] TF 3-37 AR managed to start crossing the berm at 5:37 a.m. CPT Torrance's company crossed half an hour late, because it could not find its lane through the berm. His soldiers were by no means the only ones who had trouble that morning.[62]

Getting through the berm reminded some of night moves out of assembly areas during exercises at the National Training Center (NTC) at Fort Irwin, California. Moving when it is really dark is far harder to do than it is to plan. To understand why, one must imagine a battalion with a thousand or more soldiers in two hundred vehicles moving in mist, all made worse by total darkness and minimizing communications. Drivers and commanders wearing passive night-vision devices could see very little. Gunners peering through thermal devices could see a bit better, but thermals depend on heat differences, and there were none to speak of in the lanes. In these conditions, it takes very little for things to go wrong—and things usually do. After-action reviews at the NTC then and now demonstrate the point. Since the inception of the training center, observer-trainers have invited units to consider how they can improve on clearing their assembly areas and organizing on the move. But that morning no observer-trainers took notes or photographs of units bunched up at the defiles created by the cuts in the berm. Worse still, it was so dark that no one could see the confusion as the Division groped its way ingloriously into Iraq.[63]

Eventually the Division managed to get into Iraq, its units advancing north. The plan for G-Day required them to clear the enemy's security zone and close in to attack positions near their front lines. On G+1 they would continue the attack to penetrate the enemy defenses and establish the breach. Initially the Division advanced with six battalions abreast: the Quarter Horse, TF 2-34 AR, TF 5-16 IN, TF 3-37 AR, TF 2-16 IN, and the 4-37 AR formed the lead in the attack. Overhead, the 1-1 AVN and the two air cavalry troops flew in support. The 1-34 AR, four battalions of artillery, and unit logistics trains followed the forward brigades. The 3rd Brigade, the remainder of the supporting artillery, and the rest of the Division trailed behind.

LTC Terry Bullington's planners drew a series of phase lines to enable Rhame to coordinate the advance and track progress. The planners drew Phase Line Vermont along the frontier berm. Phase Line Minnesota lay four kilometers north. Phase Line Iowa came next, seven kilometers farther on, followed by Phase Line Kansas just one kilometer north of Phase Line Iowa. The Division planned to advance at least as far as Phase Line Kansas on G-Day to clear the security zone and position for the main attack that would come the next day. Inexplicably, the planners named the next phase lines Birch and Plum rather than using the names of states; both of these lay a kilometer apart. Phase Line

Wisconsin, drawn right across the enemy's main defense, lay one kilometer beyond Phase Line Plum and three kilometers north of Phase Line Kansas. Phase Line Colorado, drawn in a semicircle, was next. At roughly five kilometers farther north, Colorado marked the initial depth of the breach designed to prevent enemy direct fire on the passage lanes. Phase Line New Jersey, also drawn in a semicircle, marked the necessary depth to prevent indirect fire into the breach area and extended roughly eighteen kilometers from the front line positions at its deepest point, about the same to the east, and seven kilometers to the west.

The Iraqi security zone extended at least ten kilometers south of its forces' front line. As a result, the attackers began discovering security forces soon after crossing Phase Line Vermont. Presumably, the Iraqis intended their security zone to preclude reconnaissance of their main positions, provide early warning, and delay attackers. At 6:15 a.m. TF 3-37 AR met the first of them. Some of the enemy behaved like they wanted to give up, others like they intended to fight, but sorting out one from the other was difficult. Often attackers held their fire to be sure they fired only on those who resisted actively. Confusion reigned in the dark and mist but, fortunately, both dissipated as the sun rose. With daylight everyone could see better, including what they had failed to see earlier. Shortly after daybreak, Gross's trail company teams captured Iraqis that his scouts and lead company teams had bypassed in the dark.[64]

About the same time, someone fired on his scouts with a light machine gun from across the Brigade's left boundary. The scouts believed Baker's 5-16 IN had fired at them, but Baker's troops later denied doing so. Baker's troops would more likely have used their twenty-five-millimeter canon or even a tank gun against Gross's Bradley-equipped scouts. Whether the Iraqis or Baker's troops had done the shooting, it illustrated the difficulty of coordinating an attack with a flanking unit in bad visibility. The incident also showed how difficult it is to know just what is happening in even the least significant events on a battlefield. Understanding battlefield events would not get any easier in the coming days.

At 8:20 a.m. LTC Dan Fake's TF 2-16 IN scouts made contact; detecting Iraqi infantry at some distance, they opened the engagement with mortars. Scout platoon sergeant SFC Harry Ennis adjusted the mortars accurately onto the infantry's dug-in position. When his platoon overran it, Ennis reported finding "nine dismounts [enemy infantrymen] in trench huddling together."[65] In this instance the situation played out as it appeared from the first.

LTC Marlin's 4-37 AR advanced by bounds. As they crossed Phase Line Kansas, Marlin's scouts called mortars on a bunker complex with an antenna sticking up, believing it to be a command post. The mortar rounds impacted only fifty meters forward of the scouts, so 1LT Lanier Ward promptly canceled the mission and prosecuted the attack with twenty-five-millimeter cannon fire. As

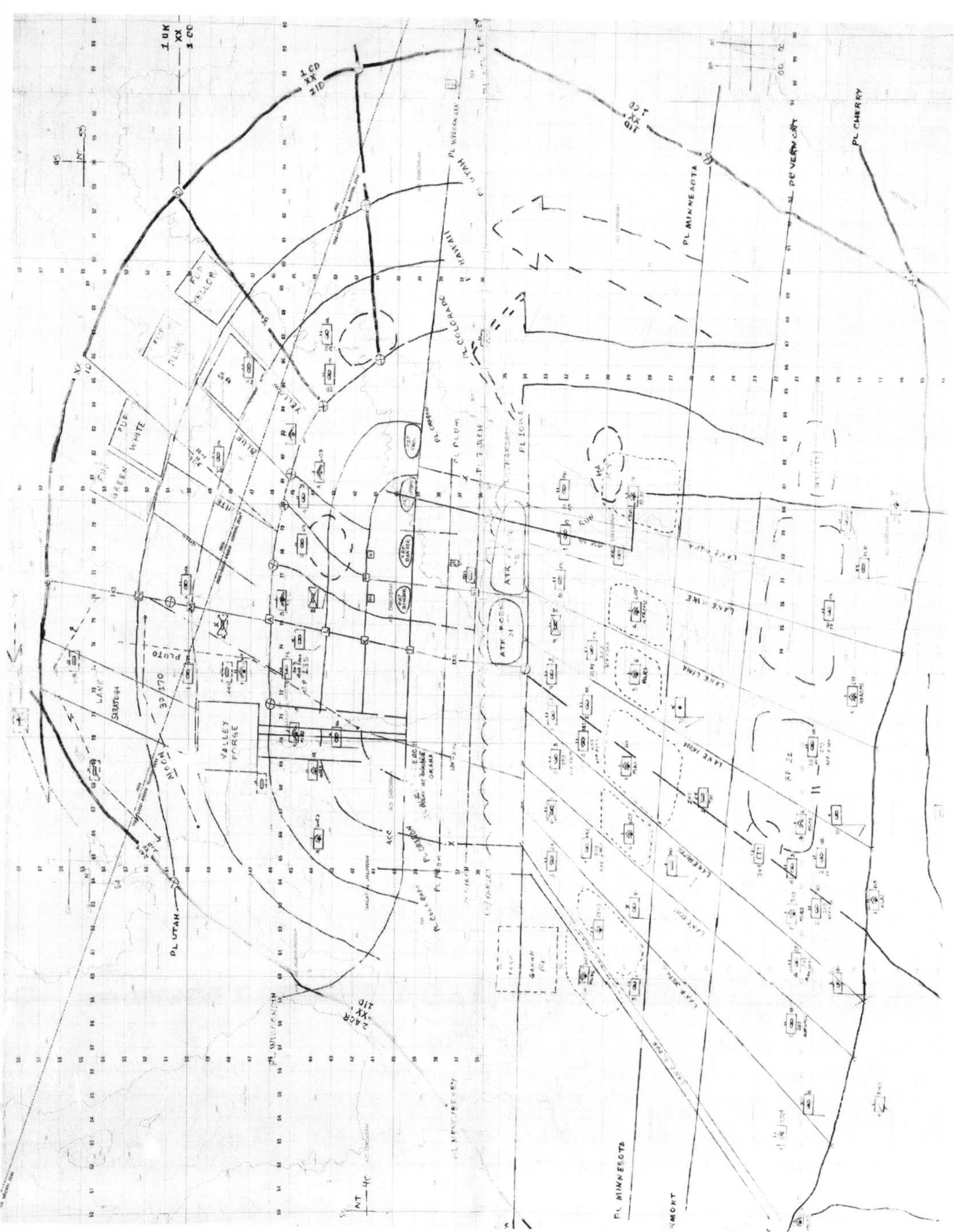

Map 7. 1st Infantry Division Operations Graphic for the penetration attack February 24, 1991. Courtesy of the McCormick Research Center, 1st Infantry Division Museum, Wheaton, Illinois. COL USA Retired Terry L. Bullington donated the original artifact, which has faded with age.

the scouts got closer to the antenna, it turned out to be a pole. Like the earlier cross-boundary firing incident, this situation turned out to be different from how it had first appeared. They found only two of the enemy, who gave themselves up. As the scouts moved into the bunker they "had a great view across the brigade front as hundreds of EPWs [enemy prisoners of war] surrendered to different units."[66]

As Ward prosecuted his contact, a tank company moved up on his right flank. Second Lieutenant Brian C. Cook, the tank platoon leader, heard "the unquestionable sound of incoming mortars."[67] Within seconds of being fired on for the first time ever, Cook found he could make judgments about mortar fire. According to him, the platoon took "a small mortar barrage."[68] As the tank company continued north, they got closer to the main defenses than intended and took small-arms fire. First Lieutenant Pete Lee's platoon quickly identified the enemy bunkers and trenches from which Iraqi troops were firing and returned fire. Behind them, Marlin described the engagement as "brief and furious."[69] Lee's troops also saw dug-in enemy armored vehicles beyond the range of their tank guns, so he called in artillery. When the artillery hit, it prompted the immediate surrender of perhaps two hundred Iraqi soldiers. Lee remembered, "No Iraqis surrendered until we opened fire and then massive amounts of EPWs surrendered."[70] These troops turned out to be Kurds, one of whom claimed to be a resident of Chicago who had returned from the states "to save his Iraqi family."[71]

COL Maggart's brigade enjoyed a similar response as they approached Phase Line Kansas around 9:30 a.m. TF 2-34 AR and TF 5-16 IN advanced abreast, and the Quarter Horse and the 1-34 AR moved into their planned attack positions to the southwest of the lead units. When Fontenot's armor task force arrived on the reverse slope of a low-lying ridge that ran east to west, north of Phase Line Kansas, he ordered the task force to move up on the ridge in order to show itself to the enemy like "Sioux Indians in a western."[72] The results were gratifying: almost immediately, enemy soldiers started streaming south across the shallow valley between their trenches and the task force, waving white flags or holding their hands up. Similar activities occurred in front of Baker's infantry. Having conducted its demonstration, TF 2-34 AR withdrew into reverse slope positions where it received the surrender of nearly 150 enemy soldiers. A similar number surrendered to Baker's troops, and within an hour both task forces had used up their capacity to process and evacuate prisoners. Short of transport, the attacking task forces resorted to using "low boy" tractor-trailers that had carried mine rollers forward to evacuate prisoners to the rear.[73]

These events proved stressful because there was real danger of firefights breaking out that could result in killing Iraqi soldiers attempting to surrender. The situation alarmed Maggart: "We had drilled our soldiers time and time again about the laws of land warfare and how to handle enemy soldiers who were trying to surrender. Here we were on the first engagement with the enemy, and we had a potentially disastrous [situation]."[74] The whole affair seemed surreal. At one point CPT John Bushyhead chastised his troops for taking photographs of surrendering Iraqis because it would embarrass them.[75] Maggart was more afraid that one of his soldiers might kill an Iraqi, while Bushyhead wanted to avoid embarrassing them. Both were right. Maggart need not have worried whether the soldiers would show compassion to their vanquished foes. With literally thousands of soldiers within sight of each other, the possibility of a tragedy was sky-high. Yet no American killed an Iraqi attempting to surrender. The Iraqi chain of command demonstrated less generosity, however; in a postwar manuscript, one American recalled "some of those who chose to surrender were cut down by their own superiors in an attempt to stop the mass capitulation."[76]

The Division achieved all of its assigned G-Day objectives by 9:45 a.m. By this time it was set on Phase Line Kansas, just out of direct-fire range of Iraqi weapons. The moment belied the estimate that well-equipped and battle-hardened Iraqis would inflict high casualties on the US Army. Indeed, the fighting on Sunday, February 24, confirmed Rhame's theory that the Iraqi 26 ID was anything but formidable. While the troops processed prisoners and refueled, events elsewhere moved rapidly.

Because the Iraqi high command believed the ground attack had begun on February 21, Saddam's inner circle perceived the attacks on February 24 as a transition to the main effort rather than its commencement. The attack of the French 6th Light Armored Division (earlier on February 24) fit the Iraqis' estimate of a coalition effort toward Baghdad via Karbala. Coalition attacks in the east against the 7th and 14th Divisions assigned to Iraqi III Corps also lay within their estimate. These attacks looked to them like the beginning of the main attack. They still believed an amphibious assault would follow. Coalition fires on Faylakah Island also tended to support their assumptions.[77]

Reports coming from units in contact did not convey just how serious an attack was under way. During the morning, foreign minister and deputy prime minister Tariq Aziz noted that "it has been 38 days since they began striking us, and they have not inflicted any losses upon us."[78] Aziz may have been whistling in the dark or merely saying what he thought Saddam wanted to hear; either way, the danger was not immediately apparent to the dictator and his inner circle. No doubt surprised and frustrated that the Soviet Union had not been able to head off ground combat, Saddam still hoped something could be salvaged.

Surprised or not, Saddam remained full of braggadocio. When he learned that the French were attacking in the west, he wondered aloud: "Attacking? Or sitting in front of their division and crying?" He went on to add, "Yes, they are asking for help and they have not even begun engaging yet." Finally, he concluded, "[French president François] Mitterrand is very despicable."[79] Meanwhile,

Saddam authorized the execution of the Tariq Project, which aimed to destroy Kuwaiti oil infrastructure. The Iraqis had already opened the pumps on a major oil terminal and poured eight million gallons of oil into the Persian Gulf; the US Air Force managed to stop that by destroying the pumps. Now Saddam's troops began setting the oil fields ablaze. Yet when confronted with American news reports claiming that Iraq was doing just what he had ordered, Saddam claimed to his advisers that only "legitimate military targets [were destroyed] in order to cause diversions."[80]

Not long after the coalition attack began that morning, CENTCOM received reports of Iraqi demolitions in Kuwait City. Accordingly, GEN Schwarzkopf thought it prudent to accelerate the attack to stop the Iraqis from razing the city entirely. Furthermore, he saw an opportunity: if the Iraqis were destroying infrastructure in Kuwait City, then it seemed likely they intended to withdraw. Schwarzkopf wanted to hit them as they moved; at 8:04 a.m. he called LTG John Yeosock and asked whether the two US corps could attack earlier than planned.[81] This was not a trivial question, because both corps were engaged as the two spoke. But the VII Corps attack aimed only to clear the Iraqi security forces from the zone of attack; the plan required the VII Corps to stop short of the breach on February 24 and attack to the breach the next day. In order to go early, artillery would have to get in position to support the breach. The UK 1 AD would also have to move into forward assembly areas a day early. LTG Yeosock believed it could be done, but wanted to poll his two corps commanders. He called Franks at 9:30 a.m., and Franks told Yeosock he thought it could be done, but wanted to survey his subordinates as well.

Rhame, too, sensed opportunity. He had already asked to go early based on the light resistance encountered in the security zone. In his opinion, there was nothing to be gained by waiting; in fact, doing so might afford the Iraqis the chance to recover. Rhame wanted to attack at 1:00 p.m. to allow the maximum amount of daylight and to avoid mounting a major night attack on the first day. Even the UK 1 AD was ready to go early despite the necessity to drive its tanks one hundred kilometers to the breach site rather than move them, as planned, on heavy-equipment transporters. The other divisions in the Corps and the 2 ACR were ready to go early as well.

Franks had reservations, because he thought it would take twelve hours of daylight to execute the penetration attack. Nevertheless, he reported to Yeosock the Corps could go early. Yeosock advised him that the attack, if it went early, would go at 3:00 p.m. If Yeosock knew, he did not say that Schwarzkopf believed the conditions on the battlefield had changed fundamentally. Consequently, no one in the VII Corps understood that a fundamental transition in the operation had occurred.[82] This led to a gap between how Franks and Schwarzkopf saw the campaign unfolding. Yeosock failed to bridge the gap, and this led to confusion and, ultimately, recrimination.

Despite wanting to go early, Rhame also polled his commanders. He called Maggart at 10:00 a.m. Only the day before he and his brigade commanders had reviewed "a success option," and now one was before them. Maggart's battalion commanders all wanted to go, and they all felt they could go by 1:00 p.m.[83] When Moreno's commanders met at around 10:30 a.m., he told them they had been "given the green light to continue the attack today and that it would be at 1300 hours."[84] No one demurred; all wanted to get on with it. The Division believed it would go at 1:00 p.m. A later time never came up. The battalions wanted to go early so they could get everything done before nightfall. There was no enthusiasm for attacking even weakly defended positions in the dark.

In his memoir, Schwarzkopf described his decision to go early as follows: "Just before noon a crucial bit of news came in: the Kuwaiti resistance radioed that the Iraqis had blown up Kuwait City's desalinization plant . . . this could only mean that the Iraqis were about to leave. And if they intended to pull out of Kuwait City, I reasoned, they intended to pull out of Kuwait."[85] He came to the conclusion that "the Iraqis were reeling. If we moved fast, we could force them to fight at a huge disadvantage."[86] He made the right decision, but failed to communicate his assessment downward or at least to assure that his subordinates at the tactical level understood that his estimate of the situation had changed dramatically. No one doubted the utility of attacking early, yet no one in the VII Corps shared his understanding of the situation.

Franks arrived at the Danger Forward command post at 11:40 a.m. There he met with Rhame, Carter, and Bullington to pass the word from Schwarzkopf via Yeosock that the Corps would attack not at 1:00 p.m. but at 3:00 p.m. Franks departed at 12:05 p.m., and radio calls set things in motion immediately.[87] COL Dodson and the various artillery commanders hustled to get guns in position to shoot preparation fires at 2:30 p.m. Dodson's fire direction center also had to compute new firing data and target sequence. Obviously they could not fire all of the targets with the desired effects in a half hour that they had planned to fire in two and a half hours.

According to Dodson, rearranging the preparation fire proved, "[e]asy to do because of the Target lay down"[88]—that is, he had organized targets into groups that would be fired sequentially so that adjusting the preparation could be done relatively quickly. Because Rhame had spoken to him earlier in the day about going early, Dodson and his staff planned for that contingency. He refined the preparation, but made sure the artillery could hit "all the primary targets in 30 minutes."[89] Listed targets stemmed from weeks of analysis and very good imagery. Fire-support officers had developed ten-digit grid coordinates for every platoon position in the two forward brigades of the Iraqi 26 ID. They discretely targeted all of the artillery batteries and air defenses; doing so enabled shooting within twenty-five meters of the center of mass of enemy positions—good enough to force their heads down. In most cases the preparation would include enough rounds to kill a third or more of any enemy at the target grid. Although Rhame had some concern that the preparation would not hit all the targets, Dodson had revised preparation fires to shift to deeper targets as the maneuver units attacked.[90] The artillery would strike all of the original targets in the course of the preparation or as fires shifted away from the point of the attack.

Planning the revised bombardment may have been fairly easy, but moving thirteen artillery battalions and several separate batteries, and revising the plan in time to fire at 2:30 p.m., was an incredible achievement. The result struck MAJ James M. Holt, executive officer of the 1-5 FA, as "Soviet-style positioning; basically, hub-to-hub artillery."[91] LTC Terry Bullington spoke for many in the 1 ID when he claimed, "Mike Dodson may be the greatest artilleryman who put an attack package together, anytime."[92] Bullington's appraisal may be hyperbolic given the massed preparations fired during World War II, but it reflects the sincere respect that those who witnessed the preparation had for the artillerymen who made it happen.

With at least two hours' notice, there remained some time for additional preparations. Fire support officer CPT Glenn Goldstein and his commander moved up on the ridge overlooking the 110th Brigade of the 26 ID. Here Goldstein adjusted the planned artillery groupings so they fell exactly on the Iraqi positions at the first two objectives. With the guns registered, Goldstein could shift fires to other targets and be assured of a high degree of accuracy.[93]

A few kilometers east, Gross ordered his two forward company team commanders to reconnoiter the enemy positions. Each went forward with three tanks. CPT Tim Norton got close enough so that, he recalls, "We could clearly see the trench line." While forward, Norton's turret halon fire extinguisher went off for no apparent reason and the turret filled with the powdery toxic gas. Norton dismissed it as "just something to make my life miserable."[94] Technically Norton should have "deadlined" his tank as non–mission capable. But he would not be left behind, and so fought his tank without the onboard extinguisher. He and the other forward commander, CPT John Long, returned satisfied that they understood the lay of the land and Iraqi positions. They had not been able to identify any minefields. Last but not least, units refueled and some moved so as to be in position to go early.

The Breach:
February 24, 1991, 2:30–4:00 P.M.

The weather improved over the course of the morning. The rain, mist, and clouds moved off to the northeast and left a clear blue sky and a bright sunny day. The wind remained from the southeast, and that favored the attackers both from the perspective of the use of Iraqi chemical weapons and the US forces' use of smoke to isolate parts of the battlefield or to screen movement. At 2:30 p.m. exactly, the ground under the Iraqi main defensive belt sprouted what appeared to be a forest of spruce trees the color of loam. This forest of explosions extended six kilometers from left to right and several kilometers deep. Thirteen artillery battalions and several separate batteries pounded targets assigned by the Division and attacking brigades. The intensity of the bombardment was such that no one could detect discrete bursts; instead, the barrage had the effect of white noise—a kind of background roar that somehow sounded less horrific than it looked. No one who saw the barrage would ever forget it; MSG Mike Schulte, a master gunner in the 1st Brigade, remembers it as "the most amazing thing I have ever seen. I will never, ever, see anything like that again."[95] COL Tony Moreno, a combat veteran of the Vietnam War, described it as "the most awesome artillery prep[aration] I have ever seen in my entire military career." Better still, Moreno noted, "The confidence it gave the soldiers was remarkable."[96]

Even before the preparation fires shifted, the assault battalions started forward as scheduled at 3:00 p.m. TF 2-34 AR attacked on the left or west with TF 5-16 IN, TF 3-37 AR, and TF 2-16 IN extending to the east. The Quarter Horse and the 1-34 AR remained in attack positions to the rear. Marlin's 4-37 AR had been on line, but now consolidated so they could follow the assault through the breach. As the assault battalions closed in on the enemy positions, a smoke blanket generated by a platoon from the 46th Chemical Company covered the western sector of the Iraqi 110th Brigade, effectively preventing about half its soldiers from being able to interfere with or even see the attack. The Division attack narrowed down to eight combined arms company teams, and tanks with mine plows preceded each; these crossed the three kilometers between the line of departure and the enemy front line in less than ten minutes. All eight companies lowered mine plows seven to eight hundred meters from the enemy trenches. Moving at slightly less than fifteen kilometers per hour, they plowed lanes about twelve to eighteen inches deep and slightly more than twelve feet wide.[97]

The initial phase of the attack moved very quickly. A few minutes after 3:00 p.m. Bushyhead's company swept over an abandoned Iraqi platoon-size outpost on a low ridge just south of the main defensive line. He deployed his tanks and Bradleys just beyond the crest of the hillock to support the attack by fire, and his task force commander pulled in behind. The low rise afforded an excellent vantage point from which to oversee the breach. Almost immediately, the Iraqis fired at least twelve 122-millimeter rounds in a preplanned concentration that landed in and around Bushyhead's formation. He ordered his troops out of the impact area, and the task force commander followed them at high speed. Obviously the Iraqis could read maps too. Just as the company displaced, someone somewhere inadvertently keyed the battalion command radio frequency. It was probably a soldier wearing a combat vehicle crewman's helmet; the switch on the helmet sometimes locked in the transmit position.

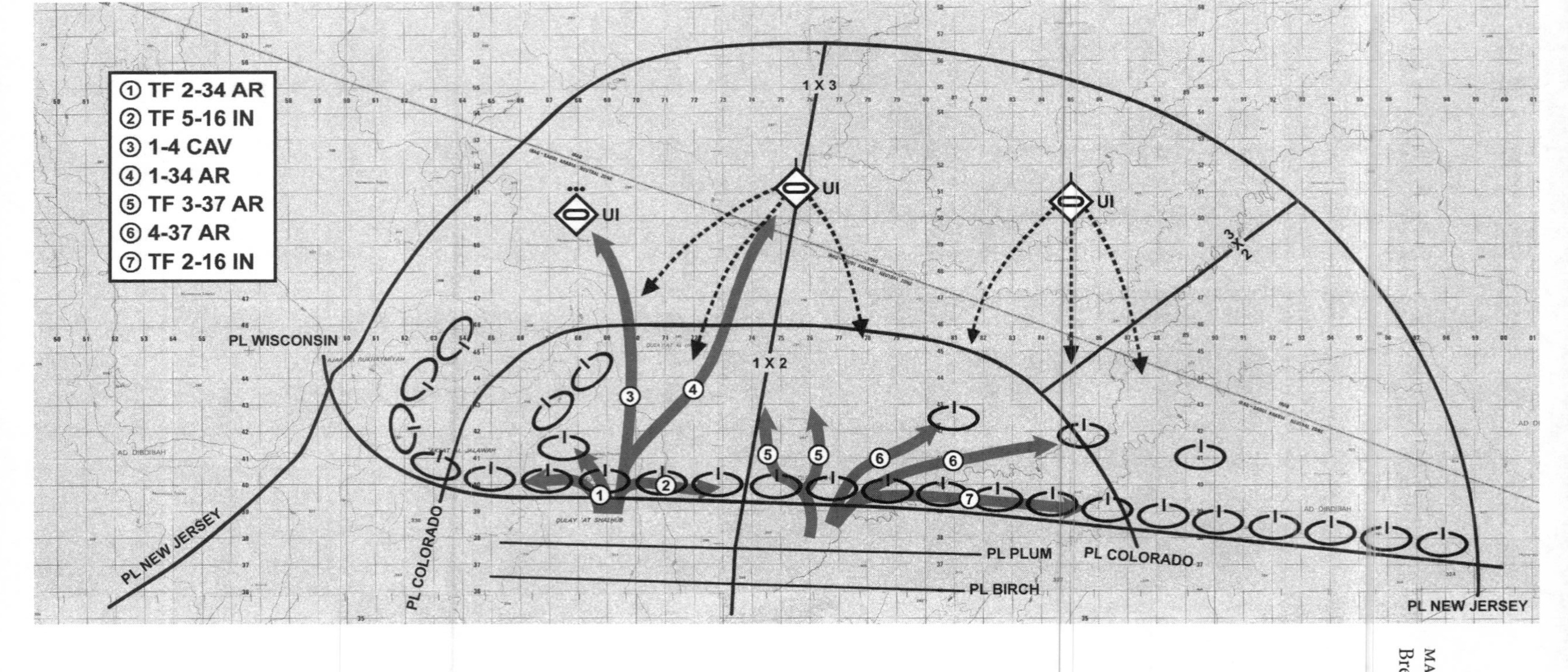

MAP 8. Penetration and Breach, February 24, 1991.

For nearly fifteen minutes, the task force could not communicate on its command network.[98]

Fontenot found the inability to communicate frustrating, to say the least, yet his troops never missed a beat. They needed no orders to execute what they had rehearsed ad nauseam. The same could be said of the entire Division. As the attack unfolded, brigade commanders had little to do with tactical execution at the tip of the spear. Their job was to listen, assess, and act when necessary. Maggart and Moreno knew when to do nothing and, better still, had the wisdom to listen rather than issue superfluous instructions. MG Thomas Rhame and his small command group moved in just to the rear of Moreno's assault battalions; Rhame, LTC Terry Bullington, CSM Fred Davenport, and MAJ Don Osterberg, the plans officer, traveled together. Rhame and Bullington each had a tank and a high-mobility multipurpose wheeled vehicle (HMMWV), and CSM Davenport had an M113 armored personnel carrier and a HMMWV. Maggart and Moreno were farther forward, and each commanded from a Bradley infantry fighting vehicle. BG Carter positioned Danger Forward where he could orchestrate the movement of follow-on forces once the attacking units established the passage lanes. But during the breach there was little any of the senior commanders could do. Companies and platoons fought within their understanding of the intended outcome.

In TF 2-34 AR, despite the locked command radio, CPT Bob Burns's and CPT Juan Toro's tank-heavy teams went in side by side, with Burns on the left and Toro on the right; both closed rapidly on their initial objective. LTC Emerson's 1-5 FA signaled that it was shifting fires from the first objective by firing white phosphorous rounds to mark both the end of that mission and the point of attack. Burns served as the "battle captain" for the assault, so Toro's troops keyed on him. As the two teams approached the first objective, Burns ordered his unit to fire a tank gun volley at the platoon they were attacking; Toro's company followed suit against the adjacent enemy platoon. The two captains had planned to fire two volleys, but Burns's volley provoked no response, so he chose not to fire the second. Toro waited a moment and then fired his second volley just prior to plowing through the Iraqi trenches. At 3:15 p.m., TF 2-34 AR managed to switch to its antijamming radio frequency and restore communications. At 3:25 p.m. Fontenot reported lanes A, B, and D clear of enemy troops and mines. CPT Johnny G. Womack's and CPT John Bushyhead's company teams entered the lanes soon thereafter. LTC Pat Ritter, closely monitoring the action, started his 1-34 AR battalion forward as soon as he heard the report.[99]

LTC Skip Baker's TF 5-16 IN also attacked with two company teams abreast. CPT Jim Nepute's tank-heavy team attacked on the left, while CPT Todd Smith's infantry-heavy team attacked on the right. CPT Rick Orth's tank-heavy team followed Nepute's. CPT Joe Thompson's infantry-heavy Team A and CPT Jerry Niland's antitank company supported by fire. At 3:16 p.m. one of Nepute's mine plows broke down. The mine roller tank following it bypassed it and continued on. With virtually no resistance, Baker's troops cleared their first lane at 3:25 p.m. Orth and Niland continued the attack to the north while the assault teams rolled out to the east and expanded the breach toward TF 3-37 AR and the 2nd Brigade.

Moreno's brigade had just crossed the line of departure at Phase Line Kansas when he halted the attack because the artillery had not shifted as planned. It took no more than two or three minutes to shift the artillery and resume the attack. Gross's task force attacked with Norton's tank-heavy Team C on the left and Long's tank-heavy Team B on the right. CPT Thomas Rouse's infantry-heavy Team A followed Norton, and CPT Mark Hammond's infantry-heavy Team D followed Long. During the planning prior to the assault, Gross and Baker shared two concerns: they were worried about fratricide, as they were attacking immediately adjacent to each other, and they had to clear to their flanks so some of their units would approach each other; they were also worried about the Iraqi 110th Brigade's reserve tank company. Located about seven kilometers north of Phase Line Wisconsin and three or four kilometers west of the brigade boundary, it could either remain in place or reposition to counterattack any penetration. It was positioned on a rise that prevented Baker's troops from seeing it. Maggart assigned Ritter the mission of destroying it, but until the 1-34 AR could get forward, the enemy tank company posed a threat.[100]

A low ridge that ran north to south created a gap between Baker and Gross that an alert enemy could exploit. Accordingly, Gross anticipated a threat from his left flank. Since neither Norton nor Long had seen mines, Gross decided not to fire his mine-clearing line charges and this enabled him to speed up the attack. As the assault company teams neared their objectives, the two trailing teams halted so they could support by fire. When Norton's company hit its section of the trench line and supporting bunkers, the Iraqi defenders fired rocket-propelled grenades and small arms at the tanks and Bradleys. His tanks opened up at short range with their main guns; resistance ceased when they destroyed the offending bunkers. Friction provided more resistance than did the unfortunate Iraqis: 2LT Roderick Hardin, leading the mine-plow platoon, found he could not lower his plow. Norton immediately committed 2LT Carl Nasatka's tank platoon in Hardin's place. Long's tankers and infantry cleared their two lanes without incident. Gross's troops quickly reduced the Iraqi position and reported all four of their lanes open at 3:30 p.m.[101]

Gross's concern with his left flank grew as the enemy continued firing across the brigade boundary. CPT Rouse's Team A began to receive artillery or mortar fire as well. Rouse believed an Iraqi observer was adjusting fire because the rounds crept closer; he wanted to get moving. Rather than wait for Norton to get the lanes cleared and marked, Rouse asked to go around to the west, across trenches and terrain west of the plowed lanes. Since neither Norton nor

Long saw any mines, Rouse believed there likely were none to be found. Gross believed the benefit outweighed the risk and authorized Rouse to bypass the lanes. Rouse began to move just as Gross reported TF 3-37 AR's lanes clear.[102]

LTC Fake's TF 5-16 IN made equally rapid progress against stiffer resistance. Prior to the attack, Fake closed to within two kilometers of the Iraqi positions astride Phase Line Wisconsin. Just prior to the artillery preparation, the 1-1 AVN fired rockets into the Iraqi positions. Following the preparation fire, Fake's two tank-heavy teams attacked, with Team A on the left and Team D on the right. CPT Morningstar's Team D drew first blood; as it moved forward, the enemy fired on the team. Morningstar's gunner saw an Iraqi tank to his front; as the captain later recalled, "About five of my tanks immediately returned fire and struck the Iraqi vehicle." An attached antitank platoon identified and destroyed a second T-55 tank some distance north.[103]

Once again friction added to the fight: one of the mine plows would not drop when released, and the plow tank commander climbed out of his turret and jumped up and down on it until it dropped. Once it went down, the commander mounted his tank and drove on unruffled, as if jumping up and down on his plow under fire was standard procedure. Once through the first Iraqi positions, the plow tanks turned on to the trenches and collapsed them by plowing along their length. Some Iraqi soldiers surrendered; a few did not. Those who did not were buried and are likely there still.[104] Similar events occurred along Phase Line Wisconsin with minor variations. TF 2-34 buried the trenches using armored combat earthmovers with a tank or Bradley traveling on either side of each bulldozer to suppress or kill enemy infantry as it buried the trench. Again some Iraqis surrendered, but others did not. More than one soldier saw the grisly aftermath, one of whom recalled "seeing body parts sticking out of the breaches."[105] The Iraqis had to choose: quit or accept the consequences.

Clearing Operations: February 24, 1991, 4:00–6:30 P.M.

As the assault company teams effected the initial penetration, follow-on forces immediately entered the lanes. The troops understood the need to maintain momentum; there was a lot to be done, and little daylight left in which to do it. By 3:30 p.m. the penetration had succeeded against four Iraqi companies, creating several noncontiguous gaps in the enemy works. Now the assault battalions and the follow-on forces set about expanding the breach toward Phase Line Colorado. Doing so would clear the ground to a depth of six kilometers across a frontage of twenty-three kilometers. As the attack progressed, Rhame planned to commit Weisman's 3rd Brigade to expand the breach to the northernmost arc of Phase Line New Jersey. For his part, Dodson had to orchestrate moving artillery forward to provide continuous support as the Division expanded the breach.

BG Carter and Danger Forward served as the "crossing force" command. Perceiving the breach as an assault crossing of a river helped in several ways. River crossings were an essential and well-practiced task in NATO; the essential steps included securing the near side and getting across to the far side, and were analogous to the breach itself. Building up on the far side and expanding required effective traffic management. Getting units across the river—or in this case through the breach—necessitated discipline and exact timing. Carter would direct traffic to assure the units moved quickly and in the desired sequence; literally thousands of vehicles had to get through. But first the two assault brigades needed to clear enough space on the far side to bring up artillery and the 3rd Brigade. Maggart had the Quarter Horse and the 1-34 AR to expand his zone; Moreno would use the 4-37 AR and TF 2-16 IN to expand east and north.

Expanding the breach began shortly before 4:00 p.m. In TF 2-34 AR, Burns's team turned west and attacked the flank of the next Iraqi company while Toro attacked north. Burns and his team attacked against negligible resistance although they took persistent fire from what he believed to be sixty-millimeter mortars. Once they overran the Iraqi company, the mortar fire ceased. Womack's team followed Toro's through the breach and then turned hard left and attacked westward, on Burn's left, overrunning two platoons of the next Iraqi company, while Burns's team destroyed the Iraqi rear platoon. Bushyhead followed Womack's troops and continued the attack northwest. LTC Ritter's 1-34 AR moved thorough the same lanes. As Company B of the 1-34 AR drove through the lanes, it was struck by artillery fire. None of the tankers were hurt, but a combat engineer, SGT Elish Jackson, was hit right between the shoulder blades by a fragment. His flak jacket stopped the fragment, but he got a nasty bruise and a burn that hurt enough that he wanted to "scream and cry." LTC Ritter's tank company drove out of the impact area. Once his battalion debouched from the breach, it attacked northeast to find and destroy the tank company that concerned Baker and Gross. The 1-34 AR started through the lanes about 3:30 p.m. and cleared them before 3:50 p.m. Maggart ordered the Quarter Horse forward at 3:30 p.m.[106]

Although on the move, the Quarter Horse could not attack north until Bushyhead defeated the enemy at an objective named 4KD, and an Iraqi mortar platoon occupied that piece of ground. This platoon fought bravely and may have fired the rounds that hit the breach lane. As Bushyhead's team attacked toward the enemy mortars, his gunners could see mines buried close to the surface through their thermal sights. It was a thin protective minefield emplaced just forward of the position. As Bushyhead would later recall, "We [Team D] came to a screeching halt with a minefield in front of us."[107] Worse still, the Iraqis remained determined to fight and fired on them. Someone reported contact. Bushyhead could see enemy gun flashes through his thermals.[108]

Since Bushyhead had no plow tanks, he brought up his mine-clearing line charge mounted on the chassis of a bridge launcher. The launcher had no radio, because radio transmissions could cause the line charge to fire accidentally, so he and the crew communicated with hand and arm signals. In short order the driver and vehicle commander had the launcher set in accord with Bushyhead's gesticulations, and when he gave them the shoot signal they fired. The line charge detonated with an earthshaking blast of dark black smoke and sand lit with a bright flash at its center. To everyone's amazement, a single Iraqi soldier emerged from the dust and smoke with his hands up.[109] The rest of the mortar platoon literally disappeared. At 4:00 p.m. Bushyhead reported Objective 4KD clear of the enemy, and the Quarter Horse raced through the lanes heading north toward Phase Line Colorado. As Wilson's first combat vehicles emerged from the lanes, they destroyed two Iraqi trucks fleeing north and a light armored vehicle. These quick engagements provoked a mass surrender of about a hundred Iraqi troops.[110]

Ritter led his battalion northeast on the Quarter Horse's right. As his tanks advanced, they were fired on from several bunkers. The battalion immediately returned fire at targets on their left and right. LTC Ritter's westernmost company got carried away and fired coaxial machine guns, accurately, at MAJ John Burdan's Bradley. Burdan, the Quarter Horse operations officer, was waiting at a point on the ground where he was supposed to make physical contact with the 1-34 AR, and he immediately began yelling on the brigade command frequency, "Cease-Fire! You are shooting at friendly units to your west."[111] Ritter got the offending company under control and continued the attack.

The 1-34 AR had two key tasks: first, they were to destroy the reserve tank company and, second, they were to destroy a bunker complex the 1st Brigade believed contained the Iraqi 110th Brigade's command post. As the 1-34 AR approached the enemy position code named Objective 5K, four F-16 fighters struck it. When the fighters left, Ritter's mortars took up the cudgels. Finally, at 5:00 p.m., the 1-34 AR called artillery on Objective 5K. After lifting the artillery, Ritter fired a round into one of the bunkers. When he did, his "lead three companies fired a near simultaneous volley."[112] Rounds from the volley came dangerously close to Norton's company, located east of the bunker complex and across the brigade boundary. That Ritter's tankers could not see those "friendlies" on the far side of the ridge had worried Gross, and apparently with good reason. By 5:15 p.m. the Iraqi 110th Brigade ceased to be a coherent fighting force; Maggart's intelligence section had been right about the command post being located at Objective 5K. Ritter's troops captured the brigade commander and those of his staff who survived the attack on the bunker complex. Of the dreaded tank reserve, no live tanks could be found.[113] Second Lieutenant Matt Green, a platoon leader in the 1-34 AR, observed of the 110th Brigade, "there wasn't a lot of fight left in those guys."[114]

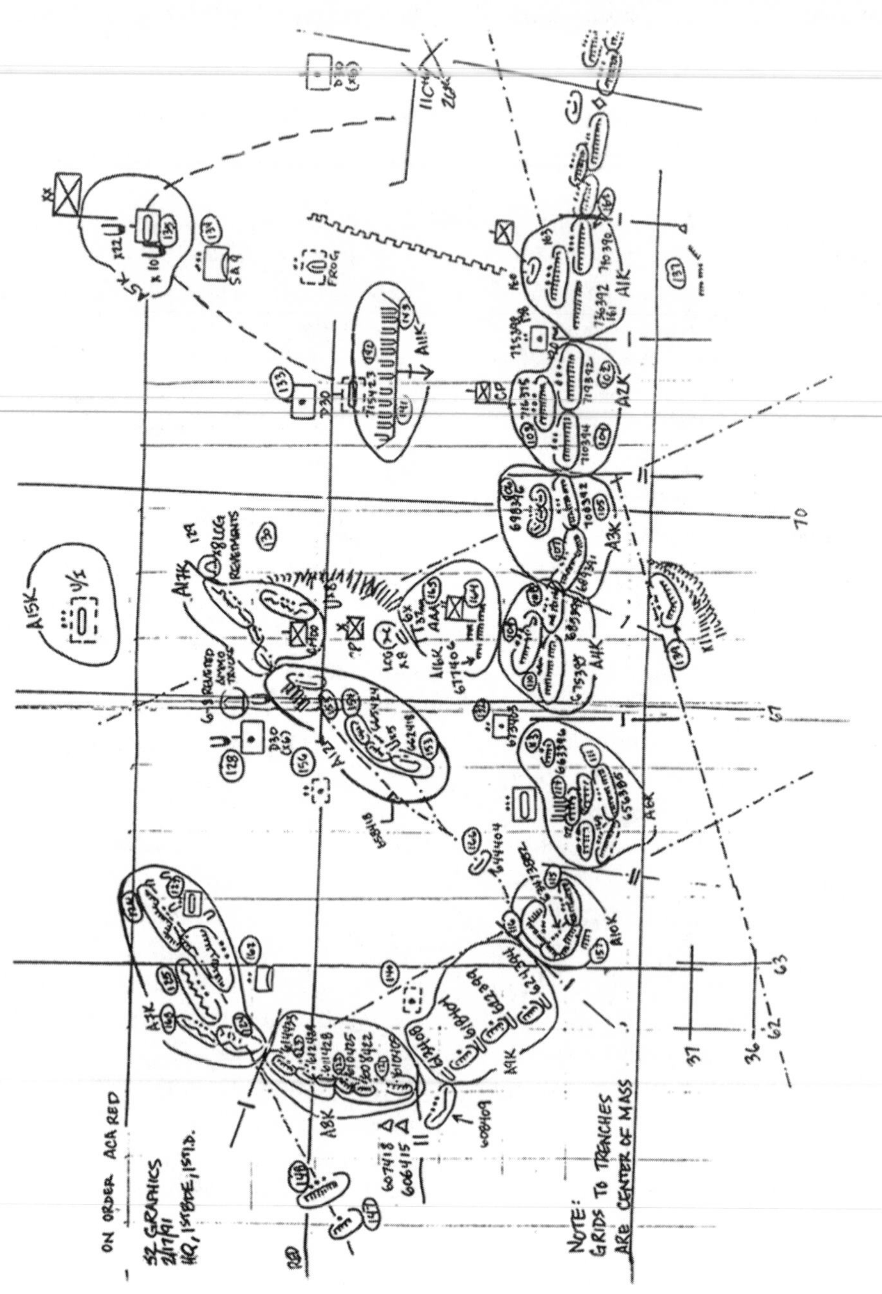

MAP 9.1 & 9.2. 1st Brigade Operations and Intelligence Graphic, February 17, 1991, juxtaposed with Captured Operations Graphic for the Iraqi 110th Brigade. The Iraqi Brigade commander complained that 1st Brigade's Graphic was more accurate than his own.

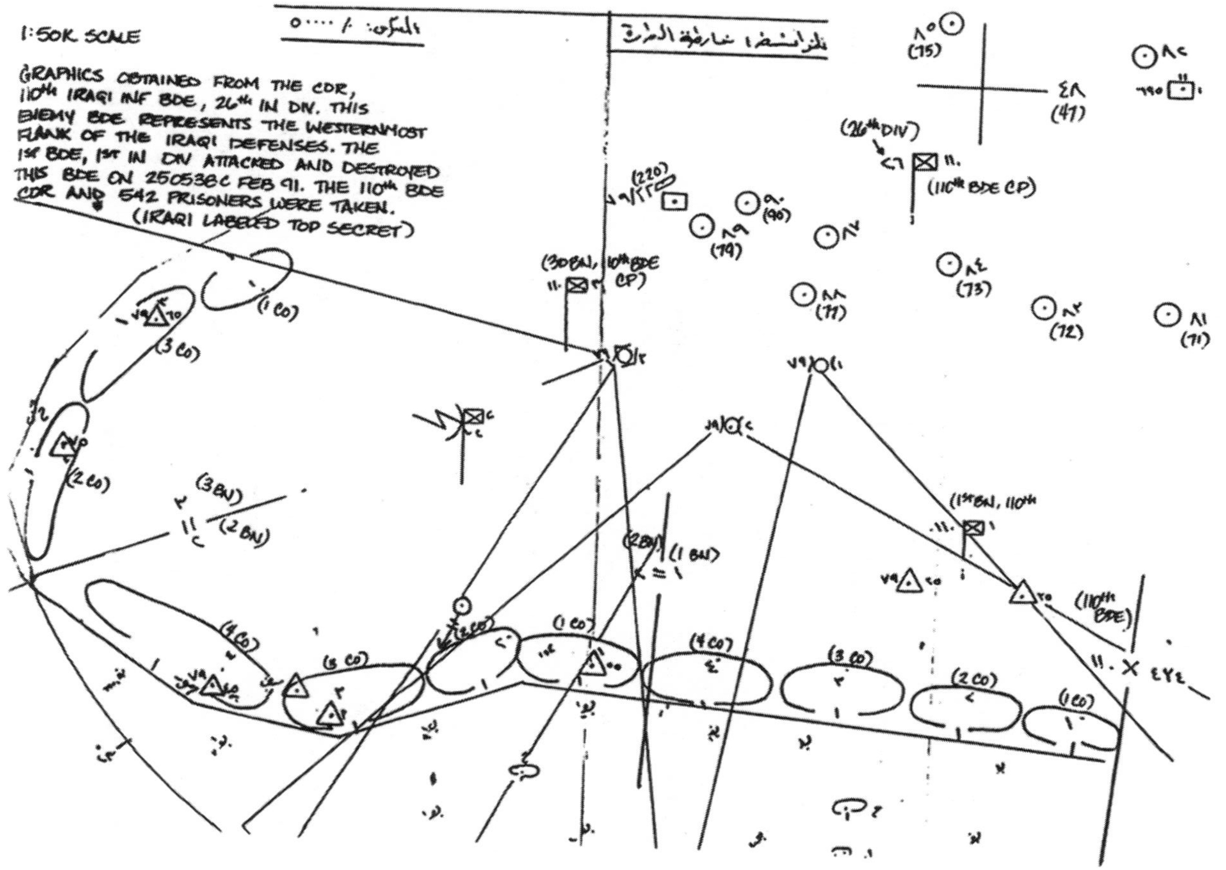
1:50K SCALE
GRAPHICS OBTAINED FROM THE CDR, 110th IRAQI INF BDE, 26th IN DIV. THIS ENEMY BDE REPRESENTS THE WESTERNMOST FLANK OF THE IRAQI DEFENSES. THE 1st BDE, 1st IN DIV ATTACKED AND DESTROYED THIS BDE ON 250538C FEB 91. THE 110th BDE CDR AND 542 PRISONERS WERE TAKEN.
(IRAQI LABELED TOP SECRET)
(26th DIV)
(110th BDE CP)
(30 BN, 10th BDE CP)
(1st BN, 110th
(110th BDE)
(3 BN)
(2 BN)
(1 BN)
(1 CO)
(2 CO)
(3 CO)
(4 CO)

Before sending the 110th Brigade's commander to the rear, Ritter relieved him of his shoulder boards and pistol. The Iraqi brigadier spoke English fluently. As they chatted, the brigadier asked Ritter how he navigated. Ritter showed off his Magellan global positioning system. Once he saw it, the Iraqi said, "we have lost this war."[115] Ritter's soldiers took possession of the brigadier's operations overlay. It compared almost exactly to the final intelligence template the 1st Brigade issued on February 17. The Division's intelligence had indeed known or concluded a great deal about their quarry.

As the Quarter Horse and the 1-34 AR expanded the 1st Brigade breach generally northward, TF 5-16 IN swept the ground to the east and just north of their initial penetration. The infantry took sporadic small-arms fire from a ridge to their northwest, labeled Objective 12K on the Brigade graphics. Baker's tanks engaged and destroyed one T-55 that may have been from the reserve tank company. Around 5:40 p.m. the 1st Brigade reached Phase Line Colorado, except in the west, where TF 2-34 AR remained about a kilometer short. There was more to be done, but the Brigade thought it was a day ahead of schedule—and it had been a very good day. That changed at 6:23 p.m., when SPC Mel Collins detonated either a mine or a dud bomblet. Unexploded artillery and air-delivered cluster munitions littered the ground in and around the breach. Baker's medics evacuated the badly wounded Collins, but he died soon afterward. He was the first Division soldier killed in action.[116]

In the 2nd Brigade, clearing the breach began in earnest when Gross authorized Rouse to lead his company team northwest around the penetration and outside the plowed lanes. Rouse moved out to secure the Brigade's western flank, close the gap with Baker's infantry, and prevent the Iraqi 110th Brigade's tank company from interfering. As it moved north, his company took small-arms and machine gun fire from Iraqi troops on the far side of the brigade boundary, and CPT Norton's company team advanced north on his right. Iraqi troops fired at both. The bunkers they occupied lay just across the boundary on the near side of a low ridge that precluded Baker's troops from engaging or even seeing the bunkers. It is unclear just who these Iraqis were; they may have been artillerymen firing from fighting positions dug to defend supporting batteries.

Thanks to prior coordination with Baker's task force, Rouse could deal with the threat and led his troops in a series of short bounds while maintaining fire on the bunkers. When the company drew near, 1LT Chris Kelzsey's infantry platoon cleared the bunkers using practically every weapon they had, including AT4 light antitank rockets and hand grenades. Rouse's tankers and infantry destroyed all of the bunkers and several trucks moving about. Shortly after 5:00 p.m. the 1-34 AR's "volley" shocked Norton and Team C. Several of the 1-34 ARs rounds went over their intended targets and seemed to pass right in front of Norton's unit. Norton got on the radio in a hurry and the shooting stopped;[117] the ridge and the tank company that worried Baker and Gross ceased to be problems.

LTC Dan Fake's TF 2-16 IN had the most to do that afternoon. Fake's task force, like TF 2-34 AR in the west, had to clear the ground along Phase Line Wisconsin out to Phase Line Colorado by the end of the day. The two flank task forces had the most enemy positions to clear. TF 2-16 IN had to attack and reduce positions for a distance of twelve kilometers to the east. By contrast, TF 2-34 AR had only six kilometers of dug-in enemy to sweep through. Moreover, TF 2-16 IN would carry the fight across the boundary of the Iraqi 26 ID and hit the right flank of the adjacent 807th Brigade of the 48 ID. Once Fake's two tank-heavy company teams penetrated the initial defenses, he turned his task force east and attacked along the flanks of the forward positions, rolling up the Iraqis from their flanks and rear.[118] Fake's troops had plenty of help, including priority of fire from Gingrich's 4-5 FA. He had plenty of targets, however, so he used his battalion mortars as well.

Hitting the trenches from the flanks enabled TF 2-16 IN to use plow tanks. With plow tanks collapsing their trenches and bunkers, "Iraqi soldiers started jumping out of their trench lines, throwing their weapons down and their hands up."[119] Methodically and deliberately, TF 2-16 IN finished off the 434th Brigade of the 26 ID, and part of the 807th Brigade. Fake's troops fought determined but weak enemy forces along the way. Artillery fire had not destroyed all dug-in vehicles that the 4-37 AR identified earlier; a few light armored vehicles remained, and Fake's troops destroyed one by tank fire and a second with an antitank missile. At 3:39 p.m. CPT Scott Rutter's infantry-heavy team attacked several Iraqi positions whose defenders would not give up. His infantrymen destroyed some bunkers with twenty-five-millimeter fire and overcame the remainder using grenades and rifles. Shortly afterward, CPT Kirk Schliefer's antitank company destroyed a tank and a ZSU-23-4 air defense artillery system.[120] As the task force approached Phase Line Colorado, they found and bypassed a surface-laid minefield. By 6:00 p.m., TF 2-16 IN reached Phase Line Colorado.[121] Along the way it had captured hundreds of prisoners and overrun the better part of three Iraqi infantry battalions.

Marlin's 4-37 AR had the mission to expand the breach to the north. He led his tankers forward as soon as the lanes were open, moving about 3:30 p.m. When Moreno called him to report the lanes clear, Marlin could see that two of them, lanes O and P, were not. Because he had positioned his battalion to use all eight lanes he "deliberately waited until lanes O and P were clear before he gave the order to move." Once moving, the 4-37 AR "shot through the lanes."[122]

Perhaps it did, but not without difficulty. The assault forces had not yet marked the lanes. When the 4-37 AR tanks reached the lanes, they found obstacles. As CPT Robert Beals, commander of A Company of the 4-37 AR, found, "There was a lot of confusion . . . TF 2-16 IN's and TF 3-37 AR's wheeled vehicles were blocking much of our movement."[123] He had planned to pass on Lanes I and J, but when his company reached Lane J, he found it blocked by an armored personnel carrier that had thrown a track. He ordered his company out of the lane and around the derelict engineer track. Almost as soon as it passed, Beals's company took fire from the right. The company engaged a number of enemy vehicles and D-30 howitzers. The tankers began destroying the howitzers with tank fire and called in the battalion mortar platoon to suppress enemy artillery. CPT Torrence's C Company came through the breach and attacked on the right. Like A Company, they soon were engaging trucks and D-30 howitzers. In the last contact of the day, one of Torrence's tankers destroyed an enemy tank. By sunset, Marlin's troops had reached Phase Line Colorado.

The Division ended the day closing on Phase Line Colorado across the zone. In the west, TF 2-34 AR had four objectives left—one just west of Phase Line Colorado and three company positions that ran in a hook almost due north from there. At 5:40 p.m., TF 2-34 AR cleared the last piece of ground short of Phase Line Colorado and prepared to continue the attack west. Throughout the Division, units prepared for the next phase of the attack to clear the zone out to Phase Line New Jersey. In the attack to expand the breach to Phase Line New Jersey, Rhame envisioned the 1st and 2nd Brigades rolling out to the flanks while the 3rd Brigade attacked to the north and northeast. Expanding would provide secure space in which the British armored division could form up. Once it had, MG Rupert Smith's division would attack east into the flank and rear of the remainder of Hamash's corps. The next step in continuing the attack required passing the 3rd Brigade and supporting artillery forward.

Just before sunset, Franks flew out to visit his unit commanders. First he landed adjacent to Rhame's small command group and got a quick update before heading off to visit Holder at the 2 ACR.[124] As Franks headed west to avoid enemy air defenses, he flew over long columns of combat support and service support units as they moved toward the breach. Once across the Division boundary, his helicopter turned north and overflew the 3 AD. To the northwest, he could see the 1 AD moving toward the Corps' Objective Purple, well north of the frontier, to attack the Iraqi 806th Brigade on Hamash's right flank. Seeing three divisions and an armored cavalry regiment in the attack is a sight few have seen. It made an impression. By the time he landed at Holder's command post, Franks had developed some reservations about the complicated tactical operations that his VII Corps would have to do during darkness if it continued the attack.

So had Holder. His unit had fought nine engagements that day and advanced more than twenty kilometers into Iraq. The two armored divisions were right behind him. He saw no reason to continue the ground attack, but thought the Corps should use attack helicopters and artillery to maintain the pressure on the Iraqis. Franks ordered Holder to slow down a bit, but to continue the attack; he then left to return to his tactical command post. On the short trip back he considered the Corps' situation. From his perspective, VII Corps had had a very good day. The Corps had taken not only all of the assigned G-Day objectives, but most of those assigned for G+1.[125]

Franks ruminated about these things as he headed back to his command post. He believed the 2 ACR would reach Phase Line Smash (a phase line drawn about 150 kilometers from the line of departure) the next afternoon. Here he intended to mass three divisions to attack and destroy the Republican Guard and Jihad Corps. The sun had set by the time he landed at about 6:00 p.m. At 6:10 Franks called Yeosock at the 3rd Army to apprise him of the Corps' situation and that he proposed to suspend the ground attack for the night, but would resume it at first light. LTG Yeosock "concurred without discussion."[126] LTG Franks and his subordinate commanders perceived that they were a day ahead of schedule and saw no need to take on complex and therefore risky night attacks on the first day of combat for most of the Corps.

In his memoir Schwarzkopf makes the case that Franks's decision reflected unnecessary caution, implying that Franks was timid and methodical to a fault. Franks made his assessment with his commanders based on their understanding of the situation and the plan. On the other hand, as historian Rick Atkinson puts it, Schwarzkopf made his assessment "four hundred miles from the front and forty feet underground."[127] GEN Colin Powell agreed with Schwarzkopf from even farther away.

The valid question is whether the Corps missed an opportunity. Early that morning, Schwarzkopf concluded that the Iraqis intended to withdraw. He was right. The Iraqis won the ensuing foot race, because they had the inside lane. Could VII Corps have begun the attack on the Republican Guard and Jihad Corps earlier? Probably. The question is whether the benefit would have been worth the cost. What is certain is a gap opened among perceptions in the VII Corps, Riyadh, and beyond.

Having made a decision, Franks called Holder and ordered him to halt for the night. Then he called a halt for the 1st and 3rd AD.[128] Once he stopped the rest of the Corps, Franks called Rhame on a satellite telephone. He wanted to know whether Rhame thought he should continue the attack to Phase Line New Jersey that night. Earlier Rhame had asked to go as early as 1:00 p.m. In the context of the decision not to attack until 3:00 p.m., Rhame could detect no underlying urgency. From his perspective, the attack went early because of local opportunity, not because Schwarzkopf had detected signs of an Iraqi withdrawal from Kuwait. Therefore, halting that night rather than mounting a night attack on the first day made sense. MG Rhame estimated that the Division could secure Phase Line New Jersey and begin passing the British around noon the next day. After hearing Rhame's assessment, Franks called MG Rupert Smith at the UK 1 AD to see whether he could go as early as noon on February 25 rather than later that day. Smith thought that he could. His division's five thousand vehicles had moved all day to get close; he wanted some time to organize and get his own artillery and the supporting artillery brigade set. Still, Smith recommended passing forward around noon on February 25. Based on these assessments, and because he believed the Corps was ahead of schedule, Franks decided to stop the 1 ID as well. He called Rhame before 6:30 p.m., telling him to halt.

The word went out to cease operations. After getting the order to stop, one commander sought Maggart out; he was hot to continue the attack. During the last moments of twilight, TF 2-34 AR's commander asserted that if he could not continue the attack, the Brigade's left flank (and for that matter the Division's left flank) would be open to the enemy. COL Maggart listened with patience, but finally ended the discussion: "Damn it we need to stop. Follow orders."[129] To some extent, events later that evening vindicated Maggart's stubborn task force commander. Concerned over the enemy positions near the boundary with the 1 ID, the 3 AD asked for and Corps approved a restricted fire line between the 1 ID and the three Iraqi positions in the hook west of Phase Line New Jersey. Essentially a restricted fire line is a boundary and, as such, it prevented TF 2-34 AR from completing the mission the next day. Despite wanting to continue when Maggart ordered him to follow orders, the recalcitrant commander felt instantly exhausted, relieved, and even grateful.[130]

The 1st Division reports describe the attack as having taken place against "light resistance." For the troops, that characterization was irrelevant. SGT Haime Edwards of the 2-16 IN's C Company, described what he felt with straightforward honesty: "Rolling into enemy lines I didn't know if I was going to survive or not. To see enemy artillery rounds landing two feet away from our vehicle, I felt I would be sick. But on the other hand, I was in charge of numerous soldiers and I couldn't let them see fear in my eyes." Edwards, like other soldiers, did what he had to do.[131] All over the Division, soldiers moved from fighting to not fighting and found it as difficult as it had been to start fighting in the first place. As the adrenaline drained out of them, exhaustion set in. Some felt sick. This postbattle phenomenon is as old as humanity, and it played out in Operation Desert Storm as it always has and likely always will. Enormous energy and hyperalertness followed by physical and mental exhaustion are the lot of soldiers in combat.

The day had gone very well throughout the theater. LTG Gary Luck's XVIII ABN Corps advanced without resistance in most of its zone. The 101 ABN had closed on Forward Operating Base Cobra and would be able to interdict the main highway from Basra to Baghdad the next day. Advancing on the Corps' right flank, the 24 ID stopped for fuel after dark well into Iraq and planned to turn east sometime on February 25. Both Arab corps had attacked successfully and halted for the night. The Marines had also achieved their first-day objectives and halted.[132]

The gap in perception between the commanders forward and those in Riyadh, hundreds of kilometers to the rear, developed when GEN Schwarzkopf perceived the Iraqi collapse but failed to communicate his assessment. It widened when Franks halted the VII Corps. Somehow Yeosock did not make it plain to Schwarzkopf that the Corps stopped that evening; either that or Schwarzkopf did not take it in. In either case, Schwarzkopf went to bed that night believing the VII Corps would attack through the night. For the moment, however, no one in the VII Corps believed that Schwarzkopf would find them wanting. MG Rhame thought the attack should have gone earlier, because everyone saw what he saw. He did not understand why the attack did not go until 3:00 p.m. According to Rhame, "For some reason we were told to hold up. Everyone knows it was time to move [early]. The enemy was broken and weakened."[133]

MAJ Mike Barefield, the operations officer at the Division main command post, reported in his journal on the day's operations quite simply: "C of S [chief of staff COL Fred Hepler] was wrought with emotion over an operation that could have produced 35% casualties actually produced none at this point."[134] (When this was written, SPC Mel Collins had not yet died.) Dodson, who with the support of BG Creighton Abrams and the Corps artillery had orchestrated such great fire support, wrote accurately, "Maneuver moved with near immunity."[135] First Lieutenant Greg Glaze was succinct; the first thing he wrote in the journal he kept for his unit was, simply, "Wow." He added that the task force "moved better than it had ever looked in any rehearsal."[136]

Rhame found time that night to write in his journal as well. February 24 was, he wrote, "A great BRO [Big Red One] day." His notes reflect his satisfaction with his troops and their achievements. Of the Iraqis he wrote, "This army was not ready for a trained and ready army. It was not ready for a combined arms fight."[137] The Corps may have stopped, but there was a lot of work to do to get units positioned to continue the attack come morning. Resupply and rearming continued. When it became likely the ground attack would go on February 24 rather than February 25, Mowery and Rhame canceled an Apache strike planned for the night of February 24–25. Instead, the 1-1 AVN would conduct an aerial reconnaissance forward of the Division. That evening, Mowery flew to the 2nd Brigade to pass the details to Moreno since the 1-1 AVN would ingress and egress the zone over the 2nd Brigade.[138]

LTC Ron Reichelderfer's 1-1 AVN took off flying north at 10:30 p.m., transited Moreno's airspace, and flew north. The Apaches flew a zone reconnaissance seeking to develop an assessment of the Iraqi 26 ID's remaining combat capability. Indeed, "they had very little contact" and returned safely, passing south through the 2nd Brigade at 12:30 a.m.[139] Reichelderfer made his report upon landing. And so ended the Division's first conventional attack since World War II.

NOTES

1. Kevin M. Woods, *The Mother of All Battles: Saddam Hussein's Strategic Plan for the Persian Gulf War* (Annapolis, MD: Naval Institute Press, 2008), 205.
2. Ibid., 202–7.
3. Ibid., 206–7. The Iraqis had detected the movement, but their locations were off. They showed part of this force in Arar, well west of where both American Corps settled. They estimated accurately the remainder of the force located in the vicinity of Rafha, Saudi Arabia.
4. Woods, *The Mother of All Battles*, 207.
5. Ibid.
6. 513th Military Intelligence Brigade Joint Debriefing Center, "The Gulf War: An Iraqi General Officer's Perspective," March 11, 1991. The author has been circumspect in citing unit commanders by name unless they are dead to avoid putting any of them at risk in the current civil war in Iraq.
7. LTC (Ret.) Keith A. Markham, telephone interview with the author, December 30, 2014.
8. COL Bert Maggart attached D Company of the 1-34 AR to the 2-34 AR to thicken the defense. D Company returned to the 1-34 AR on February 22, 1991.
9. LTG (Ret.) Thomas G. Rhame, telephone interview with the author, February 3, 2015, quoting from Rhame's personal journal, February 18, 1991.
10. Author's personal journal.
11. MG (Ret.) Lon E. Maggart, "Eye of the Storm (Duty First)," unpublished manuscript, 1992–97, 141.
12. 1LT John R. McCombs, Scout Platoon Leader, Headquarters Company, 2nd Battalion, 34th Armor, 1st Brigade, 1st Infantry Division, interviewed by MAJ Robert Cook, Commander, 326th MHD, March 27, 1991, DSIT-AS-006. See also Maggart, "Eye of the Storm," 142.
13. Maggart, "Eye of the Storm," 143; COL James Mowery, "Saudi Journal," 87; COL Michael L. Dodson, personal journal, February 18–19, 1991; COL (Ret.) Mark Landrith, telephone interview with the author, January 11, 2015.

LTC Clinton J. Ancker, personal journal, February 19, 1991, reflects the Brigade taking some time to account for what had happened, but also on preparing for the next mission.

14. LTG (Ret.) Mike Dodson, telephone interview with the author, January 11, 2016. Both soldiers accepted nonjudicial punishment.

15. Dodson interview; LTG (Ret.) Mike Dodson, personal journal, February 19, 1991. There are accounts that only five rockets had gone astray, but that seems unlikely as the launcher held six.

16. Headquarters, 4th Battalion, 5th Field Artillery, "Faithful and True: Operation Desert Storm Journal," Fort Riley, KS, n.d., 56–57.

17. Rhame interview, February 3, 2015, quoting from Rhame's personal journal, February 18–19, 1991; Mowery, "Saudi Journal," 91.

18. Mowery, "Saudi Journal," February 19, 1991.

19. Rhame interview, February 3, 2015, quoting from Rhame's personal journal, February 19, 1991.

20. Mowery, "Saudi Journal," February 19, 1991.

21. Brian (Green) Juergensmeyer, oral history, Robert R. McCormick Research Center, First Division Museum at Cantigny, Wheaton, IL, January 23, 2013. Juergensmeyer served in both the 2-34 AR and 1-1 AVN from 1988 to 1993 as Brian Green, but took the name of his wife when he married. He served with the 1-1 AVN throughout Hayles's tenure. Juergensmeyer believed that what happened was not an isolated incident, but reflected a "pattern of behavior." See also Rick Atkinson, *Crusade: The Untold Story of the Gulf War* (London: HarperCollins, 1993), 317–20.

22. Richard M. Swain, *"Lucky War": Third Army in Desert Storm* (Fort Leavenworth, KS: US Army Command and General Staff College Press, 1997), 226. Inflight reports made a big difference in confidence, at least for the author. A few days before the ground attack, the author spoke to an A-10 pilot who loitered over our objectives using binoculars to count Iraqi tanks. He reported accurately that all but one or two had been destroyed.

23. Lieutenant Colonel David F Gross, "The Breach of Sadam's [*sic*] Defensive Line: Recollections of a Desert Storm Armor Task Force Commander," unpublished manuscript, US Army War College, Carlisle Barracks, PA, 1992, 70.

24. US Department of the Army, *Division Operations*, FM 71-100 (Washington, DC: Department of the Army, 1990), 4–13.

25. COL (Ret.) Thomas Connors, BG (Ret.) David F. Gross, and MG Paul Izzo, Oral history group interview by Andrew Woods, Robert R. McCormick Research Center, First Division Museum at Cantigny, Wheaton, IL, January 22–23, 2011, 13.

26. Ibid., 57.

27. 3rd Battalion, 37th Armor, OPORD 3-91, "Desert Strike," 13 1400 Feb 91, February 1991, 2.

28. 3rd Battalion, 37th Armor, OPORD DS 4-91, 26 1400 Jan 91, January 1991, 8.

29. Markham interview.

30. Swain, *"Lucky War,"* 205.

31. 1LT Gregory G. Glaze, 2nd Battalion, 34th Armor journal, unofficial handwritten daily log, February 20, 1991.

32. Stephen A. Bourque, *Jayhawk: The VII Corps in the Persian Gulf War* (Washington, DC: Center of Military History, 2002), 143.

33. Ibid.

34. Swain, *"Lucky War,"* 204. See also Tom Clancy with General Fred Franks Jr., *Into the Storm: A Study in Command* (New York: Berkley, 2004), 304. In *Jayhawk*, Bourque reports three killed and nine wounded. I have chosen to use Swain's numbers, as he cites a 1 CD source.

35. Swain, *"Lucky War,"* 230–39. There are a number of sources from which to deduce the plan; I have chosen Swain as the least contentious in terms of agenda and because I have discussed this very idea with him at length.

36. VII Corps, FRAGO 128-91, 201200CFEB9, para. 3.a.1.

37. Maggart, "Eye of the Storm," 146.

38. MAJ Mark S. Landrith, "History: 1st Battalion, 1st Aviation Regiment, 4th Brigade, 1st Infantry Division, Desert Shield/Desert Storm," unpublished manuscript, n.d., n.p. [24–25].

39. Mowery, "Saudi Journal," 93.

40. Dodson, personal journal, February 21, 1991. Ammunition consumption rates can be found in Headquarters, 1 ID (M) DISCOM, "Desert Shield/Desert Storm Support Operations," January 15, 1992, annex P.

41. LTC Clinton J. Ancker, "2nd Armored Division (Forward) and the Gulf Conflict," unpublished manuscript, US Naval War College, Newport, RI, n.d., 135.

42. Rhame interview, February 3, 2015, quoting from Rhame's personal journal, February 21, 1991.

43. Ibid.

44. VII Corps, "Operation Desert Shield/Desert Storm," PowerPoint briefing, n.d. By February 24 the VII Corps stocked seventy-two short tons and had done so largely with reserve troops who joined the Corps in theater, with ammunition companies and truck companies, that did not complete closing on the theater until February.

45. Dodson, personal journal, February 22–23, 1991; 1 ID (M) DISCOM, "Desert Shield/Desert Storm Support Operations," annex P.

46. Order of battle files in the possession of CW3 (Ret.) Phyllis Fitzgerald; Headquarters, 1st Brigade, 1 ID, S2 graphics, February 17, 1991; 2nd Brigade,

enemy situation template, January 22, 1991; CPT Jim Stockmoe, ed., *1st Brigade, 1st Infantry Division: Desert Shield/Storm History* (Fort Riley, KS: 1st Brigade, 1st Infantry Division, 1991), 50.

47. Rhame interview, February 3, 2015, quoting from Rhame's personal journal, February 21–23, 1991.

48. LTC (Ret.) Timothy A. Norton, telephone interview with the author, April 9, 2015.

49. Woods, *The Mother of All Battles*, 209; regarding Iraqi perception of when the ground war started, see 208.

50. Ibid., 209–12.

51. LTC (Ret.) Juan E. Toro, telephone interview with the author, October 8, 2014.

52. LTC (Ret.) James A. Bell, telephone interview with the author, October 10, 2014.

53. Major James K. Morningstar, "Points of Attack: Lessons from the Breach," *Armor*, January–February 1998, 11.

54. Lieutenant Colonel David W. Marlin, "History of the 4th Battalion, 37 Armored Regiment in Operation Desert Shield/Storm," unpublished manuscript, US Army War College, Carlisle Barracks, PA, 1992, 330.

55. Author's notes, February 23, 1991.

56. Rhame interview, February 3, 2015, quoting from Rhame's personal journal, February 23, 1991.

57. Mowery, "Saudi Journal," February 23, 1991.

58. SFC Jeff Hein, personal journal, February 24, 1991.

59. Swain, *"Lucky War,"* 229. TF 3-37 AR started moving toward the berm at 5:00 a.m., and the remainder of the Division was under way within minutes.

60. Connors, Gross, and Izzo interview. Gross recounted this story in the group interview, citing admiration for COL Tony Moreno.

61. MAJ Jack Crumplar, 2nd Battalion, 34th Armor, 1st Brigade, 1st Infantry Division, interviewed by MAJ Robert Cook, Commander, 326th MHD, March 28, 1991, DSIT-AS-003.

62. Glaze, 2nd Battalion, 34th Armor journal, February 24, 1991. See also Marlin, "History of the 4th Battalion, 37 Armored Regiment."

63. This ironic mention of the NTC occurred in several interviews. See also Gross, "The Breach of Sadam's [*sic*] Defensive Line," 84–85.

64. Glaze, 2nd Battalion, 34th Armor journal, February 24, 1991. See also Gross, "The Breach of Sadam's [*sic*] Defensive Line," 85.

65. 1LT Jay C. Mumford, "Rangers in Iraq, TF Ranger, 2nd Battalion, 16th Infantry in the Persian Gulf War, 10 November 1990–12 May 1991," unpublished manuscript, August 31, 1991, 28.

66. Marlin, "History of the 4th Battalion, 37 Armored Regiment," 336–37.

67. COL Brian C. Cook, telephone interview with the author, September 10, 2014.

68. Ibid. This small mortar barrage is probably the one called by 1LT Ward that landed short of the target and close to friendly troops.

69. Marlin, "History of the 4th Battalion, 37 Armored Regiment," 344.

70. First Lieutenant Pete Lee, quoted in Marlin, "History of the 4th Battalion, 37 Armored Regiment," 347.

71. Cook interview. This story was told frequently, suggesting that it is apocryphal.

72. Author's personal journal, February 24, 1991.

73. Author's recollection. At least one Iraqi soldier had a festering leg wound caused by artillery fragments days earlier.

74. Maggart, "Eye of the Storm," 153.

75. Author's personal recollection.

76. Jeffrey K. Sanson, "Ironhorse: Alpha Co. 3rd Bn. 37th AR," unpublished manuscript, June 23, 1991, 22.

77. Woods, *The Mother of All Battles*, 212–20.

78. Ibid., 219.

79. Ibid.

80. Ibid.

81. Swain, *"Lucky War,"* 230–31; regarding the timing of the VII Corps attack, see 121–22.

82. Clancy, *Into the Storm*, 329–34; General H. Norman Schwarzkopf with Peter Petre, *It Doesn't Take a Hero: The Autobiography* (New York: Bantam, 1992), 453–54; Atkinson, *Crusade*, 391–94. See also Brigadier General Robert H. Scales Jr., *Certain Victory: The United States Army in the Gulf War* (Washington, DC: Office of the Chief of Staff, US Army, 1993), 222.

83. Maggart, "Eye of the Storm," 153–54.

84. Marlin, "History of the 4th Battalion, 37 Armored Regiment," 351–52.

85. Schwarzkopf, *It Doesn't Take a Hero*, 453.

86. Ibid.

87. 1st Brigade, 1st Infantry Division, daily staff journal, February 24, 1991.

88. Dodson, personal journal, February 24, 1991.

89. COL Michael Dodson, Commander, Division Artillery, 1st Infantry Division, interview by MAJ Thomas A. Popa, Fort Riley, KS, July 24–25, 1991, DSIT-C-068.

90. LTG (Ret.) Michael L. Dodson, interview with the author, Manhattan, KS, January 23, 2015.

91. LTC (Ret.) James M. Holt, telephone interview with the author, January 7, 2015.

92. COL (Ret.) Terry Bullington, telephone interview with the author, June 6, 2014.

93. Author's recollection. See also Maggart, "Eye of the Storm," 154.

94. Norton interview.

95. SFC (Ret.) Michael G. Schulte, telephone interview with the author, November 5, 2014.

96. COL Anthony Moreno, Commander, 2nd Brigade, 1st Infantry Division, interview by MAJ Thomas A. Popa, Fort Riley, KS, July 26, 1991, DCSIT-C-076.

97. Precise timing for all eight companies simply is not possible until the Army releases all of the records. Timings here are taken from 1st Infantry Division Main, G3, Operations, daily staff journal, February 24, 1991; and Glaze, 2nd Battalion, 34th Armor journal, February 24, 1991.

98. Glaze, 2nd Battalion, 34th Armor journal, February 24, 1991. The net was keyed at about 1505. See also Maggart, "Eye of the Storm," 155.

99. 1st Brigade, 1st Infantry Division, daily staff journal, February 24, 1991.

100. Connors, Gross, and Izzo interview.

101. Gross, "The Breach of Sadam's [*sic*] Defensive Line," 89. See also Connors, Gross, and Izzo interview.

102. Gross, "The Breach of Sadam's [*sic*] Defensive Line," 91; 1st Infantry Division Main, G3, Operations, daily staff journal.

103. Morningstar, "Points of Attack," 12.

104. Ibid.

105. LTC (Ret.) Matthew K. Green, telephone interview with the author, November 3, 2014. Green led a platoon in the 1-34 AR and saw the aftermath as the 1-34 AR passed through TF 2-34 AR on February 24, 1991.

106. 1st Brigade, 1st Infantry Division, daily staff journal, February 24, 1991; 2nd Battalion, 34th Armor daily staff journal, February 24, 1991. See also LTC Gregory Fontenot, "The 'Dreadnoughts' Rip the Saddam Line," *Army*, January 1992, 35; Stephan A. Bourque and John W Burdan III, *The Road to Safwan: The 1st Squadron, 4th Cavalry in the 1991 Persian Gulf War* (Denton: University of North Texas Press, 2007), 125. Regarding SGT Elish Jackson, see Derick Burleson, "Death Is a Constant Presence in Battle," *Manhattan Mercury*, May 3, 1991, 1. The fragment that struck Jackson was nearly three inches long and perhaps an inch in diameter; he kept it.

107. CPT Robert A. Burns and CPT John Bushyhead, group interview, Robert R. McCormick Research Center, vol. 4 (McCall to Norton).

108. LTC (Ret.) John Bushyhead, e-mail to the author, April 14, 2015. Bushyhead is unable to recall who reported contact.

109. Burns and Bushyhead interview. The author well recalls seeing the lone Iraqi soldier literally walk out of a large cloud of dust and smoke. TF 2-34 AR found antipersonnel mines and some decoys, but found no antitank mines.

110. Bourque and Burdan, *The Road to Safwan*, 125.

111. Ibid., 127.

112. 1st Battalion, 34th Armor, "1st Battalion, 34th Armor in the Ground War against Iraq: Demons in the Desert." n.d., 2.

113. COL (Ret.) George P. Ritter, telephone interview with the author, August 5, 2014.

114. Green, interview with the author, November 3, 2014.

115. Ritter, interview with the author, August 5, 2014.

116. 1st Brigade, 1st Infantry Division, daily staff journal, February 24, 1991.

117. Gross, "The Breach of Sadam's [*sic*] Defensive Line," 95–97. Connors, Gross, and Izzo interview; Norton interview.

118. Moreno interview. See also Morningstar, "Points of Attack"; and Jim Tice, "'Coming Through' the Big Red Raid," *Army Times*, August 26, 1991, 12, 16, 18, 20, and the graphic on 13.

119. Moreno interview.

120. ZSU stands for Zenitnaya Samokhodnaya Ustanovka, which translates as "antiaircraft self-propelled mount."

121. Mumford, "Rangers in Iraq," 31–32.

122. Marlin, "History of the 4th Battalion, 37 Armored Regiment," 357.

123. Ibid., 358.

124. Clancy, *Into the Storm*, 344–45.

125. Ibid., 354–53.

126. Ibid., 349.

127. Atkinson, *Crusade*, 406.

128. Ibid.

129. Maggart, "Eye of the Storm," 156.

130. Ibid. The VII Corps restricted fire line went into effect at 8:22 p.m. See 1st Brigade, 1st Infantry Division, daily staff journal, February 24, 1991.

131. SGT Haime Edwards, quoted in Mumford, "Rangers in Iraq," 31.

132. Swain, *"Lucky War,"* 236–40.

133. Rhame interview, February 3, 2015, quoting from Rhame's personal journal, February 24, 1991.

134. MAJ Michael Barefield, personal journal, February 24, 1991.

135. Dodson, personal journal, February 24, 1991.

136. Glaze, 2nd Battalion, 34th Armor journal, February 24, 1991.

137. Rhame interview, February 3, 2015, quoting from Rhame's personal journal, February 24, 1991.

138. Mowery, "Saudi Journal," 99.

139. Ibid.

FIGURE 1. Publicity photograph of 2LT Genie Thornton (right) and PFC Connie Kalvick taken by Army media during REFORGER 1973. The first two women assigned to the 1st Infantry Division created a sensation among media and senior officials. (Courtesy of COL USA Retired Eugenia Thornton)

FIGURE 2. (*Above*) 1st Division soldier preparing to guide a tank at the makeshift railhead at Fort Riley in early December, 1990. Division engineers took apart a tactical bridge to use one section of it to create a loading ramp. Loading tanks on flat cars is a dangerous and painstaking task, one made more difficult by the facilities at Fort Riley. Although the railhead had no lights, the troops loaded day and night without injury or accident. In fact they worked so effectively that they outpaced the capacity of the railway. (Col. R. R. McCormick Research Center)

FIGURE 3. (*Top Right*) On arrival in Saudi Arabia soldiers confronted the task of finding their two duffle bags among the hundreds on the ground. Many accomplished this in the middle of the night and then had to execute what they called the "duffle-bag drag," often across considerable distance. (Col. R. R. McCormick Research Center)

FIGURE 4. (*Below Right*) COL Bert Maggart 1st Brigade, pierside at Ad Daman, Saudi Arabia, January 7, 1991. The roll on/roll off vessel in the background is the *Jolly Rubino,* which brought some 8,464 short tons of equipment, including most of that for Maggart's 1st Brigade. (Courtesy of COL USA Retired Jim Stockmoe)

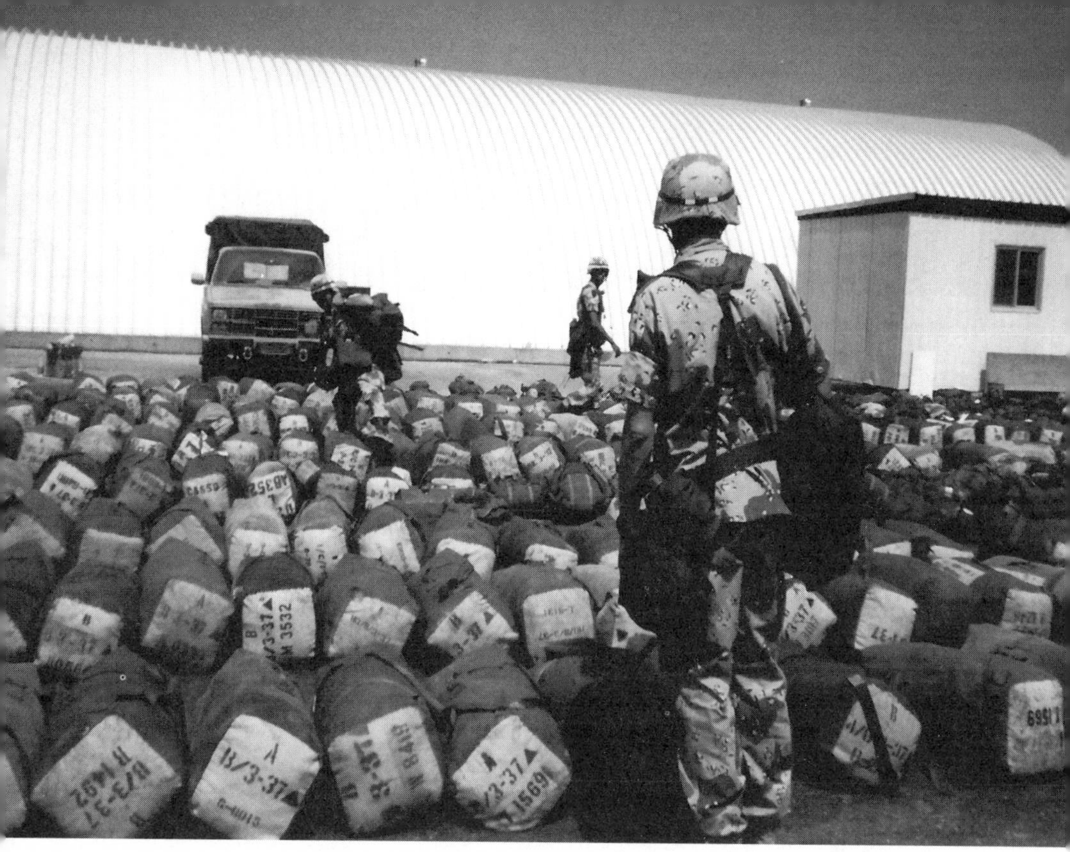
B/3-37
M 3532

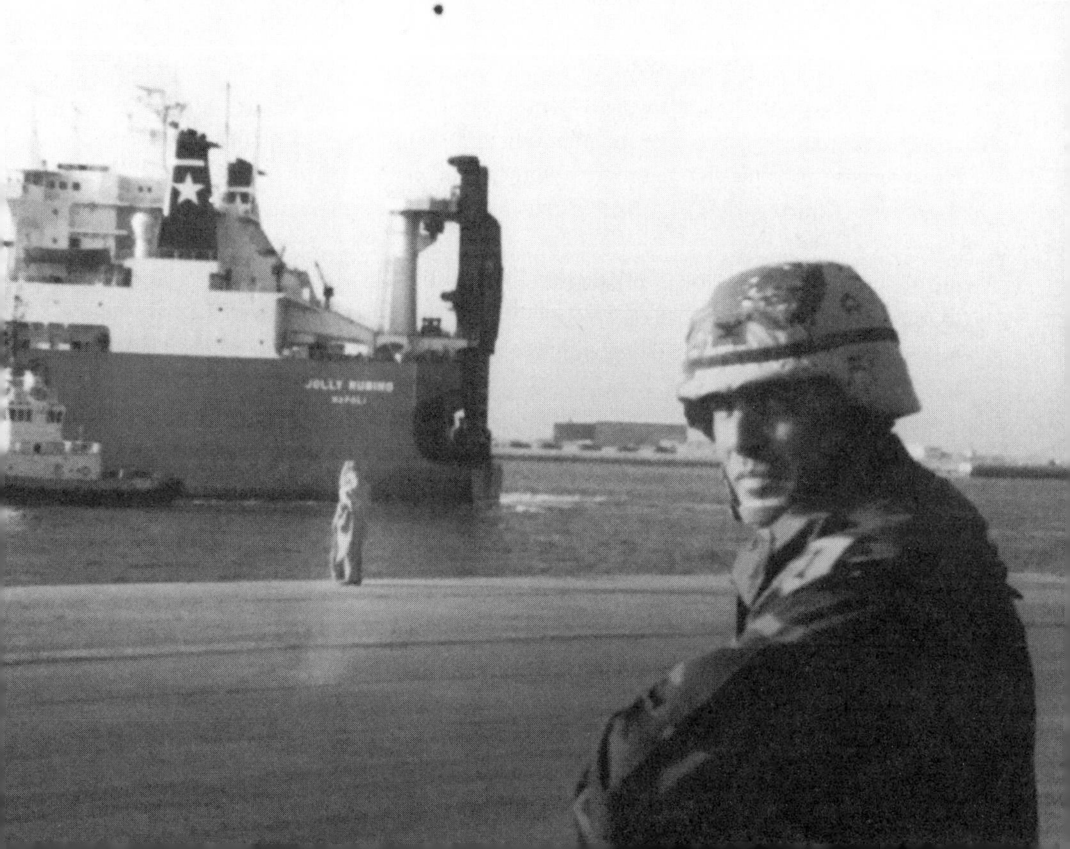
JOLLY RUBINO

FIGURE 5. (*Above*) C Company 2-34 AR on heavy-equipment transports preparing to move to the tactical assembly area on January 12, 1991. (Courtesy of Steven M. Light)

FIGURE 6. (*Top Right*) 3-66 AR troops installing a mine plow on January 25, 1991, in Tactical Assembly Area Roosevelt. None of these soldiers had ever seen or used a mine plow. Adapting to change and adopting new equipment was a constant in Desert Storm, as the Army shipped new equipment and even experimental equipment to the desert. (Courtesy of COL USA Retired Clinton J. Ancker)

FIGURE 7. (*Below Right*) Small plastic tubs like the one this young soldier is using were issued about 1 to every 8 or 9 troops. The 1st Infantry Division's soldiers washed their clothes this way for the duration of the five months they were in the field. (1st Division Museum, Fort Riley, Kansas)

DIOS NOS
BENDIGA

ARMY

FIGURE 8. A Bradley assigned to 2-34 AR scout platoon. Because the soldiers were in essence camping, they had to haul their equipment on their vehicles, as this photograph illustrates: two five-gallon water cans are hanging on the side; camouflage nets and poles are stowed above the side skirts; duffle bags and a washtub are hanging toward the rear; the combat vehicle crewman's helmet is resting on the periscope sights. Note: all combat vehicles carried two antennas whether or not they had two radios so that the enemy could not target commanders or leaders. A Howitzer can be seen on the horizon. (Courtesy of Steven M. Light)

FIGURE 9. January 1991, LT Jeff Jones loads ammunition in the assembly area. Jones is hefting the 120-millimeter depleted uranium penetrator anti-tank round. It was so effective at killing tanks that the troops called it the "silver bullet." The author observed a "silver bullet" passing through dug-in positions the length of enemy tanks and out the back. The cardboard boxes with crescents on them are MREs, or cases of meals ready to eat. Six wooden boxes of machine-gun ammunition are at the back of the turret. The tank is cluttered with useful gear. (Courtesy of Steven M. Light)

FIGURE 10. (*Above*) Task Force 2-34 AR refueling on February 14, 1991, during the 120-kilometer march to the forward assembly area. The task force advanced in company/teams abreast with each company/team in column. In this shot, Team C 2-34 AR has just about completed refueling. Each vehicle stopped long enough to refuel from the tanker and then moved forward to its place in the March column. The number 40 on the rear of the medic M 114 Armored personnel carrier identifies this track as assigned to 2-34 Armor's headquarters company. The number 41 marked A company, 42 B Company and so on. (Courtesy of Steven M. Light)

FIGURE 11. (*Top Right*) Senior commanders of the 1st Infantry Division less COL Bert Maggart of 1st Brigade. Front row left to right are: COL Dave Weisman 3rd Brigade; COL Tony Moreno 2nd Brigade; BG Bill Carter, assistant division commander maneuver; MG Tom Rhame, commanding general; and BG Jerry Rutherford, assistant division commander support. Back row left to right are: COL Mike Dodson Division Artillery; COL Jim Mowery 4th Brigade; and COL Bob Shadley Division Support Command. (Col. R. R. McCormick Research Center)

FIGURE 12. (*Below Right*) MLRS firing rockets at targets in Iraq during an artillery raid. COL Mike Dodson's Division Artillery supported by other VII Corps artillery units began firing raids on February 16, 1991, and continued doing so right until they fired the artillery preparation for the attack on February 24, 1991. (Courtesy of Steven M. Light)

FIGURE 13. (*Top Left*) Young soldier making the best of an ugly job that had to be done each morning. Tactical assembly areas could be readily located by the pyres of oily black smoke rising from the barrels containing the contents of latrines. Soon after sunup troops set fire to the muck, which they had to stir nearly continuously to keep it burning. (Col. R. R. McCormick Research Center)

FIGURE 14. (*Below Left*) CW1 Phyllis Fitzgerald Order of Battle Technician 1st Infantry Division. Fitzgerald and her team provided detailed order of battle information to support the intelligence estimate for the initial assault and subsequent operations. (Courtesy of CW3 USA Retired Phyllis Fitzgerald)

FIGURE 15. (*Above*) Final desktop rehearsal conducted at Danger Forward, BG Carter's tactical command post. MG Rhame is pointing at the map. COL Mike Dodson Division Artillery is to the left of Rhame with his back to the camera. BG Bill Carter is to Dodson's left. The four officers sitting on the left side of the table are LTC Dan Magee Executive Officer 1st Brigade, COL Bob Shadley Division Support Command, COL Dave Weisman 3rd Brigade, and COL Tony Moreno 2nd Brigade. COL Jim Mowery 4th Brigade is the officer leaning toward the map behind Weisman. (Col. R. R. McCormick Research Center)

FIGURE 16. (*Above*) Photograph taken of the Lane Marker for Lane H as 1st Brigade withdrew from Iraq in April 1991. This marker is one of three 4 x 8-foot markers emplaced to mark each of the 16 lanes. The attacking units marked the lanes at 3,000, 2,000, and 1,000 meters. Smaller markers marked the entrance to the plowed lanes. (Courtesy of Steven M. Light)

FIGURE 17. (*Top Right*) LTG Fred Franks and MG Tom Rhame review options for the employment of 1st Infantry Division on February 24, 1991. (Courtesy of LTG Frederick M. Franks Jr.)

FIGURE 18. (*Below Right*) One of several "lowboy" equipment trailers used to evacuate prisoners on February 24, 1991. The number of prisoners taken from the 26th Iraqi Division that day overwhelmed the processing capacity of the two lead brigades. (Col. R. R. McCormick Research Center)

FIGURE 19. (*Top Left*) Badly wounded American soldier being evacuated early on February 25, 1991, from TF 2-34 AR. A medical evacuation helicopter from Lone Star "Dust Off" can be seen in the background. Dr. James Goff's head can be seen at the center of the photograph. He is maintaining pressure on the wounded soldier's lacerated femoral artery. The medic aboard the Dust Off helicopter took over and maintained the necessary pressure until the helicopter reached the combat surgical hospital. (Courtesy of Dr. James Goff)

FIGURE 20. (*Below Left*) Iraqi troops, probably assigned to the 806th Brigade, seeking to surrender to TF 2-34 as it moved north on February 26, 1991. The 806th occupied positions west of where this photograph was taken. They were likely fleeing from the 1st Armored Division as it attacked north. (Courtesy of Steven M. Light)

FIGURE 21. (*Above*) TF 3-37 Armor passing one of its victims. (Col. R. R. McCormick Research Center)

FIGURE 22. (*Left*) SGT Cheryl O'Brien taking a smoke break near a Blackhawk during the ground attack. O'Brien is wearing her chemical protective overgarments. She was killed on the night of February 27–28, 1991, along with the crew and passenger of Cowboy 15. O'Brien established a sad first for women as she became the first woman assigned to the 1st Infantry Division killed in combat. (Col. R. R. McCormick Research Center)

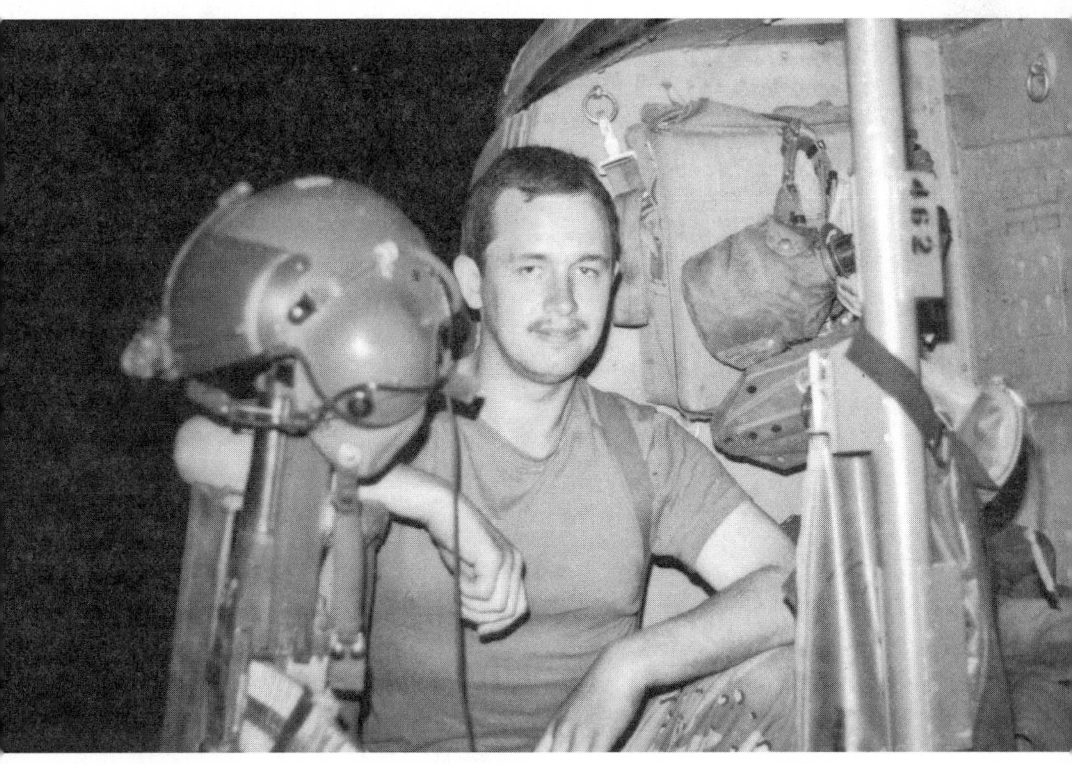

FIGURE 23. SPC Buddy Stefanoff assigned gunner of Blackhawk call sign Cowboy 15. On the evening of February 27th Stefanoff and another soldier were reconfiguring the sling load for Cowboy 15 when the crew was called on another mission. Cowboy 15 flew off with Cheryl O'Brien serving Stefanoff's stead as door gunner. Stefanoff and his teammate never saw Cowboy 15 or the crew again. An Iraqi anti-aircraft artillery crew shot down Cowboy 15 early on the morning of February 28, 1991, killing all aboard. (Courtesy of Buddy Stefanoff)

FIGURE 24. (*Above*) Iraqi Republican Guard T-72 likely destroyed by a "Silver Bullet" at Objective Norfolk in the early hours of February 27, 1991. (Author's Collection)

FIGURE 25. (*Above Right*) Turret belonging to the hull of the destroyed T-72 shown in Figure 24. When struck by either high-explosive anti-tank rounds or depleted uranium penetrators, T-72s blew up due to unprotected propellant stored in the hulls. When this happened, T-72 tank turrets typically blew off and landed right side up near their hulls. The ball bearings on which the turrets had rested, roughly an inch in diameter, flew in all directions. Many of them became collector's items. (Author's Collection)

FIGURE 26. (*Below Right*) Postwar photograph of scout platoon 1-34 AR Bradley HQ 232. Struck by a depleted uranium round fired by a B Company 1-34 AR tank, the Bradley was immediately engulfed in flames. Rapid action taken by the driver, the only soldier not wounded in the incident, prevented loss of life. SPC James Fayne evacuated his four wounded crewmates, two of whom, the scouts in the crew compartment, were badly wounded. The gunner and vehicle commander suffered only minor wounds. (Courtesy of LTC USA Retired Marvin L. Meek)

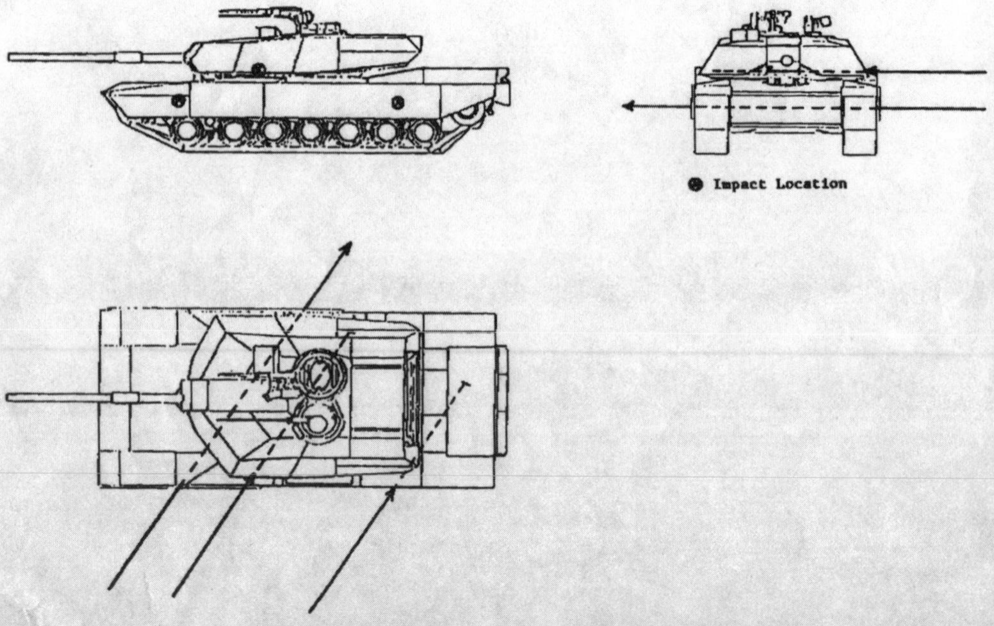

● Impact Location

FIGURE 1-10.17. (U) SHOTLINES AND IMPACT LOCATIONS.

FIGURE 27. (*Above Left*) CPT Bill Hedges' M1 Tank destroyed by 2-66 AR in the early morning hours of February 27, 1991. Three depleted uranium rounds struck tank Bravo 66 3-66 AR. SSG Tony Appleget, wounded by an artillery fragment on February 18, 1991, died in this second incident. (Courtesy of LTC USA Retired William H. Hedges)

FIGURE 28. (*Below Left*) US Army diagram of fratricide shot lines and impacts on CPT Bill Hedges' tank. (Col. R. R. McCormick Research Center)

FIGURE 29. (*Above*) Surface mining site known to the 1st Brigade as the "Valley of the Boogers." The terrain of the valley did what the Iraqis had not done: it stymied the 1st Brigade. (Courtesy of Steven M. Light)

FIGURE 30. (Above) Wreckage of Cowboy 15. Iraqi 23 millimeter air-defense artillery shot down Cowboy 15 sometime during the night of February 27–28, 1991. Cowboy 15 crashed just west of Ar Rumaylah airfield, killing all aboard. The bodies of three soldiers who died the night before when a medical evacuation helicopter crashed were also on board the ill-fated Blackhawk. The arrows indicate 23-millimeter cannon impact points. (Courtesy of Buddy Stefanoff)

FIGURE 31. (Above Right) Because he reasoned his primary task was to command his task force, LTC Dave Gross removed his 50-caliber machine gun to improve his field of vision. LTC Gross is in the commander's position on the right side of the turret. The stubby post in the middle is the tank's wind sensor. The oval shaped device at the top of the sensor is his global position system sensor. The two canisters on the left side bustle rack are ammunition canisters used to store maps. Burning wellheads can be seen in the background. (Col. R. R. McCormick Research Center)

FIGURE 32. (Below Right) Apaches assigned to 1-1 AVN refueling shortly after cease-fire on March 1, 1991. (Courtesy of Steven M. Light)

FIGURE 33. (Above Left) Iraqi delegation crossing Basra-Kuwait City highway to board US HMMWVs to be taken to Safwan Ceasefire site. The Iraqi officer in the lead of the group is Staff LTG Sultan Hashim. Tanks are those assigned to LTC Dave Gross and his operations officer MAJ Paul Izzo. (Col. R. R. McCormick Research Center)

FIGURE 34. (Below Left) Tanks and Bradleys on the move after ceasefire. Two columns pass, heading in different directions. (Author's Collection)

FIGURE 35. (Above) Mechanized infantry column preparing to move south toward Saudi Arabia in mid-April 1991. (Author's Collection)

FIGURE 36. Soldiers with Saudis in the final assembly area, where the Division prepared to return home. The Americans are 1LT Chuck Parker, SSG (first name unknown) Sweeting, 2LT Jim Enicks, and 1LT Bennie McCrae. (Courtesy of Bennie J. McRae III)

FIGURE 37. MG Thomas G. Rhame, Senator Robert J. Dole, and General Gordon R. Sullivan "troop the line" at celebration at Fort Riley, Kansas on July 4, 1991. (Courtesy of CW3 USA Retired Phyllis Fitzgerald)

CHAPTER NINE

THE MARCH UP COUNTRY

Awake at 0215 and pulling my shift on guard. There is nothing to be seen through thermals and nothing on the radios.

—Sergeant First Class Jeff Hein

Div [Division] Cont [Continued] Atk [Attack] toward PL [Phase Line] Smash.

—Major Michael Barefield

Where is the Republican Guard?

—General H. Norman Schwarzkopf

Save for the "occasional scare," as Lieutenant Colonel (LTC) Dave Marlin put it, the night of February 24–25, 1991, passed without incident.[1] COL Lon E. "Bert" Maggart's brigade saw dismounted infantry moving about the westernmost positions that lay beyond the restricted fire line. At 2:39 a.m. the First Battalion, Thirty-Fourth Armor (1-34 AR) engaged a group of three Iraqis. SSG Kevin Draper, LTC Pat Ritter's gunner, fired his coaxial machine gun at them. Ritter hoped to take them prisoner, so he ordered Draper to fire to their rear. The three went to ground, but a half hour later they moved again, this time toward the 1-34 AR's scout platoon, putting them between Ritter's position and the scouts. This time he ordered a killing burst. Draper fired and brought one of the three down. They did not move again. Later that morning, the 1-34 AR captured two survivors and buried their dead officer; it turned out they were an artillery forward observation team.[2] Similar activity occurred elsewhere, but it seemed aimless. The Iraqis were neither improving their positions nor withdrawing. Sporadic direct fire occurred, but artillery and attack helicopters carried the burden that night. Caches of Iraqi ammunition and combat vehicles set alight during the attack burned with a crackling noise punctuated by intermittent explosions.

Combat operations involve frequent transitions. Some of these are forced by the enemy. On February 25 and 26 the First Infantry Division completed the breach operation and tasks to support the VII Corps as it continued the attack. Doing so required multiple transitions. It expanded the breach to Phase Line New Jersey and assisted other units as they moved forward. There was no pause between tactical tasks; they overlapped or flowed from one to another. While it might not strike one as intuitive, sustaining offensive operations is perhaps more complex than an actual assault. Prussian military theorist Carl von Clausewitz's observations that "[f]atigue, exertion and privation constitute a separate destructive factor in war" are readily confirmed by this phase of operations.[3] Sustaining offensive operations strains logistics as well: modern mechanized forces consume enormous quantities of fuel, and ammunition must be resupplied. If not executed precisely, logistics can exert a powerful drag on an attacking formation. Additionally, the divergence of view between LTG Frederick M. Franks Jr. in the VII Corps and GEN H. Norman Schwarzkopf in Riyadh continued to grow.

Central Command and Iraqi Estimates of the Situation

By no means did the Iraqi forces enjoy a quiet night. Coalition air forces continued to attack them throughout their depth, while attack helicopters and artillery struck closer targets. The high command was optimistic as February 24 dawned, but as the day wore on, confidence waned—even among those around Saddam Hussein. At one point, one of Saddam's advisers told him that international media had reported one of Iraq's corps had been overrun. Saddam claimed, "This is lying," but the adviser maintained, "There are a lot of news reports like [this] one sir." Saddam persisted: "All of this news is wrong, but tell the news as it is. They tried to attack from different directions but everything is under control, in a good way."[4] Delusion in dictatorships is not unusual. Less than three years after the VII Corps had destroyed his unit, Ahmed Ibrahim Hamash, who had survived and been promoted to lieutenant general, claimed the Americans "didn't manage to penetrate the obstacle systems of the [Iraqi VII] corps."[5]

Despite what its members claimed, told each other, or perhaps even believed, the Iraqi high command was beginning to understand its dilemma, and it reacted to the coalition offensive both in the west and in the east. Late on February 24 the Jihad Corps ordered two brigades of the Iraqi 12th Armored Division (12 AD) southwest to occupy blocking positions west of the Wadi al-Batin, indicating concern about the US VII Corps operating west of the wadi. The situation in southeast Kuwait, defended by Major General (MG) Salah

Aboud Mahmoud's III Corps, was particularly dire. On February 24, G-Day, Mahmoud attempted several small counterattacks against the US Marines. These efforts did not restore the situation, so he planned a major attack oriented on Ahmed Al Jaber Air Base for the morning of February 25. The Marines had seized the air base, some forty kilometers south of Kuwait City, late the day before. Mahmoud planned to mount the attack using his 5th Mechanized Division (5 Mech Div) augmented with a brigade from the 8 Mech Div. The 5 Mech Div had made the attack at Al Khafji in January. A brigade of the 3 AD and the tank battalion from the 7th Infantry Division (7 ID) would conduct a supporting attack. At midnight, he briefed infamous "Chemical Ali" Hassan al-Majid on his plan. As governor of occupied Kuwait, Chemical Ali approved the plan. Mahmoud's units moved in the early morning hours to stage for the attack.[6]

In Riyadh, Schwarzkopf had gone to bed on February 24 content with the progress made during the day. On arriving at his operations center early on February 25 he found that the VII Corps had not continued the attack the night before. Indeed, on his maps the Corps appeared to have moved backward. In 1991, battle maps from platoon to unified command did not automatically reflect shared digital data; instead, staff officers indicated unit positions as reported up through the various headquarters by affixing "sticky labels" or writing with grease pencils directly on acetate-covered maps, with inevitable minor inaccuracies. The Corps had not moved backward, but neither had it moved forward. In fact, throughout the theater, only the 24 ID had continued forward that night, and it did so in the absence of enemy resistance. The Marines had fought hard on G-Day, but they, too, had halted. Nor had the two Arab Corps attacked after dark.[7] Schwarzkopf's understanding of the battle differed widely from that of LTG John Yeosock at the 3rd Army and LTG Fred Franks at the VII Corps.[8]

How this confusion or gap developed is hard to fathom. It is unlikely that Yeosock failed to appraise Schwarzkopf about VII Corps intentions. At 5:00 p.m. daily, Yeosock did an update with his principal staff officers. The notes that COL Mike Kendall, his executive officer, took at these sessions show that Yeosock reviewed with his staff the locations of the two corps, their major maneuver units, and their intentions. Furthermore, at that session, he said to his operations officer, MG Steve Arnold, "Give me a recommendation on where units should stop this evening."[9] At 7:00 p.m. Yeosock attended Schwarzkopf's Central Command (CENTCOM) battle update briefing. Just how it is that Schwarzkopf did not learn what Yeosock knew and had decided to do is unclear; it is unlikely—to the point of implausibility—that Yeosock withheld information about either his intentions or those of his two Corps commanders. In any event, the divergence of view between Schwarzkopf and Franks continued to grow.

Iraqi Actions and Reactions

Although Saddam and his inner circle may have been in denial for most of G-Day, Iraqi units responded to the threat as they perceived it. The Iraqis attempted counterattacks in several places. Of immediate interest to the VII Corps, BG Sakban Turki Mutlik attempted to move his 52 AD to blocking positions. Equipped with thirty-year-old T-55s and a mixture of Soviet Boyevaya Mashina Pekhoty (BMP) infantry fighting vehicles and Mnogotselevoy Tyagach Legky Bronirovanny (MTLB) multipurpose light-armored towing vehicles (armored personnel carriers), the 52 AD's three brigades occupied positions just to the rear of the Iraqi VII Corps' front-line divisions. Mutlik's 52nd Armored Brigade (52 AR Bde, which had the same numeral designation as the parent division) occupied the westernmost position about twenty kilometers north of the 31 ID. The 11th Mechanized Brigade (11 Mech Bde) defended some thirty kilometers farther east and nearly thirty kilometers north of the 25 ID. His 80 AR Bde was twenty kilometers northeast of the 11 Mech Bde and just west of the Wadi al-Batin. Because Franks considered the 52 AR Bde a serious threat to the breach, he had ordered his staff to "make it go away!"[10] To a large extent, Corps artillery and coalition air forces succeeded in doing just that. On the morning of February 25, the 52 AR Bde retained only fifteen tanks and fifteen BMPs—about a single battalion's strength. Despite Mutlik's order, the 52 AR Bde did not move. It is possible the brigade commander ignored his orders or was in shock; apparently he remained in his bunker that day. After his capture he complained bitterly about the constant air attacks on his unit. Thoroughly broken, the commander commented to his interrogators that when under air attack he would ask aloud, "Why don't you visit the 48th Division or the 80th Brigade?" Mutlik's 11 Mech Bde did move forward, probably to defend the approach from the Wadi al-Batin left open when the 12 AD's two brigades moved southwest.[11]

At the theater level, the Republican Guard Forces commander, LTG Ayad Futayyih Khalifa al-Rawi, issued orders at 9:30 a.m. on February 24 to reposition and reorient part of his forces to the west. It is not clear whether he issued these orders in response to the high command's assessment of the threat it perceived from the US XVIII Airborne Corps or in response to the US VII Corps attack. He had two Republican Guard divisions in the southern Rumaila oil field, the Al-Medina Armored Division to the north and the Tawakalna Mechanized Division to the south. He ordered the Tawakalna to orient to the west and southwest. He also ordered the Hammurabi Armored Division to reposition where it could backstop the Tawakalna and defend the Rumaila oil field. He did not alter the dispositions of the two remaining Republican Guard divisions located between the oil fields and Basra to the northeast.[12]

LTG Al-Rawi also exercised operational control of the Jihad Corps composed of the 10 AD and 12 AD. The 10 AD had relatively modern equipment including T-62 and T-72 tanks; the 10 AD's infantry used BMP fighting vehicles. By comparison, the 12 AD had aging Chinese-built T-55 tanks and MTLB armored personnel carriers. Al-Rawi ordered the 12 AD to blocking positions south and west of the main Republican Guard positions in the Rumaila oil field. The 12 AD moved at midnight, planning to arrive in positions to the south of the Tawakalna Mechanized Division and oriented south and southwest to block US forces moving north.

Regardless of what prompted Al-Rawi to reorient his forces, he responded in accordance with the basic contingencies assigned to the Republican Guard Forces Command (RGFC). The Republican Guard had three assigned tasks: to counterattack in the event of a penetration; maneuver in depth to defeat a coalition attack; and defend Basra. Moving the 12 AD to block an attack from the south and reorienting part of the Tawakalna Mechanized Division made sense and was consistent with the Iraqis' operational thinking and their assessment of likely coalition courses of action.[13]

American reconnaissance and surveillance focused on the Republican Guard detected not only the maneuver that Al-Rawi ordered but also the movement of the 52 AD. BG John F. Stewart Jr., the 3rd Army intelligence officer, concluded that the "Tawakalna Division of the RGFC was moving to the southwest for a meeting engagement with the [US] 2nd ACR [Armored Cavalry Regiment] and the 17th and 52nd ADs were moving to establish a defense in front of the RGFC."[14] Although 3rd Army intelligence misidentified the 12 AD as the 17 AD and was mistaken about the 52 AD's intentions, its assessment was more than adequate for planning the attack on the Republican Guard.

In the eastern part of the Kuwait Theater of Operations, the Iraqi III Corps mounted a significant counterattack. At first light on February 25 its forces rendezvoused for the operation Mahmoud had ordered the evening before. Although damaged badly at Al Khafji, the 5 Mech Div joined with elements of the 8 ID to form one wing of the counterattack; the 8th Brigade of the 3 AD augmented by a tank battalion of the 7 ID formed the second wing. At 7:10 a.m. the counterattack force advanced toward Ahmed Al Jaber Air Base in heavy fog, exacerbated by the oil fires set as part of Operation Tariq. First contact occurred at 9:00 a.m. when a T-55 tank and two armored personnel carriers penetrated a Marine tank battalion screen line. The small Iraqi unit surprised COL Richard W. Hodory, commander of Task Force (TF) Papa Bear of the 1st Marine Division (1 Mar Div), at his command post.[15]

These Iraqis could very well have overrun Hodory's command post, but they wanted to surrender. MAJ Adai, their battalion commander, not only surrendered but also gave the Marines the Iraqi III Corps' plan and warned them that the attack would come soon. Shortly thereafter, just as Adai warned, the attack began in earnest. Some ten kilometers north, the other wing of the III Corps, apparently having passed between Marine units, struck MG Mike Myatt's 1 Mar

Div command post. CPT Eddie Ray's light armored vehicle company, brought in to augment security for the command post, met the attack.[16]

The ensuing fight swelled rapidly. MG Myatt recognized the scope and scale of the attack immediately and reacted decisively. He brought to bear all of the Division's supporting assets to confront the threat to TF Papa Bear and his own command post. CPT Ray's Marines held off the Iraqis, who attacked with little coordination and even worse marksmanship. As the Iraqi attack faltered, the Marines went on the attack. CPT Ray's company swept north, destroying thirty-eight Iraqi combat vehicles and capturing three hundred of the enemy. Hodory's TF Papa Bear fought furiously for three hours and broke the counterattack by noon. Although the III Corps surprised the Marines and halted their advance on Kuwait City for a day, it achieved little else.[17] MG Mahmoud admitted as much, noting the Americans had "widened [their] area of penetration and continued to punch in deep."[18]

The unsuccessful attack constituted the only large counterattack attempted by the Iraqi Army. From then on, they fought to preserve forces or delay. Mahmoud withdrew north, planning to fight from the southern edge of Kuwait City. He reported three of his divisions' combat ineffective. He did not include the 5 Mech Div in that report, though it is unlikely much of it remained after both Al Khafji and the failed counterattack that morning. He retained six infantry divisions, the 3 AD, and what was left of the 5 Mech Div. But before he could organize a defense at Kuwait City, he received an order to withdraw toward Basra to "cover the border area."[19]

Expanding to Phase Line New Jersey

BG Bill Carter continued to direct "crossing area" activities throughout the night. Units repositioned, brought up fuel and ammunition, and processed and evacuated prisoners of war. More than a thousand prisoners had to be evacuated to free up transport and relieve guards; getting them out took considerable effort. In TF 2-16, CPT Mark Samson, the logistics officer, and 1LT Don Lannom, the adjutant, ran the operation to move some six hundred prisoners held across more than twenty square kilometers. Gathering and moving them posed a difficult logistics problem. They "pressed into service every type of vehicle they could lay their hands on, from 2 1/2-ton and 5-ton trucks to 'lowboy' heavy equipment haulers."[20] Lannom established intermediate collection points where the line companies brought their prisoners. Trucks that Samson collected hauled the prisoners from collection points to the Division "cage,"[21] but the Division needed help with transporting the prisoners from there. At 1:15 a.m. the Division heard the happy news that the 14th Military Police Brigade commander himself was on the way, leading forty five-ton trucks forward to evacuate prisoners.

MAP 10. Expanding the Penetration, February 25, 1991.

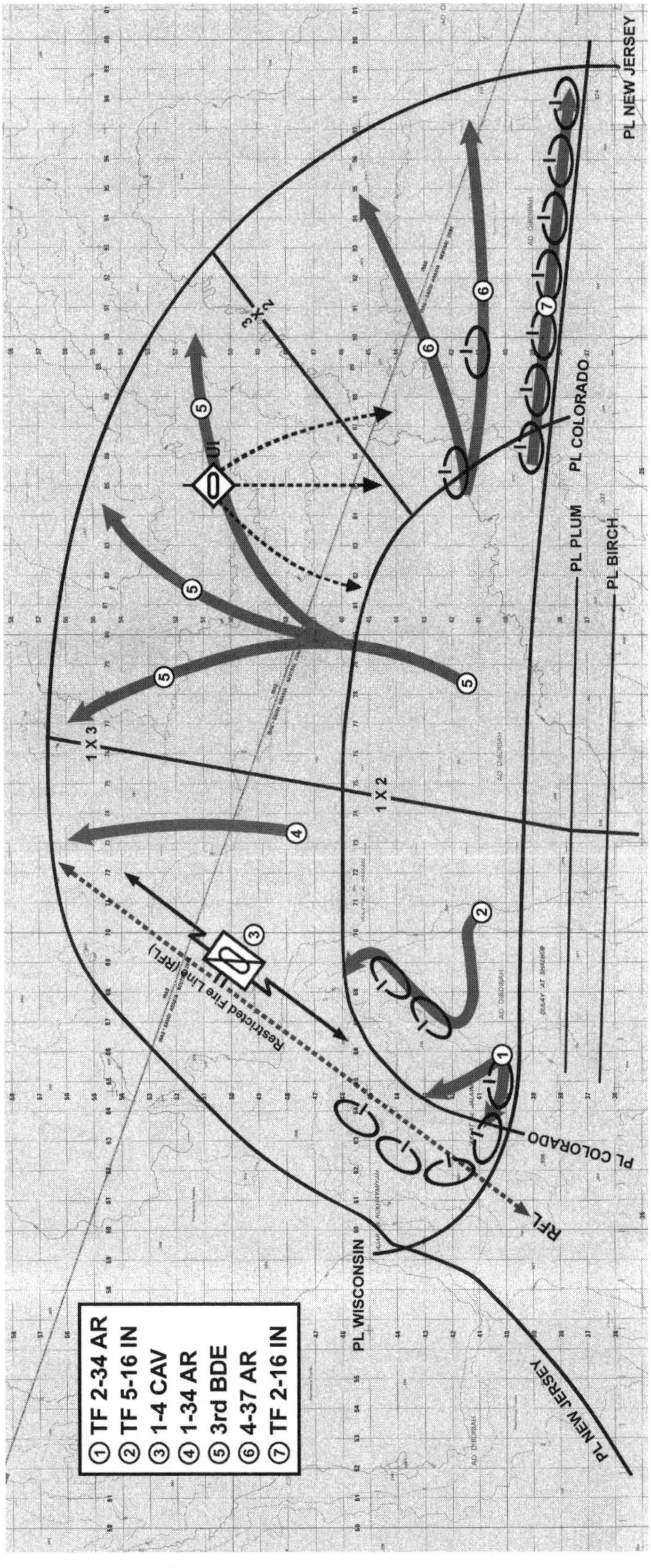

Moving prisoners, refueling, and rearming all contributed to the top priority—continuing the attack. Before the attack could begin, units had to organize to move. That included waking those not on duty, making precombat checks to ensure their equipment was ready, and getting under way in pitch-dark. Moving around in the dark in proximity of mines and dud munitions required care and some luck, and at 4:06 a.m. PFC Gussie Kostic's luck ran out. A tanker in TF 2-34 AR, he stepped on an antipersonnel landmine on his way to make sure the crew in an adjacent tank was stirring for morning "stand to." When the mine went off he shouted, "Help me! I stepped on a fuckin' mine!" Then he yelled, "Don't come here! There's fuckin' mines."[22] His crewmates ignored his advice, entered the minefield and got him out. The company's medics treated and evacuated him to the battalion aid station in an M113 tracked ambulance. At the aid station, the battalion surgeon, CPT James M. Goff Jr., stabilized him and sped him on his way. Kostic went through the medical evacuation system that led back to Fort Riley via Saudi Arabia and Germany. He made it home safely, but the danger posed by mines and duds remained acute within the breach area.[23] Not long after, the battalion operations officer set off in his tank to coordinate the attack; as he drove off, the tank exploded at least three bomblets or mines. Just moving could cause injury or damage.

The attack to expand the breach began on time at 6:00 a.m. on February 25. The mission required that every enemy soldier be killed, captured, or driven beyond Phase Line New Jersey. Expanding the breach area would achieve two things: eliminating or forcing out any Iraqis that could interfere with the passage of VII Corps units continuing to advance; and providing space for Corps artillery to get into position to support the UK 1 AD and the two US armored divisions as they attacked.

That morning, west of the breach, the 1 AD and 3 AD continued north following the 2 ACR, while the UK 1 AD prepared to pass through the breach and onto the flank of Hamash's VII Corps. Getting onto his flank was important, because Hamash's Corps comprised the westernmost part of the contiguous front line the Iraqis had developed. These evolutions conformed to the scheme the US VII Corps settled on in January and adjustments published in its Fragmentary Order (FRAGO) 138-91, issued at 8:00 a.m. on February 24. The FRAGO included a concise estimate of Iraqi intentions: "The enemy continues to defend in sector. Friendly attacks met with little return fires and many surrenders. No chemicals used in theater, no enemy air or helicopter activity. Enemy intentions appears [*sic*] to continue to defend in place."[24] Interestingly, the maneuver paragraph announced, "Plan accelerating the timelines for execution based on the enemy situation."[25]

The 1st Division attack to Phase Line New Jersey began in the west just before 6:00 a.m. CPT John Bushyhead's company team attacked the sole remaining Iraqi platoon defending the original Iraqi front line in the 1st Brigade's zone.

Simultaneously, LTC Skip Baker's TF 5-16 began to pass around TF 2-34 AR to attack its objective. CPT Juan Toro's company team fired to suppress enemy infantry on the ridge that Baker's task force was attacking. He began the engagement with coaxial and .50-caliber machine guns, and a few minutes later, his tankers opened up with tank guns. On Toro's left flank, one of his tanks pumped dense white smoke to mark the passage point for TF 5-16. By 6:40 a.m. Baker's troops had passed and were attacking northeast along the ridge. Four minutes later, Toro's troops ceased fire as Baker's units masked their line of sight. By 8:30 a.m. both task forces had concluded their attacks and turned to consolidating, taking prisoners, and destroying enemy equipment. The morning did not pass without incident. At 8:50 a.m. PFC Darrell Riley of the 101st Forward Support Battalion stepped on a mine or dud and detonated it. Medics on the scene reported him "litter urgent"; in plain English, he needed immediate attention or he would be at risk of dying, because a fragment had ripped a femoral artery.[26] CPT Goff maintained pressure to prevent bleeding until relieved by the medical evacuation helicopter crew. PFC Riley made it back and survived.

Late on February 24 the VII Corps had imposed a restricted fire line between the 1st Brigade, 1 ID and the 3 AD because the latter reported being fired on from the right and believed the fire came from the US 1 ID. In fact, the Iraqi 26 ID had three rifle companies west of the restricted fire line and oriented west. The restricted fire line made these three companies essentially untouchable, and they fired at Bushyhead's troops all day, though they were ineffective.[27] The restricted fire line impinged on freedom of maneuver as well.

LTC Bob Wilson's 1st Squadron, 4th Cavalry (1-4 CAV), still attached to the 1st Brigade, attacked to the north at 6:00 a.m. At the outset one of his cavalry platoons overran an enemy artillery battery, and SFC William Molitor captured the battery commander, who spoke some English and told Molitor that the rest of the battery wanted to surrender. Molitor agreed to accept their surrender and immediately enemy artillerymen began crowding around his Bradley intent on laying down their arms. When the cavalry troop's tank platoon came over a slight rise they saw Molitor's Bradley surrounded by enemy troops. The tankers leaped to the wrong conclusion and began firing machine guns at the crowd, which included Molitor and his crew. He and the Iraqi battery commander fled into the artillery command bunker, and the remaining troops took cover. Miraculously, no one got killed. When the firing died down, Molitor emerged cautiously and was able to explain to the tank platoon that the Iraqis wanted to surrender rather than overwhelm him.[28] The rest of the squadron reached Phase Line New Jersey without incident, but the restricted fire line precluded Wilson's troops from clearing out to the phase line. Instead, the Quarter Horse (1-4 CAV) established a screen along the restricted fire line.

LTC Pat Ritter's 1-34 AR started north at 8:04 a.m., clearing the ground as it moved. Ritter characterized the effort as a movement rather than an attack because the battalion found no enemy soldiers. His battalion had penetrated entirely through the two forward brigades of the Iraqi 26 ID; the remaining intact brigade of the 26 ID occupied positions thirty or so kilometers farther north. The Iraqis had no units in intervening space. The 1-34 AR reached Phase Line New Jersey before 11:00 a.m.; along the way, it discovered an abandoned Iraqi battery of US-made 105-millimeter howitzers. At 7:18 a.m. one of Ritter's units made contact with COL Dave Weisman's brigade as it moved into a zone of attack between the 1st and 2nd Brigades. Around midmorning, Weisman's brigade took over the center of the zone of action. At 12:00 noon, the 16/5 Lancers, the cavalry unit of the UK 1 AD, made contact with the 1-34 AR and began moving into "forming-up positions" where they would assemble to attack east.[29]

LTC Dave Gross's TF 3-37 AR saw only three enemy soldiers moving about during that first night in Iraq. Nevertheless, one ugly incident occurred. PFC Christopher Collins, one of Gross's infantrymen, was cleaning his rifle when the Iraqis fired illumination flares nearby. He moved behind his Bradley to shelter there in the event the Iraqis fired at him. Meanwhile, the Bradley's vehicle commander decided to back up to get out of the illumination. The Bradley struck Collins and ran up on his hip, causing life-threatening injuries. He needed to get to a field hospital fast. Accordingly, the task force called for air medical evacuation. A horrible series of errors ensued. Despite firing "star cluster" pyrotechnic signals to mark the site and frantic calls, the pilots from air evacuation unit known as the Lonestar Dustoff overflew it. Apparently the pilots mistook the Iraqi flares for the star clusters TF 3-37 AR used to mark the site of the evacuation. As a result, the Dustoff helicopter flew over the enemy, who promptly fired on it. Fortunately they missed, and finally the helicopter circled back, landed, and evacuated Collins.[30] The evacuation crisis provided the only excitement that night. All that remained before Gross could get his unit moving was to assist the 3rd Brigade forward.

Gross moved at 6:00 a.m. as the 2nd Brigade reserve, and not long after his task force moved out, it came under artillery fire. At first he believed the task force was being fired on by friendly artillery. LTC John Gingrich, the 2nd Brigade fire support coordinator, could find no friendly artillery firing so he reoriented fire direction radar so that he could look around. When he did so, he discovered the rounds were coming from the rear and were not being fired by friendly artillery. Gross dispatched CPT Tim Norton and his company team back to the position identified by counterfire radar. The enemy battery had fired from behind and near the Brigade boundary. Norton never found the enemy battery, but the enemy did stop firing;[31] it is likely they fired and then immediately moved on. The rest of the morning passed without serious incident, and TF 3-37 AR reached Phase Line New Jersey at noon.

LTC Dave Marlin's 4-37 AR began receiving the lead units of the 3rd Brigade shortly after 6:00 a.m. but was barely able to see them due to fog and mist. Some confusion occurred in the low visibility, and there was some intermingling with Weisman's arriving units. Marlin's battalion attacked at 9:00 a.m., generally in an arc from northeast to nearly due east. As it advanced northeast it separated from the 3rd Brigade. From north to south, the battalion advanced with the scouts in the north and A, B, and C Companies abreast. CPT Thomas D. Wock's D Company followed in reserve.[32]

Shortly after 9:00 a.m. the scouts confronted enemy infantrymen who chose to resist, but a quick fire mission from the battalion mortars convinced them to give up. Minutes later, the scouts identified enemy combat vehicles moving, and SSG Mark Firestone's gunner destroyed two with antitank missiles. As 1LT Lanier Ward would later recall, "Then all of a sudden two A-10s [US Air Force ground attack aircraft] came into the area and began to shoot at the remaining vehicles."[33] Firestone's gunner destroyed a third Iraqi vehicle. On the scout platoon's right, A Company captured two dozen of the enemy, and C Company advanced without contact, although it did spot a group of Iraqi combat vehicles beyond the range of the company's weapons. Roving A-10s destroyed them before C Company got within range.[34] CPT Joe Martin's B Company identified a complex of bunkers as it approached Phase Line New Jersey. As Martin's tankers fired main guns at the bunkers, a flight of two A-10s administered the coup de grace. Afterward, 140 Iraqis surrendered. With too few tankers to cope with that number of prisoners, Martin sent all of them, including a brigadier general, south to surrender to TF 2-16 IN. By 10:30 a.m. Marlin's battalion had reached Phase Line New Jersey.[35]

BG Carter and his command post Danger Forward continued to manage "crossing area" traffic. There had not been room enough to bring COL Weisman's troops forward the night before, and only the supporting artillery had been allowed forward. Carter permitted the 4th Battalion, 3rd Field Artillery (4-3 FA) to cross so it could fire for the two forward brigades as well as the 3rd Brigade. Unable to cross, Weisman moved as far forward as he could. The brigade command post spent the night along Phase Line Minnesota, about five kilometers north of the Iraq-Saudi frontier. The rest of the Brigade remained south of the border.[36] At first light, the 3rd Brigade headed north toward a staging area north of the breach but short of Phase Line Colorado.

Despite guides and well-marked lanes, friction intruded. For some reason, the lane on which the 3rd Brigade's TF 3-66 AR traveled that morning lacked exit markers. The task force stumbled about a bit as the lead vehicles searched for the safe lane, but it eventually reached its staging areas.[37] LTC Jim Hillman's TF 1-41 IN traveled on TF 3-66 AR's right, and LTC John S. Brown's 2-66 AR followed the two leading task forces. Brown's move was complicated by "many units, including the British . . . pushing to get ahead of schedule and jamming the lanes with vehicles moving out of sequence."[38] The traffic was so dense that some of Weisman's battalions left the lanes and took their chances moving cross-country. The confusion was such that COL Tony Moreno's troops complained of the 3rd Brigade moving through their formations. On the other hand, it looked to LTC Clint Ancker like the 2nd Brigade was moving through his. Fog, mist, and misperception all added to the friction as the events of that morning played out.

Despite the confusion, the 3rd Brigade was through the breach and across Phase Line Colorado before 9:00 a.m. The Brigade attacked north with the 1st and 2nd Brigades flanking it. Weisman attacked with TF 3-66 AR on the left and TF 1-41 IN on the right, and the 2-66 AR followed in reserve. Soon after crossing Phase Line Colorado, TF 3-66 AR ran into an Iraqi howitzer battery supported by small arms. When the Iraqi howitzers opened fire, LTC George T. Jones's tankers returned fire, overran the battery, and literally plowed under its positions. Next they discovered an abandoned artillery battery and some air defense guns. They destroyed the lot with thermite grenades and continued on.[39]

Not long after Jones's encounter, COL Weisman learned that a reconnaissance party from the 4-3 FA had mistakenly moved well forward of his leading units. Weisman ordered LTC Lanny Smith to have them dig in and await relief. The reconnaissance party went to ground northeast of Jones's TF 3-66 AR, so the armor task force went looking for the lost artillerymen. As the task force approached the isolated Americans, enemy infantry foolishly took it under fire from fighting positions near the disoriented reconnaissance party. Jones directed his tanks and Bradleys to fight with only machine guns rather than cannons to reduce the danger of hitting TF 1-41 IN, which stood just beyond the enemy. TF 3-66 AR machine gun fire drove the enemy right into TF 1-41 IN, with Hillman's troops capturing all eight of them. TF 3-66 AR recovered the members of the lost reconnaissance party, unharmed, around 10:30 a.m. The 3rd Brigade reached Phase Line New Jersey before noon, and was prepared to assist the forward passage of MG Rupert Smith's UK 1 AD.

LTC Dan Fake's TF 2-16 IN attacked on the Division's far right flank. His intelligence section reported, "There had been no major enemy movement during the night in the task force sector and a reminder that as the task force crossed the 93 north-grid line (five kilometers to our east) we would be passing into the . . . [48th] Infantry Division Sector."[40] Unencumbered by having to assist the forward passage of the 3rd Brigade, Fake used extensive artillery preparation to precede his attack. The task force moved out at 8:02 a.m., just as the last artillery rounds fell. Moreno accompanied TF 2-16 IN to assure that his brigade's main effort got the resources it needed to sustain the attack. Scouts and E Company (antitank) led in the north. South of E Company, two infantry-heavy company teams advanced in parallel with Team B on the left and Team C on the right, or south. The two tank-heavy Teams A and D followed the leading infantry teams.[41] Put another way, the four teams advanced in a box formation, with the mechanized teams forward. A few kilometers east, the commander of the Iraqi 807th Brigade saw the attack get under way. Assigned to the adjacent 48 ID, he called his division commander to report, "The Americans are overrunning the 26th IN Div and will soon hit the 807th Brigade on its flank."[42] He was right on both counts.

But the 807th Brigade had to wait until Fake's task force finished overrunning the Iraqi 26 ID. At 8:36 a.m. SSG Stephen Harriau, commander of an E-32 antitank missile track, fired at what he believed to be a command and control bunker. After Harriau's gunner hit the bunker, perhaps twenty Iraqis emerged and ran to another bunker, from which a white flag shortly appeared. On reaching the position, the antitank company discovered Harriau's missile had struck a command post, killing seven officers. CPT Kirk Schliefer's E Company accepted the surrender of "one brigadier general, one lieutenant colonel, one major, four captains, four lieutenants, and 127 enlisted men."[43] A few minutes later the task force reached the 93 easting (north-south line on the map), where it discovered a wire obstacle that ran perpendicular to their direction of attack. This tended to confirm the estimate that the 93 easting was the boundary between the two enemy divisions. As the Iraqis extended west, each division built positions or obstacles to protect its western flank until the next division arrived in the line. It is possible that because the 26 ID did not arrive until late, the 48 ID simply had not pulled down the obstacles it had emplaced to protect its flank.[44]

When TF 2-16 IN entered the 48 ID sector, it immediately made contact with active defenses. At 9:11 a.m. CPT Scott Rutter's Team C identified trenches and bunkers supported by at least three dug-in armored vehicles; he called in artillery and maneuvered to their rear. One of his Bradleys destroyed an Iraqi armored vehicle with an antitank missile at a range of more than 2,500 meters; the other two armored vehicles decamped and fled east. Team C continued to close the range, engaging the defending infantry with artillery, tanks, and Bradleys. At 9:22 a.m. Rutter lifted the artillery and ordered his troops into the assault. The attached Vulcan air defense artillery platoon let loose with twenty-millimeter Gatling guns in support of the attacking infantry. The infantry completed clearing bunkers and trench lines on foot covered by "over the shoulder direct fire" from their Bradleys. Rutter's team cleared complex defensive earthworks covering an area some one hundred by four hundred meters from the flank and rear. The fight was over by 9:44 a.m.[45]

In order to sustain the pace, Fake committed CPT Horacio Schwalm's tank-heavy Team A to take over the attack so Rutter's troops could process prisoners and consolidate their hold on the enemy positions. Whether it was the example of Team C's assault of the first position or the appearance of more American tanks, Iraqis began to surrender in droves. As he closed on Phase Line New Jersey, Schwalm reported, "They are coming out of their holes like ants."[46] In the north, CPT James K. Morningstar's Team D closed on Phase Line New Jersey as well. One of Morningstar's tank crews destroyed a T-55 tank at long range. In his zone, the Iraqis took little convincing: Team D accepted the surrender of more than two hundred enemy troops who gave up without a fight.[47] At 11:06 a.m. Fake reported to Moreno that he had reached Phase Line New Jersey; along the way, his troops had fought one major engagement, cleared a wedge-shaped piece of ground fourteen kilometers east of the start point, and captured seven hundred enemy soldiers.[48] All of this was achieved in just over three hours.

Hundreds of enemy soldiers had to be searched, disarmed, and moved. By G+1, February 25, few if any of the plastic ties used to restrain prisoners remained, but no one felt much need to restrain them. If anything, the Americans felt compassion for their vanquished foes, who seemed a miserable lot, hungry and poorly clothed.

Bomblets and mines continued to kill and maim without discriminating. After helping process prisoners, SPC John W. Knapp, a loader on one of Morningstar's tanks, trotted back toward his tank. On his way he stepped on and detonated a mine or a bomblet. Knapp had his flak vest on, but the blast "shredded his body from boots to helmet."[49] Thanks to rapid and able work by the company medic and the battalion surgeon, he survived his wounds.

COL Jim Mowery's attack helicopters supported operations during the morning, but found few targets. They ranged north, confirming the penetration, but found practically nothing north of Phase Line New Jersey. LTC Phil Wilkerson's 4th Battalion, 1st Aviation unit (4-1 AVN) focused on hauling supplies including fuel "blivets" (rubber fuel cells). His Black Hawk helicopters also brought critical repair parts forward. LTC Dave Wildes, Mowery's executive officer, began moving aviation maintenance forward so the Brigade would be able to support the attack as it moved farther north and east. Mowery wanted to get a head start, because he felt "hard pressed to keep aviation maintenance moving forward."[50] The support units of the aviation brigade, all mounted in trucks, spent the next several days struggling to keep up with the advance.

Even before the British began passing through the Division, MG Thomas G. Rhame's focus shifted to what came next. He trusted BG Bill Carter to manage the passage and BG Jerry Rutherford to run logistics, but he needed to develop better information to effect the transition to the next phase of the attack—going after the Republican Guard. Mowery provided "eyes" by flying with the daytime Apache helicopters that were conducting a zone reconnaissance. He landed at Rhame's mobile command post at 10:30 a.m. and reported the way clear north of Phase Line New Jersey. Rhame ordered him to find COL Don Holder and learn what he could from him.[51] Rhame intended to be ready to go when Franks called.

The British Are Coming: Forward Passage of the 1st Armoured Division

MG Smith and his UK 1 AD were chomping at the bit to get into the fight. As mentioned, the eager Brits had contributed to the traffic jam on the lanes earlier that morning. Just as the 1 ID's soldiers felt a duty to their tradition and history, the same was true for these British soldiers assigned to regiments whose histories predated the American Revolution. When the attack went early, Smith chose to drive his Challenger tanks one hundred kilometers rather than wait for transports to haul them; he would not permit the British division to be the cause of any delay. The UK 1 AD had spent the night of February 24 in an assembly area fifteen kilometers south of the border berm. Getting them in position to attack the flank of the VII Corps was the raison d'être for the breach.

Now that mission was coming to fruition. The 1 ID had one last task in the breach—to assist the forward passage of Smith's twenty thousand troops and seven thousand vehicles. Smith's division fielded two brigades: Brigadier Christopher Hammerbeck's 4th Brigade had two mechanized infantry battalions and one tank battalion; Brigadier Patrick Cordingly's 7th Brigade had two tank battalions and one mechanized infantry battalion. The UK Division also had the 16/5 Lancers; a target acquisition unit and an electronic warfare unit rounded it out. Two artillery groups of two battalions each provided fire support. An air defense artillery group and various support units also supported the Division. MG Smith had his own tactical air force composed of seventy-seven helicopters nearly evenly divided between utility and lift. He had corps-level hospital units and other national logistics units in support. Some six hundred guns and vehicles of the US 142 FA Brigade had to pass through the US 1 ID to reinforce the fires of the two British artillery groups. Two VII Corps artillery brigades and other Corps units also had to pass.[52]

While arguably separated by a common language, the Brits and their American cousins did speak the same doctrinal parlance. As part of NATO, both armies used many common procedures to assure interoperability of disparate allied units. One of these specified that passing units would collocate command posts with the passed unit, and passing units would send liaison teams forward. Accordingly, Smith collocated his tactical command post with Rhame's small mobile command post while British liaison teams worked with Carter's crew at Danger Forward and with the 1st and 2nd Brigades. The two British brigades mirrored Smith's effort. UK MAJ J. P. Cantwell joined COL Bert Maggart's command post on February 23 as liaison and moved with it through the breach at

9:00 a.m. on February 25. MAJ Cantwell described the scene as the command post moved "past many captured trenches and defensive positions, including burned APCs [armored personnel carriers] [that] looked to be BMPs. Hundreds of shell craters—US vehicles everywhere, guns setting up, etc. Gaps in minefields well marked."[53]

To facilitate control and mitigate the possibility of mistaken navigation, the Division established traffic control points three kilometers south of the entrances to the breach area. Here engineers emplaced four-by-eight-foot panels to mark the approach to the lanes; the panels could be seen from a distance. To enhance visibility, the letters denoting lanes were painted bright white on either a red or blue background depending on whether they were 1st Brigade or 2nd Brigade lanes. Engineers emplaced large panels at two thousand and one thousand meters and final markers one hundred meters from the point where the lanes passed through the enemy front line. Engineers also marked the entrance to each lane where it crossed suspected minefields with cerise panels normally used to signal aviators. Called VS17 panels, they could be seen from ten thousand feet away and were therefore hard to miss.[54] Finally, because mine plows had plowed the lanes to a depth of twelve to eighteen inches, the last seven to nine hundred meters of the lanes could be seen quite clearly. The assault brigades provided the last level or layer of control. Maggart and Moreno each served as a crossing-area commander in his zone; each controlled the eight lanes, and each had an engineer battalion in support. LTC Rich Jemiola and LTC Steve Hawkins served as crossing force engineers in the 1st and 2nd Brigades. They supported evacuation of damaged vehicles and repaired lanes as needed.[55]

GEN Sir Peter de La Billiere, the British national contingent commander, described the lanes from their point of view. According to De La Billiere, at 2:00 p.m. on February 25 Brigadier Patrick Cordingly's 7th Brigade was "grinding forward up the lanes cleared by the 1st (Mech) ID: the job had been brilliantly executed and the lanes were marked with tape and huge colored boards, red and blue, the size of barn doors, bearing huge capital letters, so that there was no chance of getting lost, and also the legend 'welcome to iraq courtesy of the big red one.'" De La Billiere particularly enjoyed the final touch: "Excited American soldiers waved the Challengers on their way."[56]

The business of controlling the movement of about thirty thousand British troops plus nearly half as many soldiers from three artillery brigades and support units required clarity of purpose and imperturbable character. With respect to temperament, Carter was exactly the man for the job. LTC Jim Stone, who served as Carter's de facto chief of staff at Danger Forward, described him as "relaxed; he seemed comfortable with what was going on."[57] Cool and laconic himself, anyone who found Stone "relaxed" might need to have his vitals taken. Carter ran the operation with the natural patience and skill born of experience in river-crossing operations in Europe and breaching operations at the Army's National Training Center at Fort Irwin, California. Despite some things going wrong, the passage went largely as planned because, as Stone put it, "We [the 1st Division] worked hard on the breach plan . . . we rehearsed that and rehearsed that."[58]

MG Smith's 16/5 Lancers, the counterpart to Wilson's cavalry squadron, entered the passage lanes at 12:00 noon, exactly when Rhame estimated they would. Franks's FRAGO 138-91 took Rhame at his word, specifying a start time of 12:00. The Corps' order specified completion by evening nautical twilight, or around 6:30 p.m. It is not clear just who developed this timeline, but neither Rhame nor his operations officer objected. In any case, these parameters had gone all the way up the chain to Schwarzkopf. Although both Stone and Cantwell thought it flowed well, the passage of nearly forty thousand British and American soldiers and thousands of vehicles took time—a lot of it. The advertised timeline could not be met.

The scale of such a crossing, should have led to a more cautious estimate. No one in the US Army had executed a passage of lines on this scale since World War II. Not surprisingly, the estimates of how long the passage would take were grossly inaccurate. MAJ Cantwell, for example, had to deal with problems right at the start. As he reported, "Passage of lines went very well, smooth flow initially until scattered bomblet minefield just beyond lane D found US eng[inee]r tractor blown up on mine, caused massive traffic jam." For this Cantwell found a solution: "Went down in US MP [military police] vehicle and led convoy of several hundred British vehicles across minefield to lane G, got the movement going again and was pleased to have solved the problem."[59] Problems like this cropped up throughout the passage. Each delay, however, complicated an already difficult process that occurred in two phases. First the British passed through the cleared lanes to forming up points where they organized for the attack, and then they attacked eastward from what they termed "start lines."

The 16/5 Lancers entered the passage lanes at 12:00 noon, with Cordingly's 7th Brigade not far behind. At 2:00 p.m. one of his tank battalions, the Queen's Royal Irish Hussars, crossed the start line to lead the Brigade attack. His other two battalions expected to cross their start lines beyond their forming-up positions at 4:30 p.m. Meanwhile, at 3:45 p.m., the 4th Brigade (the second of the two British brigades) started through the passage lanes. At 5:30 p.m., with the passage of his maneuver units nearly complete, Smith departed the 1 ID area. By then, his lead units had advanced twenty kilometers east of their start point.[60] The British were on their way.

Smith estimated his trail unit would clear by midnight. Cantwell thought the British had cleared the breach area by 9:40 p.m. on February 25. While they had in the 1st Brigade zone, where he was, the last of the UK 1 AD combat formations did not clear until 2:00 a.m. on February 26. Fourteen hours from the time British units started through the lanes the day before may seem like a long time, but it is not when one considers the thousands of vehicles involved. Adding to the delay, Smith's logistics could not move north until February 26 because there wasn't enough room.

The final act in the breach came early on February 26 when Carter passed responsibility for the crossing area to BG Gene Daniel, the deputy VII Corps commanding general. The VII Corps planned its main supply route to run through the breach. BG Daniel would manage traffic, assure security, and clear mines and duds to stop the steady loss of soldiers and equipment. To their dismay, Rhame ordered Fake and his troops to remain behind to provide Daniel combat troops to protect the breach area.

Smith summed up the procedure, noting, "The passage of lines went well. Particularly if we recall H Hour for my Division's passage was advanced that morning and while the two divisions were superimposed Fred Franks changed the plan—try either of those, let alone both together, at any staff college and you are sacked. It succeeded because we had talked about it together at least down to Battle Group level, we had very similar procedures and once we had learnt each other's nomenclature could fit the procedures together, we had air superiority, and HQs were collocated."[61]

Getting the job done in fourteen hours was a hell of an achievement. Believing it could be done in half that time was a mistake, one that added to the growing gap in perception among Schwarzkopf, Yeosock, and Franks. This was a physics problem, the dimensions of which the Corps and the 3rd Army had understanding, while Schwarzkopf's staff seemed to have none at all. This was not, as Yeosock was wont to say when frustrated by Schwarzkopf's often-unrealistic expectations, "a simulation."[62] MG Smith's observation that altering a detailed plan involving thousands of people comes with risks was absolutely correct, and despite the immediate confusion and subsequent recriminations it was the right thing to do.

During the course of the day, the 1st Division sought to bring its logistics forward to continue the attack if ordered. Most of the Brigade logistics waited until late on February 25 while the artillery brigades and the British moved. The bomblet and mine hazard continued unabated, causing several deaths and multiple injuries. At 3:40 p.m. an M88 recovery crew accidentally detonated a bomblet. The explosion killed one soldier outright, a second within minutes, and badly wounded a third, whom the battalion surgeon stabilized and evacuated. Elsewhere, six medics—an entire treatment team—were wounded by either a mine or bomblet. Jim Neberman, a Department of the Army civilian ammunition specialist, picked up several cluster bomblets apparently intending to haul them away for disposal. Instead, they blew up in his vehicle, killing him. By the end of the day, mines, bomblets, or enemy fire had killed three and wounded twelve. Six soldiers had been wounded and one killed on G-Day. The sad truth is, stepping on or handling US bomblets almost certainly killed and wounded more of them than had the Iraqis.[63]

Medical evacuation proved less than satisfactory. Tracked ground ambulances were most reliable, but often too slow; the best results depended on medics and battalion surgeons. In peacetime, surgeons are not assigned directly to units, so air evacuation directly from the field to the post hospital became the rule; thus, air evacuation was usually the fastest way to get a patient to a doctor. In Operation Desert Storm, however, air evacuation was often neither the fastest nor the safest method; treatment on the scene by a battalion surgeon proved best. But not everyone understood that at first; the instinct born in peacetime to call for air evacuation died hard.

Soldiers got over the shock of seeing their comrades wounded and took the proper steps to get them stabilized before evacuating them beyond battalion aid stations. More than one battalion surgeon intervened to set their inexperienced units straight. Evacuation by ground ambulance to a battalion aid station and from there by air, if necessary, proved the most effective way to assure wounded soldiers survived with the least amount of suffering. To complicate matters further, the Division had no organic air evacuation capability. A Fort Hood unit, the Lonestar Dustoff, provided that support. During the first two days, Lonestar Dustoff tended to overfly pickup points and Iraqis and thus took fire. Later, probably as a consequence of its initial experiences, the unit became overly cautious. Despite training and rehearsing hard, the Division and its supporting units still had much to learn. In combat, units either learn rapidly or suffer. Every unit in the 1 ID learned, but they often suffered in the process.

Losing soldiers to enemy fire is hard, but losing soldiers to mishaps, dud munitions, or fratricide is much harder. To survivors these losses appear avoidable and wasteful; they produce sorrow, bitterness, and recrimination. SFC Jeff Hein, a platoon sergeant, found the loss of the two M88 crewmen to bomblets very disturbing. A few hours after the tragedy, CPT Johnny G. Womack, who commanded Hein's company, brought the troops together to share with them what he knew about the incident that killed two and wounded one. He reported that one of the mechanics was "playing with one of the cluster bomb duds" and detonated it. Hein wrote in his journal, "I could see the E-7 [sergeant first class] in charge of the mechanics . . . his face showed the pain he must have felt." He added, "It's almost like losing sons when this kind of thing happens."[64] More bitter still, there was little time to mourn their sudden loss because there was too much to do. Those who knew them felt ashamed they had no time to mourn, but the mission took precedence.

Transition: Contingency Plan Jeremiah III

LTG Franks too had no time for reflection. Before the passage had begun, he turned his attention to the Republican Guard. He expected the Corps to fight three Guard divisions in the Rumaila oil field area and the two divisions of the Jihad Corps to their south. To destroy these units, he believed he needed to mass three divisions. This was based on two factors: first, he assumed that even if the air component reduced all five divisions by 50 percent, that still left a hefty capability; second, with three divisions attacking, he believed the Corps could sustain a pace that would minimize the enemy's ability to escape. Franks could, however, count only on his two armored divisions, the 1st and 3rd, because he estimated the 1st Division would emerge from the breach needing to reconstitute its combat capability. Because of that estimate, earlier he had asked for BG John Tilelli's 1 CD. Still, he had "always kept open the possibility of using the 1st IN [ID] somehow in the RGFC attack after they completed the opening-up of the breach."[65] The number of casualties estimated did not occur, the 1st Division was in good shape, and CENTCOM had not released Tilelli from the theater reserve mission. So, as it turned out, the 1st Division would continue the attack.

Corps FRAGO 140-91 articulated Franks's intent. His concept specified that the Corps would position "its tactical maneuver forces in preparation for its initial attack to destroy the RGFC." He ordered the 2 ACR, 1 AD, and 3 AD to move north to Corps Objective Collins, a featureless piece of desert one hundred kilometers north of Phase Line New Jersey. There the Corps would wheel to the east to attack the Republican Guard. Franks ordered Rhame to complete passing the British forward. Once that was done, the 1 ID would "detach a battalion task force to CORPS Rear [BG Daniel] for breach security" and assume the role of Corps reserve. The FRAGO made plain that the reserve mission would be temporary, as it specified, "On order pass through 2 ACR. Attack to destroy enemy forces in zone when committed."[66] The use of "on order" is an important distinction in the Army's lexicon; it means that the mission so described will happen at a later time.[67]

The Corps issued its order at 2:00 p.m. Rhame and his key staff huddled to plan the transition, and at 4:00 p.m. he convened his senior commanders to issue orders and intentions for the next phase of the operation—attacking the Republican Guard and continuing to the Persian Gulf. LTC Ancker took three pages of closely written notes that capture the essence of Rhame's thinking, using asterisks to mark points he and/or Rhame deemed important. Rhame began by saying the 26 ID "is dead—Good Job." He added, however, "The easy part is over. Enemy is the RGFC w/T-72 [main battle tanks armed with 125-millimeter cannons]." He reviewed the friendly and enemy situations. Of the Iraqis he noted, the "Army in Kuwait is cut off," yet "Hussein thinks he's winning." LTC Ancker put an asterisk after that point. He reported the "2 ACR along Smash [a phase line nearly one hundred kilometers north] in contact w/T-72s."[68]

Rhame focused on his "on order mission." He believed the Division would attack "the Tawakalna and/or the 17 or 12 AR." This point earned another asterisk. Rhame told his commanders they would move at 5:00 a.m. on February 26. He also issued a warning, "Watch Fratricide," and that got another asterisk. He then articulated his intentions. Ancker wrote, preceded by an asterisk, "Div Cdr wants to make contact, 1-4 CAV first. Then Bde [meant Division] fights smart. Move up Bde to fix, maneuver two Bdes to kill him [one] Bde at a time. Don't want frontal attack. We may loos [*sic*] soldiers more [*sic*] unnecessarily. At Harz hasty defense until Corps Cdr tell us. If we go to Norfolk [the Corps terrain objective], we go south [1st and 3rd AD] go north"; this was followed by still another asterisk. Rhame specified, "Execute not in a hurry," and "AVN move fwd where we can use them 2 [*sic*] find enemy at night." He paused to add, "We are on the way to the port [and home]." The staff codified his verbal orders as FRAGO 96-91,[69] and the order reflected how little the Division knew about where, who, and when it would attack.

FRAGO 96-91 articulated the key facets of Contingency Plan Jeremiah III that Rhame briefed. It specified that the 1 ID "attacks in zone . . . to destroy the Tawakalna Division." To achieve the mission, the Division first had to move nearly fifty kilometers north to Phase Line Harz. On order, it would turn east and travel another thirty-five kilometers to pass through and forward of the 2 ACR. Once forward of the cavalry, the Division would join the 1 AD and 3 AD in attacking east to destroy the Republican Guard and Jihad Corps. Rhame planned to attack with the 1st and 3rd Brigades abreast. COL Moreno's 2nd Brigade would follow in reserve. Beyond that Rhame did not specify a scheme of maneuver.

While the 1 ID expanded the breach, the rest of the Corps moved north. Ronald H. Griffiths's 1 AD attacked and destroyed the 806th Brigade of the Iraqi 26 ID on the morning of February 25. Late in the afternoon, his division closed in on an Iraqi logistics base near the town of Al Busayyah, where a commando battalion and a T-55 tank company defended the base; he left a battalion to deal with them and continued north. As the Corps turned to the east, the 1 AD moved on the left flank. The 2 ACR headed east into the security zone of the Tawakalna along the 65 easting at 12:50 p.m. Holder's regiment crossed Phase Line Smash at 1:20 p.m.. Shortly afterward, one of his squadrons destroyed most of the 9 AR Bde of the Tawakalna Mechanized Division in a short, furious fight that became known as the Battle of 73 Easting. Franks anticipated his three heavy divisions would get into position to attack late on the afternoon of February 26. Then the VII Corps would attack with the 1 AD, 3 AD, and 1st Division abreast from north to south. The 2 ACR would assume the Corps reserve mission. At 3:30 p.m. Franks met with Holder, who

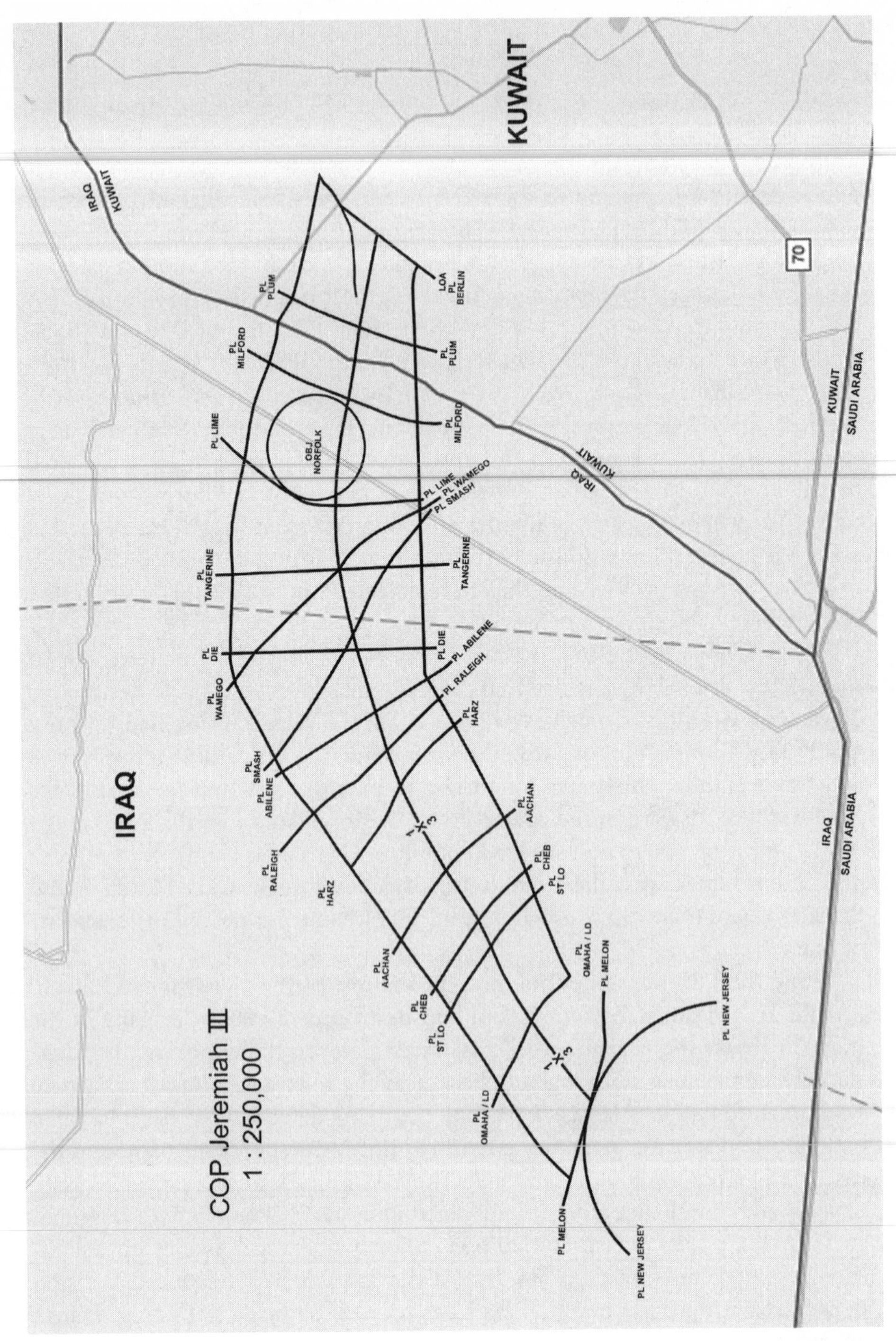

MAP 11. Graphic for Contingency Operations Plan Jeremiah III-Axis of Advance 1st Infantry Division toward Objective Norfolk, Kuwait, January 26–27, 1991. Recreated from an original artifact courtesy of the McCormick Research Center.

believed the Tawakalna was defending along the 65 easting in order to cover the withdrawal of the main body of the Iraqi Army from Kuwait. Franks told him, "Keep pressure on the Tawakalna, fix the RGFC, locate flanks, be prepared to pass 1 ID to the east."[70]

Franks's scheme seemed to be coming together. His two armored divisions would make the turn to the east by the afternoon of February 25. The 1st Division had to come a long way to catch up. The afternoon and evening of February 25 the Division staged as far north as possible. But nothing could happen right away. The trailing units of the 3 AD were still moving west of the Division's left flank, and Smith's units had not yet cleared Phase Line New Jersey.

Earlier in the day, Rhame returned LTC Bob Wilson's squadron to Division control. In that capacity, Wilson attended the 4:00 p.m. commanders' meeting. Rhame ordered Wilson to cover the Division's move and to maintain contact with the 3 AD on the left. What the squadron had to do that night illustrates what it takes to transition from one mission to the next. Wilson left the commander's meeting at 5:00 p.m. en route to his command post; on his way, he called his headquarters and issued a warning order for movement and calling for an orders briefing at 8:00 p.m. He arrived at the squadron at 5:30 p.m. He and his staff went through an abbreviated orders process and he issued guidance for his operations order. Like everyone else, the Quarter Horse had too few maps and too little time to develop and reproduce graphics for those few maps that were available. Accordingly, the plan relied on GPS waypoints; the Quarter Horse planned to move using the electronic equivalent of Hansel and Gretel's breadcrumbs. Wilson also had to get units that had been attached to him for the breach to where they needed to be next. CSM Mike Cobb took that task in hand.[71] Engineers, psychological operations units, and other combat support units were being reassigned elsewhere as the mission changed.

At 8:00 p.m. Wilson briefed the troop commanders on his scheme of maneuver, changes to task organization, and how the Squadron would sustain the operation. Shortly after 9:00 p.m. the meeting broke up. Troop commanders returned to their units and developed orders and organized to move. To accelerate the process, the troop commanders relied on standard operating procedures. This is a bit like using a playbook instead of writing detailed instructions. The ground troops could employ standard formations adjusted to specific conditions. The air troops required more detail.

The conditions added to the challenge. The night of February 25–26 was cold, overcast, and very dark. The squadron got under way at midnight and headed north to its attack position. During the move, tired soldiers made mistakes aggravated by low visibility. Maneuvering in the dark, a Bradley "threw track." This is a nasty business that can take hours to repair; the track has to be broken apart at the links and, once done, must be put back on the drive sprocket and reconnected. This is hard and dangerous work, more so in the dark.

In other cases tired drivers caused several minor collisions. Others fell asleep when they stopped, only to awake with a start as their track commander yelled at them to move. One crew woke up thinking their unit had moved without them and took off in their sixty-ton M88 tank retriever like a frightened colt, the squadron motor officer having to run them down to stop them. Although the Quarter Horse only had to move a short distance, it reached its attack position with only a couple of hours to spare before it was to move out at 4:30 a.m. on February 26.[72] The troops slept little again that night.

Throughout the Division's area, tired troops packed up and groped their way north to start points; by morning they were reeling with fatigue. Some units reached their attack positions around midnight, but most arrived even later. More than anything, the problem of transitioning from the breach to the attack demonstrated the drag of inertia. Having been on 50 percent alert since February 17, fatigue set in. No one had slept more than four hours a night, and many had slept less. Resupplying, repairing equipment, planning, and responding to enemy contact all took their toll.

That same evening, February 25, Saddam ordered his Army to withdraw from Kuwait. According to LTG Hussein Rashid Muhammad al-Tikriti, chief of staff of the Iraqi Armed Forces, the withdrawal began with a call from Saddam at 8:30 p.m., when Saddam told him, "I don't want our Army to panic. Our soldiers do not like humiliation; they like to uphold their pride."[73] During the day, LTG Sultan Hasim Ahmad al-Tai, the deputy chief of staff of the Iraqi Army, had developed a withdrawal plan and issued it prior to Saddam's call to execute. The plan required a number of difficult operations. Conceptually, it envisioned withdrawing like a sock being turned inside out. The tip would come through first, with the III Corps, defending in southeast Kuwait, departing that night. On the night of February 26 the IV Corps would follow in tandem with the II Corps. The order required Hamash's collapsing VII Corps to protect the IV Corps' flank as it withdrew. Hamash was also to coordinate closely with the RGFC. The Republican Guard and the Tawakalna in particular had to hold until the VII Corps withdrew.[74] The Iraqi withdrawal was in trouble before it started. MAJ Mike Barefield, Danger Forward's operations officer, captured the sense of what was unfolding when he concluded the operation was turning into "a run for the roses."[75]

As Rhame's units moved to staging areas, he recorded his observations on the day's events. He felt content, thinking "the hardest fight was 2nd Brigade specifically 2-16 Infantry," and believed "everything worked like clockwork." Of the Iraqis he wrote, "They either surrendered or died." About the future he was upbeat: "I expect we will be focused to destroy the Tawakalna Division of the Republican Guard. It should be much better from here on."[76]

Rhame had envisaged moving north with two brigades abreast and Wilson's cavalry squadron covering the move and reconnoitering the ground ahead.

Moreno's 2nd Brigade would follow in reserve. That plan changed at midnight, when it became clear that the British, now embroiled in a serious fight, could not clear the area by 2:30 p.m. With the 3 AD still passing in the west, there was too little space to get two brigades moving abreast. LTC Terry Bullington, the Division operations officer, did the only thing he could do: he issued a short FRAGO at 2:30 a.m., the upshot of which was "to move forward in a column of battalions instead of two brigades side by side."[77]

Ironically, in this vast desert there was too little room to move in a prudent tactical formation; the sheer size of the three divisions Franks wanted in position to strike the Republican Guard made it so. Counting only the tanks assigned to divisional tank battalions, the VII Corps fielded at least 1,044. The 1 ID had 348 tanks in its six armor battalions, nine more in the cavalry squadron, and two in the Division headquarters. Of these, twenty-eight remained at the breach site with Fake's task force. Thus, 329 tanks headed north on February 26. Moving in a column of battalions took a lot of space and a lot more time.

LTC Ritter's 1-34 AR led the Division column of eight armor and mechanized battalions, with five organized as balanced task forces. Three artillery battalions and four brigade command posts also moved in the column, trailed by several hundred trucks and trailers from brigade logistics formations. Danger Forward, Rhame's mobile command group, and the Division's main command post moved as well. With only Wilson's cavalry to its front, Ritter's battalion traveled in a "combat diamond." That meant it had three companies forward, with the lead company moving in a wedge and the other two left and right, his formation resembling an arrowhead. His command group and his mortars moved in the center of the formation while his trail company followed in a wedge—again like an arrow pointing in the direction of travel. With fifty meters between tanks, each wing of the arrowhead was just under a kilometer long. His trail company followed about even with the edges of the arrowhead. His formation was therefore more than a kilometer deep and roughly two kilometers wide.[78] The other battalions, including the artillery, took up about the same space.

The cavalry attempted to remain about ten kilometers ahead of the main body to reconnoiter the route and allow reaction time in the event of contact. Assuming roughly two kilometers of depth for each maneuver battalion and a buffer for the cavalry, the column of maneuver battalions stretched thirty kilometers. Add the artillery and various command posts, and the column length approached forty kilometers—not including the logistics train. Moving at thirty kilometers per hour, it took the column an hour and a half to pass a fixed point.

Quarter Horse moved at 5:00 a.m. with its two ground cavalry troops abreast. Allowing time for the cavalry to clear the start point with all of its impedimenta, the 1-34 AR moved at 5:46 a.m., a few minutes ahead of the planned start time. It took Ritter's battalion some time to clear the start point and get sufficiently ahead of the next battalion to create a buffer between them. Accordingly, TF 2-34 AR crossed the start point at 6:29 a.m. At exactly that moment, Ritter stopped because Wilson's cavalry had halted. That typified the progression of the approach; despite allowing an interval between battalions, the column moved in jerks for much of the morning. The lag between start times meant the column strung out for forty kilometers and more than three hours. At 8:04 a.m., slightly more than two hours after starting, the 1-34 AR had moved only fifteen kilometers.[79]

The stop-and-go forward movement occurred for several reasons. For starters, it was a cold, miserable, windy day, and for most of it rain mixed with sand pelted down, making it hard to see and assuring maximum misery for anyone outside a vehicle. As if this were not enough, the rain and smoke from oil fires reduced visibility to no less than a few hundred meters, causing everyone to move slowly and cautiously and sometimes to lose sight of other vehicles. The weather also slowed the cavalry reconnaissance ahead of the column to a pace best described as painstaking. Sporadic contact with Iraqi troops caused interruptions. And, again, whenever a column stopped, invariably some drivers and even entire crews fell asleep, resulting in still more delay.

Units also became intermingled. Because no one had enough maps, planners relied on GPS, with which the Division had little experience. They tended to set waypoints that all units followed without clear reference to map locations or regard to who owned what terrain. Units typically set straight-line azimuths from one waypoint to the next. Ancker described the effect, noting that "[shortly after starting out] . . . the artillery battalion ran into a lot of 2nd Brigade that was cutting across the zone instead of moving behind 3d Brigade. 2nd Brigade apparently was going off straight line azimuths."[80] The Division never did perfect using waypoints, and routes that crossed one another sparked confusion or worse every day. For all of these reasons, the march took far longer than hoped.

As the last of the three maneuver brigades to move, the 2nd Brigade had difficulty just getting in position to start because it had to wait for the other two brigades to clear the assigned staging area. Consequently, Moreno's force could not reposition until after midnight. The 4-37 AR, for example, moved to its staging area at 3:00 a.m. on February 26. Because the column extended so far in time and space, the 4-37 AR didn't crossed its start point until 11:00 p.m., or five hours after Ritter's battalion. Moreno did not report crossing Phase Line St Lo, only twenty kilometers north of Phase Line New Jersey, until 2:11 p.m. By then Maggart's brigade had arrived at Phase Line Harz, twenty kilometers farther forward. At 3:27 p.m. Weisman's brigade arrived at Phase Line Harz; COL Moreno caught up at 3:45 p.m.[81] The accordion effect never dissipated. The long column contributed to growing fatigue and precluded attacking the Republican Guard earlier.

Marlin's 4-37 AR moved last among the maneuver battalions and had staged farther south than any of the others. To get to Phase Line Harz, only forty-five kilometers north, Marlin's tankers traveled nearly seventy kilometers. He remembered their march with pride. The 4-37 AR traveled in a box formation of two companies forward and two trailing, and the battalion maintained orientation on Gross's TF 3-37 AR ahead of it. Marlin later wrote, "As we took off, we approached the VII Corps MSR [main supply route] and thousands of CSS [combat service support—logistics] vehicles moving north. We approached them perpendicular to their movement. We passed through them in the blink of an eye and maintained formation. It was a truly beautiful maneuver."[82]

When the 1st Division reached Phase Line Harz, it had also turned roughly forty-five degrees and oriented northeast. It was now about thirty kilometers behind the cavalry regiment. The 1 AD and 3 AD were slightly ahead, but traveling on the outside of the gentle curve the Corps made as it turned to the east. Franks's intent to effect a coordinated attack with three divisions was within reach. He wanted to get the attack under way. At 4:20 p.m. the VII Corps staff ordered the 1st Division to report when set, as "they anticipate giving us go ahead [for the attack]."[83] That word did not get down to the troops on the ground. Many of them thought they were going into reserve and probably would not be committed until the next day. As they always seem to do, events outpaced what commanders at battalion and below understood.

Franks had reviewed his concept with Yeosock that morning. After they conferred, LTC Mike Kendall, Yeosock's executive assistant, took down the details from Franks for the record. Franks proposed to attack that afternoon once the 1st Division was set. Once the 1 AD and 3 AD had established attack positions, he would bring up artillery. The 1st Division would pass through the 2 ACR on the evening of February 26 and attack the southernmost brigades of the Tawakalna Mechanized Division and elements of the Jihad Corps to clear Objective Norfolk. The 1 AD would attack the Al-Medina Armored Division in the north, and the 3 AD would take on part of the Tawakalna in center. Later the VII Corps issued an order that considered the contingencies Franks thought likely in the course of the next twenty-four hours.[84]

The ensuing FRAGO noted that Iraqi forces would "attempt to exit Kuwait to the north. RGFC units and other mobile reserves are dug in the western sector defending in place [and] covering the withdrawal of the Iraqi Forces."[85] Additionally, CENTCOM released the 1 CD from CENTCOM reserve and assigned it to the VII Corps. Franks ordered the 1 CD to be ready "to attack through 1ID to destroy enemy in zone vic[inity] OBJ Denver," a terrain objective twenty kilometers north of Kuwait City, astride the Basra–Kuwait City highway. The attack would get under way as soon as Franks believed he could launch it with all three divisions.

That time had arrived. Franks knew that the Iraqis were withdrawing from Kuwait, but now the fundamental flaw in the CENTCOM concept revealed itself. The fixing attack in the east had fixed no one. Schwarzkopf's decision to let the Marines go early on February 24 while having the VII Corps go later than it wanted to did not help. But most important, the Iraqis could run as fast or faster than the coalition could advance. Franks had four divisions attacking or ready to attack, and only one more decision to make: whether to attack as planned with three divisions abreast or alter his plan to include the 1 CD. He also considered a double envelopment in which the 1 AD would envelop from the north and the UK 1 AD from the south. When they caught up, the remaining two divisions and the 1 CD would maintain the pressure on the Republican Guard and Jihad Corps so they would be unable to maneuver. In the end, Franks rejected the second option because there had been no time for his commanders to consider it. Further, it would require the British to attack across the front of two American divisions. Finally, a double envelopment might possibly require forces to converge at night, increasing the risks of fratricide. It may have been elegant in design, but ultimately the double envelopment option was not worth the risk.[86] In addition, the 1 CD could not get in the fight soon enough, so Franks resolved to attack with three divisions as he had planned since the seminar in January.

None of these ruminations made their way down the chain of command. The 1st Division could barely communicate, as it was spread out over more than forty kilometers relying entirely on short-range tactical radios. Periodically Rhame could be heard shouting on the radio, threatening all kinds of mayhem if no one answered him. Despite many others' attempts to answer, he heard nothing. LTC Baker's task force succumbed to poor march discipline. Several logistics formations had gotten ahead of him, and he simply could not get through. Maggart made numerous agitated calls that Baker could not hear. Baker, ignorant of the brigade commander's ire, called cheery situation reports that only added to Maggart's frustration.[87]

Maggart's brigade arrived at Phase Line Harz ahead of Weisman and had begun refueling when Rhame got them both on the radio. Rhame told them that he wanted both brigades refueled and passing forward of the 2 ACR by 9:30 p.m. Both objected; neither brigade could make it by 9:30 p.m. Ancker wrote, "General Rhame, who had been pushing us hard all day, relented and gave us until 2230 hours to start the passage. He was concerned that the enemy was retreating and that we were letting him get away."[88] Rhame's assessment was not far off the mark, but entreaties could not alter the facts on the ground.

Maggart attempted to get his commanders in for a quick orders briefing. The attack would go now—and not, as they had anticipated, the next morning. At 4:05 p.m. LTC Dan Magee, the executive officer, warned the Brigade to be prepared to move at 5:00 p.m. Before the commanders could arrive, Maggart changed the start time to 5:30. Even with a half hour more, there was too little time to conduct an orders briefing. En route in a high-mobility multipurpose wheeled vehicle, LTC Greg Fontenot had not yet reached the command post to attend the orders briefing when he realized that if he continued on, his unit would have to move before he made it back from the meeting to join them. He had a testy exchange with Maggart to the effect that he could either report for the orders briefing or move his task force. Maggart let it go, and Fontenot turned back. Neither let his fatigue and frustration color his actions in execution. Fontenot barely had time to climb back on his tank before his task force had to move out. Spread out in hasty defensive positions, Maggart's brigade could not assemble and move by 5:30 p.m. But both Ritter and Fontenot moved their units not long after, traveling on "weapons tight" instructions (to shoot only when fired upon, and only with positive identification). Moving at dusk complicated matters. Maggart ordered Ritter's battalion to lead, so Fontenot's task force had to find it in the growing darkness. Ritter passed vectors and adjusted speed to enable TF 2-34 AR to locate him. Finally, one of Ritter's companies pumped smoke from its onboard smoke generators as a signal. Fontenot's scout platoon saw the thick cloud of bright white smoke and made the linkup. LTC Baker's TF 5-16 IN was still ten kilometers behind, trying to catch up.[89]

The Division now set about preparing for the passage through the 2 ACR and mounting a hasty, two-brigade night attack against the Iraqi "first team." This complicated attack would occur with few graphics and sketchy intelligence. The Division wanted to precede the attack with a bombardment like that which had been fired during the breach. The VII Corps released the 210 FA brigade from supporting Holder's cavalry and placed it in support of the 1st Division. Dodson planned to pick the 210 FA up on the fly as the Division moved forward and through the 2 ACR.[90] The weather had improved; it was cold, but the gale-force winds and driving rain had stopped. The moon was almost full, so visibility was fairly good at the outset, though later in the evening smoke from the oil fires reduced visibility.

Getting all of this done on the move and at night is much more difficult to do than it is to describe. Maggart tried to convey the challenge in a postwar article, writing, "It is difficult to describe how complicated it was to redefine the direction of attack and change formation while bouncing across the desert (in a tank or Bradley) at high speed using a 1:250,000 map."[91] The brigade had only a few 1:250,000-scale maps, but would not have had any if CPT Jim Stockmoe had not had the foresight to have them printed before the Brigade left Fort Riley. Even these maps were, however, problematic: they were black and white, and the tip of an index finger neatly covered a circle of about five kilometers, neatly masking what the finger's owner hoped to see. The use of GPS and compasses enabled the attack to occur.

Normally, Carter would have managed coordination of the forward passage of lines. But Danger Forward had not caught up. MAJ Don Osterberg or LTC Terry Bullington could have done it, but they were both in tanks traveling with Rhame and also too far back, so Rhame assigned the mission to the Quarter Horse. Accordingly, MAJ John Burdan, the squadron operations officer, traveled to the 2 ACR command post, where he met with LTC Stephen Robinette, Holder's deputy. When Burdan arrived, the Regiment's 3rd Squadron, in the center of the Regiment's line, was fighting along the 73 easting. Therefore, Burdan and Robinette thought it best to pass the 1st Brigade through the 2nd Squadron in the north and the 3rd Brigade through the 1st Squadron in the south. Neither Rhame nor Holder liked this because it would require the two brigades, at night, to then converge on each other after the passage and while in contact with the enemy. They agreed instead to pass the 1st Brigade through the 3rd Squadron in the center and the 3d Brigade through the 1st Squadron in the south.[92]

Robinette took further precautions; he withdrew the southern part of the 3rd Squadron and established the passage points back on the 70 easting, or about three kilometers west of the hardest fighting, to reduce the threat of direct fire during the passage. The 2 ACR would remain in contact with the enemy and support the 1st Division with attack helicopters and artillery. The cavalry would retain control of fires until the Division could take control of the battle as it passed through. Because they had several hours to prepare, Holder's regiment organized the passage in detail. Better still, his troops understood the task down to the platoon level. That and discipline in both units proved valuable when the passage occurred later that evening.[93]

More details became available as the Division moved forward. The 2 ACR passed coordinates for passage points and lanes and provided its assessment of enemy intentions. The Division artillery headquarters made contact with the 210 FA Brigade and absorbed what the latter knew. Division intelligence had some detailed 1:50,000-scale maps overprinted with imagery of enemy positions as of the end of January 1991 that still proved useful. The cavalry also passed on what it had learned from the better part of a day in contact with the Iraqis—who the 1st Division would be fighting, thus confirming that the Tawakalna Division was indeed in the northern part of the attack zone and the 37 AR Bde of the 12 AD was defending in the southern part of the zone.[94]

Eerie is the most useful word to describe the move to the passage points. The information about the enemy was vague; not even the 2 ACR could provide targeting data or any clear sense of just where the enemy was. As the 1st and 3rd Brigades approached the rear of the 2 ACR, they passed through and around artillery batteries still firing. The howitzers made a thumping sound that seemed muted but provided a compelling light show. Rockets from multiple-launch rocket systems leapt from their launch tubes with eye-tearing white flashes and thunderous noise. Tracked vehicles and trucks could be seen in the surreal strobe effect created by artillery and rockets. The atmosphere felt oppressive, and more than one soldier felt a sense not of real fear but of the foreboding that weighed on them. The whole effect was like Salvador Dali's melting watches—unreal and surreal. The Army had not permitted live-fire night attacks in training because they were too dangerous, yet here the troops were about to attempt just that. There is an old saw in the British Army: "You shouldn't have joined if you can't take a joke." It held true that night.

NOTES

1. Lieutenant Colonel David W. Marlin, "History of the 4th Battalion, 37th Armored Regiment in Operation Desert Shield/Storm," unpublished manuscript, US Army War College, Carlisle Barracks, PA, 1992, 383.
2. COL (Ret.) George P. Ritter, e-mail to the author, May 5, 2015.
3. Carl von Clausewitz, *On War*, trans. and ed. Michael Howard and Peter Paret (Princeton, NJ: Princeton University Press, 1984), 207.
4. Kevin M. Woods, *The Mother of All Battles: Saddam Hussein's Strategic Plan for the Persian Gulf War* (Annapolis, MD: Naval Institute Press, 2008), 226.
5. Ahmed Ibrahim Hamash, interview, *Al-Juhuriya*, January 30, 1994, n.p., translated by and courtesy of COL Reserve Pesach Malovany, Israel Defense Forces.
6. Woods, *The Mother of All Battles*, 225–26.
7. General H. Norman Schwarzkopf with Peter Petre, *It Doesn't Take a Hero: The Autobiography* (New York: Bantam, 1992), 455.
8. Richard M. Swain, *"Lucky War": Third Army in Desert Storm* (Fort Leavenworth, KS: US Army Command and General Staff College Press, 1997), 238–39.
9. COL John M. Kendall, daily memo, 242300C, February 1991; COL (Ret.) John M. Kendall, telephone interview with the author, May 5, 2015.
10. G2, VII Corps, "The 100-Hour Ground War: How the Iraqi Plan Failed," May 4, 1994, 96. The 52 AR Bde's infantry probably included both BMP infantry fighting vehicles and the far less capable MTLB armored personnel carriers. The available evidence is not conclusive. Woods's *The Mother of All Battles* is the best source for understanding the intentions of the Iraqi high command.
11. G2, VII Corps, "The 100-Hour Ground War," 14–22, 97. See also Stephen A Bourque, *Jayhawk: The VII Corps in the Persian Gulf War* (Washington, D.C.: Center of Military History, 2002), 242–43. The VII Corps G2 believed that the Iraqis remained focused on the Wadi al-Batin.
12. G2, VII Corps, "The 100-Hour Ground War," 98–99, 121. LTG Al-Rawi's order to the Hammurabi came later; they moved on February 26.

13. LTG Quais 'Abd al-Razaq al-Aa'dhmai, interview, *Alif-Baa*, December 3, 1997, n.p., translated by and courtesy of COL Reserve Pesach Malovany, Israel Defense Forces.

14. COL John M. Kendall, "The Closed Fist: VII Corps Operational Maneuver in Operation Desert Storm," unpublished manuscript, US Army War College, Carlisle Barracks, PA, March 15, 1994.

15. Woods, *The Mother of All Battles*, 226. See also Rick Atkinson, *Crusade: The Untold Story of the Gulf War* (London: HarperCollins, 1994), 411–13.

16. Woods, *The Mother of All Battles*, 226. Atkinson, *Crusade*, is the only source that names the Iraqi battalion commander and does not include his given name.

17. Woods, *The Mother of All Battles*, 415.

18. Ibid., 226.

19. Ibid., 227.

20. First Lieutenant Jay C. Mumford, "Rangers in Iraq: Task Force Ranger, 2nd Battalion, 16th Infantry in the Persian Gulf War, 10 November 1990–12 May 1991," unpublished manuscript, August 31, 1991, 33.

21. Ibid.

22. John Sack, *Company C: The Real War in Iraq* (New York: Morrow, 1995), 122–23. See also 2nd Battalion, 34th Armor, daily staff journal, February 25, 1991.

23. CPT James F. Goff Jr., telephone interview with the author, September 28, 2014. Battalion surgeons, physicians' assistants, and medics did fantastic work in Operations Desert Shield and Desert Storm, treating Americans, Iraqis, and anyone else who needed medical help.

24. VII Corps, FRAGO 138-91, 242000, n.d., published February 24, 1991. The VII Corps directed the UK 1 AD to attack the Iraqi 12 AD. In fact, the UK 1 AD struck the 52 AD and parts of the 48 ID, 31 ID, and 25 ID of the Iraqi VII Corps. See also Bourque, *Jayhawk*, 260–65, and map 17, 262.

25. Ibid.

26. 2nd Battalion, 34th Armor, daily staff journal, February 25, 1991. The 101st Forward Support Battalion provided logistics support to 1st Brigade. In this instance, the word "litter" refers to a stretcher.

27. 2nd Battalion, 34th Armor, daily staff journal, February 24, 1991.

28. Stephan A. Bourque and John W. Burdan III, *The Road to Safwan: The 1st Squadron, 4th Cavalry in the 1991 Persian Gulf War* (Denton: University of North Texas Press, 2007), 129–30.

29. 1st Battalion, 34th Armor, daily staff journal, February 24–25, 1991; COL (Ret.) George P. Ritter, telephone interview with the author, August 5, 2014.

30. COL (Ret.) Thomas Connors, BG (Ret.) David F. Gross, and MG Paul Izzo, Oral history group interview by Andrew Woods, Robert R. McCormick Research Center, First Division Museum at Cantigny, Wheaton, IL, January

22–23, 2011. See also Lieutenant Colonel David F. Gross, "The Breach of Saddam's [*sic*] Defensive Line: Recollections of a Desert Storm Armor Task Force Commander," unpublished manuscript, US Army War College, Carlisle Barracks, PA, 1992, 98–99.

31. Connors, Gross, and Izzo interview. Regarding the 3rd Brigade forward passage, see Danger Forward, daily staff journal, February 25, 1991; the entry noting the 3rd Brigade in the lanes is dated 0636, but all other sources report the actual start at 0600. See also Marlin, "History of the 4th Battalion, 37th Armored Regiment," 384.

32. Marlin, "History of the 4th Battalion, 37th Armored Regiment," 397.

33. First Lieutenant Lanier Ward, quoted in Marlin, "History of the 4th Battalion, 37th Armored Regiment," 387.

34. Marlin, "History of the 4th Battalion, 37th Armored Regiment," 392–93.

35. Ibid., 397–400.

36. Colonel (Ret.) Clinton J. Ancker, "2nd Armored Division (Forward) and the Gulf Conflict," unpublished manuscript, US Naval War College, Newport, RI, n.d., 157.

37. Ibid., 159–60. Information on lane marking come from the author's personal notes.

38. Ancker, "2nd Armored Division (Forward)," 161.

39. Ibid., 162–63; 3rd Brigade, 2nd Armored Division (Forward), daily staff journal, February 25, 1991. All times are approximate.

40. Mumford, "Rangers in Iraq," 33–34.

41. Ibid., 34. LTC (Ret.) Scott E. Rutter, telephone interview with the author, May 8, 2015.

42. G2, VII Corps, "The 100-Hour Ground War," 105.

43. Mumford, "Rangers in Iraq," 34. Mumford, the task force S2, also wrote the task force history in the summer of 1991. He believed the command post belonged to the Iraqi 48 ID. That surmise seems mistaken given that it was west of the boundary between the 26 ID and 48 ID.

44. Mumford, "Rangers in Iraq," 34.

45. Ibid., 35.

46. Ibid.

47. Ibid.

48. Ibid. See also Danger Forward, daily staff journal, February 25, 1991.

49. Mumford, "Rangers in Iraq," 35.

50. COL James L. Mowery, "Saudi Journal," February 25, 1991.

51. Ibid.

52. Tom Clancy with General Fred Frank Jr., *Into the Storm: A Study in Command* (New York: Berkley, 2004), 4–7, 350–51.

53. Major J. P. Cantwell, "Desert Storm Diary," *Combat Arms*, January 1992, 28.

54. Each combat vehicle placed a VS17 panel on its roof. The 1 ID verified with aircraft overhead that the panels could be seen from ten thousand feet; they thus served to identify friendly forces to coalition air forces.

55. From the outset the 1 ID leadership organized the breach like a river crossing. See LTG (Ret.) William G. Carter III, telephone interview with the author, December 15, 2013; COL (Ret.) Frank J. Stone, telephone interview with the author, January 31, 2015.

56. General Sir Peter de La Billiere, *Storm Command: A Personal Account of the Gulf War* (London: HarperCollins, 1992), 285.

57. Stone interview.

58. Ibid.

59. Cantwell, "Desert Storm Diary," 28.

60. 1st Brigade, 1st Infantry Division, daily staff journal, February 25, 2015. See also De La Billiere, *Storm Command*, 287. In fact, the attack occurred later that evening; Cordingly's brigade fought its first battle at night.

61. General Sir Rupert Smith, e-mail to the author, May 11, 2015.

62. Kendall interview, May 5, 2015.

63. The Army made a serious effort to account for how people were wounded or killed; there are several casualty reports and summaries, though few of them tell the same story. Sources here include the Goff interview; 1st Brigade, 1st Infantry Division, daily staff journal, February 25, 2015; and a memorandum for the Commander of US Army Personnel Command signed on March 14, 1991, by MG Rhame. This report fails to list PFC Gussie Kostic, wounded early on February 25, 1991, and the VII Corps roll-up does not include him, though an unsigned, undated 1 ID summary does include Kostic.

64. SFC Jeff Hein, personal journal, February 25, 1991.

65. Clancy, *Into the Storm*, 316.

66. VII Corps, FRAGO 140-91, n.d.

67. MG Rhame related this to the author on several occasions; he also expressed his desire that the Big Red One remain in the fight from the outset of planning. GEN Schwarzkopf retained the 1 CD as CENTCOM reserve; it appears that he wanted it available to stiffen the Joint Force Command North attack. See Kendall, "The Closed Fist," 17. Of the Egyptians, Schwarzkopf, *It Doesn't Take a Hero*, 457, notes, "They were tough methodical fighters who—like Franks—preferred to stick to a preordained plan."

68. LTC Clinton J. Ancker, personal notes, February 25, 1991.

69. Ibid.

70. 2 ACR Operations, "Operation Desert Storm 2 ACR Operations Summary 23 Feb–1 Mar 91," n.d., courtesy of LTG (Ret.) Leonard D. Holder; regarding Al Busayyah, see Bourque, *Jayhawk*, 287, and 258–95 regarding the breach and breakout.

71. Bourque and Burdan, *The Road to Safwan*, 135–36.

72. Ibid., 138–39. The Squadron actually moved two minutes early, at 4:28 a.m., on February 26.

73. Woods, *The Mother of All Battles*, 229.

74. Ibid. See also Bourque, *Jayhawk*, map 13, 190.

75. MAJ Michael R. Barefield, personal journal, February 26, 2015.

76. LTG (Ret.) Thomas G. Rhame, telephone interview with the author, February 3, 2015, quoting from Rhame's personal journal, February 25, 1991.

77. Rhame interview, February 3, 2015, quoting from Rhame's personal journal, February 26, 1991.

78. COL (Ret.) George P. Ritter, discussions with the author, on his use of the "combat diamond." Computing and determining pass time were skills absolutely required and practiced.

79. 1st Brigade, 1st Infantry Division, daily staff journal, February 26, 1991.

80. Ancker, "2nd Armored Division (Forward)," 178.

81. Marlin, "History of the 4th Battalion, 37th Armored Regiment," 411–13.

82. Ibid., 413.

83. Danger Forward daily staff journal, February 26, 1991.

84. COL John M. Kendall, "Comments on Events 25–26 February 1991," memorandum for COL Richard M. Swain, January 16, 1993. Kendall's memo cites notes he took on the days in question.

85. VII Corps, FRAGO 141-91, 261400C Feb 91, February 29, 1991. C is the time zone in which the order was published—in this case, 3:00 p.m. local time.

86. Clancy, *Into the Storm*, 460–65.

87. MG (Ret.) Lon E. Maggart, "Eye of the Storm (Duty First)," unpublished manuscript, 1992–97, 162–63. Rhame was very upset that Baker's TF 5-16 IN was so far back; Baker finally caught up after 10:30 p.m.

88. Ancker, "2nd Armored Division (Forward)," 184–86.

89. COL Gregory Fontenot, "Fright Night: Task Force 2-34 AR," *Military Review*, January 1993, 40–41.

90. VII Corps, FRAGO 140-91; Dodson, personal journal, February 26, 1991.

91. COL Lon E. Maggart, "A Leap of Faith," *Armor*, January–February 1992, 24–32.

92. COL (Ret.) Stephen H. Robinette, e-mail to the author, May 18, 2015. Robinette served as executive officer in the 2 ACR. See also Thomas Houlahan, *Gulf War: The Complete History* (New London, NH: Schrenker Military, 1999), 334–35.

93. Robinette e-mail.

94. 1 ID, FRAGO 96-91, February 25, 1991; Ancker, "2nd Armored Division (Forward)," 187–88.

CHAPTER TEN

FRIGHT NIGHT

The Attack on Objective Norfolk

Leading up to the night battle, I was amazed that we were going to actually do it. We had already begun to outrun our maps. We hadn't planned to [do this] operation and had not conducted any rehearsals.

—Captain Daniel David Pick

Images of the Operation Desert Storm ground war as a clean technological "turkey shoot" don't wash with anyone who went through the Battle of Norfolk.

—Steve Vogel, "Hell Night"

Your units could have killed many of us, but you didn't; and since I came into the hands of the American Military, I have been treated with respect and warmth.

—Iraqi Brigade Commander

In the early evening hours of February 26, 1991, as the 1st Infantry Division (1 ID) made its way forward, the VII Corps and COL Don Holder's 2nd Armored Cavalry Regiment (2 ACR) pounded the Tawakalna Mechanized Division of the Iraqi Republican Guard with artillery and attack helicopters. Earlier in the day, Holder's troops had hammered the Tawakalna 9th Armored Brigade (9 AR Bde) at the 73 easting. Before sunset, the 2 ACR withdrew to permit the 1st Division to pass forward out of contact with the enemy. The Division had too much ground to cover to make the passage in daylight. Writing about the passage after the war, COL Lon E. "Bert" Maggart observed, "The plan was relatively simple and involved a passage of lines, at night on unfamiliar terrain without any preparation and against an enemy about whom we knew virtually nothing."[1]

Several months earlier GEN H. Norman Schwarzkopf had conceived the basic outline for the developing fight, and in November had briefed the concept to his commanders. The moment for which the VII Corps had deployed to Saudi Arabia had arrived. While it was officially called the Battle of Objective Norfolk, most who fought there remember it as Fright Night, and the name is apt. The fighting that occurred on February 26 and 27, 1991, is emblematic of that for which the Cold War Army had been designed; it involved several divisions on each side and more than two thousand tanks. GEN William C. Westmoreland, GEN William E. Depuy, MG Donn Starry, MG Paul Gorman, and others had laid the foundation in the 1970s and 1980s. The Army trained and practiced for this kind of fight at the Hohenfels training area in Germany and at the National Training Center (NTC) in California.

Fright Night revealed strengths and weaknesses inherent in the late Cold War Army, and four themes emerge. First, its weapons proved superior to those of its Soviet counterparts, including the late-model Soviet tanks and infantry fighting vehicles. Second, Army training and leadership showed itself far superior to that of the opposition. Third, despite these advantages, it was hard to mount a hasty attack in poor visibility, revealing training shortfalls. Courage and persistence enabled success despite serious problems that included a high incidence of fratricide. Finally, the perception that in this battle the Americans and their coalition partners completely dominated hapless Iraqis is overdrawn. Fright Night attests to remarkable courage shown on both sides and proves the point that GEN Creighton Abrams made frequently: the US Army doesn't man equipment, it equips soldiers. American men and women—not their equipment—won the battle they call Fright Night.

Despite effective leadership and great equipment, the Division suffered four separate incidences of fratricide during the attack on Objective Norfolk. Six Americans lost their lives in these incidents, while another thirty-two suffered wounds.[2] Material costs included loss of or damage to five Bradleys and six tanks. In some ways, these fratricides seem particularly egregious given that the Division destroyed two enemy brigades, including some two hundred tanks, howitzers, and infantry fighting vehicles or personnel carriers. It is possible that the Iraqis killed none of the Americans who died that night. These four tragedies stemmed, in part, from technical limitations. First contact also played a role. Several units fought their first engagements in a night attack against enemy armor. Developed in the context of the General Defense Plan in Europe, the Army's approach to tactical gunnery played a role too. Shoot first and shoot rapidly may have been just the right approach to defend the Fulda Gap, but it was certainly not the right philosophy on Fright Night. Lastly, training to fight at night should include fighting at night; in 1990, night training seldom included night attacks.

Iraqi Forces and the US VII Corps: The Situation at Nightfall, February 26, 1991

In an early morning radio broadcast on February 26, Saddam Hussein advanced the thesis that his decision to withdraw from Kuwait concluded an "epic duel." He went on to claim that "the harvest of the Mother of All Battles [has] succeeded."[3] Kevin Woods, the premier analyst of the Iraqi records captured in Operation Iraqi Freedom, asserts that Saddam maintained this narrative from that time on. Woods's evidence is compelling; Saddam may even have believed what he said. After all, he confronted what he called "an ugly Coalition comprising thirty countries . . . under the leadership of the United States of America."[4] He considered his regime's survival against these odds a victory. It is unlikely that many of his troops heard him. If any of them had, it would have come as cold comfort; for them the die was cast.

Ordered to hold the way open for Saddam's army to withdraw to Basra, LTG Ayad Futayyih Khalifa al-Rawi had done what he could. He had repositioned his four Republican Guard divisions and the two assigned to the Jihad Corps so that all six oriented toward a threat from the west. Most were in prepared positions when the 2 ACR slammed into them. Nevertheless, Holder's regiment penetrated the Iraqi security zone by midafternoon. To add to Al-Rawi's difficulty, coalition airplanes caught the 50th Brigade, 12th Armored Division (12 AD) repositioning and decimated it. Later, advancing VII Corps troops captured the Brigade's commander and most of its survivors. To his rear, the Iraqi Army was fleeing north. During the night, the withdrawal turned into a rout on what became known as the Highway of Death. Perhaps the only advantage Al-Rawi enjoyed is that many of the troops in his forward area had yet to be engaged in a direct firefight. Coalition airmen had driven them underground but killed relatively few. Even the vaunted Republican Guard stayed away from its tanks and fighting vehicles and instead occupied bunkers. Al-Rawi's situation, already grim, deteriorated that night.

In the northern part of his sector, MG Ron Griffith's 1 AD attacked the 46th Mechanized Brigade's 12 AD around 3:00 p.m. The Tawakalna may have controlled the 46th Brigade, but it is more likely it was caught as it withdrew under pressure from the 2 ACR. Gunships from the 1 AD's cavalry squadron led the attack. At 8:30 p.m. Griffith's 3rd Brigade joined the attack. During the night, he broadened his assault, taking on the 29th Brigade of the Tawakalna and elements of the Al-Medina Armored Division.[5] The 3 AD attacked on Griffith's right. Wedged between the 1 AD and the 1 ID, it fought in a narrow zone. Shortly after 4:00 p.m. the 4th Squadron, 7th Cavalry (4-7 CAV), the divisional cavalry squadron, ran into well-prepared defenses of part of the 9 AR Bde of the Tawakalna Mechanized Division. Located on the reverse slope of a low ridge, the position denied the 4-7 CAV the advantage of their long-range weapons. The Iraqis also enjoyed the benefit of poor visibility from rain showers, gusty winds, and blowing sand. In the ensuing melee, two of the 4-7 CAV were killed, twelve were wounded, and four of its Bradleys were destroyed (the 9th Brigade destroyed two and the US 4-34 AR destroyed the other two as they converged on the fight). In return, the two US battalions destroyed at least six enemy tanks and nine of the Boyevaya Mashina Pekhoty (BMP) infantry fighting vehicles.[6]

The remainder of the 3 AD joined the fight soon after. By early evening, the two armored divisions had four brigades attacking. On the Corps' southern flank, the UK 1 AD fought through the night, leapfrogging its two brigades. The 1st Division added two brigades to the battle about midnight. The Iraqis defended with the Tawakalna and Al-Medina Divisions of the Republican Guard and the 10 AD and 12 AD of the Jihad Corps. Together these units retained eleven intact brigades. LTG Frederick M. Franks Jr. had nine line brigades and the 2 ACR, at least three of which attacked continuously. Franks and his division commanders also cycled Apache attack helicopters from his three divisions and Corps aviation units in and out of the fight. His three divisions committed more than a thousand tanks and nearly eight hundred Bradleys, a force amounting to eighteen tank battalions, eleven mechanized infantry battalions, and three divisional cavalry squadrons. Additionally, the three divisions and supporting Corps artillery fielded two hundred howitzers and nine rocket launchers. Franks envisioned hitting the Republican Guard Forces Command with what he called a "three-division fist"; the fingers came together on February 26, and he used it.[7] Al-Rawi probably had no more than seven or eight hundred tanks and about the same number of infantry fighting vehicles supported by fifteen artillery battalions with more than two hundred howitzers and guns and at least one rocket launcher battalion. By any measure, the odds favored the US VII Corps.[8]

Preparation:
February 26, 1991, 6:00–10:30 P.M.

The march to the 2 ACR's passage lanes resembled the Oklahoma Land Rush more than an organized maneuver. Ignorant of Schwarzkopf's displeasure with the VII Corps' pace, most of troops knew only that they were in a hurry; the reasons for haste that night were unknown to most of those rushing forward. Those who could hear the Division command net knew only that MG Thomas G. Rhame was as testy as a dog with a bone. Throughout the day he reprimanded his brigade commanders for not moving fast enough. According to MAJ Kevin Huddy, operations officer in the 1st Brigade, Maggart periodically got on the Division command net and explained to the commanding general just why the Brigade was moving far more slowly than Rhame wanted. According to Huddy, Maggart calmly reviewed the physics of the problem. Rhame's frustration would subside for a time, but then the cycle would begin again. He, too, knew nothing of Schwarzkopf's anger, but he wanted very much to get into the fight. Twice he sent COL Jim Mowery forward to meet with Holder. The second time, Mowery went in the early afternoon; when he arrived, Franks was at the cavalry command post. Franks asked Mowery to tell Rhame that he expected the Division to get in the fight that evening. This fit Rhame's perception. He thought the enemy had broken and that time was of the essence. Yet his outfit could go no faster, and that irked him to no end. Rhame, as Rick Atkinson has reported, had few peers "in aggressive drive."[9]

Atkinson's description of Rhame as "noisy, profane and relentless" is absolutely accurate; that word picture has provoked more than one rueful chuckle among those who worked for him. On hearing him on the radio calling for his boss, one driver wondered out loud whether "this was an ass chewing coming to us or are we going to have to drive to get it."[10] Rhame could growl and bark with the best, but he also conveyed confidence and faith in his subordinates. That night, his division did the best it could to respond with alacrity to the "pride of Winfield, Louisiana."[11] LTC Stephen Robinette, Holder's deputy, had heard the earlier conversation between Franks and Third Army commander LTG John Yeosock. As a result, he understood the reason for urgency far better than did the lieutenant colonels commanding Rhame's battalions. Robinette, who led the planning for the passage for the cavalry, had known of the passage for several hours. By early afternoon he and the regiment had the details well in hand. Robinette coordinated with MAJ John Burdan, the operations officer of the 1-4 CAV, which had been sent to get the task under way for the 1st Division. Well practiced in supporting or conducting forward and rearward passages of lines, both officers knew what had to be done. Robinette was puzzled by the 1st Division's failure to collocate its tactical command post with his as the 3 AD had done prior to their passage. But with Burdan on hand, the necessary coordination took place.

Robinette provided coordinates for the passage lanes and what combat information he had to Burdan. He also spoke by radio with LTC Terry Bullington. Bullington and Rhame, caught in traffic, were too far back to collocate with cavalry during the passage. The tactics manuals may have required a collocated command post, but Burdan and Robinette could and did handle the tasks. There was simply no time for a set piece passage such as the one at the breach. In *The Road to Safwan*, Steve Bourque and John Burdan captured the significance of this passage of lines: "Not since World War II had a United States Army armored or mechanized division conducted a passage of lines in combat. Yet, in the space of two days, the Big Red One had the opportunity to do it for a second time."[12] Robinette understood that the cavalry needed to get the 1st Division forward as rapidly as possible.

Holder and Robinette had served in cavalry units in both Vietnam and Europe. They were battle wise and understood the ramifications of supporting a forward passage of lines at night in contact. Holder focused on fighting the regiment and left the passage to his deputy. Robinette focused on three points to assure as safe and speedy a passage as possible. First and foremost, he developed effective control measures in the form of far-recognition signals and clear markings for his units. Second, by withdrawing a bit, the regiment created a shallow cleared space to afford the 1st Division the opportunity to pass through the cavalry's farthest forward unit before they were within range of enemy direct fire weapons. Finally, Holder accepted risk by physically unloading the regiment's weapons and placing them in safe mode as Rhame's units passed.

Commanders had to estimate the enemy situation quickly, plan, and issue orders on the move and then get forward as quickly as possible. More than one commander wrote notes on a kneeboard or on the turret wall of his tank, Bradley, or armored personnel carrier as it bounced, swayed, and slammed over or into obstacles on the desert floor.[13] Combat information about the identity and location of the enemy was more than a little iffy. As a consequence, the plan of attack had no elegant maneuver. Rhame ordered a straightforward frontal attack. In the north, he ordered LTC Bob Wilson to screen the Division's northern or left flank. COL Maggart's and COL Weisman's brigades would attack abreast, with Maggart in the north and Weisman in the south toward Phase Line Milford, a line about eighteen kilometers east of the passage lane exits and at the presumed depth of the enemy's main defense.[14] The Division did not further differentiate the objective, because the attack was oriented on the enemy rather than the terrain. The brigades would stop at Phase Line Milford only when they were satisfied they had destroyed the combat formations west of Phase Line Milford. In the absence of maps or identifiable terrain features, Phase Line Milford provided a reference from which notes could be made and odometers used to tick off distance. When enough satellites were available, Magellan GPS units would enable those who had one to update their position.

Wilson's 1-4 CAV had the most complicated maneuvering to do: it had to pass forward and then move out to the flank and set a screen oriented north. To maintain the screen, it might have to bound eastward as the Division advanced. Maggart's brigade would attack south of the cavalry. He originally planned to attack with his two task forces abreast, but converging logistics columns delayed Task Force 5th Battalion, 16th Infantry (TF 5-16 IN), which could not reach the passage point in time. So the 1st Brigade attacked with TF 2-34 AR in the north, where Maggart expected the most enemy infantry, and the 1-34 AR in the south. LTC Skip Baker's TF 5-16 IN troops would clear any positions the Brigade bypassed.[15]

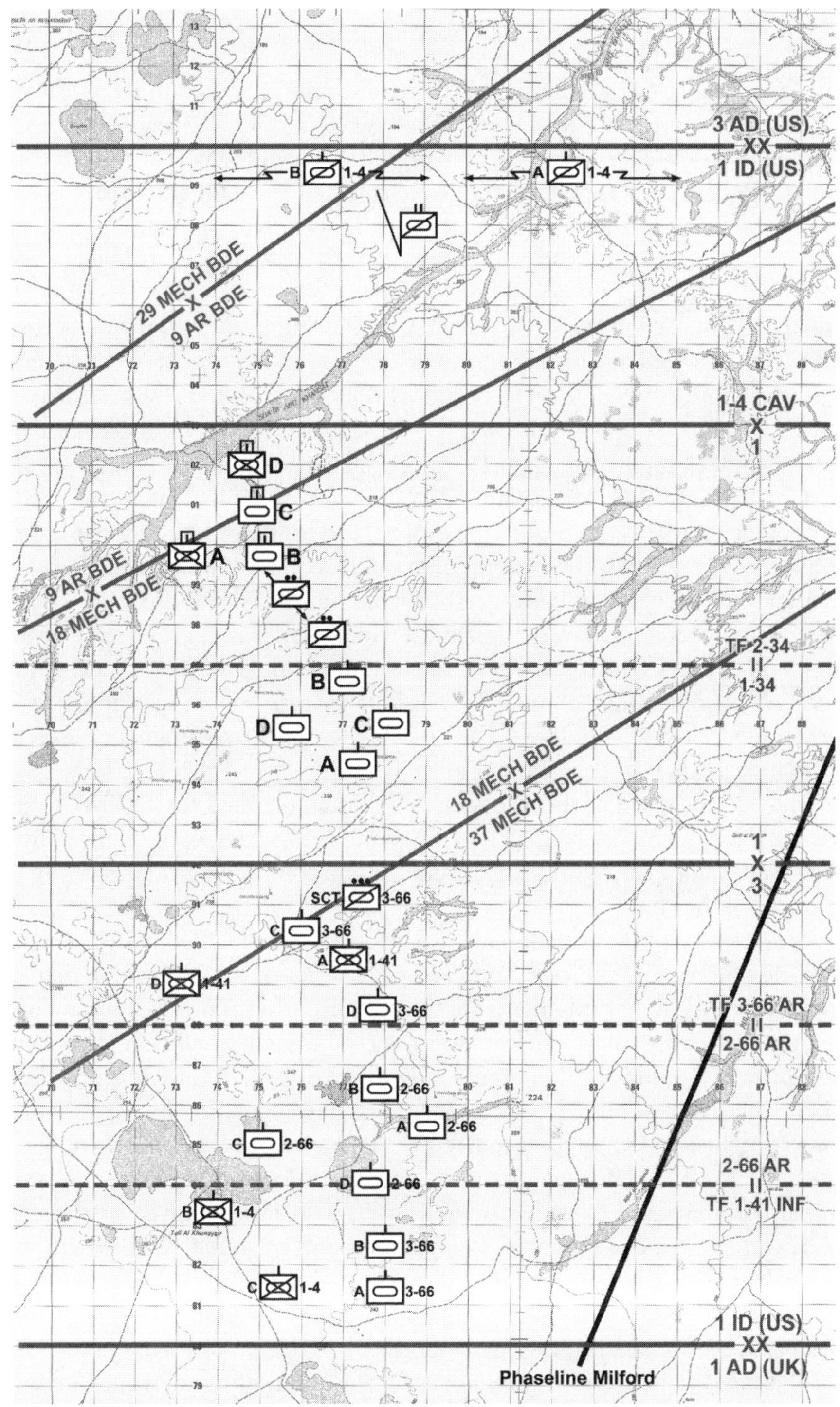

MAP 12. 1st Infantry Division "Fright Night," the Attack on Objective Norfolk, February 26–27, 1991.

In COL Maggart's 1st Brigade, LTC Greg Fontenot planned to pass forward in two columns and then attack with two tank company teams abreast, an infantry company team echeloned left to provide flank security to the north, and an infantry company team in reserve. He directed his scouts to lead the way through the passage and then move to the southern flank to maintain contact with the 1-34 AR on the right. LTC Pat Ritter decided to pass in the combat diamond he used en route and followed his lead platoon.[16]

In 3rd Brigade, COL Weisman took a more deliberate approach. Rather than transition while moving, he intended to take a short halt just east of the passage lanes where his units would transition to a brigade wedge; LTC John Brown's 2-66 AR would form the tip of the wedge. LTC George T. Jones balanced TF 3-66 AR would attack on the left, and LTC Jim Hillman's balanced TF 1-41 IN would attack on the right. LTC Jones planned to attack with a tank company on either flank and an infantry company in the center. He designated his second infantry company as his reserve. The reserve followed the company in the middle of the three forward. LTC Brown advanced in what he called mass forward, which entails three companies advancing abreast with a tank platoon in echelon on either flank. In this instance, Brown's combat support and command group traveled in the lee of the tank companies. His fourth company brought up the rear. Because the 2-66 AR would form the tip of the wedge, Brown told his troops to expect no friendlies to their front. This made sense given the intention to have the 2-66 AR at the tip of the wedge. LTC Hillman planned for TF 1-41 IN to attack in a box formation, led by two pure tank companies, each followed by a pure infantry company with combat support and command group traveling in the center of the "box."[17]

Preparations within the battalions and below occurred in the dimly lit interiors of moving combat vehicles. Tired and often irritated by getting incremental and often contradictory fragments of information as they moved, commanders, operations officers, junior officers, and noncommissioned officers sorted out just how they would solve the problem. Few had sufficient time to study their task or a map to consult. And few of them had participated in mounted force-on-force night attacks and none in live-fire night attacks because, as mentioned earlier, the Army had deemed them too dangerous to practice. More than one commander marveled at being ordered to do in combat something thought too dangerous in peacetime. As they planned and prepared, soldiers groped among their gear for chemical lights of various colors so their vehicles could be identified. Different colors or combinations would also identify company formations. In a few cases, finding chem lights entailed climbing on top of vehicles to root around in bags and storage boxes for the right colors, all while moving.

Hoping to learn more about the enemy and where they would actually execute the forward passage, most battalion commanders violated Army planning principles by not issuing their final orders until shortly before the forward passage. The 1st Brigade's experience is illustrative of the process that night. By 7:25 p.m. both the 1-34 AR and TF 2-34 AR were traveling some thirty kilometers west of the intended line of departure. Baker's TF 5-16 IN remained stuck behind an "extensive convoy" twenty kilometers farther back. Maggart began the planning process with a very basic warning order, and CPT Troy Krause scribbled the essence of that order in the Brigade daily staff journal on the sideboard that served as the desk in the M577 command post track. The note read simply, "Go through Norfolk + set on Milford + prepare to move on to Kuwait."[18]

Maggart had designated Ritter's 1-34 AR as the base, so TF 2-34 AR conformed to his movements. At 8:00 p.m. Maggart ordered Ritter to make contact with the 3rd Brigade, moving up on the southern flank as the Division turned east toward the 2 ACR. As the Brigade made the turn, the 2-34 AR, which was moving on the outside, or left, asked Ritter to slow down several times in order to keep the 1-34 AR in sight. Five minutes later the Brigade issued the final waypoints that Huddy had calculated in the turret of his Bradley. Ritter reported finding the 3rd Brigade's left flank nearly simultaneously.[19] At 8:35 p.m. the Brigade announced the passage of lines would occur at 10:00 p.m. That proved impossible. The 1-4 CAV, ahead of the 1st Brigade, begin passing the 2 ACR at 9:30 p.m. At 10:30 p.m., LTC Scott C. Marcy's squadron fired a green star cluster to mark the linkup point at grid 700000 (Cartesian coordinates from lines drawn on the map to enable relative locations), and the 1st Brigade readily identified this pyrotechnic signal. Maggart ordered, "Ok guys let's roll em!"[20]

Maggart stayed on his command net, focused on the passage, while his staff sought to learn more about the enemy. CPT Jim Stockmoe, the Brigade's intelligence officer, provided what he could. At 9:45 p.m. the Brigade issued an intelligence summary by radio that identified an enemy brigade defending in the 1st Brigade zone. The summary described the opposition as a mechanized brigade composed of a tank battalion equipped with T-55s and two mechanized infantry battalions equipped with BMPs. Furthermore, the summary reported that the enemy brigade belonged to the 17 AD (though little of this was accurate).[21] The 1st Brigade also issued overlays based on imagery of enemy positions in the area taken on January 26; they had to be delivered by hand. SFC Michael Schulte and his driver, SPC John Tabb, performed that service for TF 2-34 AR. The two took a harrowing drive across the desert in a high-mobility multipurpose wheeled vehicle using compass headings. To their considerable relief, they reached the task force tactical operations center just before the attack began and without having been shot.[22]

Battalion and task force commanders likewise planned with too little combat information or intelligence. The graphics from contingency operations plan

Jeremiah III and information from Holder's cavalry made the attack feasible in the time allowed. Company commanders and platoon leaders had little choice but to conform to general and sometimes vague instructions from above. Commanders could do little more than decide which formation to use. In the absence of adequate information, relying on formation battle drills practiced ad nauseam in training and again in the tactical and forward assembly areas was all that could be done. In any case, maneuvering in formation, like ships at sea, works effectively in the open desert. Tired leaders still had to tell their units and crews something. The exchange between SFC Ralph E. Martin and his tank crew, while pithy and profane, illustrates both the problem and the ultimate simplicity of the solution.

SFC Martin led the 3rd platoon, C Company, 1-34 AR. Ritter had great confidence in Martin, as did his company commander, CPT Jim Bell. Martin served as the tip of the arrow in C Company that in turn served as the tip of the arrow in Ritter's combat diamond formation. As Martin and his crew prepared to go through the passage lane, he shared with them what little he knew based on the terse order that had come down the chain. PFC Greg Hafford recorded the crew's internal communications, in which they can be heard discussing the mission. SFC Martin's gunner, SGT George "Mac" McAlister, having heard the fragmentary orders, asks what they are going to do. SFC Martin responds, "Let me get my head together guys." And after a moment, in a voice laden with emotion, he says, "This is what we are going to do. We are going to fight until we fucking die." To which one of his crew responds, "This is fucked up." And indeed it was.[23]

They pulled themselves together. The problem was a hard one, but the solution was as simple as Martin had said. Another crewmember summed it up nicely; his understanding of the situation was that the cavalry had the Iraqis on the run and that their crew and the rest of the Division would keep them on the run all the way to Baghdad if necessary. SFC Martin concluded his briefing by cautioning his team about itchy trigger fingers. In particular, he was concerned about the battalion scouts. Afterward, they went about organizing themselves to lead the platoon and the battalion while watching over the scouts. Ritter intended to leave his scouts out front to find the enemy.[24] He expected Martin to stay in contact with them and back them up as required. Simple, really, but as military theorist Carl von Clausewitz observed, the simplest things in war are difficult.

The Passage of Lines: February 26–February 27, 1991, 10:30 P.M.–12:15 A.M.

Just before the passage, in what was only partly an attempt at gallows humor, Fontenot called Maggart to say, "I have some concerns about this attack. If I am alive tomorrow morning, I would like to talk to you about this operation." Ritter asked to be included. Maggart responded using his commanders' call signs: "Dreadnought 6, Demon 6, this is Devil 6. If I'm alive tomorrow, I will be more than happy to discuss this operation with you both."[25] With that, the 1st Brigade started passing through the 2 ACR. Less than ten kilometers south, Weisman's 3rd Brigade also began its passage. Both began passing at 10:30 p.m. Ten minutes into the passage, Corps artillery fired one last mission at targets within the "goose egg" on maps labeled "Norfolk."[26]

Despite the confusion and poor communications, the passage went comparatively well. The Quarter Horse (1-4 CAV) passed through the 2 ACR without incident, and established a screen oriented north just over six kilometers north of its boundary with the 1st Brigade. The 1st Brigade passed more or less through a single passage point at grid 700000.[27] If there were marked lanes, the Brigade missed them and literally oozed through gaps in the 2 ACR. The 1-34 AR passed through in combat formation, literally leaving no room for TF 2-34 AR. Time was of the essence to enable a coordinated attack, so Fontenot's task force passed in two columns. A tank company team led each of the columns. His two infantry company teams followed, trailed by combat support units including engineers, mortars, and air defense. The Brigade moved with weapons "hold," meaning that even if fired upon, no one could return fire without express permission from his battalion commander.[28] Maggart had one problem with no immediate solution. LTC Harry Emerson's 1st Battalion, 5th Field Artillery (1-5 FA) had reached a position from which he could cover the passage of lines, but he would need to move to provide fire support as the Brigade moved east. COL Mike Dodson, the Division artillery commander, originally planned to use LTC John Gingrich's 4-5 FA to reinforce Emerson's battalion, but the 4-5 FA was too far back. Instead, Dodson used the 6-41 FA from the supporting Corps artillery brigade to reinforce Emerson's direct-support battalion. That battalion had to travel some to get in formation, but it arrived in time to make it possible for Emerson to follow the two lead battalions through and remain in supporting range. There were no clearly identified targets, so Maggart did not ask Emerson to fire a bombardment during the passage.[29]

The 3rd Brigade began the passage with confidence that they knew where to go and how to pass, but like that the 1st Brigade issued, their order could only be described as vague. COL Weisman ordered "a night attack to clear the enemy in zone up to Phase Line Milford."[30] Choosing the word "clear" required his troops to destroy all enemy formations of platoon size and larger within the zone. This was a tall order, and one unlikely to be executed efficiently at night. At the start Weisman, like Maggart, lacked artillery support. LTC Lanny Smith's 4-3 FA could range no farther than the 78 northing, or barely eight kilometers from the passage points. To solve this problem, Dodson assigned the 3-17 FA, a Corps artillery battalion, to reinforce the 4-3 FA, but they too were poorly positioned and could range only five kilometers east of the passage lanes. COL Weisman and LTC Smith decided to use the 3-17 FA to answer calls for fire initially. Smith would follow the maneuver units, so he could support the attack as it continued east. Weisman, like Maggart, had no targets, so he also fired no preparatory fires, although he had artillery available in the event he needed it.[31]

The weather—gloomy, gusty, and stormy all day—abated somewhat during the evening, though the night remained cold and misty. MAJ Andy Dean, the 2-66 AR operations officer, remarked that the visibility was like "looking in a closet with sunglasses on."[32] The sky was further obscured by what appeared to be low cloud cover but was actually smoke from the Kuwait oil rigs set ablaze by the Iraqis as part of Operation Tariq. The dense smoke from the burning rigs had blown downwind more than one hundred kilometers.

Corps attack helicopters were attacking deep in the 1st Division zone but planning to return during the passage of lines when Mowery's attack battalion would enter the fight. At 10:30 p.m. COL Moreno's 2nd Brigade had not yet closed on the lead brigades, but was close enough to assume the mission of either if ordered. When the 1st Brigade slowed at the passage, TF 5-16 IN caught up. At midnight, as the Division's lead units cleared the 2 ACR, Holder ordered his regiment to clear their weapons. The cavalry had accomplished their mission.[33] The passage of lines was by no means flawlessly executed. There was plenty of friction, but not enough to foil the passage; units did what they had to do to get the job done. Such information as they had the 2 ACR faithfully passed on. Until the very last moment they kept the pressure on the Iraqis.

Tracers, muzzle blasts, the eye-searing flashes of multiple-launch rocket system pods rippling off, and a cacophony of noise marked the passage. Although the 1st Division fired no bombardment, the Corps and the 2 ACR fired steadily. Howitzers and rockets produced a kind of strobe effect that made the night seem dark blue rather than black as night. The desert floor reflected muzzle flashes and the light from explosions, adding an orange hue. The weird light made by guns and rockets lingers in the minds of those who saw it.

The effect truly was eerie. In 1992 Maggart described the transition clearly and vividly: "At the exact point of the passage in the TF 2-34 AR zone, a T-72 tank that the cavalry had destroyed earlier that evening still burned brightly, filling the air with the pungent smell of burning oil, rubber and flesh." Maggart's description is accurate, with one exception; he did not get close enough to see the tank commander of the T-72 who remained at his post, shriveled and shrunken in death, with flames licking at his corpse. COL Maggart wrote, "The burning T-72 signaled the end of combat as we had known it—against dismounted infantry—and the beginning of what was to be absolute mounted warfare at is most basic level—tank against tank."[34]

The 1st Brigade Falters: February 27, 1991, Midnight to 2:00 A.M.

All of the brigades passed forward along the 70 northing into the space the cavalry cleared, some three kilometers forward of their front-line positions. The cavalry warned passing units to expect contact soon after exiting the lanes. As TF 2-34 AR passed, Fontenot ordered his scouts to move south to maintain contact with the 1-34 AR. 1LT John McCombs and SSG Jerry Ellis, his platoon sergeant, each led a scout section. Ellis's three tracks clung to CPT John Tibbets's B Company and kept a radio on his command net. McCombs and his section kept in physical and radio contact with CPT Juan Toro's tank-heavy team B in TF 2-34 AR and with the 1-34 AR on its right. The team also had a radio on Tibbets's net. The scout platoon ceased to be a reconnaissance asset and became instead the means to assure flank coordination and preclude the two task forces from firing on each other. Units throughout the Division employed similar techniques.

In the 1-34 AR, CPT Marv Meek served as "battle captain," supporting MAJ Chris Stewart, who ran the command post. Meek kept one of the battalion's operations center radios on TF 2-34 AR's command frequency, and the two units also used the 1st Brigade's intelligence net to maintain contact. Units made similar arrangements throughout the Division. Army doctrine required coordination from higher headquarters to lower, and from leftmost unit to the right. Thus, the 1-34 AR communicated with TF 3-66 AR on its right and so on down the line to TF 1-41 IN.[35] That night units exceeded doctrine and coordinated both left and right.

The 1-34 AR exited the passage point ahead of TF 2-34 AR by about five minutes. Once through, 1LT Glenn Burnham's scouts led Ritter's battalion to the southeast away from the passage point and into their zone. As it moved, the 1-34 AR drew away from Fontenot's unit and almost immediately ran into Iraqi infantry. CPT Brian Himmelberg's D Company trailed the rest of the 1-34 AR as the fourth point in its combat diamond. As his company moved into the zone, it came upon enemy troops in the rear of Tibbets's company. D Company dispatched the enemy with machine-gun fire, and soon thereafter Tibbets's company ran over two more enemy soldiers.[36]

Because TF 2-34 AR had moved through the lanes in columns, it needed to transition to a fighting formation. CPT Bob Burns's tank-heavy company team served as the base unit for the passage, though Toro would form the base once the attack began. This meant that everyone else conformed to Burns's movements. Toro led the column on the right, and Burns the column on the left. As he exited the passage lane, Toro began changing his formation from three platoons abreast, each in column, to two tank platoons abreast, each on line. His infantry came on line behind the two tank platoons. He took a position on the right of the Bradley platoon and his executive officer on the left to afford the thin-skinned Bradleys some additional protection. He then moved to the right, or south, to remain in contact with the scouts who provided the linkage to the 1-34 AR. As Toro's team inclined to the right, it made room for Burns's tank-heavy Team C to come up on his left, or north, with CPT John Bushyhead's infantry-heavy Team D on Burns's left. CPT Johnny G. Womack's infantry-heavy Team A followed in reserve, with the remaining combat and service support formations trailing.[37] Once sure the task force had cleared the last of the 2 ACR, Fontenot advised, despite his Choctaw ancestry, that "we are in Indian country. Arm your weapons."[38]

To get into position Burns intended to move far enough north to have room to change formation and then turn east. Once heading east he would have enough room to bring each of his two tank platoons on line; as they formed into line, they would come abreast of each other. Burns's infantry platoon would form a line in the rear of the formation. Bushyhead conformed as Burns exited the lane and headed to the left. As they turned north, the two companies, Burns's Team C and Bushyhead's Team D, went over a small rise and were lost from sight. Toro, the scouts, the TF 2-34 AR command group, the reserve company, and the task force combat support formations formed up, heading east.[39]

Somehow Burns failed to turn east. It was pitch-dark, and there were no visible terrain features on which to orient. There were too few satellites to obtain a GPS fix or even a direction of travel, so he had no indications of his error. Several times a day, the Magellan GPS units were useless. These outages occurred at the least opportune times, and this was one of them. Maybe Burns was distracted, or tired, or both, but for whatever reason he failed to make the turn to the east.

Not long after the two companies disappeared over the rise, Womack came on the command frequency confused because he had seen the two companies head north. Fontenot called Burns to ask his location and why he was not moving east. Burns claimed he was eastbound. Realizing something was amiss, Fontenot stopped. Toro and the scouts were stuck trying to maintain contact with the 1-34 AR. Toro asked whether to keep moving or stop and was told to keep moving, but slowly. Fontenot and Burns debated just who was heading in the wrong direction until Burns decided he would check; that meant getting off the tank and moving away from it so that the tank's metal would not interfere with his compass. But before he could get off the tank, SPC Scott Medine intervened. A trained scout, Medine served as Burns's loader. He pointed out that he could use a compass as well as Burns and the commander needed to stay on the tank. Burns agreed, and Medine dismounted to the rear of the tank and moved away, staying in the tracks the tank made to avoid mines. This was a sporting process, as Bushyhead had reported five hull-down enemy vehicles two kilometers forward of the column. Medine took the bearing and climbed back on board. He told Burns that they in fact were headed north—indeed, Burns had led the two companies astray.[40]

At the same time, Bushyhead's executive officer, 1LT Helmut Derra, asked to fire an antitank missile at a target identified as an enemy tank. Fontenot denied permission, believing that in the absence of any effective enemy fire and with two companies out of position TF 2-34 AR had no business shooting at anything. CPT Bushyhead had firm control of Team D and covered the flank and rear of Burns's team so that much was going as planned. TF 2-34 was on the verge of unhinging the 1st Brigade attack without a shot having been fired. Before that could occur, things got busier and then worse. First, moving to get into the zone of attack, the 1-34 AR scouts destroyed what they identified as a quarter-ton truck. About the same time, the Brigade passed on an alert that friendly aircraft were returning and would pass over the Brigade as they headed west.[41]

It was roughly thirty minutes after midnight. With the 1-34 AR already in light contact and both units still attempting to transition to the attack, they now had to worry about low-flying friendly attack helicopters. To the south, Weisman's brigade made contact with T-55 tanks. The brigade and battalion nets were alive with reports. In the midst of this, a tank crew in the 3rd Platoon, B Company, 1-34 AR, reported that it could see a possible ZSU-23-4 at a range of 1,570 meters and asked for permission to engage. The Soviet-made ZSU-23-4 (ZSU stands for Zenitnaya Samokhodnaya Ustanovka) is a powerful, short-range air defense system ideal for shooting down low-flying Apache helicopters. CPT Tibbets was alarmed that the ZSU would do just that, and he cleared the crew to fire if they were certain of their target. On a recording of the 1-34 AR command net, he can be heard reporting to Ritter that B Company "observed what appeared to be a ZSU at 1,570 meters. We have engaged." As he concludes his report and before Ritter can respond, a voice in the background on Tibbets's command net yells, "We got it." The next voice heard on the tape shouts that a scout has been hit. Ritter immediately yells for a cease-fire. Practically the next call is from TF 2-34 AR, wanting to know at what the 1-34 AR is shooting.[42]

The 1st Brigade attack came to a halt; both forward units were in trouble, one having suffered an apparent fratricide and the other "floundering around forward of friendly troops (2 ACR)."[43] Traveling with TF 2-34 AR, Maggart could see for himself what it needed to do. As he waited for Ritter to report, a second Bradley was hit. Chaos followed. Soon Ritter came on the command net and accused TF 2-34 AR of shooting both. Maggart, adjacent to Fontenot's tank and just behind Toro's company, could see that none of them had fired and said so. With the argument settled, or at least deferred, Maggart asked the two commanders to estimate when they could resume the attack. Both thought they could get going in a half hour. Time was of the essence. Maggart could hear on the Division command net that Weisman had a fight to the south, but he calmly told his two rattled commanders to do what they had to do.[44]

It is unlikely that what happened that night will ever be known with certainty. That a tank from B Company, 1-34 AR, shot one of its own scouts is one of the few incontrovertible facts. The scouts in that Bradley escaped with their lives, because it was climbing a slight rise. The sabot round penetrated the back of the Bradley and went through the floor—somehow without killing anyone. It passed through with such high energy that the Bradley caught fire and burned fiercely, but the crew got out with light burns and fragment wounds. The accident stemmed from a number of mistakes and errors in judgment. First and foremost, the thermal sights in use that night were by no means as good as many believed they were. It remains true today that what can be detected by thermals often cannot be identified with certainty. To compound the problem, several soldiers reported that Bradleys, when seen from oblique angles with their guns slightly elevated and hatches open, looked like Soviet ZSU air defense artillery. To the tank crew that night, the Bradley clearly looked like a ZSU. Alerted to the passage of friendly air traffic, Tibbets rightly wanted the supposed ZSU destroyed. He made a reasonable tactical decision given his crew's apparent certainty of what it saw, but that turned out to be a serious mistake. Like everyone else, he and his tankers were beginning their fourth day with little or no sleep. Misidentification and error stemming from fatigue contributed to this misfortune.

Arguably, Ritter made a mistake when he chose to lead with scouts. But if it was mistake, he is not the only one who erred. At least one other battalion commander originally led with his scouts, pulling them in only after contact. Ritter chose to lead with his scouts because he was in a movement to contact. He did not have a good picture of the enemy. Army movement to contact doctrine recommends making contact with a small force. Furthermore, he knew the scouts had better thermal imaging systems than did his tanks. The M1 Thermal Imaging System (TIS) was a compromise, based on costs, that produced images with less fidelity than either the thermal system on the older M60A3 tank or the Bradley Integrated Site Unit (ISU). None of these thermal systems worked with anything like the fidelity movie directors show. Finally, the Iraqis up to that point had not shown themselves to be aggressive. With the ISU, the scouts could expect to identify the enemy first.[45] Seen in this context, however flawed it may have looked after the fact, Ritter's choice made sense.

What happened next produced doubt and sowed suspicion and hard feelings within the Brigade. First Lieutenant Burnham maneuvered toward the stricken Bradley, seeking to shield it from enemy fire. He remained rightly concerned about the enemy to his front. Burnham's platoon had already destroyed an Iraqi quarter-ton truck. He wanted to assure security and to support evacuating the crew. Because fires from the stricken Bradley and the light truck his platoon had destroyed had "washed out" his ISU, he abandoned his thermal viewer. Instead, he stood on his turret seat so he could see out the hatch to guide his driver and platoon. His gunner, SGT David Douthit, remained on the ISU waiting for the thermal to come back on line. Heading east, Burnham pulled into position near the burning Bradley. He saw gun flashes to his left front at about the eleven o'clock position. Then he saw three tracers inbound. Colorblind, he knew only that there were three and not whether they were red, as all American tracers were, or green, as were most Iraqi tracers. He heard one round go over his head. The next penetrated the turret, went through the nape of Douthit's neck, ricocheted off the Bushmaster cannon, and rebounded from the turret wall. Burnham noticed the round illuminate the inside of the turret as it passed. The projectile retained sufficient energy after hitting the turret wall to strike Burnham on the inside of his left thigh, penetrating his femur and passing through his leg. He "heard the bone break," yet he wanted "to confirm my leg was broken. I put my weight on it and the bone moved."[46]

Burnham was not out of the fight yet, as he tried "to control what was going on."[47] When he sat back in his seat, he could see Douthit still on the ISU but obviously dead. He got on the battalion command net and gave a calm, straightforward, and accurate report. Confusion and fear could be heard in some of the voices that night. LTC Ritter heard them too, but whatever he felt, he understood that first and foremost he had to restore order. Ritter exuded calm as he issued instructions in a deliberate cadence that settled his unit, beginning with his highly agitated scout platoon sergeant. He then ordered Bell and Tibbets forward to secure the scene while medics and others moved to assist. The tone on the command net changed from panicky to professional and businesslike. Companies B and C secured the site, while medics and other soldiers worked to get the wounded back to the battalion aid station. The scout platoon sergeant withdrew the remaining four scout tracks in good order.[48]

The battalion surgeon and his team stabilized the six wounded soldiers in the first Bradley. They flew out on the first of two air evacuation missions.[49] Burnham's platoon sergeant escorted the ambulance that brought him and Douthit back to the battalion aid station. Burnham refused morphine, believing he would have to make a report.; the surgeon assured him he would not, and gave him his first pain relief in the hour since he had been wounded. He flew out on the second mission. The final insult of the night occurred when the helicopter crew chief inadvertently used Burnham's injured leg to lever him up into the aircraft; Burnham shoved the offending soldier into the back of one the pilots' seats. But he was on his way home, and soon fell fast asleep.[50]

Burnham believed then and now that Iraqi fire killed Douthit and wounded him. Some believed then and now that an American fired the fatal round. Toro and his Team B were northwest of Burnham's Bradley when it got hit. Right after it happened, Toro's southernmost tank crew took a range to the stricken Bradley and recorded it as being at seventeen hundred meters. Toro believes he saw the rounds that struck Burnham's track and is convinced a Bradley fired them. He observed what he perceived as a five-round ranging burst that struck short followed quickly by a three-round burst, and he believes that at least one of these rounds struck Burnham's track. Several others in TF 2-34 AR reported seeing rounds fired from the rear of Ritter's formation. In the 1-34 AR, several observers reported the rounds came from TF 2-34 AR. Others thought the rounds came from their own rear, and still others thought the rounds came from "way over to the left."[51] On weapons hold, no one in TF 2-34 AR had yet received permission to shoot. Neither Maggart nor Fontenot, traveling near Toro's company, saw anyone in TF 2-34 AR fire. The task force scouts were strung between Toro's right flank and Tibbets's left flank. It is technically possible that one of Toro's Bradleys or one of McCombs's scouts did the shooting.[52] There are several other less plausible theories.[53]

While the 1-34 AR dealt with its loss, TF 2-34 AR worked to get organized. Burns decided the safest way to rejoin would be to turn toward the 2 ACR rather than toward the enemy. In his view, "it was just simpler to continue the turn" through 180 degrees and safer. During the discussion about what to do next, an Iraqi machine gunner loosed off a few rounds. The burst endangered no one, but it served to amp up the stress. Burns needed some help finding the task force. To orient him, Toro fired a red star cluster. That helped, but it also alerted nearby Iraqis, who proceeded to fire small arms at Toro. Not long after, Burns asked for another star cluster. Toro agreed, but accidentally fired an illumination flare. The enemy used the light it provided to fire on him again. Burns liked that illumination flare better than the star cluster and thus asked for still another, and Toro accommodated him. After this second illumination flare burst, Toro saw something near his tank. "It was like the ground was moving," he recalls. He was seeing enemy infantry; his company was in the midst of an enemy position. In no time, enemy soldiers climbed aboard Toro's tank. He was surprised to see his loader, SPC Jeffrey Paluch, use his rifle to shove one of the Iraqis off the tank. He wondered why he had not shot the man. He could see a second enemy standing in front of the tank's coaxially mounted machine gun brandishing an AK-47. He shouted at his gunner to fire "coax." The gunner could see no target, and said so. Toro shouted again for him to shoot. His gunner fired, and the enemy soldier went down. Sensing movement, Toro turned and discovered another Iraqi coming over the back of his turret. He fired all fourteen rounds in his nine-millimeter pistol before the soldier fell backward off the tank.[54]

Blissfully unaware of Toro's problems, Burns asked for still another pyrotechnic, and this time Fontenot provided the signal. SFC Fletcher Harley fired a green star cluster that produced no enemy reaction. As the two disoriented companies closed on the task force, Burns asked that one last pyrotechnic be fired; Fontenot agreed. SFC Harley miscounted the tapes used to designate colors and launched an illumination flare. Fortunately, the flare made it possible for Fontenot's tank crew to see the heavy machine gun rounds fired at them. One of Toro's tanks destroyed the enemy machine gun.[55] Mercifully, Burns could now see Toro, and passed Fontenot, heading east to assume his position. Bushyhead remained, as ordered, on Burns's left.

As Burns and Bushyhead closed the final few hundred meters they identified enemy troops in trenches between them and Toro. CPT Burns hoped they would surrender, as he felt he was too close to Toro's troops to fire safely. He moved up toward the closest trench when an Iraqi soldier emerged from a hole right in front of him. Still worried about firing his machine gun, he had his driver run over the Iraqi. Another enemy came around to the right rear of the tank and raised a rocket-propelled grenade (RPG). SGT Gary Hartzell, the gunner on the infantry platoon leader's track to Burns's rear, concluded he could not wait for permission to fire. He fired a burst of three twenty-five-millimeter high-explosive rounds—each the equivalent of a small grenade. The RPG gunner disappeared. At that point both sides opened up with small arms fire, producing a bizarre web of tracers going in all directions. In minutes it was over. A dozen or so Republican Guard soldiers surrendered, and Burns saw "many dead in the trenches."[56]

Around 1:30 a.m. the 1st Brigade attack got under way again. It had taken more than forty minutes to get going again after the mishaps. The night already seemed interminable and yet the attack had just gotten under way. The Brigade struggled for nearly three quarters of an hour due to a navigation error, poor communications, misidentification of targets, and a handful of brave but foolhardy enemy infantry. The Tawakalna Division had an opportunity of which it did not take advantage. The 1st Brigade, now joined by TF 5-16 IN, got itself under control and moving again.

An All-Around Fight in the 3rd Brigade: February 26–February 27, 1991, 10:30 P.M.– 3:00 A.M.

The 3rd Brigade started through its lanes at 10:30 p.m. COL Weisman's team had done a first-rate job of coordinating the passage; all three of his maneuver units moved to their assigned contact points and through the lanes virtually without incident. LTC Jones's TF 3-66 AR passed through the northernmost lanes nine kilometers south of where Maggart's brigade passed. Jones's zone of action extended left to right from the 92 northing south to the 88, or only four kilometers, a very narrow zone for an armor unit. In fact, each of Weisman's units had only four kilometers in which to maneuver. Jones's task force entered its zone literally on the boundary with LTC John Brown's 2-66 AR. Jones had to move northeast to get into his zone. The lanes assigned to the 2-66 AR channeled it onto the boundary with TF 1-41 IN. Brown also had to slant to the northeast to reach his zone. LTC Hillman's lanes put TF 1-41 IN more or less in the center of its zone. At 11:00 p.m. the 3rd Brigade began clearing the 2 ACR.

After passing through, Weisman intended to halt long enough for the Brigade to assume a wedge formation. Brown's 2-66 AR would lead, while Jones's TF 3-66 AR trailed in the north and Hillman's TF 1-41 IN trailed in the south. Despite good coordination and hitting the lanes as planned, the Brigade had some difficulty as it exited. In TF 3-66 AR, CPT Hans Meinhardt's mechanized infantry followed D Company through the lane. As it exited, the company needed to move north and then east to follow the other infantry company in the center of the formation. As Meinhardt headed north, he saw American tanks moving his way with "gun tubes pointed at him."[57] A veteran of the NTC, he knew what was likely to happen next would not be good. Accordingly, he stopped and had his "base" platoon turn on its taillights to clearly orient his troops as they turned away from the tanks and headed east. Almost immediately, they could see enemy bunkers. Rather than let his troops fire on them, possibly endangering friendly troops ahead of him, he ordered them to dismount and clear the bunkers on foot.[58] It took time.

Jones's operations officer MAJ Bruce Kidder and one scout section operated on the northern flank to maintain contact with the 1-34 AR to mitigate the risk of fratricide. Kidder's tank became the leftmost or northernmost vehicle in the Brigade. He traveled along the boundary, or as near as possible with the vagaries of satellite availability for his GPS or using a compass. LTC Jones advanced with a tank company in the north, an infantry company in the center, and a tank company in the south; CPT Meinhardt remained in reserve. LTC Jones followed the center company, and used his second scout section to maintain contact with the 2-66 AR to the south.[59]

LTC Brown's 2-66 AR debouched from the lanes in good order. The battalion formed up with three companies abreast, and with each of the flanking companies refusing their flanks by having one of their tank platoons travel in echelon. LTC Brown intended to keep the battalion in close order because his zone was tight. Like Jones, he needed to move northeast. Brown's battalion never fully cleared the boundary with TF 1-41 IN. His C and D companies moved along it and sometimes strayed across. Like everyone else, the 2-66 AR often had too few satellites to obtain accurate positions and no readily identifiable terrain on which to orient. The conditions led to the battalion crowding the boundary throughout the night.[60]

For LTC Hillman's task force the passage started well; guides met his units and led them through the lanes. Nevertheless, the task force had trouble as it exited. Hillman's scouts passed through ahead of the rest of the task force and established a screen as planned. In accordance with the Brigade's plan, Hillman called a halt behind the screen to organize for the advance and await the word to go. His combat units passed in two columns. In the north, or left, CPT Bill Hedges's tank company led, followed by the task force mortars then CPT Lee Wilson's infantry company. In the south, CPT Garry Bishop's tank company led, followed by CPT Mike Sanders's infantry company. Combat support and service support units followed.[61]

Things went awry when Wilson's track broke down in the northernmost lane. He ordered the company to halt while he moved to an operable vehicle. He went first to his maintenance track, but that vehicle had no night-vision capability. Rather than riding the maintenance track until it cleared the lane, Wilson then did what he probably should have done from the outset: he executed his standing "jump" plan and displaced 2LT Mickey Williams, the leader of the 2nd Platoon. His Bradley, Bravo 26, could handle three radio frequencies simultaneously, specifically to enable it to serve as the commander's designated back up. Wilson's arrival at Bravo 26 caused some shuffling around; Williams moved to Bravo 21, where he displaced SSG Alonzo Pierce, and Pierce moved to the gunner's seat and his gunner squeezed down into the "hell hole," a narrow passage from the crew compartment to the driver's compartment. While all of this was taking place, 2LT Chip Bircher, who was leading the company, watched the tanks and mortars he was following go out of sight. With nothing and no one in view, Wilson ordered Bircher to head east. It now developed that Wilson had left his Magellan GPS unit aboard his broken-down track. Bircher tried to navigate by dead reckoning. He crept along, making frequent stops so that his wingman could dismount to use his compass to check their bearing.[62] Rain and blowing sand rendered the tank and Bradley thermals nearly worthless. Wilson never reached the position Hillman intended before the Brigade moved.

Practically from the moment the Brigade started moving it confronted active enemy, a combination of the 18th Mechanized Brigade (18 Mech Bde) of the Tawakalna and the 37 AR Bde of the 12 AD. Firing broke out first in Jones's zone, but rippled south down the line. To the north, Kidder could see both friendly and enemy tanks firing. The 3rd Brigade fought "dismounted infantry in dug in positions" supported by "tanks and armored personnel carriers, mostly in well-sited, hull- and turret-down positions."[63] Jones's task force took on a BMP company two kilometers east of the lane exits. The 2 ACR may have destroyed some of the enemy, but those who remained had plenty of fight.[64] During the night, TF 3-66 AR fought the lion's share of tanks, infantry fighting vehicles, and armored personnel carriers in Weisman's zone.

Brown's 2-66 AR also found enemy infantry within two kilometers of exiting the lanes. Iraqi RPG teams posed a particular threat as they let tanks go by so they could fire at their flanks and rear. LTC Brown's gunner, SSG Mathew Sheets, machine-gunned no fewer than six would-be tank killers.[65] The 2-66 AR also destroyed a handful of Soviet-made Mnogotselevoy Tyagach Legky

Bronirovanny (MTLB) multipurpose light-armored towing vehicles, BMPs, and four or five T-55s. CPT Duncan Robinson's B Company encountered the first enemy tanks and destroyed two pairs of T-55s in rapid sequence. The fighting was confusing and often at close range, so Robinson maintained tight control, telling his company, "No one shoots a round from their vehicle unless the target is verified by another vehicle."[66] The 2-66 AR was keyed-up, tired, and sometimes disoriented, as was everyone else that night.

In TF 1-41 IN both tank companies, moving in the lead, fended off RPG teams within two kilometers of the exits. Weisman's brigade had a fight on its hands. But it had other troubles as well. Bircher, despite his best efforts to head east and catch up to Hedges, actually drifted south as both tank companies edged northward, prosecuting contacts. Eventually Bircher encountered a halted M1 tank. He dismounted and discovered to his chagrin that it belonged to the executive officer of A Company, 3-66 AR, one of the two tank companies attached to TF 1-41 IN. Instead of making contact with the right rear of the lead company on the left, Bircher had found the left rear of the lead company on the right; he had inadvertently led his company to the wrong side of the formation. About the time Bircher discovered his error, Bishop's motor sergeant reported seeing Wilson's Bradleys to Bishop, who passed this information on to Hillman.[67]

Bircher returned to his track, unaware of this report. He called Wilson, telling him where they were and that they needed to head north. Finally he asked whether Hillman knew there had been a break in contact with the company they were to follow. Wilson told him not to worry. Consequently, Bircher believed Wilson had not told Hillman, which shook his confidence. Bircher led the company slowly north, perpendicular to the axis of advance. Next he asked for Wilson to arrange a signal with Hedges. Wilson told him not to worry about a signal. At approximately 1:45 a.m. Bircher's lead Bradley stopped and reported M1 tanks at "10 o'clock," about two thousand meters distant.[68] He passed the report up. Wilson's company was moving north and nearing the boundary with the 2-66 AR.

About this time Wilson talked to Hedges. He could see the tanks at the rear of Hedges's company. Apparently he believed Bircher was seeing the same tanks. In fact, Bircher's lead crew was probably reporting tanks from either Brown's C or D companies moving on the flank. Eager to get in formation, Wilson ordered "key on me,"[69] and moved off at a high rate of speed with Williams's 2nd Platoon in tow. Wilson headed northeast, accelerating past Bircher's platoon. Bravo 26 and Bravo 21, widely known to be the fastest Bradleys in the company, pulled away rapidly. As they traveled north, Williams bobbed up and down in his turret. First he would peer through the thermals, then stand with his head outside the turret so he could check the orientation of the platoon. Unhelpfully, Pierce suggested that he "sit his little ass down so he didn't get his head shot off."[70]

Bircher still had not moved to follow Wilson. His platoon sergeant, SFC Paul Sedgwick, reminded him they needed to get moving. The 3rd Platoon took off well behind and left of Wilson, Williams, and the other two tracks in the 2nd Platoon. The 1st Platoon had followed William's platoon. Bircher had not seen Hedges, but Sedgwick had. He could see "an M88, a tank and an M113." He could also see "machine gun and tank fire all over the place, as well as a number of T-55s." According to him, "The T-55s were visible at a range of about 400–500 meters from the flashes of tank main gun fire and from burning Iraqi vehicles."[71]

The burning tanks he saw were probably those that Robinson's company of the 2-66 AR had destroyed earlier. If so, he misestimated the range by about fifteen hundred meters—something that was not hard to do at night. Wilson's company had to maneuver around and over a trench line. As the company moved, Sedgwick saw an RPG fired at Wilson that landed short and skipped off the ground. He called out an incoming fire warning on the company net and scanned for targets.[72] Wilson saw a flash to his left and then "a round, moving too slowly to be a tank round, headed in my direction. I was sure this was an RPG and it impacted to the front and left of the Bradley and skittered across the ground in front of me."[73] PFC Dennis Skaggs, who was driving Bravo 26, saw it also, and thought the RPG looked "like a burning road wheel rolling on the ground."[74] Williams saw the RPG and saw small arms rounds bouncing off Wilson's track.

Seconds later Sedgwick, Bircher, Williams, and others saw a high-velocity round hit Bravo 26. The impact blew Wilson from the turret through the open hatch. He landed head first on the front slope of his vehicle. Immediately another high-velocity round hit Bravo 21, catapulting Williams from his seat. Next, two RPGs hit Sedgwick's track, Bravo 32, as he maneuvered left of Bravo 26. The first RPG brought Bravo 32 to a halt and wedged the crew compartment ramp and door shut. The second hit an ammunition can and gear stowed on the turret. When the warhead blew up, it burned Sedgwick and peppered him with metal fragments. Despite the damage, however, Bravo 32 could stay in the fight. Next a tank round struck Bravo 33, gouging a groove across the engine deck and destroying the engine.[75]

Bircher and his troops believed the 2-66 AR fired the rounds. He estimated one or two platoons had volley fired. A call for a cease-fire went out immediately, and Hillman repeated the cease-fire on the Brigade command net. When Brown echoed the call on his net, the firing stopped. In less than a minute, four Bradleys had been struck. B Company went from merely lost to being in serious trouble. The Halon fire extinguishers worked on Bravo 26, so it did not burn, but SFC Skaggs could neither lower the ramp nor open the door. Suffering from burns, he rummaged in the storage boxes for the Bradley's sledgehammer and he and SGT Joseph Dienstag, the gunner, pounded the door open so the infantry could escape. Dienstag remembered that when they got the door open, "a big puff of smoke came out the back and you could smell burning."[76] Some of the infantrymen needed help. A tank-round penetrator had amputated both of SPC Anthony Kidd's feet as it flew through the compartment, and Dienstag and Skaggs removed him from the Bradley. A trained combat lifesaver, Skaggs worked feverishly on Kidd to stop the bleeding and to get an intravenous feed started to maintain blood volume. Despite his own fear and pain, he succeeded; Skaggs and Dienstag managed to get Kidd on an ambulance alive. The other six infantrymen on board suffered burns and shrapnel wounds, from spall or stored ammunition that caught fire.[77]

Unlike Bravo 26, Bravo 21 caught fire immediately and burned fiercely. Williams was out cold on the ground, and his gunner was injured. Bravo 21's driver, PFC Kevin Pollack, though literally on fire, stayed at his post until he could lower the ramp; Skaggs, who witnessed Pollock's effort, described him as "engulfed in flames."[78] The ordeal on Bravo 21 had just begun. Several of the wounded could not move, so Bircher and his soldiers attempted to get them out. They managed to evacuate three soldiers when a secondary explosion blew the rescue party off the track. Undaunted, they returned and evacuated SGT David Crumby Jr. but could not rescue SPC Manuel Davilla. Someone used a fire extinguisher to keep the flames at bay, but it was too late.[79]

Major William S. Knoebel called Hillman to report that the tactical operations center was hearing reports on the logistics frequency that Wilson's company had been hit. Nothing was coming on the command net from the company, so Knoebel switched a radio on to its frequency. Within minutes he called Hillman to say that Wilson's company had three vehicles on fire and the company commander was down. The next call came from the company fire support officer, 1LT Jeff Wasmer: "Stalwart 6 [Hillman's call sign] this is Bushmaster Gunner. We're hit, we're hit really bad we need you down here, need you down here really bad." Wasmer's call affected Hillman like a blow, but he had Knoebel take charge since he was closer.[80] LTC Hillman ordered Hedges to send a tank platoon back to secure the site, and CPT Hedges assigned the mission to 2LT Bob Arndt. His executive officer, 1LT Bob Finnegan, had a Magellan GPS unit, so he led Arndt's platoon to the site.

Meanwhile, Bircher and the infantry with him on his Bradley organized the treatment and evacuation of the wounded. SFC Sedgwick, in accordance with company standard operational procedure, pulled his track in the lee of Bravo 26 to use it as cover. Once in position, he elevated his missile launcher and dismounted his infantry to organize security. CPT Wilson found him and asked that he call the company's tracked ambulance forward. The medics responded immediately. En route, an Iraqi soldier emerged from a trench and aimed his weapon, but the medics ran over him before he could fire. The 1st Platoon swept the area out to five hundred meters to clear it of the enemy.[81]

Arndt arrived to find tracks burning and American infantry firing into bunkers as they cleared the area around the site. He had no idea what had happened; all he knew was that he was to provide security. At first he thought the burning vehicles were those of the enemy. Only when he pulled his platoon into a tight "coil" around the three burning tracks did he realize that at least one of them was a Bradley. As Arndt and his tankers pulled in, they perceived hostility from the infantry, but once the infantry recognized the tanks came from Hedges's company the tension lifted. Arndt and his platoon had routinely gone to the field with them back home in Garlstedt, Germany;[82] they knew each other.

By 2:30 a.m. those who required evacuation and the three killed outright departed for the battalion aid station in three tracks—an ambulance and two personnel carriers. Meanwhile, company mechanics had repaired Wilson's Bradley, and his crew reached the company just in time to lead the convoy of wounded to the aid station using the Magellan he had left on board. As they withdrew, someone, almost certainly an Iraqi, fired an illumination flare. Under the glare the enemy fired four or five mortar rounds that landed around the derelict vehicles. Wilson was standing with Sedgwick when the mortar rounds impacted. Exhausted, they did not respond, but continued to sip the coffee Sedgwick's gunner had given them. B Company had had three killed outright, and at least twenty were wounded. Kidd died three days later. Wilson, suffering from shock and concussion, was hors de combat, as was his company.[83] LTC Hillman resumed the attack without them.

Enemy RPGs and the 2-66 AR had devastated B Company. The tragedy occurred for several reasons. First, the enemy, undeterred by the odds, got their licks in. Second, it was the 2-66 AR's first fight. Brown's tankers took pride in their gunnery; they were fast and accurate and they reacted to Wilson's approach and the RPG ambush fast—too fast. For obvious reasons, the soldiers in the 2-66 AR did not and do not want to believe they did the shooting. Some who acknowledged shooting argued they were blameless. One thesis advanced in explanation is that the tank crews perceived the RPG strikes on Wilson's Bradleys as muzzle flashes of guns firing at them. CPT Robinson reported he could identify the vehicles that got hit as Bradleys from his position twenty-two hundred meters away. The tanks that destroyed the Bradleys were closer.[84]

The question is why they fired at muzzle flashes. What was the threat? It seems likely the tankers saw the approaching Bradleys as threatening. CPT Wilson was moving north and then northeast across the direction of the attack, and his disorientation likely contributed to the unease in the 2-66 AR. After the war, 3rd Brigade operations officer LTC Clint Ancker led a study focused on understanding what happened and why. His team developed charts showing relative positions of the combatants during the course of the fight. They show B Company heading into the 2-66 AR's zone, passing from C Company's right to left. To C Company, the Bradleys appeared to be a counterattack force maneuvering on the battalion's flank. Apparently they mistook Wilson's Bradleys for BMPs and fired on what they thought were muzzle flashes. They, too, were exhausted and unable to navigate with confidence. Arguably the Brigade was attacking on too narrow a frontage, but given the uncertainty of the threat, putting maximum force forward made sense. Iraqi and American units were intermingled when the four Bradleys got hit. In such a melee, the likelihood of inadvertently hitting friendlies rises exponentially. Precisely that had happened the previous afternoon in the fight between the (Iraqi) 29th Brigade and the US 3 AD units.

The 2-66 AR also had its hands full—first with aggressive antitank teams and then with bypassed units. Support troops in the battalion's combat trains became embroiled in a fight in a bunker complex through which C Company, 2-66 AR, had passed earlier. According to CSM Vincent Conway, "there were rounds flying all over," and the support troops "saw lots of activity in the bunkers." After seeing green tracers to the rear of the combat trains, Conway told Brown he was going back to investigate. His sojourn led him near Wilson's company, where he saw RPGs strike both Wilson and Williams. He saw a third RPG fired (possibly the one that hit Sedgwick). CSM Conway, his driver SPC James Delargy, and SGT John Rowler, a photographer from Public Affairs, dismounted and went on foot to where they saw the last RPG fired. They found and surprised eight Iraqi soldiers, including an RPG gunner, and killed them.[85]

Having done what they set out to do, the unlikely patrol headed back to their vehicle. As they made their way they "heard an explosion and saw an Iraqi tank burning."[86] CSM Conway could see a second Iraqi tank in front of the burning T-55 and noticed "the turret moving ever so slowly. As a matter of fact, I took a few seconds just to make sure it was moving."[87] He decided to destroy it. Conway and Delargy set off to kill the tank; Rowler stayed back to return fire on a bunker whose occupants had fired at them. En route, Conway killed two more of the enemy. Arriving at the T-55, he climbed aboard and dropped two incendiary grenades in a hatch. Before he could dismount, the explosion in the turret blew him off the tank. Unhurt, he and Delargy returned to find Rowler still exchanging fire with the Iraqis in the bunker. CSM Conway destroyed it with two grenades, and his fire team killed four more Iraqis as they emerged. Of the action, Rowler observed, "God, I was only here to take pictures."[88]

The 3rd Brigade dealt with the fighting to its rear, evacuated the wounded, and continued east. Hillman wanted to go to B Company but "could not go back without abandoning the forward force so we continued the attack."[89] It was a hard night; one of Jones's company commanders, CPT Tim Ryan, described the night as "target after target after target."[90] Brown's battalion had all it wanted. MG Rhame watched from the line of departure, just about on the boundary between the two brigades. During the day he had been impatient to get into the fight; that night he was the soul of patience as Maggart and Weisman fought their brigades. There was little he could do to help. What he could see told him what he needed to know: "There were tremendous hits and fireballs all over the skyline."[91] The night seemed interminable, yet when TF 1-41 IN evacuated its wounded it was only 2:30 a.m.[92]

The 1st Brigade Breaks Through: February 27, 1991, 2:00–6:00 A.M.

COL Maggart, moving with TF 2-34 AR, had a close view of the fighting. Both of his lead battalions fought steadily through the night. The intelligence overlay CPT Stockmoe issued, based on month-old imagery, turned out to be very useful, showing a great many unoccupied positions that the Iraqis had prepared as alternates. The Tawakalna occupied them when Al-Rawi repositioned them to orient west. Initially, Fontenot's task force fought against the remnants of the Iraqi 9th Brigade, destroying a tank, four BMPs, and a good number of infantry within three kilometers of the passage point. Beyond that point, TF 2-34 AR crossed the boundary between the 9 AR Bde and the 18 Mech Bde of the Tawakalna. LTC Ritter's 1-34 fought through the 18 Mech Bde and perhaps part of the rear echelon of the 37 AR Bde of the 12 AD. Although tactically ineffective, the Republican Guard and 12 AD troops fought bravely. Several tank crews actually had to repel boarders. Tank gunnery standards never included firing pistols and rifles from a tank or shoving an enemy off a tank with business end of rifle, but all of these things and more happened that night. Task force infantry dismounted and fought two furious engagements without loss.[93]

At roughly 2:00 a.m., just as intelligence imagery had promised, TF 2-34 AR made contact with the better part of a mechanized infantry battalion equipped with BMPs supported by T-55s and T-72s. Additionally, the task force destroyed a few MTLBs and even a Soviet-made Bronetransportyor (BTR) armored personnel carrier. Shortly after, Ritter's battalion reported that prisoners had confirmed the presence of T-55s, T-72s, and BMPs.[94] This combination made little sense, as the Iraqis did not usually mix different kinds of tanks and infantry carriers in this way, but it reflected the intermingling of the 18 Mech Bde of the Tawakalna with the 37 AR Bde of the 12 AD.[95]

Despite the information on the overlay and warnings from the operations center, the task force struggled as it transitioned to hasty attack. It had only just concluded a dangerous fight with enemy infantry when it detected a number of targets, some of which were moving. LTC Fontenot managed the attack by advancing in short bounds. He intended to close the range down to fifteen hundred meters before firing and halt. Once in position, he planned to divide targets among the subordinate units, and once targets were assigned, he planned to direct the company teams to fire platoon or section volleys to maximize shock and preclude coherent reaction. Contacts did not always play out as planned. In at least one instance, the task force troops crested a slight rise and found the enemy literally in front of them. Moreover, gunners and tank or Bradley commanders who could see hot spots wanted to shoot on sight. Most of them understood intellectually that the enemy's infrared projectors and viewers could not detect them at the ranges their own systems could detect the enemy, but confidence in that knowledge was hard to maintain in practice. Many thought the deliberate advance endangered their lives. Their fear and stress could be heard on the radio, but they obeyed.[96]

Generally the scheme worked. In the hour after the confusion that surrounded exiting the passage, TF 2-34 AR claimed ten T-55 tanks, twenty-five BMPs, and ten trucks of various kinds.[97] Still, it struggled to keep pace with the number of enemy targets. The command net crackled with reports of azimuths and ranges to various targets. CPT Bushyhead's Team D fought the bulk of these contacts. Having been told to expect BMPs, at first it reported everything it destroyed as BMPs. To the team's surprise, when it passed by the enemy vehicles it had destroyed, many of them turned out to be tanks. Bushyhead cajoled, urged, and led his team as it destroyed both mounted and dismounted enemy in its path. During one particularly hot firefight, he expressed his confidence in his troops by saying he was "going to have a cigarette [he did not smoke] and chill out, you guys keep hosing these fuckers."[98]

To prevent fratricide, Fontenot and Ritter developed a system based on azimuths of fire. Bushyhead controlled fires on the task force's left flank by restricting fires north of a specific azimuth. That mitigated the risk to the Quarter Horse. CPT Toro managed the problem in the south. This system was unreliable; for it to work effectively, crews had to know the azimuth of fire. If enough satellites were up, Magellan GPS worked well. If not, someone had to dismount and use a compass. Once a tank or Bradley crew had an azimuth, it could aim its gun in that direction and "follow it." With fully stabilized turrets crews could follow their guns, provided they could get frequent updates using either a Magellan or a compass. This approach worked fairly well and partially compensated for the fact that neither tanks nor Bradleys had the means to find direction on board.[99]

At first TF 2-34 AR, like other units, assumed that a cold target meant that the vehicle in question had been destroyed or was unoccupied. That changed quickly after the task force identified eight enemy tanks. Because none of them showed heat, Fontenot told his troops not to shoot, believing that the Air Force had killed them. SFC Ellis intervened to say he could see enemy troops moving around; further, he could see some of them climbing aboard. Bombing had driven Iraqi crews away from their combat vehicles, but had killed relatively few. Soon everyone learned to shoot enemy combat vehicles whether they glowed in the thermal sights or not.[100]

Although TF 2-34 AR infantry dismounted more than once that night, Fontenot kept the infantry on their tracks when possible. As the task force swept through the mechanized battalion's position, it drove by burning combat vehicles it had destroyed minutes earlier. Killing the tracks did not always solve the problem. Passing through burning infantry fighting vehicles, TF 2-34 AR found trenches, wire, and aroused infantry. Bushyhead recommended, "We have the infantry sweep this place and get the little fuckers out of here." But some Iraqis wanted to surrender, while others did not. Fontenot told him, "No, I am afraid my own people will shoot my own infantry. What you need to do is get these little assholes moving west." Then he amplified, his thoughts: "I know. We will just bypass them, if they come out just shoot at them with coax."[101]

Fighting through the enemy mechanized battalion position took a good hour. The enemy position was only two kilometers wide and a bit over two kilometers deep, but it seemed chock full of "bad guys." Bushyhead complained on the command net about the number of BMPs, noting, "Every time we light one up, there's another sighted."[102] During this fight, Burns noticed his loader linking belts of 7.62-millimeter ammunition to reload the ready stowage for the coaxial machine gun. The turret was filled with hazy acrid smoke billowing up from the weapon. It burned his eyes and had the pungent aroma of ammonia common to the propellant in the ammunition. He could see the barrel glowing pink. To his amazement his gunner had fired several hundred machine gun rounds. CPT Womack's company team in reserve destroyed several bypassed enemy vehicles and helped "herd along" Iraqi troops who wanted to surrender; that meant simply disarming them and sending them westward. His company also had the advantage of perspective and found targets others could not see.[103] Everyone in TF 2-34 AR—and, for that matter in the Division—had to cope with trenches, unexploded bombs, bomblets, an occasional minefield, and large bomb craters. Some craters extended thirty feet in diameter and ten feet deep. Just moving required patience and skill. By 4:30 a.m. TF 2-34 AR was in the midst of an Iraqi logistics support area, trying very hard to avoid exploding ammunition. Fontenot asked for and received permission to stop shooting into supply trucks. Maggart agreed, and ordered Baker to clear the logistics area as his task force came through.[104]

All the while, advancing against lighter opposition and despite having to evacuate the wounded scouts, the 1-34 AR pulled farther away. LTC Ritter's battalion advanced steadily, generally along the 96 northing across a frontage of about two kilometers. The scouts' ordeal finally ended at 2:18 a.m. when they reached the battalion aid station escorting the tracked ambulance carrying Burnham. It had been nearly an hour since he had been hit, and still he led his platoon for much of that time.[105]

Ritter's operation is a model of how battalions fought that night. The command net resonated with calm and cool instructions. His executive officer, operations officer, and intelligence officer occasionally entered the net to pass information or effect coordination. CPT Marv Meek and CPT Wes Jennings, Ritter's watch officers, monitored the units on the battalion's flanks. His four company commanders collaborated effectively. Nearly stunned by the way things began, the 1-34 AR adjusted and continued its mission both efficiently and effectively.

Ritter's tankers destroyed a mechanized battalion supported by tanks. Most of the Iraqi infantry fought from trenches and bunkers. Ritter's force machine-gunned those who resisted, but disarmed those who sought to give up and sent them west. At 3:30 a.m. the 1-34 AR was within two kilometers of Phase Line Milford, having penetrated the depth of the 18 Mech Bde and the rear of the 37 AR Bde. LTC Ritter issued orders to assume a hasty defense with B, C, and A companies abreast, facing east, and CPT Himmelberg's D Company to the rear of the other three, oriented west. The scout platoon rejoined the battalion when it escorted the battalion trains forward to resupply the companies. The battalion desperately needed fuel; four tanks had run out during the night. The 1-34 AR reported destroying fifteen tanks, eight BMPs, five BTRs, one ZSU, and one MTLB. It disarmed and sent to the rear at least a hundred enemy soldiers.[106]

TF 2-34 AR arrived at Phase Line Milford at 6:30 a.m., having destroyed four more tanks, six more BMPs, three BTRs, and various trucks in the preceding hour. It reported destroying fifteen tanks, forty armored personnel carriers, and twenty trucks. It bypassed and reported numerous trucks and supply dumps that proved too hazardous to cope with in the dark.[107] Between them, the 1-34 AR and TF 2-34 AR finished off the Iraqi 9 AR Bde, destroyed the 18 Mech Bde, and perhaps took out part of a battalion assigned to the 37 AR Bde. LTC Skip Baker's TF 5-16 IN did its share also. Moving behind the two lead task forces, Baker's troops destroyed eleven Boyevaya Razvedyvatelnaya Dozornaya Mashina (BDRM) Soviet combat reconnaissance patrol vehicles, two BMPs, sixteen MTLBs, eleven trucks, and hundreds of small-arms weapons. Unlike the two armor units, Baker's infantry actually counted its prisoners and reported taking 144. Baker arrived at Phase Line Milford after 7:00 a.m.[108]

Maggart's brigade had accomplished its mission. It had come with a price, but by any reasonable estimate the cost was low. There was no time to rest and no time to reflect—it seemed likely the attack would resume, and soon—so the Brigade brought up its logistics and began to rearm and refuel.. The tanks in the two balanced task forces were nearly out of fuel. Ammunition consumption in the two lead battalions reflected a furious fight. For example, TF 2-34 AR fired 299 tank rounds, 1,889 twenty-five-millimeter cannon rounds, ten antitank missiles, 3,300 .50-caliber rounds, 11,400 7.62-millimeter rounds ,and slightly less than five thousand 5.56-millimeter rounds.[109]

The Quarter Horse Screens the Left Flank: February 27, 1991, 1:30–8:00 A.M.

As the brigades began their fight, LTC Bob Wilson's 1-4 CAV entered their zone. The 2 ACR continued to engage targets as the squadron cleared their lanes, producing some angst but no delay. CPT Ken Pope and A Troop led the way, with CPT Mike Bills's B Troop following. The two troops moved northeast and established a stationary screen about ten kilometers north of TF 2-34 AR. To the north, LTC Terry Tucker's 4-7 CAV screened the 3 AD's right flank. The Quarter Horse found coordinating with the 4-7 CAV difficult, as it used a 1:100,000-scale map while the Quarter Horse used a 1:250,000. The 4-7 CAV also used a different location device than Magellan GPS units. For soldiers deep in the throes of sleep deprivation, resolving these small differences nearly exceeded their capacity.[110] The squadron understood the risks associated with operating a screen at night, with the 4-7 CAV attempting the same thing across the invisible line that constituted the boundary between two divisions. To diminish the chance for fratricide, the 1-4 CAV and the 4-7 CAV traded unit frequencies and locations. They also made face-to-face contact and maintained radio communications throughout the night. LTC Wilson accepted risk by moving aggressively to establish the screen well to the east. Once set, the cavalry could operate a stationary screen, thus reducing the chance of drawing fire. Finally, he and the troop commanders enforced tight fire control based on lessons learned in January and February during their first contacts.[111]

LTC Wilson's cavalry settled in with B Troop on the left and A Troop on the right, both oriented north. The early part of the night passed quietly, although both troops had light contact. CPT Bills's troop identified what he thought were dug-in tanks. Not surprisingly, he had "an uneasy feeling" about his position.[112] His platoons could see worrisome enemy activity including Iraqi RPG teams moving toward where enemy dug-in tanks might be. Shortly afterward, they identified a T-55 as it pulled out of "hide"; one of the troop's tanks killed it.[113] As CPT Pope's A Troop moved into position it had contact as well. Pope encountered what he believed to be an Iraqi logistics element. The troop's Bradleys destroyed an ammunition truck, a few other vehicles, and several supply tents.[114]

Conscious of a gap between the two troops, Wilson and Burdan moved out to investigate. In two Bradleys, and accompanied by the fire support officer in his personnel carrier, they moved past Bills's troop and turned north into the gap, creeping forward, Burdan leading. His driver reported "someone standing on a berm to our left." Burdan looked left and through his night-vision goggles he could see a T-72 tank dug in to turret defilade—only the turret could be seen above the surface. He shouted "Tank!" on the command net and reversed; Wilson and his fire support officer backed up as well.[115] Apparently the Iraqis heard the movement but could not see them; in any case, the enemy did not fire. Wilson called Bills for help. In minutes, 2LT Adrian Lowndes's platoon arrived supported by two tanks. Lowndes's tanks and Bradleys destroyed five tanks, several other vehicles, and an unknown number of infantry.[116] Even so, there seemed to be more enemy tanks still out there.

Wilson withdrew. His job was to screen the flank, not to become decisively engaged. He and Burdan concluded they had found an enemy "kill zone" or engagement area defended by infantry and tanks. He decided to deal with them at sunrise, and at 6:00 a.m. the squadron attacked east with the two ground troops abreast, each supported by aerial scout weapons teams. They immediately made contact. Pope's A Troop, attacking on the left, killed two T-72s soon after getting under way; the Troop continued the attack, destroying a number of bunkers and enemy vehicles including BMPs, BTRs, and artillery. Iraqi artillery fired preplanned concentrations at the Troop, but their rounds impacted behind it. A scout weapons team swept the area ahead and killed more of the enemy. Bills's troop attacked on the right, supported by a second airborne scout weapons team. It rolled through a number of small enemy positions.[117] The Quarter Horse reached Phase Line Milford by 7:15 a.m.

Wilson and Burdan had one more adventure. They motored back to the "gap" where Burdan thought his gunner had killed a BMP; on arriving at the scene, they discovered the BMP was actually a T-55. As they headed back to Phase Line Milford they surprised a T-72. The Iraqi tank commander dropped inside his turret and started traversing. Burdan's gunner fired a missile from two hundred meters, but it grounded. LTC Wilson's gunner fired a second missile and destroyed the tank. Having satisfied their curiosity, the two returned to the task of preparing for the next mission.[118] It was not yet 8:00 a.m.

The 3rd Brigade Finishes the Fight: February 27, 1991, 3:00–6:00 A.M.

LTC Hillman described TF 1-41 IN's fight as one of "constant but light resistance." This does not imply there was no resistance, nor does it mean insignificant resistance; it simply means the Iraqis had relatively few tanks and armored vehicles. His task force "machine gunned a lot of Iraqis."[119] In the northern part of the Brigade zone, LTC Jones's TF 3-66 AR fought at least two BMP mechanized infantry companies supported by at least one T-72 tank company and a few T-62 tanks. His infantry dismounted several times to clear bunkers and trenches. Task Force 3-66 AR also used mine plows on bunkers and trenches. Jones's troops destroyed part of the 18 Mech Bde of the Tawakalna. His task force also fought part of the 37 AR Bde of the 12 AD. By 3:00 a.m. TF 3-66 AR crossed Phase Line Milford and attacked an Iraqi artillery group composed of two howitzer battalions and some Soviet-made multiple rocket launchers just beyond.[120]

LTC Brown's 2-66 AR had gotten ahead of TF 3-66 AR, having fought through fewer tanks and BMPs in the early going, but as they moved east

Brown's tankers encountered plenty of opposition. The battalion destroyed at least eight tanks and a number of MTLBs belonging to the 37 AR Bde, as well as significant number of air defense and field artillery weapons. Mostly, though, the 2-66 AR fought through ground that was crawling with infantry. At one point, Brown ordered his crews to operate with closed hatches and within twenty-five meters of each other so they could use machine guns to sweep Iraqi infantryman off each other's tanks. More than a dozen of his tanks fell into trenches or collapsed bunkers. Some recovered on their own power; others had to be towed out. Once during the attack, CPT Brad Dick turned to look over his shoulder for his fire support officer and saw that "the sky was full of tracers and they were all green."[121] Brown's troops fought a 360-degree battle. The redoubtable Conway and the battalion's logistics troops won the battle in the rear. The 2-66 AR crossed Phase Line Milford and occupied defensible ground shortly before 3:00 a.m.[122]

In the south, TF 1-41 IN fought through and destroyed what amounted to two MTLB-equipped infantry companies supported by a handful of tanks. Hillman's two tank companies advanced abreast and were pretty well on line with the 2-66 AR. B Company remained where Brown's tanks had fired on them, supported by Arndt's tank platoon. C Company was about three kilometers behind the two tank companies dealing with the detritus of the 37 AR Bde, including multiple bunkers and trenches. Like the rest of the 3rd Brigade, TF 1-41 IN had crossed Phase Line Milford;[123] the phase line was not, however, their objective.

MG Rhame intended Phase Line Milford as a means of orienting the force. His order required the brigades to destroy the enemy in zone. Although Weisman reached Phase Line Milford at 2:30 a.m., his brigade had not penetrated the enemy. His units could still see enemy forces to the east. Both the Tawakalna and the 12 AD had oriented to southwest, with the result being that the Iraqi front line trace extended from northwest to southeast. As the Division advanced, the attacking brigades perceived that they were driving though successive defensive belts. In fact, they attacked nearly on the flank of these units. For that reason, Maggart's brigade penetrated the enemy prior to reaching Phase Line Milford. In Weisman's zone, the enemy extended a bit farther east. Accordingly, he continued the attack beyond Phase Line Milford.[124]

Despite trying their best to maintain alignment to mitigate the possibility of fratricide, the 3rd Brigade failed to do so. Jones had difficulty maintaining contact with the 2-66 AR and had lost contact with the 1-34 AR altogether; this was in part because the Iraqi troops in the Tawakalna and the 12 AD fought with remarkable courage. Some attempted to board tanks and Bradleys in every one of the forward battalions. It happened at least twice in TF 1-41 IN. Hillman personally observed one such incident, seeing three Iraqis clamber aboard one of Hedges's tanks. Unable to help, he watched another tank fire a "brief burst of coax." The burst of machine gun fire had a salutary effect as it "dropped two of the Iraqis";[125] the third jumped from the tank and ran off. Fighting infantry supported at night rendered close alignment difficult, if not impracticable. If bypassed enemy troops found the courage to attack tanks and Bradleys from the rear, someone had to deal with them, which played havoc with parade ground precision in maintaining formations.

COL Weisman was not unaware of the problem. As his operations officer observed, with enemy both forward and to their rear, the situation was, as Ancker put it, getting "out of hand."[126] The enemy defenses included trenches, wire, and in some instances mines. On at least one occasion, gunners in the 2-66 AR saw through their thermals buried mines that retained enough heat to be seen.[127] Avoiding obstacles and mines played havoc with neat formations; maintaining alignment in the absence of identifiable terrain features in the dark is a daunting task. Unit formations tended to melt away for another reason. CPT Dick described an accordion affect in his company: tanks seemed to come together of their own volition, and Dick would order corrections, but soon the tanks drifted back. What he experienced happened all over the battlefield. The phenomenon stemmed from pure atavistic urges. Tank and Bradley commanders had good reason to be fearful, and thus instinctively sought comfort from each other, but as they did, tanks and Bradleys became clumped together.[128] Stress coupled with poor visibility and small firefights directly affected tactically sound formations.

Pyres from burning combat vehicles could be seen at all points of the compass. From north to south, tracers streaked across the horizon, some moving in flat lines like laser beams, others moving in slowly described arcs. Exhausted but hyperalert, soldiers experienced time distortion thanks to the biochemistry of "fight or flight." Gunners who had had trouble sensing sabot rounds in peacetime training found that night that they had no difficulty seeing the same rounds moving at more than a mile per second; they found it easy to track them all the way to impact. Many described armored vehicles glowing white hot at the point of impact, and reported watching the metal cool to orange when the stricken vehicle typically exploded. The resulting plume of orange flame looked viscous, as though it was plasma or molten metal.[129] Such sights did little to assure neat alignment and orientation of combat vehicles.

The 3rd Brigade reached the depth of the Iraqi positions around 3:30 a.m. As it did, it found fewer enemy. Even so, the troops remained hyperalert; they were not yet sure they were done, even if they were beginning to think they might be nearing the end of that night's fighting. In Jones's TF 3-66 AR, fighting had petered out. In Brown's 2-66 AR, the situation remained unclear. Both Dick's A Company 2-66 AR and CPT Jeff Ingraham's D Company 2-66 AR had prosecuted contacts that led them south. In fact, Ingraham's company apparently drifted south of the boundary with TF 1-41 IN, Dick's company, about a kilometer east advanced along the boundary.[130]

A discussion ensued on the Brigade command net over whether it was time to stop and consolidate. The forward-most companies in the Brigade were scattered along the 85 and 86 easting in Brown's and Hillman's zones of action just across Phase Line Milford. They needed to decide whether they had penetrated the depth of the enemy and if they had destroyed the formations through which they had fought. Fundamentally they agreed the job was done, but where to stop was more problematic. According to Hillman, Brown was concerned about enemy infantry in the rear area and wanted to withdraw to deal with them. Hillman asked to consolidate where he was, and Weisman concurred. LTC Hillman "told the company commanders we were as far as we were going to go that night, to set [make final moves to establish positions] . . . and report the GPS locations."[131]

Hillman's companies began to transition from attack formations to establishing defensive positions. They would be moving for a few more minutes before settling in for the remainder of the night. CPT Hedges's company was not quite two kilometers southeast of Ingraham and just over two kilometers north of Bishop's company. He was leading his company from the tip of a wedge formation, and his 3rd Platoon, less one tank, was in echelon left to his left rear. The 2nd Platoon traveled in echelon on his right. Second Lieutenant Arndt's platoon and 1LT Finnegan, Arndt's executive officer, had not returned from supporting Wilson's company. CPT Bishop's company was moving in a wedge about two or three hundred meters farther east and to Hedges's right. Hedges's 1st Platoon formed the tip, with the 3rd Platoon in echelon left and the 2nd Platoon in echelon right. Bishop followed the 1st Platoon, tucked up inside the formation.[132] Hillman followed Hedges. By then, the task force commander believed they had run out of enemy vehicles and "had mostly enemy dismounts (infantry) to our front."[133]

Both tank companies had just descended into a shallow depression. As Hedges tank Bravo 66 neared the bottom of the depression, his driver steered left and up a slight rise to avoid an obstacle. To the east, Iraqi infantry were firing small arms at Bishop's company. Hillman could see Bishop's tankers firing both .50-caliber and coax machine guns. He watched Hedges's tank climb the rise and stop. Next he saw "[w]hat I thought was an RPG round come in from the left front of the tank. It traveled in a slow arching path and struck the front of the tank and skittered away. It caromed off of the tank and did not explode."[134]

Within seconds, a sabot round fired by one of Dick's platoon leaders struck Bravo 66. Hillman saw the tank shudder, "and then saw sparkles, like glitter [super-heated metal fragments ejected from the target on impact—tankers call it splash] thrown into a beam of light. . . . Not half a second later I could see a glow from inside the tank which illuminated the TC [tank or track commander]."[135] The sabot round killed the gunner, SSG Tony Appelget, instantly. Hillman thought he saw Hedges struggling with something in the turret; it is possible he was trying to get at Appelget. The loader, PFC Chris Sigler, climbed out of his hatch. Sigler and Hedges jumped from the tank and began moving away; Hedges's driver, SPC Marlon Stith, got out as well. As the crew moved away, Hillman saw the tank shudder a second time "and a fireball come out of the open hatches."[136]

When his platoon leader's tank fired, Dick traversed so he could see the target. Located to the left and rear of the firing tank, Dick had nearly the same perspective, but from a greater range. As the turret came around, he saw the second round the crew fired hit the turret ring of the target tank. When he peered through his sight he saw a "perfectly clear M1 like you saw in the book."[137] He called for a cease-fire, but there was no response. Terrified the tank would fire again, he called on the platoon net and ordered his gunner prepared to fire his 7.62-millimeter machine gun on the platoon leader to get his attention. Finally, the lieutenant answered.

Hedges and his crew got down and stayed down. Hillman started forward to help, when suddenly "there was hellacious tank fire from the left, a second tank was hit."[138] On Hedges's right, Bishop's troops could see muzzle flashes. SFC Steve Jaramillo, platoon sergeant in Bishop's 3rd Platoon, saw the 2-66 AR firing and hitting its target two or three times. At the time, he did not realize the target was Hedges's tank. He called for a report. As he finished, he saw what looked "like a missile coming at him [Jaramillo] . . . I felt the tank shake and it started shutting off. When I looked back there it was all smoky and it smelled. I knew it was time for us to evacuate."[139] Jaramillo ordered his crew to exit on the right side of the tank, away from the firing, and to move off fifty meters. The Halon fire suppression system worked. The crew had time to evacuate, but then Jaramillo decided to retrieve his "things." Jaramillo saw a "white flash and the next thing I know I was sitting on the ground . . . and I see the tank on fire and I don't even know where I am."[140]

In quick succession, Bishop saw a round pass literally over his head and tank rounds strike two more of his tanks. He did not know quite what was happening or who was shooting at him, but he ordered his company to execute their ambush drill. His troops responded quickly. They made a high-speed half turn to the rear and then doubled back toward the firing. Meanwhile, 2LT Arndt, returning from his mission in the rear, arrived within sight of the "fight." He could see the 2-66 AR firing machine guns, and he believed they were shooting at the damaged and burning tanks in his company. LTC Hillman called for a cease-fire on the task force net and nothing happened, so he repeated the call on the brigade net and "like magic the firing stopped. All of this happened in less than 30 seconds." LTC Hillman reported to Weisman that he "thought it was fratricide."[141] As Bishop returned to the depression, he saw soldiers on foot coming toward him. At first he believed they were Iraqis who had fired at them just before the tank rounds hit. He considered ordering his company to fire, but "something told him" not to shoot. They were no threat, so he told his troops to hold their fire. The "dismounts" turned out to survivors from the fratricide.[142]

LTC Hillman moved his Bradley forward to cover the survivors. The tank fire had stopped. He, too, could see some of Brown's tanks firing machine guns, but it looked to him like they were shooting to suppress the enemy. He had his driver lower the Bradley ramp and ordered the two infantrymen in back to dismount. When he tried to follow, he could not move. He had wound himself up tight in microphone cords, a night-vision device "dummy cord," and God knows what else. When he finally untangled himself and dismounted, Hedges was the first tank crewman he met.[143] COL Weisman halted the 3rd Brigade in place to sort out where his units were and just what was happening; the Brigade then used a combination of pyrotechnics and mortar illumination rounds to determine where everyone was. Although the enemy remained nearby, the Brigade consolidated where it was and awaited daylight to continue the attack.

In response to Hillman's second crisis, the Brigade called the air evacuation unit known as Lonestar Dustoff to evacuate four urgent and five ambulatory patients with fifteen more wounded on the ground. The 507th Medical Evacuation Company launched its first aircraft almost immediately. A second, with pilots 1LT Dan Graybeal and CWO1 Kerry Hein, medic SSG Michael Robson, and crew chief SPC Nick Wright, took off about 4:00 a.m. Soon after takeoff, something went wrong. In the midst of briefing a third crew, MAJ Greg Griffin saw his second aircraft at about five hundred feet altitude with its searchlight on. It bobbed up and down several times and then hit the ground hard. The explosion and fire lit up the aviation brigade's laager. SPC Wright unbuckled his seat belt when the helicopter landed hard—very hard. Before he could open his door, an explosion blew him through it. SPC Wright returned to the burning helicopter and struggled to free Hein. A second explosion blew him clear and ended his rescue attempt. Hein died in the second explosion.[144]

One last action concluded the fighting. In TF 3-66 AR, CPT Hans Meinhardt had left a section of his 2nd Platoon in the rear to assist in evacuation of captured Iraqis. Around 5:00 a.m. he called 2LT Larry L. Chaney and ordered him to rejoin the company. Around this time, A Company, 1-34 AR, reported seeing two T-62 tanks to its front. MAJ Glynn Slay, the operations officer, had the battalion while LTC Pat Ritter slept. Slay told A Company to keep watching, but he did not clear it to fire. Over the next half hour, the enemy tanks appeared several more times. Meanwhile, Chaney, in Bradley Delta 26, accompanied SSG Angel Moreira in Delta 21, and headed east with their infantry contingent. They drifted north into the 1-34 AR's zone.[145]

Around 5:30 a.m. they passed fifteen hundred meters south of A Company; at about 6:00 a.m., still heading east, they came upon a group of Iraqis off to their north who seemed "willing to surrender."[146] They wheeled to the left and headed north across A Company's front. Short of the Iraqi troops, Chaney halted the Bradleys in a position to cover the enemy. He and the two squads with him dismounted and went forward to secure the Iraqis. An enemy infantrymen to his rear opened fire, and some of the surrendering enemy now changed their minds, retrieving their weapons and joining the fight. Chaney and his troops went to ground and returned fire. Someone on the other side fired an RPG. Machine gun fire began impacting around A Company. The tankers believed the fire came from the T-62s they had seen earlier. MAJ Slay "could see the tracers coming in our direction and position. I had soldiers out of the vehicles and in danger. I ordered Company A to fire on the approaching tanks. The Company A XO [executive officer] executed."[147]

A Company fired at least five tank rounds at the Bradleys, hitting Delta 26 first. SSG Moreira got hit next and managed to report only that he was hit. SSG Moreira and two soldiers had remained on Delta 21. Apparently, only one soldier remained on Delta 26. The round that struck Delta 21 killed SPC James Murray and wounded Moreira and his gunner, and enemy fire wounded a fourth soldier. Chaney and his dismounted infantry withdrew to the southeast. Bradleys traveling with the 1st Brigade's logistics arrived soon after and fired on Chaney and the Iraqis both. The firing made both Chaney and the nearby Iraqis "surrender." As yet, no one in TF 3-66 AR knew where Chaney might be. At 6:10 a.m. the 1-34 AR reported two T-62s destroyed.[148] Slay soon learned the unpleasant truth.

The fighting at Objective Norfolk ended. The 3rd Brigade destroyed the 37 AR Bde of the 12 AD. Sadly, nothing the enemy had done had stopped the 3rd Brigade, but fratricide had; friendly fire destroyed or damaged five Bradleys and six tanks. A combination of friendly and enemy fire killed six and wounded thirty-two Americans. Precisely what happened and why may never be fully known. The internecine firefights in the two brigades marred the end of a hard night's work. No American planned on shooting other Americans that night, so how did it happen?

A number of factors contributed to creating the conditions that led to fratricides. Two of the three formations in the 3rd Brigade fought their first fight that night. Mistakes are made in first contacts and first battles, including this one. Visibility was horrendous; CPT Dick described the weather as "raining mud." Rain, blowing sand, clouds, and smoke from burning oil wells and burning combat vehicles all played tricks with visibility. The Army had arguably the best night-vision capability in the world, but that capability included tradeoffs. US night vision was good, but crews could see and hit things beyond the ranges they could positively identify. Fatigue played a role as well. More than one tank crew saw things that were not there or saw things they expected to see rather than what they were actually seeing. Confirmation bias occurred that night, as it had before and would thereafter.

Orientation and navigation were difficult, and this contributed to the problem. The 3rd Brigade had too few Magellans, a problem exacerbated by determined Iraqi infantry and tankers who often occupied reverse slope positions and/or let Americans pass them by and would then fire at the Americans' flanks. This created an impression that enemy fire might come from any direction, and thus discouraged dismounting to use a compass, so for much of the time tank and Bradley crews could neither be sure of where they were or in what direction they were pointing. In his investigation, Weismann found "no dereliction of duty nor malicious intent"; the fratricides happened due "to the confusion, the excitement the 'fog of war' and reaction of young soldiers to their first real contact with the enemy during the conduct of a tremendously difficult mission."[149] It could have been worse, and it *would* have been worse if the two tank companies the 2-66 AR fired on had returned fire. It would have been worse if Wilson's company had launched antitank missiles at the tanks that fired at them. In all three cases, the victims could see that their tormentors were other Americans. LTC John Brown may have said it best when he concluded his tank crews saw "what they expected to see."[150]

It is important to note that the 3rd Brigade destroyed forty BMPs and MTLBs, at least thirty tanks, about forty howitzers, five rocket launchers, and nearly a hundred trucks. They killed or captured hundreds of Iraqi soldiers. By any measure, their attack on Norfolk achieved its objectives—and at low cost. Furthermore, American soldiers attempted to accept surrender in many cases in which other Iraqis continued to fight. What happened to 2LT Chaney was not an isolated incident. That, too, could have been worse.

Throughout Fright Night the Division had done what it was asked to do and now prepared to continue the attack east. There was no postmortem, and no time to ponder the events of the night. The VII Corps summary for February 27 described the operation in the laconic language of bureaucracy everywhere. According to the G2, "VII Corps has turned the western flank of the Iraqi defenses and is about to penetrate and exploit through the Republican Guards."[151] By sunup on February 27, the 1 ID had penetrated the Republican Guard. Later that morning, the 3 AD and the 1 AD finished off the Tawakalna Division and destroyed the Al-Medina.

NOTES

1. COL (Ret.) Stephen H. Robinette, telephone interview with the author, June 15, 2015; 2 ACR Operations, "Operation Desert Storm 2 ACR Operations

Summary 23 Feb–1 Mar 91," n.d.; MG (Ret.) Lon E. Maggart, "Eye of the Storm (Duty First)," unpublished manuscript, 1992–97, 167.

2. It is possible that the Iraqis killed only one of the six: SGT David Q. Douthit.

3. Kevin M. Woods, *The Mother of All Battles: Saddam Hussein's Strategic Plan for the Persian Gulf War* (Annapolis, MD: Naval Institute Press, 2008), 231.

4. Ibid.

5. Stephen A Bourque, *Jayhawk: The VII Corps in the Persian Gulf War* (Washington, DC: Center of Military History, 2002), map 20, 340–41. The 12 AD had been charged with covering the Republican Guard. One of its brigades, the 50th, had been virtually destroyed by air attack. The 2 ACR had been pushing the remaining two brigades back since 6:00 a.m. See Thomas Houlahan, *Gulf War: The Complete History* (New London, NH: Schrenker Military, 1999), 363–67. Based on the type of equipment and number of tanks that the 3rd Brigade, 1 AD encountered, Houlahan assessed that the Al-Medina had positioned at least some of its units with the Tawakalna. His assessment is likely correct given the orders Al-Medina had to reinforce the Tawakalna. Units from the Jihad Corps were also intermingled with the Republican Guard. This did confuse attacking units, but it had no real effect on the outcome.

6. Houlahan, *Gulf War*, 373–76.

7. Tom Clancy with General Fred Franks Jr., *Into the Storm: A Study in Command* (New York: Berkley, 2004), 293, 337. The author calculated these numbers in 1992 while assigned as chief of the Commanders' Planning Group at the US Army's Training and Doctrine Command (TRADOC). Data for the analysis came from various after-action reports; the UK liaison officer to the US Army Armor School at Fort Knox, KY (whose name I failed to write down and thus have forgotten); and COL Charles T. Rogers, UK liaison officer at TRADOC. The author had no way of ascertaining equipment availability that night, so the numbers are not exact. The best source on Iraqi forces is G2, VII Corps, "The 100-Hour Ground War: How the Iraqi Plan Failed," May 4, 1994. Houlahan, *Gulf War*, offers plausible theories on Iraqi actions and unit positions. It is not yet possible to speak with the authority about the Iraqis and it may never be possible because some records were lost as some Iraqi units literally ceased to exist, including the Tawakalna, which never reconstituted. The 50th Brigade of the 12 AD succumbed to air strikes on the morning of February 26 and is not included in the count of available Iraqi brigades.

8. There are number of sources of order of battle information; the source cited here is Bourque, *Jayhawk*. The numbers for the VII Corps do not include the UK 1 AD, as it was still overrunning the Iraqi VII Corps in the south. The

author has estimated Iraqi numbers based on orders of battle in G2, VII Corps, "The 100-Hour Ground War."

9. LTC (Ret.) Kevin L. Huddy, telephone interview with the author, June 15, 2015. See also Rick Atkinson, *Crusade: The Untold Story of the Gulf War* (London: HarperCollins, 1994), 395.

10. Huddy interview.

11. Atkinson, *Crusade*, 395

12. Stephen A. Bourque and John W. Burdan III, *The Road to Safwan: The 1st Squadron, 4th Cavalry in the 1991 Persian Gulf War* (Denton: University of North Texas Press, 2007), 140.

13. MAJ Andrew K. Dean wrote grids and information on the turret wall of his tank; LTC (Ret.) Andrew K. Dean, telephone interview with the author, August 27, 2014. The author wrote notes directly on his map and asked MAJ Larry Steiner, the battalion executive officer, to attempt to keep things in order inside a moving command post vehicle.

14. Phase Line Milford was not a straight line, but rather a shallow concave curved depicted on 1:250,000-scale graphics for Contingency Operations Plan Jeremiah III.

15. Maggart, "Eye of the Storm," 164.

16. Formation descriptions stem from conversations with each commander and from sketches they provided. LTC (Ret.) Marvin Meek provided an overlay contemporary to the fight depicting in detail movement of the 1-34 AR across the Norfolk battlefield and periodic movement of TF 2-34 AR. The overlay is 1:50,000-scale and imposed on a terrain analysis graphic prepared in February 1991 based on imagery.

17. Colonel (Ret.) Clinton J. Ancker, "2nd Armored Division (Forward) and the Gulf Conflict," unpublished manuscript, US Naval War College, Newport, RI, n.d., 183–93, 283–85. See also 2nd Armored Division (Forward), "The Battle for Objective Norfolk, 2nd Armored Division (FWD), 26–27 February 1991," n.d.; this briefing reflects data collected in a postcombat "staff ride" to the Norfolk battlefield. Ancker and his brigade engineer literally identified global position grids to each combat vehicle destroyed on the battlefield including their own. BG (Ret.) Brown provided a letter and a paper that includes a sketch of his mass forward formation.

18. 1st Brigade, 1st Infantry Division, daily staff journal, February 26, 1991; LTC (Ret.) Bradley C. Dick, telephone interview with the author, December 12, 2014. See also COL Lon E. Maggart, "A Leap of Faith," *Armor*, January–February 1992, 24–32; and COL Gregory Fontenot, "Fright Night: Task Force 2-34 Armor," *Military Review*, January 1993, 38–52.

19. Maggart, "A Leap of Faith," 25–27. See also Fontenot, "Fright Night," 40–42.

20. Maggart, "Eye of the Storm." See also Maggart, "A Leap of Faith," 25–27; and Fontenot, "Fright Night," 40-42.

21. Fontenot, "Fright Night," 42–43.

22. Ibid.; SFC (Ret.) Michael E. Schulte, interview with the author, November 5, 2014; LTC John D. Tabb, interview with the author, October 30, 2014.

23. CPT James A. Bell and SFC Ralph E. Martin, group interview, Ad Dammām, Saudi Arabia, May 4–5, 1991, Robert R. McCormick Research Center, vol. 4 (McCall to Norton). Recording of Martin's tank crew intercommunications and the 1-34 AR command net, night of February 26–27, 1991, courtesy of LTC (Ret.) Marvin Meek.

24. Bell and Martin interview; COL (Ret.) G. Patrick Ritter, telephone interview with the author, August 4, 2014.

25. Maggart, "A Leap of Faith," 24.

26. 1st Brigade, 1st Infantry Division, daily staff journal, February 26, 1991.

27. Grids are Cartesian coordinates derived from eastings (north-south lines measured from west to east) and northings (east-west lines measured from south to north).

28. Author's notes; recording of the 1-34 AR command net, courtesy LTC (Ret.) Meek.

29. LTC (Ret.) James M. Holt, telephone interview with the author, January 7, 2015.

30. Ancker, "2nd Armored Division (Forward) and the Gulf Conflict," unpublished manuscript, US Naval War College, Newport, RI, n.d., 189.

31. Ibid., 190.

32. LTC (Ret.) Andrew K. Dean, telephone interview with the author, August 27, 2014.

33. Robinette interview; 2 ACR Operations, "Operation Desert Storm 2 ACR Operations Summary."

34. Maggart, "A Leap of Faith," 27–28. The dead tank commander and the aroma of the battlefield are unforgettable. 1st Battalion, 34th Armor, daily staff journal, February 26, 1991.

35. LTC (Ret.) Marvin L. Meek, telephone interview with the author, January 2, 2015; LTC (Ret.) Bruce Kidder, interview with the author, Lansing, KS, September 14, 2014; COL William S. Knoebel, telephone interview with the author, June 15, 2015.

36. Brian S. Himmelberg, telephone interview with the author, June 19, 2015.

37. Fontenot, "Fright Night," 43–44; LTC (Ret.) Juan E. Toro, telephone interview with the author, June 19, 2015.

38. 2nd Battalion, 34th Armor, D Team. TF 2-34 AR radio net during the night of February 26–27, 1991, transcript by SPC James Clemens, n.d.

39. Fontenot, "Fright Night," 44–45.

40. Fontenot, "Fright Night," 45; COL (Ret.) Robert A. Burns, interview with

the author, Leavenworth, KS, April 16, 2014. See also group interviews, Robert R. McCormick Research Center, vol. 4 (McCall to Norton).

41. 1st Battalion, 34th Armor, daily staff journal, February 27, 1991; Task Force 2-34 AR, daily staff journal, February 27, 1991; 2nd Battalion, 34th Armor, D Team, TF 2-34 AR radio net, Clemens transcript.

42. 1st Brigade, 1st Infantry Division, daily staff journal, February 27, 1991; 1st Battalion, 34th Armor, daily staff journal, February 27, 1991; Task Force 2-34 AR, daily staff journal, February 27, 1991; recording of the 1-34 AR command net, courtesy LTC (Ret.) Meek; LTC (Ret.) John R. Tibbets, telephone interview with the author, June 15, 2015; Himmelberg interview.

43. Fontenot, "Fright Night," 45.

44. Author's recollection; Maggart, "A Leap of Faith," 28; recording of the 1-34 AR command net, courtesy LTC (Ret.) Meek.

45. At Fort Riley the 1 ID had long required what the troops called a TIS festival, which occurred every night on tank gunnery ranges for soldiers to determine just what they could see at various ranges through the TIS. In February 1991 CPT Toro noticed that M1 tanks, when seen from behind at ranges of two thousand or more meters, looked almost exactly like BRDM target panels. The author held a TIS festival shortly after so crews could see that phenomenon.

46. Glen D. Burnham, telephone interview with the author, June 28, 2015.

47. Ibid.

48. Recording of the 1-34 AR command net, courtesy LTC (Ret.) Meek.

49. Ibid.; Tibbets and Himmelberg interviews; Ritter interview; 1st Battalion, 34th Armor, daily staff journal, February 27, 1991.

50. Burnham interview.

51. Recording of the 1-34 AR command net, courtesy LTC (Ret.) Meek.

52. Ibid.; map with timings and grid coordinates to various events that evening prepared by LTC (Ret.) Marvin L. Meek from 1st Battalion, 34th Armor, daily staff journal, February 27, 1991; Toro and Tibbets interviews; Fontenot, "Fright Night," 45–46; 2 Battalion, 34th Armor, D Team, TF 2-34 AR radio net, Clemens transcript .

53. One theory is that MAJ Kevin Huddy did the shooting, but he claims he never fired a round during the war. The Brigade's Bradley master gunner served as Huddy's gunner, but it is exceedingly unlikely that he did the shooting. If he had he would almost certainly have fired using doctrinal technique; he knew to fire a ranging round, followed by two rounds in adjustment, and then a killing burst of three rounds. Some claimed Maggart's gunner fired the killing round, but his cannon was inoperable. Houlahan, *Gulf War*, 338–39, concludes that Toro's mechanized infantry platoon did the shooting. The truth is that no one really knows.

54. Toro interview; Fontenot, "Fright Night," 45–46. The timing of these incidents remains unclear.

55. Author's recollection; Burns interview; 2nd Battalion, 34th Armor, D Team, TF 2-34 AR radio net, Clemens transcript; Burns and Bushyhead group interview.

56. Author's recollection; Burns interview; 2nd Battalion, 34th Armor, D Team, TF 2-34 AR radio net, Clemens transcript; Burns and Bushyhead group interview.

57. Ancker, "2nd Armored Division (Forward)," 194. LTC (Ret.) Hans N. Meinhardt, telephone interview with the author, May 26, 2015.

58. Meinhardt interview.

59. COL (Ret.) George T. Jones, telephone interview with the author, March 11, 2014; Kidder interview; Ancker, "2nd Armored Division (Forward)," 191.

60. BG (Ret.) John S. Brown, interview with the author, Denver, September 25, 2015. BG Brown wrote several letters to the Army's Combat Identification Task Force. One in particular is vital to understanding the operations of his battalion during Fright Night; see LTC John S. Brown to MAJ Bill Hammond, October 10 [1991]. The letter includes six attachments labeled annexes A–F. There are several sketches, including Brown's "mass forward" formation in which two platoons in each of the flank companies moved in echelon thus refusing the flanks of the battalion. Annex F, titled "A Speculative Comment," suggests his soldiers saw what they expected to see. Letter provided courtesy of BG John S. Brown. The author experienced a similar phenomenon in his unit.

61. Lieutenant Colonel James L. Hillman, "Task Force 1-41 Infantry: Fratricide Experience in Southwest Asia," unpublished manuscript, US Army War College, Carlisle Barracks, PA, 1993, 11. The order listed is partly supposition. LTC James L. Hillman, interview with the author, Fort Bliss, TX, June 8–10, 1992; COL (Ret.) John E. Bircher, interview with the author, Fort Leavenworth, KS, August 6, 2014.

62. CPT Lee Wilson, interview, Checkpoint Bravo Highway 8, Iraq, April 12, 1991; Bircher interview; COL Maurice L. Williams, telephone interview with the author, August 26, 2014. See also Wilson's sworn statement as part of Headquarters, 3rd Brigade, 2nd Armored Division (Forward), "Operation Desert Shield," APO NY 09758, March 10, 1991, an informal investigation of the night attack conducted by the 3rd Brigade on February 26–27, 1991.

63. Ancker, "2nd Armored Division (Forward)," 192; see also Task Force 2-34 AR, "Battle for Objective Norfolk 26–27 Feb. 91," 1991.

64. Ancker, "2nd Armored Division (Forward)," 192; "Battle for Objective Norfolk 26–27 Feb. 91."

65. Steve Vogel, "Hell Night: For the 2nd Armored Division (Forward) It Was No Clean War," *Army Times*, October 7, 1991, 8, 14–16, 18, 24, 69. Vogel's soldier interviews produced insightful commentary.

66. CPT Duncan Scott Robinson, Commander, Bravo Company, 2-66 Armor interview with unidentified interviewer, unspecified location, June 6, 1991, in the collection of COL (Ret.) Clint Ancker.

67. Bircher interview. COL Garry P. Bishop, telephone interview with the author, December 3, 2014.

68. Bircher interview.

69. Ibid.; Wilson interview.

70. Williams interview.

71. SFC Paul Sedgwick, interview, Ar Rumaylah Airfield, Iraq, April 14, 1991.

72. Ibid.

73. Wilson interview.

74. Vogel, "Hell Night," 16.

75. Wilson interview; witness statement n.d.; Bircher, Sedgwick, and Williams interviews. Bravo 31 is not listed as destroyed in any record the author could find; it was beyond TF 1-41 IN's capacity to repair it, so it was exchanged for an operational float.

76. Vogel, "Hell Night," 14.

77. Wilson interview; Sedgwick and Bircher interviews.

78. Vogel, "Hell Night," 14.

79. Ibid.; Bircher interview.

80. Hillman interview.

81. Wilson interview.

82. LTC Robert J. Arndt, telephone interview with the author, June 29, 2015.

83. Wilson interview; Sedgwick interview. Sedgwick did not report himself wounded.

84. Robinson interview; Brown to Hammond, October 10, [1991]. See also Vogel, "Hell Night," 18.

85. CSM Vincent Conway, interview, site unknown, May 31, 1991.

86. Vogel, "Hell Night," 18.

87. Ibid.; Conway interview.

88. Vogel, "Hell Night," 18.

89. Ibid.

90. Ibid.

91. LTG (Ret.) Thomas G. Rhame, telephone interview with the author, February 3, 2015.

92. Times cited are based on various interviews and on Hillman, "Task Force 1-41 Infantry."

93. Task Force 2-34 AR, daily staff journal, February 27, 1991; Toro interview; 1 LT Steven M. Light, e-mail to the author, July 17, 2015.

94. 1st Battalion, 34th Armor, daily staff journal, February 27, 1991; Task Force 2-34 AR, daily staff journal, February 27, 1991; recording of the 1-34 AR command net, courtesy LTC (Ret.) Meek.

95. 1st Battalion, 34th Armor, daily staff journal, February 27, 1991; Task Force 2-34 AR, daily staff journal, February 27, 1991. For equipment breakouts of the Tawakalna and the 12 AD see G2, VII Corps, "The 100-Hour Ground War," tabs L-9 and L-10. The Tawakalna fielded BMPs and T-72s, and the 37 AR Bde of the 12 AD fielded T-55s and MTLBs; the BTRs may have been assigned to support units.

96. See John Sack, *Company C: the Real War in Iraq* (New York: Morrow, 1995).

97. Task Force 2-34 AR, daily staff journal, February 27, 1991.

98. 2nd Battalion, 34th Armor, D Team, TF 2-34 AR radio net, Clemens transcript .

99. Task Force 2-34 AR, daily staff journal, February 27, 1991; 2nd Battalion, 34th Armor, D Team, TF 2-34 AR radio net, Clemens transcript.

100. Task Force 2-34 AR, daily staff journal, February 27, 1991; 2nd Battalion, 34th Armor, D Team, TF 2-34 AR radio net, Clemens transcript; author's recollection.

101. Task Force 2-34 AR, daily staff journal, February 27, 1991; 2nd Battalion, 34th Armor, D Team, TF 2-34 AR radio net, Clemens transcript; author's recollection.

102. 2nd Battalion, 34th Armor, D Team, TF 2-34 AR radio net, Clemens transcript.

103. "Battle Debrief: Battle for Objective Norfolk," in CPT Jim Stockmoe, ed., *1st Brigade, 1st Infantry Division: Desert Shield/Storm History* (Fort Riley, KS: 1st Brigade, 1st Infantry Division, 1991), 85–86.

104. Task Force 2-34 AR, daily staff journal, February 27, 1991; Fontenot, "Fright Night," 48; Maggart, "A Leap of Faith," 29.

105. 1st Battalion, 34th Armor, daily staff journal, February 27, 1991.

106. Battle damage assessment for the 1-34 AR—and, for that matter, any of the 1 ID units—is suspect. The 1st Battalion, 34th Armor, daily staff journal, February 27, 1991, for example, reports far less battle damage than does the 1-34 AR's postwar after-action review. The author used the numbers reported in 1st Battalion, 34th Armor, "1st Battalion, 34th Armor in the Ground War against Iraq: Demons in the Desert," n.d.

107. Task Force 2-34 AR, daily staff journal, February 27, 1991; Fontenot, "Fright Night." The author cannot say with certainty just what the task force destroyed that night. None of the reports jibe.

108. Stockmoe, ed., *1st Brigade, 1st Infantry Division: Desert Shield/Storm History*, 92–93.

109. Author's notes, entry titled "Ammo Consumption at Norfolk." The note does not reflect grenades or pistol ammunition. Many tank commanders fired their pistols. Shooting a .50-caliber handgun at night is not permitted in peacetime because it has no night-vision sight.

110. Bourque and Burdan, *The Road to Safwan*, 148–49.

111. LTG (Ret.) Bob Wilson and LTC (Ret.) John Burdan, e-mails to the author, January 20, 2016.

112. Bourque and Burdan, *The Road to Safwan*, 150. MG Michael A. Bills, telephone interview with the author, February 2, 2015.

113. Bourque and Burdan, *The Road to Safwan*, 151.

114. Ibid., 150; LTC (Ret.) John Burdan, e-mail to the author, January 22, 2015.

115. Bourque and Burdan, *The Road to Safwan*, 151–53.

116. Ibid., 153.

117. Ibid., 156; LTC (Ret.) Kenneth W. Pope, telephone interview with the author, February 3, 2015.

118. Bourque and Burdan, *The Road to Safwan*, 157.

119. Hillman interview.

120. 2nd Armored Division (Forward), "The Battle for Objective Norfolk, 2nd Armored Division (FWD)." The author relied on the 3rd Brigade's postwar analysis for numbers of combat vehicles.

121. Dick interview.

122. 2nd Armored Division (Forward), "The Battle for Objective Norfolk, 2nd Armored Division (FWD)."

123. Ibid.

124. Ibid.; G2, VII Corps, "The 100-Hour Ground War," 117–20. The 1st Brigade did not produce a detailed postwar analysis, but did go back and survey the enemy positions. What it found is very similar to what the 3rd Brigade reported.

125. Hillman interview.

126. Ancker, "2nd Armored Division (Forward)," 219.

127. Brown interview.

128. Dick interview. The author experienced this in his own task force; the accordion effect that Dick described in his company was not unusual.

129. Author's recollection.

130. 2nd Armored Division (Forward), "The Battle for Objective Norfolk, 2nd Armored Division (FWD)." The timeline is difficult to construct here in the absence of complete access to the records. The author has a copy of the 3rd Brigade's daily staff journal, but the entry for February 27, 1991, is missing. The best source is Ancker, "2nd Armored Division (Forward)," but it does not cite times.

131. Hillman interview.

132. 2nd Armored Division (Forward), "The Battle for Objective Norfolk, 2nd Armored Division (FWD)"; Bishop interview; Dick interview; Ancker, "2nd Armored Division (Forward)," 221.

133. Hillman interview.

134. Ibid.

135. Ibid.

136. Ibid.; Dick interview. Hillman took in these details, because like everyone else he was experiencing time distortion.

137. Dick interview.

138. Hillman interview.

139. MSG (Ret.) Steven Jaramillo, telephone interview with the author, December 19, 2014.

140. Ibid. The second round appears to have been a sabot round. Jaramillo suffered at least one fragment wound, burns, a broken jaw, and lost nine teeth. His gunner suffered burns and his driver suffered fragment wounds; only the loader survived without injury.

141. Hillman interview.

142. Bishop interview.

143. Hillman interview.

144. LTC (P) Greg A. Griffin, "Personal Experience Monograph, Commander 507th Medical Company (AA) Desert Shield/Storm," unpublished manuscript, US Army War College, Carlisle Barracks, PA, 2000, 9–12. See also 4th Brigade, 1st Infantry Division, 1st Battalion, 1st Aviation Regiment, daily staff journal, February 27, 1991.

145. Ancker, "2nd Armored Division (Forward)," 223–26. The 1-34 AR position is drawn on an intelligence overlay of the Iraqi Tawakalna Division, 12 AD, and 17 AD prepared from coverage on January 23, 1991. MAJ Glynn Slay Jr., S3, 1-34 AR, witness statement appended to Headquarters, 3rd Brigade, 2nd Armored Division (Forward), "Operation Desert Shield," APO NY 09758, March 10, 1991 (informal investigation of the night attack conducted by the 3rd Brigade on February 26–27, 1991); this investigation did little to shed light on what happened that night, but it is all that was done. There is no report of T-62s in the 1-34 AR daily staff journal until 6:10 a.m., when A Company reported destroying two T-62s. Around 7:00 a.m. the journal reflects reports indicating that A Company had destroyed two Bradleys.

146. 2LT Larry L. Chaney, witness statement appended to Headquarters, 3rd Brigade, 2nd Armored Division (Forward), "Operation Desert Shield."

147. Slay statement.

148. Chaney statement. See also Headquarters, 1 ID (Mech), Memorandum for Commander PERSCOM Operation Desert Storm Casualties/Injuries, March 14, 1991. No two official casualty lists agree. The author is fully confident only of the number of Americans killed.

149. Headquarters, 3rd Brigade, 2nd Armored Division (Forward), "Operation Desert Shield," 4.

150. Brown interview. See also Brown to Hammond, October 10 [1991], annex F, "Speculative Comment."

151. G2, VII Corps, "The 100-Hour Ground War," 125.

CHAPTER ELEVEN

GO FOR THE BLUE

The Way Home

You have got to be shitting me. Why a cease-fire now?

—Lieutenant General Cal Waller

Mission first, soldier second, self last.

—Private First Class Martha Hill

We passed through burning vehicles bunkers and dead bodies. The burning vehicles caused secondary explosions and because of this we avoided getting too close.

—Lieutenant Colonel Dave Marlin

On February 27, 1991, the morning after Fright Night, none of those dozing in tank turrets or the infantry compartments of Bradleys understood the war would end a day later. Decisions on terminating the war occurred at several levels, but none of them were made in combat vehicles. Iraqi soldiers played no role in deciding how to end the war, either; they streamed north in a pell-mell flight that widened from four paved lanes on the Basra–Kuwait City highway to a dozen and more streams of traffic. Periodically, coalition airmen savaged the pathetic streams, turning them into rivulets. Defeat and panic shredded what little cohesion existed. Though victorious, the US VII Corps began to experience the effects of three days of nonstop moving and fighting. Winning is far better than losing, but even winning wears down the victors.

The gap in perceptions and expectations between the VII Corps and Central Command (CENTCOM) continued. On the occasion of their first meeting in November, GEN H. Norman Schwarzkopf found LTG Frederick M. Franks Jr.

insufficiently enthusiastic. His discomfort grew to full-fledged disapproval on the second morning of the ground offensive.[1] Now Schwarzkopf wanted the VII Corps to cut off the fleeing Iraqi Army. The great Prussian military theorist Carl von Clausewitz argued that the "real fruits of victory are won only in pursuit." GEN Schwarzkopf could see the "real fruits of victory" were within his grasp if the VII Corps would move as fast he liked. Although his mission did not require the absolute destruction of the Iraqi Army it did require, in his view, the destruction of the Republican Guard, and now he feared some in the Guard would get away. He had not imagined Saddam Hussein ordering a withdrawal, nor had he considered the command and control system would unravel due in part to what Clausewitz called "the disorganizing effects of victory." According to Clausewitz, at the end campaign, "the winning side is in almost as much disorder and confusion as the losers, and will, therefore, have to pause so that order can be restored, stragglers collected, and ammunition distributed."[2] GEN Schwarzkopf's frustration grew as the war ended in a way he failed to anticipate.

With respect to the 1 ID, Clausewitz's appreciation certainly applied. On February 26, the Division transitioned from movement to contact to hasty attack to pursuit and exploitation. These changes proved difficult to effect and occurred more slowly than expected in Riyadh and Washington. Lack of fuel, fatigue, confusion, and misperception led to honest mistakes compounded by enemy action. Nevertheless, the 1 ID lunged toward the coast on February 27. To do so, the troops overcame logistics shortfalls, and the enemy, to do their part in concluding the ground offensive. The end, when it came, was almost unexpected, and with it came recrimination born of fundamentally differing points of view.

Iraqi and CENTCOM Estimates: Wednesday, February 27, 1991

In January 1992, MG Ahmed 'Abdallah Saleh, commander of the Tawakalna Mechanized Division, gave an interview to an Iraqi journalist. In it he discussed his division's fight with the benefit of hindsight and American accounts. He remarked that two US armored divisions and one US mechanized division attacked his troops. Close enough, although he failed to mention the 2nd Armored Cavalry Regiment (2 ACR). According to Saleh, the fight "was very fierce and both sides used all types of weapons they possessed." After six hours of fighting, he claimed the Americans ceased their attack and "failed to renew the contact with them [his Division] because of the dense fire" of his units.[3] In the Iraqi official history, LTG Ayad Futayyih Khalifa al-Rawi credited the Tawakalna with "obliging him [the enemy] to interrupt his [attack] on al Basra."[4]

Despite his complimentary remarks, Al-Rawi suffered no illusions about how his force had done; he understood the Tawakalna no longer existed as a fighting organization and reported the situation with surprising candor.[5] He informed the Iraqi high command that coalition forces had reached Highway 8, the main Basra–Baghdad highway. He apprised the high command of serious attacks against both the Adnan and Nebuchadnezzar Divisions and asked that "an armored division be sent immediately to close the gap created by the near loss of the Tawakalna Ala Allah [the name translates as 'Rely in God']." The high command understood he was in trouble. At 11:30 a.m. his superiors reassigned the 10th Armored Division (10 AD) from the II Corps to the Republican Guard.[6] Although by now Kuwait was lost, Al-Rawi arranged the defense of Basra using the Adnan, Hammurabi, and Nebuchadnezzar Divisions and other units as they became available. The Iraqis had difficulties throughout the theater. The UK 1 AD attack that had started late on February 25 continued nonstop, and by the morning of February 27, the British had demolished the Iraqi VII Corps. They defeated in turn the 48th, 31st, 25th, and 27th Infantry Divisions. In the east, the Iraqis continued the flight from Kuwait.[7]

Kevin Woods's *The Mother of All Battles* is the most authoritative source on Iraqi planning and operations during the conflict. Woods makes plain the fundamental misapprehension Iraq and the United States had of each other. This was important, because the Americans dominated coalition thinking and, for the most part, almost always mistook Iraqi intentions. The Iraqis, on the other hand, never got it right. On February 27 the divergence of views between the chief protagonists could be measured in parsecs. Saddam realized on February 24 that he could not hold Kuwait; from then on, he focused on saving his Army and defending Iraq. Once he ordered the forces in Kuwait to withdraw, CENTCOM's plan became irrelevant, predicated as it was on an attack to fix the Iraqis in Kuwait. The attack from the Marines and Arab forces by no means prevented the Iraqis from moving. In any case, the Iraqis first withdrew and then bolted for home.

LTG Al-Rawi's thinking and Saddam's directives make clear that they assumed Schwarzkopf would attempt to seize the oil fields southwest of Basra and then Basra itself. They further supposed coalition forces would continue on to Baghdad to topple the regime. Despite this grim estimate, Woods argues they did not yet see themselves as defeated. Saddam and his advisers believed they could defend Iraq. This may sound implausible in retrospect, but it seemed entirely reasonable to them. As Woods proposes, "Given Iraqi notions of what the coalition's ultimate military objectives were, at least some in the regime saw reason for cautious optimism."[8] Regime survival constituted victory and looked likely.

GEN Schwarzkopf, whatever Saddam presumed, had no mandate to seize Basra, let alone Baghdad. Simply stated, Saddam could not believe that the enormous force assembled by the coalition would be used to attain limited objectives. What the Iraqis thought likely was out of bounds for the coalition because the disparate aims of the coalition's members precluded such great ambition. Schwarzkopf's mandate required two things: he was to drive the Iraqis from Kuwait and destroy their offensive capability. Iraq and the United States miscalculated based on their inability to achieve any empathy for each other.[9]

At daybreak on February 27, Arab and Marine units drove into Kuwait City. On the northern flank, LTG Gary Luck's XVIII Airborne (ABN) Corps reached Highway 8, essentially cutting off the Iraqis from Baghdad. This only mattered if the coalition aimed to continue the attack beyond the original purpose. LTG Franks's VII Corps had overrun the Republican Guard's forward defenses and was within striking distance of the Basra–Kuwait City highway. Schwarzkopf "felt confident that this war was going to end very soon. Central Command's Army corps were now moving inexorably east, like the piston in an enormous cider press. We were driving the enemy into the pocket across the Euphrates from Basra."[10] That same morning he ordered his staff to begin planning to send the troops home. Late in that day, he asked LTG John Yeosock, who commanded the two Army corps, "How much longer do you need to finish the Republican Guard?" Yeosock answered, "One more day. They'll be done for by tomorrow night."[11] Because Schwarzkopf believed destroying the Republican Guard essential to precluding an Iraqi offensive capability, Yeosock believed he would have February 28 to complete the task. Schwarzkopf enjoyed the day and prepared "the mother of all briefings."

"Go For the Blue": February 27, 1991, 7:30 A.M.–Noon

Far to the north of Riyadh, bleary-eyed troops found some fuel and food, but few found rest. MG Thomas G. Rhame and his mobile command group spent the night in the rear of COL Dave Weisman's brigade near its boundary with COL Lon E. "Bert" Maggart's brigade. BG Bill Carter displaced Danger Forward into the center of what had been the Iraqi 18th Brigade's position. Danger Forward arrived and established communications at 4:15 a.m., just to the rear of Maggart's maneuver units; Carter felt it was not safe farther forward. At first the area in which he chose to stop did not appear safe either; the command post was nearly overrun with Iraqis whom Maggart's troops had caught up in the fight and disarmed, but had not escorted to the rear. Sending Iraqis to the rear without escort reflected the lack of infantry and military police required to manage high numbers of prisoners that no one had imagined likely.[12] This failure also reflected the growing conviction among the troops that the Iraqis would cause no trouble, and increasingly they felt sorry for their counterparts.

Carter was neither as trusting nor under the same pressure. The small group of soldiers who supported the tactical command post assumed responsibility for the human flotsam of the battle; they herded the captured Iraqis into revetments prepared for tanks and infantry fighting vehicles that the 18th Brigade had not occupied, and by dawn they had more than four hundred prisoners.[13] MAJ Mike Barefield, Carter's operations officer, described this and the aftermath of the battle. To him the scale of the fight was apparent from the "burning wreckage." He estimated Maggart's brigade destroyed "at least sixty armored veh[icles]/numerous personnel bunkers/stores/trucks."[14] The stream of Iraqis continued unabated to the point that Danger Forward, having given away most of its available food and water, adopted the 1st Brigade's practice and directed the Iraqi soldiers to evacuate themselves. This they could do so merely by pointing the way.

Around 6:30 a.m. the Corps' commander landed at Danger Forward. Franks, like everyone who fought at Objective Norfolk, found the sight of the battlefield stunning:

> As far as we could see, there were burning vehicles. Tanks without turrets burning. BMPs burning and overturned. Some equipment obviously hit by LGBs [laser guided bombs] as the tanks without turrets and the hulls were almost flattened. Trucks were on fire. Black smoke rose in small columns from burning vehicles littering the sand. Iraqi dead lay on the battlefield. We could see picking their way through all of this, the logistics support trucks of the 1st IN Division support command commanded by Colonel Bob Shadley, attempting to keep up the pace to bring needed fuel.[15]

Soldiers in the 1st Division might quibble with one of Franks's observations. During the fighting, the Division's tankers learned that, when hit, T-72s exploded catastrophically; their turrets blew off, spewing wreckage in all directions. Every T-72 struck generated a fiery, horrific sight. Curiously, the turrets tended to come down right side up. Although equipped with a formidable 125-millimeter cannon, the T-72 proved to be the least survivable tank on the battlefield. It fired semifixed ammunition with its propellant stored in the turret and not in a separate compartment. Every time a US tank round or antitank missile hit a T-72, it produced a blaze that would have frightened Dante. Tank and Bradley gunners could attest that many of the tanks they destroyed looked just like the ones Franks assumed bombs had killed.

With the aid of a map board, Carter reviewed the operation. He told Franks, "It was a tough fight last night. We think we have broken through . . . [the Division is] continuing east toward Denver," a terrain objective eighty kilometers east of phase line Milford.[16] He reported, "About 8 KIA [killed in action] and maybe thirty wounded."[17] Franks then asked him to raise Rhame on the radio. Franks and Rhame had a quick conversation, during which Rhame estimated the Division could reach Phase Line Denver by nightfall. Franks told him to "Attack to Denver. I'll give details to Bill." Then Franks, Carter, and Carter's planners turned to a 1:100,000-scale map. Franks looked at the map and seized on a phrase he felt would get through to minds clouded by fatigue. He pointed at the Persian Gulf on Carter's map and ordered Carter to "Attack east. Go for the Blue on the map."[18] The injunction to "Go for the Blue" made it down to the attacking battalions. The order had a galvanizing effect on those who heard it. He was right: "Go for the Blue" would penetrate sleep deprivation.

Franks departed Danger Forward around 7:15 a.m. No one needed to urge Rhame to attack, but none of his Brigades could go just then. As Rhame remembers it, "We had reached our limit of advance in terms of fuel."[19] Most of the Division needed fuel desperately after nonstop movement and combat during the preceding twenty-four hours. Most units had refueled the previous afternoon or evening, but the M1 tank, for all of its tremendous attributes, had one glaring weakness: it burned fuel at prodigious rates. Unreliable transfer pumps aggravated the problem. There are two separate fuel cells in the M1. A tank with an inoperative fuel pump forces a tank with that problem to operate with half the designed fuel capacity. During the night, some tanks ran out of fuel and had to be left behind. Still, Rhame believed enough fuel could be found to get as far forward as Phase Line Berlin, forty kilometers east of Phase Line Milford.[20]

At Phase Line Berlin, the Division would have to have time and resources to refuel fully. Only then could it continue the attack to Phase Line Denver and ultimately cut the Basra–Kuwait City highway, fifty kilometers farther east. There it would cut off any remaining Iraqi units and attain Franks's objective. The Division's zone would drive across the narrow neck of Kuwait along the border with Iraq. Rhame understood Franks perfectly; this was about keeping the Iraqis on the run and cutting off those heading north. He had three variables to manage: time, fuel, and the enemy.

Meanwhile, COL Jim Mowery's Apache helicopter crews could keep the pressure on the Iraqis. The Apaches of the 1st Infantry Division, 1st Combat Aviation Brigade (1-1 AVN) would lead the Division in a "movement to contact." At 7:00 a.m. CPT Tim Linderman's day company launched and headed east. The Apaches destroyed more than twenty armored vehicles before they, too, had to refuel. With the weather threatening, Mowery and his pilot, CWO Terry Morgan, took off to reconnoiter the Basra–Kuwait City highway forward of the ground units. MG Rhame wanted to know if the Iraqis were using the highway. Mowery and Morgan flew the road but saw no "stream of enemy vehicles" moving north and detected no radar supported air defense artillery.[21] The question was, had the Iraqis already escaped, or did the lack of traffic suggest there might still be time to cut the road before the Iraqis could get out? Cutting off the Iraqis depended on the ground troops because the weather grounded the attack helicopters after Mowery's mission.

Rhame knew there was no time to lose. Having penetrated the depth of the Iraqi positions, the Division had to exploit success. As Field Manual FM

71-100, *Division Operations*, asserts, "Exploitation may follow the deliberate or hasty attack to destroy the enemy's ability to reconstitute an organized defense or to conduct an orderly withdrawal."[22] Rhame recognized the transition at 4:00 a.m. In a note written that morning, he reviewed the night's fighting against the Iraqi 18th and 37th Brigades: "These units simply don't exist anymore . . . as the [Iraqis] broke I could see we had to press him [the enemy] quickly and fast."[23]

He did not need to thumb through the manual. He knew what came next: pursuit. FM 71-100 defined pursuit as "a natural extension of the exploitation. It differs from exploitation in that its primary function is to complete the destruction of the enemy force which is in the process of disengagement."[24] LTG Yeosock's two Army corps constituted an "encircling force"; the Marines and the Arab forces advancing up the coastal highway formed "the direct pressure force." The VII Corps had to continue to attack east if it was to have a chance to destroy the Republican Guard. LTG Al-Rawi had largely ruined that chance. He sacrificed the Tawakalna and Al-Medina Divisions and the Jihad Corps in order to withdraw the Adnan, Hammurabi, and Nebuchadnezzar Divisions. He used them to establish a bridgehead south of the Euphrates River near Basra, to hold the door open for the Iraqi Army to get out.

After his radio conference with Franks, Rhame asked his commanders how quickly they could get moving. LTC Bob Wilson was in good shape and about ready to move; COL Maggart needed until 10:00 a.m. COL Tony Moreno estimated he could roll at 8:30 a.m.; COL Weisman reported 8:00 a.m., but then revised his estimate to 8:30 a.m. Rhame knew Maggart's brigade had "fought long and hard."[25] Task Force 2nd Battalion, 34th Armor (TF 2-34 AR) had only arrived at Phase Line Milford at 6:30 a.m. Task Force 5th Battalion, 16th Infantry (5-16 IN) was still dealing with bypassed enemy units and completing the destruction of a large logistics base five kilometers short of Phase Line Milford. He accepted Maggart's estimate and ordered Moreno to pass through Maggart and assume his zone of action. The Division would attack with Moreno on the left and Weisman on the right; the two brigades began moving at 8:30 a.m. Rhame told Maggart, "You are now the Division Reserve. Be refueled by 1000 and follow the 2nd Brigade to PL Berlin. Be prepared to continue the attack east."[26]

By this time, the word *prepare* had become a euphemism for "hurry up." There was no time to "prepare." None of the units issued written orders. The war had become, in Army parlance, "push to talk": commanders pushed the talk switch on their microphones and talked. Commanders and operations officers had neither the time nor a place to think about the mission. Few of the soldiers making plans and issuing orders would have escaped criticism in a staff college exercise, but they got moving quickly. Tired commanders issued orders to equally worn-out subordinates on short-range FM radios with less information than they had the night before. On the best day in the best conditions, radios are a poor means to communicate intentions with accuracy. Conveying subtlety in intention is virtually impossible.

Maggart made his arrangements on his estimate of the condition of his units. LTC Pat Ritter's 1-34 AR assumed a hasty defense on Phase Line Milford at 4:00 a.m. It passed for well rested. Task Force 2-34 AR had finished its fight barely an hour earlier and needed more time. Maggart decided to resume the attack with LTC Skip Baker's TF 5-16 IN taking TF 2-34 AR's zone of action on the Brigade's left. LTC Ritter's 1-34 AR would remain on the right. TF 2-34 AR would form the reserve. Maggart arranged a rendezvous with Baker to issue orders face-to-face. Traveling east to the rendezvous, Baker and his operations officer, MAJ Brian Zahn, ran into a southbound T-55. Another of Baker's Bradleys dispatched the T-55 before it could kill the commander and his operations officer. In the process of avoiding the tank, Zahn injured himself badly enough to require evacuation. The delay to evacuate him, though short, exacerbated matters. Worse still, Baker could not refuel by 10:00 a.m. Maggart had to revise his plan and use TF 2-34 AR. Baker's task force remained in reserve.[27]

At 4:00 a.m. the 3rd Brigade, less B Company of the 1-41 IN, assumed a hasty defense about four kilometers east of Phase Line Milford. COL Weisman's brigade was "well rested." Fuel available varied by unit. Too little time and too little fuel necessitated rationing, but most of the Brigade's combat vehicles got some fuel. Task Force 1-41 IN's fuel trucks arrived in enough time to pump some fuel, but not to top off. LTC George T. Jones's fuel trucks, however, could not be found. His command sergeant major was leading the logistics column. Traveling in the dark across contested ground and without a Magellan GPS unit, he drifted south and arrived at TF 1-41 IN instead of TF 3-66 AR. The sergeant major immediately turned his convoy north and made his way to the thirsty tanks, arriving just in time for each tank to get a sip of fuel. The Bradleys had to do without. LTC John Brown's 2-66 AR refueled without incident.[28]

Because the 3rd Brigade had been meticulous about properly evacuating prisoners, it still had hundreds of them. Nevertheless, it managed and made the start time. Weisman headed east within the same formation used the night before: Jones, Brown, and LTC Jim Hillman attacked abreast. CPT Lee Wilson's company remained to secure the Brigade's logistics, because the rear area still crawled with enemy. Most wanted to surrender, but some still wanted to fight.[29]

COL Moreno's brigade had followed Maggart's the night before. Although technically in the rear, the 2nd Brigade fought pockets of bypassed enemy. Moreno's soldiers were not well rested even by the low standards in the Division; furthermore, the Brigade had just enough fuel to reach Phase Line Berlin and could have trouble there, since more than half of the 4-37 AR's fuel trucks had gone missing. Moreno got under way on time, but not without excitement. He designated LTC Dave Gross's TF 3-37 AR as the base for the attack. LTC

Dave Marlin and the 4-37 AR would conform to his movements. As was their wont at critical moments, the GPS units took a hiatus.[30]

This had serious implications that no one realized at first. In the absence of at least three satellites, the Magellan usually showed "searching for satellites." Sometimes, however, it gave constant course corrections that led the user in a gradual but steady right-hand curve. Whatever the cause, Gross headed off in in the wrong direction. Marlin found this alarming and kept querying his colleague about the course. So did Moreno, who Gross thought "got a little hyper."[31] Marlin eventually halted and watched TF 3-37 AR complete a circle before heading east. Once Gross headed east, Marlin's battalion had to drive at breakneck speed to reach the line of departure. Gross beat him there, at which time Marlin became the target of Moreno's encouragement. The delays mounted and frustration rose, but at 9:45 a.m. the 1st Brigade reported that the 2nd Brigade had cleared its positions heading east.

Only the 1st Squadron, 4th Cavalry (1-4 CAV) got under way without incident. CPT Ken Pope's A Troop led, followed by CPT Mike Bills's B Troop; the squadron executed a moving flank screen. The two troops bounded east, occupying a series of hasty positions oriented to the north to provide early warning and some delay in the event of an enemy counterattack. The Division attack ordered at 8:30 a.m. finally got moving at 9:30 a.m.[32] As Clausewitz observed nearly two hundred years earlier, "Fatigue, exertion, and privation [fuel, in this instance] constitute a separate destructive factor in war."[33] All of these played a role that morning.

Weisman's brigade made contact almost immediately. Task Force 1-41 IN actually began the action before the attack got under way. Preparing to move out, Hillman spotted an Iraqi tank to his front. He asked his operations officer to confirm identification. MAJ Glenn Hulse confirmed that it was an Iraqi tank. Hillman's gunner launched a missile that went awry. Seeing this, Hulse's gunner fired an antitank missile and destroyed the tank. When the Brigade started moving, a second T-55 tank debouched from a concealed position and sprinted east. It did not outrun a sabot round fired by the 2-66 AR. Next, a Bradley gunner in TF 3-66 AR killed a third tank with an antitank missile.[34]

Things calmed down until Brown's 2-66 AR started across the Wadi al-Batin and into Kuwait, at which point enemy artillery impacted in and around the battalion. Brown's tankers drove out of the artillery barrage at high speed east toward the enemy across the wadi and into Kuwait. This far north, the wadi is shallow swale rather than the rugged, deep gully it is in Saudi Arabia. As the 2-66 AR exited the wadi, it discovered a bunker complex and engaged and hit an armored vehicle moving among them. The stricken track turned out to be British. Fortunately, no one was killed, though two British soldiers were wounded. Not surprisingly, those British soldiers who had them flew large

Union Jacks henceforth. After this final incident, Weisman's brigade advanced rapidly against light resistance. Concerned about yet another fratricide, Weisman put his unit on tight weapons control. Disarming Iraqis and dispatching abandoned enemy vehicles took some time, but the Brigade made it to Phase Line Berlin around 11:00 a.m., desperate for fuel.[35]

COL Moreno's brigade recovered quickly from its difficulty navigating. Moving forward, it passed numerous abandoned enemy tanks and BMPs. Moreno's troops crossed the Wadi al-Batin, entered Kuwait, and continued east without encountering resistance until they approached Phase Line Berlin. Here Gross's TF 3-37 AR caught up with a dozen or more Iraqi tanks. Gross could hear tank guns firing, but he could not see the fighting, which was off to his north. To his front, he watched two Bradleys cross a gentle rise. An enemy tank on the far side fired at and missed both vehicles. Prudently, the Bradleys reversed back up the slope at full speed. One stopped before the other within Gross's field of view. That crew raised their missile launcher even as the Bradley rocked back on its suspension. When the launcher locked down, the gunner fired. Gross watched, fascinated, as the antitank missile streaked a distance of no more than ninety meters and struck the enemy tank, which went off "like a Roman candle shooting up."[36]

TF 3-37 AR had caught up with the enemy across its front. The task force found it had entered the target area of a Kuwaiti army tank range. Now, as the melee moved east, the soldiers had to distinguish between enemy tanks and derelicts used as "hard targets" on the range. In a bizarre and confusing fight, TF 3-37 AR killed more than a dozen enemy tanks using tank guns and Bradley antitank missiles.[37]

LTC Marlin advanced without resistance, but not without incident. He expected that once past the 1st Brigade, "everything to our front was the enemy,"[38] but he nonetheless cautioned his troops to report what they saw and to clear fires. Not long after crossing the line of departure, his scouts observed what he thought were enemy vehicles at long range. First Lieutenant Lanier Ward reported and obtained clearance to shoot. As Ward's scouts prepared to fire, one of his Bradley commanders identified the targets as US artillery. Next Marlin's tankers avoided shooting the 1st Brigade's command post, as it wandered across his front, traveling perpendicular to the axis of advance.[39]

The 1st Brigade crossed the line of departure at 10:41 a.m., helped by frequent requests for an estimated time of departure from the commanding general. Once the Brigade moved, Rhame wanted to know when it would reach Phase Line Berlin. He kept the pressure on both the Iraqis and his own troops; time was of the essence. Too tired to do the necessary math, Maggart asked Fontenot to plug the numbers into the formula *time of arrival equals distance divided by rate*. Frequent computation of the estimated time of arrival failed to speed things up. Traveling the forty kilometers to Phase Line Berlin seemed to take forever. For three days, the desert had been filled with death and destruction; now, following the 2nd and 3rd Brigades, it seemed comparatively empty. The lack of activity proved as nerve-racking as constant contact had been. Approaching the Wadi al-Batin, Fontenot told his troops, "When we get to Phase Line Plum, we'll be in Kuwait, this thing will be close to being over if we just take care of ourselves." Making mistakes due to fatigue was a serious concern. As the task force entered Kuwait, Fontenot instructed, "Concentrate or you're going to hurt somebody, possibly one of us." He reminded them, "We're still on weapons hold, I'll need a note from your mother and an excuse from me before you can shoot. Guidons . . . welcome to Kuwait."[40]

The Attack to the Northeast: February 27, 1991, Noon–5:30 P.M.

As the 1st Brigade moved east, Rhame ordered Maggart to pass forward of Moreno and continue to the 30 northing about ten kilometers forward of Phase Line Berlin. The remainder of the Division would then form on either side of the 1st Brigade. Maggart only knew that the three brigades would attack abreast. However, Rhame intended to attack in a Division wedge, with the 1st Brigade forming the tip; Moreno's 2nd Brigade and Weisman's 3rd Brigade would form the left and right wings. Somehow this information did not get disseminated or, if it was, it was widely misunderstood.

As he approached Phase Line Berlin, Maggart spoke to Moreno to coordinate passing. Moreno instructed him, "Pass your unit by the burning T-55 tank on the left."[41] Discrete lanes and markers that characterized the high-fidelity passage at the breach had now gone by the wayside. As a marker, Moreno's burning tank proved inadequate. As TF 2-34 AR approached the site of TF 3-37 AR's recent fight, Fontenot called Gross to confirm the rendezvous. LTC Gross announced that he was "by the burning tank." Fontenot responded, "Okay, partner. I see a bunch of burning tanks up there. Which one of those burning tanks is it?"[42] In the end, TF 2-34 AR found the right burning tank, as did the 1-34 AR. Having refueled while the others attacked, Maggart's brigade passed forward at 1:41 p.m.

By the time the 2nd Brigade reached Phase Line Berlin, the 4-37 AR was running on fumes. Because his fuel trucks had not turned up, Marlin needed help. Task Force 2-34 AR provided what it could. Clausewitz argued that offensive operations eventually culminate. In his view, friction assured that offensive operations could not be sustained indefinitely. The longer the offensive lasted, the more likely it would culminate, even in the absence of resistance. In Clausewitz's day and since, offensive operations often culminated logistically. Attacking forces run out of gas figuratively and/or literally. The 1st Division did not quite culminate at midafternoon on February 27, but it teetered on the edge. Running on the inside of the VII Corps' wide turn to the east, the Division had driven roughly 240 kilometers since 5:38 a.m. on February 24. And it had fought two major engagements along the way.

Sustaining the attack grew more difficult as it continued, simply because the distances grew longer. Understanding how supplies, in particular fuel, are brought forward is crucial to understanding how close the Division came to culminating in the last day and half of the ground attack. Logistics Base Echo, where the Division Support Command drew supplies, now lay three hundred kilometers to the rear. Fuel convoys originated even farther south.[43] Each of the Division's three maneuver brigades consumed 80,000–100,000 gallons of fuel daily; the Corps' two armored divisions, moving on the outside of the turn, used even more fuel. The 1 AD had to go farther than the rest of the Corps. As a consequence, Old Ironsides stopped at sunup, as it was about to run out of fuel. The 3AD sent enough to keep it moving, barely.[44]

Supplies move in loops—or at least that is doctrine. In theory, the way the loops work is simple. The fuel system required the VII Corps Divisions to back-haul empty fuel trailers to a supply point. There they would drop off empties and replace them with full fuel trailers. In Operation Desert Storm, the system worked this way, although the Corps delivered fuel all the way to the divisions when it could. In the 1st Division, COL Bob Shadley pushed fuel forward to reduce the burden. MAJ Michael Sevcik served as the support operations officer in the support battalion that provided for the 1st Brigade. Sevcik remembered getting 80,000–100,000 gallons in each push. As he put it, supporting the attack meant "game on."[45]

Within the brigades, battalions drove 2,500-gallon tankers to brigade support areas, where they topped off from Corps or Division 5,000-gallon tankers and returned to their units. The interlocking loops reduced line haul, or total travel distance, for each of the echelons. Fatigue, breakdowns, and navigation errors prevented zero defects execution. Some convoys, like those in TF 3-66 AR and the 4-37 AR, got lost. In others, drivers fell asleep at the wheel, ran into other trucks, or drove into some unexpected obstacle. The danger of driving into bomb craters was very real, but not something that had been imagined in training. Despite everything, logistics troops sustained the attack.[46]

To reduce line haul distances and distribute fuel forward, the 2nd Corps Support Command (COSCOM) supporting the VII Corps planned intermediate logistics bases along the planned zone of operation. On February 25, the 2nd COSCOM units moved out to establish Logistics Base Nellingen some sixty kilometers north of the border. Even with three million gallons of fuel stored at Logistics Base Echo and the capacity to haul three million gallons more, the Corps needed Logistics Base Nellingen. Each day, the VII Corps consumed at least two million gallons of fuel. To put this in perspective the VII Corps used twice as much fuel as World War II's famed Red Ball Express hauled on its best day.[47]

Logistics Base Nellingen could not be built, however, until combat and combat support units passed through the breach. MAJ Jim Martin, who helped build Nellingen, found the delay irritating but the mission exhilarating. While waiting to go forward on February 25, he wrote that it would "be massive if the war is not over before we get there. The convoy we're taking is massive." His convoy included the 300th Supply and Services Battalion, the 136th Water Battalion, the 4th Transportation Battalion, an explosive ordnance detachment, military police, and a contingent from the COSCOM Headquarters.[48] MAJ Martin and the Corps support troops began operating Logistics Base Nellingen late on February 26. That reduced the distance for fuel trucks from LTC Tom Waterman's 701st Main Support Battalion. Waterman had fifty-four 5,000-gallon tankers to support long haul. Each of the brigade support battalions fielded twenty 5,000-gallon tankers.[49] The Division had a capacity of more than a half million gallons of fuel in the tankers assigned to the Division Support Command. This total did not include the minimum authorized capacity of more than a quarter of a million gallons in the maneuver battalions alone.

Despite the best efforts of the logisticians at midday on February 27, the brigades had barely enough fuel. While the 2nd and 3rd Brigades refueled, the 1st Brigade pressed on. Soon after, Ritter's battalion overtook two Iraqi tanks and dispatched them without pausing. The Brigade reached the 30 grid line without further contact and slowed so the other two could form up on either side. There remained some confusion. Rhame, Carter, and the handful of troops who traveled with them may have understood what came next, but few others in the Division understood any more than "Go for the Blue." Determined to do just that, the Division continued east as fast as it could go, on the edge of culminating and barely in control.

At this point, the command and control system depended on "push to talk," with occasional face-to-face coordination. According to Maggart, the only time he could talk to Rhame reliably during a fight was on February 24. Often, orders reached units secondhand through relays. Franks could fly anywhere he liked, and when weather permitted he did so, as it was the best way for him to issue orders and assess his units. But commanding that way did not allow his Division commanders the chance to "eavesdrop" on instructions to others that provided context. In fact, Rhame had little choice in the matter. The VII Corps had moved too far, and too rapidly, for the command and control systems then available to provide a conference with his key subordinates. Further, he had no reliable means to communicate orders and intentions digitally. The Corps had not issued a written order since midnight on February 26, and that order was overcome by events before the sun rose.[50] The 1st Division had the least modern communications systems in the Corps, and it was now starting to show.

Before making his rounds early on February 27, Franks considered employing a double envelopment of the Iraqi operational reserve using the 1 AD and the UK 1 AD. Apparently he did not share his thinking with Carter in their morning meeting, but after visiting Carter, he decided instead to use the 1st Division as the southern enveloping force. Using the 1st Division would be far simpler than asking MG Rupert Smith to disentangle himself in the south and attack across both the 1st Division and the 3 AD. Once the 1 AD refueled, it would envelop from the north. Franks's planners drew an overlay illustrating the double envelopment. Shortly before noon, COL Stan Cherrie took off with the overlay to explain the plan to Rhame.[51] In the end, Cherrie briefed Carter, because Rhame was beyond reach in a tank far forward.

No one below the Division level received that overlay. Even if overlays had been issued, hardly anyone had maps to put them on. According to LTC Clint Ancker, when the 3rd Brigade moved out that morning, it posted its last 1:50,000-scale map sheets, which portrayed the ground only as far east as the Wadi al-Batin—figuratively, the edge of the world. At one point Rhame called a grid over the radio to Weisman and told him, "If you'll look at those coordinates, you'll see a tower." Weisman retorted that he was using a renumbered and blank 1:50,000-scale map sheet showing only grid lines and so could not see what Rhame thought he could. Rhame opined it was fine since there were so few geographical features anyway.[52] Operations now depended on GPS without the benefit of maps that could aid developing a common view.

Now LTG Franks introduced a far more complicated plan than attacking straight east, as he had ordered in the morning. This double envelopment plan required the 1st Division to make yet another turn; now it would turn from attacking east, as ordered at 7:15 a.m., to attacking northeast oriented on the northern part of the "goose egg" labeled Objective Denver. Rhame intended to bring all three brigades up and attack in a Division wedge. In the absence of terrain on which to orient the three brigades, he had somehow to turn without unraveling the formation. Just who besides Rhame and Carter understood exactly what the plan entailed is uncertain. The Division staff passed waypoints for the brigades to plug into their Magellans but provided little other guidance or information. The Division's planners did not do this maliciously but instead because giving more guidance just wasn't possible. Everything was moving fast.

COL Maggart's brigade reached the 30 grid line just before 2:00 p.m., with the other two on its heels. The weather, which had already shut down air operations, progressively worsened, as it seemed to do each day. Scudding clouds, blowing sand, and large raindrops reduced visibility and kept all but a handful of committed or foolhardy pilots on the ground. Push-to-talk warfare entered a new phase, with three brigades converging on waypoints that did not offset their routes. Those who still had maps to use had no control measures they could post on them. Confusion resulted.

At approximately 2:00 p.m. the 1st Brigade angled northeast, with TF 2-34 AR on the left and the 1-34 AR on the right. At least one company team in

TF 2-34 managed to drive through a minefield without setting off any of the mines. CPT Steve Youngberg of A Company, 1st Engineer Battalion (1 EN), chose not to lead his company through the same minefield; he reported the minefield and had his company mark it, so those who followed did not need to depend on luck. In low visibility CPT John Howell, the battalion motor officer, drove forward of the task force. When he realized his error he turned back and was nearly mistaken for the enemy. When the task force saw him, it considered shooting but, mindful of fratricide, waited. Howell escaped with his life when he was finally identified. Fifteen minutes later the 1st Brigade ran straight into defensive positions protected by a berm that extended across the zone. Both forward units immediately began a hasty breaching operation. LTC Ritter's battalion started through within four minutes, and LTC Fontenot's task force took a minute longer. During the breach, the assaulting units destroyed three tanks and a BMP.[53]

Things happened fast after this skirmish, because the 2nd Brigade overtook the 1st Brigade. LTC Gross's task force came up at high speed on Fontenot's left and moved slightly ahead. Effectively, TF 3-37 AR forced Fontenot's task force to its right, crowding the 1-34 AR in turn. LTC Ritter's battalion had to adjust as well. Next, Marlin's battalion motored through Fontenot's trailing units. Gross and Marlin were not acting in a cavalier fashion but were instead following waypoints in low visibility and moving quickly in order to catch up. Since they could not see clearly, they closed more rapidly than they otherwise would have. The waypoints neither accounted for the size of task forces nor defined routes, zones, or boundaries. No one in stationary command posts developed orders; all of this was done on the move by hand. That afternoon, the Division discovered yet again that although the shortest distance between two points is a straight line, it is not necessarily the right path to take. Even the relatively simple geometry needed to bring the three brigades together without incident was too much for tired plans officers.

To compound matters, the pursuit now caught up with the fleeing Iraqis. First Lieutenant Craig Borchelt's scout platoon in the van of TF 3-37 AR maneuvered in and around little moguls of dirt and slag on the edge of a surface mining operation that may have appeared on 1:50,000-scale maps. No one standing in a tank or Bradley turret had the necessary map sheets so the surface mining operation came as surprise. Visibility averaged no more than fifteen hundred meters and often closed down to half that. The already rough ground was further broken up by abandoned fighting positions, interfering with clear sight lines.[54] Borchelt's Bradleys appeared and reappeared as they made their way across the left front of TF 2-34 AR.

The close proximity of friendly forces alarmed Maggart because "the potential for fratricide increased exponentially."[55] Before his thinking went further, an enemy tank "exploded in a huge fireball about 200 meters directly to my left front."[56] The excitement had just begun. What happened next did so nearly simultaneously and thus much faster than one can describe it. Fontenot's task force precipitated a melee with a retiring Iraqi armor unit, with Borchelt's scouts between the two. The task force was moving in box formation, two tank teams forward and two infantry teams following.

CPT Bob Burns's Team C formed the left front corner of the box. Several of his tank crews reported seeing two enemy tanks. It is likely these tanks had just withdrawn from the defensive positions TF 2-34 AR and the 1-34 AR had cut their way through. Burns could see some of Borchelt's Bradleys, but he saw neither of the enemy tanks. He refused to let his thoroughly alarmed tank crews fire until he was satisfied that no friendlies stood in harm's way; this had been the injunction from his task force commander. Just then, at 2:45 p.m., SSG Norman L. James, tank commander of Charlie 12, saw a third enemy tank. James slewed his tank cannon on to the target he had seen from his perch in the tank commander's hatch. He asked his gunner, SPC Marc Penn, to identify. James remained with his head up outside the turret searching for other targets. Penn identified the tank "lased" it and received a range return of 690 meters. James could not break into the command frequency to report because another crew was reporting a fourth tank. Burns now had four or more enemy tanks nearby and moving among the TF 3-37 AR scouts he could see. He struggled to make sense of what he could see versus what he was being told. Then Penn and James saw their enemy tank reposition and traverse its turret toward a friendly. James could wait no longer and ordered Penn to fire. Penn did as he was told, and the tank blew up.[57]

SPC Penn's tank lay exactly on the line of sight between Fontenot and one of Borchelt's Bradleys. Neither Fontenot nor Burns had seen the tank, a T-55. At nearly the same time that Penn fired, the T-55 fired as well. Its round passed through the task force, shedding sparks as it went, but missed everyone. What Fontenot perceived was that someone fired and his troops returned fire and hit the Bradley that he could see. Believing James had killed a TF 3-37 AR scout, Fontenot yelled for a cease-fire on his command net and reported on the Brigade command net that "one of my guys fired on friendly unit to his left. They fired on us. We returned fire. I think it's a Bradley." Then more firing broke out, so he said, "these might be bad guys [and] I'm going lower [back on the TF 2-34 command net]."[58]

LTC Gross's task force found more of the enemy and began firing to their right at targets that TF 2-34 AR could not see, but were across its front. The task force could hear staccato cracks of 105-millimeter cannons and see flashes dimly through mist, dust, and banks of smoke. Marlin's battalion added to the cacophony by firing literally between friendly tanks. Fontenot's troops detected three more enemy tanks moving, but had no clear line of sight to fire. The enemy tanks disappeared north into the gloom. In less than five minutes, Gross's tanks dispatched perhaps twenty enemy tanks. One of Fontenot's tanks killed at least one more, as did the 4-37 AR. CPT John Tibbets, who could see only three Iraqi tanks, commented on Ritter's command net, "I think of three Brigades against three T-55s as overkill."[59] Ritter chose not to comment. Tibbets, like everyone else that afternoon, could not see the whole fight.

In short order, the 2nd Brigade reported that TF 2-34 AR had not shot a Bradley, and SSG James rightly went from goat to hero. Burns took some heat from his troops for tightly controlling fires as Fontenot had ordered. Some believed he had unnecessarily risked their lives, but James understood. Burns could have shifted responsibility for the order to his commander, but chose instead to behave as though the order was his own. He understood that, given the demonstrated ineptitude of Iraqi tankers, the risk of fratricide outweighed the threat.

COL Moreno continued his attack to the northeast. The 1st Brigade halted while its leadership considered what to do next. Both Ritter and Fontenot wanted to take a short halt and let the 2nd Brigade separate. In the few minutes since the fight began, visibility had closed to five hundred meters or less. Maggart called Rhame and explained the situation, telling Rhame he wanted to halt until the other brigades cleared. The commanding general, far enough forward to see the confusion for himself, concurred. The Division would have to attack in a wedge some other time. The 1st Brigade waited at the edge of the surface mining operation while the 2nd Brigade disappeared in the deepening murk on the left and the 3rd Brigade disappeared on the right.[60] By 3:30 p.m. daylight faded; low clouds, rain, blowing sand, and the smoke generated by the oil fires the Iraqis had set created an eerie early twilight.

TF 3-37 AR completed the task of destroying the enemy armor the 1st Brigade had assaulted from the march. The quarry in which the fight began was big and mazelike. LTC Gross's executive officer MAJ Tom Connors claimed, with fair accuracy, that the quarry was "about the size of Detroit;"[61] the thing was so big it seemed impossible to find a way around it. Gross managed to skirt the very edge of the quarry, but to those not as fortunate, it seemed an enormous and unearthly collection of holes, berms, and slag piles, like moguls on a giant's ski slope, unearthly in the growing darkness, an eerie moonscape. Gross's 3-37 AR continued northeast. Behind him and to the left of TF 2-34 AR, Marlin's battalion made its way through the edge of the quarry. In near darkness with no roads through the maze, unit integrity broke down. LTC Marlin, who had a Magellan, eventually led his battalion, single file, out of the morass and followed in Gross's wake.[62]

Around noon that day Rhame grudgingly granted the 3rd Brigade time to refuel, but exhorted it to get moving as soon as possible. He knew the Division was running out of time if it was to cut off any of the Iraqis fleeing Kuwait. Both because of time and available supply, the Brigade decided to ration fuel.

Weisman's logisticians hoped to pump one hundred gallons in every tank. They could not achieve that goal, so the Brigade would need to fuel again—and soon. Still low on fuel, the 3rd Brigade moved out and traveled on Moreno's right. It came up the 2nd Brigade's right flank without incident, but made contact soon after when Hillman's two tank companies destroyed several Iraqi tanks. The Brigade then also passed through part of the Kuwaiti Army's tank range complex, where target berms, hard targets, and spent training projectiles further complicated things.[63]

Traveling in separate tracked vehicles, Weisman and Ancker followed Brown's 2-66 AR. The 2-66 AR formed the tip of the wedge formation Weisman favored. Forward of them, one of Brown's tanks seemed to disappear in a ball of flame. Weisman said to Ancker over the radio, "Uh oh, I think we just lost a tank!"[64] They had not. Instead, one of Brown's tanks "crested a small rise and come [*sic*] face to face with an Iraqi [tank] at 25 meters." Both tanks traversed as quickly as they could. The 2-66 AR crew won the race.[65] Brown's tankers polished off four more T-55s in quick succession. Not long after, as night fell, Weisman halted his brigade before it ran completely out of fuel. MG Rhame reluctantly accepted what he could not change, but told Weisman to be ready to continue the attack at first light. The troops assumed hasty defense short of their part of Objective Denver. The Brigade had advanced one hundred kilometers and picked off the tail end of the withdrawing Iraqis.[66] Just as Clausewitz had once theorized, the 3rd Brigade's attack culminated logistically.

The Quarter Horse Cuts the Basra Road

Early on February 27, Wilson eavesdropped on the radio conversation between Rhame and Franks. He heard Rhame tell Franks he would get to Objective Denver by nightfall. The goose egg named Objective Denver would cut the highway to Basra and effectively complete the southern wing of Frank's double envelopment. Wilson's mission required him to screen the Division's left flank, but doing so was not, in his mind, an end in itself—getting to Denver was. The Quarter Horse moved northeast virtually unopposed. An airborne scout weapons team searched the area ahead within the limits imposed by weather. Unimpeded by the enemy, Wilson outpaced the three brigades. Around 4:00 p.m. the Quarter Horse (1-4 CAV) lost radio contact with the rest of the Division. To the south, Moreno's brigade was finishing off an enemy tank battalion and moving along the edge of the mining operation. Maggart's brigade was wending its way through the quarry. Weisman's brigade missed the quarry and continued to advance against light contact until it ran short of fuel.[67] All three brigades were well to Wilson's rear. He knew none of this, and could talk to no one who did.

In the absence of radio contact Wilson had to decide what to do. He rightly concluded that the squadron had gotten ahead of the Division. His choices were obvious. He could drive on to Denver, fulfilling Rhame's commitment to the Corps commander, but he might put the Division at risk of a counterattack on its flank. He could also defer the decision to Rhame by remaining in place securing the left flank until Rhame got close enough to reach by radio. Wilson, his operations officer, John Burdan, and the two ground troop commanders, Pope and Bills, met on the ground and mulled over their options, eventually deciding to continue to Denver. Meeting the Corps commanders' intent seemed to them to trump the security of the Division's flank and, as there had been no sign of enemy activity, the threat seemed minimal. Because Wilson's scouts could still fly, he did not realize that weather south of him had shut down visibility, effectively grounding helicopters. So he was mistaken in the belief that he could use his helicopters to let the Division know where he was and what he was doing when such became necessary.[68]

At 4:30 p.m. the Quarter Horse reached the northern end of Objective Denver and moved to cut the Basra highway. Wilson's squadron was in sight of the road that linked Basra with Kuwait City; it was fourteen kilometers south of the junction between that highway and the major highway that ran from Basra to Baghdad. The town of Safwan was eleven kilometers to the north. The rest of the Division was at least thirty kilometers south. To cut the road, he ordered Bills and B Troop to secure the west side of the highway and sent Pope and A Troop to occupy ground on the east side. Doing so would enable the squadron to block traffic in either direction.[69]

As the two ground troops approached the highway, a D Troop Cobra attack helicopter identified and destroyed two tanks with antitank missiles. SSG Gerald Broennimann, leading A Troop as it angled across to the east side of the highway, killed a BMP. "Fight's on" accurately described what came next. Pope's 1st and 2nd Platoons attacked northeast across the highway, while the 3rd Platoon and the troop's mortars crossed farther south and then turned north. Second Lieutenant James Copenhaver, the 1st Platoon leader, finished blocking the highway when his gunner killed a T-55 moving north on the highway. One of his tanks killed a second. His platoon sergeant, SFC William Molitor, identified two more, and his gunner destroyed both. When the firefight subsided, a dozen pyres marked destroyed enemy tanks and fighting vehicles.[70]

By nightfall, 1-4 CAV had all it could handle. Wilson, Pope, and Bills met briefly to organize a 360-degree defense of the newly established roadblock. Their plan was straightforward. A Troop defended from "12-6" and B Troop from "6-12." In the nineteenth century the 4th Cavalry Regiment earned a reputation as Indian fighters; now it literally circled the wagons against Iraqis heading north, desperate to get out of Kuwait.[71] To exacerbate matters the forward element of the 1-4 CAV had broken into three groups. The group at the highway included both ground troops. MAJ Bill Wimbish, the executive officer; Burdan, the operations officer; and the Squadron command post settled in eight kilometers southwest of the roadblock. Wimbish and Burdan could not move the command post because the weather had forced down the last airborne scout weapons team, so the pilots of the two aircraft had no choice but to land at the command post. Wimbish could not leave the two helicopters, so the command post remained where it was. Wilson did order Burdan forward to join him. CPT Doug Morrison led the third group. Morrison, who commanded the headquarters troop, was bringing logistics forward. As he neared the road, he could see the red and green tracers from the fight. Morrison called Bills to let him know he was coming and asked that Bills not "shoot me."[72]

Combat in the Rear: Wednesday, February 27, 1991

Since the Gulf War of 1991, it is not uncommon for soldiers and others to describe the contemporary battlefield as more complex than Desert Storm. The language used in the AirLand Battle doctrine, in place during Operation Desert Storm, contributes to the myth. AirLand Battle did describe the battlefield geometry of close, deep, and rear. Fire-control measures, including a fire support coordination line, a coordinated fire line, and a restricted fire line, convey linear geometry. The 1st Division communicated orders using these terms. Lanes, lines of departure, and phase lines also suggest precision and linear geometry. This geometry was just that descriptive. Cold War planners writing the General Defense Plain in Germany did not expect rear areas to be secure, nor did they expect to fight along continuous lines. The battlefield then and now was complex. Bypassed enemy units, line crossers, civilians on the battlefield, and special operations forces assured complexity about close, deep, and rear combat operations before, during, and since Desert Strom.

The Iraqis did develop a continuous front line from the coast of Kuwait to west of the Wadi al-Batin. The bulk of the two US Army Corps employed in Desert Storm went around the end of that line. To the north of the main defense, Al-Rawi built a length of contiguous line through which the VII Corps attacked on February 26–27. But the VII Corps had too few troops and too little time to "clear" its zone of attack consistent with the speed GEN Schwarzkopf demanded. As a result, there was no secure rear area north of the border berm. For that matter, bypassed enemy remained active for several days after the cease-fire. The danger was real enough that soldiers technically in the rear fought combat actions. The redoubtable CSM Vincent Conway, who with two other soldiers led the fight in 2-66 AR's rear during Fright Night, is perhaps the best case in point.

When the Division transitioned from exploiting the penetration of the Republican Guard to the pursuit, notions of front and rear made little sense. Both the difficulty of navigating and the lack of delineation between front and rear can be seen in the story of the 4-37 AR's missing fuel trucks. Late on February 25, when 4-37 AR support platoon leader 1LT Craig Thompson prepared to haul fuel forward to the 4-37 AR, he made an error in entering data in his Magellan GPS unit. When he realized his mistake, he returned to a known point, entered the correct data, and headed back with thirteen fuel trucks, arriving at his battalion's logistics base ("trains") on February 27. On his sojourn, he collected many vehicles that had been left along the way, either because they were in need of repair or for some other reason. When he reached the Brigade's rear area, Thompson assembled an impressive column that included the "lost" fuel trucks, supply trucks, and combat vehicles: three tanks, two Vulcan air defense artillery tracks from the 2nd Battalion, 3rd Air Defense Artillery, and two Bradleys from the 1-4 CAV.[73]

SSG William J. McCormick III and his tank, Alpha 12, joined the column and moved with it at 11:00 a.m. on February 27 to rejoin the battalion. McCormick coordinated the defense of the convoy with the other tank and track commanders, operating on a common radio frequency and organizing to fight. The tanks were battle ready except for one crew that failed to update its bore sight. At 7:00 p.m. the column hit a large group of Iraqi soldiers moving into trenches. The column halted, and McCormick brought a second tank up and maneuvered on the enemy, scaring twenty-two Iraqi troops into giving up. The crews disarmed the Iraqis and turned them over to a military police platoon that was traveling in the column. As the column prepared to resume moving, McCormick heard a Vulcan twenty-millimeter cannon firing to his rear. The Vulcan crew reported they had fired at Iraqi infantry. At about the same time, one of the Bradleys saw a T-72.[74]

McCormick and his teammate raced back to the column to cope with the T-72, but before they got halfway there, the Bradley struck it with a missile. They continued on up the column to resume their positions when McCormick's gunner identified a T-55 on the move. The enemy tank fired at the head of the still halted column, but missed. McCormick maneuvered to a firing position. His gunner, SGT Otis Harris Jr., killed the T-55 with a single round at 1,330 meters. Finally the column moved on and completed its journey through the rear area and reached the 4-37 AR early on February 28.[75]

On the morning of February 27, CPT Lee Wilson's B Company of the 1-41 IN had a brief fight some fifty kilometers to the rear of the 3rd Brigade. Not long after first light, SFC Paul Sedgwick, although lightly wounded, led an assault on a bunker, throwing in two grenades and killing all eleven occupants. Skirmishes in the rear and newly discovered Iraqis seeking to surrender produced large numbers of prisoners that nearly overwhelmed the 3rd Brigade's logistics troops; by 3:20 p.m. they had three hundred prisoners of war in the brigade support area. Some in the Brigade staff wanted to give them what food and water they had and send them on their way, but the Brigade provost marshal pointed out that they had assumed responsibility for their prisoners and should do no such thing. The problem grew larger. By 5:00 p.m. the 3rd

Brigade's trains had 450 Iraqis on hand, with 350 more on their way from forward units. The support battalion had only five hundred meals-ready-to-eat (MREs) on hand. Iraqi prisoners were literally eating them out of house and home.[76] Prisoners and enemy wounded stressed brigade trains, but mindful of the resolute provost marshal's reminder, it discharged its responsibility.

The 1st Brigade Culminates in the Valley of the Boogers

Within a half hour of seeing the other brigades disappear into the growing murk, Maggart ordered his brigade deeper into the surface mining operation. Although no one knew how large it was, nobody thought to seek permission to go around the quarry, believing they would get through it shortly. LTC Ritter assumed the lead as surface mining pits and mounds closed in on all sides. The mounds varied in size, but they were big enough and steep enough to force even tracked vehicles to go around them. Maneuver space narrowed as the Brigade continued, and soon it slowed to a crawl as it went deeper into what some soldier called the Valley of the Boogers. Just who coined the phrase is unknown, but it caught on. It has been used with perfect understanding ever since and is as surely a part of the Division's history as more romantically named battlefields. In the dark, the Valley of the Boogers seemed malevolent and scary. One minute the ground was more or less flat, and the next it was riven with mounds of dirt, ore, or who knows what. There was no apparent pattern in the mining.

Ritter's lead platoon found a trail that ran more or less in the right direction and took it. Barely wide enough for tanks, it appeared darker than the ground around it and proved to be hard-packed earth with a coating that reeked of crude oil. Jockeying for position, the companies of the two lead battalions merged, quite without intending to do so. No one wanted to be left behind, so control evaporated. CPT Juan Toro described what happened: "We were down to two battalions moving in column by intermixing columns, one of their [the 1-34 AR's] tanks, one of my tanks, one of their tanks, one of my tanks and so on."[77] Second Lieutenant Chuck Parker thought moving through the Valley of the Boogers "was very scary, because going through the maze you'd have like 12 feet of dirt 12 feet wide. And then you'd drop on the side for like 20 or 30 feet."[78]

The Brigade groped its way at a snail's pace, obstructed only by the terrain. Along the way, tank and Bradley commanders could see well-sited but unoccupied two-step firing positions for tanks or BMPs. These positions had one level that placed the entire fighting vehicle below the surface, with a second level the enemy could drive up on in hull defilade. These positions were much better than any they had seen before. At 6:20 p.m. satellite signals became iffy. Inexplicably, Ritter's receiver could still get signals from the necessary three, so he assumed the lead of the extended, intermingled column. A few minutes later he passed an abandoned Soviet-made Mnogotselevoy Tyagach Legky

Bronirovanny multipurpose light-armored towing vehicle. This was the only sign of an Iraqi presence since the earlier fight. In nearly three hours since the fight at midafternoon, the Brigade had traveled only twelve kilometers. COL Maggart, whose Bradley had broken down around 3:30 p.m., was on the move again, but ten or so kilometers behind Ritter.[79]

The "road" grew worse as the sun set and the murky afternoon transitioned to starless, inky night. Compass and satellites were the only means of determining direction. Drivers drove by feel; even with night-vision devices, they could see little. Ritter's driver managed to keep his tank on the road for a time by "steering away from the lean," but he eventually drove off the road and nosed down hard into one of the many pits that alternated with the equally ubiquitous mounds of spoil from the pits. As the tank slid downward, the angle grew so steep that Ritter's loader began sliding down the roof of the turret. Ritter grabbed his right leg and held on while the driver gunned the tank in reverse. Half climbing and half collapsing on the shoulder of the "road," he managed to get back up on the road just as Iraqi infantry assaulted the tank.[80] It was 6:30 p.m. and, though no one yet knew it, the Brigade had culminated.

The loader climbed back in his hatch and fired his M240 machine gun, while Ritter drew his M16A2 rifle.[81] The weapon was brand new, issued when the unit deployed. Although Ritter had qualified with the M16, the M16A2 was new to him. For twenty years he had known the M16 fired either single shot or automatic. In his excitement, he forgot the M16A2 fired single shot or three-round bursts. He wanted very much to kill the guys trying to mount his tank, so he turned the selector switch to what he believed was automatic fire, squeezed the trigger and fired a three-round burst. It killed the closest Iraqi, but the weapon stopped firing. He jacked the bolt back to clear his "jammed" weapon and fired another three-round burst that killed a second enemy soldier. His weapon "jammed" again, and he concluded that his new rifle was broken. With rounds traveling in all directions, he threw it aside and took up the AK47 he had liberated after the breach. Now he had an automatic weapon. Everyone on his tank was shooting except for the driver.[82]

To Ritter's rear and flank, the rest of the Brigade sat in single file in an S curve that extended about three kilometers. Because of the curving column, few could fire in support. SFC Ralph Martin's platoon could occasionally fire to either side of Ritter's tank. Farther back, other Iraqi infantry now appeared, but the main fight occurred at the head of the column and continued virtually all night. Maggart called Fontenot and asked him to report. Fontenot told him the Brigade had halted in single file, with no way to move forward and no way to maneuver. Still far enough back to have room to move, Maggart did not immediately grasp the problem. But eventually, "it was clear to me that we had driven into a tanker's worse [*sic*] nightmare . . . there was no room to maneuver and no room to shoot."[83] Maggart solicited Ritter for a second opinion. When Ritter answered the radio, Maggart could hear his machine guns rattling away. He said only, "Boss I am very busy right now. I will call you later!"[84]

During a short lull in his personal fight, Ritter took a call from Fontenot, who proposed to arrange their intermingled units for defense while Ritter resolved the contact. Maggart intervened, recommending a herringbone defense, and at 6:34 p.m. the Brigade set about assuming the position. A herringbone is a defensive formation units can use when ambushed or stopped on a road, though it had not been used in combat or even practiced much since the Vietnam War. Ritter was too busy to issue orders, so Fontenot coached their two battalions into position. (Baker's TF 5-16 was farther back and not affected.) Simply put, in a herringbone defense, tracked vehicles pivot to face in alternating directions on a road. The vehicle farthest forward—in this case, Ritter's tank—orients to the front. From there back, vehicles alternate, with one facing right front, the next left front, and so on. The vehicle farthest back faces in the direction the column came. This is an appropriate reaction to ambush on a narrow road if the unit is unable to drive through the "kill zone." Since no could move until Ritter resolved the fight, a herringbone was a good choice.[85]

Mindful that Rhame wanted to push on, Maggart reasoned further with Fontenot. Worn out and concerned about additional antiarmor ambushes, Fontenot agreed they could go on if they must. However, with the Brigade intermingled and no way to maneuver, he recommended they halt. Maggart got the picture, and around 7:00 p.m. he proposed to the commanding general that the Brigade stop. Rhame agreed, for two reasons: first, he, too, was in the morass or maze of surface mines and could see for himself the difficulty of moving, let alone fighting and moving; and second, the VII Corps ordered a halt just before Maggart called Rhame. Explicitly the Corps specified "all units to remain in place."[86]

The VII Corps issued the order to buy time to plan the next stage of the attack. In his memoir *Into the Storm,* LTG Franks described the increasing friction as the VII and XVIII ABN Corps turned east. From north to south, the 24 ID, the 1 AD (with the 1 CD behind it), the 3 AD, the 1 ID, and the UK 1 AD all were in some measure of contact and fighting. Six heavy divisions were attacking on a frontage of barely one hundred kilometers. LTG Franks's corps was fast running out of maneuver space; when he ordered the double envelopment, he had complicated matters. By late on February 27, the complicated maneuver combined with the scale of the attack became problematic. Although the 1 ID had transitioned from exploitation to pursuit, the same was not the case elsewhere. Both the 1 AD and 3 AD attacking east had not yet fully penetrated the Al-Medina and Tawakalna Divisions.

Franks intended only a short halt while planners developed new boundaries for the divisions. Tired staff officers at the Corps tactical command post ordered the halt, but failed to come back with instructions on the route and the order to resume the attack. The order to stop went out, but the Division did not come to a halt immediately. The Quarter Horse continued maneuvering to establish a sound defense of the roadblock. The 3rd Brigade culminated not long after due to lack of fuel. The 2nd Brigade was still moving northeast about twenty kilometers south of the cavalry and clear of the surface mine operation.[87] Mistakes made by tired people succeeded in doing what the enemy had not: they stopped the Division attack.

LTG Yeosock, despite working hundreds of miles away in Riyadh, sensed the growing friction and congestion. At his 5:00 p.m. evening update, he observed he was "[r]unning out of maneuver space in the VII Corps sector with five heavy divisions."[88] At 7:40 p.m. he ordered the Corps to "hold." The confusion between the 1st Division and the VII Corps no longer mattered. LTG Yeosock specified limits of advance or stop orders for the rest of the VII Corps. The gas already seeping from the bag now escaped rapidly: only momentum and inertia kept the Corps moving for a time.

"We Gotta Save Bobby": The 2nd Brigade Grinds to a Halt

COL Moreno avoided the worst of the Valley of the Boogers and continued northeast around 3:00 p.m. His brigade destroyed the tank battalion flushed out by the 1st Brigade. During the melee, TF 3-37 AR overran a "bunker complex" and captured a number of Iraqi soldiers including a brigadier general, the chief of administration of the 27 ID, one of the divisions manning the Iraqi defenses along the frontier.[89] From then until 6:00 p.m. the Brigade moved against no resistance. At 6:00 p.m., just after dark, one of CPT Tim Norton's tank platoons destroyed two enemy tanks. Norton's company destroyed five more tanks and three enemy armored vehicles soon after. First Lieutenant Randall Shannon, the task force fire support officer, hit the next tank. As Gross's task force moved, Shannon discovered a dug-in Iraqi tank oriented to take flank shots and maneuvered his track closer to it. He then dismounted with an AT4 short-range antitank missile launcher and moved to within fifty meters of it. Shannon dispatched the tank at close range, but barely escaped being burned by the blast from the catastrophic explosion that resulted.[90]

After the brawl with the tanks, Moreno found "no cohesive defense. You're running into a couple of tanks here, a couple of tanks there."[91] He knew he was through the last of the "organized" resistance, but he could also sense the Division attack was unraveling. By 6:00 p.m. the 2nd Brigade and two artillery battalions were out in front of the 1st Brigade. Moreno mistakenly believed he was perhaps ten or twelve kilometers ahead of the 3rd Brigade. In fact, Weisman had not yet stopped moving, but was behind. Also, both Moreno and Marlin had seen British units cross to their front, most assuredly outside their zone this far north. Later he observed that "about four kilometers in front of me a tank engagement begins and I know of no friendlies to my front."[92] Moreover, Gross and Marlin were not in close proximity to each other. Accordingly, Moreno closed his brigade up about 7:00 p.m. and sought "clarification of the boundaries and the friendly forces around us." This required relaying messages through several stations to reach Rhame, who was stuck in the quarry about fifteen kilometers back. Moreno convened an orders group at the command post of LTC Larry Adair's 6th Battalion, 41st Field Artillery. Assigned to the VII Corps artillery, Adair's battalion was reinforcing the Division artillery and generally following the Division. Adair had missed the mining operation altogether. He had his impedimenta, including his tactical operations center.[93]

Marlin left for the meeting with the understanding that the Brigade would halt for the night. He expected the meeting would review defensive measures, including his own mission to defend the two artillery battalions. He almost did not make it to Adair's command post, later noting, "It was so dark my driver drove into a deep pit."[94] Marlin's tank dropped about six feet; the impact shook the crew up, but they managed to get out of the hole and make it to the meeting. When Gross found the command post he was surprised: "Out of the clear blue there's a battalion TOC [tactical operations center] . . . Larry's got his TOC set up there and he's got his artillery battalion in direct lay [prepared for direct fire defense], because he didn't know where anybody else was."[95]

So Moreno and his commanders met in Adair's TOC. He began by asking Adair, "Can I use your radio?" Adair's headquarters troops had erected the RT 292 antenna, which greatly improved reception and transmission. LTC Adair said, "Sure I need help too."[96] When Moreno got on the division command net, LTC Bob Wilson, far ahead on Objective Denver and astride the Basra highway, interrupted with, "Hey I'm out here, I'm cut off. I need tanks; I need tanks now." Moreno told Wilson, "Bobby, we'll come as soon as—we got to get fuel, we got to get fuel. We'll be there."[97] Marlin had a side conversation with the brigade commander, during which Moreno said, "We gotta save Bobby."[98]

Out of fuel and desperate to relieve Wilson, Moreno gave up any ideas he may have had about waiting for the rest of the Division. He wanted to attack as soon as he could find fuel, and hoped to move about 7:30 p.m. Thanks to Adair's long antenna, he was able to reach Rhame. By this time Rhame had orders to hold at a limit of advance south and west of Moreno. Because of the limit of advance, Rhame told him, "Okay, I want you to withdraw 12 kilometers."[99] Gross claims that Moreno attempted a classic Army dodge upon receiving unwelcome orders by radio: the recipient simply claims the sender is coming in broken and unreadable.[100]

If Moreno tried that, it did not work. Moreno, every bit as aggressive in a fight as Rhame, debated the point with his commanding general. This was no trivial matter. He knew that Rhame's inclination was the same as his. He objected to giving up ground he had fought to take, saying, "I'm not willing to give it [the ground] back up and then have to fight through it again tomorrow." Not surprisingly, Rhame found that convincing. He told Moreno, "Okay hold your position."[101] But Moreno did not give up just yet. Rhame had not known of Wilson's dilemma, so Moreno followed up by saying, "We can get to Bobby Wilson in an hour and a half from attack time." The back and forth went on for a bit, because Rhame also wanted to "save Bobby." Rhame sought permission from the Corps but got none. Finally he told Moreno, "Do not move again until you hear my voice."[102] No one, least of all Rhame, liked leaving Wilson and his troops to their own devices.

The "Mother of All Briefings" and Unintended Consequences

At 9:00 p.m. GEN Schwarzkopf presented the now famous "mother of all briefings" to assembled journalists. When the news conference began, he knew the end was near. Earlier in the day, he and GEN Colin Powell had agreed to end the war late on February 28. Doing so would afford Yeosock's two Army corps time to complete the task of destroying the Republican Guard. He knew the VII Corps had destroyed the Tawakalna Division, most of the Al-Medina, and had eviscerated the Jihad Corps. The Adnan, Nebuchadnezzar, and Hammurabi Divisions remained more or less intact. CENTCOM had not yet accomplished the mission Schwarzkopf inferred from the guidance he had been given. As he began his remarks, Schwarzkopf had no reason to imagine the arrangement he reached with Powell on when to terminate the war would change.[103]

Schwarzkopf began the briefing in his persona as commander in chief of CENTCOM. He was businesslike, direct, and well rehearsed. In a half hour he reviewed the history of the campaign from the arrival of the first troops through the fighting going on that night. He made a point of telling his audience the fighting continued and sternly advised them combat is not a "Nintendo game." He asserted that the two Army corps had pushed what was left of the Republican Guard into what he called the Basra Pocket. He used charts to illustrate this point and others. After a crisp, even dazzling briefing, he took questions. He alternated between stern and avuncular, and it was clear he was enjoying himself. During the give-and-take with reporters he warmed to his task and made several unequivocal statements that had far-reaching consequences. First he said, "We've accomplished our mission." He then went on to add, "The gate is closed. There is no way out of there." He further claimed

Iraq could no longer threaten the region. Not surprisingly, several reporters pressed him about whether it was time to stop. It dawned on him that he may have gone too far. GEN Schwarzkopf attempted to soften his earlier hubris by insisting work remained to be done.[104]

In Washington, even more remote from the fighting, the enthusiasm for continuing the war ebbed rapidly. About 2:30 p.m., or a half hour after the "mother of all briefings," Powell provided an update to President George H. W. Bush and his key advisers. According to him, the president wondered aloud whether the war should stop, since it seemed the coalition had accomplished what it had set out to do. The images from the so-called Highway of Death stimulated concern about whether the coalition was going too far. The scenes on television suggested great slaughter. No one favored pounding the seemingly hapless Iraqi troops from the air. Furthermore, the UN mandate did not require destroying the Republican Guard or the Iraqi Army; the coalition existed only to restore Kuwait. Still, despite the growing unease among the allies and ugly images on television, President Bush was prepared to continue the fight. According to Rick Atkinson, in his book *Crusade*, the president asked Powell whether he wanted another day. Despite having agreed earlier to fight another day, Powell chose not to make the case to continue; instead he called Schwarzkopf from the Oval Office to solicit his opinion. At the outset of the call he told his field commander, "The thinking is we should end it today." Quite rightly, Atkinson found this was not "a formulation that invited demurral."[105] Of course, Schwarzkopf acquiesced. On the basis of the information he had, and the mandate, the president decided to declare a cease-fire.

In Washington all that was left to decide was when to stop and when to tell Schwarzkopf to make it so. Originally the decision makers thought they would declare a cease-fire effective at 5:00 a.m. local in Iraq on February 28. Schwarzkopf called Yeosock at 11:00 p.m. on February 27 to tell him the war would end at 5:00 a.m. What Schwarzkopf wanted to know was whether the orders to stop would get to the troops in time. LTG Yeosock thought so, but he frequently reminded those around him, "There are eight echelons between me and the guy in the tank."[106] He wanted to issue clear orders and intentions, because he understood that stopping the war would be far less straightforward than starting it had been. Just how the thing ended would not be up to those in Washington or Baghdad; rather, it lay in the hands of coalition and Iraqi troops on the ground.

Merely deciding a time to stop shooting does not end ambiguity, uncertainty, and danger on the battlefield. Richard M. Swain's *"Lucky War"* is the best operational narrative of what transpired between Washington, Riyadh, and the troops in the field. Swain shows that just as in the child's game of Crack the Whip, the troops eight echelons down from Yeosock experienced high levels of centrifugal force. Depending on how you count them, the "guy in the tank" was at least twelve echelons removed from the Oval Office. At 11:10 p.m. Yeosock called Franks, the seventh echelon from the guy in the tank, and told him to stop his attack—including deep operations—because a cease-fire was in the offing. At 2:00 a.m. on February 28, the 3rd Army followed up with Fragmentary Order 67, *Potential Temporary Cease-Fire*. Using the words *Potential* and *Temporary* may have been intended to assure that the VII and XVIII ABN Corps remained instantly ready to attack. If so, it did not work. According to Swain, "both Corps" took the order to mean cease-fire at 5:00 a.m. and not cease-fire maybe. When COL Stan Cherrie got the word, he thought, "I'm going to live through this son of bitch";[107] his feelings likely reflected those of all 146,000 soldiers in the VII Corps. By the early morning hours, the VII Corps, practically out of fuel anyway, came to a halt, presuming a cease-fire at 5:00 a.m.[108]

The "guy in the tank" knew only that he had been told to stop. Meanwhile, deep in the heart of the Valley of the Boogers, the 1st Brigade and Iraqi infantry continued to bang away ineffectually at each other. The Iraqis raised the ante a bit by firing a few mortar rounds, but with no better results. Alone astride the highway to Basra, the Quarter Horse continued to take prisoners, hoping very much that someone would soon come to help them. The cavalry heard a roaring noise all night that to them suggested the Iraqi Army was bypassing their roadblock. Both the 2nd and 3rd Brigades still needed fuel. Across the battlefield, some young officers and noncommissioned officers could no longer make radio contact with their commanders and thus continued to execute their last order.

This is the situation in which 1LT Dave Carter, the support platoon leader in TF 2-34 AR, found himself. At midday on February 27, Carter's platoon passed fuel to both TF 2-34 AR and the 4-37 AR. Afterward, he led his fuel trucks back to the brigade logistics trains, where fuel had arrived from Log Base Nellingen. There they topped off their tankers and slept for a few hours. After nightfall they set off to rejoin the task force, knowing it would need fuel at first light. Carter contacted TF 2-34 AR by radio and headed for the grid, northeast of the Valley of the Boogers, where the task force logisticians claimed they would be by sunup. Carter's GPS took him by the shortest route to that point, but arrived to discover that the task force was nowhere to be seen. (In fact, it was still stuck in the Valley of the Boogers.) Prudently, he found a place from which he believed his platoon could defend themselves and literally circled the wagons.[109]

Carl von Clausewitz's description of the disorganizing effects of victory can be seen at work both in the desert and in the conversations among decision makers. Experiences similar to Carter's played out across the theater, because the pursuit intermingled with the pursued. Many commanders could not say just where their units were; some had strung out during the pursuit, while others had separated into small groups. This was the essence of the problem for Yeosock and his corps commanders. First they had to get everyone stopped, and then they had to find out where everyone was. Finally, they had to pass instructions. Even if the coalition proved able to stop and locate its troops, no one could assure the other side could do the same. Ending the war seemed in some ways more difficult than fighting it. Washington and Riyadh contributed to the disorganization by issuing equivocal orders. Finally, the possibility of being the last one killed in a short war did not have broad appeal.

Deciding where to establish positions to support the final phase of the operation, separating the combatants and defending Kuwait, had to be done with imperfect information and in very little time. When Franks took the call from Yeosock, he asked, "Why now?" Yeosock responded, "I already told the CINC [commander in chief] we needed another day. But I'll try to get this clarified."[110] The Corps issued its own orders. Franks believed that, with the confirmation about cease-fire, "air went out of the balloon." The Corps may well have culminated when the *Potential Temporary Cease-Fire* order went out. Exhausted, Franks went to sleep. Not long after, Cherrie lay down under a poncho to ward off mist and intermittent rain.

Meanwhile, Washington decided to crack the whip once more. Sometime between midnight and 3:00 a.m. Powell called Schwarzkopf to tell him the cease-fire would be at 8:00 a.m. rather than 5:00 a.m. According to Powell, stopping at 8:00 a.m. would make Desert Storm "a hundred hour war."[111] The thousands of soldiers, sailors, airmen, and marines who had been in the desert since August and those who started shooting on January 17 may well have objected to that pithy epithet, but no matter. As Schwarzkopf put it, "I had to hand it to them: they really knew how to package an historic event."[112]

Reminded by his chief of staff that a large chunk of the Republican Guard remained at large, Schwarzkopf called back minutes later. He told Powell, "If we call this cease-fire we're going to see Republican Guard T-72s driving across pontoon bridges."[113] After checking, Powell told Schwarzkopf that the White House could live with some tanks getting away. Schwarzkopf turned to the final "crucial matter to resolve: where to halt the ground advance."[114] He directed the taking of one last objective: he told Yeosock he wanted the junction of the Basra–Kuwait City highway and the Basra–Baghdad highway blocked if it could be done without a big fight. Yeosock promised nothing, but thought that the 1st Division could reach the junction prior to 8:00 a.m.[115] Schwarzkopf issued this order to reduce the number of enemy T-72s that got away.[116]

Schwarzkopf awakened Yeosock at 3:00 a.m., and Yeosock woke Franks at 3:15 a.m. Cherrie took a call from BG Steve Arnold, his counterpart at the 3rd Army, at the same time. Yeosock notified Franks that the ceaseCfire would occur at 8:00 a.m. rather than 5:00 a.m. Just hours before, the emphasis had been on avoiding contact and assuring no one got hurt, but now the emphasis had changed: Yeosock wanted maximum destruction of the enemy by 8:00 a.m. In fact, the order to achieve maximum destruction actually came from

CENTCOM. Furthermore, Yeosock passed on Schwarzkopf's order—that he wanted the VII Corps to get to the road junction near Safwan. According to Cherrie, Arnold was emphatic about the need for the VII Corps to stop enemy traffic using the junction through which he claimed the Iraqis were escaping. LTG Franks thought the order puzzling. Given that the 1 ID had cut the road south of the junction, he did not see how the junction north of the roadblock mattered. He also complained that this was the third Army-level order in twelve hours. Changing tasks for a corps of more than 146,000 people is not a trivial matter.[117] Unlike ships at sea, which can turn relatively quickly, the same cannot be said of a fully mounted corps in combat. Once stopped, a large combat formation mimics Newton's law of inertia. In his notes on the order Yeosock's executive officer wrote that it was not "guidance translated into action quickly."[118]

But orders were orders. COL Cherrie looked at the last known locations of Corps units. Unlike Yeosock, he concluded that no one could reach the junction by 8:00 a.m., thus issuing an order to take it made no sense. He and Franks decided that stopping enemy traffic through the highway junctions was the critical task. If they could do that they would meet the intent. The quickest way to achieve the desired result was to use Apaches to attack enemy traffic passing through the highway interchange. Franks ordered the rest of the Corps "to attack in the same direction with the same objectives we had been using prior to the early evening adjustments."[119] The Corps issued the order by radio at 4:06 a.m., specifying 5:00 a.m. as the time of the attack. Franks acted in good faith given the conditions; he ordered the possible rather than attempt the impossible. But centrifugal force and friction now combined to confound him.

At Danger Forward, the record of the order is a handwritten entry scrawled on the Daily Staff Journal, "Jayhawk 6 [Franks] gave notice to Danger 7 [Carter] that the DIV Will move to highway. Danger 7 gave notice to Danger 6 [Rhame]." BG Carter indeed passed the order to Rhame, still stuck in the Valley of the Boogers. Rhame responded succinctly, "You mean they want us to move the entire Division in one hour! What insanity."[120] He told Carter to tell the Corps that the Division would attack at 6:00 a.m. He understood the intention was to resume the attack east to assure the highway from Kuwait City was cut. No mention of an attack north had been made in the order radioed from the VII Corps.

At 5:02 a.m. the VII Corps advised the 1st Division that the 11 AVN would attack the road junction. Corps wanted to assure clear air space and that no friendlies were nearby. At 5:07 a.m., upon learning the location of the Quarter Horse, the Corps canceled the 11 AVN attack and directed the Division to use its Apaches instead. At 5:10 a.m. the Division ordered the 4th Brigade to reconnoiter the highway north up to the junction and to attack any enemy traveling on the highway or through the interchange. COL Mowery understood that the mission required his attack helicopters to "destroy all enemy moving north of the division sector occupied by the ground forces."[121] In practical terms, that meant everything north of the 1-4 CAV on Objective Denver to the highway intersection. At 5:15 a.m. Cherrie issued coordinates assigning a new boundary that included the junction but with no order to take it. This chunk of ground was truly weird, as it formed a small box "perpendicular to the current division orientation." The duty officer at the 1st Division did record an additional order to "reconnoiter to the coastal highway just short of the junction."[122] For perfectly understandable reasons, only Apaches were going to attack the highway interchange. The Corps assumed that the 1 ID would seize the junction in due course. MG Rhame, on the other hand, planned to attack east in accordance with what he understood he was to do.

MAJ Mark Landrith, the 1-1 AVN operations officer, developed the plan. The attack battalion planned to launch at 5:30 a.m. and head east to the Basra–Kuwait City highway, forward of the advancing ground forces. The attack battalion's zone of action was north of the 1-4 CAV and included the junction, although attacking the junction itself was not the purpose: destroying any enemy traffic was. LTC Ron Reichelderfer committed his entire battalion. Weather had kept the attack battalion on the ground the night before, so his pilots had slept some. Landrith would lead with B and C Companies. Reichelderfer originally planned to follow with A Company, but instead flew in tandem with Mowery to reconnoiter the highway ahead of the battalion. About fifteen kilometers west of the highway, the weather grew worse until the battalion was "almost hovering." Landrith estimated that the ceiling dropped down to "50 feet and the visibility was less than 1/4 mile."[123] Up to this point, the battalion had had no contact, although it had managed by gesture to cause several Iraqis to throw down their weapons. He saw one Apache crew hover low enough over a bedraggled group of Iraqis to drop MREs and water.[124] Visibility was so bad that the attack battalion diverted to their planned assembly area short of the Basra–Kuwait City highway. To get there the 1-1 AVN resorted to using a technique that required more courage than sense.

CW3 Larry "Caspar" Le Blanc flew their aircraft so Landrith could control the fight. When the murk closed in to the point where he could no longer be sure of seeing the ground over the nose of his aircraft, Le Blanc turned the Apache ninety degrees to the direction of flight and continued sideways. Looking out of the side of his canopy, Le Blanc could see the ground. Landrith described the method on the command net. The attack battalion adopted it and groped its way east at about forty knots. This was slow going, but preferable to crashing or giving up. After an amazing piece of flying, the 1-1 AVN neared the assembly area with the cease-fire time nearly at hand. Landrith acquired and identified several enemy vehicles near the patch of ground where the battalion intended to land. Shortly before 8:00 a.m. he destroyed two tanks, a

Soviet-made Bronetransportyor armored transporter, and an air defense artillery piece with his thirty-millimeter cannon.[125]

Meanwhile, Mowery had lifted off at about 7:00 a.m. in an OH-58D scout helicopter. He struggled with the same awful weather the attack battalion faced but linked up with Reichelderfer and found a way through the murk to the 1-4 CAV. There the weather seemed better. He and Reichelderfer flew the highway north, destroying three tanks en route to the interchange. Once they reached the junction they remained in the area until about 9:00 a.m. but saw no enemy vehicles. In fact, the main body of Iraqis had gone through before Wilson cut the highway from Kuwait City the prior afternoon. Most of the Iraqis who survived the attacks on the highway had already escaped, as had the three Republican Guard Divisions that withdrew during the night of February 26–27.

On his way south to land at the assembly area, Mowery checked in with his tactical command post. He was told that Rhame wanted to see him because the Apache battalion had fired at the command group. COL Mowery climbed to a higher altitude so he could reach Rhame by radio. When he did, the conversation "was ugly."[126] It turned out that the command group had been near the enemy vehicles Landrith destroyed. MG Rhame thought his small group was next. After Mowery explained what happened, "the subject was dropped." Tired people ordered hither and yon, and guns firing, do not make for calm, reasoned discussions.

COL Maggart's brigade missed the 6:00 a.m. time of attack for two reasons. First, as soon as it became light enough to see, the enemy—which had been bellicose the night before—gave up in droves. Among them an Iraqi lieutenant asked LTC Fontenot if he could be allowed to take his fourteen soldiers to their home in Nasiriyah. Fontenot told the officer that with more than two hours until cease-fire it was too dangerous to walk the sixty kilometers to Nasiriyah. After disarming the lieutenant and his group, the task force gave them cigarettes, water, MREs, and directions to the rear.[127]

Second, the Brigade needed time to untangle and get clear of the surface mining operation. Maggart did tell Rhame he could not mount a coordinated attack at 6:00 a.m., but he determined the Brigade would do what it could. Maggart ordered each of his three maneuver units to send a company forward as soon as it could be separated from the gaggle. This took time. Ritter was at the head of the column, so one of his companies would go first. Ritter and Fontenot arranged between them for Fontenot to separate the units. Fontenot found a wide spot in the trail where he could wave by 1-34 AR vehicles and shunt off his own. CPT Jim Bell's C Company moved first. He cleared the Valley of the Boogers and broke out into open, flat desert just before 6:30 a.m. He had spent the night only a kilometer short of the exit from the infernal quarry. After a night in the Valley of the Boogers, the flat, open desert looked good. The rest of the battalion followed minutes later. At 6:25 a.m. Ritter's gunner hit a T-55, and soon after bagged another. Shortly after, Fontenot launched his scouts and CPT Toro's Team B under the command of MAJ Jack Crumplar to find and secure Carter's support platoon. At 7:23 a.m. the Division ordered cease-fire immediately. At 7:37 a.m. Fontenot quit playing traffic cop when LTC Skip Baker reached his position. With the trail out of the quarry clear, the Brigade continued east, desperate for fuel.[128]

Maggart got under way in his high-mobility multipurpose wheeled vehicle (HMMWV), having had enough of his Bradley for a while. As he headed out he passed Rhame's group, also preparing to move. Once clear of the Valley of the Boogers, Rhame headed off to his firing incident with Landrith. Maggart arrived at the 1st Brigade's designated objective after the 8:00 a.m. cease-fire and ahead of his battalions. There he found an Iraqi armor unit in a defensive formation oriented west. He cautiously approached the enemy tanks with only his HMMWV driver covering him. The tanks had been abandoned. Maggart "seized" his Brigade's last objective personally.

COL Moreno's day began at 4:15 a.m. with a call from Rhame. They went back and forth for about fifteen minutes, but the gist was straightforward: Rhame wanted to know whether Moreno could cut the Basra–Kuwait City highway. When Moreno replied, "Absolutely," Rhame asked, "Can you cut the road before 8:00?" Moreno responded, "Without a doubt." To this Rhame ordered an "attack."[129] He also gave Moreno operational control of the 1-4 CAV. At last, the 2nd Brigade could "save Bobby." Moreno passed his orders to his outfit, which included the two maneuver units led by Gross and Marlin, the two artillery battalions led by Adair, and Gingrich and Hawkins's 1 EN. He planned to attack with the 4-37 AR out front and TF 3-37 AR trailing on Marlin's right. He chose to attack in echelon, "anticipating that the greatest threat was going to be people trying to get out of the way."[130]

Marlin moved out in dense fog and oily black smoke at 5:30 a.m., Moreno and his command group at 5:45 a.m., and Gross at 6:00 a.m. A few minutes later, unable to see his two armor formations, Moreno asked them to report their GPS locations and discovered he was ahead of the tanks and Bradleys. Worse still, they expected only enemy to their front. Asking everyone not to shoot, he stopped to let his 2nd Brigade catch up. Soon after, Norton's company team pulled up alongside him and thereafter the Brigade continued on as intended, reaching the highway at roughly 7:00 a.m., dispatching several enemy tanks along the way. At 7:23 a.m. the 2nd Brigade received the cease-fire order. Within an hour, it detained two thousand Iraqi soldiers, and it would take in one thousand more during the course of the day.[131]

Shortly after 4:00 a.m. COL Dave Weisman issued his order for the 3rd Brigade to attack at 6:00 a.m. Weisman planned to seize the Kuwaiti Army barracks located on the Basra–Kuwait City highway. Weisman understood the job was to cut off retreat "and destroy as much enemy equipment as we could before the cease-fire."[132] His brigade attacked at 5:30 a.m., led by Brown's scout platoon. The scouts located and bypassed some enemy armor, but passed their grid coordinates. At 6:00 a.m. the rest of the Brigade moved out in their customary wedge. LTC Brown's battalion killed the enemy tanks his scouts reported. There was no further contact, although the Brigade cleared bunkers and destroyed a great many abandoned tanks, BMPs, and artillery as it headed east. At 7:15 a.m. Weisman's troops reached the barracks and secured both sides of the highway.[133]

The 3rd Brigade used up what little fuel it had to reach the highway. When fuel caught up, Jones pumped 490 gallons into his two fuel tanks. With a capacity of 505 gallons, Jones had been virtually running on fumes. The 3rd Brigade arrived on the edge of an inferno of thirty wellheads set afire by the Iraqis. The sky was black with oily smoke. The image was grim; to Ancker it looked like "the set from a science fiction movie about the apocalypse or the aftermath of Armageddon." The sun, when it was visible, appeared as a dull disk behind a curtain of black. At 7:30 a.m. the 3rd Brigade was given a cease-fire order. The Brigade turned to the task of coping with hundreds of Iraqi soldiers clamoring for food and water and "began the job of occupying Kuwait, helping to enforce the peace, and providing what assistance we could to the victims of the war."[134]

The 1-4 CAV spent an uneasy, sleepless night astride the highway. No great horde of Iraqis attacked the squadron, but Iraqis headed north steadily. Some wanted to give up, and others wanted to fight their way through. Using night-vision devices, the cavalry troopers tried not to shoot those who wanted to give up. In *The Road to Safwan*, Steve Bourque and John Burdan point out that "it was difficult to differentiate one group of Iraqis from another."[135] LTC Wilson worried about the proximity of the Republican Guard. It was probably best that he did not know how much of the Hammurabi Division was positioned nearby. Some Hammurabi units were no more than fifteen kilometers north of him, in and around the airfield at Safwan. LTG Yeosock's staff at the 3rd Army estimated that the Iraqis had eighteen heavy battalions (armor or mechanized infantry) and twelve infantry battalions in and around Basra, less than thirty kilometers farther north.[136] The Quarter Horse would have been at risk in the event of a counterattack.

During the night the cavalry killed some Iraqis but captured far more. At dawn, the 1-4 CAV counted two thousand Iraqi prisoners of war in its "pen." A kerfuffle had occurred during the night when some of the Iraqi troops "grumbled and grew rebellious." What happened next resolved the matter. One of the troopers on guard carried an "over-and-under" combination M16 and forty-millimeter grenade launcher. Intending to fire a warning shot with his M16 he accidentally fired a grenade that exploded at the edge of the prisoners' pen. According to Bourque and Burdan, "From then on, the prisoners gave the guards no trouble."[137] Wilson's surgeon concluded that several wounded prisoners might die if they could not be evacuated. Air evacuation unit Lonestar Dustoff tried twice to get through, but the weather forced it to turn back both times. Squadron surgeon MAJ Roger Hansen and his medics kept the wounded prisoners alive, and they were evacuated on February 28. During the night, Hansen and his soldiers treated some 450 wounded prisoners.[138]

At dawn, Wilson's troopers could see Safwan Mountain twelve kilometers to the north. The mountain loomed nearly five hundred feet above the surrounding desert. From there, an observer could see how isolated Wilson and his troops were. The cavalry could also see the devastation of the oil fields to the east. The roaring sound heard during the night had not come from Iraqis escaping north but from burning wellheads. COL Moreno and his brigade arrived soon after the cease-fire. He had agonized over not being allowed to "save Bobby." When he saw B Troop commander CPT Mike Bills, Moreno dismounted and hugged him. Then he got on with moving units in to help the cavalry deal with the many prisoners they had taken. And so the shooting war came to an end.

NOTES

1. General H. Norman Schwarzkopf with Peter Petre, *It Doesn't Take a Hero: The Autobiography* (New York, Bantam, 1992), 380–83, 455–60.

2. Carl Von Clausewitz, *On War*, trans. and ed. Michael Howard and Peter Paret (Princeton, NJ: Princeton University Press, 1984), 263, 531.

3. Ahmed 'AbdallahSaleh, interview, *Al-Qadisiyah*, May 3, 1992, translated by and courtesy of COL Reserve Pesach Malovany, Israel Defense Forces.

4. Kevin M. Woods, *The Mother of All Battles: Saddam Hussein's Strategic Plan for the Persian Gulf War* (Annapolis, MD: Naval Institute Press, 2008), 236.

5. Ibid.

6. Ibid., 238–39.

7. Ibid., 236–39. See also Stephen A. Bourque, *Jayhawk: The VII Corps in the Persian Gulf War* (Washington, DC: Center of Military History, 2002), 314–15, 376–80.

8. Woods, *The Mother of All Battles*, 239.

9. See Woods, *The Mother of All Battles*, chaps. 8 and 10. As Woods notes, because the coalition did not continue the attack, Saddam concluded he had won after all (241).

10. Schwarzkopf, *It Doesn't Take a Hero*, 466–67. This is proof positive of the gap between line units three hundred miles to the north and the headquarters in Riyadh. Schwarzkopf gloated that the VII Corps had attacked all night and

had not lost a tank, and that is decidedly inaccurate. In the race to publish, GEN Schwarzkopf got it wrong.

11. Ibid., 467.

12. MAJ Michael R. Barefield, personal journal, February 27, 1991.

13. LTG (Ret.) William G. Carter III, telephone interview with the author, July 6, 2015.

14. Carter interview.

15. Tom Clancy with General Fred Franks Jr., *Into the Storm: A Study in Command* (New York: Berkley, 2004), 500. A Boyevaya Mashina Pekhoty, or BMP, is a Soviet-made infantry fighting vehicle

16. Ibid.; Carter interview.

17. Clancy, *Into the Storm*, 500.

18. Ibid., 504.

19. LTG (Ret.) Thomas G. Rhame, telephone interview with the author, February 3, 2015, quoting from Rhame's personal journal, February 27, 1991. Rhame kept rough notes in a memo book during the day; when he had time, he transcribed the notes to his journal. He does not recall when he transcribed the notes from February 26–27.

20. Ibid.

21. COL James L. Mowery, "Saudi Journal," February 27, 1991.

22. US Department of the Army, *Division Operations*, FM 71-100 (Washington, DC: US Department of the Army, 1990), 4–27.

23. Rhame interview, February 3, 2015, quoting from Rhame's personal journal, February 27, 1991.

24. US Department of the Army, *Division Operations*, 4–28.

25. Rhame, interview, February 3, 2015, quoting from Rhame's personal journal, February 27, 1991.

26. MG (Ret.) Lon E. Maggart, "Eye of the Storm (Duty First)," unpublished manuscript, 1992–97, 175.

27. Ibid., 175.

28. LTC Clinton J. Ancker, "2nd Armored Division (Forward) and the Gulf Conflict," unpublished manuscript, Naval War College, Newport, RI, n.d., 227–28.

29. Ibid.

30. COL (Ret.) Oscar J. Hall, telephone interview with the author, July 13, 2015. Hall served as the logistics officer for the 4-37 AR. The support platoon leader made a not uncommon error: at night, and tired, he mistakenly entered the wrong grid zone designator. He faithfully followed his GPS directions to coordinates that took him west toward Syria rather than north toward the 4-37 AR. He did not realize his error until he saw the sun rising to his rear rather than on his right. He turned and led his troops on a fifty-hour sojourn to find the battalion, picking up numerous lost or recently repaired 2nd Brigade vehicles

on his way. The missing trucks rejoined the battalion early on February 28. See also COL (Ret.) Thomas Connors, BG (Ret.) David F. Gross, and MG Paul Izzo, oral history group interview by Andrew Woods, McCormick Research Center, First Division Museum at Cantigny, Wheaton IL, January 22–23, 2011.

31. Connors, Gross, and Izzo interview.

32. Rhame interview, February 3, 2015, quoting from Rhame's personal journal, February 27, 1991. LTC David W. Marlin, "History of the 4th Battalion, 37 Armored Regiment in Operation Desert Shield/Storm," unpublished manuscript, US Army War College, Carlisle, PA, 1992, 430–40; 1st Brigade, 1st Infantry Division, daily staff journal, February 27, 1991; Connors, Gross, and Izzo interview.

33. Clausewitz, *On War*, 207

34. Ancker, "2nd Armored Division (Forward)," 236–37.

35. The 3rd Brigade killed at least two tanks as it crossed the line of departure. Ancker, "2nd Armored Division (Forward)," 232; LTC James L. Hillman, interview, Fort Bliss, TX, June 8–10, 1992.

36. Connors, Gross, and Izzo interview.

37. Ibid.

38. Marlin, "History of the 4th Battalion, 37 Armored Regiment," 441.

39. Ibid., 440–41.

40. 2nd Battalion, 34th Armor, D Team, TF 2-34 AR radio net during the night of February 26–27, 1991, transcript by SPC James Clemens, n.d.; times are not annotated, provided by LTC (Ret.) John Bushyhead. D team was a mechanized infantry company team composed of two mechanized infantry platoons from D Company, 5-16 IN, and one tank platoon from C Company, 2-34 AR. "Guidons" is the pro word, meaning "all stations," that precedes instructions for all subunits.

41. Maggart, "Eye of the Storm," 177.

42. Connor, Gross, and Izzo interview.

43. Headquarters, 1 ID (M) DISCOM, "Desert Shield/Desert Storm Support Operations," January 15, 1992, 4 and annex O. See also 2nd COSCOM, "Operations Desert Shield/Storm: Logistics in Motion," postwar operations briefing.

44. Clancy, *Into the Storm*, 509–10.

45. COL (Ret.) Michael C. Sevick, interview with the author, Leavenworth, KS, April 3, 2015.

46. Headquarters, 1 ID (M) DISCOM, "Desert Shield/Desert Storm Support Operations," annex O. The 1 ID DISCOM issued 1,020,000 gallons of diesel fuel during the four days of the attack. COL (Ret.) Michael C. Sevcik, interview with the author, Leavenworth, KS, April 3, 2015.

47. The Red Ball Express Operated in France in 1944 and managed about 800,000 gallons a day. Fuel usage for the Corps is extrapolated from data cited

in Headquarters, 1 ID (M) DISCOM, "Desert Shield/Desert Storm Support Operations," annex 0.

48. MAJ James B. Martin, personal journal, February 26, 1991.

49. Headquarters, 1 ID (M) DISCOM, "Desert Shield/Desert Storm Support Operations," 4–5. The 701st also supported the 4th Brigade and Division artillery. Direct support artillery battalions brought organic tankers forward.

50. The VII Corps issued fragmentary order (FRAGO) 144-91 at midnight on February 26, 1991 and FRAGO 145-91 at 3:00 a.m. on February 28, 1991.

51. Clancy, *Into the Storm*, 514–15.

52. Ancker, "2nd Armored Division (Forward)," 240–41.

53. 1st Brigade, 1st Infantry Division, daily staff journal, February 27, 1991. Author's recollection regarding 1LT John Howell escaping being shot.

54. Connors, Gross, and Izzo interview; author's recollection. See also John Sack, *Company C: The Real War in Iraq* (New York: Morrow, 1995), 176–79.

55. Maggart, "Eye of the Storm," 178. MAJ (Ret.) Lon E. "Bert" Maggart, telephone interview with the author, July 16, 2015.

56. Maggart, "Eye of the Storm," 178.

57. Sack, *Company C*, 179–83.

58. 1st Brigade, 1st Infantry Division, daily staff journal, February 27, 1991. This same quotation can be found in Sack, *Company C*, 182–83.

59. 2nd Battalion, 34th Armor, D Team, TF 2-34 AR radio net, Clemens transcript.

60. For the author this was easily the most frightening moment since TF 2-34 AR fired its first shots on February 17. Maggart, "Eye of the Storm," 178–79; 2nd Battalion, 34th Armor, D Team, TF 2-34 AR radio net, Clemens transcript.

61. Connors, Gross, and Izzo interview.

62. Marlin, "History of the 4th Battalion, 37 Armored Regiment," 455.

63. Ancker, "2nd Armored Division (Forward)," 238–39, 242.

64. Ibid., 242.

65. Ibid., 243.

66. Ibid., 244.

67. Stephen A. Bourque and John W. Burdan III, *The Road to Safwan: The 1st Squadron, 4th Cavalry in the 1991 Persian Gulf War* (Denton: University of North Texas Press, 2007), 164–71.

68. Ibid.

69. Ibid., 169–70.

70. Ibid.

71. Ibid., 172–73.

72. Ibid., 173.

73. Marlin, "History of the 4th Battalion, 37 Armored Regiment," 451–54; Hall interview.

74. Marlin, "History of the 4th Battalion, 37 Armored Regiment," 452–53, taken from a statement written by SSG William J. McCormick II. There is a map at 454, but it seems inconsistent with the statement.

75. Ibid.

76. Ancker, "2nd Armored Division (Forward)," 230–37.

77. Company B, 2nd Battalion, 34th Armor, 1st Brigade, 1st Infantry Division: CPT Vaughn [Juan] E. Torro [Toro], Commander; 1LT Val [Lavelle] Jenkins, Executive Officer; 2LT Richard A. Shinaman [Schueneman], 2nd Platoon Leader; 1LT Charles N. Parker Jr., 3rd Platoon Leader; and 2LT James L. Jenicks [Enicks], 1st Platoon Leader. Interviewed by MAJ Robert Cook, Commander, 326th MHD, March 29, 1991. DSIT-AS-008..

78. Ibid.

79. 1st Battalion, 34th Armor, daily staff journal, February 27, 1991; Maggart, "Eye of the Storm," 179.

80. COL (Ret.) George P. Ritter, telephone interview with the author, August 8, 2014; COL (Ret.) George P. Ritter, personal journal, February 27, 1991.

81. The loader's weapon is a 7.62-millimeter pedestal mounted machine gun.

82. Ibid.

83. Maggart, "Eye of the Storm," 179.

84. Ibid.

85. 1st Brigade, 1st Infantry Division, daily staff journal, February 27, 1991; Task Force 2-34 AR, daily staff journal, February 27, 1991. Just when things happened is unclear, but it is clear that Maggart ordered the formation shortly after 6:30 p.m. Author's notes.

86. Danger Forward, daily staff journal, February 27, 1991.

87. For some time Franks remained unaware that no one at the Corps had called the 1 ID to continue to move. The 1 ID asked for permission to move about 7:30 p.m., and a Corps staff officer denied permission. See Bourque, *Jayhawk*, 376.

88. LTC John M. Kendall, Daily Memo 242300C, February 27, 1991, 3.

89. As chief of administration, Moreno was responsible for logistics and maintenance in the 27 ID. His role combined that of BG Jerry Rutherford, who served as assistant division commander for support, and COL Bob Shadley, the division support commander. See 513th Military Intelligence Brigade Joint Debriefing Center, report no. 5.

90. MAJ James K. Morningstar, "Task Force 3-37 AR in Operation Desert Storm," n.d., 20–21. See also Connors, Gross, and Izzo interview.

91. COL Anthony Moreno, Commander, 2nd Brigade, 1st Infantry Division, interview by MAJ Thomas A. Popa, Fort Riley, KS, July 26, 1991, DSIT-C-076.

92. Ibid. It is hard to say who this might have been. It is very unlikely the combatants included British troops.

93. Moreno interview DSIT-C-076. See also Bourque, *Jayhawk*, 469; Connors, Gross, and Izzo interview; and Marlin, "History of the 4th Battalion, 37 Armored Regiment," 457.

94. Marlin, "History of the 4th Battalion, 37 Armored Regiment," 458.

95. Connors, Gross, and Izzo interview.

96. Ibid.

97. Ibid.

98. Marlin, "History of the 4th Battalion, 37 Armored Regiment," 458.

99. Connors, Gross, and Izzo interview.

100. Ibid.

101. Moreno interview DSIT-C-076.

102. Ibid.

103. Reading Powell's and Schwarzkopf's accounts of what happened reveals a great deal about both of them. Both believed the war needed to go twenty-four more hours. Schwarzkopf, understandably elated about the success of the war to this point, went too far. Powell had the opportunity to make the case for continuing the war twenty-four hours, but chose not to do so. See Schwarzkopf, *It Doesn't Take a Hero*, 468–70; and Colin Powell with Joseph E. Persico, *My American Journey* (New York: Random House, 1995), 520–22.

104. Schwarzkopf, *It Doesn't Take a Hero,* 469–72. The complete briefing and Q and A can be seen at various sites on the Internet. The entire affair took just under fifty-eight minutes.

105 Rick Atkinson, *Crusade: The Untold Story of the Gulf War* (London: HarperCollins, 1994), 471.

106. COL (Ret.) John M. Kendall, telephone interview with the author, July 28, 2015.

107. BG (Ret.) Stanley F. Cherrie, telephone interview with the author, July 30, 2015.

108. Richard M. Swain, *"Lucky War": Third Army in Desert Storm* (Fort Leavenworth, KS: US Army Command and General Staff College Press, 1997), 284–85.

109. David S. Carter, telephone interview with the author, July 29, 2015.

110. Clancy, *Into the Storm*, 539.

111. Schwarzkopf, *It Doesn't Take a Hero*, 470.

112. Ibid.

113. Ibid., 471.

114. Ibid., 472.

115. Ibid.

116. Ibid.

117. Cherrie interview; Swain, *"Lucky War,"* 285–86; Clancy, *Into the Storm*, 538–40.

118. Kendall, Daily Memo 242300C.

119. Clancy, *Into the Storm*, 544–45.

120. Maggart, "Eye of the Storm," 181.

121. Mowery, "Saudi Journal," February 28, 1991.

122. Swain, *"Lucky War,"* 287–89. Rhame interview, February 3, 2015.

123. MAJ Mark S. Landrith, "History, 1st Battalion, 1st Aviation Regiment, 4th Brigade 1st Infantry, Desert Shield/Desert Storm," unpublished manuscript, n.d., n.p. [35].

124. Ibid.

125. Ibid., n.p. [35–36].

126. Mowery, "Saudi Journal," February 28, 1991.

127. Author's recollection. The Iraqi lieutenant spoke English with a slight Oxbridge accent and seemed genuinely to care for his troops.

128. 1st Brigade, 1st Infantry Division, daily staff journal, February 28, 1991; Maggart, "Eye of the Storm," 181–82.

129. Moreno interview DSIT-C-076.

130. Ibid. It is not clear from this interview just where Steve Hawkins's battalion was in this formation.

131. Moreno interview DSIT-C-076.

132. Ancker, "2nd Armored Division (Forward)," 246.

133. Ibid., 247–48.

134. Ibid., 249–50.

135. Bourque and Burdan, *The Road to Safwan*, 178.

136. Ibid., 179. See also G2, VII Corps, "The 100-Hour Ground War: How the Iraqi Plan Failed," May 4, 1994, 134–35.

137. Bourque and Burdan, *The Road to Safwan*, 179.

138. Ibid., 182.

CHAPTER TWELVE

SAFWAN AND HOME

To all the Volunteers of the "family support group," My family and I want to sincerely thank you for your support, care & concern for my son . . .

—Ann Delaney

Read report from Iraqi generals. We were assessed to be bad to the bone.

—Major Mike Barefield

It's an obscenity that we celebrate.

—Elizabeth McAlister

AT 7:23 A.M. on February 28, 1991, the VII Corps ordered an immediate cease-fire in reaction to a report of fratricide, but also to be sure the Corps met the 8:00 a.m. unilateral cease-fire announced by President George H. W. Bush. The decision to end the war when it did was taken in Washington, DC. When GEN Colin Powell asked GEN H. Norman Schwarzkopf whether he had an objection to stopping, Schwarzkopf acquiesced. He did so without complaint even though he had not, by his own definition, finished the job. He deferred to Powell's political judgment. If, as Prussian military theorist Carl von Clausewitz argued, war is an extension of policy by other means, then the war ended just as it should have and just when it should have. President Bush's policy and the UN mandate required two things: forcing Iraq from Kuwait; and destroying its conventional offensive capability. The limited aims to which the coalition could agree had been achieved. The speed with which the end came in 1991 surprised the troops in the field and revealed that neither Riyadh nor Washington had really thought through how the war should end.

Shortcomings within the theater command structure produced confusion remedied by troops on the ground. Most important, the cease-fire did not conclude the mission but instead led to another transition. The operation now entered phase 6 of the operations plan: defend northern Kuwait. In January, few commanders at any level had given any thought to what would happen after the fighting. Because they were soldiers, they focused on the fight. Commanders in the field did understand how to defend, but they had not considered what else had to be done. Planning for war termination was, to say the least, inadequate. The troops adjusted, made do, or acted instinctively—and got it mostly right.

The transition that occurred after the shooting stopped drove postwar operations. This war, like most wars, did not produce an unambiguous conclusion politically or in the field. Neither did it end neatly; the area remained dangerous. Dangers ranged from unanticipated combat operations to the hazards of mines, unexploded ordnance, and accidents. Confusion during the last day of the war produced a dangerous incident at the Iraqi border town of Safwan. Resolving this unnecessary crisis without a shot being fired may be the best operation the Division executed. In the months following the cease-fire, the Army learned it had paid insufficient attention to what the institution later called military operations other than war. The aftermath of wars is replete with misery and confusion, and victorious armies have moral obligations to both friend and foe. In 1991 the US Army was not ready to meet those obligations. For its part, the Division adapted and mostly got it right, sometimes in spite of orders.

Getting there in an operational deployment is less than half the fun. Going home after Operation Desert Storm was a joy for most, though nearly a thousand soldiers stayed behind to complete processing equipment for shipment and loading it. Their story is told here in less detail than it deserves. On July 4, 1991, the 1st Infantry Division (1 ID) celebrated its homecoming. That celebration is the logical conclusion to both its service in the desert and to its history since April 15, 1970, when it returned from Vietnam.

Saddam Hussein's Thesis: Not Losing Is Winning

In considering why President Bush unilaterally declared a cease-fire, Saddam Hussein theorized that he "probably said to himself, 'It is very apparent that he [Saddam] is going to cause us damage.'"[1] In *The Mother of All Battles*, Kevin Woods follows Saddam's development of the idea that the war ended because the United States did not have the stomach to continue it. Saddam amplified his thinking by claiming too that Iraq had stood successfully against overwhelming odds. He seems even to have believed his claims. It is equally clear that he did not fully appreciate just how grim the Iraqi situation had become. The 513th Military Intelligence Brigade's Joint Debriefing Center reports, developed from thorough interrogation of captured Iraqi senior officers, show that the commanders of Saddam's front line and tactical reserve formations did not share his view. The ferocity of the air campaign and the speed of the ground offensive surprised and overwhelmed them. Saddam had not seen what they had. Still, his assessment made sense from his point of view. Why would Bush declare a unilateral cease-fire if the US and coalition forces were in command of the situation? Neither Saddam nor his senior military officers fully understood the depth of the thrashing they had taken at the tactical level.

The cease-fire did suggest ambiguity about the outcome. LTG Ayad Futayyih Khalifa al-Rawi managed to extract the bulk of the Adnan, Hammurabi, and Nebuchadnezzar Divisions of the Republican Guard from Kuwait on February 27 and position them on the south side of the Euphrates River, from where they could defend Basra and the major avenue of approach to Baghdad. He and the high command, including Saddam, assumed that the United States would attempt to take Basra and then Baghdad. Not surprisingly, they perceived that the Army, especially the Republican Guard, had stood up to the "strongest and wealthiest country in the world." Despite public pronouncements by Schwarzkopf and Powell about its destruction, enough of the Iraqi Army survived to assure the regime's survival. Saddam concluded that Bush "decided on a cease-fire, in order for him [President Bush] to control the cease-fire situation."[2]

Closing on Phase Line Denver: February 28, 1991

Shortly after the cease-fire, MAJ Mark Landrith and the bulk of the 1st Infantry Division, 1st Combat Aviation Brigade (1-1 AVN) landed at its planned assembly area. He and the Apache helicopter crews gathered within sight and sound of the burning Iraqi combat vehicles Landrith destroyed. They shook hands, congratulated each other, and enjoyed the moment. Looking around, he could feel a "sense of relief and pride . . . a great weight had been removed and it was time to lighten up just a little." Throughout the Division, soldiers shared "an air of accomplishment and satisfaction."[3]

But no one had time to enjoy the feeling for more than a moment. Coalition troops had cease-fire orders, but just what the Iraqis might do remained, as yet, unknown; it would take time for the word to get out. Iraqi and coalition units were still moving, and in close proximity. Any number of bad things could and would happen. Not far from where Landrith and the pilots of the 1-1 AVN landed, the 2nd Squadron, 3rd Armored Cavalry Regiment (3 ACR) was preparing to move. Assigned to the XVIII Airborne (ABN) Corps, the 3 ACR operated on the XVIII ABN's flank. At 9:23 a.m. the regiment ordered the 2nd Squadron to secure the crash site of an unidentified American helicopter that had gone down west of the Ar Rumaylah Airfield.[4]

At 9:45 a.m. the Squadron headed east with G, E, and F Troops abreast from north to south. Minutes later the 3 ACR ordered the 2nd Squadron to go beyond the crash site and establish a screen along the 98 northing beyond the airfield. Furthermore, the orders required it "not to engage in direct fire unless fired upon."[5] If the regiment actually believed the mission could be concluded peacefully, it was mistaken. An Iraqi armor company, an infantry company, and at least a battery of air defense artillery defended the airfield. The Iraqi infantry opened fire at 10:27 a.m. The Iraqis should have begun the fight with tanks, because they fought with little coordination; the cavalry quickly overran the airfield and captured or killed its defenders. By noon, it was consolidating east of the airfield.[6]

The 3 ACR tentatively identified the helicopter as belonging to the 1st Division based on uniform patches they found on the bodies. Black Hawk tail number 78-23015, radio call sign Cowboy 15, lay in pieces both large and small along a debris field that stretched five hundred meters to the west of the airfield. COL Jim Mowery learned of the crash at noon; soon after, he and an "accident" investigation team flew the fifty kilometers to the crash scene. En route he learned there were nine dead. The cavalry also found a body bag containing the remains of a tenth soldier; he had been killed the night before, along with two others, when a helicopter from the Lonestar Dustoff air evacuation unit had crashed. Mowery's investigation team later found the other two body bags at the western end of the debris field.[7]

Just what happened may never be known, but the crash added an unpleasant first. Cowboy 15 went missing the previous day as the aviation brigade displaced into Kuwait. On the afternoon of February 27, Cowboy 15 landed around 5:30 p.m. at an intermediate staging area to assist in moving people and supplies to the next assembly area, located in Kuwait. Specifically, they were asked to haul a pallet load of AT-4 antitank missiles and several soldiers. CW1 George Swartzendruder, the pilot in command, took one look at the pallet and concluded that it was too heavy. He detailed door gunner and mechanic SPC Buddy Stefanoff and another soldier to break the pallet into two smaller loads.[8]

While Stefanoff and his colleague began working on the pallet, SGT Cheryl O'Brien showed up with her gear to ride to Kuwait. She took Stefanoff's place at one of the two door guns. Stefanoff objected, but O'Brien insisted. Events overtook the argument over who would man the door gun. Swartzendruder received orders to return to an assembly area about forty kilometers south to retrieve the bodies of three soldiers killed the night before when the air ambulance went down. CW1 Swartzendruder left the two soldiers working on the pallet, each with a bottle of water and a meal-ready-to-eat (MRE), and told Stefanoff he would be back for them in an hour. Cowboy 15 spooled up and flew south; Stefanoff never saw them again.[9]

Around nightfall, Cowboy 15 headed back north, but flew well north of the Division's zone, across the zones of the 3 AD and 1 AD and north of the boundary with the XVIII ABN Corps. How is it they never returned to pick up Stefanoff and the other soldier remains unknown. COL Phil Wilkerson and his

Black Hawk crew found the two—dehydrated, hungry, and fearful that no one would ever find them—three days later on March 2.[10]

Cowboy 15 did retrieve the bodies and an additional passenger as ordered. What happened after that is unclear. It is likely the crew made a mistake in entering navigational data on their long-range navigation device. Cowboy 15 took off after dark en route to pick up the two soldiers working on the pallet, but never found them. Instead Cowboy 15 overflew them and continued about one hundred kilometers too far north.[11]

At some point the pilots must have realized their error, because Cowboy 15 eventually turned east and flew into the air defenses at Ar Rumaylah Airfield. Iraqi air defense artillery shot it down with twenty-three-millimeter cannon fire about four kilometers west of the single runway. The twenty-three-millimeter air defense cannon fired explosive rounds. The first entered the helicopter just aft of the pilot's head, and it is possible that that round killed everyone on board. At least three more rounds struck in quick succession. The helicopter flew its last heading, shedding parts and metal for five hundred meters, and crashed. Anyone still alive died on impact. The loss of Cowboy 15 is easy to explain: Iraqi gunners shot it down. But how Cowboy 15 happened to be where it was when it was hit will puzzle and sadden those who knew the crew for the rest of their lives. The legacy of Cowboy 15 is ambiguity, uncertainty, and nine dead.

As a consequence, SGT O'Brien, who took SPC Stefanoff's place as the door gunner on Cowboy 15, was the first woman assigned to the 1 ID to be killed in combat. According to her peers and superiors, she was confident, competent, and determined. She wanted to serve and wanted to fly that mission as door gunner. Like those with whom she flew, O' Brien accepted the risks that came with that choice.

After MG Thomas G. Rhame made his way out of the so-called Valley of the Boogers, he headed east. He arrived at the Highway of Death around 9:00 a.m., as yet ignorant of the loss of Cowboy 15. What he saw stunned him; the evidence of panic, looting, and devastation along the highway defied description. A young artilleryman in the 4th Battalion, 5th Field Artillery (4-5 FA) summed up the ugly panorama as well as it could be done. Like his commanding general, he was stunned: "The shock of seeing so much death felt like a hammer hitting me in the pit of my stomach. The odor the bodies emitted was a mixture of burning fat and rubber. Severed or blown off limbs were lying here and there."[12]

The toll of destroyed and abandoned vehicles included Iraqi combat gear and hundreds of stolen cars and trucks they had hoped to bring out of Kuwait. Most of the vehicles were filled with loot that varied from the mundane to the strange. LTC Clint Ancker examined several abandoned combat vehicles; they were "crammed with civilian goods that gave all the appearance [of] having been looted from both stores and private homes. The floor of one tank was covered with dishes and glasses."[13] The destruction and looting of buildings was equally chilling: Iraqis had pulled wire and outlets out of walls, took light fixtures, and stripped off flooring; they seemed indiscriminate, hauling away anything that could be carried. In one oil company complex, nothing that could be moved remained in any of the buildings—not even the baseboards. As the final insult, Iraqi soldiers had defecated more or less in the center of every room.[14]

To those who saw it, what the Iraqis did to Kuwaiti villages and oil facilities along the Highway of Death was as stunning as the images of the highway itself. The media focused on the woebegone Iraqi soldiery and not on what they did to Kuwait. As with the looting of Kuwaiti buildings, the Iraqis generally destroyed what they could not take; setting fire to the oil wells in Operation Tariq was only the most visible act of destruction out of an untold many. Although he was no poet, Rhame felt the need to record his "impressions." He summed up inelegantly but accurately, "Kuwait was trashed and pillaged by Iraq." He went on to say his command post was adjacent to fifty-nine burning wellheads, adding, "The man [Saddam] is a madman." He described acres of destroyed Kuwaiti infrastructure ranging from power distribution yards to buildings. The quantity of destroyed and abandoned Iraqi combat equipment amazed Rhame. What impressed him most, however, was the fact that there were "hundreds and hundreds of tons of ammunition everywhere."[15]

Hundreds of tons of ammunition had the potential to prove problematic, but if undisturbed, abandoned ammunition posed little immediate danger. On the other hand, thousands of thirsty and hungry Iraqi soldiers posed an immediate problem. LTC Bob Wilson and the 1st Squadron, 4th Cavalry (1-4 CAV) survived a tense night, fearing that the Iraqis trying to fight their way out might overwhelm them. Occasional firefights heightened that concern. Instead, securing and supporting the enormous number of prisoners proved far more challenging. COL Tony Moreno inherited the problem when Rhame subordinated the Quarter Horse to him. Moreno dispatched a mechanized infantry company to help.[16] He soon had enough prisoners to challenge even his more robust resources.

At 10:00 a.m. the infantry company commander attached to the Quarter Horse (1-4 CAV) reported 2,064 prisoners in the cavalry's improvised enclosure.[17] Providing proper care presented immediate difficulties. If the 1st Division came close to culminating on February 27, it almost certainly reached culmination on February 28. Fuel, water, and food were all in short supply. Rhame estimated that the Division had four thousand prisoners on hand, but his estimate was low. Moreno's 2nd Brigade alone had at least four thousand prisoners when the cease-fire went into effect.[18] COL Bert Maggart's brigade had several hundred in various stages of being evacuated to the rear, and COL Dave Weisman's troops had still more.

Weisman's brigade captured one hundred prisoners of war at its final objective and had hundreds more in a "cage" back at Norfolk, with the brigade military police platoon waiting for transportation to become available for evacuation. Many Iraqi soldiers were already suffering from dehydration when they were captured. The platoon made do by asking passing units for food and water. Out of contact with the Division, the platoon did raise the VII Corps tactical command post.[19] The Corps sent help.

LTC Dave Gross had problems of a different kind. His Task Force 3rd Battalion, 37th Armor (TF 3-37 AR) had nearly seventeen hundred prisoners. Gross decided to have his armored combat earthmovers plow up berms to build prisoner of war enclosures. But when the tactical dozers started working, one group of Iraqis became agitated to the point of "riot." MAJ Paul Izzo concluded that the prisoners believed the Americans intended to kill them. He theorized they thought the dozers were digging mass graves. And his theory proved correct: the prisoners calmed down once they understood they would not be killed. It was also plain that they "hadn't been fed in while." The task force had no food to spare, but Izzo asked volunteers to give what they could and would later remember, "People gave up their MREs to feed these guys."[20] Treating sick and injured prisoners proved more difficult. Saddam had "taken diabetics off the street and put them in uniform," and seventeen of these unfortunates were in various stages of insulin shock; by the time the medics identified them, it was too late for some. The US Army did not deploy insulin-dependent diabetics, so TF 3-37 AR had no ready means to treat insulin shock.[21]

Despite having fought them, most US soldiers felt sympathy for their enemy. Coping with thousands of prisoners and treating their wounded and sick were not the only challenges. The Division had outrun its logistics; vehicles that had broken down and then been repaired were trying to catch up, and unit maintenance teams spread out across the battlefield to repair and recover equipment. CW3 Jim Logan's experience exemplifies that of other maintenance officers. He and his trail party caught up late on the afternoon of February 28; they did so by replacing the fuel pump in a Bradley so it could move on its own. But they were also towing a track—ironically, an M88 recovery vehicle. Logan spent the night of February 28 with his unit, but then headed back to recover two engineer vehicles that had died of old age. Both were of venerable vintage and had done well to hang in as long as they had. They short-tracked one and towed the other.[22] (Short tracking requires taking the track apart and rehanging it around those road wheels that are still supported by serviceable torsion bars. Shortening the track is backbreaking work, and not something crews practice.)

A number of soldiers repaired vehicles themselves or made temporary repairs adequate enough to move on. Several crews traveled two, three, or four days alone and unable to communicate, and by hook or by crook, they found their units. The sojourn of 2LT Adrian Lowndes and part of his platoon from B Troop of the 1-4 CAV demonstrates sheer cussed determination to rejoin the fight. On the morning of February 27, one of his tanks broke a torsion bar; the squadron had no torsion bars on hand, so the platoon short-tracked the tank. CPT Mike Bills left Lowndes with one section of Bradleys to provide security and told him to catch up when he could.[23]

The tankers worked until late that night, but did not finish until midmorning on February 28. The detachment then headed east at its top speed of twenty kilometers per hour. At noon, they scrounged a hot meal from a unit of the 2 ACR, which passed along the happy news of the cease-fire and gave them directions. They moved on after their meal, but halted at nightfall to avoid running over a mine or into a wadi; better to spend another night in the desert than risk further damage. Finally, on March 1, they rejoined the Squadron.[24]

SGT Thomas T. Tuttle towed a broken-down howitzer through all four days of the ground offensive. "I have heard of towing equipment from a war, but never through a war," Tuttle would later comment. "A 114 [an inoperable howitzer] saw more miles backwards than forward; all the way through three countries!"[25] Tuttle towed A 114 all the way to the Division's final objective. Everywhere, soldiers did what they had to do, often in small groups, without GPS, and sometimes even without a map. They accomplished amazing feats of navigation traveling under dangerous conditions across hundreds of kilometers of unforgiving desert.

Division logistics struggled to keep up with the combat forces, often without success. To do their jobs, they needed to stop, because breaking rations, repairing equipment, and issuing fuel can only be done when stationary. Just to keep up, however, many units couldn't afford to stop or, when they did, had to move again too soon for their technicians to complete the necessary work. Additionally, the pace of the advance outstripped available transportation capacity. By February 28 the logistics formations had people and equipment strung out along the route as far back as the original division support area in Saudi Arabia. Logistically, the Division culminated on February 28. It had been a hard four days. The 1 ID had consumed more than a million gallons of diesel fuel during the ground offensive. At cease-fire, COL Bob Shadley's support command had only 20,000 gallons of fuel on hand, far short of 250,000 gallons used on each of the preceding four days. During the same four days, the troops and their prisoners consumed 980,000 gallons of bulk water and a half million two-liter bottles of water. The support command had water, but insufficient means to get it where it was needed.[26] The logisticians had reached the end of their rope. Shadley needed time and trucks to get forward

By sundown, most of the Division had arrived along the Basra–Kuwait City highway. That night, those not required for duty slept. COL Maggart may have set the record for hours slept that night. He unrolled his sleeping bag on a cot near his Bradley and collapsed into a deep sleep despite the roaring noise and smoke of the oil fires. To his surprise and pleasure, no one woke him to take a radio call or report shots fired. In fact, no one woke him for the morning alert known as stand-to. He slept straight through for eighteen hours.[27] He may have set the record, but all of those who could sleep slept hard—really hard.

Scapegoats, Safwan, and Cease-Fire: March 1, 1991, 3:00 A.M.–5.00 P.M.

There were very few well-rested soldiers anywhere in the theater that evening. GEN Schwarzkopf's effusive "mother of all briefings" and confusion between the 3rd Army and VII Corps ensured another sleepless night for many. After taking the decision to end the war, President Bush directed that cease-fire negotiations occur within forty-eight hours of the cease-fire order. That left little time to select a site. With unabashed hubris, Schwarzkopf considered holding the conference aboard the USS *Missouri*. Fortunately, his staff convinced him that getting all of the conferees aboard was too hard, so he asked LTG John Yeosock to recommend a site. From a list of three, Yeosock chose Jalibah Air Base, which LTG Gary Luck's XVIII ABN Corps had captured on February 27. But sometime after midnight on February 28, Yeosock called Schwarzkopf to report that the air base was unsuitable, because it had a lot of "unexploded ordnance spread around it."[28] Schwarzkopf was not amused; he had already reported Jalibah to Powell. Without consulting Yeosock, he then chose the airfield north of the border town of Safwan on the Basra–Kuwait City highway near the interchange he wanted attacked that morning. It was not on the list of recommended sites.[29]

In *"Lucky War,"* Richard M. Swain has described what followed as "the most painful and least creditable period for the Desert Storm high command, one which like most errors of the high command, would be redeemed by the soldiers on the ground."[30] Schwarzkopf did order Yeosock to "take" the road junction near Safwan. But he issued muddled orders that permitted more than a little wiggle room. He ordered the 3rd Army to seize Safwan, but only if it could avoid "a big fight you can't finish on time [0800]."[31] At 11:00 p.m. on February 27, he told Yeosock "to be out of contact by 0500." At 3:00 a.m. he woke Yeosock to order him to resume the attack and take the junction. Order followed by counterorder yielded, as it always does, disorder. Orders that can be misunderstood will be.

Yeosock's staff issued equivocal orders as well. The 3rd Army directed the VII Corps "to destroy enemy armored vehicles and seize road junction [near Safwan] to block Iraqi withdrawal [while making] maximum use of AH-64s and Air Force assets."[32] No one, including Schwarzkopf, ordered anyone to seize Safwan Airfield, yet any unit seizing the junction would almost certainly pass through or around the town and the nearby airfield. BG Steve Arnold, the 3rd Army operations officer, called COL Stan Cherrie to make sure he understood the intent was to destroy enemy units going through the junction.

The staff officer who wrote the order at the 3rd Army no doubt meant for ground troops to seize the junction. But, as written, air assets could achieve the intended results. Furthermore, the order could not be executed in the time permitted. The order and Arnold focused on the enemy and not the terrain. That is how both LTG Frederick M. Franks Jr. and Cherrie understood it—or, rather, misunderstood it. They both understood what the verb *seize* meant, but they believed the enemy was the object and not the junction itself. Finally they were told unequivocally to avoid a big fight and finish by 8:00 a.m. Only Rhame's division was close enough even to try for the junction, and neither officer believed that it could seize the junction by 8:00 a.m. They chose to do what could be done. They would use Apaches to strike enemy forces passing through the road junction. It is a fact that the VII Corps never did take the junction with ground troops. It is also a fact that they did not report taking it.

COL Jim Mowery and LTC Ron Reichelderfer flew to the junction and found no Iraqis. To be clear about context, Powell and Schwarzkopf had ordered an offensive mounted by no less than nine divisions in two corps to stop. Four hours later, they wanted all nine to resume the attack, but for a duration of no more than four hours. Rhame's response to the order he received accurately characterizes high-level orders that night: "insane."

Nothing was said about Safwan on February 28. Around 1:30 a.m. on March 1 Yeosock called LTG Franks and asked if the 1st Division "could determine if the airfield near Safwan was secure for use as the conference site."[33] He likely knew the answer when he called. The Corps daily staff journal recorded the answer: "1 ID has not had eyes on airfield. Area in vicinity has extensive damage to personnel and equipment."[34] Yeosock then asserted he had issued a written order to seize Safwan. This was the first Franks knew of any interest in Safwan or its airfield. When the report made it to Schwarzkopf, he (in his own words) "came completely unglued."[35] A man who bullied subordinates as a matter of course, he responded with a pyroclastic flow of dire threats. As the eruption subsided, he demanded investigations and ordered Safwan Airfield and Safwan Mountain "occupied." He specified that it be done without "a major firefight" and without "any troops put at risk to cover the asses of officers who failed to do the job in the first place."[36]

As the 1st Division duty officer, MAJ Stephen A. Bourque, author of *Jayhawk: The VII Corps in the Persian Gulf War*, witnessed the next scene in this ugly comic opera. Soon after Yeosock and Franks concluded their conversation, a VII Corps staff officer called. MAJ Bourque took the call and "[f]or almost ten minutes the division's duty officer confirmed to several corps staff officers that no one in the division was near Safwan and that unit locations had not changed since the report he rendered at 7:00 p.m."[37] Suddenly an exasperated Franks got on the phone and shouted, "Do you know who this is?" MAJ Bourque did. Franks yelled, "Get Rhame on the line now!" This was no time to send a messenger, so Bourque sprinted the fifty yards to Rhame's tent across "fire illuminated sand." He awakened the exhausted general, who had just fallen asleep; the time was 2:00 a.m.[38]

MAJ Bourque sat beside Rhame as the next scene played out. He confirmed what Franks knew: the Division had not seized Safwan, the airfield, or the junction and had not been ordered to do so. After some time Rhame asked what his orders were. Franks ordered a reconnaissance of the area, but noted that the "intent is to not take any casualties."[39] This incident occurred because of muddled orders and inaccurate or misunderstood reports, and because Schwarzkopf preferred not to call Powell and tell him he needed to change the cease-fire meeting site a second time. Further, Schwarzkopf believed Yeosock, Franks, Rhame, or all three had disobeyed him. To him this was personal—he did not intend to be embarrassed twice in one day. Yet his orders also required no casualties and no shooting without his permission.[40] Perhaps he truly believed that his reputation and his conviction about his subordinates made it acceptable to put lives at risk. This guidance was impossible to follow, or at the very least unlikely to be followed, as it suggested that soldiers would not be able to return enemy fire without permission.

The comic opera had to run its course. At 2:40 a.m. Rhame radioed Wilson and told him to move as quickly as he could to reconnoiter the ground north to the airfield. Further, if he could do so without a fight, Wilson was to secure the airfield. Rhame authorized Wilson to return fire if fired on. He could tell him nothing of consequence about the enemy. The purpose of the mission was to learn which Iraqi units might be defending the airfield. Next, he ordered COL Mike Dodson to provide artillery support, and Dodson assigned the mission to LTC John Gingrich's 4-5 FA at 4:00 a.m. In the meantime, Rhame decided against attempting this mission in the dark. He ordered a start time of 6:15 a.m.[41]

At 6:00 a.m. Rhame called Moreno to the command post. When he arrived, Rhame brought him up to date, including relating the various caveats. He ordered Moreno to secure the area including the airfield, the road junction, and the town of Safwan. To do that he was to use his two battalions, the 1-4 CAV and 4-5 FA, and LTC Skip Baker's TF 5-16 IN from the 1st Brigade. Rhame told him to move at 10:00 a.m. On the ride back to his command post, Moreno issued a warning order and developed his concept for the operation. He decided to advance north toward Safwan with TF 3-37 AR on the left and the 4-37 AR on the right. He intended to use Baker's task force to envelop the airfield from the left or west.[42]

Gingrich described the Safwan mission as "a strange battle." When he got the order, all he knew was that the 1-4 CAV had a mission to secure an airfield. Gingrich wondered, "What airfield and why." Further, he did not "know the commander's intent. We did not have any graphics nor a scheme of maneuver.

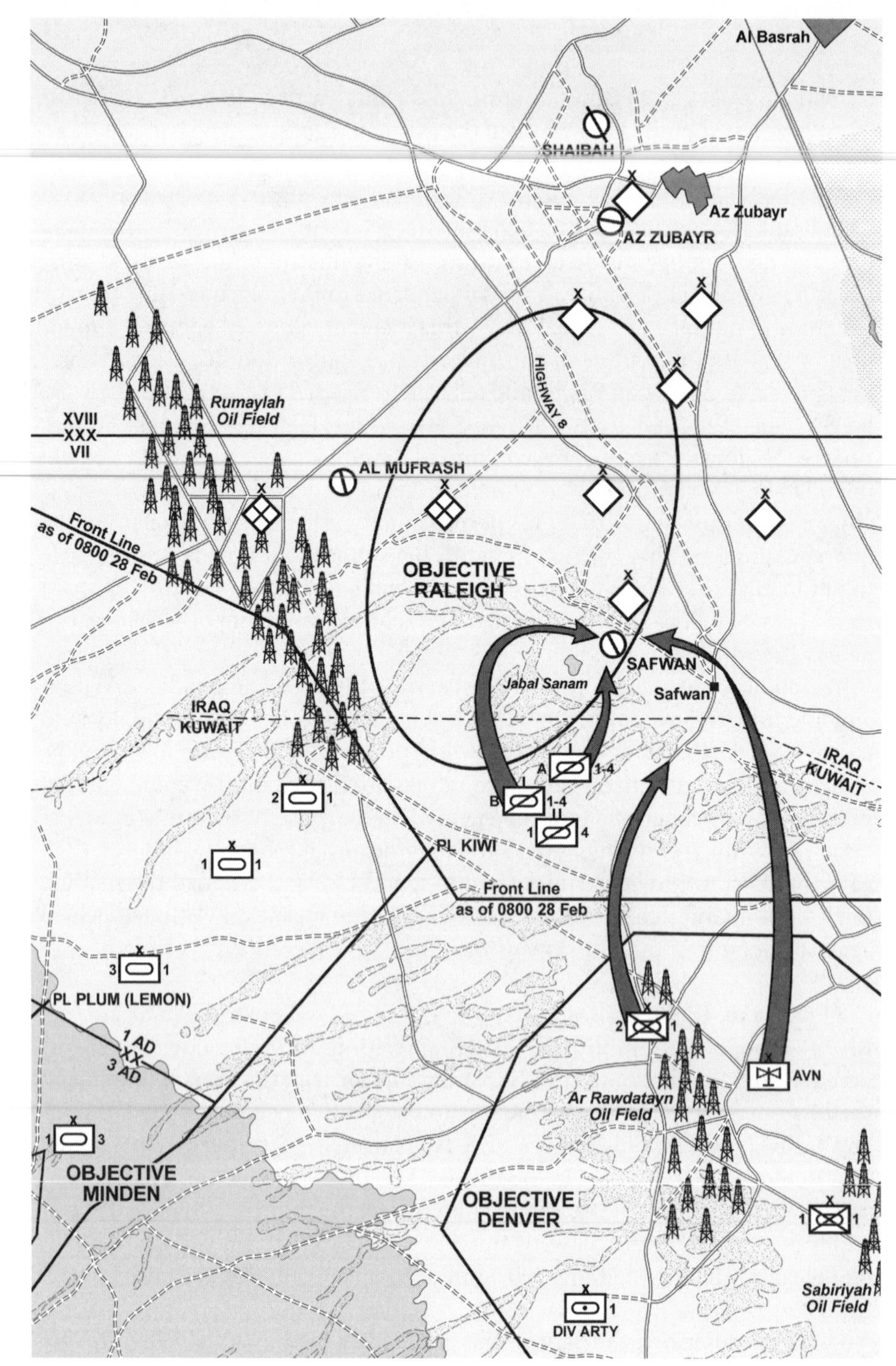

MAP 13. Movement on Safwan, March 1, 1991. Recreated from Map 26, Stephen A. Bourque, *Jayhawk! The VII Corps in the Persian Gulf War.*

We did not have a solid handle on what was going on."[43] Whatever doubts Gingrich and Wilson may have entertained did not interfere with getting started. As Gingrich put it, "time was short, I put these thoughts [questions] aside for now."[44] Both headed north toward the Safwan Airfield at 6:15 a.m. The cavalry moved cross-country with air cavalry scouting the ground ahead of the two ground troops. B and A troops advanced abreast, with B Troop on the left. Several kilometers farther south, Gingrich's 4-5 FA traveled parallel to the Basra–Kuwait City highway toward a location from which it could support the 1-4 CAV. En route, Gingrich diverted to the 2nd Brigade command post, where Moreno filled in some of the blanks.[45]

The Quarter Horse crossed the asphalt strip at the airfield at 7:15 a.m. LTC Wilson's air cavalry saw no Iraqis on Safwan Mountain just west of the airfield. Approximately 350 feet high, Safwan Mountain dominated the surrounding area. The two ground troops and aerial scouts quickly estimated that the Iraqis had a brigade-size armor force on the north side of the airfield. LTC Wilson reminded his troops not to shoot, but to continue moving slowly. The cavalry came to a halt on the north side of the airfield, well within range of enemy tanks and Soviet-made Boyevaya Mashina Pekhoty infantry fighting vehicles. LTC Wilson briefed Rhame by radio, and LTC Rhame directed Wilson to use his air cavalry to scout the road junction. In due course, airborne scout weapons teams reported more Iraqis near the interchange.[46]

About 8:15 a.m. Gingrich and the 4-5 FA survey party reached the area from which they could support Wilson. As they began to mark out positions for the howitzers, they observed enemy troops "picking up their weapons and getting into the prone position." To the small group with him, Gingrich announced, "We are about to have an international incident." He had his troops withdraw a short distance. He then told the survey party, "I'm going to talk to them. Apparently they have not gotten the word of the cease-fire." One or more of his troops wondered, "Is the Colonel crazy?"[47] As he marched out toward the Iraqis, he made a show of disarming. After handing his pistol to one of his officers, he continued alone, and "then a big Iraqi soldier met the Colonel and they shook hands."[48] The big Iraqi turned out to be the colonel who commanded a second Iraqi brigade, this one centered on Safwan. The Iraqis insisted they were in Iraq and would not leave.

At 8:30 a.m., as Gingrich began his negotiation, Wilson prepared to meet with the Iraqis near the airfield. He, too, went on foot and met with a "well-fed and well-dressed Iraqi" wearing the uniform flash of the Republican Guard. This officer was also a colonel. Wilson told him he had to withdraw his units from the airfield and surrounding area, and the Iraqi colonel departed to seek guidance from his superiors. As he did, an Iraqi tank platoon advanced on Wilson, who had returned to his Bradley. The tanks leveled their gun tubes. Wilson withdrew one hundred yards. By this time, an Apache helicopter company had arrived overhead. Wilson asked the Apaches to "buzz" the airfield, and when they did the Iraqi tanks withdrew. Next, Mowery landed and accompanied Wilson to his second meeting. This time both swore to the Iraqi colonel that the entire Division was behind them. Mowery promised to "[d]arken the skies with Apaches and to kill every single one of them if they were not gone in two hours."[49] On hearing this news, the colonel departed to seek still more guidance.

As tricky and dangerous as these meetings were, the human side emerged as well. Because Wilson's troops gave nearby Iraqi troops food, their commander insisted on brewing tea for them in return. Negotiations like that conducted by Wilson and Mowery also took place at lower levels as well. Things went reasonably well. At 9:00 a.m. the Quarter Horse reported the Iraqi commander was allowing the 1-4 CAV to copy his graphics. On the other hand, Gingrich's situation remained tenuous, with both sides pointing guns at each other.[50]

At 10:00 a.m. Moreno and his brigade started for the airfield. They reached the scene of Gingrich's confrontation at 11:00 a.m., and Moreno took over. He soon learned that the Iraqi infantry hailed from Tikrit, Saddam's hometown. They believed that if they withdrew, their families would be killed. To Moreno, it was clear that the Tikriti troops hoped to find a way out of their predicament. In the midst of this, BG Bill Carter arrived by helicopter. Moreno met him and asked that he stay out of it. He reasoned that if the US side had a general, then the Iraqis would want one as well, and this would slow the negotiation process. Carter readily agreed and joined Wilson and Mowery at a point from which he could monitor the action and keep Rhame apprised.[51]

Moreno asked the Iraqi infantry to find an officer to meet with him. Meanwhile, apprised of the confrontations, Yeosock called Central Command (CENTCOM) for instructions. Schwarzkopf was sleeping, and no one would awaken him. Rhame and Moreno continued to work to negotiate the Iraqis out of the airfield and the town. At 12:30 p.m. two Iraqi generals and a civilian official arrived to talk to Moreno. At roughly the same time, Yeosock spoke with Schwarzkopf, the latter presumably refreshed from his nap. He told Yeosock he would check with Powell about using a site other than Safwan if necessary.[52]

An hour later, Schwarzkopf called Yeosock back to say that no change was possible. Powell "was upset that the road junction had not been taken, because the contrary had been reported to the White House. Moving talks to an alternate site now was out of the question."[53] Thus, after Schwarzkopf decided that risking lives for the sake of using the airfield made no sense, Powell said no. Apparently now Powell's ego required the talks to take place at Safwan Airfield. The Iraqis had to be seen off so that Powell would not have to change the site a second time. COL Moreno's discussions with the Iraqis produced no relief. The Iraqis in the delegation claimed they needed to consult with their superiors and would return at 3:00 p.m.

At 3:00 p.m. Yeosock called Rhame directly. He said, "We must have the airfield . . . I want you to go into the airfield at Safwan with overwhelming combat power and force the Iraqi units out." He loyally passed on, without comment or attribution, additional requirements that came from Schwarzkopf, such as "attempt to avoid contact and request permission from the commander-in-chief before initiating offensive action."[54] This was yet another equivocal order. But surrounding the airfield was offensive action; what Schwarzkopf wanted to avoid was firing the first shot. No one could guarantee the results of this kind of contradictory order. Essentially, the order required a bluff for which neither Powell nor Schwarzkopf would take responsibility. This kind of order is known colloquially as bet your bars—as in, you lose your commission if you get it wrong. It had only one purpose: to assure that neither Colin Powell nor H. Norman Schwarzkopf would suffer embarrassment. But Rhame had not waited on Yeosock, Franks, or Schwarzkopf to issue unequivocal orders.

Tired of "more and more guidance" coming down from the higher headquarters, he moved to end the standoff on his own. An hour or so before Yeosock called, Rhame flew north and met with Moreno. At 2:30 p.m. he issued a succinct order uncluttered with parameters that could not be guaranteed. He ordered Moreno to tell the Iraqis to get out by 4:00 p.m. or they would be killed. He was back at his command post in time to receive Yeosock's irrelevant instructions. Moreno was the perfect choice to deliver that kind of ultimatum. Swarthy and powerfully built, he looked more like a pirate in an Errol Flynn movie than the sophisticated intellectual he was. He, too, had had enough. In minutes, his brigade moved out, drove around the Tikriti infantry company, surrounded the town, and linked up with the Quarter Horse. At 3:00 p.m. he rode his Bradley right up to the Iraqi delegation, where it rocked to a stop. As he disembarked, he cut his lip on his binoculars. Bleeding, he confronted them. One Iraqi began to read a statement, but Moreno stopped the proceedings by hawking a gobbet of blood on the ground and announcing, "If you don't leave by 1600 hours we will kill you." If that was insufficiently dramatic, a company of US tanks rolled up, gun tubes leveled and cannons traversing back and forth like dogs scenting the air.[55]

For a moment Moreno feared one of the tanks might actually run into the Iraqi delegation's car. He yelled "Stop" and the closest tank nearly stood on its nose. He turned back to the senior general and said, "See, my soldiers are eager for a fight. They are willing to fight and if you give us a chance, we'll kill every one of your soldiers and you're the man that's going to be responsible for their deaths." There followed minor quibbling about the time of departure. Moreno gave them until 4:20 p.m., a deadline they met. The offending infantry company withdrew, and the 2nd Brigade positioned itself around the road junction north of the town. As they left, the Iraqi senior officer thanked Moreno "for not killing my soldiers."[56] That ended what Gingrich rightly called "a strange battle."

Negotiations, Consolidation, and Clearing Roads: March 1–3, 1991

In his memoir, Schwarzkopf claimed he called Rhame soon after the standoff ended at Safwan. He described how he "wanted to orchestrate the Iraqis' arrival." He recalled telling Rhame to intimidate and impress the Iraqis to "make sure they come in the proper frame of mind." Of Rhame's response he wrote, "I could almost hear him grinning over the phone."[57] According to Rhame, that conversation never occurred. Rhame took a call from Schwarzkopf the day before the ground attack, but this one never happened. He did get plenty of guidance and understood the intent, but he never heard it from Schwarzkopf himself.

Rhame ordered Carter to prepare Safwan Airfield for the cease-fire talks. Yeosock and Schwarzkopf's logisticians were to provide tents, tables, chairs, and other amenities by convoy. That evening Rhame wrote sardonically that it was "a great plan; all the convoys are lost."[58] The required equipment arrived eventually. Carter organized the work, but Moreno's brigade did the bulk of it. Nevertheless, Carter had plenty to do, as more and more staff officers arrived with equipment or claimed to speak for the Corps, 3rd Army, or CENTCOM. At one point a cargo helicopter carrying tents blew down those that had already been erected. Eventually Carter had a short discussion with Franks to the effect that he had too many bosses. Franks solved that problem.

Operations at Safwan Airfield had high visibility, but there was much more to be done throughout the Division. Recovering people and equipment continued. Upon cease-fire, the VII Corps took measures to assure the Iraqis did not attempt to return to Kuwait or counterattack in Iraq. These measures included patrolling, maintaining high alert levels, and preparing local defenses. Concluding combat operations safely and cleaning up the mess created by the fighting took precedence over everything save making sure things went well at Safwan. Corps fragmentary order (FRAGO) 147-91, issued at 10:00 a.m. on March 1, required units to "locate and reduce bypassed forces" by persuasion.[59] Negotiations or at least discussions with Iraqi units occurred throughout the Corps area. Remarkably, no skirmishes occurred. Clearing unexploded munitions and destroying tons of abandoned enemy equipment were also key tasks. FRAGO 148-91, issued later that day, identified enemy equipment the VII Corps was to acquire for intelligence organizations to exploit. The list was extensive and ranged from missiles to communications security equipment.[60] Finally, the Division had to clear unexploded munitions, vehicles, and human remains from nearly seventy kilometers of the four-lane highway that connected Basra to Kuwait City.

Clearing the highway was an enormous task. The Division also had to rid the area of ammunition and unexploded ordinance. Both of these operations were dangerous and largely without precedent. Getting rid of ammunition posed a particular problem. The Iraqis had cached several million tons of it in the Division zone. The thousands of unexploded submunitions that lay around Iraqi installations and defensive positions posed an even greater danger. Finally, hundreds of vehicles and thousands of small arms had to be destroyed. The Division dug into the task that very day.

LTC Steve Hawkins's 1st Engineer Battalion (1 EN) cleared the area in and around the northernmost twenty kilometers of the Basra–Kuwait City highway. LTC Rich Jemiola's 9 EN worked the rest of the zone. LTC Hawkins's troops cleared 25 square kilometers in two days, destroying 404 pieces of enemy equipment, including sixty-one tanks and forty-one armored personnel carriers. They also destroyed 2.5 million tons of ammunition.[61] LTC Jemiola's engineers, supported by combat units from the 1st Brigade, cleared the area to the south of hundreds of combat vehicles, trucks, cars, and artillery pieces. Their first task was to clear a long enough stretch of highway on which C-130 transport planes could land to deliver food and water.[62]

To clear Safwan Airfield, the VII Corps dispatched an explosive-ordinance disposal unit that supervised the safe disposal of unexploded bombs and submunitions that covered a lot of the ground around the airfield. No undamaged buildings remained. In fact, Safwan was no more suited for the negotiations than Jalibah, but neither Schwarzkopf nor Powell had any interest in choosing another site. Moreno's troops worked around the clearance operation to build the negotiations site, centered on a large tent equipped with conference tables and chairs. They also erected tents to provide facilities for the conferees, their entourages, and the media. A mess hall that served fresh food appeared as if by magic. The VII Corps and 22nd Support Command provided the necessary equipment.[63]

Hundreds of soldiers working through the day and that night completed the work by sunup on March 2. Franks arrived early to satisfy himself that all was ready to go. He was pleased with the effort, even the large sign that welcomed attendees to Iraq courtesy of the big red one. Of it he wrote that "it was unit pride working . . . yet it was also a historical fact."[64] All was ready, but the meeting was postponed until 11:00 a.m. Sunday, March 3.

After being notified of the delay, Franks discussed the uproar over the highway interchange with Rhame and Carter. Carter learned for the first time that Schwarzkopf wanted written explanations, including one from him. He flatly refused to comply. He had received no order to take Safwan and refused to cooperate with an "investigation." The whole affair had the ring of "rounding up the usual suspects." Hundreds of miles away, in Riyadh, Yeosock took full responsibility for the debacle and asked to be the only officer in charge of explanations. In the end, Schwarzkopf relented in part. Only Yeosock and Franks would explain why the junction had not been taken. Not yet privy to the outcome of Yeosock's remonstration, Franks and Rhame departed to visit subordinate units. Carter and the team at the airfield returned to the task of assuring that everything would be ready for the negotiations.[65]

The following morning, helicopters arrived carrying various luminaries, hangers-on, and a large contingent of media. The brigade was told to "expect about 4 helicopters, prepare for 8, with an outside chance of 12." LTC Jim Cook, Mowery's deputy commander, thought the number of helicopters could actually go as high as fifty. In the end, some sixty helicopters, including seventeen CH-47 cargo helicopters flew in.[66] Schwarzkopf and His Royal Highness General Khaled bin Sultan, who commanded all the Arab troops in the coalition, were the lead dignitaries. Even before the Iraqis arrived, Safwan Airfield made quite a sight.

During the preparation, Carter gave explicit instructions to Moreno on the impression he was to create. On Sunday morning, March 3, Moreno orchestrated the affair as Carter had instructed. COL Moreno met the Iraqis at the wretched highway intersection. They arrived in four cars escorted by a dozen tanks. There were eight in the Iraqi delegation including the officer that Moreno had ordered out of Safwan. LTG Sultan Hashim Ahmad al-Jabburi al-Tai, the Iraqi Army's operations and logistics officer, led the delegation. LTG Salah Abbud Muhammad, commanding general of the Iraqi III Corps, served as deputy. Representatives from the other services and commands in the Basra region rounded out the contingent.[67]

Two of Gross's company teams were on hand, so Moreno was not without capability of his own. The Iraqi delegation left their vehicles and boarded four high-mobility multipurpose wheeled vehicles (HMMWVs). Mounted in their tanks, Gross and Izzo pulled up on either side of the column of HMMWVs, while Moreno and his operations officer, MAJ Pete Lawson, followed in their Bradley fighting vehicles. LTC Gross led off with the four HMMWVs within the cordon formed by the four armored vehicles. He rapidly increased the speed to about seventy kilometers per hour. The formation sped on to the airfield, where they drove through a gauntlet of Apache helicopters parked along the runway with more flying overhead and fighters orbiting above them. The Quarter Horse tanks and Bradleys were in defensive positions in and around the airfield.[68]

The cavalry marked its territory with panache. CPT Bills's Bradley, Bravo 66, was parked adjacent to the negotiating tent to serve as a "getaway vehicle" for Schwarzkopf and Prince Khaled if something untoward occurred. The Squadron's colors, with streamers commemorating campaigns dating to before the Civil War, stood on one side, while B Troop's red and white guidon stood on the other side.[69] Camera crews and media personalities crowded around, haranguing one and all for insight on the talks. Among them Tom Brokaw stood out. He mingled with the troops and let them use his satellite phone to call home.

The cease-fire discussions concluded in an hour, and Moreno and Gross returned the Iraqi delegation to the junction. They departed soon after, leaving behind a tank that would not start. Using literal interpretation of their instructions, the 2nd Brigade destroyed the derelict tank. Back at the airfield, Khaled shook hands with some of the troops and left. Schwarzkopf shook hands with a few soldiers as well. Then he and Carter, who had worked for him in a Pentagon assignment, went to a tent nearby where they "shot the breeze" for a few minutes. Since most of the helicopters had flown off, Hawkins's engineers resumed their work blowing up enemy equipment and ammunition. The first explosion startled Schwarzkopf, who asked Carter, "What the hell is that? I don't want to die here." Carter explained, and they talked a few more minutes with no mention of the highway intersection. Then Schwarzkopf left, and the troops began tearing down the site.[70]

Much has been written since about the negotiation at Safwan, but little of that is central to this story. The Division did what it was asked to do. Schwarzkopf believed the 1 ID "had carried out my instructions with a vengeance."[71] These efforts did not escape the attention of the lead Iraqi negotiator. In his opinion, "the Americans had prepared a military show to flex their muscle and display arrogance. They had a force of more than a brigade, maybe close to a division just to provide protection for the area. The soldiers were fit with large physiques, as if they were handpicked and brought there to impress us."[72]

Carter worried that the US made a mistake by not demanding that Saddam or Tariq Aziz, his foreign minister and deputy prime minister, represent Iraq.[73] LTG Sultan was a staff officer and junior to Schwarzkopf and Prince Khaled. Carter thought it did not look right. However it looked, Sultan did very well for Saddam when he got Schwarzkopf to allow Iraqi helicopters to fly. A few days later, Iraqi gunships slaughtered Shia rebels. Neither the controversy over Safwan nor studied effort to humiliate the Iraqis reflects well on the United States. Muddled decision making at CENTCOM, the 3rd Army, and the VII Corps produced incoherent orders, sometimes coupled with guidance that made execution unlikely without unnecessary risks.

When Are They Coming Home?

Practically from the moment President Bush announced the cease-fire, soldiers' families demanded to know when their soldiers were coming home. For those who worked on behalf of soldiers and their families the task was often difficult. Family support groups, no matter how well organized and led, confronted serious challenges from family members who either could not or would not cope. Those family members who could not cope proved most burdensome, but most of these learned how with help from their family support group, the Family Support Center at Fort Riley, or the installation staff in Garlstedt, Germany.[74] Those who would not cope or made unreasonable demands sometimes were dealt with summarily. One spouse created debts her family could not afford and then demanded her family support group pay the debt. The answer to that demand was easy: No! Three young wives went to a Topeka television station where they claimed neither the Army nor their family support group would help them. When the television station followed up, it learned that none of these young women had called on their family support group, a unit representative, the Family Support Center, or their unit rear detachment.[75]

In Garlstedt, COL Paul Baerman eventually had to confront a spouse who abused volunteers who managed her unit's family support group. Sometimes spouses vented with no particular complaint, but only to lash out at someone in authority. Linda Rhame recalled one town hall meeting at which COL Gary LaGrange had taken enough abuse and declared that "the venting will cease or the meeting will cease." Most spouses and family members rose to the challenge with some help and education, but some never did.[76]

There were enough real problems to challenge young spouses, and family support groups helped solve a great many. These ranged from a child having a psychotic episode to a spouse not knowing how to run a household budget. The Family Support Center and family support groups located and provided interpreters for spouses who spoke little or no English so they could do basic things like see a doctor. Many of the spouses missing their soldiers were young and had never before been away from home; some chose to live temporarily with parents or other family members, but many stayed in Kansas or Germany with none of their family nearby. Most family support groups also supported the parents of both married and unmarried soldiers. Being kept in the information loop boosted the morale of those spouses and family members not living either at Fort Riley or Garlstedt, as well as that of their soldiers.[77]

Access to accurate, timely information was nearly impossible. From the time the Division cut off access to telephones in mid-February until a few soldiers made calls on Tom Brokaw's satellite phone, no one heard up-to-date information about the 1st Division. That might not have been a problem except for CNN, which generated a lot of information. Some reasoned that if CNN could provide what appeared to be current information, then surely the Army could. CNN's coverage suggested more clarity and timeliness than existed in fact. Coverage of ground forces remained problematic partly because the Army restricted coverage to assure operational security. CENTCOM also closely managed access. For all of these reasons, news was largely devoid of unit-specific content.

Families ached to know whether their soldiers were safe. Reporting and tracking casualties therefore assumed high importance. The Army knew how devastating mistaken reporting could be and understood that fraudulent reporting occurred as well. Telling families how the Army made notifications helped prepare them for fraudulent reports. The Army uses a uniformed team to notify families of casualties. Still, two young wives from the 2-34 AR received calls from people claiming to be Army officials. Both were told their husbands had been killed in action. Fortunately, both remembered how the system was supposed to work and called their family support group. After checking with the rear detachment, they were told that the US Army had issued no such report.[78]

Worse still, the Army made mistakes. Wounded on February 27, 2LT Mickey Williams suffered burns and shrapnel wounds. He received immediate care in Iraq and Saudi Arabia, and within days he was flown to the Army hospital in Landstuhl, Germany. His spouse had gone home to Columbus, Georgia, to stay with her parents. She received a visit from an official Army notification team who told her that Mickey had been killed in action. About an hour later, someone from the 3rd Brigade rear detachment called to say he had been wounded. She related to the caller what the Army notification team told her. The chagrined unit representative promised to check and get back to her. Her father, a combat veteran wounded in Vietnam, advised her to give it some time. Steadied by him, she was better prepared when the unit called to confirm her husband was wounded, not dead. A day or two later, Mickey himself called. Grateful and upset at the same time, she asked, "Where the hell are you? They told me you were dead."[79]

Tracking wounded and seeing to their needs brought little credit to the Army's medical commands. Williams's sojourn from Objective Norfolk was difficult, but the medical professionals did their best and took good care of him. In March, when doctors at Landstuhl were ready to release him, the hospital made no provision for clothing. Williams went to the post exchange, where he bought flip-flops, a sweatshirt, and sweat pants for the daylong ride in an Army van back to Garlstedt. CPT Bill Hedges was more fortunate; his soldier sister-in-law, who served as a nurse, bought him underwear and socks and he made do. He was flown to Rhein-Main Air Base, where he discovered there was no means to get him home. Hedges made his way to the commercial airport on the other side of the main runway. There he rented a car and drove to Garlstedt. At least one unit learned of a wounded soldier from the soldier himself. The young man called the rear detachment after arriving at Irwin Army Hospital in Fort Riley.[80]

Correcting misinformation and attempting to quell rumors occupied a lot of time. *The Sandblaster*, published biweekly from January to June 1991, updated families in Garlstedt on the operations and activities of the 3rd Brigade. COL Baerman used it to provide information and to quell rumors, and his frequent town hall meetings and visits to unit family support groups supplemented that effort. Baerman also penned an advice column under the pseudonym Desert Debbie; he often wrote the letters himself and then answered the questions posed. For example, he provided a detailed answer to Wondering in Wyoming, who wanted to know when the unit would return. Desert Debbie began by saying, "This question has been asked a thousand times in a thousand ways since the end of the ground war," and then reviewed the variables that affected the Brigade's return. Baerman, as Debbie, concluded, "We in Garlstedt are estimating on or about 1 June."[81]

No matter how hard Desert Debbie, Gary LaGrange, or family support groups tried to stem them, rumors abounded. One family support group leader, tired of having to respond to rumors, took action. She set up her answering machine to respond with a salutation that said, "Do not call me with another rumor."[82] Her answering machine message went on to advise callers that if they had not heard it from her, then it was a rumor. When discussing the home front with her husband, Linda Rhame opined, "I am not sure you could handle the women Gary LaGrange had to handle."[83]

But LaGrange's and Baerman's efforts paled by comparison to those of Pearl Speer and the host of volunteers who worked for nothing beyond their commitment to their spouses and units. Donna Baer, married to SFC Ted Baer, ran the family support group for her husband's infantry platoon. Donna Baer felt a sincere duty to the young infantrymen and families in Ted's company and she saw her effort as part of her "primary support to her soldier."[84] Perhaps. Peggy Waterman, who served the 701st Main Support Battalion, spoke for all who volunteered when she said, "Lord knows we tried."[85]

The energy expended to help family members learn how to cope proved worthwhile, as many of them became capable, independent, and great additions to the force of volunteers helping others. Those who would not cope were a distinct if noisome minority. Those on the home front bonded as surely as the troops in the field did. What families and the Army learned is that in a volunteer force they are not a burden but rather, if educated and supported, are capable of contributing to cohesion of the force—especially in long deployments.

Postcombat Operations: March 4–23, 1991

Rumors abounded not only at home but in the field. If plans were developed for postcombat operations, none made their way down to the battalion/task force level. There is a saying in the Army so old it is an aphorism: Plan for victory! The coalition achieved catastrophic victory for which no plan existed. Not surprisingly, contradictory orders and rumors resulted. LTC Ancker described the continuous flux in orders as "[t]he saga of 'what is today's version of the truth.'"[86]

Consolidation occurred as the natural continuation of the mission. Rearming, recovering broken-down equipment, refitting, and preparing to renew combat operations are ongoing in any combat mission. Renewing the attack to destroy the Republican Guard bridgehead on the Euphrates River remained a possibility if the coalition did not reach a permanent cease-fire agreement with the Iraqis. Refitting included comparatively novel activities. At one point, the US Air Force airdropped bottled water by parachute. That effort produced only wet spots, so the Division cleared a stretch of the Basra–Kuwait City highway. COL Shadley named the strip Danger International Airport after the 1 ID call sign and, beginning on March 5, several C-130 aircraft landed there to bring in food and water.[87]

After the initial cease-fire negotiations at Safwan, the Division focused on the defense of northern Kuwait. Initially that meant occupying defensive positions and clearing the battlefield. Without truly understanding the implications, the Division also undertook humanitarian operations. BG Carter and the 2nd Brigade began that task around Safwan. Iraqi civilians, cut off from their government and not welcome in Kuwait, suffered immediately as they had no safe water supply. BG Carter witnessed people drinking water from drainage ditches, and called on the 2nd Brigade to provide water and food. At first CENTCOM opposed providing aid to Iraqi civilians, and GEN Schwarzkopf sent a senior staffer to see what Carter was doing. After the visit, CENTCOM confirmed Carter's decision as consistent with what was required of an occupying force under international law.[88] Like it or not, the 1 ID was an occupying force and would be until Iraq and the coalition reached an agreement that would permit the coalition troops to withdraw.

The "first in, first out" policy complicated matters. In practice, that meant units would go home in the same order as their arrival. This decision had no operational basis, but reflected the idea of what was fair. The service chiefs and the public wanted the troops brought home as quickly as possible. To achieve this goal, the VII Corps and XVIII ABN Corps assumed responsibility for all of occupied Iraq—most of Iraq south of the Euphrates River. The two sides also agreed to a buffer zone of two kilometers on either side of the line of demarcation. This assured that combatants confronting each other were at the edge of direct-fire range, close enough to see each other but far enough apart to reduce the possibility of an incident.[89]

The 3rd Army and VII Corps shuffled units to maintain a screen along the demarcation line when the XVIII ABN Corps began to withdraw in accordance with "first in, first out." For the 1st Division, operations after the cease-fire fell into three discrete phases. Starting on March 3 the Division screened a demarcation line from west of Safwan to the Iraqi naval base at Um Qsar, about thirty kilometers east; this first phase ended on March 23 when the 3 AD assumed the sector so the 1st Division could withdraw. During the second phase, the Division assumed the role of Corps reserve. The final phase began on April 7, when the Aviation Brigade with the Quarter Horse back under Brigade control assumed the 2 ACR's share of the demarcation line so the latter could withdraw. This last phase ended on April 12 when the parties signed the cease-fire agreement.

Until March 10 the Division occupied the area immediately around Safwan with the 2nd Brigade. To the south, the 1st and 3rd Brigades occupied areas of operation that extended from west of the Basra–Kuwait City highway to the coast. Moreno's troops also established Checkpoint Charlie at the infamous road junction; the checkpoint was named after the famous crossing point between the US sector in West Berlin and Soviet sector of East Berlin. In the beginning there was very little traffic through Checkpoint Charlie, but traffic grew when civilians began to move. It was virtually impossible to sort out who was moving through the checkpoint; some people coming south were Kuwaitis who had been released. It is likely some of the people moving around appeared to be Iraqi deserters and later some people came south as a consequence of the short-lived Shia uprising.[90]

The Brigade also provided security for a nearby "peace tent" where Iraqi delegates met periodically with coalition representatives regarding cease-fire issues or with VII Corps representatives regarding local issues. COL Mowery's aviation brigade conducted an aerial screen of the ground east of Safwan to the coast at Um Qsar. The basic tasks included preventing Iraqi troops from crossing the demarcation line, recovering equipment, destroying Iraqi equipment, and clearing mines and/or unexploded ordinance.

The engineers acquired a lifetime's experience in demolition in less than a month, though not without incident. LTC Hawkins caught his troops competing to see who could blow the Iraqi tank turrets highest. On March 5, engineers demolished an Iraqi tank literally across the Basra–Kuwait City highway from the 4-37 AR's command post. The tank cooked off for hours, endangering everyone around it. LTC Hawkins and LTC Jemiola took matters in hand; both instituted stringent safety requirements. They also developed better ways of doing business. For example, attempting to detonate crated ammunition succeeded mostly in blowing unexploded projectiles over a wide area. They learned to uncrate ammunition and arrange it to assure it exploded without scattering, and also to detonate it in comparatively small amounts.[91]

The maneuver units in the brigades scoured their areas for Iraqi equipment, ammunition, and unexploded ordinance. They buried and marked the graves of dead Iraqi soldiers, and they supported humanitarian operations as required. The routine shifted on March 9 when the VII Corps began to relieve the XVIII ABN Corps and the 1 CD. As these units departed, the VII Corps area of responsibility nearly doubled. The next day the VII Corps ordered the Division to "assist the American Red Cross in their mission to assist Kuwait refugees."[92] The Red Cross established a refugee center in Kuwait just south of Safwan and near the Basra-Kuwait City highway. The order to support was vague. In fact, the Red Cross wanted very little except transportation. Checkpoint Charlie, to the north, provided indirect support by taking guns, grenades, and drugs from those heading south to the refugee center. The effort to clear the ground of dud munitions enabled the safe operation of the center.[93]

Occasionally the Iraqis, either by intent or accident, challenged the demarcation line. On March 10, Iraqi troops crossed the line east of Safwan and established a roadblock on a secondary road in the 2nd Brigade's sector. COL Moreno ordered LTC Marlin to confront them and see to it that they left. LTC Marlin got plenty of help. The Division provided Wilson's air cavalry to scout the ground, supported by Apaches on call, and Moreno assigned Marlin priority of fires from the 4-5 FA. Marlin issued orders that evening and executed a "tabletop" rehearsal with the aviators, artillerymen, and tankers slated to execute the mission.[94]

The 4-37 AR set out at 6:00 a.m. on March 11 with two tank companies, scouts, and mortars supported by the air cavalry. MAJ Bernard Dunn, a VII Corps foreign area officer, accompanied Marlin to negotiate with the Iraqis. Marlin's executive officer in his main command post also had plenty of help: BG Carter, COL Moreno, and COL Dodson were on hand, as were LTC Wilson, LTC Gingrich, and LTC Bob Westholm, who was slated to relieve Marlin when he changed command that summer. Marlin's troops reached the offending Iraqis without incident before noon. Following six hours of negotiations that went nowhere, Dunn, with Marlin's concurrence, issued an ultimatum to the Iraqis: leave or fight.[95] They chose to leave. In retrospect, this little contretemps seems trivial, but every armed confrontation had the potential to end in tragedy. The 1st Division responded to each by making a show of force, fully prepared to fight if need be. If fighting broke out, Marlin could expect immediate support.

On March 13 all three brigades reset with one battalion on the screen line, one performing clearing operations, and the third maintaining equipment and training in the event of renewed combat operations. LTC Ancker thought the emphasis on continuing training was an important comment on "the ethos the Army had instilled in its commanders and NCOs."[96] Additionally, training kept the troops alert and reinforced standards of conduct in operations and in "field discipline" supported by the theater-wide motto, "Not one more life."

When the 3-66 AR explored the Um Qasr sector, they discovered ammunition storage sites containing Chinese-made Silkworm and French-made Exocet antiship missiles. The US Navy and intelligence specialists arrived, eager to examine the find. Farther south, the Division unearthed a huge Iraqi storage depot. The depot included everything from equipment for individual soldiers, such as boots, equipment harnesses, and clothing, to hundreds of tons of ammunition. There were abandoned antiaircraft sites, maintenance facilities, motor pools, two division headquarters, and two corps headquarters.[97] There was literally enough gear lying around to equip a small army.

Practically from the moment the 2nd Brigade secured Safwan, civilians in the hundreds showed up. There were refugees attempting to return to Kuwait, Iraqi soldiers hoping to surrender, Iraqi deserters posing as refugees, and injured, sick, or wounded people of all sorts. LTC Marlin's battalion inherited the problem when it established Checkpoint Charlie at the road junction. On March 4, he brought his battalion aid station forward in order to provide medical support to returning American prisoners of war who were to be returned via Checkpoint Charlie. Although the former prisoners were returned by another route, Marlin's medical staff had plenty of other customers.[98]

Doctors and medics at Checkpoint Charlie spent much of their time treating horrific wounds caused by unexploded munitions. Seriously ill Iraqis and Kuwaiti refugees also sought help, some having fled the Shia uprising in Basra that began in early March, which aggravated matters. When LTC Pat Ritter's battalion assumed the mission, the problem grew too large for his aid station; the 101st Support Battalion augmented the 1-34 AR with two more doctors and additional equipment. Ritter and his troops saw a great many ugly things, but one image stuck with him. He recalled seeing a young boy who had been hit in his hand by fire from a large-caliber machine gun. When the medics washed the child's hand Ritter could see through the hole in his palm. The surgeons and medics tried to break up the sad routine of death and pain with happy outcomes; they even delivered a baby.[99]

Training and postcombat operations continued apace. Simultaneously, units began studies focused primarily on the fighting at Norfolk, or as the troops thought of it, Fright Night. Units from the platoon level to the 3rd Army conducted after-action reviews designed to assess performance that would lead to training, doctrine, or acquisition solutions to improve execution. Study groups arrived from the United States, ranging from historical detachments from the Army's Center of Military History who wanted to do postcombat interviews to hardware developers who wanted to know how well a particular piece of equipment had performed. Most of the reports were published with limits to civilian access. On the other hand, the studies developed in congressional hearings or by the General Accountability Office were made available as they were completed; the office's report on the Hayles incident remains available. Hayles unfortunate fratricide incident is the most thoroughly investigated fratricide of the war.

Homeward Bound: March 23–July 5, 1991

The arrival of teams looking for insights on how well various systems and equipment had performed in the field signaled that a return home was on the horizon. On March 21 the Division began withdrawing from the demarcation line, moving out of Kuwait to Assembly Area Allen in southern Iraq. Here the focus changed to preparing equipment for the long road march to the port. On April 1 Baker led his tankers, infantrymen, and a contingent of engineers south to clear routes back to a nondescript bit of desert north of King Khalid Military City in Saudi Arabia. At this truly undistinguished piece of desert that the planners named Assembly Area Heubner, the focus shifted once more.[100] Here the troops focused on preparing to go home.

Here the team that had fought together began to break up. On April 6, BG Jerry Rutherford, who had served nearly three years as an assistant division commander at Fort Riley and reprised this role in the desert, gave up command of the 2nd AD (Forward). The next day, Rutherford was promoted to major general and took command of the 3 AD, where he had begun his career. Because Rutherford was well respected and liked, a great many soldiers found a way to get to the ceremony. His change of command served as a celebration of the Cold War army. Present were representatives from both the VII Corps and the 3rd Army, and the French and British divisions and several other coalition partners sent representatives. MG Rutherford got a well-deserved celebration before taking the 3 AD back to Germany, where he would soon draw it down as part of the post–Cold War "peace dividend."

The parties involved signed the formal cease-fire agreement on March 12; the 1-1 AVN and the Quarter Horse withdrew that day. LTC Wilson's troops enjoyed the distinction of supplying the bookends to combat operations. From January 24 to April 14, with only about two weeks' respite, they conducted combat operations ranging from security to all-out combined arms fighting. They were justifiably proud. On March 14, the 2nd Brigade started south, followed the next day by the 1st Brigade and the bulk of the 3rd Brigade.[101]

A flood of irritating instructions that reeked of peacetime regulation further confirmed that the end was near. The VII Corps and 3rd Army found it necessary to exhort commanders to ensure their troops drank enough water and avoid accidental discharge of weapons. At one point the VII Corps ordered all helicopters grounded for a briefing on "safety in the desert" and a maintenance inspection. COL Mowery was incredulous: "What do they think we do everyday?"[102] COL Maggart expressed amazement at how quickly commanders whose judgment in combat had seemed adequate now had to contend with detailed instructions on simple matters. The peacetime folderol irritated Mowery and practically everyone else. Despite his grousing, Mowery understood that while the war may have ended, in some ways the most dangerous part of the mission was just beginning. As he put it, "All that can happen now are bad things. Nothing good can occur, only everyday accomplishments." He was concerned also with "go home itis." Mowery may have found the emphasis on safety irritating, but he knew mitigating carelessness took work.[103]

Getting home required several steps. Ammunition had to be downloaded, accounted for, and repacked; equipment, some of which had gone missing, had to be located, repaired, and prepared for shipment. Every piece of equipment and every stitch of clothing had to be cleaned. Every vehicle, trailer, and piece of equipment had to pass a US Department of Agriculture inspection to avoid bringing various desert denizens home. Nematodes, in particular, horrified agriculture inspectors. Some things could not be shipped at all. Tents and canvas covers of any kind could not be brought home. Some equipment purchased in theater had to be left behind because it did not meet US Environmental Protection Agency standards. Cleaning equipment produced one of the most incongruous sights of the war. The Division built wash racks and hauled in water and pumps to permit at least a rough wash of equipment prior to heading back to the ports. Crews power-washing tanks with high-pressure wands miles from the nearest source of water provided grist for laughter among the soldiers. The sight must have puzzled those desert dwellers who saw it.

Many Army administrative requirements had to be met. Individual soldiers hastily transferred into combat units to bring them up to strength had to be returned from whence they came. Breaking up wartime task organization also occurred at Assembly Area Heubner. COL Weisman's 3rd Brigade moved to the assembly area, but reverted to the control of BG Gene Blackwell, who had assumed command of the 2nd AD (Forward) from Rutherford. BG Carter, to his despair, became assistant division commander for both support and maneuver—or, as he phrased it, the "S and M." Mundane tasks such as inventorying and accounting for property had to occur, including explaining why one should not have to pay personally for gear damaged or lost in the fighting. To some, the list of requirements or "gates" that had to be met seemed longer than the list to go to war. but with so much to do, the time passed rapidly. Most units spent only a week or ten days getting through the "gates" and were on their way to the port.

Traveling back to Ad Dammām, Saudi Arabia, proved far less harrowing than had the trip out. By this time, CENTCOM and the 3rd Army had sufficient infrastructure to make the trip to the port less difficult and dangerous. Most important, there were enough US heavy-equipment transporters to haul tanks and other tracks safely. The 3rd Army established a convoy support center about halfway to the port where convoys could refuel and make needed repairs; troops appreciated that the center also provided food, restrooms, and a place to rest. By now there were adequate strip maps and military police patrols that could help. Better still, most of the troops were spared the long road trip. US Air Force C-130s flew the bulk of them south from King Khalid Military City. The first week of May found most of the Division back near the port of Ad Dammām, preparing to confront the last two obstacles to going home.[104]

Some six thousand vehicles needed to be cleaned a second time. Washing at Assembly Area Heubner had cleaned the exteriors reasonably well, but the interior of vehicles also had to be cleaned. This more thorough effort happened near the port. Washing occurred at several sites. Most of the washstands were makeshift and used salt water. Washing to Department of Agriculture standards was no trivial matter: everything had to come out of every vehicle to be cleaned. For example, crews pulled the engine and transmission of every tracked vehicle and power-washed those components and the hulls. The process continued 24 hours a day, seven days a week until all six thousand vehicles passed inspection. This was brutal, hot work that took each battalion roughly ninety-six continuous hours to complete. When inspectors cleared a vehicle, it was moved to a "sterile" area. After that, no one, including even a unit commander, was admitted to the sterile area.[105]

Once a unit's equipment passed into the sterile area, the only thing left was to fly home. Generally, that occurred within two or three days. The flow home moved rapidly and generally efficiently. On May 10, 1991, Rhame brought the Division's colors home to Fort Riley. In a ceremony with less pomp but the same symbolism of that when the Division returned from Vietnam in April 1970, he and CSM Fred Davenport unfurled the colors symbolizing the Division's return. By the end of the next week, only the 750 soldiers loading the Division's equipment remained in Saudi Arabia.

BG Bill Mullen's 1 ID (Forward) had unloaded and staged the VII Corps equipment as it arrived. The divisions managed the return of their equipment. MG Rhame left Carter to oversee the final stages of redeploying the troops and equipment. LTC Scott Lingamfelter, the Division Artillery executive officer, remained to command a provisional port support activity. Lingamfelter's port support activity would plan loads, move equipment, load it, and lash it down aboard ships. Carter ran interference, but left execution to Lingamfelter and his team. Rhame had issued one proviso: he wanted the job done and the troops home by the Fourth of July. Lingamfelter thought the chief problem was that no one in the port support activity had any idea how to plan and load all the varied ships, from Military Sea Lift Command roll-on/roll-off ships to some "tramp break-bulk civilian freighter."[106] He was mistaken, for his team included CPT Renee Miller, who was trained in surface transport operations and had worked at Military Traffic Management Command's ocean terminal in Bayonne, New Jersey, and later at Pusan, Korea; she understood how the system was supposed to work. CPT Gene Malik, also assigned to the port support activity, claimed CPT Miller was the main reason why the port support activity finished on time. Miller was sufficiently tough and aggressive that Lingamfelter's sergeant major nicknamed her the Hammer.[107]

Even with the Hammer's expertise, Lingamfelter and his troops waged "logistics combat." They learned their jobs fast, fought for ships, and were ready when a ship became available to load it efficiently and safely. They set a record for the port when they loaded 1,530 pieces aboard the Norwegian-flagged

Nosac Rover in fifty-four hours.[108] They worked under cloudless skies in stifling holds to chain down trucks, tanks, and whatever else needed to come aboard. With ambient temperature in the low 100s, "The temperature below deck is at least 115–120 degrees. Soldiers are soaking wet. We must drink bottle after bottle of water. When you walk out into 100 degree weather it feels like it's 65 degrees."[109]

The port support troops finished the job and flew home on two flights. LTC Lingamfelter was the last 1 ID soldier to leave Saudi Arabia; he boarded the DC-10 that took him home at 10:06 a.m. on the Fourth of July. Once on board, he wrote in his journal, "This is my final entry in this saga. Tonight I will be reunited with my family."[110] In fact, he got home at 2:00 a.m. on July 5. Going home was an incredible experience. Returning soldiers were stunned by the enthusiastic support of their fellow citizens. Many 1st Division flights came through Bangor, Maine, and others through Newark, New Jersey. The people of Bangor became justly famous for the airport receptions they hosted, but receptions at Newark among the supposedly jaded city dwellers were just as enthusiastic as those in Bangor. Garlstedt, Germany had an active antiwar movement that vigorously protested Operation Desert Shield/Storm, but the antiwar protestors eschewed protesting during the troops' return, "Because that would have been rated as a personal attack."[111] They remained opposed to war, but not opposed to the soldiers themselves and expressed sorrow for those who died. However, the bulk of the German community and the 3rd Brigade's partnership units welcomed the US troops home as though they were their own.[112]

Fort Riley soldiers landed at the one-time air base at Forbes Field in Topeka. The arriving troops processed through a dilapidated relic of a hangar that had apparently not been maintained since World War II. Soldiers from several arriving aircraft reported seeing a middle-aged man wearing military memorabilia commemorating service in Vietnam. He stood silently by the airfield perimeter fence, occasionally waving to the returning troops. At least one saw him in tears; the Desert Storm homecoming seemed to be a homecoming for him as well. PFC Martha Hill spoke for her fellow troopers when she told a reporter, "I can't believe we have this much support. I am surprised and I am happy."[113] All of those who served took pleasure in the wholly unexpected outpouring of support from their fellow citizens.

NOTES

1. Kevin M. Woods, *The Mother of All Battles: Saddam Hussein's Strategic Plan for the Persian Gulf War* (Annapolis, MD: Naval Institute Press, 2008), 240.

2. Ibid., 240.

3. MAJ Mark S. Landrith, "History, 1st Battalion, 1st Aviation Regiment, 4th Brigade, 1st Infantry, Desert Shield/Desert Storm," unpublished manuscript, n.d., n.p. [37]. There is some debate over just when the VII Corps directed the cease-fire. The Danger Forward duty officer logged the message at 7:25 a.m., with an effective time of 7:23 a.m. A cease-fire order did go out followed by a "resume the attack" message. That second message never reached the 1 ID. In any case, it is hard to see the point of the second order given scheduled cease-fire at 8:00 a.m. See Tom Clancy with General Fred Franks Jr., *Into the Storm: A Study in Command* (New York: Berkley, 2004), 549–50.

4. CPT A. A. Puryear and LT Gerald R. Haywood II, "Ar Rumaylah Airfield Succumbs to Hasty Attack," *Armor*, September–October 1991, 17.

5. Ibid.

6. Ibid., 18–19.

7. COL James Mowery, "Saudi Journal," February 28, 1991.

8. Buddy A. Stefanoff, telephone interview with the author, August 5, 2015; Jed Dunham, "Black Hawk Found: The Final Flight of Black Hawk 78-23015 Operation Desert Storm, February 27, 1991," unpublished manuscript, n.d. The soldier who was left with Stefanoff asked that his name be withheld.

9. Stefanoff interview; Dunham, "Black Hawk Found." There is confusion over just where Stefanoff and his colleague were left. Stefanoff believes they were left at a rally point named Allen, north of an assembly area the 4th Brigade labeled Iraq 1. Dunham believes they were left at Iraq 1. The author believes that Stefanoff has it right.

10. Buddy A. Stefanoff, e-mail to the author, October 15, 2015.

11. The flight path of Cowboy 15's last flight is not known.

12. Headquarters, 4th Battalion, 5th Field Artillery, "Faithful and True: Operation Desert Storm Journal," unpublished manuscript, Fort Riley, Kansas, n.d., 79.

13. COL Clinton J. Ancker, "2nd Armored Division (Forward) and the Gulf Conflict," unpublished manuscript, Naval War College, Newport, RI, n.d., 252.

14. This account is based on a visit to the campus of an oil company facility the author made on about March 2, 1991, but is consistent with stories others told.

15. LTG (Ret.) Thomas G. Rhame, telephone interview with the author, August 4, 2015, quoting from Rhame's personal journal, February 28, 1991.

16. Stephan A. Bourque and John W. Burdan III, *The Road to Safwan: The 1st Squadron, 4th Cavalry in the 1991 Persian Gulf War* (Denton: University of North Texas Press, 2007), 186. See also COL Anthony Moreno, Commander, 2nd Brigade, 1st Infantry Division, interview by MAJ Thomas A. Popa, Fort Riley, KS, July 26, 1991, DSIT-C-076.

17. Bourque and Burdan, *The Road to Safwan,* 186.

18. Rhame interview, August 4, 2015.

19. Ancker, "2nd Armored Division (Forward)," 249–50.

20. COL (Ret.) Thomas Connors, BG (Ret.) David F. Gross, and MG Paul Izzo, oral history group interview by Andrew Woods, McCormick Research Center, First Division Museum at Cantigny, Wheaton, IL, January 22–23, 2011.

21. Ibid. Izzo believed that all seventeen might have died. TF 3-37 AR had no means to provide the necessary care.

22. CW4 (Ret.) James D. Logan, telephone interview with the author, August 3, 2014; James D. Logan, e-mail to author, August 10, 2014.

23. Bourque and Burdan, *The Road to Safwan*, 161. Broken torsion bars are fairly rare, as is short-tracking a tank. The author experienced broken torsion bars more than once, but in twenty-eight years of service never had to short-track a tank. Second Lieutenant Lowndes, in the Army for less than a year, had to do it in combat. Thank God for noncommissioned officers and well-illustrated technical manuals!

24. Bourque and Burdan, *The Road to Safwan*, 180, 189, 198.

25. Headquarters, 4th Battalion, 5th Field Artillery, "Faithful and True," 83.

26. Headquarters, 1 ID (M) DISCOM, "Desert Shield/Desert Storm Support Operations," January 15, 1992, A-2, M-1, O-1; MG (Ret.) Robert D. Shadley, e-mail to author, August 12, 2015.

27. MG (Ret.) Lon E. Maggart, "Eye of the Storm (Duty First)," unpublished manuscript, 1992–97, 187.

28. General H. Norman Schwarzkopf with Peter Petre, *It Doesn't Take a Hero: The Autobiography* (New York: Bantam, 1992), 474. In his memoir Schwarzkopf claims the call took place at 2:00 a.m., but given the times of conversations at the 3rd Army, VII Corps, and 1 ID, that must be mistaken.

29. Richard M. Swain, *"Lucky War": Third Army in Desert Storm* (Fort Leavenworth, KS: US Army Command and General Staff College Press, 1994), 293.

30. Ibid., 293–95.

31. Schwarzkopf, *It Doesn't Take a Hero*, 472.

32. Stephen A. Bourque, *Jayhawk: The VII Corps in the Persian Gulf War* (Washington, DC: Center of Military History, 2002), 389. For a full discussion of the events surrounding the whole miserable affair see Bourque, *Jayhawk*, 393–406.

33. Swain, *"Lucky War,"* 295.

34. Ibid.

35. Schwarzkopf, *It Doesn't Take a Hero*, 475.

36. Ibid., 476.

37. Bourque, *Jayhawk*, 400; Stephen A. Bourque, telephone interview with the author, August 12, 2015. Bourque still seemed surprised by the whole affair of that night and the name-calling that ensued.

38. Bourque, *Jayhawk*, 400; Bourque interview. Swain, *"Lucky War,"* 295, puts the call from Yeosock in a window between 1:25 a.m. and 3:00 a.m. Based on the 1st Infantry Division Main, G3, Operations, daily staff journal time for VII Corps' call, Yeosock must have spoken to Franks prior to 2:00 a.m.

39. Bourque, *Jayhawk*, 400–402. Bourque and Burdan, *The Road to Safwan*, 192.

40. Swain, *"Lucky War,"* 295.

41. Rhame interview, August 4, 2015; COL Michael L. Dodson, personal journal, March1, 1991. See also Lieutenant Colonel John R. Gingrich, "Battle for Safwan, Iraq," unpublished manuscript, US Army War College, Carlisle Barracks, PA, 1992, 2; and US Army Central Command, "Southwest Asia Deployment," in Valorous Unit Award, 1st Squadron, 4th Armored Cavalry Regiment, May 4, 1991, http://www.history.army.mil/html/forcestruc/vua_citations.html.

42. Moreno interview DSIT-C-076.

43. Gingrich, "Battle for Safwan, Iraq," 2.

44. Ibid., 3.

45. Ibid., 5–7.

46. Ibid.; Bourque and Burdan, *The Road to Safwan*, 194–95.

47. Headquarters, 4th Battalion, 5th Field Artillery, "Faithful and True," 87.

48. Ibid.

49. Bourque and Burdan, *The Road to Safwan*, 195; Mowery, "Saudi Journal," March 1, 1991.

50. Bourque and Burdan, *The Road to Safwan,* 197; Gingrich, "Battle for Safwan, Iraq," 13–20. Things remained tense for John Gingrich throughout the negotiations.

51. 1st Infantry Division Main, G3, Operations, daily staff journal, March 1, 1991. Swain, *"Lucky War,"* 297; LTG (Ret.) William G. Carter III, telephone interview with the author, July 1, 2015.

52. Swain, *"Lucky War,"* 298–99.

53. Ibid.

54. Bourque, *Jayhawk*, 405.

55. Ibid.; Moreno interview DSIT-C-076; Rhame interview, August 4, 2015, quoting from Rhame's personal journal, March 1, 1991.

56. Moreno interview DSIT-C-076.

57. Schwarzkopf, *It Doesn't Take a Hero*, 478.

58. Rhame interview, August 4, 2015, quoting from Rhame's personal journal, March 1, 1991.

59. G3, Fragmentary Order 147-91.

60. G3, Fragmentary Order 148-91.

61. BG (Ret.) Steven R. Hawkins, telephone interview with the author, August 19, 2015; 1st Engineer Battalion, "1st Engineer Battalion: Desert Storm, January 17, 1991–April 11, 1991," 19.

62. Lieutenant Colonel Richard W. Jemiola, "The 9th Engineer Battalion in Operation Desert Storm," unpublished manuscript, US Army War College, Carlisle Barracks, PA, 1993, 18–19. Jemiola's totals include destruction carried out after March 3. He reported 245 combat vehicles, 117 Air Defense guns, 23 howitzers, 303 trucks, 473 bunkers, and hundreds of tons of ammunition. Small arms totals were so high that no one really kept track of them.

63. 1 ID, Fragmentary Order 151-91.

64. Clancy, *Into the Storm*, 570.

65. Carter interview; COL (Ret.) John M. Kendall, telephone interview with the author, August 19, 2015. Kendall heard Yeosock make the case successfully that MG Rhame bore no responsibility for the confusion.

66. Mowery, "Saudi Journal," March 4, 1991. Colonel Mowery elaborated further in an e-mail to the author, January 31, 2016.

67. Moreno interview DSIT-C-076; Mowery, "Saudi Journal," March 4, 1991; Woods, *The Mother of All Battles*, 244. There were eight in the delegation, but Woods does not name the other delegates.

68. Moreno interview DSIT-C-076; Carter interview.

69. Bourque and Burdan, *The Road to Safwan*, 200.

70. Carter interview.

71. Schwarzkopf, *It Doesn't Take a Hero*, 483.

72. Woods, *The Mother of All Battles*, 245.

73. Carter interview.

74. Most units that fought with the 1 ID came from Fort Riley or Garlstedt, but units came from other installations in Germany and from Fort Hood, Texas. National Guard and Army reserve units also served with the 1 ID.

75. Dana H. Fontenot, interview by Betty Rutherford, Lansing, KS, July 30, 2006; Dana H. Fontenot, interview with the author, Lansing, KS, August 19, 2015.

76. COL (Ret.) V. Paul Baerman, telephone interview with the author, November 12, 2014; COL (Ret.) V. Paul Baerman, telephone interview with the author, August 21, 2015; Dana Fontenot, personal recollections; Fontenot interview, July 30, 2006; Linda Rhame, interview by Andrew Woods, Robert McCormick Research Center, First Division Museum at Cantigny, Wheaton, IL, June 21, 2015.

77. BG (Ret.) John S. Brown, Mary Elizabeth Brown, BG (Ret.) Lloyd T. Waterman, and Peggy Waterman, group interview with the author, Denver, CO, September 25, 2014.

78. Fontenot interview, July 30, 2006.

79. COL Maurice L. Williams, telephone interview with the author, August 26, 2014.

80. COL Maurice L. Williams, telephone interview with the author, August 26, 2014; LTC (Ret.) William H. Hedges, telephone interview with the author, November 30, 2014.

81. [COL V. Paul Baerman,] "Dear Desert Debbie," in 2 AD, Public Affairs Office, *Sandblaster*, March 27, 1991, 7.

82. Linda Rhame interview.

83. Ibid.

84. Donna Baer and 1SG (Ret.) Ted A. Baer, telephone interview with the author, August 8, 2015.

85. Browns and Watermans group interview.

86. Ancker, "2nd Armored Division (Forward)," 259.

87. Maggart, "Eye of the Storm," 196; Shadley e-mail.

88. Carter interview.

89. Brigadier General Robert H. Scales Jr., *Certain Victory: The United States Army in the Gulf War* (Washington, DC: Office of the Chief of Staff, US Army, 1993), 325. The 3rd Army's two corps occupied a rhombus-shaped area in southern Iraq bounded by Rafha, Saudi Arabia, and the Kuwait border at its southwestern edge and by Samawah, Iraq, to the coast south of the Euphrates at its northeastern edge. Occupied Iraq extended roughly 250 kilometers east to west and 150 kilometers north to south. US forces also operated in northern Iraq in response to a humanitarian crisis during the Kurdish uprising. Operation Provide Comfort lasted through May 1991.

90. For a description of the purpose for Checkpoint Charlie and the activity Maggart witnessed there, see Maggart, "Eye of the Storm," 207–10, 212–13.

91. 1st Engineer Battalion, "1st Engineer Battalion: Desert Storm"; Jemiola, "The 9th Engineer Battalion."

92. 1 ID, Fragmentary Order 160-91; 1 ID, Fragmentary Order 161-91.

93. Maggart, "Eye of the Storm," 213.

94. Lieutenant Colonel David W. Marlin, "History of the 4th Battalion, 37th Armored Regiment in Operation Desert Shield/Storm," unpublished manuscript, US Army War College, Carlisle Barracks, PA, 1992, 582.

95. Ibid., 591. The incident lasted most of the night.

96. Ancker, "2nd Armored Division (Forward)," 268.

97. Ibid., 268–69; Bourque, *Jayhawk*, 425. The 1 ID discovered the depot on March 9; some of the equipment and ammunition went to the Kuwaiti forces.

98. Marlin, "History of the 4th Battalion, 37th Armored Regiment," 544.

99. COL (Ret.) George P. "Pat" Ritter, telephone interview with the author, August 8, 2014. See also Bourque, *Jayhawk*, 415–16, 428–33.

100. Assembly Area Heubner was named for MG Clarence R. Heubner, who had commanded the 1 ID from 1943 to 1944, a time that included the invasion of Normandy. In January 1945, Heubner left the 1 ID to assume command of the V Corps.

101. Ancker, "2nd Armored Division (Forward)," 299. Assembly Area Allen was named for MG Terry D. Allen, who commanded the Division from 1941 to 1943, a time that included the invasion of northern Africa. Bourque and Burdan, *The Road to Safwan*, 227.

102. Mowery, "Saudi Journal," April 5, 1991.

103. Maggart, "Eye of the Storm," 227; Mowery, "Saudi Journal," April 12, 1991.

104. The Saudi cities of Ad Dammām, Dhahran, and Al Khobar are all adjacent to each other. Redeployment activities of one kind or another occurred in all three.

105. Marlin, "History of the 4th Battalion, 37th Armored Regiment," 765–75.

106. COL (Ret.) L. Scott Lingamfelter, "The Port Support Activity (PSA): The Non-Standard Mission of All Non-Standard Missions," unpublished manuscript, 2015, 1. This is an eleven-page manuscript COL Lingamfelter prepared from his personal journal and notes at the author's request.

107. MAJ (Ret.) Renee L. MacDonald (née Miller), telephone interview with the author, October 23, 2015. CPT Eugene J. Malik, telephone interview with the author, September 9, 2015.

108. Lingamfelter, "The Port Support Activity (PSA)," 1, 6–7.

109. Ibid., 9.

110. Ibid., 11. Lingamfelter, Malik, and Miller all raved about the endurance and persistence of the men and women who loaded and secured equipment for the voyage home.

111. *Osterholzer Kreisblatt*, March 9, 1991, 1; translation (citation incomplete) courtesy of the 2nd AD (Forward) Public Affairs Office.

112. The local paper reported the activities of the Brigade weekly. The community hosted events for families and a celebration on the Brigade's return.

113. Patrice Macan, "From Storm Front to Home Front: Soldiers Welcomed," *Fort Riley Post*, March 15, 1991, 9.

CHAPTER THIRTEEN

EPILOGUE: YOU LEFT YOUR MARK

I don't want to have to come back here in four or five years. I don't want my children back here doing this.

—Sergeant James Weaver, CNN report April 1991

I would go back again if I had to.

—Private First Class Stacy Owen, May 1991

Desert storm had a cathartic, even redemptive effect in the United States. Victory in the desert seemed to many to cast off the specter of Vietnam. There was reason for optimism. The Cold War had ended with the United States and the Soviet Union collaborating on a soft landing. The coalition formed to oust Saddam Hussein from Kuwait succeeded at comparatively low cost. Liberal democracy seemed triumphant and Churchill's vision of the sunny uplands of peace within reach. But even at the moment of victory, President George H. W. Bush seemed uncertain about just what the outcome meant. At a news conference on March 1, 1991, he admitted, "I haven't felt this wonderfully euphoric feeling that many of the American people feel." What worried Bush is that, unlike World War II, there was no "definitive end." He went on to add, "And now we have Saddam Hussein still there—that man that wreaked havoc on his neighbors."[1]

President Bush had hoped to build a "new world order" founded on the work done with the Soviet Union and on the basis of the goodwill among the coalition that ousted Saddam, but his vision of a new world order characterized by stability and peaceful cooperation did not materialize. Instead, instability and conflict came to characterize the post–Desert Storm environment. Although this narrative has focused on the 1st Division it has done so in context.

In that vein, the strategic implications of Desert Storm matter. What had been achieved and what did it mean?

When coalition forces ejected Iraq from Kuwait they achieved the United Nations mandate. The coalition, and the United States in particular, mounted Operation Restore Hope in northern Iraq and built refugee camps in southern Iraq and Kuwait to support returning Kuwaitis, third country nationals, and Iraqis fleeing the brutal suppression of the Shiite uprising. Coalition forces destroyed much of Iraq's capacity to threaten its neighbors. The 1st Division alone shattered several Iraqi divisions. In *Jayhawk: The VII Corps in the Persian Gulf War*, Stephen A. Bourque asserts the coalition "destroyed 3,300 Iraqi tanks, 2,100 other armored vehicles, and 2,200 artillery tubes."[2] As many as 50,000 Iraqi troops lost their lives in the fighting and another 80,000 surrendered. The Iraqi Army may have lost as many soldiers to desertion as they did killed or captured. US forces, however, failed to destroy the Republican Guard.

Still, the US Army felt vindicated on several counts. The Bradley infantry fighting vehicle and the M1 tank, both of which had been criticized, proved themselves superior in every way to their Soviet counterparts. Results in the field vindicated post–Vietnam revision of doctrine and the enormous investment in training simulations and the National Training Center. In the summer of 1991, the US Army was the preeminent land force in the preeminent defense establishment in the world. There were indications of change in the character of warfare evidenced by the growing importance of technology and the renewed requirement for post-combat operations devoted to humanitarian ends.[3]

Critics emerged soon after the victory in the Gulf. Perhaps the most common criticism was about why the war was fought. Some argued the war had been waged exclusively over access to oil. In fact, the coalition formed to eject Iraq from Kuwait did so to assure access to oil, but also out of genuine concern about Saddam's ultimate intention. Oil security aside, many nations believed the invasion of one sovereign nation by another should not be allowed to stand. Other critics suggested the war ended too soon and that Saddam should have been toppled. There was neither energy nor mandate to go on to Baghdad. In *The Generals' War*, Michael Gordon and Bernard Trainor described the end as "untidy." In *Lucky War*, Richard M. Swain defined the outcome more clearly, "limited and Coalition wars are seldom entirely satisfactory to any one participant."[4] In his memoir, GEN H. Norman Schwarzkopf noted that despite postwar criticism not a "single head of state, diplomat, Middle East expert, or military leader . . . advocated continuing the war and seizing Baghdad."[5]

From the outset, caveats of the participants constrained operations. For example, no Arab forces could be used in the "left hook." Although Arab states provided substantial forces, they all stipulated their troops could not be used to invade Iraq. They were willing to commit forces to defend the Saudi frontier, but they would not violate Iraq's border. Accordingly, in January 1991 Syrian and Egyptian divisions defending the Saudi frontier with Iraq moved to positions farther east from which they eventually attacked into Kuwait.

Those who argued more could and should have been done failed to explain how. The coalition formed to force Iraq from Kuwait would do no more than it did. What was achieved in 1990–1991 remains impressive and possible only because of a coalition that formed for a limited scope of operations. In the *Gulf Conflict, 1990–1991: Diplomacy and War in the New World Order*, Lawrence Freedman and Efraim Karsh illuminate both the promise and limits of the imagined new world order.[6] They show that coalition forces achieved the United Nations mandate only because of "active cooperation with the West by the Soviet Union and by more passive acquiescence from China."[7] Freedman and Karsh assert that such cooperation in the future would depend "on the general state of the international system."[8] The general state of the international system has not enabled as broad a coalition since.

Freedman and Karsh suggested presciently, "The West may not find conflicts with the principles so clear-cut, enemies so ready to take on Western military power on its own terms and circumstance so favourable [sic] to its application."[9] In the first few years after Desert Storm, it was hard to find an assessment as pessimistic as theirs. Other observers claimed a revolution had occurred in military affairs. The most often heard idea at the time was that information, or knowledge-based warfare, had come to the fore. Alvin and Heidi Toffler exemplified this train of thought in *War and Anti-War: Survival at the Dawn of the 21st Century*. They believed operations in the spring of 1990 showed the beginning of knowledge-based systems they characterized as "Third Wave" warfare.[10] In 1991 and for several years thereafter, many people in the United States believed that technology had changed the character of warfare, generally in favor of the American armed forces.

Other observers concluded that the United States and the weapons technology demonstrated in Desert Storm constituted a serious threat to their interests. In *War in the Gulf: Lessons for the Third World*, Indian Brigadier V. K. Nair made a compelling case for that view. He called the United States "the technological giant." Nair went on to point out that the United States had "'willy nilly' and progressively conducted offensive military operations against Libya, Grenada, Panama, and Iraq." He asserted that, given US aggression and weapons, "developing countries especially the threshold powers, need to review their threat perceptions."[11] In his assessment published in 1991, Nair proposed lines of inquiry that might enable a lesser power to survive American aggression, including, among other things, electronic countermeasures, passive means to protect key sites, improved missile-guidance technology, and tandem warheads for the ubiquitous RPG.[12] The moral for Third World countries is the one

Freedman and Karsh suggest and consistent with Nair's advice. No foe should take on the United States on "its own terms." It is a lesson that radical Islamists learned well.

Iraqi: Not Losing = Winning

US lessons-learned teams began their work before the war started and continued through to the culmination of the operation. After the cease-fire they descended on units in the field en masse. The Iraqis, too, sought to learn lessons from the tactical to the strategic level. Kevin Woods, in the *Mother of All Battles*, observed that the Iraqi lessons-learned efforts were "continuous, even if not always honest."[13] The Republican Guard, for example, held a conference in August 1990 to reflect on their just completed invasion and occupation of Kuwait. At an Army level conference in November 1991, Saddam began a national level lessons-learned conference with a strategic overview. He reviewed operations and strategy beginning with the war with Iran through what he thought of as the Second Gulf War. In his view, Iraqi performance in combat varied widely, but he exulted in the performance of the Republican Guard. He claimed they deserved to be seen alongside "Napoleon's guard."[14]

Despite the hyperbole, he understood well enough the chief problem—many Iraqi soldiers either did not fight or fought ineffectively. In a lessons-learned conference in May 1991 Saddam described, with frustration, an American cross-border raid that took place prior to the ground attack. He recalled that, "two Chinook helicopters," landed near a division but the commander proved "incapable [of] dispatching ten soldiers to go and fire at those aircraft to defeat them." Of this commander he said, "I feel even stones are more flexible than them [sic]."[15]

Sessions that did not include Saddam produced more candid assessments. At one such conference an Iraqi general admitted leadership problems in the military, but thought there were also "political leaders who failed in their responsibility."[16] Another general pointed out "if there are negative points [observations/lessons], then according to the permission of the political or military leadership we can also teach them."[17] Saddam, the elephant either figuratively or literally in the room at every lessons-learned conference, genuinely desired officers to use their initiative. He could not see that the environment of fear and uncertainty that he had created precluded initiative.

Clearly some of Saddam's judgments about the war stemmed from the fact that he expected to fight for survival after the bombing began on January 17, 1991. Instead, the coalition did not seek to turn him out and chose not to interfere in the Shia uprising that occurred after the cease-fire. That led him to reach conclusions that seem unwarranted from the point of view of outsiders. One of the most unsettling images from that time is a video of "Chemical Ali" stomping on the head of a "rebel suspect." The savage repression of the uprising was no secret in the spring of 1991. Because the coalition stopped short of overturning the regime and stood aside during the insurrection, Saddam and his minions concluded they had won. From their point of view, what other explanation could there be for the flaccid response of the United States in particular?

In March 1991, Saddam offered his assessment on the Gulf War's outcome. According to him, "The strongest scientific, technological, and military powers and the highest financial and economic potential existing in the region and the world without any exception. They all got together against us and did not succeed despite what happened. They did not dare attack Baghdad."[18] Saddam never veered from this view. Given the military strength of the coalition, his conclusion has merit. Saddam misjudged the coalition's willingness to drive his army from Kuwait. Equally important, he did not understand why the coalition chose not to attack to seize Baghdad. The United States and Saddam each continued to misread the intentions of the other right up until US forces seized Baghdad in 2003.

1st Infantry Division: Lessons Learned

Thanks to enormous combat capability, US miscalculation in 1990–1991 had fewer deleterious effects than did Saddam's. The US Army provided much of that capability in the form of well-equipped and well-trained units. Excellence in units stemmed from both good equipment and the training revolution of the 1970s. The training revolution produced a culture of learning from mistakes. In *The Commanders*, Bob Woodward pondered the changes wrought by GEN William E. Depuy. According to Woodward, "Relentless training was at the heart of the new [post Depuy] Army." Of the NTC he wrote, "Mistakes were practically encouraged. 'Learning through failure' became the unspoken motto of these rigorous exercises."[19]

Training was so much a part of Army culture that practically as soon as the shooting stopped units sought opportunities to train. According to LTC Clint Ancker, 3rd Brigade Operations Officer, "we were constantly seeking ways to train within the constraints."[20] For the Army, training always had two parts. Doing was part one and learning part two. After-action reviews were the method for "learning through failure." The US Army differed from Saddam's by performing after-action reviews and collecting lessons from the bottom up.

Within days of cease-fire, despite ongoing operations, both the active process of identifying lessons and conducting reviews began. It was an instinctive response. On March 4th, COL Dave Weisman's 3rd Brigade did a "full blown AAR [after-action review] of the War." The AAR, "went for six and a half hours . . . it became the basis for the first cut at a written narrative and detailed after-action review on the brigade's activities during the war."[21] In his unpublished memoir of the war, Clint Ancker wrote that this process had "become widely known because of the Army's use of it at the National Training Center."[22]

Ancker thought it unfortunate that, unlike at the NTC, the process could not include hearing from the opposing forces.

Something very like what Ancker described occurred from company level all the way up through Third Army and ultimately within the Army's commands in the United States. The process occurred more or less simultaneously at all echelons. Reports always incorporated observations from subordinate formations and usually listed them discretely so that the reader could readily identify sources. The almost universal tendency to find more flaws than success reflected the way the Army trained at the NTC. After-action reviews focused analyses on battle-operating systems. Because training was not one of the battlefield-operating systems, it was not assessed as part of execution. Nevertheless training emerged as central to success in postwar reviews.

The 1st Division published numerous studies and after-action reviews. MG Tom Rhame signed the first of them on April 19, 1991. "Operation Desert Shield and Desert Storm Command Report" is a chronology, graphics of operations, and contact summary reporting what units the Division fought and where. It includes a battle damage assessment claiming 558 tanks, 468 personnel carriers/Infantry fighting vehicles, 212 artillery pieces, 268 air defense weapons destroyed, and 11,425 prisoners captured.[23] The reviews and reports that followed the "Command Report" concentrated on observations and recommendations based on analysis of performance and/or the efficacy of systems.

Units believed they defeated the Iraqis because they were well trained and well rehearsed. In particular, they credited the NTC as crucial to success. In May 1991 Rhame spoke for most of his soldiers and leaders when he said, "If it were not for the NTC we couldn't have done what we did."[24] In a letter, written on March 7, 1991, that accompanied his battalion's AAR (after-action review), LTC Skip Baker attributed success to "task force and company drills—practiced and rehearsed before hand."[25] Baker, his peers, superiors, and subordinates agreed that training, whether in Germany or in the California desert, drove success. One soldier is supposed to have said that fighting the Iraqis was easier than fighting the opposing forces at the NTC.

The Division uniformly raved about how effective certain technology proved. The first lesson in the 1st Brigade AAR trumpeted GPS as the "real hero of the operation." GPS enabled the Division to maneuver effectively across the almost featureless desert of southern Iraq. Several important technological innovations permitted the 1st Division to breach the obstacles and prepared defenses of the 26 (Iraqi) Division with ease. Baker wrote, "No. 1 man, dismount . . . has been the bane of an Infantryman's existence for fifty years when an obstacle must be breached. The M1 tank (with mine plow), the CEV (with rake) and the MICLC (mine clearing line charge) [sic] AVLM (armored vehicle launching MCLC) have shown that heavy task forces so equipped can breech [sic] even sophisticated obstacles with speed and under armor protection."[26] The combat systems Baker described worked so well that infantrymen seldom dismounted during the assault phase of the breach—to the point that some Infantrymen complained after the war they had not been allowed to do their jobs.[27]

The Bradley and the M1 received nearly universal accolades. Despite great performance, faulty fuel pumps and high-fuel consumption were definite shortcomings for the M1. Nevertheless the M1 tank proved itself the most lethal and survivable ground-combat system on the battlefield. Survivability stemmed in large measure from armor, the weight of which came at a cost in fuel. Only other M1 tanks damaged or destroyed it. The M1 was so quiet it could literally sneak up on enemy positions. The Bradley, however, was noisy. Its transmission made a high-pitched noise. Bradleys on the move could be heard a long way off. But the biggest complaint lodged against the Bradley was that antitank missiles stored on board tended to blow up or burn if penetrated. On the other hand the Bradley replaced the far more vulnerable M113. Even when a Bradley caught fire comparatively few crew members died as a result. In Desert Storm, the Bradley gave mechanized infantry a lethal antitank capability and improved survivability over the M113. In short, the Army's ground maneuver combat systems were a success.

Battlefield surveys provided additional grist for conclusions about US technology. COL Bert Maggart led a large group of officers back to the Objective Norfolk or Fright Night battlefield on March 23, 1991. Among other things, they found that most of the BMP kills that TF 2-34 AR reported were actually T-72 tanks. Just why they were misidentified is unclear, but they confirmed in Maggart's mind that the "resolution of the thermal equipment at extended ranges is imprecise."[28] The misidentification also stemmed in part from the intelligence estimate that opined TF 2-34 AR was attacking mechanized infantry. Soldiers across the battlefield that night saw what they expected to see. But what Maggart noticed reinforced the idea that even outstanding technology had limits. Humans still needed to make judgments.

LTC Clint Ancker, and MAJ Lou Marich, the 3rd Brigade engineer, a small survey party, and security team headed for the Norfolk battlefield on March 29, 1991, and spent four days surveying it. They produced a detailed analysis that included discrete grid coordinates for every enemy vehicle and its orientation. From that they developed a logical template of enemy formations showing company and battalion positions. Equally important, they developed similar data for every damaged or destroyed American vehicle. The 3rd Brigade survey is the best and most accurate artifact of its kind in the 1st ID.[29]

Both 1st and 3rd Brigade battlefield reviews confirmed the effectiveness of US tank and missile technology. COL Maggart gained an "appreciation for the power of the 120mm ammunition. The damage inflicted on the T-72 tanks stuck by either 120mm HEAT (high explosive anti-tank) or SABOT ammunition was nothing short of catastrophic."[30] By the time Maggart led his officers back to the battlefield, they were using the term "Silver Bullet" to describe the SABOT round. Soldiers were amazed at the destructive power of both the 105-millimeter and 12-millimeter variants of the Silver Bullet. COL Maggart wrote that the result for Iraqi tanks was consistently "after tangling with the Silver Bullet—a great pile of junk where the hull of the tank had been moments before."[31]

The 1st Brigade survey concluded that bombing produced rather less damage than claimed. They found many impressive craters produced by "dumb" (not laser guided) bombs. They were as large as fifteen feet deep and thirty-five to forty-feet across. Dumb bombs destroyed few tanks. However, where bombs struck tanks there was little left.[32] Whether or not bombs destroyed tanks is not of great importance. It was enough that bombing, as confirmed by the Iraqis themselves, drove the enemy from their tanks to bunkers.

The surveys provided further grist for the detailed after-action reviews of the AirLand Battle battlefield operating systems. These included: maneuver; mobility, countermobility and survivability; fire support; air defense; intelligence; combat service support; and command and control. Combat operations revealed shortcomings in all of the battlefield operating systems, but the most serious problems emerged in maneuver, fire support, intelligence, combat service support, and command and control. The after-action reviews asserted that technology alone would not serve to address all the shortcomings, but effective technology was central to success.

The Division claimed in its AAR that it maneuvered effectively. Indeed it had. On February 24th two brigades conducted a penetration attack, including passing forward a second set of attacking units to deepen the penetration. The following day, 3rd Brigade passed forward and the Division expanded the breach in a three-brigade attack to Phase Line New Jersey. That same day, they passed forward artillery units and other combat support formations to support the Corps advance. That afternoon, 3rd Brigade assisted the forward passage of the First Armoured Division (UK). That night, the 1st Infantry Division staged for a 100-kilometer movement. On February 26th it moved forward, passed through the 2 ACR in contact, and attacked from the march throughout that night. On February 27th, it made two internal passages of lines as it transitioned from exploitation to pursuit ending astride the Basra–Kuwait City highway on the morning of February 28th.[33]

The aviation brigade took particular pride in the attack battalion's execution of its cavalry role in reconnaissance.[34] Reconnaissance however was not the primary role for which the battalion trained. The Army's Apache transition training emphasized attacking across the forward line of troops against Soviet second-echelon formations. The battalion's training tasks had cavalry missions well down the list. Conditions in the desert and decisions made at Central Command (CENTCOM) restricted attacking well forward of friendly formations. The attack battalion adjusted and executed these missions effectively. Finally, the attack battalion made several hasty attacks successfully.

Units offered multiple observations on fighting, navigating, and identifying targets at night. The consensus was that the M1 Abrams tank and the M2 Bradley fighting vehicle conveyed decisive advantages when fighting at night, but that both needed an identification friend or foe device installed on every vehicle.[35] There were other observations concerning night fighting. One concluded, "More training is required by units executing night attacks to avoid fratricide and maintain orientation on the objective."[36] Ironically, for safety reasons, units did not attack at night at the NTC. Safety was not the foremost concern when LTG Frederick Franks ordered a night attack with three divisions. MG Rupert Smith (UK) led the way in VII Corps night attacks. The British made their first attack of the war at night. Despite the risks, more training at night seemed like a good idea then and now.

But there were other problems with maneuver. Insufficient and inadequate maps, too few GPS devices, a lack of positive means of identifying friend from foe, and no direction-finding devices on tanks and Bradleys all attracted criticism and specific recommendations. Most recommendations proposed technological solutions. Command and control in the 1st Division suffered from technological shortfalls as well. Fragile short-range communications perfectly adequate in the defense failed in fast-moving offensive operations. LTC Baker said it succinctly in a handwritten letter appended to his report when he wrote, "The age and relative fragility of our communications systems, especially tactical FM (frequency modulated radios), became a monumental problem from which we never fully recovered."[37]

The Division offered twenty observations in the fires battlefield operating system. Several concerned developing targets and assessing battle damage. Two findings suggested using remotely piloted vehicles to support targeting and battle damage assessment. Determining the effect of fires proved difficult throughout the short campaign. Most of the fires findings reflected technical problems associated with supporting fires in fast-moving offensive operations. Few of these findings came from maneuver battalions. Still, against a better-led and more-determined enemy, fires may have played a greater role after the breach than it had against the Iraqis. The Army's transition from defending in Europe to fast-paced offensive operations remained incomplete, something other findings show.[38]

The Division offered thirteen observations on intelligence. Maps emerge as one of the two chief irritants. The number one complaint was, "Current Intel [ligence] Systems are not responsive to the tactical commander," but there was more. The report went on to complain, "Divisions often have to send Intel [ligence] officers to Army and EAC [echelons above corps] to personally sort through imagery to get current critical intelligence Information."[39] Finally, intelligence from above often proved untimely and of little use at the tactical level. The lesson labeled, "Intelligence Systems And Analysts Must Be Focused To A Specific Commander is revealing about the way intelligence is managed." This "lesson" complained about higher-level intelligence sections noting, "Much critical Information at the division level was found discarded at higher levels, because it was too detailed for that level commander."[40] Precisely because intelligence sections look inward to the commander they support, the brigades made the same complaint about the division and the battalions about the brigade. An artillery battalion found the intelligence estimates provided by the brigade they supported so wanting that "several times during the operation the British were the best source of intelligence we had."[41] The Division reported insufficient capacity to manage prisoners on the scale encountered and the means to exploit them for tactical information.[42] This problem also directly affected logistics and maneuver. The Division described the Long Range Surveillance Detachment (LRSD) as the "Wrong Unit with the Wrong Mission."[43] To his credit CPT John Schatzel, who commanded the detachment, agreed. The LRSD was still another artifact of a design optimized to defend in Europe rather than to operate in the offensive.

The Division report took little notice of a major complaint by the battalions who breached the enemy front lines. Of the use of Dual Purpose Improved Conventional Munitions, one commander wrote, "No one in 1st Brigade wanted DPICM fire where we wanted to go, but the Corps Artillery Commander prevailed. Result was 2 dead and 3 WIA in my task force alone."[44] Artillery units firing DPICM on Soviet Armor attacking in NATO made sense. It made far less sense in the offense.

The Division report offered no less than twenty-five observations on logistics. As organized and equipped, it had insufficient means to haul water and fuel. The AirLand Battle concept explicitly required the units to sustain offensive operations over long distances, but units remained organized and equipped for defensive combat. In execution, "Only by use of captured equipment was the division able to adequately supply the force with water for drinking, cooking and personal use."[45] In his report Rhame was less critical of the logistics system's abject failure to supply parts than his subordinates. Even COL Bob Shadley admitted, "Very little class IX [repair parts] reaching the division."[46] The repair parts system failed miserably. Lack of transport and automation and communications problems compounded logistics problems. As a consequence, VII Corps and 1st Division outran their logistics.

Battalion commanders were passionate in their criticism of the logistics system. Several commanders riffed on the theme of "if you don't have it with you, you won't see it."[47] What troubled battalion commanders about combat service support or logistics was what they perceived as an attitude problem. One commander complained, "that at every level we encountered business as usual bureaucracy."[48] There were harsher comments. One of the most pointed came from a logistics unit. The 498th SPT Battalion's internal AAR noted a "9 to 5" mentality in some of its troops. Specifically, the review observed, "Many times soldiers did not contribute to the mission simply because they were not on shift."[49] There were many complaints about the culture of logistics units that besmirched the incredible efforts of the great majority of logistics soldiers.

More than anything else, the lack of transport and an inability to track requisitions and parts led many battalion commanders and their soldiers to conclude that the combat service support battlefield operating system was broken. At cease-fire, the 1st Division probably could have continued a few more hours but in effect it had culminated. This point is missed or ignored in virtually every history of Desert Storm. The ground offensive could not have continued as some have claimed it should without reorganizing, reorienting, and resupplying.

The Division's assessment of command, control, and communications draws clear differences between the import of technology and leadership in combat. The Division lacked the equipment and structure imagined necessary to execute AirLand Battle. The AirLand Battle tenets of agility, initiative, synchronization, and depth depended on effective command, control, and communications. The technical means available varied from obsolete to obsolescent. Rhame and his commanders recognized their deficiencies in equipment. Low-power, frequency-modulated radios lacked the range to facilitate high-speed operations over long distance. The Division had few long-range communications systems. COL Dave Weisman's brigade from 2nd AD (Forward) had Mobile Subscriber Equipment (MSE). MSE was the most modern tactical communications in the Army, but it had serious limitations. Most important was that only the subscriber enjoyed mobility. The system also depended on fixed line of sight radios. Weisman's brigade had to give up MSE in order to communicate with the 1st Division, which did not yet have it. Tactical satellite radio was the best system available, but there were too few of these to afford effective communications. For Rhame to use a tactical satellite radio he had to travel to the Danger Forward command post.

Inadequate frequency-modulated radios, too few tactical satellite radios, and a shortage of multichannel tactical satellite terminals to provide telephone communications did not prevent the Division from operating within the AirLand Battle concept. MG Rhame and his commanders understood their limitations and developed the means to mitigate them. They operated when they had to without graphics, maps, and communications. Doing so underscored the validity of the concept. In a paragraph of his command report entitled "Intent is Key When Communications Fail," Rhame made several important points. First, he asserted that, "Communications will fail during fast moving operations covering long distances." Indeed they had. In the absence of reliable communications, soldiers were expected to operate within the intent articulated by their next higher commander's concept of operation. MG Rhame cited LTC Bob Wilson as an example of operating within intent, "Though out of radio contact with the division commander, the cavalry squadron of the 1ID continued his mission to cut a critical escape route of the enemy."[50]

Wilson's conduct was the rule rather than the exception. Task Force (TF) 2-34 AR, for example, made the assault on February 24th with its command frequency jammed. Though unable to communicate, TF 2-34 breached the enemy defense and cut four lanes without incident. Effective cross-talk at Norfolk contributed to success and precluded even more incidents of fratricide. Equally important, commanders and staffs did not lose focus when disaster struck. On the recording of SFC Ralph Martin's internal communications, his stress and anxiety can be heard in one moment and his determination in the next. Leadership still mattered in 1991. Soldiers and leaders sometimes had to reach deep. At Norfolk, 1-34 AR lost two Bradleys in short order. There was a moment when the battalion might have descended into chaos. Instead, LTC Pat Ritter restored order and ultimately confidence by his calm demeanor and clear instructions.

What Ritter achieved that night goes beyond intent. One can plainly hear the moment he recovered his composure in the recording of his command net. Confidence, at least in his voice, replaced anxiety. In the next moment the listener can hear and sense the transition from a shaken unit to a calm, confident, and aggressive one. LTC Ritter's skill and courage and his soldiers' loyalty and courage carried them beyond momentary fear and potential panic. The timber of their voices reveals the underlying mental basis of the tenets of agility and initiative. Agility and initiative stem not from hardware, but rather what Carl von Clausewitz called moral factors. These are, "the skill of the commander, the experience and courage of the troops and their patriotic spirit."[51] Though written nearly 200 years earlier, this observation remained relevant in 1991.

Listening to the recording of Ritter's command net a quarter of a century later drives the point home. LTC Ritter and his troops developed confidence based on experience developed in training. That led to them overcoming the intense fear spawned by the awful realization in battle that both the enemy and their friends were shooting at them. Units may be afforded advantage because of how they are equipped and structured, but in the end agility comes from within the minds of those assigned. Initiative, too, is a matter of the mind and not material. No one required Specialist (SPC) Scott Medine to volunteer to climb down off his tank in the middle of a fight to examine a compass that same night, but he did.

MG Rhame and his commanders offered a second overarching observation on the importance of command in the context of limited communications and scale and scope of control. Collectively, the Division believed that assigning tasks by echelon reduced the burden of control. Rhame relied on intent communicated in directives to exert command. BG Bill Carter and BG Jerry Rutherford affected both control and command in their respective domains. Carter communicated with Corps to keep Franks abreast of the situation, while Rutherford personally intervened when he thought it necessary. But control is more a matter of discipline, standards, and orders issued with supporting graphics. Rhame felt within his rights to harangue commanders as they moved to the sound of the guns, but once they joined the fight, he left them alone. As he saw it, his job was to concentrate forces and "synchronize the supporting weapons systems allocated to him."[52]

Similarly, brigade commanders managed fires and logistics, freeing their battalions to fight tactical engagements. The division of labor could be adjusted as required and aimed to prevent task force and battalion commanders from being "swamped by the requirement to control or employ too many weapons systems. The task force commander should fight the direct fire battle supported by his organic indirect fire weapons."[53] At Norfolk for example, Maggart made adjustments. When both of his battalions ground to a halt soon after the passage, he asked for their estimates of what it would take for them to solve their problems and left them to it. Once he knew what they needed to do and how long they needed to do it he could coordinate as required within the Division or with the 2 ACR. Later, when the brigade came upon a large Iraqi logistics support area, he committed his reserve to clear it. This maneuver freed up the lead units to continue the attack.

During the same action, Weisman organized the fight and arranged continuous artillery support. After the passage, the brigade took a short halt to get into their planned formation. Later he changed the formation from attacking in wedge to attacking on line, because he believed the latter formation would be safer. Otherwise, he let his subordinates run the fight. When Carter arrived on the scene at Safwan, Moreno headed him off. Moreno told Carter if he intervened at that point he might complicate matters. Carter accepted Moreno's judgment without question. Knowing when to do nothing is as important as knowing when to intervene. Being comfortable with delegating during a life-and-death struggle is difficult. Doing so is invaluable to producing units and commanders capable of agility and initiative. The 1st Division demonstrated agility and initiative throughout Desert Shield and Storm, because its commanders could step aside for subordinates.

The 1st Division reflected the values its soldiers shared. While some of these are difficult to articulate, they are inculcated and felt. In some cases they are artifacts of culture peculiar to the 1st Division. MG Rhame remarked, during the intense preparation to deploy, that the Division motto was much on his mind. Writing about it twenty-five years later seems odd, even ridiculous. Why should a motto matter? "No Mission too Difficult, No Sacrifice too Great—Duty First," were words that meant something to him and to the young men and women with whom he served. Soldiers are often motivated by what to others seem to be trivial symbols and "tribal" aphorisms. Even taking on the breach felt right, because it meant the Big Red One would attack first. Danger Forward and going first was part of the Division's mystique, its essence.

With the exception of the Korean War, the 1st Infantry Division had been the first to fight. What did that mean? Rhame recalled visiting with a tank crew a few days before the ground offensive. He asked a young tanker how he felt about doing the breach. The young soldier pointed at his officer who could be seen perched behind his .50 caliber machine gun. "Sir," he said, "You see that lieutenant? Where he goes, I go." To Rhame that summed it up. They were in this thing together. Soldiers wanted to be with units they valued. Several aging Vietnam veterans tried to get back into 1st Division units to go to Desert Storm—it meant that much. SGT David Douthit wanted to go to war with his old outfit and paid for it with his life. Commitment to the Division motto and unit pride really do exist.[54]

The 1st Division's tradition of going first was well known. Many soldiers did not know the Division's history in North Africa and Sicily, but all of them knew about Omaha Beach. Inculcating a sense of obligation to the unit's traditions and each other is a necessary part of building cohesion, something by which every good unit is characterized. The benefit can be seen at work in TF 1-41 after the potentially catastrophic fratricides at Norfolk. It is no accident that Hillman's troops did not panic and recovered rapidly from not one but two shocking incidents of fratricide. Cohesion, courage, and responsiveness are essential to effective command. Communications and control, on the other hand, may be necessary, but are in and of themselves insufficient.

An Ugly Lesson: Friendly Fire

In the wee hours of February 27th, someone killed SGT David Douthit and badly wounded 1LT Glen Burnham. On March 17th, Ritter reported to Maggart that investigators from the Army Material Command had concluded that an Iraqi 14.5mm round had killed Douthit and wounded his platoon leader. Of this report, Maggart wrote, "I hadn't yet made up my mind about the requirement for all this high-tech detective work on fratricides. There were some things best left unknown."[55] It is no exaggeration to say that when LTC Ralph Hayles hit two US combat vehicles with Hellfire antitank missiles, he deeply affected thinking in the Division. After that incident, nearly every time a round was fired at a 1st Division unit, they assumed a friendly unit was firing at them. Assuming fratricide became nearly instinctive. That assumption was exacerbated by actual instances.

The 1st Division investigated "friendly fire" but without the level of intensity soldiers expected. Moreover, these investigations depended on imperfect information and the results were not widely circulated. LTC Ancker's detailed survey of the Norfolk battlefield is the best and most complete effort of its kind. Yet to this day no one is certain who in the 3rd Brigade killed and wounded other Americans. Only CPT Brad Dick unequivocally admitted that his company had done so. Dick's company fired on CPT Bill Hedges's company and probably at CPT Garry Bishop's company but had nothing to do with the mayhem inflicted on CPT Lee Wilson's company earlier that night. Dick's admission does not mean that no other units from 2-66 AR fired on TF 1-41. It is certain others did.

During ground offensive, the 1st Division lost 5 tanks, 5 Bradleys, a Black Hawk, and an air ambulance from a supporting unit. Of these, Iraqi air defenses accounted for the Black Hawk, Cowboy 15, and, if the Army Material Command investigators had it right, an Iraqi heavy machine gun destroyed Burnham's Bradley. It is not clear what caused the air ambulance to go down. Friendly fire accounted for the others. The investigations that followed failed to satisfy. Fisticuffs ensued within 3rd Brigade following their return to Germany and there is continued bitterness today. Twenty-five years later a man who soldiered with Dave Douthit observed, "Fratricide is a fact of war; but covering it up is dishonorable." He is not alone in his anger. He remains convinced that another American killed Douthit rather than a 14.5-millimeter round. To him the cause of these incidents is obvious, "It's about training."[56]

There is no evidence to support the allegation that the 1st Division failed to investigate adequately. The perception stems from two problems—the reports themselves were not transparent and they were insufficiently conclusive. It is true however that opinion on fratricide investigation varied between those who saw combat in Vietnam and those who did not. The men who fought in Vietnam suffered far more both from enemy and friendly fire than those whose first combat experience was Desert Storm. The Vietnam veterans were not cavalier about friendly fire, but they shared Maggart's view that some things are best left unknown. Some genuinely believed that knowing would hurt families more than it would help.[57] Unlike the Hayles incident, there was no time to do an immediate analysis of fratricide events that occurred during the attack. The investigation of the incidents of February 27th were not attempted until days or, in some cases, even weeks later. Forensic investigation was done and reasonable conclusions reached without directly identifying who did the shooting that killed or wounded fellow soldiers. Eyewitness accounts seldom agreed, and angles of fire and locations of firing vehicles could not be determined with accuracy.

Tanks and Bradleys do not have gun cameras so there was no incontrovertible evidence as there was in the Hayles case. For all of these reasons it was impossible to determine with certainty either the shooters or the positions from which they fired. There is little evidence that soldiers sought to avoid responsibility for their actions. Certainly 1-34 AR freely admitted to the tragedy of shooting at the lost platoon from Delta Company 1-41 IN. The tank crew that hit the first Bradley in the early morning hours of February 27th came forward. LTC John Brown acknowledges that his battalion fired on friendlies. It is likely that there were crews who fired on Americans who did not come forward.

So why did these incidents happen? What happened at Norfolk reflected the culture of the armor branch—shoot first and shoot fast. Gunnery standards stemmed from GEN Donn Starry's legitimate ideas about the central battle against the Soviet Union in West Germany. Speed was essential in the central battle. On the other hand, the genuine and realized risk of fratricide at the NTC suggested accurate identification trumped speed, particularly at night. Soldiers who trained in the California desert tended to learn that lesson. To drive it home, Fort Hood–based III Corps, the headquarters with training oversight of the 1st Division, required the inclusion of "friendly" targets in the gunnery target array. If a crew shot one of these targets, they were disqualified. This approach changed gunnery culture, at least in III Corps.

US Army, Europe, had not instituted this practice by 1990. There is a correlation between fratricide and crews not tested at Fort Irwin. The 2-66 AR produced the bulk of the known fratricides in 1st Division. They had not trained at the NTC and were steeped in the gunnery culture of US Army, Europe. Gunnery in Europe was also influenced by an annual tank platoon gunnery competition held in NATO since 1963. Not until 1977, did a US unit even place. Winning the trophy for the best tank platoon gunnery in NATO was a major goal for units in Europe. That contest focused on speed within a defensive context. American tank units in Europe expected to fight outnumbered against rapidly advancing Warsaw Pact units. Not surprisingly the Army's standard gunnery program rewarded speed and did not require sorting out friend from foe.[58] The correlation between training approach driven by conditions in Europe and fratricide is not high enough to prove causation, but it is suggestive.

The M1 Abrams Thermal Imaging System or TIS contributed to the problem. With TIS, crews could see and shoot accurately at targets beyond the ranges at which they could positively identify what they were seeing. The lack of onboard compasses exacerbated the problem. At night, on flat terrain with no recognizable features, identifying boundaries and fire-control measures depended on an effective navigation and compasses. Poor navigation put CPT Lee Wilson's company at risk when it moved north toward 2-66 AR and perpendicular to the direction of the attack. LTC John Brown's tankers had good cause to perceive Wilson's company as a threat. Wilson's company wandered about the battlefield without alerting LTC Hillman let alone flank units. This too contributed to the tragedy. Onboard compasses might have saved Wilson from honest mistakes that led to death and wounding of his soldiers.

Beyond Desert Storm

US forces came home from the desert every bit as quickly as they had gotten there. Soldiers, sailors, airmen, and Marines paraded in June down the broad avenues of the nation's capital and a few days later down the canyon-like streets of New York City amid a shower of confetti and ear-splitting cheers of New Yorkers who stood within touching distance of the marching units. Truly it was a celebration to behold. Practically before the streets were cleaned, the Army continued to draw down in size. Within a year, Army divisions that had fought or sent troops to Operation Desert Storm no longer existed. The VII Corps Headquarters that fought the biggest tank battle in history stood down in March 1992. By 1995, the Army's budget had declined by roughly one-third. Eight of its active duty divisions had cased their colors. That year 510,000 soldiers served on active duty, down from 770,000 in 1989.[59]

In *Kevlar Legions*, BG (Ret.) John Brown, who commanded 2-66 AR during Desert Storm, chronicles the transformation of the US Army from the end of the Cold War in 1989 through 2005. He covers the decisions the Army leadership took with respect to lessons learned in the desert in the context of reductions in forward-deployed forces. Although neither would claim credit for what transpired, GEN Gordon R. Sullivan and GEN Frederick M. Franks Jr. had the greatest immediate impact on the post–Cold War, post–Desert Storm Army.[60]

Sullivan succeeded Carl E. Vuono as chief of staff of the Army. He selected the VII Corps Desert Storm commander to run the United States Army Training and Doctrine Command (TRADOC). After commanding 1st Division from 1988 to 1989, Sullivan served for a year as the Army operations officer. Then he served a year as Vuono's vice chief. By the time he became chief he knew the ins and outs of the institutional Army and Defense Department. Although he had never served in the Pentagon as a field-grade officer, Franks was well prepared to run TRADOC. He served with Donn Starry in the 11th Armored Cavalry Regiment in Vietnam, where he was badly wounded. Later he worked for Starry at TRADOC and served as deputy commandant at the US Army Command and General Staff College. He knew combat and doctrine development as well as anyone in uniform.[61]

Simply put, Sullivan aimed to find a way to avoid allowing Army readiness to decline to the point reached in the summer of 1950 in Korea. His mantra was "No more Task Force Smiths," a reference to the sad condition of the first units hurriedly deployed to the peninsula following Korea's invasion of the south. He therefore emphasized readiness, while doing what he could to address the basic problems that surfaced in the desert and to modernize where he could. Franks believed that Desert Storm was a Janus-like war. That provided insights into how fighting would change. Both understood they were not going to buy another "Big Five" weapons program.

Sullivan and Franks made three major contributions to changing the post–Cold War/Desert Storm Army while preserving readiness. In 1993, they published a revision of the AirLand Battle doctrine that made explicit the new requirement for strategic lift to support force projection and also sought to describe a range of operations the Army might conduct including outright war, lesser conflicts, and peacetime. They believed that "operations other than war" could occur during peacetime or periods of conflict short of war and so they devoted an entire chapter of the basic operations doctrine of the Army to Operations Other than War. Unsatisfactory tactical logistics and the complexity of managing logistics from the continental United States to the theater led them to add a chapter on logistics. Finally, they included a chapter describing both the physical and human dimension of combat. Operations in Somalia, Haiti, Rwanda, and Bosnia would follow before the Army had fully developed supporting doctrine, but the 1993 Operations Manual set the stage for transition.[62]

Sullivan made a compelling case for investment in strategic mobility in the Department of Defense. Sealift delivered 95 percent of all cargo and 99 percent of all petroleum products to the theater during Desert Shield and Storm. Buying sealift is the province of the Navy. The maritime service had not invested much in sealift since the end of World War II, with the result that only 12 of 44 Ready Reserve Force ships met their readiness timeline to deploy. Only 6 of the next 27 mobilized made their timeline.[63] Chartering vessels made the deployment possible and that is the course the Navy preferred, but Sullivan stuck to his guns and the secretary of the Navy supported him. The secretary of defense aided matters by assigning service resources to United States Transportation Command. Some 16 vessels have been procured.[64] Sullivan and strategic transporters in the US Air Force actively supported the development and acquisition of the C-17 Globemaster that replaced the C-141 Starlifter.[65] The Army also invested in strategic mobility. As a result, Sullivan could argue years later that, "If you go through the United States now and look at all installations all the way from Fort Hood to Fort Campbell, to Fort Bragg, Fort Drum, Fort Riley, you will see all new rail heads."[66] The new railheads are well illuminated and able to support loading multiple battalions simultaneously. The goal was to enable state side army installations to support strategic force projection.

Because they understood there would be no money forthcoming to invest in replacing obsolescent equipment such as the M113 personnel carrier, Sullivan and Franks looked for the means to improve combat capability at least cost. The idea of digitally linking Army forces emerged from a series of experiments. The potential of the idea perhaps was driven home most forcefully in a trip Franks made to the NTC in the fall of 1992. Franks observed the operations of a platoon of M1A2 tanks equipped with a digital link known as the Inter-vehicular Information System (IVIS). In *Kevlar Legions* John Brown described Franks's reaction to what he saw as an epiphany. Franks spoke at length with SFC Phil

Johndrow and his soldiers. He learned that IVIS provided them with GPS navigation and a near-real-time display of their respective positions as well as the means to see other combat vehicles and to send short messages.[67]

From this visit, Franks concluded that digitally linking other combat systems could be done and that the way forward was not to buy proprietary systems exclusive to a single weapons system. The digitization idea took form in an acquisition program called Force XXI that sought to take advantage of "off the shelf" technology in a coordinated way. Force XXI led to digital communications hardware and software ranging from better fire-coordination software to in-transit visibility. Force XXI technology literally enabled fighting vehicles to see each other and to send graphics and texts. Sullivan and Franks argued these digital links would increase lethality of the force, enable higher tempo of operations, and improve survivability. Force XXI bore fruit in the invasion of Iraq in 2003. On several occasions during that campaign, digital links prevented fratricide.[68]

Homecoming: July 4, 1991

The 1st Division had not fully realized the benefits of the equipment and structure that stemmed from Starry's AirLand Battle until Desert Storm. Still, it exemplified the end of the Reagan buildup and the renaissance that began in summer 1969. Fully mechanized, albeit not fully modernized, it demonstrated the benefit of the doctrine and training revolutions of the 1970s and 1980s. Because of the focus on the NTC, it was committed to realistic, demanding training. As a REFORGER unit, it kept one eye on the General Defense Plan for Europe and literally kept its bags packed. Together these requirements led to a culture based on the rapid deployment and adaptability on arrival. Far more lethal than its Vietnam predecessor, it was also manned by willing and well-qualified volunteers, men and women, rather than conscripts.

A male-only domain in 1970, by 1990 women served throughout the Division. It had been too few years since Women's Army Corps stood down for any of them to command battalions, but they played other important roles. As the G1 or personnel officer, MAJ Rose Walker served on a par with her male colleagues LTC Terry Ford (G-2, Intelligence), LTC Terry Bullington (G-3, Operations), and LTC John Andrews (G-4, Logistics). MAJ Sylvia Marable led the Division forward when COL Bob Shadley sent her out from the initial assembly area to establish Division Support Area Junction City in January 1991. CW1 Phyllis Fitzgerald led the analytic effort to identify the enemy at the breach, and it was CPT Nancy Morales who personally brought intelligence out to the brigades. Women held essential positions throughout the Division Support Command. According to CPT Gene Malik, one of them, CPT Renee Miller, was decisive in getting the Division's equipment loaded and shipped home. Genie Thornton, who paved the way, took vicarious pleasure in the success women enjoyed in her old division. SGT Cheryl O'Brien earned the respect of those with whom she worked and established a sad first when, sharing the hazards of the battlefield, she was killed on Cowboy 15.

The Division that came home from the desert differed in all these ways from the one that came home in April 1970. But in other ways it retained much that would have made it familiar to the Doughboys who brought the colors home in 1919 or to those in the Division who served in the occupation of Germany or fought in Vietnam. The soldiers who came home in 1991 took pride in their history and believed they added laurels of their own. They had their moment on the Fourth of July 1991.

Fort Riley enjoyed a beautiful midsummer day that year on Independence Day. It was the kind of day John Denver imagined when he wrote, "Blue is just a Kansas summer sky." It was cloudless and comprised of hues that varied from powder blue on the horizon to deep blue at altitude. The soldiers of the 1st Division and the 937 Engineer Group stood side-by-side on an emerald green parade ground with a salute battery adjacent.[69] Sand-colored uniforms, deep green, and amazing blues produced intense contrasts. It was the kind of day that shunted recollections of searing heat and numbing cold that often characterize the weather at Riley. The air crackled with expectation among the several thousand family members, friends, and curious locals on hand to participate in a celebratory review to welcome the troops home.

Guests, senior officers, and NCOs not required on the field occupied seats on the reviewing stand. BG Bill Carter served as commander of troops and Rhame as host. GEN Gordon Sullivan and Senator Bob Dole joined Carter as part of the reviewing party. Senator Nancy Landon Kassebaum attended, as did representatives from state and local government. LTG (Ret.) Dick Seitz and LTG (Ret.) Marvin D. "Red" Fuller were the senior retired officers present. LTG Fuller commanded the 1st Division from August 1974 to May 1976. MG (Ret.) Calvert P. Benedict, who commanded the Division from May 1976 to May 1978, and MG (Ret.) Neal Creighton, who commanded from December 1982 to June 1984, were among those on the reviewing stand. There were several preliminaries to the review. On behalf of the Society of the First Infantry Division, Rhame presented scholarships to SFC Gary E. Streeter's teenage daughters. SFC Streeter died aboard Cowboy 15. His family reminded those present that "low casualties" sounds fine except to the families of those who died. Senator Kassebaum presented a Senate resolution recognizing the Division's accomplishment in the desert. Now serving as chief of staff, Gordon Sullivan hung two battle streamers on the Division's colors and awarded Rhame a Distinguished Service Medal.

Rhame, Sullivan, and Senator Dole climbed aboard a HMMWV while the Division band played Garry Owen—the regimental air of the 7th Cavalry. Escorted by Carter, they rode down the lines of the assembled battalions of the 1st

Division and 937th Engineer Group and returned to the reviewing stand. Each made short remarks. Rhame took a moment to read LTC Scott Lingamfelter's last report rendered at noon Saudi time that day: mission accomplished and the last 1st Division soldiers were on their way home. Sullivan spoke about the Army's diversity. He told the audience what binds American soldiers together is that they, "Believe in America and are proud to be American."[70] Bob Dole, himself a wounded combat veteran, spoke last. First he read a letter from President Bush. The president wrote, "Our pride in the Big Red One and all of our armed forces is equaled only by what they accomplished."[71] Dole told the soldiers, "You left your mark on the Iraqi Republican Guard." But with exquisite timing, the Republican Party senator added, "Boy I wish they would change that name."[72]

Following Dole's remarks, the Division passed in review. Straight ranks, in step, wearing "chocolate chip" Desert Uniforms, regiments as old as the American Revolution and as young as the aviation units formed in the mid-1950s marched past. They saluted the old soldiers and honored guests and in turn received their accolades. The review marked the end of an era and a celebration innocent of cynicism. It was unabashedly patriotic and as thick with sentimentality as a film by Capra or Ford. It was perfect. It was a day of poignant potential unsullied by foreboding.

NOTES

1. Quoted in Michael R. Gordon and General Bernard E. Trainor, *The Generals' War: The Inside Story of the Conflict in the Gulf,* (Boston: Little, Brown and Company, 1995), xv.

2. Stephen A. Bourque, *Jayhawk!: The VII Corps in the Persian Gulf War* (Washington D.C.: Center of Military History, 2002), 455.

3. See BG Robert H. Scales, Jr., *Certain Victory: The United States Army in the Gulf War* (Washington, D.C.: Office of the Chief of Staff, US Army, 1993), makes the Army's case.

4. Richard M. Swain, *"Lucky War": Third Army in Desert Storm* (Fort Leavenworth, KS, US Army Command and General Staff College Press, 1994 according to Ch. 12), 324.

5. GEN H. Norman Schwarzkopf with Peter Petre, *It Doesn't Take a Hero: General H. Norman Schwarzkopf, The Autobiography* (New York, Bantam Books, 1992), 497.

6. Lawrence Freedman and Efraim Karsh, *The Gulf Conflict, 1990–1991: Diplomacy and War in the New World Order* (Princeton, NJ: Princeton University Press, 1993).

7. Freedman and Karsh, *Gulf Conflict*, 441.

8. Ibid.

9. Ibid., 442.

10. Alvin and Heidi Toffler, *War and Anti-War: Survival at the Dawn of the 21st Century* (Boston: Little Brown and Company, 1993).

11. Brigadier V. K. Nair, *War in the Gulf: Lessons for the Third World* (New Delhi: Lancer International, 1991), 97.

12. Ibid., 100–111, 121.

13. Kevin M. Woods, *The Mother of All Battles: Saddam Hussein's Strategic Plan for the Persian Gulf War* (Annapolis, MD: Naval Institute Press, 2008), 262.

14. Ibid., 300.

15. Ibid., 266. Saddam is likely referring to air assault raids made by 101 ABN Div and 82 ABN Div in mid-February. Scales, *Certain Victory,* 198–200.

16. Ibid., 268.

17. Ibid., 269.

18. Kevin M. Woods, David D. Palkki, and Mark E. Stout, eds., *The Saddam Tapes: the Inner Workings of a Tyrant's Regime, 1978–2001* (Cambridge, United Kingdom: Cambridge University Press, 2011), 214.

19. Bob Woodward, *The Commanders: The Pentagon and the First Gulf War, 1989-1991* (New York: Pocket Books, 1991), 128.

20. COL (Ret.) Clinton J. Colonel Ancker, "2nd Armored Division (Forward) and the Gulf Conflict," n.d., 268.

21. Ibid., 258.

22. Ibid.

23. Headquarters, 1 ID (Mechanized) "Operation Desert Shield and Desert Storm Command Report, April 19, 1991, BDA totals.

24. Video of news conference in the possession of the McCormick Research Center, Wheaton, IL.

25. Headquarters 1st Brigade, 1 ID, "Lessons Learned, Operation Scorpion Danger," March 14, 1991. 1st Brigade, "Lessons Learned," Memorandum, handwritten attachment.

26. 1st Brigade, "Lessons Learned," Memorandum.

27. The author had a spirited postwar discussion during an after action review with several young soldiers who were upset they had not had more chances to fight. They were told they could be as angry as they liked as long as they were alive.

28. MG, (Ret.) Lon E. Maggart, "Eye of the Storm (Duty First)," unpublished manuscript, 1992-97, 223.

29 Ancker, "2nd Armored Division," 283–87.

30 Maggart, "Eye of the Storm," 223.

31. Ibid.

32. Ibid., 224–25, author's recollection.

33. Headquarters, 1 ID Mechanized, "Operation Desert Shield," 4–6. See also 1 ID timeline attached to the command report. Details are from chapters 7–11.

34. 4th Brigade, "Operation Desert Shield/Desert Storm," n.d.

35. Headquarters, 1 ID (Mechanized), "Lessons Learned During Operation Desert Shield/Storm," 2.

36. Ibid., 3.

37. 1st Brigade, "Lessons Learned."

38. Headquarters 1 ID (Mechanized), "Lessons Learned," 4–9.

39. Headquarters 1 ID (Mechanized), "Lessons Learned," 9.

40. Ibid., 10.

41. 4-3 FA, After Action Review, Ancker collection. This AAR is incomplete as it lacks the cover letter. See also 1st Brigade, "Lessons Learned," 10–12.

42. Ibid., 11.

43. Ibid., 10.

44. 2-34 AR, "Operation Desert Strom AAR," appended to 1st Brigade "Lessons Learned."

45. Ibid., 13.

46. Headquarters 1 ID (M) Division Support Command, "Desert Shield/ Desert Storm Support Operations," Fort Riley, KS, January 15, 1992, 6. See also Annex Q.

47. 1-34 AR, After Action Review, submitted with 1st Brigade "Lessons Learned." This was a common theme within battalion reports.

48. 2nd Battalion, 34th Armor," Operation Desert Storm AAR," submitted with 1st Brigade "Lessons Learned."

49. 498th Support Battalion, "After Action Review," March 10, 1991, Ancker collection.

50. Ibid., 21.

51. Carl Von Clausewitz, *On War*, trans. and ed. by Michael Howard and Peter Paret (Princeton, NJ: Princeton University Press, 1984), 186.

52. Ibid., 23. In frequent interviews both Rhame and Carter asserted there was little they could do once they allocated resources and the brigades joined the close fight.

53. Ibid., 23.

54. LTG (Ret.) Rhame has recounted this tale several times, most recently to the author at the 1 ID museum in Wheaton, IL, on February 6, 2016. Vietnam veterans contacted several units. The author remains in touch with a Vietnam-era medic who wanted to go to war a second time with the 2-34 AR. There is little hard evidence, but a visit to a reunion provides ample anecdotal evidence. Several COHORT units were assigned to 1 ID. D/5-16 IN had soldiers who had served together for three years. They remain a tight group with their own reunions to this day. The observation on SGT David Douthit is from soldiers

who served with him.

55. Maggart, "Eye of the Storm," 217.

56. This quotation is from a telephone interview done in August 2015. It is on file at the McCormick Research Center. I have chosen to leave out this soldier's name not at his request, but in deference to the sensibility of others.

57. The author heard this often enough to believe it, although the data is anecdotal.

58 The contest took its name, Canadian Army Trophy, from the Silver trophy donated by the government of Canada.

59. John Sloan Brown, *Kevlar Legions: The Transformation of The US Army, 1989–2005* (Washington, D.C.: Center of Military History, 2011), is the best source to understand the rapid transition the US Army achieved at the end of the Cold War.

60. Ibid. See Brown, "The Sullivan Years."

61. GEN (Ret.) Gordon R. Sullivan interview, ed. by COL John R. Dabrowski, Ph.D., oral history, US Army Military History Institute, Carlisle Barracks, PA, n.d. This interview recounts his career and thinking while Chief of Staff of the Army. Tom Clancy with General Fred Franks, Jr. *Into the Storm: A Study in Command* (New York: Berkley Books, 2004) is the best source on Franks and his thinking. The edition cited includes his thoughts on the implications of Operation Iraqi Freedom written in the year following the invasion of Iraq in 2003.

62. Headquarters, Department of the Army, FM100-5 *Operations*, (Washington, D.C.: Department of the Army, 14 June 1993).

63. Brown, *Kevlar Legions*, 94. See also James K. Matthews and Cora J. Holt, *So Many, So Much, So Far, So Fast: United States Transportation Command and Strategic Deployment for Operation Desert Shield/Desert* Storm, (Washington, D.C.: Joint History Office, 1992).

64. Sullivan interview. See also Brown, *Kevlar Legions*, 94–97. For a list of Fast Sealift vessels see Military Sealift Command website. Military Sealift Command is the Naval component of US Transportation Command.

65. Sullivan interview. Brown, *Kevlar Legions*, 96–97.

66. Sullivan interview. The author can attest to the quality of the railheads at both Fort Riley and Fort Hood.

67. Brown, *Kevlar Legions*,122. See full discussion 118–24. See also Clancy, *Into the Storm*, 631–35. As chief of the Command Planning Group at TRADOC, the author accompanied GEN Franks on this and other trips. Because GEN Franks's mind was tending in this direction I am not prepared to claim he had a moment like Saul had on the road to Damascus. I can say he found the promise of digital links compelling.

68. COL (Ret.) Gregory Fontenot, LTC E. J. Degen, LTC David Tohn, *On Point: The US Army in Operation Iraqi Freedom* (Washington, D.C.: Office of

the Chief of Staff US Army, 2004). Regarding Force XXI see chapter 1. A system called Blue Force Tracker enabled units to see their combat systems on a digital display. The author watched units attacking in Baghdad on a monitor in Fort Leavenworth, KS. For me that was an epiphany.

69. 937th Engineer Group was brigade-size headquarters stationed at Fort Riley from 1975 to 2005. Several Corps units reported to the Group during peacetime. It deployed prior to the 1st Division to Saudi Arabia where it supported the XVIII ABN Corps and Third Army. The 937th Engineer Group deactivated at Fort Riley in 2005.

70. These observations and this quotation are taken from a Public Affairs video of the review in the 1 ID Archives in Wheaton, IL.

71. Ibid.

72. Ibid.

BIBLIOGRAPHY

BOOKS

Adan, Avraham (Bren). *On the Banks of the Suez: An Israeli General's Personal Account of the Yom Kippur War.* London: Arms and Armour, 1980.

Arburish, Said K. *Saddam Hussein: The Politics of Revenge.* London: Bloomsbury, 2005.

Aron, Raymond. *The Imperial Republic: The United States and the World.* Englewood Cliffs, NJ: Prentice Hall, 1974.

Atkinson, Rick. *Crusade: The Untold Story of the Persian Gulf War.* London: HarperCollins, 1994.

Bacevich, Andrew J. *American Empire: The Realities and Consequences of U.S. Diplomacy.* Cambridge, MA: Harvard University Press, 2002.

Baker, James A., III, with Thomas M. DeFrank. *The Politics of Diplomacy: Revolution, War and Peace, 1989–1992.* New York: Putnam's, 1995.

Baker, William G. *Arabs, Islam, and the Middle East.* Dallas: Brown, 2003.

Bell, William Gardner, ed. *Department of the Army Historical Summary, Fiscal Year 1971.* Washington, DC: Center of Military History, 1973.

Bin, Alberto, Richard Hill, and Archer Jones. *Desert Storm: A Forgotten War.* Westport, CT: Praeger, 1998.

Bohm, Walter. *REFORGER: Vehicles of the US Army during Exercises, "Return of Forces to Germany."* Vol. 1, *1969–1978.* Erlangen, Germany: Tankograd, 2008.

———. *REFORGER: Vehicles of the US Army during Exercises, "Return of Forces to Germany."* Vol. 2, *1979–1985.* Erlangen, Germany: Tankograd, 2008.

———. *REFORGER: Vehicles of the US Army during Exercises, "Return of Forces to Germany."* Vol. 3, *1986–1993.* Erlangen, Germany: Tankograd, 2008.

Bolger, Daniel P. *Dragons at War: Land Battle in the Desert.* New York: Ballantine, 1986.

Bourque, Stephen A. *Jayhawk: The VII Corps in the Persian Gulf War.* Washington, DC: Center of Military History, 2002.

Bourque, Stephen A., and John W. Burdan III. *The Road to Safwan: The 1st Squadron, 4th Cavalry in the 1991 Persian Gulf War.* Denton: University of North Texas Press, 2007.

Brown, Gordon S. *Coalition, Coercion and Compromise: Diplomacy of the Gulf Crisis, 1990–91.* Washington, DC: Edmund A. Walsh School of Foreign Service, Georgetown University, 1997.

Brown, John Sloan. *Kevlar Legions: The Transformation of the US Army, 1989–2005.* Washington, DC: Center of Military History, 2011.

Bunting, Josiah. *The Lionheads.* New York: Braziller, 1972.

Bush, George, and Brent Scowcroft. *A World Transformed.* New York: Vintage, 1999.

Carhart, Tom. *Iron Soldiers: How America's 1st Armored Division Crushed Iraq's Elite Republican Guard.* New York: Pocket Books, 1994.

Chapman, Anne W. *The National Training Center Matures, 1985–1993.* Fort Monroe: VA: Military History Office US Army Training and Doctrine Command, 1997.

———. *The Origins and Development of the National Training Center, 1976–1984.* Fort Monroe, VA: Office of the Command Historian, US Army Training and Doctrine Command, 1992.

Chubin, Shahram, and Charles Tripp. *Iran and Iraq at War.* Boulder, CO: Westview, 1988.

Cincinnatus [pseud.]. *Self-Destruction: The Disintegration and Decay of the United States Army during the Vietnam War.* New York: Norton, 1981.

Clancy, Tom, with General Fred Franks Jr. *Into the Storm: A Study in Command.* New York: Berkley, 2004.

Clancy, Tom, with General Chuck Horner (Ret.). *Every Man a Tiger.* New York: Putnam's, 1999.

Clausewitz, Carl von. *On War.* Translated and edited by Michael Howard and Peter Paret. Princeton, NJ: Princeton University Press, 1984.

Clay, Steven E. *Blood and Sacrifice: The History of the 16th Infantry Regiment from the Civil War through the Gulf War.* Wheaton, IL: Cantigny First Division Foundation, 2001.

Cohen, Elliot. *Citizens and Soldiers: The Dilemmas of Military Service.* Ithaca, NY: Cornell University Press, 1985.

De La Billiere, General Sir Peter. *Storm Command: A Personal Account of the Gulf War.* London: HarperCollins, 1992.

Doughty, Major Robert A. *The Evolution of Tactical Doctrine, 1946–76.* Leavenworth Papers No. 1. Fort Leavenworth, KS: Combat Studies Institute, 1979.

Dunnigan, James F., and Austin Bay. *From Shield to Storm: High-Tech Weapons, Military Strategy, and Coalition Warfare in the Persian Gulf.* New York: Morrow, 1991.

Dunnigan, James F., and Raymond M. Macedonia. *Getting It Right: American Military Reforms after Vietnam to the Gulf War and Beyond.* New York: Morrow.

El Shazly, Lt. General Saad. *The Crossings of the Suez.* San Francisco: American Mideast Research, 1980.

Fisher, Ernest F., Jr. *Guardians of the Republic: A History of the Noncommissioned Officer Corps of the U.S. Army.* New York: Ballantine, 1994.

Fontenot, Gregory. "Junction City–Fort Riley: A Case of Symbiosis." In *The Martial Metropolis: US Cities on War and Peace*, edited by Roger W. Lotchin, 35–60. New York: Praeger, 1984.

Forty, Simon. *American Armor: 1939–45 Portfolio.* Harrisburg, PA: Stackpole, 1981.

Freedman, Lawrence. *A Choice of Enemies: America Confronts the Middle East.* New York: Public Affairs, 2008.

Freedman, Lawrence, and Efrain Karsh. *The Gulf Conflict in 1990–1991: Diplomacy and War in the New World Order.* Princeton, NJ: Princeton University Press, 1993.

Freidman, Norman. *Desert Victory: The War for Kuwait.* Annapolis, MD: Naval Institute Press, 1991.

Gabriel, Richard A., ed. *Fighting Armies: Antagonists in the Middle East: A Combat Assessment.* Westport, CT: Greenwood, 1983.

Gabriel, Richard A., and Paul L. Savage. *Crisis in Command: Mismanagement in the Army.* New York: Hill and Wang, 1978.

Gaddis, John Lewis. *Strategies of Containment: A Critical Appraisal of Postwar American National Security Policy.* New York: Oxford University Press, 1982.

Gehrig, Stephen P. *From the Fulda Gap to Kuwait: U.S. Army, Europe, and the Gulf War.* Washington, DC: Center of Military History, 1998.

Gole, Henry G. *General William E. DePuy: Preparing the Army for War.* Lexington: University Press of Kentucky, 2008.

Gordon, Michael R., and General Bernard E. Trainer. *The Generals' War: The Inside Story of the Conflict in the Gulf.* New York: Back Bay Books, 1995.

Gorman, Paul F. *The Secret of Future Victories.* Fort Leavenworth, KS: US Army Command and General Staff College Press, 1994.

———. *Strategy and Tactics for Learning: The Papers of General Paul F. Gorman.* Fort Leavenworth, KS: Combat Studies Institute, 2004.

Gray, Colin S. *The Sheriff: America's Defense of the New World Order.* Lexington: University Press of Kentucky, 2004.

Griffith, Robert K. *The US Army's Transition to the All-Volunteer Force, 1968–1974.* Washington, DC: Center of Military History, 1997.

Haas, Richard N. *War of Necessity, War of Choice: A Memoir of Two Iraq Wars.* New York: Simon and Schuster, 2009.

Herbert, Paul. *Deciding What Has to Be Done: General William E. DePuy and the 1976 Edition of FM 100-5, Operations.* Leavenworth Papers 16. Fort Leavenworth, KS: Combat Studies Institute, 1988.

Hiro, Dilip. *The Longest War: The Iran-Iraq Military Conflict.* London: Routledge, Chapman and Hall, 1989.

Henderson, William Darryl. *The Hollow Army: How the U.S. Army Is Oversold and Undermanned.* New York: Greenwood, 1990.

Hofmann, George F., and Donn A. Starry, eds. *Camp Colt to Desert Storm: The History of the U.S. Armored Forces.* Lexington: University Press of Kentucky, 1999.

Houlahan, Thomas. *Gulf War: The Complete History.* New London, NH: Schrenker Military, 1999.

Houppert, Karen. *Home Fires Burning: Married to the Military for Better or Worse.* New York: Ballantine, 2005.

Johnson, Rob. *The Iran-Iraq War.* Basingstoke, England: Palgrave Macmillan, 2011.

Karney, Benjamin R., and John S. Crown. *Families under Stress: An Assessment of Data, Theory, and Research on Marriage and Divorce in the Military.* Santa Monica, CA:, RAND, 2007.

Kaslow, Florence W., and Richard I. Ridenour, eds. *The Military Family: Dynamics and Treatment.* New York: Guilford, 1984.

Khalani, Avigodor. *Heights of Courage: A Tank Leader's War on the Golan.* London: Greenwood, 1984.

Kitfield, James. *Prodigal Soldiers: How the Generation of Officers Born of Vietnam Revolutionized the American Style of War.* New York: Simon and Schuster, 1995.

Klein, Gary. *Sources of Power: How People Make Decisions.* Cambridge, MA: MIT Press, 1998.

Kuzmarov, Jerry. *The Myth of the Addicted Army: Vietnam and the War on Drugs.* Amherst: University of Massachusetts Press, 2009.

Malovany, Pesach. *The Wars of Modern Babylon: A History of the Iraqi Army from 1921 to 2003.* Lexington: University Press of Kentucky, forthcoming.

Matthews, James K., and Cora J. Holt. *So Many, So Much, So Far, So Fast: United States Transportation Command and Strategic Deployment for Operation Desert Shield/Storm.* Honolulu, HI: University Press of the Pacific, 2002.

Maulucci, Thomas W., Jr., and Detlef Junker, eds. *GIs in Germany: The Social, Economic, Cultural and Political History of the American Military Experience.* New York: Cambridge University Press, 2013.

McDonough, James R. *The Defense of Hill 781: An Allegory of Modern Mechanized Warfare.* Novato, CA: Presidio, 1988.

Metz, Stephen. *Iraq and the Evolution of American Strategy.* Washington, DC: Potomac Books, 2008.

Meyer, General Edward C. *E. C. Meyer, General United States Army, Chief of Staff, 1979–1983.* Washington, DC: US Department of the Army, n.d.

Morden, Bettie J. *The Women's Army Corps, 1945–1978.* Washington, DC: Center of Military History, 1990.

Mylander, Maureen. *The Generals: Making It, Military-Style.* New York: Dial, 1974.

Nye, Joseph S., Jr., and Roger K. Smith. *After the Storm: Lessons from the Gulf War.* Lanham, MD: Madison Books, 1992.

Olsen, John Andreas. *John Warden and the Renaissance of American Air Power.* Washington, DC: Potomac Books, 2007.

Orgill, Andrew. *The 1990–1991 Gulf War: Crisis, Conflict and Aftermath.* London: Monsell, 1995.

Pagonis, William G., and Jeffrey L. Cruikshank. *Moving Mountains: Lessons in Leadership and Logistics in the Gulf War.* Boston: Harvard Business Review Press, 1982.

Palmer, Dave Richard. *Summons of the Trumpet: US-Vietnam in Perspective.* Novato, CA: Presidio, 1978.

Patai, Raphael. *The Arab Mind.* New York: Scribner's, 1976.

Pollack, Kenneth M. *Arabs at War: Military Effectiveness, 1948–1991.* Lincoln: University of Nebraska Press, 2002.

———. *The Persian Puzzle: The Conflict between Iran and America.* New York: Random House, 2004.

Powell, Colin, with Joseph E. Persico. *My American Journey.* New York: Random House, 1995.

Record, Jeffrey. *Hollow Victory: A Contrary View of the Gulf War.* Washington, DC: Brassey's, 1993.

Romjue, John L. *The Army of Excellence: The Development of the 1980s Army.* Fort Monroe, VA: Office of the Command Historian, US Army Training and Doctrine Command, 1993.

———. *From Active Defense to AirLand Battle: The Development of Army Doctrine 1973–1982.* Fort Monroe, VA: Historical Office, US Army Training and Doctrine Command, 1994.

Romjue, John L., Susan Canedy, and Anne W. Chapman. *Prepare the Army for War: A Historical Overview of the Army Training and Doctrine Command, 1973–1993.* Fort Monroe, VA: Office of the Command Historian, US Army Training and Doctrine Command, 1993.

Sack, John. *Company C: The Real War in Iraq.* New York: Morrow, 1995.

Said, Edward W. *Orientalism.* New York: Vintage, 1979.

Scales, Brigadier General Robert H., Jr. *Certain Victory: The United States Army in the Gulf War.* Washington, DC: Office of the Chief of Staff, US Army, 1993.

Schubert, Frank N., and Theresa L. Kraus, eds. *The Whirlwind War.* Washington, DC: Center of Military History, 1993.

Schwarzkopf, General H. Norman, with Peter Petre. *It Doesn't Take a Hero: The Autobiography.* New York: Bantam, 1992.

Starry, Donn A. *Press On! Selected Works by General Donn A. Starry.* 2 vols. Edited by Lewis Sorley. Fort Leavenworth, KS: Combat Studies Institute Press, 2009.

Stewart, Richard W. *American Military History.* Vol. 2, *The United States in a Global Era, 1917–2003.* Washington, DC: Center of Military History, 2009.

Swain, Richard M., ed. *Selected Papers of General William E. DePuy.* Fort Leavenworth, KS: Combat Studies Institute, 1994.

———. *"Lucky War": Third Army in Desert Storm.* Fort Leavenworth, KS: US Army Command and General Staff College Press, 1997.

Summers, Colonel Harry G. *On Strategy II: A Critical Analysis of the Gulf War.* New York: Dell, 1992.

USA Today. Desert Warriors: The Men and Women Who Won the Gulf War. New York: Pocket Books, 1991.

US News and World Report. Triumph without Victory: The Unreported History of the Persian Gulf War. New York: Random House, 1992.

Ward, Steven R. *Immortal: A Military History of Iran and Its Armed Forces.* Washington, DC: Georgetown University Press, 2009.

Warden, John A., III. *The Air Campaign: Planning for Combat.* Rev. ed. New York: iUniverse.

Wawro, Geoffrey. *Quicksand: America's Pursuit of Power in the Middle East.* New York: Penguin, 2010.

Weigley, Russell F. *History of the United States Army.* Bloomington: Indiana University Press, 1984.

Wheeler, James Scott. *The Big Red One: America's Legendary 1st Infantry Division from World War I to Desert Storm.* Lawrence: University Press of Kansas, 2007.

Williams, William Appleman. *The Tragedy of American Diplomacy.* New York: Dell, 1959.

Wilson, John B. *Maneuver and Firepower: The Evolution of Divisions and Separate Brigades.* Washington, DC: Center of Military History, 1998.

Woods, Kevin M. *The Mother of All Battles: Saddam Hussein's Strategic Plan for the Persian Gulf War.* Annapolis, MD: Naval Institute Press, 2008.

Woods, Kevin M., Williamson Murray, Elizabeth A. Nathan, Laila Sabara, and Ana M. Venegas. *Saddam's Generals: Perspectives of the Iran-Iraq War.* Alexandria, VA: Institute for Defense Analysis, 2011.

Woods, Kevin M., David D. Palkki, and Mark E. Stout, eds. *The Saddam Tapes: The Inner Workings of a Tyrant's Regime, 1978–2001.* Cambridge: Cambridge University Press, 2011.

Woodward, Bob. *The Commanders*. New York: Pocket Books, 1991.

Zatarain, Lee Alan. *Tanker War: America's First Conflict with Iran, 1987–1988*. Philadelphia: Casement, 2008.

UNPUBLISHED MANUSCRIPTS

Ancker, COL Clinton J. "2nd Armored Division (Forward) and the Gulf Conflict." US Naval War College, Newport, RI, n.d.

Benson, Kevin C. M. 2010. "Educating the Army's Jedi: The School of Advanced Military Studies and Introduction into the U.S. Army Doctrine 1983–1994." PhD diss., University of Kansas, November 27, 2010.

Brown, LTC John S. "Desert Reckoning: Historical Continuities and the Battle of Norfolk, 1991." US Naval War College, June 19, 1992.

———. "The Hundred Hour End Point: An Operational Assessment." US Naval War College, Newport, RI, 1991.

———. "The Siege of Kuwait." US Naval War College, Newport, RI, November 7, 1991.

Continental Army Command. "Noncommissioned Officer Education and Professional Development Study." Defense Technical Information Center, Fort Monroe, VA, 1971.

Craig, Colonel Walter M., Jr. "Operation Desert Shield–Desert Storm: First Infantry Division, Ft. Riley, Kansas." US Army War College, Carlisle Barracks, PA, 1992.

Dunham, Jed. "Black Hawk Found: The Final Flight of Black Hawk 78-23015 Operation Desert Storm, February 27, 1991." n.d.

Gentry, MAJ Gary M. "Planning Consideration for the Use of Prepositioning of Material Configured in Unit Sets." MMAS thesis, US Army Command and General Staff College, Fort Leavenworth, KS, June 1992.

Gingrich, Lieutenant Colonel John R. "Battle for Safwan, Iraq." US Army War College, Carlisle Barracks, PA, 1992.

Griffin, LTC (P) Greg A. "Personal Experience Monograph, Commander 507th Medical Company (AA) Desert Shield/Storm." US Army War College, Carlisle Barracks, PA, 2000.

Gross, Lieutenant Colonel David F. "The Breach of Sadam's [*sic*] Defensive Line: Recollections of a Desert Storm Armor Task Force Commander." US Army War College, Carlisle Barracks, PA, 1992.

Hawkins, Major Glenn R. "United States Army Force Structure and Force Design Initiatives, 1939–1989." Washington, DC: Center of Military History, 1991.

Headquarters, 4th Battalion, 5th Field Artillery. "Faithful and True: Operation Desert Storm Journal." Fort Riley, KS. n.d.

Hillman, Lieutenant Colonel James L. "Task Force 1-41 Infantry: Fratricide Experience in Southwest Asia." US Army War College, Carlisle Barracks, PA, 1993.

Jemiola, LTC Richard W. "The 9th Engineer Battalion in Operation Desert Storm." US Army War College, Carlisle Barracks, PA, 1993.

Kendall, COL John M. "The Closed Fist: VII Corps Operational Maneuver in Operation Desert Storm." US Army War College, Carlisle Barracks, PA, March 14, 1994.

Landrith, MAJ Mark S. "History, 1st Battalion, 1st Aviation Regiment, 4th Brigade, 1st Infantry Division, Desert Shield/Desert Storm." n.d.

Lingamfelter, COL (Ret.) L. Scott. "The Port Support Activity (PSA): The Non-Standard Mission of All Non-Standard Missions." 2015.

Maggart, MG (Ret.) Lon E. "Eye of the Storm (Duty First)." Manuscript based on personal journal, 1992–97.
Marlin, Lieutenant Colonel David W. "History of the 4th Battalion, 37th Armored Regiment in Operation Desert Shield/Storm." US Army War College, Carlisle Barracks, PA, 1992.
Mumford, First Lieutenant Jay C. "Rangers in Iraq: Task Force Ranger, 2nd Battalion, 16th Infantry in the Persian Gulf War, 10 November 1990–12 May 1991." August 31, 1991.
Petro, Captain James M. "Operations of the 5th Battalion, 16th Infantry Regiment (1st Infantry Division) during Breaching Operations of the Iraqi Main Defenses, 24–28 February 1991 (Operation Desert Storm)." US Army Infantry School, Fort Benning, GA, December 1991.
Robbins, Cpt. Douglas C. "Operation Desert Storm, Battle of Norfolk, Scout Platoon Task Force 5-16." Monograph, Infantry Officer Advanced Course, Fort Benning, GA, 1991.
Sanson, Jeffrey K. "Ironhorse: Alpha Co. 3rd Bn. 37th AR." June 23, 1991.
Schiller, CPT Stephen M. "Fratricide: Operation Desert Storm." US Army Infantry School, Fort Benning, GA, June 25, 1993.
Stewart, BG (P) John F., Jr. "Operation Desert Storm: The Military Intelligence Story, A View from G2, 3d US Army," April 1991.
Stockmoe, MAJ Jim. "Brigade Intelligence Operations in the Gulf War, Then and Now." n.d.
Whitaker, CPL Kevin W. "Memories of Long Range Surveillance." Student paper. n.d.

PERIODICALS

'Abdallah, Saleh Ahmed. Interview. *Al-Qadisiyah*, May 3, 1992, n.p.
Al-Aa'dhmai, LTC Quais 'Abd al-Razog. Interview. *Alif-Baa*, December 3, 1997, n.p.
Atkeson, MG Edward B. "Iraq's Arsenal: Tool of Ambition." *Army*, March 1991, 22–30.
Bainbridge, Sergeant Major of the Army (Ret.) William G., and Colonel (Ret.) Karl R. Morton. "US Army Sergeants Major Academy: The Founding." *Army*, January 2005, 40–49.
Bleda, Paul R. "Realtrain: A Critique." *Army*, November 1972, 34–37.
Bloomfield, Gary. "Food Stamps Could Ease Inflationary Pains: Many Junior Enlisted Families Are Barely Surviving." *Fort Riley Post*, January 11, 1980, 1.
———. "Fort Riley GIs Are Moonlighting to Off-set Low Pay and Inflation." *Fort Riley Post*, October 19, 1979, 1.
Blumenson, Martin. "The Army Women Move Out." *Army*, February 1978, 14–23.
Brown, Ginger. "Guard/Reserve Vital to Mission." *Fort Riley Post*, January 3, 1986, 1.
Burleson, Derick. "Death Is a Constant Presence in Battle." *Manhattan Mercury*, May 3, 1991, 1, 12.
Cantwell, Major J. P. "Desert Storm Diary." *Combat Arms*, January 1992, 28.
Cartwright, Carl. "Rail Loading Underway." *Fort Riley Post*, November 30, 1990, 1.
Durie, Brigadier I. G. C., CBE. "1st Armored Division Artillery On Operation Granby." *Journal of the Royal Artillery* 18, no. 20 (1991): 16–29.
Easterly, Jana. "Annual Military Pay Raise Isn't Enough: Wives Work to Help Make Financial Ends Meet." *Fort Riley Post*, October 19, 1979, 2.
———. "Operation Manhattan: We Had It All Together." *Fort Riley Post*, October 26, 1979, 45.
Eisenberg, Steve. "Adverse Conditions Don't Slow Division Soldier." *Fort Riley Post*, September 16, 1998, 1, 4.

"11 Division Plan Is Quashed." *Army*, December 1971, 6.

Fontenot, LTC Gregory. "The 'Dreadnoughts' Rip the Saddam Line." *Army*, January 1992, 28–36.

———. "Fear God and Dreadnought: Preparing a Unit for Confronting Fear." *Military Review*, July–August 1995, 13–24.

———. "Fright Night: Task Force 2-34 Armor." *Military Review*, January 1993, 38–52.

Garvin, Ed. "Fort Riley's 1990 Budge Absorbs Cuts." *Fort Riley Post*, February 16, 1990, 1–2.

———. "Warfighter Challenges the Big Red One." *Fort Riley Post*, March 7, 1990, 1–2.

Gatty, Bob. "Congress on the Move: GI Housing: Changes in the Wind." *Army*, April 1978, 27–29.

Gohmin, Janet. "Support Battalion Makes Heavy Haul." *Fort Riley Post*, January 22, 1989, 2.

Hamash, Ahmed Ibrahim. Interview. *Al-Juhuriya*, January 30, 1994, n.p.

Harrison, S. L. R. "America's 1969 Option." *NATO's Fifteen Nations*, April–May 1969, 14–16.

Henson, Robert. "Devil Strike XIII: Soldiers Comment on National Training Center." *Fort Riley Post*, March 8, 1988, 1.

Howell, Beth. "Every Devil Strike Soldier Learned Something." *Fort Riley Post*, February 12, 1982, 1.

Jupa, Richard, and James Dunnigan. "The Republican Guard Loyal, Aggressive, Able." *Army*, March 1991, 54–62.

Lemnitzer, Lyman L. "Fulcrum for the Future." *NATO's Fifteen Nations*, February–March 1969, 72.

Lowrey, Vernon. "Initial Observations by Engineers in the Gulf War." *Engineer*, October 1991, 42–48.

Ludvigsen, Eric C. "CATTS: Simulating a Realistic Enemy." *Army*, January 1977, 26–28.

Killebrew, CPT Robert B. "Volunteer Army: "How It Looks to a Company Commander." *Army*, March 1971, 19–22.

Kindsvatter, LTC Peter S. "VII Corps in the Gulf War: Deployment and Preparation for Desert Storm." *Military Review*, January 1992, 2–16.

Macan, Patrice. "From Storm Front to Home Front: Soldiers Welcomed," *Fort Riley Post*, March 15, 1991, 9.

———. "Vehicles Loaded." *Fort Riley Post*, December 7, 1990, 4.

Maggart, COL Lon E. "A Leap of Faith." *Armor*, January–February 1992, 24–32.

May, LTC Theodore S. "Training Devices Become 'Big Business.'" *Military Review*, September 1976, 79–84.

McNamara, Robert S. Excerpt from Defense Posture Statement of Robert S. McNamara, *Army Digest*, July 1968, 44.

Meseke, Mark M. "Reduction in Force Impact Reduced." *Fort Riley Post*, June 10, 1988, 4.

Morningstar, Major James K. "Points of Attack: Lessons from the Breach." *Armor*, January–February 1998, 7–13.

Newman, Maj. Gen. A. S. "The Forward Edge: A Volunteer Army Is More Fun, But . . ." *Army*, April 1971, 59–60.

"Non-Essential Spending Curtailed." *Fort Riley Post*, August 31, 1990, 4.

Osterholzer Kreisblatt, March 9, 1991, 1. Translation provided courtesy of the 2nd AD (Forward) Public Affairs Office.

Parson, Lew. "Gallant Eagle 80: The Best Exercise of Its Kind—No Better Place to Train. *Fort Riley Post*, April 4, 1980, 1.

Puryear, CPT A. A., and LT Gerald R. Haywood II, "Ar Rumaylah Airfield Succumbs to Hasty Attack." *Armor*, September–October 1991, 16–20.
"Redesignation Completed." *Fort Riley Post*, April 17, 1970, 1–2.
Resor, Stanley R. "Small Budgets Big Mission Will Demand Adroit Steering." *Army Green Book*, October 1970, 17–22.
Rosenberg, Larry. "121st Hard At It in NTC Desert." *Fort Riley Post*, August 26, 1983, 1.
Rutherford, COL Wilson R., III, and MAJ William L. Brame. "Brute Force Logistics." *Military Review*, March 1993, 61–69.
Schrecengost, Dave. "Based on Historical Data: This Was the Safest Even for Big Red One Soldiers." *Fort Riley Post*, November 23, 1988, 3.
———. "REFORGER Safety Successful, Exceeds Goal." *Fort Riley Post*, November 23, 1989, 3.
———. "Troops Continue Redeployment." *Fort Riley Post*, October 14, 1988, 1.
2 AD, Public Affairs Office. *Sandblaster*. Newsletter. Garlstedt, Germany. Bound volume, personal collection of COL (Ret.) V. Paul Baerman, Monument, CO.
Seminara, Mark. "River Crossing Exercise Challenges Soldiers." *Fort Riley Post*, September 13, 1985, 1.
Skinner, Tom. "Secretary of Defense Pays Visit to Post." *Fort Riley Post*, July 27, 1990, 1.
Smith, General Sir Rupert. "A Commander Reflects." *Journal of Military Operations*, Winter 2012, 4–7.
Stephens, Lori. "Discipline Developmental Preparation." *Fort Riley Post*, November 30, 1990, 1.
Sullivan, Kevin. "The (Plastic) Key to Understanding Iranian Martyrdom." *Real Clear World*, May 3, 2013, 1.
Swain, COL Richard M. "Reflections on the Revisionist Critique: Ground Operations in the Gulf War." *Army*, August 1996, 25–31.
Taylor, GEN Maxwell D. "Is an Army Career Still Worthwhile?" *Army*, February 1973, 10–13.
Tice, Jim. "'Coming Through' the Big Red Raid," *Army Times*, August 26, 1991, 12, 16, 18, 20.
"Unit Deploys, Others Prepare." *Fort Riley Post*, September 7, 1990, 1.
"Valor." *Army Digest*, June 1970, 71.
Vogel, Steve. "Hell Night: For the 2nd Armored Division (FWD) It Was No Clean War." *Army Times*, October 7, 1991, 7–8, 14–16, 18, 24, 69.
———. "Numbness, Chills Strike Witnesses," *Army Times*, August 26, 1991: 4, 6.
Wilson, LTC Robert. "Tanks in the Division Cavalry Squadron." *Armor*, July–August, 1992, 6–11.

PRIMARY SOURCES

Official Publications

Central Intelligence Agency, Directorate of Intelligence. *Operation Desert Storm: A Snapshot of the Battlefield*. IA 93-10022. Washington, DC: Central Intelligence Agency, 1993.
Combat Studies Institute. *Sixty Years of Reorganizing for Combat: A Historical Trends Analysis*. CSI Report 14. Fort Leavenworth, KS: Combat Studies Institute, 1999.
Korpanty, Robert S., PE. *Rail Deployment at CONUS Installations during Operation Desert Storm*. MTMCTEA Report OA 91-4a-26. Fort Eustis, VA: Military Traffic Command Transportation Engineering Agency, 1992.

US Army. *Tanking in the Desert.* Fort Knox, KY: Armor Center, 1990.

———. *US Army Deaths and Prisoners of War (POW) in the Persian Gulf War, 1990–1991: Historical Resources Branch Fact Sheet.* Washington, DC: Center of Military History, n.d.

US Army Intelligence Agency. *How They Fight: Desert Shield Order of Battle Handbook.* Washington, DC: US Army Intelligence Agency, 1990.

———. *Identifying the Iraqi Threat and How They Fight.* Washington, DC: US Army Intelligence Agency, 1990.

US Army War College. *Study in Military Professionalism.* Carlisle Barracks, PA: US Army War College, 1970.

US Department of the Army. *Division Operations.* FM 71-100. Washington, DC: US Department of the Army, 1990.

———. *A Guide to Establishing Family Support Groups.* Pamphlet 608-47. Washington, DC: US Department of the Army, 1988.

———. *Operations.* FM 100-5, 1976 ed. Washington, DC: US Department of the Army, 1976.

———. *Operations.* FM 100-5, 1982 ed. Washington DC: US Department of the Army, 1982.

———. *Operations.* FM 100-5, 1986 ed. Washington DC: US Department of the Army, 1986.

———. *A Review of Education and Training of Officers.* Washington, DC: US Department of the Army, 1978.

———. *Tank Gunnery.* FM 17-12. Washington, DC: US Department of the Army, 1972.

US Department of Defense. "Operations Desert Shield/Desert Storm." Timeline. http://www.gulflink.osd.mil/timeline/time2.htm.

US General Accounting Office. *Operation Desert Storm: Apache Helicopter Fratricide Incident.* Washington, DC: US General Accounting Office, 1993.

US Senate. 1991. *Operation Desert Shield/Desert Storm: Hearings before the Committee of Armed Services United States Senate, 102 Congress First Session.* Washington, DC: GPO.

Unit Records, Memoranda, Briefings, and Other Documents

Conflict Records Research Center

Located on the campus of the National Defense University at Fort McNair in Washington, DC, the Conflict Records Research Center houses several collections of captured Iraqi documents and other media including recordings. There are two major collections: one on Saddam Hussein and one on al-Qaeda. There are nearly 60,000 pages and two hundred hours of Saddam on tape in the Saddam Hussein collection. For the present the records at the center are the best means of documenting the Iraqi perspective during Saddam's regime. Documents are organized according to a taxonomy based on metadata that define the source, the kind of media, and general information. Thus, SH defines a work as coming from the Saddam Hussein Collection, IZAR is a document or transcript pertaining to the Iraqi Army, and GMID is a document from the Military Intelligence Directorate. The Conflict Records Research Center proved able to provide limited support at the outset of this effort, but it is essentially hors de combat at present due to budget constraints.

The Art of War: The Training for War Manual—Basic Iraqi Army Operations and Training Manual. SH-IZAR-D-001-417.
"Discussion Regarding Cease Fire in 1st Gulf War." SH-PWDN-D-000-534.
"A Dossier on the Role of Iraqi AF in 1st Gulf War." SH-AADF-D-000-396.
42nd Armor Brigade. "Emergency Plan for Dealing with Enemy Landings at Chosen Targets." Counter-Paratroop Plan Number 3. SH-AFGC-D-001-141.
General Military Intelligence Directorate. "Tracking of Coalition Forces Movement in the Theater." SH-GMID-D-000-957.
"Instructions to Withdraw Iraqi Army from Kuwait." SH-PWDN-D-000-406.
"Iraqi Report on the 1st Gulf War." SH-MISC-D-000-952. Includes complaints on the influence of the American Israel Public Affairs Committee.
"Iraqi Study of 1991 Gulf War." SH-MISC-D-000-641.
"Meeting between Saddam Hussein and Advisors on the Potential for War with US in 1990." SH-SHTP-A-000-848.
"Meeting between Saddam Hussein and His Military Commanders after the First Gulf War." SH-SHTP-V-000-237.
"Memoranda on Invasion of Kuwait and Coalition Operations to Liberate Kuwait." SH-GMID-D-000-998. Includes assessment of Iraqi and coalition morale.
"Overview of Iraqi Army Basic Tactics and Organization." SH-AADF-D-000-597.
Report on Republican Guard fighting in Kuwait in 1st Gulf War. SH-PWDN-D-000-346.
Various telegrams, memoranda, and intelligence reports on the First Gulf War, August–September 1990. SH-MISC-D-000-901.
"Warnings of Imminent Ground Attack." SH-GMID-D-001-798.

First Infantry Division

As the following lists show, there is no consistent naming convention used in 1st Division documents. I have cited credited authors and titles as they appear. Daily staff journals are records kept at each command post and staff section. Unless otherwise specified, all of the citations are from the operations section.

First Brigade, First Infantry Division

1st Brigade, 1st Infantry Division. Recording of Brigade Operations and Intelligence frequency on February 24, 1991.
———. Daily staff journal, February 24–28, 1991.
———. "SPOT Report for General Gordon R. Sullivan." March 2, 1991.
Headquarters, 1st Brigade, 1st Infantry Division. Graphics. February 17, 1992.
Headquarters, 1st Brigade, 1st Infantry Division (Mechanized). "Order Desert Storm-4, 26 1800 Jan 91." This is the operations order for the assault executed on February 24, 1991.
Stockmoe, CPT Jim, ed. *1st Brigade, 1st Infantry Division: Desert Shield/Storm History.* Fort Riley, KS: 1st Brigade, 1st Infantry Division, 1991.

Fifth Battalion, Sixteenth Infantry

5-16 Infantry. Daily staff journal, January 31–March 6, 1991.
Headquarters, 5-16 Infantry (Mechanized), 1st Infantry Division (Mechanized). "Frago #7 to Desert Ranger 3, 22 1600 Feb 91." TF 5-16 INF operations order for the assault executed on February 24, 1991.
TF 5-16 IN. "Frago #8 To OPLAN Desert Ranger 3." TF 5-16 IN fragmentary order to attack, Objective 12K, February 25, 1991.

First Battalion, Thirty-Fourth Armor

1st Battalion, 34th Armor. *Annual Historical Supplement FY 91.* Fort Riley, KS: 1st Battalion, 34th Armor, 1991.

———. "Centurions in Operation Desert Storm." n.d. This document was likely part of the unit's valorous unit award nomination.

———. Daily staff journal, February 24–28, 1991.

———. "1st Battalion, 34th Armor in the Ground War against Iraq: Demons in the Desert." n.d.

Second Battalion, Thirty-Fourth Armor

Glaze, 1LT Gregory G. 2nd Battalion, 34th Armor journal. Unofficial handwritten daily log, November 8, 1990–April 13, 1991. Glaze made entries nearly every day, and the commander made frequent but not daily entries. This journal was intended to add depth to the daily staff journal required by regulation.

2 Battalion, 34th Armor. "Army Logistics: Failure in Combat." n.d. Unsigned submission to 2-34 AR after-action review included in after-action record without comment.

———. "Attack on Objective Norfolk." March 26, 1991.

———. "Battle Debrief: Battle for Objective Norfolk." n.d. Unsigned record included in 2-34 AR after-action review.

———. "Breach of Enemy Positions, 24 and 25 February, 1991." March 13, 1991.

———. Company C radio net recording. n.d. John Sack Collection, Howard Gotlieb Archival Research Center, Boston University. The recording came into the possession of John Sack, although he may not have been the sole source of the recording.

———. Daily staff journal, November 8, 1990–April 13, 1991.

———. "Desert Lore #1." March 24, 1991.

———. "Desert Lore #2: Tactics and Techniques." March 23, 1991.

———. "Operation Desert Storm AAR." March 8, 1991.

2 Battalion, 34th Armor, D Team. TF 2-34 AR radio net during the night of February 26–27, 1991. Transcript by SPC James Clemens. n.d.

Task Force 2-34 AR. "Battle for Objective Norfolk 26–27 Feb. 91." 1991. Valorous Unit Award recommendation. Packet is incomplete, but includes daily staff journal and supporting documents such as ammunition consumption and prisoners captured.

———. Order DSA-4-91. January 26, 1991.

———. "Valorous Unit Award Recommendation Breach: 23–25 Feb. 91." 1991. Narrative, orders, daily staff journal, and supporting documents associated with the breach.

First Engineer Battalion

1st Engineer Battalion. "1st Engineer Battalion: Desert Storm, January 17, 1991–April 11, 1991." Unit journal. n.d.

Fourth Brigade, First Infantry Division

4th Brigade, 1st Infantry Division, 1st Battalion, 1st Aviation Regiment. Daily staff journal, February 24–March 1, 1991.

———. "Operation Desert Shield/Storm Unit History: 8 November 1990 to 25 May 1991." 1990–91.

4th Brigade, 1st Infantry Division (Mechanized). "Desert Storm Highlights." n.d.

4th Brigade, Tactical Operations Center. 4th Brigade daily staff journal, February 21–March 1, 1991.

Headquarters, 4th Brigade, 1st Infantry Division. "4th Brigade Operation Desert Shield/Storm." n.d.

Reichelderfer, LTC Ronald R. "Valorous Unit Award." November 18, 1991.

Headquarters, First Infantry Division

Danger Forward [1st Infantry Division Tactical Command Post]. Daily staff journal, January 15–March 5, 1991.

Headquarters, 1 ID (Mech), Memorandum for Commander PERSCOM Operation Desert Storm Casualties/Injuries, March 14, 1991.

1st Infantry Division. "Desert Storm." n.d.

———. "Desert Storm Mission." n.d.

———. "Firing Incident O/A 0100 17 February 1991." February 17, 1991.

———. "1st ID, Scorpion Danger." n.d.

———. *Fort Riley KS, Home of the 1st Infantry Division (Mechanized): Annual Historical Supplement FY 85.* Fort Riley, KS: 1st Infantry Division, 1985.

———. *Platoon Kills Battalion (PKB) Situational Training Exercise: Live Fire Exercise Handbook.* Fort Riley, KS: 1st Infantry Division (Mechanized), 1999.

———. *Redeployment of the First Infantry Division: After Action Report.* n.d.

———. Tactical Command Post daily staff journal, February 24–March 1, 1991.

1st Infantry Division Main, G3, Operations. Daily staff journal, January 28–March 5, 1991.

1st Infantry Division (Mechanized). "Big Red One: Logistics Readiness: Deployment through Reconstitution." January 13, 1992.

———. "Danger Homecoming." Operations Plan 150–91. King Khalid Military City, Saudi Arabia. April 10, 1991.

———. "Operation Desert Shield/Storm Briefing." September 17, 1991. There are several variations on this briefing, some of which have different information. Many of these are not dated. Some versions are identified only by who gave the briefing or the audience. I have chosen to list only the base briefing and a variation used by COL Gary LaGrange.

Headquarters, 1st Infantry Division. "Platoon Gunnery Proficiency." August 16, 1990.

———. *Operations Plan Keystone Blue Jay: Redeployment of the 1st Infantry Division: AAR.* APO 96345. Fort Riley, KS: Headquarters, 1st Infantry Division, 1980.

Headquarters, 1st Infantry Division (Forward). *Desert Shield/Storm After-Action Report: VII Corps Debarkation and Onward Movement.* Fort Riley, KS: Headquarters, 1st Infantry Division (Forward), 1991.

Headquarters, 1st Infantry Division (Mechanized). *Operation Desert Shield and Desert Storm Command Report.* Fort Riley, KS: Headquarters, 1st Infantry Division (Mechanized), 1991.

———. "Operation Desert Shield and Desert Storm First Look Chronology of Events." March 14, 1991.

Headquarters, 1st Infantry Division (Mechanized) and Fort Riley. "Republican Flats—Setting the Azimuth." February 21, 1989.

———. *Iraqi Threat Handbook.* Fort Riley, KS: Headquarters, 1st Infantry Division (Mechanized) and Fort Riley, 1990.

Second Brigade, First Infantry Division

Second Battalion, Sixteenth Infantry

Headquarters, 2nd Battalion, 16th Infantry Regiment. 1991. "Task Force 2-16 Infantry Valorous Unit Award Nomination." June 26, 1991.

2 Bde, 1st Infantry Division (Mechanized). Opord 3-91. n.d.

Third Battalion, Thirty-Seventh Armor

Morningstar, MAJ James K. "Task Force 3-37 Armor in Operation Desert Storm." n.d.

3rd Battalion, 37th Armor. "Mine Plow Exercise: Lessons Learned." January 18, 1991.

———. "EPW Update." Message 27, 11 1849 Z Feb 91. February 1991.

———. "History of Task Force 3-37 Armor: Operation Desert Storm, Valorous Unit Award Narrative and Vignettes." n.d.

———. OPORD DS 4-91. 26 1400 January. January 1991.

———. OPORD 3-91, "Desert Strike." 13 1400 Feb 91. February 1991.

First Infantry Division Artillery

4-5 Field Artillery, Tactical Operations Center. 4-5 FA daily staff journal, February 18–March 11, 1991.

———. "Battle Book for the Company FSO." Standard operating procedures contemporary to Desert Shield/Storm. n.d.

Headquarters, 4th Battalion, 5th Field Artillery, plans and orders issued during Operation Desert Shield/Storm, including overlays.

———. Newsletters published for family support group.

First Infantry Division, Support Command

Headquarters, 1 ID (M) DISCOM. "Desert Shield/Desert Storm Support Operations." January 15, 1992.

513th Military Intelligence Brigade

The 513th was the theater intelligence brigade assigned to support US Central Command. COL Stuart Herrington operated the Joint Debriefing Center, where the unit debriefed captured Iraqi Officers. Some of the Debriefing Center records are declassified and may be found at the Army Historical and Education Center in Carlisle, Pennsylvania. The collection there includes Joint Debriefing Center Reports 53–74. For a summary, see 513th Military Intelligence Brigade Joint Debriefing Center, "The Gulf War: An Iraqi General Officer's Perspective," March 11, 1991, in the Robert R. McCormick Research Center at Cantigny in Wheaton, Illinois. While these records are declassified, some of them contain the names of Iraqi general officers. In the interest of protecting their safety, I have not cited the names of those known to be alive. Few of the records in either of these collections apply specifically to the units the 1st ID attacked, although several are summaries that may include officers from those units. The Joint Debriefing Center Records support insight into the Iraqi point of view.

Second Armored Division (Forward)

Ancker, COL (Ret.) Clinton J. Personal Collection. n.d. Ancker served as G3 in the 2nd Armored Division (Forward). He kept approximately seven linear feet of records, memoranda, notes, and periodicals relating to the 2nd Armored Division (Forward) and the 1st Infantry Division (Mechanized). The bulk of the records are in eight three-ring binders amounting to several thousands of pages. The contents are as follows:

Book 1: After-action reviews.
Book 2: Handouts provided to the participants of in the Gulf War Illness Conference hosted by the Department of Defense in 1997.
Book 3: After-action reviews and notes made by LTC Ancker.

Book 4: Letters, postwar notes and news stories.

Book 5: Memoranda varying from VII Corps Information sheets, Center of Military History Information Papers, and miscellaneous information handouts on everything from culture in Saudi Arabia to precombat inspection checks.

Book 6: Lessons learned, grid coordinates to enemy positions and combat vehicles at Objective Norfolk, TF 1-41 INF Valorous Unit Award packet.

Book 7: Combat interviews and documents pertaining to TF Rafha mission.

Book 8: Miscellaneous orders, fact sheets, and documents.

G2, 2nd Armored Division (Forward). "Operation Desert Storm Battle Reconstruction." Charts. n.d.

Headquarters, 2d Armored Division (Forward). "Operations Desert Shield/Storm Intelligence After Action Review, Lesson Learned." June 18, 1992.

Headquarters, 3rd Brigade, 2nd Armored Division (Forward). "Operation Desert Shield." APO NY 09758. March 10, 1991. Informal investigation of the night attack conducted by the 3rd Brigade on February 26–27, 1991.

2nd Armored Division. n.d. "The Hundred Hour War."

2nd Armored Division (Forward). "The Battle for Objective Norfolk 2nd Armored Division (FWD) 26–27 February 1991." n.d.

———. "Blackheart." October 9, 1992.

———. Briefing script. n.d.

———. Memorandum for G3, external after-action comments, Operation Desert Storm. March 11, 1991.

———. "Task Force Iron After-Action Report." n.d.

3rd Brigade, 2nd Armored Division (Forward). Daily staff journal, January 29, 1990–February 28, 1991.

———. "TF Iron Intelligence Operations." February 18, 1991.

2nd Armored Cavalry Regiment

Headquarters, 3rd Squadron, 2nd Armored Cavalry Regiment. Memorandum for record, Operations Desert Shield and Desert Storm, March 30, 1992.

2 ACR Operations. "Operation Desert Storm 2 ACR Operations Summary 23 Feb–1 Mar 91." n.d.

———. Sketches. n.d.

US Army Central Command, Third Army

Fragmentary Orders 153-91 through 240-91. Collected by BG Stanley F. Cherrie, G3, VII Corps, The documents were declassified after a page-by-page review in 1995. Subsequently, they were reviewed and marked by the Center for Army Lessons Learned in 1997, in accordance with the Department of Defense Declassification Instructions Issued in 1992. The Fragmentary Orders (FRAGOS) cover the period January 3, 1991–March 1, 1991. These include FRAGOS 1-91 through 240-91, less FRAGOS 11-91, 20-91, 21-91, 23-91, 33-91, and 39-91.

US Army Central Command. Valorous Unit Award, 1st Squadron, 4th Armored Cavalry Regiment. May 4, 1991. http://www.history.army.mil/html/forcestruc/vua_citations.html.

US Army Training and Doctrine Command

Deputy Chief of Staff for Training and Schools, US Army Training and Doctrine Command. *How to Win Outnumbered.* January 8, 1974. http://usacac.army.mil/cac2/CSI/docs/Gorman/03_DCST_1973_77/05_74_TanksWinOutnumbered_8Jan.pdf.

Romjue, John L. *A History of Army 86.* Vol. 1, *Division 86: The Development of the Heavy Division, September 1978–October 1979.* Fort Monroe, VA: Historical Office, US Army Training and Doctrine Command, 1980.

———. *A History of Army 86.* Vol. 2, *The Development of the Light Division, the Corps and Echelons above Corps, November 1979–December 1980.* Fort Monroe, VA: Historical Office, US Army Training and Doctrine Command, 1982.

US Army Sergeants Major Academy. *Self Study of the US Army Sergeants Major Academy.* Fort Bliss, TX: US Army Sergeants Major Academy, 1985.

———. *Annual Historical Review, 1 January 1987–31 December 1987.* Fort Bliss, TX: US Army Sergeants Major Academy, 1988.

US Army Training and Doctrine Command. *US Army Operational Concepts: The AirLand Battle and Corps 86.* Pamphlet 525-5. Fort Monroe, VA: US Army Training and Doctrine Command, 1981.

———. *Desert Storm Conference Report.* Fort Monroe, VA: US Army Training and Doctrine Command, 1992.

VII Corps

G2, VII Corps. "The 100-Hour Ground War: How the Iraqi Plan Failed." May 4, 1994.

G3. Fragmentary Orders. Collected by BG Stanley F. Cherrie, G3, VII Corps. The documents were declassified after a page-by-page review in 1995. Subsequently, they were reviewed and marked by the Center for Army Lessons Learned in 1997, in accordance with the Department of Defense Declassification Instructions Issued in 1992. The Fragmentary Orders or FRAGOS cover the period January 3, 1991–March 1, 1991. These include FRAGO 1-91 through 240-91 less FRAGOS 11, 20, 21, 23, 33, and 39.

"Ground Transportation Management for VII Corps during Operation Desert Shield/Desert Storm." n.d.

Headquarters, VII Corps. "VII Corps Master Gunners Conference." Operation Desert Storm. March 1991.

VII Corps. "Air Operation Center." Daily situation report. February 16, 1991.

———. "Air-Ground Operations in Desert Storm." n.d.

2nd Corps Support Command

2nd COSCOM. "Operations Desert Shield/Storm: Logistics in Motion." n.d.

INTERVIEWS

Author's Interviews

Group Interviews, in Person

Brown, BG (Ret.) John S., Mary Elizabeth Brown, BG (Ret.) Lloyd T. Waterman, and Peggy Waterman. Denver, CO. September 25, 2014.

Fitzgerald, SFC (Ret.) Keith E. and CW3 (Ret.) Phyllis A. Fitzgerald. Junction City, KS. January 24, 2015.

Speer, Pearl I., and COL (Ret.) William L. Speer. Milford, KS. June 25, 2014.

Individual Interviews, in Person

Bircher, COL John E., IV. Fort Leavenworth, KS, August 6, 2014.
Bodenheimer, LTC (Ret.) Jim. Leavenworth, KS, January 29, 2014.
Brown, BG (Ret.) John S. Denver, CO, September 25, 2014.
Burns, COL (Ret.) Robert A. Leavenworth, KS, April 16, 2014.
Camarena, LTC (Ret.) Mark. Leavenworth, KS, October 22, 2014.
Carlton, Bradley. Junction City, KS, October 31, 2013.
Cherrie, BG (Ret.) Stanley F. Leavenworth, KS, September 27, 2013.
———. Leavenworth, KS, February 10, 2014.
———. Leavenworth, KS, February 11, 2015.
Dowdy, LTC (Ret.) James D. Fort Leavenworth, KS, December 9, 2014.
Fitzgerald, SFC (Ret.) Keith E. Junction City, KS, January 24, 2015.
Fitzgerald, CW3 (Ret.) Phyllis A. Junction City, KS, January 24, 2015.
Fontenot, Dana H. Lansing, KS, August 19, 2015.
Githerman, COL (Ret.) Larry W. Fort Riley, KS, November 20, 2013.
Hillman, COL (Ret.) James L. Fort Meade, MD, April 23, 2014.
Hoeffner, Linda S. Fort Riley, KS, October 31, 2013.
Kidder, LTC (Ret.) Bruce L. Lansing, KS, September 20, 2014.
LaGrange, COL (Ret.) Gary L. Manhattan, KS, June 26, 2014.
McCurry, LTC (Ret.) William K. Leavenworth, KS, January 27, 2015.
Rhame, LTG (Ret.) Thomas G. Alexandria, VA, April 23, 2014.
Riddle, MAJ (Ret.), Duane H. Fort Leavenworth, KS, April 22, 2015.
Samson, LTC (Ret.) Mark A. Leavenworth, KS, May 29, 2015.
Schatzel, LTC (Ret.) John A. Leavenworth, KS, November 25, 2014.
Sevcik, COL (Ret.) Michael C. Leavenworth, KS, April 3, 2015.
Shannon, LTC Randal S. Wyandotte, KS, October 14, 2014.
Wildes, COL (Ret.) David. Washington, DC, April 25, 2014.

Individual Telephone Interviews

Arndt, LTC Robert J. June 29, 2015.
Barefield, LTC (Ret.) Michael R. December 10, 2014.
Baer, Donna, and 1SG (Ret.) Ted A. Baer. August 11, 2015.
Bell, LTC (Ret.) James A. October 1, 2014.
Bills, MG Michael A. February 2, 2014.
———. September 26, 2014.
Bishop, COL (Ret.) Garry P. December 3, 2014.
Boles, MG (Ret.) Vincent E. April 9, 2015.
Bullington, COL (Ret.) Terry W. October 29, 2013.
———. June 6, 2014.
———. June 24, 2014.
———. November 20, 2014.
———. December 21, 2014.
———. January 2, 2015.
Burnham, Glen D. June 28, 2015.
Bushyhead, LTC (Ret.) John E. October 13, 2014.
Carter, David S. July 29, 2015.
Carter, LTG (Ret.) William G., III. December 5, 2013.

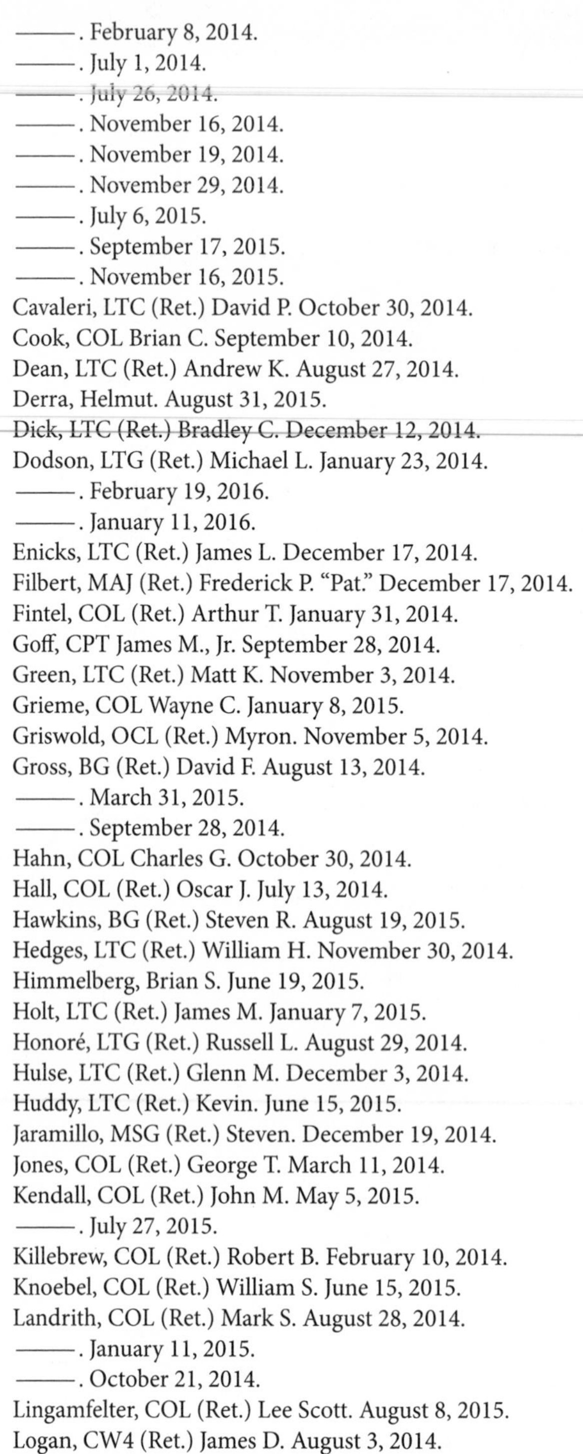

———. February 8, 2014.
———. July 1, 2014.
———. July 26, 2014.
———. November 16, 2014.
———. November 19, 2014.
———. November 29, 2014.
———. July 6, 2015.
———. September 17, 2015.
———. November 16, 2015.
Cavaleri, LTC (Ret.) David P. October 30, 2014.
Cook, COL Brian C. September 10, 2014.
Dean, LTC (Ret.) Andrew K. August 27, 2014.
Derra, Helmut. August 31, 2015.
Dick, LTC (Ret.) Bradley C. December 12, 2014.
Dodson, LTG (Ret.) Michael L. January 23, 2014.
———. February 19, 2016.
———. January 11, 2016.
Enicks, LTC (Ret.) James L. December 17, 2014.
Filbert, MAJ (Ret.) Frederick P. "Pat." December 17, 2014.
Fintel, COL (Ret.) Arthur T. January 31, 2014.
Goff, CPT James M., Jr. September 28, 2014.
Green, LTC (Ret.) Matt K. November 3, 2014.
Grieme, COL Wayne C. January 8, 2015.
Griswold, OCL (Ret.) Myron. November 5, 2014.
Gross, BG (Ret.) David F. August 13, 2014.
———. March 31, 2015.
———. September 28, 2014.
Hahn, COL Charles G. October 30, 2014.
Hall, COL (Ret.) Oscar J. July 13, 2014.
Hawkins, BG (Ret.) Steven R. August 19, 2015.
Hedges, LTC (Ret.) William H. November 30, 2014.
Himmelberg, Brian S. June 19, 2015.
Holt, LTC (Ret.) James M. January 7, 2015.
Honoré, LTG (Ret.) Russell L. August 29, 2014.
Hulse, LTC (Ret.) Glenn M. December 3, 2014.
Huddy, LTC (Ret.) Kevin. June 15, 2015.
Jaramillo, MSG (Ret.) Steven. December 19, 2014.
Jones, COL (Ret.) George T. March 11, 2014.
Kendall, COL (Ret.) John M. May 5, 2015.
———. July 27, 2015.
Killebrew, COL (Ret.) Robert B. February 10, 2014.
Knoebel, COL (Ret.) William S. June 15, 2015.
Landrith, COL (Ret.) Mark S. August 28, 2014.
———. January 11, 2015.
———. October 21, 2014.
Lingamfelter, COL (Ret.) Lee Scott. August 8, 2015.
Logan, CW4 (Ret.) James D. August 3, 2014.

MacDonald, MAJ (Ret.) Renee L. (née Miller). October 2, 2015.
Maggart, MAJ (Ret.) Lon E. "Bert." July 16, 2015.
Malik, CPT Eugene J. September 22, 2014.
———. September 9, 2015.
Marcy, COL (Ret.) Scott C. September 10, 2014.
Markham, LTC (Ret.) Keith A. December 30, 2014.
McCaffrey, GEN (Ret.) Barry R. March 10, 2014.
McCombs, LTC (Ret.) John. October 3, 2014.
Meek, LTC (Ret.) Marvin L. January 2, 2015.
Medine, Scott E. August 24, 2015.
Minehardt, LTC (Ret.) Hans N. May 26, 2015.
Moore, COL (Ret.) Bill R. October 9, 2014.
Moreno, COL (Ret.) Anthony A. August 12, 2014.
Mowery, COL (Ret.) James L. April 4, 2014.
Mullen, BG (Ret.) William J., III. January 20, 2014.
Norton, LTC (Ret.) Timothy. April 9, 2015.
Orlov, COL (Ret.) William S. January 17, 2014.
Orth, COL (Ret.) Richard K. December 23, 2014.
Osterberg, COL (Ret.) Donald A. October 14, 2014.
Peay, GEN (Ret.) J. H. Binford, III. October 30, 2014.
Phillips, COL (Ret.) Gary E. February 10, 2015.
Pike, COL Daniel W. May 5, 2014.
Pope, LTC (Ret.) Kenneth W. February 3, 2015.
Rhame, LTG (Ret.) Thomas G. November 11, 2013. Rhame read journal entries to author in a series of telephone interviews.
———. February 16, 2014.
———. April 24, 2014.
———. October 21, 2014.
———. November 6, 2014.
———. November 7, 2014.
———. December 16, 2014.
———. December 19, 2014.
———. December 31, 2014.
———. February 2, 2015.
———. February 3, 2015.
———. July 6, 2015.
———. August 4, 2015.
Ritter, COL (Ret.) George P. August 4, 2014. Ritter read journal entries to author in a series of telephone interviews.
———. August 5, 2014.
———. August 8, 2014.
———. May 8, 2015.
Robinette, COL (Ret.) Stephen H. June 16, 2015.
Rutherford, LTG (Ret.) Jerry A. December 16, 2014.
Rutter, LTC (Ret.) Scott E. May 8, 2015.
Sanderson, Thomas K. September 18, 2015.
Schenk, BG (Ret.) Donald F. November 8, 2014.

———. November 15, 2014.
Schulte, SFC (Ret.) Michael G. November 5, 2014.
Shadley, MG (Ret.), Robert D. August 1, 2014.
Sorkness, SFC (Ret.) Steven M. September 23, 2014.
Stefanoff, Buddy A. August 5, 2015.
Stockmoe, COL (Ret.) James L. November 18, 2014.
Stone, COL (Ret.) Frank J. January 31, 2015.
Strickland, MAJ (Ret.) Jacob D. August 7, 2014.
Smith, COL (Ret.) Robert L. October 8, 2014.
Stavnes, COL Robert P. October 8, 2014.
Sullivan, GEN (Ret.) Gordon R. April 21, 2014.
Talley, LTC (Ret.) James R. November 6, 2014.
Tabb, LTC John D. October 30, 2014.
Teener, Douglas R. July 31, 2014.
Thornton, COL (Ret.) Eugenia. May 5, 2014.
Tibbets, LTC (Ret.) John R. June 15, 2015.
Toro, LTC (Ret.) Juan E. October 6, 2014.
———. October 8, 2014.
———. June 19, 2015.
Waterman, BG (Ret.) Lloyd T. October 28, 2014.
Whitfield, (Ret.) Steven K. November 4, 2014.
Wilkerson, COL (Ret.) Philip L. October 22, 2014.
Williams, COL Maurice L. August 26, 2014.
Wilson, LTG (Ret.) Robert. April 14, 1991.
———. February 6, 2014.
Winstead, LTC (Ret.) Mark D. June 20, 2015.
Zahn, COL (Ret.) Brian R. September 12, 2014.
———. November 22, 2014.

Center of Military History and Military History Institute, Fort McNair, Washington, DC

Center of Military History catalog numbers are sequenced without regard to alphabetical order. Although these interviews were transcribed, they were never edited. Reading them without fully understanding context, including Army jargon, may prove difficult.

Andrews, LTC John, G-4, 1st Infantry Division. Interview by MAJ Thomas A. Popa. Fort Riley, KS, July 24, 1991. DSIT-C-066.

Arnold, BG Steven L., G-3, Third Army and ARCENT HQ. Interview by Major Larry G. Heystek, Commander, 44th Military History Detachment. Riyadh, Saudi Arabia, November 19, 1990.

Bracket, MAJ Mike, G-3 Training, 1st Infantry Division. Interview by MAJ Thomas A. Popa. Fort Riley, KS, July 23, 1991. DSIT-C-065.

Buffington, LTC Edwin L., Commander 101st Forward Support Battalion, 1st Infantry Division. Interview by LTC William H. Taylor. Carlisle Barracks, PA, December 13, 1991. DSIT-MHI-003.

Bullington, LTC Terry, G-3, 1st Infantry Division. Interview by MAJ Thomas A. Popa. Fort Riley, KS, July 24, 1991. DSIT-C-067.

Dodson, COL Michael, Commander, Division Artillery, 1st Infantry Division. Interview by MAJ Thomas A. Popa. Fort Riley, KS, July 24–25, 1991. DCSIT-C-068.

Ford, LTC Terry, G-2, 1st Infantry Division. Interview by MAJ Thomas A. Popa. Fort Riley, KS, July 23, 1991. DSIT-C-064.

Franks, GEN Frederick, Commanding General, VII Corps. Interview by unknown person. October 31, 1991. DSIT-MH1-011.

Gingrich, LTC John R., Commander, 4th Battalion, 5th Field Artillery, 1st Infantry Division. Interview by COL Terry L. Nienhouse. Carlisle Barracks, PA, November 18, 1991. DSIT-MHI-013.

Hawkins, LTC Steven [Stephen], Commander, 1st Engineer Battalion, 1st Infantry Division. Interview by MAJ Thomas A. Popa. Fort Riley, KS, July 26, 1991. DSIT-C-078.

Maggart, COL Lon, Commander 1st Brigade, 1st Infantry Division. Interview by MAJ Thomas A. Popa. Fort Riley, KS, July 25, 1991. DSIT-C-073.

Marlin, LTC David W., Commander, 4th Battalion, 37th Armor, 2nd Brigade, 1st Infantry Division. Interview by COL Terry L. Nienhouse. Carlisle Barracks, PA. November 8, 1991. DSIT-MHI-026.

Moreno, COL Anthony, Commander, 2nd Brigade, 1st Infantry Division. Interview by MAJ Thomas A. Popa. Fort Riley, KS, July 26, 1991. DSIT-C-076.

O'Donnell, MAJ Jim, Chief, G-3 Operations, 1st Infantry Division. Interview by MAJ Thomas A. Popa. Fort Riley, KS, July 25, 1991. DCSIT-C-072.

Rhame, MG Thomas, Commanding General, 1st infantry Division. Interview by MAJ Thomas A. Popa. Fort Riley, KS, July 26, 1991. DCSIT-C-077a.

Shadley, COL Robert D., Commander, Division Support Command, 1st Infantry Division. Interview by MAJ Thomas A. Popa. Fort Riley, KS, July 25, 1991. DCSIT-C-071.

Wilson, LTC Robert, Commander, 1st Squadron, 4th Cavalry, 1st Infantry Division. Interview by MAJ Thomas A. Popa. Fort Riley, KS, July 28, 1991. DCSIT-C-080.

VII Corps Desert Shield/Desert Storm Interview Tape Collection

The 326th Military History Detachment conducted interviews in Task Force, 2nd Battalion, 34th Armor, thus including some interviews of soldiers assigned to A and D Companies of the 5th Battalion, 16th Infantry. Although these interviews were transcribed, they were never edited. Reading them without fully understanding context, including Army jargon, may prove difficult. The Center of Military History (CMH) assigned catalog numbers without regard to alphabetical order. Although the original CMH inventory sheet list the interviews as having taken place in Iraq, the 2-34 AR interviews actually occurred in northern Kuwait.

TF 2-34 AR by the 326th Military History Detachment

Group Interviews

Bradley Crew, 2nd Platoon, Company D, 5th Battalion, 16th Infantry, 1st Brigade, 1st Infantry Division: SSG Ronald E. Cline, Bradley Commander; SGT Calvin J. McCloy, Gunner; PVT Christopher S. Hunt, Rifleman; and PFC Barry T. Hyso, Driver. Interviewed by SSG Gerry A. Albin, 326th MHD. March 29, 1991. DSIT-AS-019.

Company A, 5th Battalion, 16th Infantry, 1st Brigade, 1st Infantry Division: CPT Johnny Womack, Commander; 1LT Jeffrey E. Smitherman, Executive Officer; and 1SG

Benjamin O'Sullivan, First Sergeant. Interviewed by MAJ Robert Cook, Commander, 326th MHD. March 29, 1991. DSIT-AS-014.

Company B, 2nd Battalion, 34th Armor, 1st Brigade, 1st Infantry Division: CPT Vaughn [Juan] E. Torro [Toro], Commander; 1LT Val [Lavelle] Jenkins, Executive Officer; 2LT Richard A. Shinaman [Schueneman], 2nd Platoon Leader; 1LT Charles N. Parker Jr., 3rd Platoon Leader; and 2LT James L. Jenicks [Enicks], 1st Platoon Leader. Interviewed by MAJ Robert Cook, Commander, 326th MHD, March 29, 1991. DSIT-AS-008.

Company C, 2nd Battalion, 34th Armor, 1st Brigade, 1st Infantry Division: CPT Robert A. Burns, Commander, and 1SG Robert P. Harn Jr., First Sergeant. Interviewed by MAJ Robert Cook, Commander, 326th MHD. March 28, 1991. DSIT-AS-012.

Crew of Tank B-23, 2nd Platoon, Company B, 2nd Battalion, 34th Armor, 1st Brigade, 1st Infantry Division: SSG Vincent E. Baker, Tank Commander; SGT Franklin C. Cooper, Gunner; SPC Charles L. Williamson Jr., Loader; and PVT James E. Strink, Driver. Interviewed by SPC Kirk L. Maynard, 326th MHD. March 29, 1991. DSIT-AS-009.

Crew of Tank C-?, Company C, 2nd Battalion, 34th Armor, 1st Brigade, 1st Infantry Division: SSG Norman L. James, Tank Commander; CPL Mark J. L. Penn, Gunner; PFC Josh Simpfle, Loader; and SPC David M. Means, Driver. Interviewed by SPC Kirk L. Maynard, 326th MHD. March 28, 1991. DIST-AS-013.

1st Platoon, Company B, 2nd Battalion, 34th Armor, 1st Brigade, 1st Infantry Division: SSG John McKinn Jr., Tank Commander; SGT William F. Wright, Gunner; and SPC L. M. Henry Jr., Driver. Interviewed by SPC Kirk L. Maynard, 326th MHD. March 29, 1991. DSIT-AS-010.

Mortar Platoon, Headquarters Company, 2nd Battalion, 34th Armor, 1st Brigade, 1st Infantry Division: SPC Aaron J. Weaver, Assistant Gunner; CPL Michael T. Newbauer, Squad Leader; and PVT Patrick R. Vozza, Driver. Interviewed by SPC Kirk L. Maynard, 326th MHD. March 28, 1991. DSIT-AS-005.

Scout Platoon, Headquarters Company, 2nd Battalion, 34th Armor, 1st Brigade, 1st Infantry Division: SSG Rex T. Pentland, Team B Section Sergeant; SGT Willy F. Davis, Bradley Cdr; SGT John M. Glover, Bradley Cdr; SSG Jerry L. Ellis, Scout Platoon Sergeant; and SSG Sylvain R. Ronneburg, Team A Section Sergeant. Interviewed by SSG Gerry A. Albin, 326th MHD. March 28, 1991. DSIT-AS-007.

3rd Platoon, B Company, 2nd Battalion, 34th Armor, 1st Brigade, 1st Infantry Division: SGT James F. K. Besso, Gunner; SPC Gary Schaeffer, Loader; and SPC Holschwander, Driver. Interviewed by SSG Gerry A. Albin, 326th MHD. March 29, 1991. DSIT-AS-011.

3rd Platoon, Company A, 5th Battalion, 16th Infantry, 1st Brigade, 1st Infantry Division: SPC Adrian A. Collier, Team Leader; PFC Larry W. Robbins, Driver; PFC Gary W. Owens, Driver; and PVT Jon-Paul M. Bockman, SAW Gunner. Interviewed by SSG Gerry A. Albin, 326th MHD. March 29, 1991. DSIT-AS-016.

Individual Interviews

Bushyhead, CPT John E., Commander, Company D, 5th Battalion, 16th Infantry, 1st Brigade, 1st Infantry Division. Interviewed by MAJ Robert Cook, Commander, 326th MHD. March 29, 1991. DSIT-AS-017.

Crumplar, MAJ Jack S-3, 2nd Battalion, 34th Armor, 1st Brigade, 1st Infantry Division. Interviewed by MAJ Robert Cook, Commander, 326th MHD. March 28, 1991. DSIT-AS-003.

Depot, 1 LT Barry Gerard, Mortar Platoon Leader, Headquarters Company, 2nd Battalion, 34th Armor, 1st Brigade, 1st Infantry Division. Interviewed by MAJ Robert Cook, Commander, 326th MHD. March 27, 1991. DSIT-AS-004.

Fontenot, LTC Gregory, Commander, 2nd Battalion, 34th Armor, 1st Brigade, 1st Infantry Division. Interviewed by MAJ Robert Cook, Commander, 326th MHD. March 29, 1991. DSIT-AS-001.

McCombs, 1LT John R., Scout Platoon Leader, Headquarters Company, 2nd Battalion, 34th Armor, 1st Brigade, 1st Infantry Division. Interviewed by MAJ Robert Cook, Commander, 326th MHD. March 27, 1991. DSIT-AS-006.

Peterson, 2LT Joseph W., 1st Platoon Leader, Company D, 5th Battalion, 16th Infantry, 1st Brigade, 1st Infantry Division. Interviewed by SPC Kirk L. Maynard, 326th MHD. March 29, 1991. DSIT-AS-018.

Steiner, MAJ Laurence M., Jr., Executive Officer, 2nd Battalion, 34th Armor, 1st Brigade, 1st Infantry Division. Interviewed by MAJ Robert Cook, Commander, 326th MHD. March 29, 1991. DSIT-AS-002.

Robert R. McCormick Foundation: Interviews by Research Staff or Funded by the McCormick Foundation

Group Interviews

Connors, COL (Ret.) Thomas, BG (Ret.) David F. Gross, and MG Paul Izzo. Oral history group interview by Andrew Woods. Robert R. McCormick Research Center, First Division Museum at Cantigny, Wheaton, IL. January 22–23, 2011.

Group Interviews. May 4–5, 1991. Ad Dammām, Saudi Arabia. These interviews, resourced by the Robert R. McCormick Research Center, are not dated explicitly nor are interview participants always identified fully. Excerpts of some of these interviews were used in the A&E TV documentary *Journals of War*. The interviews are on compact discs organized in five volumes:

Vol.1. MG Thomas G. Rhame, Commanding General, 1st ID.
Vol. 2. Colonel Gregory Fontenot, Commander, 2-34 AR, and Colonel Anthony A. Moreno, Commander, 2nd Brigade
Vol. 3. Dodson to Peters: Fourteen interviews (COL Michael Dodson, Commander, Division Artillery, and thirteen others).
Vol. 4. McCall to Norton: Six interviews
Vol. 5. Hart to Lee: Four interviews.

Individual Interviews

Desautel, LTC (Ret.) Joe. Wheaton, IL. June 6, 2015.

Long, LTC (Ret.) John, III, Commander B Company 3-37 AR. Wheaton, IL. July 2, 2008.

Mowery, COL (Ret.) James L. Wheaton, IL. October 25, 2010.

Rhame, Linda. Interview by Andrew Woods, Robert R. McCormick Research Center, First Division Museum at Cantigny, Wheaton, IL. June 21, 2015.

Rhame, LTG Thomas. Robert R. McCormick Research Center, November 1, 1997.

Schulte, SFC (Ret.) Michael G. Interview by Andrew Woods. June 14, 2013.

Watts, LTG (Ret.) Ronald L. Interview by Andrew Woods, Society of the 1st Division Reunion, Colorado Springs, CO. August 22, 2008.

Second Armored Division (Forward) Interviews

Listed as interviews, these documents seem to be transcribed and edited narrative statements made by the subjects; the original handwritten narratives accompany some of the interviews. These interviews were almost certainly done in southern Iraq.

Conway, CSM Vincent. May 31, 1991.
Jones, LTC G[eorge T.], Commander, TF 3-66. June 4, 1991.
Pick, CPT Daniel David, S2, 3-66 Armor. June 6, 1991.
Robinson, CPT Duncan Scott, Commander, Bravo Company, 2-66 Armor. June 6, 1991.
Sedgwick, SFC Paul. Ar Rumaylah Airfield. April 14, 1991.
Wilson, CPT Lee. Checkpoint Bravo, Highway 8. March 12, 1991.
Wilson, CPT Lee, Commander, B Company, 1-41 Infantry. April 13, 1991.

US Army Military History Institute, Senior Officer Oral History

General Gordon R. Sullivan. Oral History interview. Edited by Colonel John R. Dabrowski. Carlisle Barracks, PA: US Military History Institute.

Additional Interviews from Various Sources

Fontenot, Dana H. Interview by Betty Rutherford. Lansing, KS, July 30, 2006.
Hillman, LTC James L. Fort Bliss, TX, June 8-10, 1992.

PRESENTATIONS AND BRIEFINGS FROM VARIOUS SOURCES

DePuy, GEN William E. Speeches, US Army Training and Doctrine Command, Fort Benning, GA. May 22, 1974.
Franks, GEN Frederick M., Jr. "VII Corps in Desert Storm." Presentation to the School of Advanced Military Studies, Fort Leavenworth, KS, n.d.
Harrington, COL Stuart A. "The Gulf War: An Iraqi General Officer's Perspective." Presentation to the US Army War College, Carlisle Barracks, PA, 1991.
Kryschtal, COL Myron. "Desert Logistics." Postwar briefing. n.d.
LaGrange, COL Gary. Fort Riley garrison briefing, presented at Fort Benning, Georgia. A handwritten note suggests that LaGrange gave this briefing on March 15, 1991. It includes force modernization and deployment data not found in the Division operations briefings.
Robert R. McCormick Research Center. Desert Shield/Desert Storm Commanders Workshop, Robert R. McCormick Research Center, First Division Museum at Cantigny, Wheaton, IL, May 16, 2009. Recordings of a daylong workshop with 1st Infantry Division commanders, including, LTG (Ret.) Thomas G. Rhame, CG, 1st ID, Desert Shield/Desert Storm; LTG (Ret.) Jerry A. Rutherford, Assistant Division Commander–Support, Desert Shield/Desert Storm; LTG (Ret.) Michael Dodson, Commander, Division Artillery, Desert Shield/Desert Storm; LTG (Ret.) David S. Weisman, Commander, 3rd Brigade, 2nd Armored Division Desert Shield/Desert Storm; LTG (Ret.)

Robert Wilson, Commander, 1-4 Cavalry, Desert Shield/Desert Storm; BG (Ret.) David F. Gross, Commander, 3-37 Armor, Desert Shield/Desert Storm; BG John S. Brown, Commander, 2-66 Armor, Desert Shield/Desert Storm; BG (Ret.) Lon E. Maggart, Commander, 1st Brigade, Desert Shield/Desert Storm; COL (Ret.) Anthony A. Moreno, Commander, 2nd Brigade, Desert Shield/Desert Storm; COL (Ret.) James L. Mowery, Commander, 1st Aviation Brigade, Desert Shield/Desert Storm; COL Terry Bullington (Ret.), G3, 1st ID, Desert Shield/Desert Storm; and COL (Ret.) Gregory Fontenot, Commander, 2-34 Armor, Desert Shield/Desert Storm. This workshop focused questions raised by the McCormick Foundation researchers on the 1st Infantry Division's preparation and execution of Operations Desert Shield and Desert Storm.

Rhame, MG Thomas G. McCormick Research Center briefing, May 31, 1991.

Thornton, COL (Ret.) Eugenia. "I'll Shoot You Myself: One Woman's Journey in 'This Man's Army.'" Presentation to the Delaware Humanities Forum, Wilmington, Delaware, 2000.

PERSONAL NOTES AND JOURNALS

Ancker, LTC Clinton J. Personal journal. February16–25, 1991.

Barefield, MAJ Michael R. Personal journal. January 2–April 29, 1991.

Cherrie, COL Stanley F. Personal journal. January–March, 1991.

Dodson, COL Michael L. Personal journal. December 29, 1990–April 25, 1991.

Fontenot, LTC Gregory. Personal notes. August 1990–May 1991.

Hein, SFC Jeffrey. Personal journal. February 24–25, 1991.

Martin, MAJ James B. Personal journal. December 16, 1990–April 6, 1991.

Meek, CPT Marvin. Personal journal. January 25–February 4, 1991.

Mowery, COL (Ret.) James L. "Saudi Journal." December 1990–May 1991.

Osterberg, COL (Ret.) Donald A. Personal journal. 1991.

Rhame, MG (Ret.) Thomas G. Personal journal. 1991.

Sullivan, GEN (Ret.) Gordon R. Sketchpad and personal notes. 1990–91. Archive, Military History Institute, Army Historical and Education Center, Carlisle Barracks, Pennsylvania.

E-MAILS TO THE AUTHOR

Burdan, LTC (Ret.) John. January 20, 2016.

Bushyhead, LTC (Ret.) John E. April 14, 2015.

Emerson, LTC Harry. January 30, 2014.

Green, LTC (Ret.) Matt. December 23, 2014.

Higgins, MG (Ret.) George. November 21, 2014.

LaGrange, COL Gary. December 28, 2015.

Light, 1LT Steven M., July 17, 2015.

Mowery, COL (Ret.) James L. January 3, 2016.

Rhame, LTG (Ret.) Thomas G. December 21, 2015.

Ritter, COL (Ret.) George P. May 5, 2015.

Robinette, COL (Ret.) Stephen H. May 18, 2015.

Shadley, MG (Ret.) Robert D. August 12, 2015.

Smith, GEN Sir Rupert (UK). May 1, 2015.

Stefanoff, Buddy A. October 15, 2015.
Thornton, COL (Ret.) Eugenia. August 14, 2014.
Watts, LTG (Ret.) Ronald L. September 9, 2014.
Wilson, LTG (Ret.) Robert. January 3, 2016.
———. January 20, 2016.
Wishart, LTG (Ret.) Leonard. September 10, 2014.

MISCELLANEOUS DOCUMENTS

Brown, BG (Ret.) John S. "3rd Brigade 2nd AD Forward Iraqi Wpn Systems Destroyed by Direct Fire up to Objective 3 (Battle of Norfolk 26–27 Feb 1990)." n.d.

Brown, LTC. John S. Letter to the editor of the *Army Times*. n.d.

———. Letter to MAJ Bill Hammond, Operation Desert Storm Study Group, October 10, 1991. Accompanied by a memorandum for BG Robert H. Scales, director of the Operation Desert Storm Study Group, November 13, 1991.

———. Video script. n.d.

Bullington, COL (Ret.) Terry W. "The First Infantry Division in Desert Shield/Desert Storm: Notes by Terry Bullington," Undated letter to the author, received June 16, 2014.

———. Map, scale 1:50,000, with graphic overlay depicting the approach and breach zone through Phase Line New Jersey, 1990. First Infantry Division Museum at Cantigny, Wheaton, IL.

Bullington, LTC Terry W. "Notes for Presentation to Military and Civilian Groups after Desert Storm." Robert R. McCormick Research Center, First Division Museum at Cantigny, Wheaton, IL.

Deputy Chief of Staff for Personnel. "Letter of Instruction." June 16, 1997.

"Family Support Group Formation Planning Meeting." Notes. August 28, 1990. Possession of Dana H. Fontenot.

Hand-drawn positions of Iraqi and US forces depicting fratricide event of February 27, 1990 involving B Company, TF 1-41 IN and C Company, 2-66 AR. n.d.

Kendall, COL John M. Daily Memo 242300C. February 1991.

Shadley Collection, McCormick Foundation, First Infantry Division Museum at Cantigny, Wheaton, IL.

Unsworn statements concerning fratricide event involving TM D, TF 1-41 IN, and Company C, 2-66 AR, taken from SPC Dably Anderson, Robert L. Culpepper (rank not identified), SFC Barrington Arnold, SGT José Hernandez, SGT Shoen D. Parsley, and SSG Wayne Williams, February 27, 1991.

US Army Military Personnel Center, slide presentation, Worldwide Conference, December 1985.

The White House. "Persian Gulf Security Framework." Presidential Directive NSC 63. January 15, 1981.

———. "U.S. Policy toward the Iran-Iraq War." National Security Decision Directive 114. November 26, 1983.

———. "U.S. Policy toward the Persian Gulf." National Security Decision Directive 26. October 2, 1982.

INDEX

Note: page numbers in italics refer to figures; those followed by n refer to notes, with note number. "fig." numbers refer to the photograph section following p. 282.

B

D

E

F

G

H

I

J

K

L

M

N

O

P

R

S

T

U

V

W

Y

Z